*"In this new ecological age
of developing global community
and interfaith dialogue,
the world religions face what is perhaps
the greatest challenge that they
have ever encountered.
Each is inspired by a unique vision of the divine
and has a distinct cultural identity.
At the same time, each perceives the
divine as the source of unity and peace.
The challenge is to preserve their
religious and cultural uniqueness
without letting it operate as a cause
of narrow and divisive sectarianism that
contradicts the vision of divine unity and peace.
It is a question whether the healing light
of religious vision will overcome the social
and ideological issues that underlie
much of the conflict between religions."*

STEVEN C. ROCKEFELLER,
Spirit and Nature, p. 169

A
SOURCEBOOK
for the
Community *of* Religions

Joel D. Beversluis

Project Editor

The Council for a Parliament of the World's Religions • Chicago, 1993

G

Additional copies of this book may be ordered from the
Council for a Parliament of the World's Religions
at its address above or from:

The SourceBook Project
1039 Calvin SE
Grand Rapids, MI 49506 USA

Send $15.00 (US) per copy by check or money order to either
address. Add $2.00 per copy for shipping and handling in the
United States, and $3.00 to other countries, worldwide.

Discounts are available for quantity purchases: Send $12.00
each for orders of four or more copies, plus shipping costs.
Libraries and trade and wholesale outlets should write or call
for more information: (616) 452-1828.

ISBN 0-9637897-0-8

Library of Congress Catalog Card No.: 93-90678

ACKNOWLEDGEMENTS

Grateful acknowledgement is due the following for use of their
copyrighted materials:

Albert LaChance. Excerpts from the Preface and Introduction
to *Greenspirit: Twelve Steps in Ecological Spirituality*,
published in the USA, 1991, by Element, Inc., 42 Broadway,
Rockport, MA 01966; and in Great Britain in 1991 by Element
Books Ltd., Longmead, Shaftesbury, Dorset. Used with
permission.

Beacon Press. From *Spirit and Nature* by John C. Elder and
Steven C. Rockefeller. Copyright 1992 by John C. Elder and
Steven C. Rockefeller. Reprinted by permission of Beacon
Press.

College Theology Society. "The Cosmology of Religion" by
Thomas Berry, in *College Theology Annual Volume*, #34,
edited by Dr. Paul Knitter. Used with permission.

GAIA Books Ltd. *The Gaia Atlas of First Peoples* by Julian
Burger; A Gaia Original, copyright 1990 Gaia Books Ltd., 66
Charlotte Street, London W1P 1LR UK. Published in the US
by Doubleday/Anchor. Used with permission.

GIA Publications, Inc. "Chant for the Universe: An Interfaith
Anthem." Music by Richard Proulx, copyright 1992. Chicago,
Illinois. (Text by Rabbi Bronstein and Ronald Kidd, copyright
The Council for a Parliament of the World's Religions.) Used
with permission.

International Association for Religious Freedom. "Religious
Freedom," by Robert Traer. Published in the IARF *World*,
January 1993. Used with permission.

International Religious Foundation, Inc. "The One, the Other,
the Divine, the Many in Zulu Traditional Religion of Southern
Africa," by Lizo Doda Jafta, in *Dialogue and Alliance*, Summer
1992. Used with permission.

Inter Religious Federation for World Peace. "African
Traditional Religion," by Darrol Bryant. The General
Programme, IRFWP New Delhi Congress, 1993. Used with
permission.

IUCN/UNEP/WWF. *Caring for the Earth. A Strategy for
Sustainable Living*. 1991, Gland, Switzerland. Used with
permission.

Kosei Publishing Company. "A Dual Awakening Process" by
Dr. Ariyaratne, printed in *Dharma World*, July/August 1992;
and the editorial by Kazumasa Osaka and other quotations
from *Dharma World*, Jan./Feb. 1993. Used with permission.

Millennium Institute. "The Role of the Faith Traditions," and
other excerpts by Dr. Gerald O. Barney, Jane Blewett and
Kristen Barney. From *Global 2000 Revisited*. Copyright 1993
Millennium Institute. Used with permission.

National Conference of Christians and Jews. "The World
House," published Spring 1992. Chicago. Used with
permission.

Open Court Publishing Company. "General Introduction," by
Richard Hughes Seager, to *The Dawn of Religious Pluralism*,
edited by Richard Hughes Seager and published in Association
with the Council for a Parliament of the World's Religions.
Copyright 1993. Used with permission.

Orbis Books. *The Desert is Fertile*, by Dom Helder Camara.
1983. Maryknoll, New York. Used with permission.

SCM Press Ltd., London, UK:
        "Conclusions" of *Pilgrimage of Hope*, by Marcus
Braybrooke. 1992 (US rights: Crossroad Publishing Co.). Used
with permission.
        Portions of Chapters 1 and 2 of *Stepping Stones to
a Global Ethic*, by Marcus Braybrooke. 1992. Used with
permission.
        Four excerpts from articles in *A Dictionary of Religious
Education*, edited by John M. Sutcliffe. 1984. Used with
permission.

The Tablet Publishing Co., Ltd. "The New Consciousness," by
Bede Griffiths. Printed in the January 16, 1993 issue of *The
Tablet*, edited by John Wilkins. London, UK. Used with
permission.

World Conference on Religions and Peace. *Prayers from
Religion for Peace: Proceedings of the Kyoto Conference on
Religion and Peace*, edited by Dr. Homer Jack. Copyright
WCRP 1973. Used with permission.

World Council of Churches. "We Will Not Hang our Harps on
the Willows," by Barbel Von Wartenberg-Potter. Copyright
1987 WCC Publications, Geneva, Switzerland. Used with
permission.

World Happiness and Cooperation. "A World Core
Curriculum," by Robert Muller, from *Essays on Education*; and
"Decide to be a Spiritual Person" by Robert Muller.
Reproduced by permission of World Happiness and
Cooperation, P.O. Box 1153, Anacortes, WA 98221.

Table of Contents

In Appreciation

*"Representatives of many faiths
have gathered here in the spirit of
mutual tolerance and respect, and in
the hope that life on earth might
continue in this same spirit.
This Parliament of the World's
Religions, envisioned and enacted here
in Chicago, is a more reliable
launching pad for global harmony,
I believe, than other and previous
approaches. I doubt, for instance, that a
new world order can spring forth whole,
like Venus from the head of Zeus, after
indiscriminate bombing
or during a crusade!*

*"It is so important to dramatize in
our age that there are many forms
revelation has taken or takes,
and thus also many ways to salvation.*

*"If the leaders of this Parliament have
opened their minds and hearts wider
than before, it is right and meet for all of
us, in and beyond this historic assembly,
to follow their example, slowly, perhaps,
but surely."*

JANE BLAFFER OWEN,
New Harmony, Indiana

*M*any individuals and organizations contributed to the publication of this book. In particular, I must express my sincere appreciation to:

the numerous contributors for their essays, articles, poems and information, generously provided;

the members of the Board and staff of the Council for a Parliament of the World's Religions, especially Jim Kenney and Daniel Gómez-Ibáñez who supported and helped guide the process;

Jane Blaffer Owen, of New Harmony, Indiana, who underwrote a significant portion of the printing costs;

Peter Wege, of the Wege Foundation, who provided funds to give a copy to each of the Delegates to the Assembly;

Brother Wayne Teasdale, whose enthusiasm and hands-on assistance of many kinds enriched the book and the process;

friends at the Institute for Global Education, who provided assistance of heart, hand and resources;

friends in the Grand Rapids Interfaith Dialogue Association, who present a model of interreligious harmony and insight;

friends and colleagues at my place of employment, for patience in my absence and for their assistance and advice;

Walter Bakes, for assistance with final proofreading and corrections;

Willem Mineur and David Lubbers, for the cover design and photograph;

and especially to those closest to me:

the Creating and Sustaining One;

my parents, who have provided life-long Christian nurture and other tangible assistance;

my children and their spouses and their children's children . . . , whose futures provide motivation for this work;

Gwendolyn, my wife, whose encouragement, love and gardens are a blessing to me.

JOEL BEVERSLUIS

Note

Foreword

Dr. Robert Muller

Former Assistant Secretary-General of the United Nations, Chancellor of the University for Peace in Costa Rica (Emeritus), and author of numerous books, speeches and articles about global issues, the United Nations and education. Dr. Muller was recently awarded the Albert Schweitzer International Prize for the Humanities because of his lifelong dedication to peace.

*T*he centennial—and second—Parliament of the World's Religions is one of the greatest events taking place at the end of this century and millennium. This *SourceBook*, prepared for the Parliament and the evolving community of religions, is a most important building block of the "Global Cathedral of Spirituality and Religions" to be erected in the next millennium. In it we seek the fulfillment of humanity's extraordinary destiny in the unfathomable and mysterious universe.

Celebrations and a rare date like the year 2000 provoke unusually deep thinking and taking stock, both retrospection and envisioning the future. Two other similar events are already being planned: the 50th anniversary in 1995 of the first universal political organization on this planet, the United Nations, and the 100th anniversary in 1999 of the first World Peace Conference in The Hague in 1899.

From all perspectives—scientific, political, social, economic and ideological—humanity finds itself in the kindergarten of an entirely new age: the global, interdependent, universal age, an incredibly promising age, a truly quantum jump, a cosmic event of the first importance that is perhaps unique in the universe; this is all due, principally, to advances in science and technology. Most people, governments and institutions are bewildered by this phenomenon. They see the future with anxiety. They turn and cling to the past which they know better and where they feel more secure. As a result, the world is a mess, a courtyard of globally uneducated children.

But we will make it! We are learning. One leap of progress is happening after another: the decolonization of the planet in less than 40 years; no world war in a half century; the end of the cold war; a universal organization of all nations of Earth with 32 specialized agencies and world programmes covering practically everything under the sun—and beyond the sun; one world conference after the other, attended by heads of states in person; a successful European Community after millennia of bloody, divisive wars; 15 other communities in the making around the world; and I could go on with my list.

When I look back at my 40 years of world service at the United Nations, I can hardly believe the changes. Coming from war-torn and disputed Alsace-Lorraine, I think now I am dreaming. My grandfather knew three wars and had five nationalities in his lifetime, without leaving his village. My father knew two wars, was twice a French soldier and once a German soldier. I knew one war which made us twice refugees. Half of my cousins wore French uniforms, the other half German; we might have killed each other. Later, as I watched events from the UN, I was convinced on numerous occasions that another world war would break out. As a young official I was told that decolonization would take from 100 to 150 years. I was asked why I had joined the UN, and told that I would lose my job because it would not survive more than ten years. Today I am convinced that with all we have learned and achieved, there will be an acceleration in the solutions to our world's problems. From being a pessimistic young man when I joined the UN, I have become its "Optimist-in-Residence."

Nevertheless, one dimension has been missing from this extraordinary journey, a dimension lamented by Secretaries-General Dag Hammarskjöld, U Thant and Javier Perez de Cuellar: the spiritual dimension, the highest, deepest, most common, universal and binding dimension of all. What science, politics, economics and sociology were trying to achieve, the religions knew long ago by virtue of transcendence, elevated consciousness and union with the universe and time. This dimension is still missing, yet it is urgently needed in world affairs.

Hence the crucial importance of the Parliament of the World's Religions. The common heritages and their spirituality can be the greatest single contribution to a better world. Though an atheist, André Malraux has said that "the third millennium will be spiritual or there will be no third millennium." Dag Hammarskjöld, a rational economist and world observer, said "I see no hope for permanent world peace. We have tried and failed miserably. Unless the world has a spiritual rebirth, civilization is doomed."

Religions are still accused of hindering peace, human progress and brotherhood. How often have I heard, after one of my speeches, "Mr. Muller, we agree with most of what you said, except one: forget about religions. They are one of the main trouble-makers and dividing factors in the world." Yet I stubbornly continue to preach about the spiritual and religious dimension. Like it or not, this new age we are entering will be an age of communities and of cooperation; it will be an age of family (celebrated by the UN in 1994), and of the family of nations. The family of religions cannot be absent; its absence could mean the retrocession and evanescence of religions, left behind by rapidly growing political, economic, scientific, ecological and sociological globalization.

Religions and spiritual traditions: the world needs you very much! You, more than anyone else, have experience, wisdom, insights and feeling for the miracle of life, of the Earth and of the universe. After having been pushed aside in many fields of human endeavor, you must again be the lighthouse, the guides, the prophets and messengers of the ultimate mysteries of the universe and eternity. You must set up the mechanisms to agree, and you must give humanity the divine or cosmic rules for our behavior on this planet.

*T*his remarkable *SourceBook* tells it all. Its table of contents is a lucid eye-opener to the world and to the participants in the Parliament. I relish reading it and reciting its scope: 1. The Centennial—Legacies of the Parliaments, and Religions and Critical Issues; 2. Religions of the World—Who we are and what we stand for; 3. Forming a Community of Religions—Dialogue, Understanding, Cooperation, and Moving toward a Global Ethic; 4. Looking Toward the 21st Century—New Voices, Warnings, Visions and Strategies, The Next Generation, and, most important, What Can I Do?

The book looks to be a monumental work at this juncture of history. I ask for it and its visionary editor, Joel Beversluis, and for the Parliament's numerous other contributors, all the gratitude, protection and blessings of the heavens where the prophets and spokesmen and -women for peace in the universe must be smiling and rejoicing. The work of the Parliament can be a tremendous building block for the great Temple of Earth which awaits completion in the third millennium. I pray that its deliberations and results will be among the most significant contributions to the reflection and actions taking place around the world in preparation for the year 2000 and the next century.

As an invited participant in the Assembly of Religious and Spiritual Leaders—an honor of which I am unworthy—and nourished by 40 years of world-wide experience, reflection and love for this miraculous planet and its genial human race, my answers to the four important questions on the agenda are enthusiastically and unreservedly positive:

1) Yes, the world's religious and spiritual leaders can and must come to agreement about ways to continue interreligious collaboration for peace, the relief of suffering and the preservation of the planet;

2) Yes, the members of the Assembly can and must endorse and bring plans and common projects to their communities and to their nations' leaders;

3) Yes, the members must take up the question of an ongoing Parliament or Council of religious and spiritual leaders as a network of organizations devoted to finding solutions to the shared problems of the human community;

4) Yes, the members of the Assembly can and should endorse statements such as the Parliament's Declaration of Global Ethics, the Universal Declaration on Non-Violence and similar statements.

*Y*es, if we put together our energies, our minds, our hearts and our souls, keeping always before our eyes the images of the poorest, most suffering, downtrodden brothers and sisters on this planet, we can make this Parliament the most significant, hope-engendering event at the end of this millennium. A large part of the world has its eyes turned on us. Let us reverberate the light, hope and benefits of a spiritual union of all the world's religions for the good of humanity and of our lovely planet. Let us build the community of religions—which is an idea whose time has come. This Parliament must be remembered in history as the birthplace of a world-wide spiritual Renaissance and as the fulfillment of the dreams of so many people, including this participant.

My Dream 2000

I dream
That on 1 January 2000
The whole world will stand still
In prayer, awe and gratitude
For our beautiful, heavenly Earth
And for the miracle of human life.

I dream
That young and old, rich and poor,
Black and white,
Peoples from North and South,
From East and West,
From all beliefs and cultures
Will join their hands, minds and hearts
In an unprecedented, universal
Bimillennium Celebration of Life.

I dream
That the year 2000
Will be declared "World Year of Thanksgiving"
By the United Nations.

I dream
That during the year 2000
Innumerable celebrations and events
Will take place all over the globe
To gauge the long road covered by humanity
To study our mistakes
And to plan the feats
Still to be accomplished
For the full flowering of the human race
In peace, justice and happiness.

I dream
That the few remaining years
To the Bimillennium
Be devoted by all humans, nations and institutions
To unparalleled thinking, action,
Inspiration, elevation,
Determination and love
To solve our remaining problems
And to achieve
A peaceful, united human family on Earth.

Introduction

Joel D. Beversluis

Project Editor, A SourceBook for the Community of Religions; works in academic publishing and in the peace, justice and ecology movements; is currently studying religions at Western Michigan University.

Audience and context

*T*his *SourceBook* was created first of all as a resource tool for those who would participate in the Parliament of the World's Religions, in Chicago, late summer 1993. The Editor and the Council staff believed that the Parliament's workshops, deliberations and resolve would be enhanced by access to a wide range of foundational information and resources.

Beyond that audience, this book addresses a larger community which, many observers believe, is—or should be—forming among the religions. Ultimately, however, this book addresses the broad context of the Earth, which is in deep distress. This wider reach complements the program of the Parliament since its mission, like religion itself, encompasses the whole community of the Earth.

The SourceBook embodies the conviction that one of many essential tasks for the religions of the world is to create a new community, one which embraces both our differences and similarities. It must be clear, however, that we are not proposing a super-religion or deliberate syncretism among religions. Rather, the Parliament and this book defend the integrity of diverse traditions and stand for the value of pluralism within our societies. Furthermore, it is not the task of the Council nor of this Editor to make theological statements about ultimate truth or "true" religion.

Nevertheless, the selection of these materials does inevitably reflect some of the Editor's values and beliefs as well as some of those shaping the program of the Parliament. Likewise, the others who have contributed to the book are expressing their distinctive beliefs and values. In all cases, our goal is not to subsume those beliefs under one system but to engage each other and the reader in respectful dialogue about them. Through their inclusion in this book, the contents provide great potential for such interaction regarding diverse religious traditions, issues, scriptures and prayers, dialogue, ethical considerations, and responses to issues in our personal and corporate lives.

The numerous systems of the Earth—including human culture—are undergoing unprecedented challenges. As we move across and above the face of the earth, with increasingly creative and destructive powers, humans stand at a nexus point. We can see many challenges and opportunities converging around us, and the future is quite uncertain out the other end of a darkening funnel. If we are to find light in this *co-nexus* of ecology, spirituality, economics, politics and social factors, we must make major changes in our perceptions and behavior. That kind of transformation will probably require—and receive—substantial assistance from the Divine. Are these outrageous expectations? History and this book affirm that personal and communal awakenings, which clearly lie within the domain of the spiritual traditions and religions, are not only desirable but possible!

The SourceBook also witnesses to the understanding that the human species must give birth to bold visions guided by ancient wisdom *and* by the enlightened application of contemporary knowledge and strategic organization.

The contents

*M*y goal in compiling this book was to bring a wide range of foundational information to one context—the Parliament of the World's Religions—and one publication. Some of the materials are previously printed but scattered among many organizations and publications. They and the many new essays and articles are designed to supplement the Parliament's agendas.

The contents include work from many perspectives and approaches: historical, reflective, critical, visionary and strategic. They demonstrate on-going conversations among people of religious orders and institutions, scholars, scientists, philosophers, parliamentarians, and leaders of organizations and movements for change. Some of the materials document the history and evolution of powerful ideas.

Part of the value of this collection of diverse materials is as a resource and reference tool; more substantially, however, its value lies in the integration of the contents by readers who perceive them as parts of a larger and significant narrative. The plot of that story may be briefly summarized as follows:

PART 1: **The Centennial**
Reflections on the legacies of the past 100 years of interfaith relations and on the context and goals of this Parliament.

PART 2: **Religions of the World**
Portraits of who we are and what we stand for, as people of many traditions, spread across the Earth.

PART 3: **Forming a Community of Religions**
These things we have done and are doing together to form a community which is moving toward a global ethic with cooperative responses to critical issues.

PART 4: **Looking Toward the 21st Century**
Voices old and new offer warnings, strategies and visions of the future for our children and theirs.

To discover the book's scope in detail, readers should examine the table of contents. Though the book does follow a certain logic, it need not be read front to back. Indeed, readers should follow their interests and browse among its nuggets of various kinds.

Due to the nature of the subjects, overlap among the

contents in different parts of the book is inevitable. If there is an underlying theme, it is the interconnectedness of our needs and aspirations, embracing our differences, and expressed by a magnificent chorus of voices. In the germinating community of religions, these elements are the waters and the catalysts of growth and life.

A challenge

Due in part to the media, to labor-saving devices, and to our styles of leisure, we can easily become spectators of life. Our scientific and liberal educations and even our religious lives are so colored by the inclination to observation and analysis that we grow accustomed to thinking that good thoughts—and good reading—are nearly equivalent to good deeds.

This book and the Parliament are parts of a process, but substantive change of any kind is difficult. If it helps readers move into more demanding and rewarding forms of reflection and action, this book will have accomplished its goals. If it is only providing good information, the reader still has work to do (see Part 4D).

In presenting who we humans claim to be and hope to become, the *SourceBook* seeks to identify our tasks, acknowledge our strengths and promote the many gifts among us. Like the Parliament itself, this book is designed to nurture and expedite a process which will never be complete. There is no better time to begin it than in this year of interreligious cooperation and understanding.

A personal note

In the summer of 1992 this book called out to me for publication. Many authors and editors of new books think that, of course, and often it is true. Poets, prophets, composers, and artists have confirmed that the muse strikes where it is welcome, the spirit moves where it will, and we become instruments of a greater work. I was fortunate to have the time, interests, skills, technology, friends and relatives to assist me in doing what needed to be done.

I am very grateful for the unique opportunity of compiling this *SourceBook*. Among the rewards in a project like this is the interaction with many generous contributors. They provided their articles but also personal support and validation of the book's goals; most important, however, is their witness to the significance of the mission of this Parliament. By participating in this book, the contributors are already giving substance to the community of religions.

Now, literally and figuratively, it is in your hands.

PART 1

The Centennial

A. Legacies of the Parliaments

B. Religions and the Critical Issues

"We meet on the mountain height of absolute respect for the religious convictions of each other; and an earnest desire for better knowledge of the consolations which other forms of faith than our own offer to their devotees. The very basis of our convocation is the idea that the representatives of each religion sincerely believe it is the truest and the best of all; and that they will, therefore, hear with perfect candor and without fear the convictions of other sincere souls on the great questions of the immortal life."

HON. CHARLES CARROLL BONNEY,
Opening Address at the
World's Parliament of Religions,
September 11, 1893

"The first Parliament has left Chicago with a legacy and an unfinished agenda. Thus in 1988 a group of people of different faiths from Chicago began meeting to plan a centenary celebration of the Parliament in 1993."

from an unpublished short history
of the Council for a Parliament
of the World's Religions

INTRODUCTION TO THE
1993 Parliament of the World's Religions

Dr. Daniel Gómez-Ibáñez
Executive Director, Council for a Parliament of the World's Religions

> "*Our goal in creating the 1993
> Parliament of the World's Religions is
> to extend and build on a century of
> interfaith dialogue. We invite people to
> find ways communities can live
> peacefully and sustainably together,
> communicating and understanding,
> respecting one another's diversity, and
> protecting the common ground which
> nourishes all life.*
>
> *Persons should come to the
> Parliament above all to listen to one
> another, to be challenged to find new
> ways of living together, and to seek a
> new vision for the future.*"
>
> from *The Invitation*
> to the Parliament

History and Vision

*T*he Council for a Parliament of the World's Religions was
formed in the spring of 1988 to prepare for a centennial celebration of the
World's Parliament of Religions held in Chicago 100 years ago. As the
centerpiece and the most remarkable of the many congresses that were
held at the World's Columbian Exposition, the 1893 Parliament was the
first formal public meeting of representatives of the major religions in the
history of the world. It marks the beginning of interfaith dialogue and
cooperation in the modern world, and is recognized in many countries for
its significance as the first time that representatives of Asian religions
spoke to Western audiences. It has also been called a watershed event in
American religious history.

The culmination of years of activity and planning, this commemoration
recognizes and appreciates that past, but it is focused upon the present and
the future. The Parliament is as much for people who cannot attend as it is
for those who are present. It is intended to be a catalyst for dialogue,
understanding, introspection and reflection. . . a spark to ignite changes in
the ways we live and relate to each other.

Great changes are the result of deeply significant experience. Sometime
people are forced to change by extreme circumstances. But profound change
also happens when people are inspired by an irresistible call from within, a
call which often echoes the songs and visions of dreamers, poets, prophets or
saints. The Parliament must open the gates of vision.

The 1993 Parliament

*B*eginning on Saturday, August 28 and running through
Sunday, September 5, the Parliament will support reflection, dialogue,
understanding and response, within and among persons and within and
among institutions. It will bring together a great variety of people: willing
listeners, coming not out of curiosity but because they are caring people
who want to act in the world. The attendees will include persons who can
inspire and influence others.

The 1993 Parliament is a forum where people can speak and listen easily,
free from fear. It stands for collaboration and respect. At the same time it
will challenge all to think more broadly, whatever their starting point. It will
be a place where inspiration can happen.

The 1993 Parliament extends an extraordinary dialogue which occurred
100 years ago. The time is right for this gathering. It coincides with a
growing awareness of the limitations of our technological and political
ingenuity. It responds to a growing confidence in the power of spiritual
understanding and the desire for wisdom.

Because we face enormous challenges, we will ask of ourselves challenging
questions. These are intended to engage us all, despite our differences. For
example, we ask:

What is the place in our faith traditions of new revelation, wisdom or
understanding concerning human participation in our common future on
Earth?

What does the wisdom of our faith traditions teach us about hatred and violence against those who differ in faith, culture, race or gender?

What do we or our faith traditions offer as an alternative vision for living peacefully and sustainably together with others and with the Earth?

The Parliament will support reflection, dialogue and understanding on these and other important issues, within and among persons and within and among institutions. Every part of the program is designed to prepare people to make choices and to act from within a spiritual framework.

A legacy for the future

The centenary of the 1893 World's Parliament of Religions offers a unique opportunity for the community of religions to come together in a spirit of harmony and friendship. While commemorating the original Parliament, we strive to build in its foundation an atmosphere of peace and unity, truth and clarity. We work to establish interfaith understanding and cooperation at the local level, and we are committed to addressing issues of global significance as the world moves into the 21st century.

There are many ways to learn, many approaches to change, many visions for collaboration. The Parliament welcomes all—whatever their paths may be—who want new experience and understanding of the world's faiths and of the critical issues facing the global community.

"I regret that I will not be able to join you at this commemoration, but I wish you and your colleagues success in organizing meaningful and productive discussions. All of us need a sense of community and receptivity to each other's concerns and beliefs as much and more, now, as a hundred years ago. I hope that in trying to capture the imaginative spirit of enquiry in the Parliament of 1993, we may rediscover the humane and tolerant core of all religions."
P. V. NARASIMHA RAO,
Prime Minister of India

Although she was unable to attend the Parliament, H. H. Mata Amritanandamayi also sent a message:
"Darling children, these are times when the language of power alone is understood, so we have to be strong. Then only the world will pay heed to us, listen to our wisdom and strive to assimilate this knowledge in daily life. Only through unity can we acquire strength. Each one of us should foster the feeling that, despite differences in dress, language and tradition, we are all children of the Universal Mother.

Children, your labor in this direction indeed is the greatest sacrifice (yangya), highest austerity and most pious pilgrimage. Amma's grace is always with her children. May the Lord bring fulfillment to your noble efforts."
H. H. MATA AMRITANANDAMAYI,
Hindu spiritual leader and singer of *bhajans* (devotional songs), in Kerala, India

A Legacy Worth Celebrating

Dr. Richard Hughes Seager

Lecturer in Religion at Harvard University

When the World's Parliament of Religions convened in Chicago in September of 1893, it drew together a wide spectrum of religious and spiritual leaders and attracted more than 150,000 spectators to its numerous public presentations. Since the published record of the numerous speeches has been out of print for decades, the Research Committee of the Council for a Parliament of the World's Religions decided to resurrect a portion of the texts. Working with Dr. Seager, they compiled a representative selection of the more than 194 papers, speeches, poems and sermons delivered during the 1893 Parliament. Their work is published in *The Dawn of Religious Pluralism: Voices from the World's Parliament of Religions, 1893,* **edited by Richard Hughes Seager. The following essay is the "General Introduction" to that volume, published by Open Court Publishing Company in association with the Council for a Parliament of the World's Religions. –Ed.**

I

*I*n the mid-1880s, New York, St. Louis and Chicago were engaged in a stiff competition for the honor of playing host to the World's Columbian Exposition—the nation's salute to the 400th anniversary of Christopher Columbus's discovery of the New World. After lengthy public debate and private lobbying, Washington gave the nod to Chicago, then still the "great metropolis of the West" and a city rebounding from its devastating Great Fire of 1871.

New Yorkers were skeptical about the ability of a city best known for its slaughterhouses, grain and lumber exchanges, and sprawling, smoky railroads to mount a suitably august world's fair, so national promoters of the Exposition set as their standard the most important fair since London's Crystal Palace Exposition of 1851—Paris's 1889 *Exposition Universelle.* As a result, the World's Columbian Exposition was a synthesis of Chicago "can-do" energy and a canon of taste established by the more Francophilic East: its displays of invention, commerce, science and industry were housed in an ensemble of "palaces," a *Beaux Arts* tour de force designed by leading New York architects such as Stanford White and Richard Morris Hunt. The Exposition was itself a technological triumph; the latest techniques of steel-span construction were used to erect a neoclassical vision—the fair was popularly known as the White City, Magic City or Dream City—on a 700-acre parcel of undeveloped dunes and wasteland on the shore of Lake Michigan, seven miles south of the city's business district.[1]

In September of 1889, when plans for the fair were just getting under way, Charles Carroll Bonney, a Chicago lawyer and a layman in the Swedenborgian church, proposed that the Exposition Corporation sponsor a series of international congresses to complement the material triumphs and technological marvels that formed the substance of the Exposition's displays. "Something higher and nobler," he wrote, "is demanded by the enlightened and progressive spirit of the age." In October of the same year, a committee of Chicago businessmen, clerics and educators issued a plan for an international convention "more widely representative of 'peoples, nations, and tongues' than any assembly which has ever yet been convened."[2]

Bonney was named president of a proposed convention called the World's Congress Auxiliary, which grew under his direction to include 20 different departments devoted to, among other things, women's progress, the press, history, fine arts, public health, medicine and surgery, engineering, temperance, government, social reform, and religion. To house the convention, the city of Chicago, the Chicago Art Institute and the Exposition Corporation constructed the Memorial Art Palace (now the Art Institute) in downtown Chicago. The Auxiliary eventually sponsored 200 different congresses, which drew an estimated 700,000 people in the course of the Columbian summer of 1893. Of them all, the Congress of Religion—the World's Parliament of Religions in particular—drew the most attention, the most applause and the best press.[3]

Bonney selected John Henry Barrows, minister at Chicago's prestigious First Presbyterian Church, to chair the World's Congress Auxiliary's Department of Religion. Barrows headed a local committee consisting of P. A. Feehan, Chicago's Roman Catholic archbishop; Emil Hirsch, a radical Reform rabbi; and 14 local Protestant ministers from as many denominations. Jenkin Lloyd Jones, a liberal Chicago Unitarian, was named executive secretary. Under their leadership, 45 different religions and denominations and organizations such as the Evangelical Alliance and the Free Religious Association, together with special-interest groups such as Jewish women and African-American Catholics, agreed to hold their meetings under the auspices of the Department of Religion.

In the eyes of the leaders of the Department of Religion, the World's Parliament of Religions was the capstone of the entire proceedings. In the midst of the many denominational congresses and other meetings, the Parliament was scheduled as a 17-day-long event that was referred to in the Department's organizational literature as "a series of Union Meetings."[4] In his progress report of 1892, John Henry Barrows went so far as to suggest that "it is our expectation that the Parliament of Religions will be the most important, commanding and influential, as surely it will be the most phenomenal fact of the Columbian Exposition."

II

World's Columbian Exposition, World's Congress Auxiliary, World's Parliament of Religions—as the names suggest, the vision of the Chicago promoters was global, inclusive and expansive. In an early preliminary report issued by the General Committee, Bonney set the agenda and tone for the proceedings when he wrote that the mission of the Parliament was "to unite all Religion against all irreligion . . . to present to the world in the Religious Congresses to be held in connection with the Columbian Exposition of 1893, the substantial unity of many religions in the good deeds of the religious life." The World's Parliament of Religions would be the occasion for the religions of the world to set forth "their common aims and common grounds of union." It would help to secure "the coming unity of mankind, in the service of God and of man." John Henry Barrows, who stood well to the theological right of Bonney, expressed similar, if more grandly vague, sentiments in his own report when he quoted a verse from Tennyson's *Locksley Hall*, which became a kind of unofficial motto of the Parliament:

Till the war-drum throbb'd no longer, and
  the battle-flags were furl'd
In the Parliament of man, the Federation
  of the world.

The fact that the majority of the delegates on the floor were from the United States should not detract from the Parliament's significance. No small part of its historic importance rests with the way in which the assembly forced a confrontation between the hopes and aspirations of people in the American religious mainstream and the concerns of peoples overseas.

The roster of delegates who presented papers at the Parliament or sent

"The very conception of a Parliament of Religions . . . is in itself a sign of the times in which we live, and is worthy of the great nation from which it emanates."

ALI BILGRAMI,
Deccan, India

"The project is an admirable one, and it ought to receive the encouragement of all who really love truth and charity and who wish to further their reign among mankind."

BISHOP JOHN J. KEANE, Rector,
The Catholic University of Washington

"I trust that your largest hopes concerning the Parliament may be fully realized. I am not surprised that narrow-minded men, in our own church even, should oppose it. There are some good bigots who imagine that God will not cease working until he has made all men Presbyterians. . . ."

S. J. NICHOLLS,
formerly Moderator of the General
Assembly of the Presbyterian Church

them is impressive. Among Protestant presenters alone, one finds evangelicals B. Fay Mills, George Pentecost and Luther Townsend; new theology men Lyman Abbott and Theodore Munger; Social Gospel advocates Washington Gladden and Albion Small; and Unitarians Thomas Wentworth Higginson, Edward Everett Hale and Julia Ward Howe. The Catholic delegation included James Cardinal Gibbons, the leader of the American Catholic community; John Keane, Rector of Catholic University; and Monsignor Robert Seton, onetime chamberlain to Pope Pius IX and nephew of the now-sainted Elizabeth Seton. The Jewish delegation included Isaac Meyer Wise, Kaufmann Kohler and Emil Hirsch—leaders representing a spectrum of positions in the then-dominant Reform movement—as well as Henry Pereira Mendes of New York's prestigious Sephardic Temple Shearith Israel and Alexander Kohut, both of whom represented the rising tide of the Conservative movement in Judaism. Friends, Shakers and a variety of less-venerable sectarian movements were also heard from on the Parliament floor.

The Parliament was also successful in achieving its global reach. Eastern Orthodox Christianity had representatives, official and unofficial, from Greece, Armenia, Syria and Russia. Protestant missionaries spoke on the state of the religions of Asia, and the Department of Religion secured papers from comparative religion scholars such as F. Max Müller, J. Estlin Carpenter, C. P. Tiele, and August and Jean Réville. Leading delegates from the religions of Asia made the most important international contributions: P. C. Majumdar of the Hindu reform group the Brahmo-Somaj; Vivekananda, a young Bengali ascetic destined to be leader of the Ramakrishna Math, an important Hindu revitalization movement; and Anagarika Dharmapala, the founder of the Maha Bodhi Society and leader of a movement to unite Buddhist forces in Asia.[5]

It is also instructive to consider those parties that were underrepresented at the Parliament or were not there. On the domestic scene, Mormons were simply not invited to the Parliament. Native American religions were represented by one, brief, highly general paper presented by an academic anthropologist in the Parliament's scientific section. African-Americans made only two official presentations, one by a bishop in the African Methodist Episcopal church and a second by a Unitarian laywoman. The Parliament was hailed as a breakthrough for women in religion, but under close examination most Protestant women on the floor were from the liberal religious traditions, either Universalists or Unitarians. Several Jewish women who subsequently rose to prominence in their community presented papers, but there were no female delegates, in or out of orders, in the Catholic delegation.

Aside from a strong dose of Anglo-Saxon triumphalism, issues linked to the question of ethnicity were also muted. The Catholic delegation was overwhelmingly Irish; no delegates presented issues that concerned the Germans, Poles, Italians and other national minorities that were important, often controversial, elements in the burgeoning immigrant community. Similarly, the delegates from Judaism, although voicing alarm about the rise of anti-Semitism both at home and overseas, did not include any representatives from central European and Russian immigrant communities that were growing rapidly in U.S. coastal cities. The question of racism was raised in the course of the Parliament by both African-Americans and Asians, but the overall tenor of discussion at the Parliament was theological and spiritual rather than political, although the political implications of Christian missionaries overseas was an issue that on a number of occasions disrupted the generally irenic spirit of the assembly.

Exclusions were even more conspicuous on the international scene. The so-called tribal or primitive religions had no representation, aside from an

6

occasional "scientific" paper, paternalistic or negative in tone, presented by Americans or Europeans. Neither the continent of Africa nor of South America had any significant representation, the latter a particularly conspicuous absence given that the celebration of Christopher Columbus's achievements was the occasion for the event. Among the major religious traditions of the world, Islam was seriously underrepresented, a development perhaps attributable to the fact that Sultan Abdul Hamid II did not accept the call for Islamic delegates issued by the Department of Religion and refused to become involved with the planning for the assembly. The delegates from the Asian religions were selected with an eye to what a century ago were considered "the ten great religions of the world." As a result, relatively modern groups such as the Sikhs and distinctive regional variants of a religious tradition such as Tibetan Buddhism had no representation at the assembly.

III

And yet, the global and inclusive composition of the Parliament, however limited by today's standards, made the assembly a first-of-its-kind event in the history of the world, a fact that makes it a challenge to generalize about its overall significance.

It is first of all important to think about the Parliament as simultaneously an American and a world event. Second, it is important to keep in mind that the quest for unity that played a central role in setting the tone for the assembly had an explicitly theological agenda. Given these considerations, one cannot avoid the conclusion that the Parliament—an event that set out to explore the common grounds for national and world religious unity—turned out to be a revelation of the plurality of religious forces on the domestic and international scenes.[6]

The centennial of the Parliament marks its discovery, not its rediscovery, as an event in American religious history.[7] For almost a century, its voluminous papers have not drawn the attention of students of American religious history. But the Parliament now provides an excellent case study for scholars who are interested in the ongoing process of revisioning religion in American history.

The Parliament, with its diverse and prominent Protestant delegates, together with its distinguished representatives from Catholicism and Judaism, is proof that the foundations for the "triple melting pot" that Will Herberg described in the 1950s were already firmly laid.[8] The quest for unity among Jews and Christians at the Parliament pointed to that short-lived heyday in the post–World War II world, when America confidently called itself a Judeo-Christian nation.

Standing as it does on the threshold between the 19th and 20th centuries, the assembly can be viewed, to paraphrase Sidney Mead, as representing a second "hinge" of American religious history.[9] The revolutionary era marked a first hinge, when Protestantism, then the overwhelmingly dominant faith, reorganized itself in response to the ideas of the Enlightenment, the ideals of the American Revolution and the mandates of the new Constitution. The Parliament marks a second, different kind of hinge—another turning point in national history—when two major immigrant communities and their religious institutions of Catholicism and Judaism were coming of age as forces to be reckoned with in the subsequent history of the United States. The Parliament, in short, represents the incipient broadening of and diversification in the American religious mainstream.

The absence or underrepresentation of other domestic groups only serves to underscore the degree to which the Parliament was a harbinger, not of unity, but of plurality; a kind of plurality that would not become conspicuous in America until Herberg's triple melting pot had become obsolete by the late 1960s. A comparable national assembly today would be incomplete without far more attention given to the variety of African-American religions, the Native American traditions, the varied women's spiritualities and the myriad movements in the nation, be they Christian-based, post-Christian or Asian. One would also expect to find representatives from the highly varied ethnic communities within Catholicism and Judaism and from those many Asian religious traditions that have taken root in the United States, some more than a century ago, some quite recently.

The idea of plurality also serves as the link between the significance of the Parliament on the domestic and global scenes. The assembly set out in pursuit of the foundations of religious unity; it sought, in the words of Barrows's report, "to indicate the impregnable foundations of Theism." But the real theological situation as it unfolded on the Parliament floor pointed not to a single foundation for global theism, but to the multiplicity of God concepts in the various religions. Primitive Biblical monotheism, Darwin-inspired evolutionary theism, and a kind of latter-day Deism were conspicuously different kinds of theology espoused by American Christians alone, while Jews argued for the primacy of the Hebrew "God-idea." The Asians contributed to the discussion Vishnu in his incarnation as Krishna; the Shinto *kami;* the Confucian Shang-Ti; the Divine Mother of the Hindus; the nonpersonal, immanental theology of the Jains; and the essentially nontheistic soteriology of the Buddhists. According to Parliament delegates, "God" was said to be revealed through the Christian and Hebrew Bibles, the *Koran,* the *Vedas* and all the great literature of the world, and through science, nature and the grace bestowed on the devotee by the *guru.*

The Parliament was not only a revelation of the plurality of the religious forces in the world at large. It also marked the beginning of a full-scale Asian mission to the Western nations, a development that would in time add a significant Eastern presence to the domestic scene.

The World's Parliament of Religions of 1893 was infused with the optimistic progressivism and postmillennial hope that was a conspicuous feature of the religious landscape in many quarters at the turn of the century. Most parties looked forward to the dawn of a new era, a better era, with the dawn of the 20th, perhaps the Christian, century. The Parliament is a valuable witness to this era, an era before the schism between fundamentalists and liberals in the old Protestant mainstream, before the triumph of ultramontanism and antimodernism and the rise of Zionism and conservativism in the Catholic and Jewish communities, respectively. It was an era in which the confidence of the Western, Christian nations had not yet been shattered by World War I and the great empires not yet disbanded by the success of the 20th-century wars of liberation.

The Parliament was a harbinger of, a prelude to, perhaps the first exercise in what we now call globalization and multiculturalism. Indeed, its failure to achieve world religious unity—its inclusivism was tainted by racism and ethnocentrism and its platform flawed by facile theological assumptions—should not be allowed to overshadow its actual accomplishments. It is remarkable in the first place that such a Parliament was convened at all. More importantly, the assembly stands at the forefront of the ecumenical, dialogue and interfaith movements that have been an important and conspicuous part of the religious world in the twentieth century.[10]

Perhaps most importantly, the World's Parliament of Religions of 1893 provides us a century later with a valuable witness to where we have been in the past and to what we have aspired. It serves as a kind of bottom line against which we can measure what has and has not been achieved over the course of a century in the way of interreligious and intercultural understanding. In the papers presented on the Parliament floor, we can recognize the way in which the world, the parties considered worthy of inclusion and the ground rules for discussion have changed radically over the course of a century.

Above all, the Parliament is a century-old legacy worth celebrating—with many qualifications, to be sure—and worth adding to by mustering the best that we can offer at its centennial, all the while cognizant of our limited perspective on what will be considered of genuine, lasting significance by those who look back and evaluate our hopes and aspirations from the end of the 21st century. ✿

NOTES

1. For information on the World's Columbian Exposition, see Reid Badger, *The Great American Fair: The World's Columbian Exposition and American Culture* (Chicago: N. Hall, 1979); David Burg, *Chicago's White City of 1893* (Lexington: University Press of Kentucky, 1976); and Brooklyn Museum, *The American Renaissance, 1876–1917* (New York: Brooklyn Museum, 1979).

2. The best source for the planning and organization of the Department of Religion and Parliament is Charles Carroll Bonney, "The Genesis of the World's Religious Congresses of 1893," *New Church Review* 1 (January 1894): 73–100. Quoted material from Barrows and Bonney in the introductory essay is drawn from this article. Reports on the various denominational meetings can be found in John H. Barrows, ed., *The World's Parliament of Religions: An Illustrated and Popular History of the World's Parliament of Religions, Held in Chicago in Connection with the World's Columbian Exposition,* 2 vols. (Chicago: Parliament Publishing Company, 1893); and Walter R. Houghton, ed., *Neely's History of the Parliament of Religions and Religious Congresses at the World's Columbian Exposition* (Chicago: Neely Publishing Company, 1894). In addition, a number of denominations published proceedings of their meetings. For the planning and organization of the other congresses sponsored by the World's Congress Auxiliary, see Bonney, "The World's Congress Auxiliary of the World's Columbian Exposition," Appendix A, in *Report of the President to the Board of Directors of the World's Columbian Exposition* (Chicago: Rand McNally, 1898).

3. Burg, *Chicago's White City of 1893,* 284–85.

4. *Programme of the World's Religious Congresses of 1893,* preliminary edition (n.p., n.d.).

5. One of the few discussions of the Asians at the Parliament is found in Joseph Kitagawa, "The World's Parliament of Religions and Its Legacy," Eleventh John Nuveen Lecture (Chicago: Privately printed by the University of Chicago Divinity School, 1983).

6. For a more extensive discussion of this, see Richard Hughes Seager, "Pluralism and the American Mainstream: The View from the World's Parliament of Religions," *Harvard Theological Review* 82:3 (1989): 301–24.

7. The Parliament is discussed at some length in Carl T. Jackson, *The Oriental Religions and American Thought* (Westport: Greenwood Press, 1981), 243–61; Paul A. Carter, *The Spiritual Crisis of the Gilded Age* (DeKalb: Northern Illinois University Press, 1971), 199–221; Martin E. Marty, *Modern American Religion* (Chicago: University of Chicago Press, 1986), vol. 1, *The Irony of It All,* 17–31.

8. Herberg called Protestantism, Catholicism and Judaism "equilegitimate subdivisions" of mid-20th-century American religious life. Will Herberg, *Protestant-Catholic-Jew: An Essay in American Religious Sociology* (Garden City, NY: Doubleday, 1955), 227.

9. Sidney Mead, *The Lively Experiment: The Shaping of Christianity in America* (New York: Harper & Row, 1976), 52.

10. Marcus Braybrooke, *Inter-Faith Organizations, 1893–1979: An Historical Directory* (New York: Edwin Mellen Press, 1980), 7–8.

"*There are few things which I so truly regret having missed as the great Parliament of Religions, held in Chicago as a part of the Columbian Exposition. Who would have thought that what was announced as simply an auxiliary branch of that exhibition could have developed into what it was; could have become the most important part of that immense undertaking; could have become the greatest success of the past year, and I do not hesitate to say, could now take its place as one of the most memorable events in the history of the world? Even in America, where people have not fully lost the faculty of admiring, and of giving hearty expression to their admiration, the greatness of that event seems to me not yet fully appreciated.*"

PROFESSOR F. MAX MULLER
of Oxford University, and editor of the
50-volume *Sacred Books of the East*

Early Dreams and Plans for the Centennial

Ronald R. Kidd

Executive Director of the Institute for World Spirituality; founder and Director of the Bultasa Zen Group

Serving as Administrator of the Council for a Parliament of the World's Religions from 1988 to 1990 gave Ronald R. Kidd a unique vantage point from which to describe the early dreams and plans. In this short history, the author reveals the visions and realities, the successes and the failures of the first several years of planning for and commemorating the centennial. What comes clear is the dream that the centennial would not be a one-time event, but a process that would make a lasting contribution to interfaith relations throughout Chicago's diverse religious community. –Ed.

*E*arly planning for the centennial of the Parliament of the World's Religion yielded a valuable crop of ideas and principles. A few have been incorporated into current plans, but many, I suspect, came before their time. The following short history of our organizing efforts focuses on these ideas and visions rather than on narrative, characters, scenes or plot. I write this to recall what seems valuable and may otherwise be lost, and to pass along to those who organize the next great interfaith events some ideas which may issue in a new generation of this work.

1. *The first* prises de position

*T*wo realizations dawned upon the early organizers as we embarked upon designing the project itself—a rather terrifying step beyond the stage of merely dreaming about it. As I remember those early meetings at the Vedanta Society, at Meadville/Lombard Seminary, and at the Chicago Bahá'í Center in spring and summer of 1988, the contributions of Gene Reeves stand out. Through his work with Meadville/Lombard and the International Association for Religious Freedom, he brought experience with international interfaith gatherings and with the state of affairs between religions; two principles which governed our early work were, I believe, part of his contribution.

The first was to look at Chicago, which had been the setting for the first Parliament of Religions. To all evidence, nothing of the kind had happened. Chicago lived on, religion separated from religion, without any particular interfaith activity (although much Christian ecumenical dialogue has occurred in the last decades). Only recently are there interfaith gatherings, thanks in large part to Rev. Stan Davis's initiatives with the National Council of Christians and Jews, notably in their annual Thanksgiving service. Christian-Muslim dialogues had been formed as well as Jewish-Christian encounters.

But, to all appearances, the 1893 Parliament of Religions left no impact whatsover on the city of Chicago.

We concluded that, whatever we might do to plan a world event for the centennial, our first focus should be on the religions of Chicago, to assure that the centennial would yield a more vital legacy than its predecessor. In fact, some even said it would be a fitting centennial if we were to do nothing at all on a world-wide scale, but instead leave to our city and its populations a vital network of interfaith relations.

Our second underlying realization was that virtually all of the world's religions are, in 1993, resident in the city and metropolitan area of Chicago. A hundred years ago, the organizing committee wrote 10,000 letters to invite delegates from the religions of the world to Chicago. A hundred years later, they are all here: Jew and Buddhist, Muslim and Sikh, Zoroastrian and Jain, Hindu and Bahá'í. A world class spectacle may be wonderful for a thousand reasons, but the basic elements of a parliament are already here. We just don't yet know each other and we rarely talk together. Only the *parliament*, the place to *parler* is needed.

As we moved a little further along in thinking through our tasks for the centennial, we began to see that in so many ways the wonderful 1893 Parliament was a "no-brainer." Bring the people together, let them say what they want to say, and you've made history by the very fact that it had never been done before.

Today the situation is quite different. On the broad national and international fronts, *information* about other religions—as distinct from contact, communication and community—is available from sources ranging from encyclopedia articles, to basic college courses in comparative religion, to television series on symbols and myths. It seemed clear—and here again I remember Gene Reeves's voice in the lead—that something very different was called for in 1993. A gallery of monologues explaining the basic positions of one's religion, no matter how fine, may give delight and indeed help some to learn what they otherwise would not, but it would hardly advance the state of interfaith relations. We felt that, just as the original parliament broke the ground for interfaith relations on a world scope, the centennial should do no less than inaugurate a new era in interfaith relations.

Much of the early dreams for the Parliament stem from a weekend series of meetings which the first Board and Program Committee held at Crystal Lake, Illinois, in the late summer of 1988. This planning was advanced and supported in good measure by Stan Davis, who was gently urging us to take stock of where we were and to begin to formulate plans as to where we might go. These were brainstorming sessions; little intricate planning was done and few resolutions adopted. Yet a growing sense emerged that the centennial should be truly a move into new dimensions, presenting a unique moment in history for all who came to Chicago (and all, we thought, who would watch via satellite around the world; we were not victims of timid dreams!)

Two strong suggestions for the centennial came from those discussions. The first was, I believe, Jim Kenney's—his presence stands out in memory and his ideas were strong, imaginative and articulate. The idea was that instead of speakers telling the basic tenets of their religions in sequence, we could use this gathering of significant religious leaders to help advance the consensus which exists—sometimes clearly, sometimes in shadow form—among the world's religions in regard to social and planetary needs and goals. Perhaps, we proposed, we can help advance the thinking and the articulation of the leaders of the great religions of the world as we face the human and material challenges of the 21st century. The themes we talked about were peace, war, homelessness and refugees, gaps between the North and the South, the impact of science on religious worldviews, relations between the races, the diminishing resources of the planet, and the needs of the teeming populations of the world. The point was not to politicize the centennial nor to forsake religion in favor of ethics; it was rather to mobilize the *religious* inspiration and power of the centennial's participants toward unified positions in these immediate challenges which religious people face at the end of this 20th century.

Further, we wanted there to be ample opportunity for participation in one another's religious services, liturgies, periods of meditation, ceremonies and so forth. Ritual is often where a religion is *enacted;* theology, on the other hand, talks *about* religion. We wanted to provide a chance to observe and even, where appropriate, to share in the actual expressions of religious symbol, rite and ceremony. We wanted the centennial to be itself a *religious* event and not just a week of talk *about* religions.

It was Dr. Paulos Mar Gregorios who had urged us, very early in our history, to offer extensive opportunity to experience one another's religion rather than only words about one's religious beliefs. Based on a visit several of us had with him, I recognized Metropolitan Gregorios as a great leader and a man of deep and thorough-going spirituality; he was subsequently invited to be keynote speaker at the Inaugural Ceremonies for the Parliament at Rockefeller Chapel in November 1989.

We also spoke at Crystal Lake about an "Olympics of the Spirit," a phrase which particularly pleased Daniel Gómez- Ibáñez, who led us through these sessions with gracefulness, sensitivity and direction. Indeed, much of the credit for the success of these early planning meetings is due to his adroit leadership. Our use of the phrase was not to indicate competition or ranking, but rather to conjure up an image of festival and spectacle by assembled multitudes, each representing one's own "colors"—religion, in this case, as well as culture and nationality.

Even before the Crystal Lake meetings, we had looked carefully at the name by which we would be known. We tried several variations. A *world's* Parliament? Without a world's fair (as in 1893), it hardly seemed appropriate to see the world as agent. And would it be mainly a Chicago event? Maybe it wouldn't be an international event at all. Another version was "Parliament of World Religions," but this seemed to exclude the more local and indigenous religions such as African, Shinto or Native American whom we very much wanted to welcome in 1993, however sparse and token their presence in 1893. So the final name incorporated a measure of modesty in not claiming the world's authority with a will to exclude no religion. So—despite feeling it was somewhat unwieldy—we became "the Council for a Parliament of the World's Religions." As far as I remember, no one objected to the term "Parliament," no matter how metaphorically we proposed to use it. Its use was too well sanctioned by history, by John Henry Barrows' inspiration from the line of Tennyson's poem; it had to be the centennial of the *Parliament* of religions.

2. *The first panorama of the centennial*

*T*he scope we envisioned for the several years of the centennial was first drawn out in a Saturday meeting at Common Ground in Deerfield. Daniel Gómez-Ibáñez, Jim Kenney and Ron Kidd met to try to put down where we were after the first meeting at Crystal Lake and to flesh out the next steps: How can we bring all these grand themes, aspirations, and visions into a *plan?* (It was felt, we learned later, that others should have been invited to this session, and that is no doubt a just criticism. At the time we had little idea of what we were up to; it seemed easier to think things out with only three people. A second Crystal Lake weekend 18 months later added detail and involved Board members more deeply in the planning process.)

The first stage of the process, we thought, would be local, since much discussion at Crystal Lake elaborated on this theme from the earliest planning. We set out plans to involve congregations in the Chicago area in several sets of activities: interfaith worship services in their own congregations; interfaith dialogue groups between members of congregations (with a facilitating committee of those somewhat more experienced); interreligious social action programs for the homeless, the addicted and the poor; a broad-based project on science and religion; and, later, an interfaith meditation group.

We formed committees which went out, each in their own fashion, to begin the grassroots work. Overall, we found little interest among the congregations. Interfaith worship services were held, but announcements of our availability to design these services for other churches and temples brought no invitations. The interfaith meditation group met at various meditation centers once a month for nearly two years, and occasionally attracted as many as 20 or 30 participants. But, bit by bit, attendance dropped off until only a small handful remained—often only the host group and one or two others. This program came to a halt due to lack of interest.

An interfaith retreat program was more successful. We held several retreats at the Franciscan Retreat in Cedar Lake, Indiana. The format then changed to an Introduction to Meditation workshop which maintained some of the qualities of a retreat, including the practice of silence and a focused process.

The dialogue committee encountered lack of interest when it went out to the congregations. Swami Sarveshananda, who had initiated the whole centennial effort, himself set up dialogue programs which continued with small numbers of participants for some time. One was held between the Vedanta Society and the First Presbyterian Church of Chicago (the home congregation of John Henry Barrows, the chairman of the first Parliament); the second was between the Vedanta Society and the Zoroastrian Community. A series of visits was arranged between members of the Bahá'í community of Evanston and members of Wat Dhammaram, a Thai Buddhist temple on the southwest side. Introductory visits were made, some personal invitations family to family ensued, and some plans involved children from the two communities. The series came to an end when the Bahá'í organizers moved. Later, the chair of the dialogue committee saw it rather as an opportunity for the members to develop ideas and theories about dialogue; and a subsequent chair reorganized the effort so committee members would themselves visit different temples and churches to learn about different religions. Thus the early dream of hundreds of congregation-to-congregation dialogues had but few realizations.

The science and religion group met with some regularity, debated the issues with vigor, occasionally got close to making plans for programs, but then disbanded. The social action group, too, met several times and debated its mission with some care and profundity. People working on the streets were not too excited by the prospect of groups of disparate religions descending upon them to help out for a few hours before they regained their surburban *patria*. Former Chicago Alderman Dick Simpson once scolded the Board for its lack of planning to do something about the poor, the homeless and needy right here in Chicago. He saw the centennial as a chance to pull religions together for immediate action and questioned whether all our talk would miss the point if we never rolled up our sleeves and worked for those in evident need. Perhaps the only real enthusiasm for concrete social projects came from some Muslims who were working with homeless people; they felt cut off from members of other religions involved in the same work and welcomed the chance to get to know one another and to learn what others are doing. The social action committee stopped meeting before any concrete projects were undertaken.

It seemed clear that only handfuls of people were interested enough in the local, grassroots dimensions to make something happen at that level. Perhaps we need the media blitz of a world-scale centennial to awaken, city-wide, to the challenge of interfaith relations at the truly local level. Those potentially interested, we learned, were often those with strong commitments to a particular religion and its practice, organizations and programs. For them, there was also family, job and—at best, in priority number four—interfaith work. Perhaps we tried too much too soon. One or two goals, strongly espoused and persistently worked for, might have created at least some interfaith activity across the city. The dream of Crystal Lake, in which hundreds of congregations might meet in dialogue and where interfaith services would be common in churches and temples, has not happened. Most of Chicago was as unaware of the centennial a year before its advent as it was of the original Parliament five years after it closed.

A second layer of activity leading up to the centennial and designed to bring more people into the process (in all senses) was to have been a series of conferences. A subcommittee of the Program Committee identified five broad areas which we thought summed up the critical issues with which religions of the world had to be concerned if they were to be relevant to the needs of human beings in the late 20th and early 21st centuries. These were: the earth; the human community (including race, gender issues, and the family); economics and justice; science and religion; and "Power, Politics and Liberation" (the minorities, the dispossessed, those without voice who struggle for voice). We wanted to ask the religions of the world to address these concerns not by designing appropriate strategies or gathering momentum for UN resolutions or governmental programs. Rather, we wanted to ask religious leaders to address them from the wealth of inspiration in their own traditions—scriptures, stories, heroes and saints; to begin to see what religious men and women could do about them; and to see if we might move toward common calls for action. We did not wish to ignore sociological and political considerations; but we wished to be, length and breadth, a parliament of *religions*.

In order to begin these enormously important conversations, in order to acquaint ourselves with the tasks of organizing colloquia and with the speakers who, it seemed to us, had something significant to say, and to involve issues-oriented Chicagoans in this process, we proposed holding conferences twice a year. We also considered ways of making this material available to centennial delegates, and we realized that long, involved conversations on all these issues have been going on all over the world for decades. The conferences would help to bring us of the Parliament up to date, so that the centennial might be able to move the discussion on to new areas and break new ground.

Only one conference was held. In terms of attendance, it was a moderate success, with about 125 participants, and was hosted by the Center for the Study of Values at De Paul University, a Parliament cosponsor. Gerald Barney gave the keynote address and laid out in sharp contours the challenge we face in providing for the increasing population of this world with limited and diminishing resources. A lively debate was enjoined by panelists, who took issue with Dr. Barney as much as they agreed with him. The afternoon sessions, in which each of the five "critical issues" subgroups held their own programs, were lively and, at times, controversial; discussion was vigorous.

Not long after the first conference, the Board of Directors of the Council took deep account of what was happening—or, more accurately, what was not happening—financially. They reached the difficult decision to close the office we had opened, to abolish the position of administrator and to discontinue the series of conferences. When the organization began to reform itself some six to nine months later, attention concentrated on the centennial rather than on the various plans for wider local participation. Time and financial restraints dictated a leap in focus to 1993.

By way of postscript to these stories of dreams and frustrations, it is worth emphasizing the importance of what we set out to do. Most conferences must operate in time constraints that render impossible any more than a nudge to the ongoing discussions which they pick up for those few days. What we tried to do was to involve the congregations across a major city with each other and to join those great and already mature conversations about the Great Issues of Our Time. We wanted to bring the unique inspiration of the world's religions into these debates in a way which would move the whole movement into a new day. The plan's ambitions exceeded our capabilities. The dream remains solid gold.

3. First sketches for the centennial

Our early planning sessions also yielded basic plans for the centennial itself. These have been superceded by events. None of us, for example, ever entertained the slightest notion that cosponsors and others would propose 900 separate speeches and events for the week of the centennial. It is clear, too, that what we had in mind would require a very strong organizing hand, and that requires, among so much else, staff and money. I want to describe what we dreamed not because I think it would have been so much better; I suspect it would have been, but it may well not be possible at this time. Rather, I write this as a vision which may inspire someone else down the line and give

him or her courage to take interfaith conferences into a new level of complexity, discourse, and common action.

The original dream asked the religions of the world to *share discourse*. We planned, it is true, for separate religious services, many particular artistic events, and meditational observances for each tradition. But the major discourse was to be common: the religions of the world speaking not in successive monologues, but addressing, from their wisdom, revelation and histories, the common issues.

This was so much the vision that on several occasions, when there were questions about when the great leaders in the world religions and heads of particular bodies would speak, and how, and where, I would answer that the various religious groups would have their own liturgical or other religious ceremonies, and denominational discourse would occur in denominational religious settings. The Parliament was organizing directed, common discourse.

The early plans also envisioned four great, simultaneous programs running through the weekdays of the Parliament: the Congresses on Critical Issues, worship services and religious ceremonies, a festival of the arts, and a contemplative vigil.

The plan was to hold Congresses on each of the five "critical issues" treated in the preparatory conferences. These would run mornings and afternoons through the week, consisting of major presentations and working groups. In the evenings, each "issue" would have a quasi-plenary where world-class speakers would make their presentations.

Among our many plans for the congresses were to present summaries from the six semi-annual conferences and to compile and edit calls for action made during the congresses. These "calls for action" would then become a focal point of the closing plenary sessions, planned then to last at least two days.

The second major area of programs was to have been religious services, services of worship and ceremonials. We wanted to encourage cosponsors to bring their best and finest to Chicago: Benedictines of St. Pierre-qui-Vire to sing daily Lauds and Vespers at Holy Name Cathedral, for instance. But we wanted also to invite the Navajo to sing the Blessing Way, Tibetan monks to construct a *Kalacakra* sand *mandala,* Taoist priests to present rituals perhaps never before presented in the Western world, and so on. It would have been at these events that the great teachers of the many religions and denominations would speak.

The third set of programs was to have been an ongoing festival of the arts. We were eager to enlist the museums of Chicago, the Chicago Symphony, the Lyric Opera and others. We talked about commissioning works for the centennial. Richard Proulx, composer of the "Chant for the Universe"* which was written for the Inaugural (words are by Rabbi Herbert Bronstein and myself) expressed his interest in expanding his piece into a contata. We thought of presenting Glass's opera on

*printed in Part 4

Gandhi, and we talked to staff at the Art Institute about special exhibits of religious art. But we were interested as well in popular art: Gospel choir competitions, rock concerts, Margy Maclain's Chicago Traditions (devoted to ethnic art). We had hoped to present several major artistic productions each day.

In our plans we called the final ongoing program a "contemplative vigil." One goal was to designate a central sanctuary in which members of religions with contemplative or meditative observances would assist, each for an assigned period of time, 24 hours a day throughout the Parliament. Another part of the plan would have invited communities to hold their own "vigils" in their own centers, with participants from other religions where appropriate. Finally, we wanted to ask these same communities to invite their colleagues around the world to unite with us from the first moment of the Parliament to the last. In this way, we dreamed of shoring up all the words and analyses, all the activities, all the prayer with an underlying foundation of contemplation and silent awareness.

The closing plenary that we envisioned was to present the various calls to action from the Congresses and also to present in some way excerpts or short resumés of the outstanding speeches of the Congresses. We also talked of presenting a program designed and rehearsed in youth groups during the week. The "Declaration of Human Values," as we were calling it, would have overlapped some of the calls to action from the congresses, but we wanted both parts at this culminating point of the centennial. Finally, we pictured the leaders of the great religions of the world united in calling down blessing upon the 21st century.

4. Conclusions

*E*lements of our early visions call for remembering.

- We wanted to focus initially on the city of Chicago and its religions; these may need the centennial to awaken congregations to the possibilities of mutual involvement in worship services, in dialogue and in facing together the social challenges of our city. Our vision, to leave Chicago with a richer and more vital legacy than the first Parliament, remains an important dream.

- Our intent was to wade into the vast and complicated discussions of how best to meet the needs of the human population and the planet in the 21st century, to animate that conversation with the particular inspiration of the religions of the world, and to engage the members of the religions in real and spiritual ways of solution.

- The dream of having the centennial itself be a genuinely religious event deserves to be said again and again. The hour of meditation each morning and the half-hour interfaith religious service each evening may be treated by participants as incidentals, as local presentations of great charm and cheer, or as significant religious enactment. But these observances may also give some present life to our earlier dreams of a series of ceremonies, rituals and contemplative vigils.

All of this remains valid and important, however changed the scope of the centennial may be. The conversation continues; the present centennial will make its contribution, but we must see beyond the symbolic presentations of this summer into the wide expanse and demands of life itself.

The Vision Beckons
From Parliament of Religions to Global Concourse of Religions

Dr. Paulos Mar Gregorios

Metropolitan of Delhi (the Orthodox Syrian Church of the East), and President for Asia, World Council of Churches.
Dr. Gregorios delivered this speech at the Inaugural Ceremonies of the Centennial at Rockefeller Chapel, November 1989.

*F*or me this is a great privilege indeed, to inaugurate the centenary celebrations of the World's Parliament of Religions. The World's Parliament of Religions, convened in this historic city of Chicago a century ago, held aloft a torch which helped us see a vision. We are far today from having realized it; but to renew that vision is the purpose of my few words this evening.

It is a perennial yearning of the human race to find its own unity. To this, I believe, the 1893 Parliament responded. Of course, the Columbian Exposition was there with all the glory of the technology which had just come into being in the last two decades of the last century. But along with all that urban/industrial, scientific/technological progress, in the mind of humanity there was another yearning—the yearning for that which binds humanity together, the unity of humanity on a spiritual basis and not just on the basis of a mere technological/industrial civilization. That is the vision before us today. Technology and modern civilization are not that which will unite us ultimately. That civilization has made it possible for us to come together, to communicate with each other, but that civilization cannot, alas, provide the necessary foundation for the spiritual unity of mankind. It is in search of that foundation that we—a hundred years later—begin these celebrations.

1. Religions and the secular world

*I*n 1893, perhaps the purpose was to fight irreligion. Today, that cannot be our purpose. We do not want to fight. Religions have done their share of fighting in the past. We shall not fight wars, but wage peace. Because a thousand million secular people without belief are also human beings, we are not going to fight them. Religions should never gang up against something called irreligion. No, that shall not be our purpose. Our purpose shall be to provide a multi-faceted foundation on which, in mutual respect, the cultures of the world can come together and live in a global concourse of religions.

And we shall *not* take the Golden Rule as our uniting principle as they did a hundred years ago. That was in fashion at the end of the last century, when American liberal Christianity had lost its spiritual moorings and could only find this little plank of the Golden Rule to hold on to. That is not what is before us. What is before us is a rich, deep, penetrating, respectful understanding of each other's religions. Not a common religion which puts everything into one pot; we do not want a religion which unites all religions. What we want is a Global Concourse of all Religions, to which the unbeliever shall not be a stranger, but shall be wholly welcome. That is the vision we need to recreate.

You know, in the Soviet Union, which was supposed to be the most anti-religious expression of secular forces, today the accent is totally different. Marxists have recognized that the values which shall unite humanity and shall make it possible for nations to live together in peace cannot come out of a secular ideology, but will have to come from a moral vision of humanity as a global phenomenon. And, as a result of that, they are now openly apologizing for their attitude towards religion in the past. Last August [1989] the Central Committee of the World Council of Churches met in Moscow. Two hundred people were invited to the Kremlin for a reception. At that reception, the Prime Minister of the Soviet Union, Mr. Ryzhkov, made a 20-minute address in which he openly stated that the Party and government in the Soviet Union were wrong in their attitude towards religious people in the past, and asked us, literally, to forgive them.

That is the world in which we live, where even secular people are turning towards religion to find meaning and hope. The unfortunate part of it is that religions are not quite ready to face that challenge, because the kind of exclusivistic traditional religion on which most of us have been nurtured is not able to cope with the crying need of humanity for meaning.

2. A Global Concourse of Religions

*A*nd that is the fundamental purpose of a permanent Parliament of Religions which will come out of these celebrations which we inaugurate this evening. I call it a "Global Concourse of Religions." You may later on agree to call it a Parliament; I would not quarrel. Parliament literally means *a talking shop*. That is all right. But what I would like to see is a *concourse*—a flowing together, a running together—of all religions: active, dynamic, without losing their identity, but in relation to each other, understanding each other, with mutual respect, and moving toward certain specific goals.

Let me say something now which I hope can be

understood: so long as Western civilization or Western Christianity dominate the World Parliament or Concourse, it will not work, because the identities of the other religions bear strong hostility toward both Western Christianity and Western civilization for their aggression against the cultures of the world. Western civilization has been a largely one-way mission, in which both the civilization and the church claimed to know the truth and refused to listen to aspects of truth in the experience of the rest of humanity. And, therefore, I want to say this from the heart: I love my Western brethren and sisters; I love my Western Christian brethren and sisters also. But where they dominate, an impasse prevails which does not allow the other cultures of the world to function. They are helplessly dominant. Men or women, they cannot do anything but dominate. And, therefore, the most important thing for a Global Concourse of Religions is for the Western civilization and Western Christianity to be humble and courteous enough to take a back seat.

The West has contributions to make, of course. Especially, their capacity to organize is unparalleled— even by the Japanese! And so we will need your help in the organization of such a Global Concourse of Religions. But can you do it without dominating, quietly, and let others be free to do it their way? Try! Then we might be able to use your God-given capacity in our common work, not as a leader, but in a more modest way. Otherwise, we would find the rest of the cultures of the world still inhibited by fear that they would be steam-rolled by Western civilization, Western Christianity and their values and approaches. This is a very fundamental thing that I wanted to say on this occasion.

3. Justice, peace and environment

A second fundamental thing that I wanted to say is that this Global Concourse of Religions must be committed not just to dialogue with each other, but to the future of humanity as a whole. If religions cannot get into that question of the welfare of all humanity, those great values to which they bear witness will not make much sense to vast millions of the people of this world. On the one hand, all religions have to develop a deep spiritual commitment, the re-creation of the deepest levels of meaning for human existence in a personal and communal spirituality. But equally important is the other pole: the commitment to the welfare of humanity, the commitment to justice, the commitment to peace, the commitment to an environment that promotes life rather than threatens to extinguish it, the commitment to eliminate toxic drugs and nuclear weapons. Three foci for such a Global Concourse are: justice, peace and the environment. Those must be three overarching goals of any global concourse that we shall set up. If it is not so, then most of the people of the world will say, "Well, another organization of religious people to talk among

themselves about things which are interesting to them, but not of immediate concern to us."

I would say that the cry for justice is the most heart-rending cry of humanity, and if religion is not relevant to justice in the world, religion is not worth having. If religion is an escape from the struggle for justice, then it's not worth much for most of the people in this world. Many would rather do away with religion altogether. And to touch on the issue of justice is also to touch on the fact that, among perpetrators of injustice, the religious people have more often been on the side of the oppressor than on the oppressed. This is what has made religion repulsive to many people. The reason why the secular humanist movement had to arise in the West was because the Christian religion lost its humanist vision. Because religion supported the cause of the oppressor, the slave owner, the exploiter, therefore a rival secular morality had to arise in this civilization. That is why we don't need to fight secularism, but rather should learn from it. We need to learn those great human values to which all people of good will stand committed, values which come out of our various religious heritages, but which the religions are not practicing today. If that doesn't happen, if this is going to be simply a talking shop for the old-style religion, then the Global Concourse may not make much sense to most people.

We all can talk about peace. Christians will say "Christ is the Prince of Peace." Hindus can say "*shanti, shanti, shanti.*" Jews can say "*shalom.*" Muslims can say "*salaam.*" All mean peace. Wonderful. But until recently, most of the wars in the world came out of religious conflicts. The last two world wars were, perhaps, not like that, but in the history of humanity religion has too often been the cause of war while talking about peace. And, therefore, we will have to shift our emphasis from talking to action for peace.

In each religion there are two levels. One level is exclusivistic and expansionist. That is to say, each religion says, we have the truth and if you want to have the truth, join us. That is the exclusivist, expansionist, lower type of religion. All religions have that lower type.

But in religions there is also a higher type, a type which is universal in its orientation, which is all-embracing in its love, which is non-discriminating between members of its own community and those outside. That good, humanistic, open tendency in all religions will have to be brought to the top. It is there. It only needs to be emphasized further. Only that way will we promote Peace on Earth.

4. Three concerns: a supranational spirit, security and science

Let me mention some of the areas where I think this Global Concourse of Religions will have to put some emphasis. First of all, ailing and alienated humanity is desperately in need of transcending national loyalties. For the last 200 years, the nation has often been our identity, and our loyalties have been to one's own nation's interests over against the interests of other nations. We will have to move out of this kind of identity. History is pushing us to move out of national parochialism into a universal humanism. That global perspective is in every country, just beginning to break out, but the governments are not able to embody that principle. Governments still give higher priority to national interests than to human interests. There is where religion has to play a major role, in changing the very attitude of governments so that they no longer think of national interests except in the context of universal human interests. Religion must help each nation and people to move beyond national, tribal, regional parochialisms, to give priority to their global humanity over nation and region and race.

A second thing to which humanity is aspiring is called *comprehensive global common security*—C.G.C.S. This is a concept which the religions have to pick up and develop in the world. What does this mean? This means, first, security without weapons, security based on trust. We must move in that direction. We cannot go on arming ourselves to the teeth and destroying and wasting our resources in a blinding and senseless militarism, which pervades all nations in the world, including my own country, India. We must move out of the concept that it is behind the guns and rockets that one finds national security. We must move internationally towards that same kind of mutual trust by which people within one nation today trust each other and do not have to be pointing guns at each other in order to live in security. We must learn to trust each other, and to live in a global community as responsible citizens. Again, this means a fundamental shift in the way human beings think. I believe religion has a responsibility in moving the human race out of national patriotism to patriotism of the globe—the love of humanity, planetary patriotism.

Let me say a third fundamental thing and then I shall stop. The hardest job that religions have is in liberating science and technology from being inhibiting factors and destructive factors. You know, in the medieval times, we black-robed clergymen had the final authority, at least in Europe. When there was a dispute, it was the clergy who gave the final verdict. That's gone, those days when one could say, "*Roma locuta est, causa finita est,*" "Rome has spoken, the cause is finished." Today it seems that the role of the black-robed clergy is assumed by the white-robed scientist at his computer or in his laboratory, so that today the phrase is, "*Scientia locuta est, causa finita est*"; "Science has said the last word, nothing further can be discussed." I think just as the clerical dictatorship of the medieval ages was overthrown, science's doctrinaire authoritarianism will have to be overthrown. But science itself cannot be abandoned. Science itself is the best tool that has come the way of man. Unfortunately, science and technology are now prisoners—prisoners of either profit-minded large corporations or destruction-minded defense establishments. They are the ones who finance science today, and they control research, and research is oriented either towards making a fast buck in business or the most effective way of exterminating people. Those are the two directions in which scientific research is now moving: making money for the corporations, or killing people. That is where the urban/technological culture we celebrated once has now led us.

We must emancipate science, both from its authoritarianism and from its orientation toward profit and war. And there, again, I believe religions have a major role to play. But religions shall not attack science, only show science its limitations and its enslavement and try to emancipate it from its limitations, so that the same science and technology can now be applied to finding bread for the hungry, shelter for the homeless, clothing for the naked, transportation, communication—the basic needs of humanity. And in that process, science itself will become an ally of religion, not the hostile enemy of religion. And religion also will not have to regard science as an enemy, but as an ally. That is the kind of orientation that I would like to see for a Global Concourse of Religions. But it shall not abandon its primary role, which the *Upanishad* spoke about: "*Tamaso ma jyotirgamaya, asato ma sadgamaya, mrityormamritam gamaya.*" That is, "from darkness to light, from untruth to truth, from death to life." That is our primary orientation, but along with that, these three other orientations would have to be kept, and to that kind of vision, I beseech you, my beloved brothers and sisters, to give your commitment to act and your committed prayer. May God bless you!

Global Humanity Between the Poles

In his original text, Metropolitan Gregorios added a treatment of transcendent value and earthly reality; this was omitted from the spoken inaugural address, but is included here because of its intrinsic interest and important teaching. –Ed.

*H*umanity exists between two poles—its transcendent origin and ground, on the one hand, and, on the other, the world with which it is integrally related. The latter point is easier to grasp, though often forgotten. If the sun did not shine, my life on earth could not exist. And that sun is a point in a multi-billion star galaxy of galaxies in which all things are interconnected. The earth, with its oceans and lakes, rivers and wind-systems, mountains and clouds, birds and trees, animals, and other humans is an integral part of my life. My life could not exist if that universe did not sustain and support it. And only one dimension of that vast and complex universe is open to our senses. I become a human being only by interacting with the earth—consciously through work and unconsciously through my breathing and blood circulation, through my food-and-drink intake and elimination systems, and through the thousand other unconscious processes going on in my body and mind, as well as around me.

Now something has happened to the way we interact with our earth. We came upon a developed science/technology and the big-machine industrial system only about a century ago. In fact, the World's Parliament of Religions was convened in connection with the Columbian Exposition of America's industrial-technological achievements. Electricity came only in 1878, the telephone in 1876, the typewriter in 1873 and the railways and telegraph in 1866. There was an air of excitement about the new technology which revolutionized our interaction with the earth and our environment. Justified excitement, indeed, but what a mess our industrial system has got us into!

Our problem today is that the earth is reacting rather negatively to our high-handed industrial-technological handling of it. In fact, all the three problems we confront today—injustice, war and environmental deterioration—are directly related to our technologically based industrial system. We have been too unrestrained and immature in our greedy handling of the earth and in our relationship with human beings on it. The Western version of the Christian religion bears a large share of the responsibility of bringing humanity to such a predicament. *Hubris* and greed, desire for domination and property, have ruined the human race and its environment, exposing us and all life to the risk of extinction.

The religions of the world have now to work together to redeem humanity from its present precarious predicament. We need to liberate humanity from the secular trap in which it has been unconsciously caught. Modern science and the technology based on it, as well as the political economy that undergirds it, have developed in a secular framework where humanity as dominating subject and the world as passive object have been the only two factors that mattered. God or the transcendent has become an unnecessary hypothesis in our science and technology, in our universities and schools, in our political institutions.

This is the secular trap from which humanity needs emancipation. It is not simply a question of bringing God in through the window. Philosophical theisms are all too philosophically weak to stand. It is not simply at the intellectual or conceptual level that the Transcendent has to be reaffirmed.

The various religions of the world have honored and cherished the experience of the transcendent throughout human history, despite the scathing secular attack. We have done so through our doctrines and practices, through our prayers and rituals, through our mystic quests and experiences, through our compassion for humanity and our devotion to the Source and Ground of all being.

Of course, in religion, too, we have made a mess of things. We have made religion an instrument of our greed for political power and for economic advantage. We have allowed the most ungodly and inhuman practices in the name of religion. We have fought wars and destroyed each other in the name of God and religion. We have used our crusades and our *jihads* to plunder and pilfer the wealth of other peoples.

Religion, too, needs emancipation. We as humanity now stand alienated by our own evil practices from both poles of our existence, from the transcendent Source and Ground of our being and from the earth and society in which we have been placed.

The two redemptions, the overcoming of the two alienations, i.e., in the two realms of transcendent religion and humanitarian dealing with our earth—the double salvation for which humanity yearns—must become the top concern of the Global Concourse of Religions. The two emancipations can come only as a single package. It is only as our religions cease being negative and exclusive that our science/technology and our political economy can also become more human.

To me, this is the vision that beckons. We shall not abandon critical reason, but we shall go beyond it to find a kind of reason that is more compassionate, more humane, more acknowledging of transcendence. We do not abandon our national loyalties, but we shall go beyond them to keep global human interests above our national interests. We do not abandon our own particular religious loyalties; but we shall deepen them in dialogue and concourse with other religions in order to find those deeper roots in each religion which affirm the unity of global humanity and which affirm the transcendent Love in which we all live and move and have our being.

As I humbly inaugurate this opening of the Centenary celebrations, let us also move to common prayer, that all humanity may be brought into a single concourse and all of us acknowledge together in various idioms the Transcendent Love, Wisdom and Power that really unites us. ✿

"*We do not abandon our own particular religious loyalties; but we shall deepen them in dialogue and concourse with other religions in order to find those deeper roots in each religion which affirm the unity of global humanity and which affirm the transcendent Love in which we all live and move and have our being.*"

DR. PAULOS MAR GREGORIOS

Making the Connections Within the Community

The Rev. Dirk Ficca

Director of Outreach for the Council for a Parliament of the World's Religions

During the 14 months leading up to the Parliament event, I have assisted the various religious and spiritual communities of metropolitan Chicago as they made plans to host those who will have gathered to commemorate the centenary. Among their goals is to present "the living face" of their various religious and spiritual traditions to the world.

This local connection is only fitting. For, if, in 1893, the world came to Chicago, today the people of the world live in Chicago. In 1993 in metropolitan Chicago, there are: 80,000 Hindus attending 17 temples; more Muslims than Jews; more Thai Buddhists than Episcopalians; over 600 Zoroastrians; significant numbers of Bahá'ís, Native Americans and of first-generation Sikhs and Jains; large populations of mainline Roman Catholic, Orthodox and Protestant Christians. As I traveled around the metropolitan area to visit these communities, it has been my unique opportunity to learn about their religious and spiritual traditions, not out of a book or from a lecture, but by getting to know the people who embody them, who live them out, right here in Chicago.

In order to facilitate the participation of these local communities in the Parliament, Host Committees have been formed in 14 traditions: Bahá'í, Buddhist, Christian (Anglican, Roman Catholic, Orthodox, Anglo-Protestant and African–American Protestant), Hindu, Jain, Jewish, Muslim, Native American, Sikh and Zoroastrian. Among the many tasks assigned to Host Committees has been fundraising, publicity and encouraging registrations for the Parliament event. Most importantly, the Council has looked to these Committees to represent their particular religious or spiritual traditions to the Parliament and, through the Parliament, to the world.

Several reasons underlie the Council's dependence on these local communities.

One is the acknowledgement that the living expression of a particular religious or spiritual tradition is its highest expression.

Another has been the great practical value of having local religious and spiritual communities make contact with the speakers and plan the programs, workshops and cultural presentations that will best represent their tradition in the Parliament forum.

Finally there is the hope that an ongoing metropolitan interreligious organization will emerge to continue the dialogue and cooperation between the local religious and spiritual communites that has developed amidst the planning for the Parliament. Chicago is one of the only cities of its size in North America that does not have an active, metropolitan-wide, constituency-based interreligious forum. For such a forum to emerge, by which the collective religious and spiritual community could have a greater voice in matters of moral and social concern at the local level, would be a tremendous legacy for what lies ahead in Chicago in the next 100 years.

It has been said: "All politics are local." The organizing strategy behind the Parliament says essentially the same thing about matters of religion and spirit.

"*Most of the people I've talked with want to encounter the 'living face' of the world religions, of Buddhism, of Islam, of Zoroastrianism, of Native American spirituality and the rest. . . by encountering the people of those religions and spiritual traditions. In other words, the desire is not so much to learn about Hinduism or Judaism or Catholicism as world religions in an abstract or academic sense, but to encounter Hindus and Jews and Catholics.*"

DIRK FICCA, from *Making the Connection: Out of the Office and into the Trenches*, printed in the *CPWR Journal*, April 1993

Cosponsors of the 1993 Parliament of the World's Religions

The cosponsors listed below are supporting one of the world's most comprehensive interfaith organizations. Cosponsorship reaches beyond Chicago because the Council is working to increase understanding among all the world's communities of faith.

Cosponsorship was open to groups that could work as partners with the CPWR. Organizations with a measure of stability and standing in their communities were invited to endorse the mission of the Council, support its work financially and with the numerous tasks, and

participate in the programs and planning of the Parliament. Cosponsors were asked to respect the right of others to the expression of their opinions and to cooperate with and understand others rather than try to convince or convert them. Cosponsorship by so many diverse groups does not, of course, imply that these organizations endorse the beliefs or objectives of others.

The list of cosponsors as of June 1993 follows on the next page.

List of Cosponsors

African American Leadership Partnership, *Chicago*
American Academy of Religion, *Atlanta, Georgia*
American Buddhist Congress, *Chicago*
American Humanist Association, *Amherst, New York*
American Islamic College, *Chicago*
American Jewish Committee, *New York City*
American Jewish Congress, *Chicago*
Anthroposophical Society in America, *Chicago*
Anti-Defamation League of B'nai B'rith, *Chicago*
Anuvrat Global Organization (Anuvibha), *Jaipur, India*
Association of Unity Churches, *Lee's Summit, Missouri*
Badarikashrama, *San Leandro, California*
Bahá'í International Community, *United Nations, New York*
Bharatiya Temple, *Flint, Michigan*
Brahma Kumaris World Spiritual University, *Mt. Abu, India and Chicago*
Buddhist Council of the Midwest, *Evanston, Illinois*
Buddhist Peace Fellowship, *Berkeley, California*
Buddhist Society of Compassionate Wisdom, *Chicago*
C.I.R.C.E.S. International, Inc., *Plainfield, Indiana*
Call to Action, *Chicago*
Catholic Theological Union, *Chicago*
Center for Respect of Life and Environment, *Washington, DC*
Center for the Study of Values, *DePaul University, Chicago*
Center for Yoga and Christianity, *Pacific Grove, California*
Central Conference of American Rabbis, *New York, New York*
Chicago Association of Reform Rabbis, *Chicago*
Chicago Center for Religion and Science at Lutheran School of Theology, *Chicago*
Chicago Dharmadhatu (Shambala Center), *Chicago*
Chicago Disciples Union (Disciples of Christ), *Oak Park, Illinois*
Chicago Theological Seminary, *Chicago*
Circle Sanctuary, Inc., *Mt. Horeb, Wisconsin*
City of God, *Moundsville, Virginia*
Christian Laity of Chicago, *Evanston, Illinois*
Church of Jesus Christ of Latter-Day Saints, *Salt Lake City, Utah*
Church of the International Society of Divine Love, Inc., *Austin, Texas*
Church of the New Jerusalem—Swedenborgian, *Bryn Athyn, Pennsylvania*
Common Ground Center, *Deerfield, Illinois*
Community Renewal Society, *Chicago*
Conscious Choice Magazine, *Chicago*
Covenant of the Goddess, *Berkeley, California and New York City*
Earthkind, U.S.A., *Washington, DC*
EarthSpirit Community, *Medford, Massachusetts*
Episcopal Diocese of Chicago, *Chicago*
Ethical Humanist Society of Chicago, *Evanston, Illinois*
Evangelical Lutheran Church in America, *Chicago*
Evangelical Lutheran Church in America, Metropolitan Chicago Synod, *Chicago*
Federation of Jain Associations in North America, *Cincinnati, Ohio*
Federation of Zoroastrian Associations of North America, *Hinsdale, Illinois*
Fellowship in Prayer, Inc., *Princeton, New Jersey*
Fellowship of Isis, *Enniscorthy, Ireland*

First Baptist Church, *Evanston, Illinois*
First Unitarian Universalist Association, *Ann Arbor, Michigan*
Focolare Movement, *Chicago*
Free Daist Communion, *Middletown, California*
Fung Loy Kok Institute of Taoism, *Denver, Colorado*
Gayatri Pariwar-Yugnirman, *Hardwar, India and Niles, Illinois*
General Convention, The Swedenborgian Church, *Newton, Massachusetts*
Gobind Sadan USA, *New York City*
Greater Chicago Broadcast Ministries, *Chicago*
Greek Orthodox Diocese of Chicago, *Chicago*
Guru Gobind Singh Foundation, *Rockville, Maryland*
Hindu Temple of Greater Chicago, *Lemont, Illinois*
Humane Society, International, *Washington, DC*
Humane Society of the United States, *Washington, DC*
Hyde Park/Kenwood Interfaith Council, *Chicago*
Illinois Conference on Churches, *Springfield, Illinois*
Institute for Ecumenical and Cultural Research, *Collegeville, Minnesota*
Institute for Twenty-First Century Studies, *Arlington, Virginia*
Institute for World Spirituality, *Chicago*
Institute of Jainology, *London, United Kingdom*
Institute of Muslim Minority Affairs, *London, United Kingdom and Jeddah, Saudi Arabia*
Integral Yoga International, *Buckingham, Virginia*
Inter-Religious Federation for World Peace, *Ashtead, United Kingdom and New York City*
Interfaith Ministries, *Wichita, Kansas*
International Assembly of Spiritual Healers and Earth Steward Congregations, *Seattle, Washington*
International Association for Religious Freedom, *Frankfurt, Germany*
International Association for Religious Freedom, United States Chapter, *Abington, Pennsylvania*
International Church of Metaphysics, *Windyville, Missouri*
International Coordinating Committee on Religion and the Earth, *Greenwich, Connecticut*
International Council of Christians and Jews, *Heppenheim, Germany*
International Council of Community Churches, *Palos Heights, Illinois and Durham, North Carolina*
International Mahavir Jain Mission, *Blairstown, New Jersey*
International Society of Divine Love, *Austin, Texas and Vrindaban, India*
Islamic Research Foundation for the Advancement of Knowledge, *Louisville, Kentucky*
Jain Society of Metropolitan Chicago, *Bartlett, Illinois*
Joseph Campbell Society, *Evanston, Illinois*
Kashi Church Foundation, *Sebastian, Florida*
Kiwanis Club of Downtown Madison, *Madison, Wisconsin*
Korean Chungtho Buddhist Mission Center, *Jersey City, New Jersey and Seoul, Korea*
Lakeside Buddha Sangha, *Evanston, Illinois*
Lyceum of Venus of Healing, *Ayer, Massachusetts*
Madison Quakers; Madison Monthly Meeting of the Religious Society of Friends, *Madison, Wisconsin*
Maha Bodhi Society of India, *Calcutta, India and Mt. Lavinia, Sri Lanka*

McCormick Theological Seminary, *Chicago*
Meadville–Lombard Theological School, *Chicago*
Monastic Interreligious Dialogue, *Saint Joseph, Minnesota*
Muslim Community Center, *Chicago*
National Association of Diocesan Ecumenical Officers, *St. Louis, Missouri*
National Association of Humane and Environmental Education, *East Hadden, Connecticut*
National Conference of Christians and Jews, Chicago and Northern Illinois Region, *Chicago*
National Council of the Churches of Christ in the USA, *New York City, New York*
National Spiritual Assembly of the Bahá'í of the United States, *Washington, DC*
National Spiritual Association of Churches, *Lily Dale, New York*
Native American Center, *Madison, Wisconsin*
Noble Thoughts Development Foundation, *Glendale Heights, Illinois*
North American Conference on Christianity and Ecology, *Washington, DC*
North American Interfaith Network, Inc., *Buffalo, New York*
Northwestern University Dept. of Religion, *Evanston, Illinois*
Office of Religious and Cultural Affairs of the Central Tibetan Administration, *Dharamsala, India and New York City*
Peaceworks International Center for the Dances of Universal Peace, *Fairfax, California*
Presbyterian Church (U.S.A.), *Louisville, Kentucky*
Presbytery of Chicago/Presbyterian Church (USA), *Chicago*
Religious Education Association, *New Haven, Connecticut*
Ribbon International, *Centerport, New York*
Roman Catholic Church, Archdiocese of Chicago, *Chicago*
Saint Benedict Center Interfaith Dialogue Group, *Madison, Wisconsin*
Saint Isidore's Roman Catholic Church, *Bloomingdale, Illinois*
Samaya Foundation, *New York, New York*
Science of Spirituality (Sawan Kirpal Ruhani Mission), *Naperville, Illinois*
Self-Realization Fellowship, *Los Angeles, California*
Shalom Ministries, *Chicago*
Sikh Religious Society of Chicago, *Chicago*
Spertus College of Judaica, *Chicago*
Spiritual Assembly of the Bahá'í of Chicago, *Chicago*
Spiritual Growth Network, *Lexington, Kentucky and Danville, Illinois*
Sri Annamacharya Project of North America (SAPNA), *Floosmoor, Illinois*
Sri Aurobindo Association, *Berkeley, California*
Sri Chinmoy Center, *Chicago*
Sukyo Mahikari, *Brooklyn, New York*

Swedenborg School of Religion, *Newton, Massachusetts*
The Center for Women, the Earth, the Divine, *Ridgefield, Connecticut*
The Graymoor Ecumenical and Interreligious Institute, *New York City, New York*
The Jabala Center, *Bloomingdale, Illinois*
The Liberal Catholic Church, *Evergreen Park, Illinois*
The Monthly Aspectarian, *Morton Grove, Illinois*
The Church of the New Jerusalem—Swedenborgian, *Bryn Athyn, Pennsylvania*
The Organization for Universal Communal Harmony (T.O.U.C.H.), *Chicago*
The Society of the First Presbyterian Church of Lake Forest, *Lake Forest, Illinois*
The Temple of Understanding, *New York City*
The Theosophical Society in America, *Wheaton, Illinois*
The Theosophical Society, *Pasadena, California*
The World Fellowship of Buddhists, *Bangkok, Thailand*
Union of American Hebrew Congregations, *New York City, New York*
Unitarian Universalist Association, Central Midwest District, *Oak Park, Illinois*
Unitarian Universalist Association of Congregations, *Boston, Massachusetts*
United Church of Christ, Illinois Conference, *Westchester, Illinois*
United Church of Christ—Chicago Metropolitan Association, *Chicago*
United Lodge of Theosophists, *Los Angeles*
United Methodist Church—Northern Illinois Conference, *Chicago*
Unity School of Christianity, *Unity Village, Missouri*
Universal Peace Sanctuary, *Seattle, Washington*
Vaishnava Center for Enlightenment, *Okemos, Michigan*
Vedanta Society of Madison, *Madison, Wisconsin*
Vishwa Hindu Parishad of America, *Berlin, Connecticut*
Vivekananda Foundation, *Alameda, California*
Vivekananda Vedanta Society, *Chicago*
Wat Dhammaram (Thai Buddhist Temple), *Chicago*
Wat Thai of Washington, DC, *Silver Spring, Maryland*
Winnetka Congregational Church, *Winnetka, Illinois*
Women of Faith Resource Center, *Chicago*
Won Buddhism of America, *Flushing, New York*
World Alliance of Reformed Churches, *Geneva, Switzerland and LaGrange Park, Illinois*
World Conference on Religion and Peace, *New York City*
World Congress of Faiths, *London, United Kingdom*
World Inter-Faith Education Association (Canada), *Victoria, British Columbia*
Yoga Journal, *Berkeley, California*

Spiritual Dimensions of the Environmental Crisis

Dr. Daniel Gómez-Ibáñez

Executive Director, Council for a Parliament of the World's Religions

*I*n the spirit of the Parliament of the World's Religions, I wish to begin this discussion of the critical issue of environment, and its relationship to spiritual matters, with a Sanskrit invocation from the *Vedas*. I ask those of you who are not Hindus to understand that any invocation must arise from one tradition or another, and to reflect on the relevance of these words for your own tradition or to reflect on their meaning for the earth and for those of us who would restore it to health. This is a chant for peace from the *Yajur Veda*.

Om
Dyauh Shantir Antariksham Shantih
Prithivii Shantir Aapah Shantir
Oshadayah Shantih Vanaspatayah Shantir
Vishvedevaah Shantir Brahma Shantis
Sarvam Shanti Shantireva Shanti
Saa Maa Shantiredhi

Yajur Veda 36, 17

May there be peace in the heavens, peace in the skies
   and peace on earth.
May the waters be peaceful.
May the grasses and herbs bring peace to all creatures,
   and may the plants be at peace also.
May the beneficent beings bring us peace,
   and may the way of all creation bring peace
   throughout the world.
May all things be peaceful, and may that peace itself bring
   further peace.
May we also bring peace to all.

*T*he attention given to the environment has varied enormously over the last few decades. In 1990, however, over 100 million people observed Earth Day and in some way gave thanks for the earth that sustains us all. One hundred million people are about two percent of humankind—more than enough to start a revolution! Since then, newspapers and television networks of all political shades have been featuring the plight of the earth, and this ten-year period is widely held to be the decade of the environment.

We have made some progress since 1970. The rate of growth of the earth's population has begun to slow down, although the numbers of people added each year—nearly 90 million this year—are unprecedented and still rising. The United Nations predicts that the total world population will stabilize around the end of the 21st century at somewhere between eight and 13 billion

persons.[1] The margin of error is about the same as the present population of the world: five billion persons. It is in the developing countries that population growth will be greatest and where increasing demand for energy and material goods will put enormous strains on the earth's resources of air, water and soil. Twenty years ago, leaders in those nations often voiced the cynical attitude that the environmental concerns of the industrialized nations were yet another ploy to keep the developing regions in a state of subjugation. But today that attitude is giving way to the realization that environmental problems are indeed a threat to every country and perhaps especially threatening to the welfare of developing regions.

In wealthy countries, people now nearly unanimously say they support environmental causes. In the United States, 80 percent of those questioned in a June 1989 *New York Times*/CBS News poll agreed that protecting the environment is so important "that requirements and standards cannot be too high and continuing environmental improvements must be made regardless of cost." Forty-three percent had agreed with the statement in September 1981.[2] Laws protecting the environment have been passed in most developed countries, and in Germany the Green Party has significantly changed the political landscape, if not yet the physical landscape. Even the normally conservative and complacent business community is awakening to environmental issues. Articles about the environment appear frequently in periodicals such as *Business Week, Fortune, Forbes, The Economist* and *The Wall Street Journal*.

Despite these encouraging signs, by most measures we have failed during the last 20 years to improve the health of the planet on which we all depend. The rate of extinction of species has quickened, not slowed. At least two or three species are lost irretrievably each day. Not only are we strangling the creation's genetic diversity, but entire ecosystems are being ravaged. Deforestation and erosion are destroying the once pristine Himalayas. Deserts are spreading in Africa south of the Sahara. We are losing 20 hectares of tropical forest each minute—an area the size of Ohio every year. The rate is increasing. Eighty percent of all Amazonian deforestation has occurred in the last ten years.[3]

In industrialized regions, forests, lakes and fields suffer increasingly from acid precipitation. There have been ominous decreases in crop and forest yields recently. Production, consumption and dissipation of toxic chemicals have increased since 1970. We have a landfill crisis, an ocean dumping crisis and an air quality crisis. The energy efficiency of Western economies increased during the last two decades, but after a brief slowdown around 1980, overall energy use continued to climb. Carbon emissions from fossil fuels increased worldwide by about 40 percent, 1970–1990.[4] The increase in atmospheric carbon dioxide may be causing significant global warming. We may not know enough about the earth's climate to know exactly what we are doing to it, but many scientists are deeply concerned. In my opinion, the uncertainty itself is cause for concern, and restraint is the prudent response.

And finally, as if these and other assaults on life were not enough, global spending on weapons and military activities has nearly doubled (in constant dollars) in 20 years. Each year we spend about one trillion dollars on arms which, if ever they were used, would lay waste to the entire biosphere.[5] We should be spending the money instead on healing the earth; and if we are to survive, we soon will need to do so.

These threats to creation are not just numerous or widespread, they encompass the whole ecosphere, and this emergence of the universal scale of our influence is what distinguishes our activities from those of previous generations. The natural resources we are consuming are no longer simply local, such as deposits of minerals, or tracts of forest, prairie or marsh. They now include the global reserves of air, water, soil and genetic material on which we all depend.

Furthermore, our environmental problems are intertwined with and in a real sense indistinguishable from the other great afflictions of the world. The divisions which wound the human community, such as racism, sexual discrimination or xenophobic nationalism; the grotesque coexistence of affluence and poverty; the prevalence of all kinds of violence, oppression and exploitation; and the alienation of individuals: these ills, like our environmental problems, all have common origins in the vision which increasingly has guided human affairs during the last two centuries.

In most of our daily affairs, in our prognoses for the human condition and in prescriptions for making the world a better place to live in, we accept or assume this vision. It is the vision in which material progress produces increasing happiness and well-being.

For millennia people have had faith in progress, or at least believed that progress was the birthright of humankind, but it is only relatively recently that we have come to associate progress almost exclusively with increases in *material* prosperity. When the great teachers of the world, Christ, Buddha, Mohammed, Krishna, Confucius, Lao-Tzu and others, point the way to joy and fulfillment, they are not talking about money and material goods, but today these have become the nearly universal talismans of goodness and wealth. In the Sermon on the Mount, Christ puts the issue clearly, but few have

listened. ". . . Where your treasure is, there will your heart be also."[6]

Many individuals understand that spiritual growth brings greater freedom and more lasting happiness than material growth, but as a society we are reluctant to admit that premise in our collective, corporate or political debates on the purposes of society or the future of the world.

A result of this vision of a purely material prosperity is that we usually use material, that is economic, criteria to allocate worldly resources. The familiar concepts of economics—calculations of costs and benefits, rent, the laws of supply and demand, rights of property (ownership), the concept of a free market—are defended in the delusion that an economy somehow operates independently of cultural or spiritual biases. On the contrary, the economy is an especially clear reflection of our spiritual or metaphysical priorities. One brief example will make this point.

Before the British colonized Nigeria, the land in that part of West Africa was not a commodity. Land was an attribute of the community or kinship group which inhabited it, but it was not property. It could not be owned (in the European sense), much less bought or sold. Land was associated with the group perhaps similarly to the way we associate last names with families. Boundaries were correspondingly fluid. In fact the idea that something so essential as land might be an object of trade was beyond the experience of many non-Western peoples.

Not understanding how the landscape mirrored West African attitudes, the British simply saw this state of affairs as primitive and as a hindrance to economic progress. So they surveyed the land, determined ownership on the basis of occupation, set up a system of cadastral records, and issued titles to parcels of land. Suddenly it became possible to own land, to buy and sell it, to use it as collateral, and to enforce rights of property against others. Thinking they had done the Nigerians a great service, the British proceeded to purchase the land for farms and plantations and to develop the colonial economy. The Nigerians reacted with bewilderment. They were dispossessed before they could understand what was happening to them. One can only imagine the social and cultural upheaval which this bit of European "progress" caused. Of course the British assumed that the money they paid Nigerians for the land was appropriate compensation. The whole process was sustained and enforced by the British legal system—another "gift" to the colonies.[7]

European settlers produced a similar effect in North America, though without resorting to the niceties of surveys and titles. Here is the response of Chief Seattle, speaking in 1855: "How can you buy or sell the sky, the warmth of the land? The idea is strange to us. If we do not own the freshness of the air and the sparkle of the water, how can you buy them?"[8]

I give this example simply to make the point that

attitudes we take for granted have enormously important consequences for the way we treat the earth and the way we treat each other. Reducing the earth's resources and creatures to the status of commodities has made it difficult to discuss or even to recognize their transcendent values—to put a "value" on diversity, or beauty, or life itself, which can somehow be compared with the "values" of the conventional transactions of the marketplace, such as building a road or a factory, or sales of automobiles, television sets or tuna fish.

Conventional economists assume that markets are indeed able to put a price on sunsets, for example, because people willing to pay for an unobscured view will do so, forcing the factory owner to build elsewhere. But not everyone who wants to see the sunset can afford to buy the view. Further, many potential "customers" have no access to the market, hence no say in determining the sunset's "value," for the simple reason that they have not been born yet. They are the future generations for whom we ought to be holding this beautiful earth in trust. Their welfare, or the beauty they inherit, depends on our willingness to defer our own gratification for the sake of theirs. (Sadly, the marketplace simply mirrors our intentions: in fact many of us heavily discount the future. The proof is our willingness to pay very high rates of interest to be able to satisfy our desires immediately.) A few economists, like Nicholas Georgescu-Roegen, Kenneth Boulding, Herman Daly and E. F. Schumacher have worked to construct an economics grounded in environmental realities and designed for a sustainable future, but they are as yet a small voice in the wilderness.[9]

Society's powerful, materialistic vision of progress seems to leave little room for the gentler, more loving vision which also finds a home in us. This is the vision of the heart and spirit we all share: the vision in which progress means caring for creation, for each other, for the earth and the environment we live in; building a peaceful community and world; and living harmoniously together, with fairness and justice. With such a vision we are moved by love.

But the modern, materialistic vision of progress depends on self-interest as the motivation for transactions, rather than love. So it can only be maintained by coercion—usually tacit, sometimes explicit. Coercion is violence to the spirit as well as to creation. Listen to the words of Wendell Berry, written 20 years ago:

Do we really hate the world? Are we really contemptuous of it? Have we really ignored its nature and its needs and the problems of its health? The evidence against us is everywhere. It is in our wanton and thoughtless misuse of the land and the other natural resources, in our wholesale pollution of the water and air, in strip mining, in our massive use and misuse of residual poisons in agriculture and elsewhere, in our willingness to destroy whole landscapes in the course of what we call "construction" and "progress," in the earth-destroying and population-destroying weapons we use in our wars, in the planet-destroying weapons now ready for use in the arsenals of the most powerful and violent nations of the world. It is in our hatred of races and nations. It is in our willingness to honor profit above everything except victory. It is in our willingness to spend more on war than on everything else. It is in our unappeasable restlessness, our nomadism, our anxiousness to get to another place or to "the top" or "somewhere" or to heaven or to the moon.

Our hatred of the world is most insidiously and dangerously present in the constantly widening discrepancy between our power and our needs, our means and our ends. This is because of machinery and what we call efficiency. In order to build a road we destroy several thousand acres of farmland forever, all in perfect optimism, without regret, believing that we have gained much and lost nothing. In order to build a dam, which like all human things will be temporary, we destroy a virgin stream forever, believing that we have conquered nature and added significantly to our stature. In order to burn cheap coal we destroy a mountain forever, believing, in the way of lovers of progress, that what is of immediate advantage to us must be a permanent benefit to the universe. Fighting in Vietnam in the interest, as we say and would have ourselves believe, of the Vietnamese people, we have destroyed their villages, their croplands, their forests, herded the people into concentration camps, and in every way diminished the possibility of life in that country; and the civilian casualties are vastly greater than the military. In order to protect ourselves against Russia or China, or whoever our enemy will be in ten years, we have prepared weapons the use of which will, we know, involve our own destruction and the destruction of the world as well. Great power has always been blinding to those who wield it.[10]

A great danger in this materialistic and mechanistic view of the universe is that even when we see the problems it has wrought, we often assume that the solutions are to be found only in the same material realm, perhaps because we forget to consider any other possibility. For example, in the many stories on the environment which have appeared in the business press recently, the most frequently cited reasons for our environmental ills are ignorance, inefficiency, misapplied technology, population growth, institutional inertia and lack of political will. All these reasons are true, but they are symptoms, not the root causes, of our failure to create a friendly and sustainable world.

Similarly, most proposals for cleaning up the environment focus on technical fixes. We want more miles-per-gallon, aerosols and refrigerants that don't destroy the ozone, more efficient homes and factories, and non-toxic pesticides. All these things will help. We have used science and technology to get us into this predicament and I think we will use science and technology to get us out.

But the greatest help and the only lasting solution to the violence we do to the world and to each other will arise from an ethic based on compassion and love rather than self-interest. Aldo Leopold's vision of a land-ethic is one expression of this truth: "In short, a land ethic changes the role of *Homo sapiens* from conqueror of the land community to plain member and citizen of it. It implies respect for his fellow-members, and also respect for the community as such."[11]

But the hour is late. The signs of our heedlessness, selfishness and fear are all about us. This beautiful earth, mother to us all, groans beneath the blows. The trends are worrisome rather than reassuring. For the first time in many generations our children are no longer confident of being able to live in a better world. Have we reached the end of hope?

I think not. We only reach the end of hope when we abandon our claim to being whole human beings. If we believe that the future will be simply a projection of past trends, then we yield it and ourselves helplessly to the notion that our destiny has already been determined by the destructive processes we have set in motion.[12]

We cannot assume that only one possible future lies before us without being guilty of idolatry, because to do so would amount to worshipping our present technological civilization, submitting to the thralldom of the machine rather than accepting our responsibility to control it. We would be guilty of forgetting the importance of human consciousness, of divine purposes and transcendent visions which might call us to a different destiny. There are many instances when the path of history has taken an unforeseeable turn because of the passions and convictions of dreamers, heroes and saints. We stand at such a place today and the earth calls us to recognize and create a new way forward.

Against the strength, even the apparent omnipotence, of the machine, we need to call forth a power that is greater still, the power of compassion and love. In place of self-interest let us cultivate selflessness. We must be willing to restore the primacy of the heart, and to make every intention and every action an expression of kindness and love.

In all the world's religions we find the ethic of loving kindness, compassion and relatedness. In some, this earth and all upon it are sacred because they are created by God: "The earth is the Lord's and the fulness thereof, the world and those who dwell therein . . ."; or because creation is a reflection of God's glory: "The heavens are telling the glory of God; and the firmament proclaims his handiwork." "O Lord, how manifold are thy works! In wisdom hast thou made them all; the earth is full of thy creatures."[13]

All creation is part of the divine, only differentiated by our power to respond. From the Hindu *Isha Upanishad*:

The Spirit moves, and it moves not. It is far, and it is near. It is within all, and it is outside all. Who sees all beings in his own Self, and his own Self in all beings, cannot hate. To the seer, all things have truly become the Self. What delusion, what sorrow, can there be for the one who sees this unity?

The words of Black Elk, a holy man of the Oglala Sioux:[14]

My friend, I am going to tell you the story of my life, as you wish; and if it were only the story of my life I think I would not tell it; for what is one man that he should make much of his winters, even when they bend him like a heavy snow? So many other men have lived and shall live that story, to be grass upon the hills.

It is the story of all life that is holy and is good to tell, and of us two-leggeds sharing it with the four leggeds and the wings of the air and all green things; for these are children of one mother and their father is one Spirit.

*A*nd from the great vision he had when he was a boy:

. . . I was seeing in a sacred manner the shapes of all things in the spirit, and the shape of all shapes as they must live together like one being. And I saw that the sacred hoop of my people was one of many hoops that made one circle, wide as daylight and as starlight, and in the center grew one mighty flowering tree to shelter all the children of one mother and one father. And I saw that it was holy.

*L*isten again to the voice of Chief Seattle:[15]

Every part of this earth is sacred to my people. Every shining pine needle, every sandy shore, every mist in the dark woods, every clearing and humming insect is holy in the memory and experience of my people. . . . We are part of the earth and it is part of us. The perfumed flowers are our sisters; the deer, the horse, the great eagle, these are our brothers. The rocky crests, the juices of the meadows, the body heat of the pony, and man—all belong to the same family. . . . What is man without the beasts? If all the beasts were gone, men would die from a great loneliness of spirit. For whatever happens to the beasts, soon happens to man. All things are connected.

Here is a metaphor from Saint Paul: "God has arranged the body so that . . . each part may be equally concerned for all the others. If one part is hurt, all parts are hurt with it."[16]

Ecologists know that everything is connected to everything else. That is one of Barry Commoner's "four laws of ecology." Other scientists also are moving towards an explanation of the universe as infinitely related. The new science of chaos and the mathematics of fractal geometry draw attention to this essential unity.[17]

Let me borrow a lesson from the teachings of a Buddhist monk, Thích Nhât Hanh:[18]

If you are a poet, you will see clearly that there is a cloud floating in this sheet of paper. Without a cloud, there will be no rain; without rain, the trees cannot grow; and without trees, we cannot make paper. The cloud is essential for the paper to exist. If the cloud is not here, the sheet of paper cannot be here either. So we can say that the cloud and the paper *inter-are*. "Interbeing" is a word that is not in the dictionary yet, but if we combine the prefix "inter-" with the verb "to be," we have a new verb, *inter-be*. Without a cloud, we cannot have paper, so we can say that the cloud and the sheet of paper inter-are.

If we look into this sheet of paper even more deeply, we can see the sunshine in it. If the sunshine is not there, the forest cannot grow. In fact, nothing can grow. Even we cannot grow without sunshine. And so, we know that the sunshine is also in this sheet of paper. The paper and the sunshine inter-are. And if we continue to look, we can see the logger who cut the tree and brought it to the mill to be transformed into paper. And we see the wheat. We know that the logger cannot exist without his daily bread, and therefore the wheat that became his bread is also in this sheet of paper. And the logger's father and mother are in it too. When we look in this way, we see that without all of these things, this sheet of paper cannot exist.

Looking even more deeply, we can see we are in it too. This is not difficult to see, because when we look at a sheet of paper, the sheet of paper is part of our perception. Your mind is in here and mine is also. So we can say that everything is in here with this sheet of paper. You cannot point out one thing that is not here—time, space, the earth, the rain, the minerals in the soil, the sunshine, the cloud, the river, the heat. Everything coexists with this sheet of paper. That is why I think the word inter-be should be in the dictionary. "To be" is to inter-be. You cannot just *be* by yourself alone. You have to inter-be with every other thing. This sheet of paper is, because everything else is.

This lesson on interdependence is at the heart of understanding. (In fact it is part of a commentary on the *Sutra* of the Heart of Wisdom.) Once you begin to see the world in this way, you are forever changed. At first you may think that seeing yourself as one with all that is might put an intolerably heavy burden on you. If everything is everything else, then everyone is responsible for everyone else too; and everyone's suffering is also our own. But this *is* the truth which sets you free, because now you know who you are and what you can do. From this heart of wisdom come compassion and loving kindness to all.

The violence we wreak on the earth is a kind of hatred done in ignorance, and it comes back to haunt us in many ways. We poison the soil, water and air, and they in turn poison us. We build terrifying arsenals, and live in fear.

But when we live fully aware of the creation and the web of life in which we humans are but a strand, we will begin to do unto the earth as we would have done unto us. It is ignorance which drives us apart from creation.

When we accept the earth as our home and mother, and all the inhabitants as our kin, then we will be able to find the peace which now eludes us. Black Elk's prayer was, "Grandfather, Great Spirit, give me the strength to walk the soft earth, a relative to all that is!"[19]

Our new awareness brings both joy and suffering, because the new-found kinship demands new responsibility. When we accept the responsibility of seeing, we learn how to love. Let me turn to Thích Nhât Hanh again:[20]

At the beginning of each meal, I recommend that you look at your plate and silently recite, "My plate is empty now, but I know that it is going to be filled with delicious food in just a moment." While waiting to be served or to serve yourself, I suggest you breathe three times and look at it even more deeply, "At this very moment many, many people around the world are also holding a plate, but their plate is going to be empty for a long time." Forty thousand children die each day because of the lack of food. Children alone. We can be very happy to have such wonderful food, but we also suffer because we are capable of seeing. But when we see in this way, it makes us sane, because the way in front of us is clear—the way to live so that we can make peace with ourselves and with the world. When we see the good and the bad, the wondrous and the deep suffering, we have to live in a way that we can make peace between ourselves and the world.

Seeing more clearly and the transcendence of self are the most fundamental teachings of all religions. Truly to restore the earth we must first restore ourselves. The inner and outer worlds are inseparable. They must be in harmony. Here is the prayer of a Sufi (Muslim) mystic, Ansari of Herat:[21]

Watch vigilantly the state of thine own mind.
Love of God begins in harmlessness.

Know that the Prophet built an external *kaaba*
Of clay and water,
And an inner *kaaba* in life and heart.
The outer *kaaba* was built by Abraham, the holy;
The inner is sanctified by the glory of God himself.

On the path of God
Two places of worship mark the stages,
The material temple
And the temple of the heart.
Make your best endeavor
To worship at the temple of the heart.

A heedless person cannot bring caring to the world. A fearful person cannot see clearly; a selfish person does not embrace the wholeness of all creation and an angry person does not bring peace to the world. We must ourselves be whole and healthy if we would heal the earth. Its peace begins with ours, at home, in our daily lives, in our peaceful hearts.

The healing of creation will not be accomplished by the judicious application of technology alone, but by a commitment which must be as intense as any religious faith. Our personal commitment to spiritual growth will lead us to ecologically responsible behavior, because it will make clear the interrelatedness of all beings.

In fact caring for creation is a commitment for which the religions of the world provide the essential teachings. Faced with unprecedented global environmental and social crises, the challenge to us all is to recover the meaning of those teachings for today, to renew our kinship with all creation, to restore the primacy of spiritual values and of communal and personal spiritual growth, and to rediscover the simple truths: that there is no separateness and therefore there can be no selfishness, and that compassion for all is the heart of understanding.

Let me close with a poem by Gerard Manley Hopkins, an English mystic poet of the late 19th century.

PIED BEAUTY

Glory be to God for dappled things
   For skies of couple-colour as a brindled cow;
     For rose-moles all in stipple upon trout that swim;
Fresh-firecoal chestnut-falls; finches' wings;
   Landscape plotted and pieced—
       fold, fallow and plough;
    And áll trádes, their gear and tackle and trim.
All things counter, original, spare, strange;
   Whatever is fickle, freckled (who knows how?)
     With swift, slow; sweet, sour; adazzle, dim;
He fathers-forth whose beauty is past change:
     Praise him.

NOTES

This essay is adapted from a lecture given on July 21, 1990, at the conference on "Spiritual Values in the Global Village," at Vivekananda Monastery, Ganges, Michigan.

1. United Nations Department of International Economic and Social Affairs, *World Demographic Estimates and Projections, 1950–2025* (New York, 1988), cited in *The Economist*, January 20, 1990.

2. *The Economist*, September 2, 1989. A poll in April, 1990 by *The Wall Street Journal*/NBC News indicated that 86 percent of respondents want to protect the environment even if it means they will have to pay higher prices. (*The Wall Street Journal*, April 20, 1990.)

3. Lester Brown, *et al.*, *State of the World, 1990* (New York: Norton, 1990)

4. *Ibid.*

5. Lester Brown, *et al.*, *State of the World, 1989* (New York: Norton, 1989)

6. Matthew, 6:21

7. See Paul Bohannan, "The Impact of Money on an African Subsistence Economy," *Journal of Economic History*, XIX (1959), 491–503; and Paul Bohannan, "Africa's Land," *The Centennial Review*, IV (1960), 439–449.

8. *Chief Seattle's Testimony* (London: Pax Christi & Friends of the Earth, 1976)

9. Nicholas Georgescu-Roegen, *The Entropy Law and the Economic Process* (Cambridge: Heard University Press, 1971); E. F. Schumacher, *Small Is Beautiful* (New York: Harper, 1973); Herman Daly, ed., *Toward a Steady-State Economy* (San Francisco: Freeman, 1973); Herman Daly, *Steady State Economics* (San Francisco: Freeman, 1977); and Herman Daly & John Cobb, Jr., *For the Common Good* (Boston: Beacon Press, 1989).

10. Wendell Berry, "A Secular Pilgrimage," in *A Continuous Harmony* (New York: Harcourt Brace Jovanovich, 1975) pp.10–11.

11. Aldo Leopold, "The Land Ethic" in *A Sand County Almanac* (New York: Ballantine, 1970) p.240.

12. See Lewis Mumford, "Prospect," in W. L. Thomas, ed., *Man's Role in Changing the Face of the Earth* (Chicago: University of Chicago Press, 1956) pp.1141–1152.

13. From Psalms 24, 19 and 104.

14. John G. Neihardt, *Black Elk Speaks* (New York: Pocket Books, 1972), pp.1, 36.

15. *Chief Seattle's Testimony*

16. 1 Corinthians, 12:24–26. Christianity has been criticized for emphasizing separation between humans and creation and for teaching that creation is subservient and intended for humankind's use and enjoyment. See Lynn White, Jr., "The Historical Roots of Our Ecologic Crisis," *Science*, v. 155 (1967), pp.1203–1207. The first two chapters of Genesis appear to support these views, although there are also thoughtful contrary interpretations. The true picture is more complex. Attitudes towards the environment are rooted in the secular culture as well as in religion, and neither the West nor Christianity have any monopoly on environmental damage or disrespect.

The Christian mystical tradition reveals the sense of relatedness and responsibility for creation. From a sermon by Meister Eckhart: "Though we talk about human beings, we are speaking at the same time of all creatures, for Christ himself said to his disciples: 'Go forth and preach the gospel to all creatures.' God poured his being in equal measure to all creatures, to each as much as it can receive. This is a good lesson for us that we should love all creatures equally with everything which we have received from God. . . . So God loves all creatures equally and fills them with his being. And we should lovingly meet all creatures in the same way." (Matthew Fox, *Breakthrough: Meister Eckhart's Creation Spirituality in New Translation* [New York: Doubleday, Image Books, 1980], p.92.)

Many Christians are deeply sensitive to the tensions between Christian doctrine and a creation in urgent need of healing. See, for examples: Gerald Barney, "The Future of the Creation: The Central Challenge for Theologians," *Word & World*, v. 4 (1984), pp.422–429; William E. Gibson, *Keeping and Healing the Creation* (Louisville, Kentucky: Presbyterian Church [USA], Eco-Justice Task Force, 1989); Thomas Beny, *The Dream of The Earth* (San Francisco: Sierra Club, 1988); Matthew Fox, *Original Blessing* (Santa Fe, NM: Bear, 1983).

17. Barry Commoner, *The Closing Circle* (New York: Knopf, 1971); see also Benoit B. Mandelbrot, *The Fractal Geometry of Nature* (New York: Freeman, 1983); James Gleick, *Chaos* (New York: Viking, 1987).

18. Thích Nhât Hanh, *The Heart of Understanding* (Berkeley, California: Parallax Press, 1988), pp.3–4. This is a commentary on the *Maha Prajñaparamita Hridaya Sutra*.

19. Neihardt, p.5.

20. Nhât Hanh, p.54.

21. Abdullah al-Ansari al-Harawi (d. 1088). This translation is by Sardar Sir Jogendra Singh, quoted in Eknath Easwaran, *God Makes the Rivers to Flow* (Petaluma, California: Nilgiri Press, 1982), p.55.

The Role of the Faith Traditions

Dr. Gerald O. Barney, Jane Blewett and Kristen R. Barney

MILLENNIUM INSTITUTE *(formerly named the Institute for 21st Century Studies)*

As part of the preparation for the Parliament of the World's Religions, the Millennium Institute prepared a substantial report on the critical issues of the 21st century. Titled *Global 2000 Revisited: What Shall We Do?*, this report was presented to several conferences in association with the Critical Issues Working Group of the Parliament. The book's contents identify and analyze a number of issues in detail; its scientifically-derived projections, based on extensive research and consultation, compel us to take these issues seriously. In addition, the authors raise fundamental questions and perspectives about the role of faith traditions in both the origin and resolution of these global concerns. The excerpts below present some of the challenges and questions that Dr. Barney, Ms. Blewett, Ms. Barney and the Council for a Parliament of the World's Religions are addressing to religious and spiritual leaders and to the congregations of the Earth. *–Ed.*

*W*e humans have begun asking questions about "sustainable development." This is an important question, but it does not go deep enough. We must also begin asking questions about "sustainable faith."

Is there a faith tradition in existence today that is practicing a way of life that provides "progress" for the whole community of life, not just the human species? Is there a faith tradition such that if everyone on earth suddenly adopted it, the human future on Earth would be assured? . . .

Sir Shridath Ramphal, former secretary general of the Commonwealth and foreign minister of Guyana, has implicitly raised this same question in the context of the "holy texts of many religions." He writes as follows in the official report prepared for the opening of the United Nations Conference on Environment and Development:

> In the language of the Independent Commission on International Humanitarian Issues. . . , the holy texts of many religions, not to mention legal traditions, philosophies and customs ". . . abound in moral injunctions that imply an ethic of human solidarity. . . . For centuries, the great religious texts have taught the essential oneness of the human race." What scriptures have not always taught is that nature is the loom on which is woven life's seamless fabric of which humanity is a significant, but not unduly dominant, part.[64]

The God I know is still speaking, and there have been at least four new revelations.

First, has been revealed that among the most destructive forces on Earth today is hatred between the followers of different faith traditions. Of the almost 50 armed conflicts in progress currently, the vast majority are motivated in significant part by hatred of the followers of one faith for the followers of another faith.[65] The arms industry—the largest industry in the world, larger even than illegal drugs and oil—is supported in significant part by the hatred of the followers of one faith for the followers of another faith.

Examples of the destructiveness of interreligious hatred are found almost daily in all major newspapers. . . . What faith is now *not* involved in acts of hatred and violence in one or more of the ethnic and religious wars currently in progress?[67]

The second new revelation comes from a 1,500-year meditation on Earth, a meditation we usually call "science." From this meditation we know that Earth is the product of a 15-billion year journey from the first burst of

Goals of the Critical Issues Working Group

"The objective of the Parliament and the later work of the Council and the Institute for 21st Century Studies [now Millennium Institute] *is to initiate a process of religious and scientific dialogue on critical issues that could change the course of history. There are, of course, more modest but still significant results that may be expected from the work. Two are especially important:*

An advance in the dialogue between science and religion. . . .

An advance on what is perhaps **the** *critical issue. . . interreligious intolerance and divisiveness on matters critical to the planetary future."*

excerpted from a paper titled "The Critical Issues: A Partnership Project of the Council for a Parliament of the World's Religions and the Institute for 21st Century Studies." (Revised 11/10/91)

creative energy. We know that we humans and all other life on Earth are intimately connected through a single, integral and continuing creation journey and that we humans are related genetically to everything that contains the DNA molecule: to eagles, apes, snakes, frogs, trees, grasses, molds, bacteria . . . . We are all cousins, and we all depend on each other through the complex bio-geo-chemical cycles of Earth. Earth is not just our home; we are Earth. Our entire physical being is made up of bits and pieces of Earth—water, air, rice, potatoes, etc.—and we, collectively, are an important part of the consciousness of Earth.[68]

The third revelation is that five billion of us individual humans, both poor and affluent, are acting today in ways that are destroying the life sustaining capabilities of Earth and thereby destroying our own prospects. Nothing survives now—no person, no species, no lake, no river, no ocean, no forest, no soil, no mountain, not even the atmosphere—unless we humans will it so.

The fourth revelation is that we humans—not as individuals, but as a species—will exercise an enormous influence on the future of Earth. There is little question that we can destroy our species and many others with us. We can create an Earth future without humans. We might also create an Earth future in which there is a rich and mutually enhancing Earth-human relationship. In effect, we humans have become co-creators with the Divine of the future of the Earth.

This fourth revelation is of some considerable import, but to my knowledge, no faith tradition has prepared us for it. No faith anticipated the development of human power over Earth's future, this enormous responsibility. To my knowledge, no faith tradition has prepared us to know ourselves not as individuals but as a species. To my knowledge, no faith tradition has provided moral precepts to guide inter-species behavior, to decide which species should cease to exist, which new species shall be created through genetic engineering (and then patented), and to judge the alternative futures humans are considering for Earth.[69]

Where can we turn with questions that deal with matters of ultimate meaning and direction, with cherished beliefs, with fears and insecurities about the future? Where can we turn to learn to act responsibly as a species? Where can we turn for insights into what possibilities there might be for a mutually enhancing human-Earth relationship in the future? Where can we turn for insights into what the original creative energy might desire our species—humans collectively—to make of Earth?

These are fundamentally spiritual questions, and they are being raised openly today in many communities, by scientists and economists, by philosphers and theologians, by historians and anthropologists, by religious and secular leaders alike.[70] Such questions are in the hearts of ordinary men and women who wonder about the future for all life and wonder how to answer their children's questions.

The questions being raised are unique to the experience and consciousness of peoples of our time, peoples who have looked into the farthest reaches of space, seen back in time to the very origins of the cosmos, have come to know Earth to be a relatively small planet in a galaxy of billions of stars and planets in a cosmos of billions of galaxies; people who have probed the core of the atom, lived with the prospect of nuclear annihilation, and now face the possibility of ecological annihilation. The questions are welling up from the human spirit struggling to be faithful to the moment. So, in hope and trust, we turn to you, the carriers of our spiritual wisdom, with our questions.

Questions for our spiritual leaders

What are the traditional teachings—and the range of other opinions—within your faith on how to meet the legitimate needs of the growing human community without destroying the ability of Earth to support the community of all life?

- What does your faith tradition teach about how the needs of the poor are to be met as human numbers continue to grow? What is the cause of human poverty?
- How are the needs and wants of humans to be weighed relative to the survival of other forms of life?

What are the traditional teachings—and the range of other opinions—within your faith on the meaning of "progress" and how it is to be achieved?

- What does your faith tradition teach about the human destiny? Is the human destiny separable from that of the Earth?
- What is your destiny, the destiny of the followers of your faith tradition? What does your faith tradition teach concerning the followers of other traditions?
- How are we to measure "progress?" Can there be progress for the human community without progress for the whole community of life?

What are the traditional teachings—and the range of other opinions—within your faith tradition concerning a proper relationship with those who differ in race or gender (conditions one cannot change), and culture, politics or faith?

- Much hatred and violence is carried out in the name of religion. What teachings of your faith tradition have been used—correctly or not—in an attempt to justify such practices?
- Discrimination and even destructive behavior of men toward women is often justified in the name of religion. Which, if any, of the teachings of your faith have been used—correctly or incorrectly—in this way?
- How does your faith tradition characterize the teachings and followers of other faiths? Do some adherents of your tradition hold that the teachings and followers of other faiths are evil, dangerous, misguided? Is there any possibility that your faith tradition can derive wisdom, truth or insight from the teachings of another faith?

What are the traditional teachings—and the range of other opinions—within your faith on the possibility of new revelation, new understanding, new interpretation, new wisdom and new truth concerning human activity affecting the future of Earth?

- Does your faith tradition envision and provide for the criticism, correction, reinterpretation and even rejection of ancient traditional assumptions and "truth" in light of new understandings or revelations?

NOTES

64. Ramphal, Shridath. 1992. *Our Country, The Planet: Forging a Partnership for Survival.* Washington, DC: Island Press. pp.202–203

65. Binder, D. and Crossette, B. "As Ethnic Wars Multiply, U.S. Strives for a Policy." *The New York Times.* February 7, 1993. p.A1

. . .

67. For a list of the 48 religious and ethnic wars now in progress on every continent, see: Binder, D. and Crossette, B. "As Ethnic Wars Multiply, U.S. Strives for a Policy." *The New York Times.* February 7, 1993. p.A1

68. See Swimme, Brian and Berry, Thomas. 1992 *The Universe Story;* Cloud, Preston. *Oasis in Space: A History of the Planet from the Beginning.* Cambridge University Press; Campra, Fritjof and Steindle-Rast, David. *Belonging to the Universe.* HarperCollins. 1991; and Wilson, E.O. *The Discovery of Life.* Belknap-Harvard.

69. While no faith tradition has gone very far in developing inter-species ethics and morality, a few individuals have made significant steps in this direction. See, for example: J. Engel, Ronald, and Engel, Joan Gibb, eds. 1992. *Ethics of Environment and Development: Global Challenge and International Response.* University of Arizona Press.

70. For examples of questions being raised by others, see: Forrester, J.W. 1971. "Churches at the Transition Between Growth and World Equilibrium." In: Forrester, J.W. 1975. *Collected Papers of Jay W. Forrester.* Cambridge, MA: The M.I.T. Press. pp. 255–269; Shiva, V. 1989. *Staying Alive: Women, Ecology, and Development.* London: Zed Books; Spretnak, C. 1991. *States of Grace: The Recovery of Meaning in the Postmodern Age.* San Francisco: Harper Collins; Hardin, G. 1963. "A Second Sermon on the Mount." *Perspectives in Biology and Medicine.* vol. vi, no. 3, Spring 1963; Hardin, G. 1968. "The Tragedy of the Commons." *Science,* vol. 162, December 13, 1968. pp.1243–1248; Vickers, G. 1970. *Freedom in a Rocking Boat: Changing Values in an Unstable Society.* Middlesex, England: Pelican Books.

For more information, contact:

Millennium Institute
1611 North Kent Street, Suite 204
Arlington, Virginia 22209-2111 USA

TEL: (703) 841-0048;
FAX: (703) 841-0050

To purchase books, contact:

Public Interest Publications
P.O. Box 229
Arlington, Virginia 22210 USA

TEL: (800) 537-9359 (US, Canada and Mexico)
(703) 243-2252 (elsewhere)
FAX: (703) 243-2489

Religions of the World

A. INDIGENOUS RELIGIONS: African Traditional Religions; First Peoples; Native Americans; Shintoism

B. WORLD RELIGIONS: Bahá'ísm; Buddhism; Christianity; Confucianism; Hinduism; Islam; Jainism; Judaism; Sikhism; Taoism; Zoroastrianism

C. (Some) FAMILIES, MOVEMENTS AND BRANCHES

Many thanks are due to the authors of these essays for their gracious responses to our invitation to make this contribution to the Parliament and to interreligious dialogue. They have written not as official representatives, and not primarily as scholars (though most of them are), but, in the majority of cases, as knowledgeable and committed participants in the traditions they describe. Their willingness to write to a pre-determined structure, on short notice and despite very busy schedules is testimony to the significance they attach to the Parliament and its goals. In addition to the essays, most authors also provided selections of scriptures, prayers or commentary valued by their traditions, and some even made original translations.

In so few pages it is impossible, of course, to provide for the diversity of the religious traditions of the earth. Imbalances regarding which traditions are included (or not), and weaknesses in the categorization are also the result of a complex and timebound process. (The Editor will redress weaknesses if future printings seem in order.)

Criteria used for representation include one or more of the following: 1) the historic, worldwide religious traditions; 2) representative indigenous traditions; 3) a presence at the first Parliament and the present one; 4) engagement in interfaith dialogue or with the critical global issues; and 5) influential movements rooted in the historic religions with a significant presence in North America. Finally, representation was also limited to those whom the Editor could reach and who could respond quickly with an essay.

The authors of new articles were invited to write short essays—portraits of the traditions—on the following: 1) Origins, beliefs, symbols and census; 2) Approach to interfaith dialogue and participation in it; 3) Critical issues and responses to them; 4) Scriptures, prayers, commentary or wisdom relating to the above.

In some cases the Editor has also included previously printed articles, reflections, scriptures or prayers which provide further insight into the self-understanding of some members of the tradition. All materials are intended to add depth to our understanding of the religions and to provide insights from them related to the challenges and opportunities we face today. *–Ed.*

The community of religions has many wondrous and under-utilized gifts among its members! The commitment, the organizational and motivational resources at their disposal, the wisdom and the insight in their heritages, and their practical experience with real life issues are a substantial cultural and spiritual legacy. Religious and spiritual leaders—and the laity as well—have the opportunity and responsibility now to bring these gifts to assemblies of the religions, to the councils of diplomacy and to the meeting rooms of corporate enterprise—for the well-being of the community of the Earth.

JOEL BEVERSLUIS, editor of
A SourceBook for the Community of Religions

A. INDIGENOUS RELIGIONS

Zulu Traditional Religion of Southern Africa

Lizo Doda Jafta

Lecturer at the Federal Theological Seminary of Southern Africa, Natal

"One of the basic human experiences is that a human being is a dependent creature; therefore, the contingency of being human demands that one should properly relate oneself to the environment upon which one depends. Thus the human sense of dependence becomes the root religion.

"One becomes aware that one did not create the universe; one found the universe already created. This awe-inspiring universe with its boundless spaces and measureless forces occasions God-consciousness. Natural events in particular are occasions of God-consciousness among the Zulu people. The changes in the clouds, the highness of the heavens, the overflowing rivers, the frightening lightnings and thunderstorms side-by-side with religious ceremonies are all occasions of God-consciousness. In these events God is experienced as the One, the Other, the Divine and the Many. The key word is experience. . . .

". . . The Zulu notion of God-consciousness . . . says that God lives in, through and beyond everything and everyone, but that God is most clearly apprehended through those spirits who are always around, below, above and in them . . . . When the Zulus see the Deity in every place and all the time, they are acknowledging the ubiquitous nature of God as well as their constant sojourn with the realm of the divine presence."

excerpted from "The One, the Other, the Divine, the Many in Zulu Traditional Religion of Southern Africa" in *Dialogue and Alliance,* Summer 1992, pp.79–89.

PORTRAITS OF
African Traditional Religions

An Introduction

Rev. Dr. Abraham Akrong

THE TERM

Since the time of Pliny the elder, who is reputed to have first used it, the term "Africa" has been a bone of contention because it means different things to different people: For many people Africa is essentially a racial group; for some, Africa is a geo-political entity carved up in the last century at the Berlin conference of 1884–85; for others, Africa is a linguistic-cultural entity that describes the life of the African peoples that belong to these communities: The Niger-Congo, the Nilo-Sahara, the Afro-Asiatic and the Khoisan linguistic groups.

Generally, today, we are conditioned to view Africa as a conglomeration of different ethnic groups bound together by the colonial divisions of Africa which still persist today, in independent Africa.

THE CONCEPT OF AFRICAN RELIGION

Related to this geo-political and cultural view of Africa is the 19th-century classification based on the so-called evolutionary theory of culture and religion. This classification of religions based on belief systems puts African religion and culture on the lowest level of the evolutionary ladder, because, it was believed, African primitive culture can only produce the most elementary and primitive belief systems. Until recently, this treatment of African religions in the Western intellectual tradition has made it impossible for African traditional religion to speak for itself except in terms of 19th-century evolutionism or the Western anthropological theories of primitive religions and cultures.

FROM HISTORY TO CULTURE

Today the liberation from the classifications of the last century has given an intellectual autonomy to African religion and culture. They can now be understood as self-contained systems that are internally coherent without reference to any grand theories. This has allowed us to face up to the plurality of religions and cultures. Therefore in any discourse about African religion we must start from the perspective of the worshipers and devotees of African traditional religion.

AFRICAN RELIGION FROM WITHIN

A study of the beliefs and practices of the African peoples leads to the theological observation that African traditional religion is a religion of salvation and wholeness. A careful analysis shows an emphasis on this-worldly salvation and wholeness as the *raison d'etre* of African traditional religion. Because Africans believe that life is a complex web of relationships that may either enhance and preserve life or diminish and destroy it, the goal of religion is to maintain those relationships that protect and preserve life. For it is the harmony and stability provided by these relationships, both spiritual and material, that create the conditions for well-being and wholeness.

The threat to life both physical and spiritual is the premise of the quest for

Prayers and Religious Expression

Dr. Darrol Bryant

Professor of Religion, Waterloo University, and a Presiding Council Member, Inter Religious Federation for World Peace

*T*he expressions of African traditional religion are manifold. They have shaped the lives of African peoples from the dawn of history down to the present time. They have lived as oral traditions in the memory and practice of countless generations. The name of God varies across traditions as do the names of the divinities and the practices of the spiritual life. The Nuer of East Africa, for example, believe that prayer is appropriate at any time because "they like to speak to God when they are happy."

A typical Nuer prayer is:

Our Father, it is thy universe, it is thy will,
let us be at peace,
let the soul of thy people be cool.
Thou art our Father,
remove all evil from our path.

For African traditional religion there is a daily intercourse between the living and the dead, the ancestral spirits. The interaction with these realities is facilitated through prayers, rites, incantations and libations. Many of these practices involve elements of nature such as water, foodstuffs like cassava or nuts, or animals like chickens in sacrificial rites. Yoruba practices involve all types of foods and drinks in their offerings. A Yoruba chant cries out:

O God of heaven, O God of earth,
I pray thee uphold my hand,
My ancestors and ancestresses
Lean upon earth and succour me
That I may not quickly come to you.

This tradition celebrates the spirits present in the natural world and seeks to maintain proper relations between the living community and the living cosmos. Drums and dancing often figure prominently in its rites and practices. There is often a great concern for healing and health. Expressions of this tradition are too diverse to allow easy generalizations.

previously printed in the General Programme,
IRFWP New Delhi Congress, 1993

INTRODUCTION, continued

salvation. The threat is so near and real because, for the African, life is a continuum of power points that are transformed into being and life is constantly under threat from evil forces. This logic of the relationality of being and cosmic life gives rise to the view that all reality is inter-related like a family. This same relational metaphysics is what undergirds the life of the individual in community.

INDIVIDUAL IN COMMUNITY

J. S. Mbiti captures this relational metaphysics succinctly in the dictum: "I am because we are and because we are therefore I am." The life of the individual comes into fruition through the social ritual of rites of passage. These rites are the process that can help the individual to attain to the goals of his or her destiny, given at birth by God. Those who successfully go through the rites of passage become candidates for ancestorhood—the goal of the ideal life. For the African, ancestors are much more than dead parents of the living. They are the embodiment of what it means to live the full life that is contained in one's destiny.

GOD, CREATION AND COSMIC LIFE

*G*od in Africa is a relational being who is known through various levels of relationship with creation. In relation to humanity, God is the great ancestor of the human race. Therefore, all over Africa God is portrayed more in terms of parent than as sovereign. In relation to the earth, God is a husband who stands behind the creative fecundity of the earth that sustains human life. God in relation to creation is the creator from whom life flows and is sustained. In relation to the divinities, God is their father who requires them to care for the cosmic processes.

UNITY AND DIVERSITY

*T*he various elements of African religion that make what I call the transcendental structure of African religion are expressed differently by the various African peoples on the basis of their social organization and environment.

A DEFINITION

*O*ne can describe African religion as a this-worldly religion of salvation that promises well-being and wholeness here and now. It is a religion that affirms life and celebrates life in its fullness; this accounts for the lively and celebrative mood that characterizes African worship in all its manifestations. ✥

A PORTRAIT OF
The First Peoples

Some of what follows was written by representatives of indigenous peoples; some was provided by non-indigenous people. Texts and quotations identified with the citation *Burger*, are from *The Gaia Atlas of First Peoples: A Future for the Indigenous World,* by Julian Burger with the assistance of campaigning groups and native peoples worldwide, some of whom are quoted below. –*Ed.*

**THE FIRST PEOPLES
in the FOURTH WORLD**

Julian Burger explains (in *The Gaia Atlas Of First Peoples*) that there is no universally agreed name for the peoples he describes as:

"*first peoples, because their ancestors were the original inhabitants of the lands, since colonized by foreigners. Many territories continue to be so invaded. The book also calls them indigenous, a term widely accepted by the peoples themselves, and now adopted by the United Nations.*"

BURGER, p.16

"*Fourth World is a term used by the World Council of Indigenous Peoples to distinguish the way of life of indigenous peoples from those of the First (highly industrialized), Second (Socialist bloc) and Third (developing) worlds. The First, Second and Third Worlds believe that 'the land belongs to the people'; the Fourth World believes that 'the people belong to the land.'*"

BURGER, p.18

*F*irst peoples see existence as a living blend of spirits, nature and people. All are one, inseparable and interdependent—a holistic vision shared with mystics throughout the ages. The word for religion does not exist in many cultures, as it is so closely integrated into life itself. For many indigenous peoples spirits permeate matter—they animate it. This led the early anthropologists to refer to such beliefs as "animist." (Burger, p.64)

Myths that explain the origins of the world remind people of their place in the universe and of their connection with the past. Some are humorously ironic, others complex and esoteric. Some, notably Aboriginal Dreamtime, speak of the creation of the hills, rocks, hollows and rivers formed by powerful ancestral spirits in the distant past. Others describe a dramatic split between the gods and humankind or the severance of the heavens and the Earth—as in the sudden separation of the Sky Father and Earth Mother in Maori legend. Others tell the story of how the earth was peopled, as in the sacred book of the Maya of Central America. Myths invest life with meaning. The rich symbolic associations found in the oral traditions of many indigenous cultures bring the sacred into everyday life—through a pipe, a feather, a rattle, a color even—and help individuals to keep in touch with both themselves and the spirit world. (Burger, p.66)

Indigenous peoples are strikingly diverse in their culture, religion, and social and economic organization. Yet, today as in the past, they are prey to stereotyping by the outside world. By some they are idealized as the embodiment of spiritual values; by others they are denigrated as an obstacle impeding economic progress. But they are neither: they are people who cherish their own distinct cultures, are the victims of past and present-day colonialism, and are determined to survive. Some live according to their traditions, some receive welfare, others work in factories, offices or the professions. As well as their diversity, there are some shared values and experiences among indigenous cultures. . . .

By understanding how they organize their societies, the wider society may learn to recognize that they are not at some primitive stage of development, but are thoughtful and skillful partners of the natural world, who can help all people to reflect on the way humanity treats the environment and our fellow creatures. (Burger, p. 15)

Partners toward a sustainable future

*A*s we awaken our consciousness that humankind and the rest of nature are inseparably linked, we will need to look to the world's more than 250 million indigenous peoples. They are the guardians of the extensive and fragile ecosystems that are vital to the wellbeing of the planet. Indigenous peoples have evolved over many centuries a judicious balance between their needs and those of nature. The notion of

A PORTRAIT OF
Native American Spirituality

Robert Staffanson

Executive Director, American Indian Institute

*N*ote a dictionary's definition of spirituality: "devotion to spiritual (i.e. metaphysical) things instead of worldly things." This definition does not apply to Native Americans because they do not recognize a dichotomy between "spiritual" and material things.

A simplistic definition of Native American spirituality would be that it is the opposite of pragmatism (i.e. short-term concern with "practical" results). While Native American spirituality is not easily defined, it has several defining characteristics:

a) **Recognition of the interconnectedness of all Creation**, and the responsibility of human beings to use their intelligence in protecting that interconnectedness. That applies particularly to the lifegiving elements: water, air and soil.

b) **A belief that all life is equal**, and that the presence of the life spark implies a degree of spirituality whether in humans, animals or plants. In their view the species of animals and birds, as well as forests and other plant life, have as much "right" to existence as human beings, and should not be damaged or destroyed. That does not mean that they cannot be used but that use has limitations.

c) **Their primary concern is with the long-term welfare of life rather than with short-term expediency or comfort.** They consider all issues and actions in relationship to their long-term effect on all life, not just human life.

d) **Their spirituality is undergirded by thankfulness to the Creator.** Prayer, ceremonies, meditation and fasting are an important part of their lives. But they ask for nothing. They give thanks: for all forms of life and for all the elements that make life possible, and they are concerned with the continuation of that life and the ingredients upon which it depends.

Traditional Native Americans believe that any of their people who lack spirituality are no longer Indian. Traditional Native Americans do not see any spirituality in our "western" world. They believe that we have a kind of mindless materialism that is destroying both us and the world we live in. ✵

VOICES OF INDIGENOUS PEOPLES: The Earth

"Every part of the earth is sacred to my people. Every shining pine needle, every sandy shore, every mist in the dark woods, every clearing and humming insect is holy in the memory and experience of my people."

A DUWAMISH CHIEF (Burger)

"The Earth is the foundation of Indigenous Peoples, it is the seat of spirituality, the fountain from which our cultures and languages flourish. The Earth is our historian, the keeper of events and the bones of our forefathers. Earth provides us with food, medicine, shelter and clothing. It is the source of our independence, it is our Mother. We do not dominate her; we must harmonize with her."

HAYDEN BURGESS,
native Hawaiian (Burger)

"One has only to develop a relationship with a certain place, where the land knows you and experience that the trees, the Earth and Nature are extending their love and light to you to know there is so much we can receive from the Earth to fill our hearts and souls."

INTI MELASQUEZ,
Inca Shaman (Burger)

---

sustainability, now recognized as the framework for our future development, is an integral part of most indigenous cultures.

In the last decades, indigenous peoples have suffered from the consequences of some of the most destructive aspects of our development. They have been separated from their traditional lands and ways of life, deprived of their means of livelihood, and forced to fit into societies in which they feel like aliens. They have protested and resisted. Their call is for control over their own lives, the space to live and the freedom to live their own ways. And it is a call not merely to save their own territories, but the Earth itself.

While no one would suggest that the remainder of the more than five billion people on our planet would live at the level of indigenous societies, it is equally clear that we cannot pursue our present course of development. Nor can we rely on technology to provide an easy answer. What modern civilization has gained in knowledge, it has perhaps lost in sagacity. The indigenous peoples of the world retain our collective evolutionary experience and insights which have slipped our grasp. Yet these hold critical lessons for our future. Indigenous peoples are thus indispensable partners as we try to make a successful transition to a more secure and sustainable future on our precious planet.

MAURICE F. STRONG,
excerpted from the *Foreword* to *The Gaia Atlas of First Peoples*, by Julian Burger.

"Man is an aspect of nature, and nature itself is a manifestation of primordial religion. Even the word 'religion' makes an unnecessary separation, and there is no word for it in the Indian tongues. Nature is the 'Great Mysterious,' the 'religion before religion,' the profound intuitive apprehension of the true nature of existence attained by sages of all epochs, everywhere on Earth; the whole universe is sacred, man is the whole universe, and the religious ceremony is life itself, the common acts of every day."

PETER MATTHIESSEN,
Indian Country (Burger)

"We Indian people are not supposed to say, this land is mine. We only use it. It is the white man who buys land and puts a fence around it. Indians are not supposed to do that, because the land belongs to all Indians, it belongs to God, as you call it. The land is a part of our body, and we are a part of the land."

BUFFALOE TIGER,
Miccosukee (Burger)

"When the last red man has vanished from the Earth, and the memory is only a shadow of a cloud moving across the prairie, these shores and forests will still hold the spirits of my people, for they love this Earth as the newborn loves its mother's heartbeat."

SEALTH,
a Duwamish chief (Burger)

"When Indians referred to animals as 'people'—just a different sort of person from Man—they were not being quaint. Nature to them was a community of such 'people' for whom they had a great deal of genuine regard and with whom they had a contractual relationship to protect one another's interests and to fulfill their mutual needs. Man and Nature, in short, was joined by compact—not by ethical ties—a compact predicated on mutual esteem. This was the essence of the traditional land relationship."

OJIBWAY MAGAZINE

ECONOMY, WEALTH AND A WAY OF LIFE

*T*he economic life of indigenous people is based not on competition but on cooperation, for survival is only possible when the community works together. Most small-scale indigenous societies have elaborate systems for sharing food, possessions, and ritualizing conflict. . . . Indigenous forms of economy cannot, of course, satisfy the needs of a burgeoning world population now nearing six billion. But the knowledge and, especially, the values of the peoples practicing them are vital. The scientific community has recently begun research into indigenous skills in resource management. But it is, above all, wisdom that is needed in Western culture—we all need to learn respect for the Earth, conservation of resources, equitable distribution of wealth, harmony, balance and modest cooperation. In 1928 Gandhi wrote:

"God forbid that India should ever take to industrialism after the manner of the West . . . It would strip the world bare like locusts." (Burger, p.42)

"An Innu hunter's prestige comes not from the wealth he accumulates but from what he gives away. When a hunter kills caribou or other game he shares with everyone else in the camp."

DANIEL ASHINI, Innu (Burger)

WAR AND PEACE

" 'Was it an awful war?'
'It was a terrible war.'
'Were many people killed?'
'One man was killed.'
'What did you do?'
'We decided that those of us who had done the killing should never meet again because we were not fit to meet one another.'"

SAN describing a war
to Laurens van der Post (Burger)

In Papua New Guinea hostilities between groups are part of the cycle of events encompassing long periods of peace and enmity. War is just one aspect of cultural life. The idea of annihilating the other group is absent; indeed, the Tsembaga and Mae Enga are known as the peoples who marry their enemies. War is a means by which the individual and the group find their identity, and is largely ceremonial. . . even on the point of war there is always a ritual means of stepping back from open confrontation. Anger can be channelled into a "nothing fight," a competition of insults and shouting. Or else it may lead to a real fight, with blows exchanged and sometimes even serious casualties. After a war a lengthy process of peace-making begins. Gifts, ceremonies and marriages establish links and obligations between the parties. (Burger, p.62)

A PORTRAIT OF
Shinto

Naofusa Hirai

Professor at Kokugakuin University, Tokyo (Emeritus); assistance was graciously provided by Professor H. Byron Earhart of Western Michigan University

About Shinto

Shinto is the indigenous, national religion of Japan. It is more vividly observed in the social life of the people, or in personal motivations, than as a firmly established theology or philosophy; yet it has been closely connected with the value system and ways of thinking and acting of the Japanese people.

Modern Shinto can be roughly classified into three types: Shrine Shinto, Sectarian Shinto and Folk Shinto.

Shrine Shinto has been in existence from the prehistoric ages to the present and constitutes a main current of Shinto tradition. Until the end of 1945, it included State Shinto within its structure and even now has close relations with the emperor system.

Sectarian Shinto is a relatively new movement based on the Japanese religious tradition, and is represented by the 13 major sects which originated in Japan around the 19th century. Each of the 13 sects has either a founder or a systematizer who organized the religious body. New Shinto sects which appeared in Japan after World War II are conveniently included in this type.

Folk Shinto is an aspect of Japanese folk belief which is closely related to Shinto. It has neither firmly organized religious body nor doctrinal formulas, and includes small roadside images, agricultural rites of individual families, and so on. These three types of Shinto are interrelated: Folk Shinto exists as the substructure of Shinto faith, and a Sectarian Shinto follower is usually a parishioner of a certain shrine of Shrine Shinto at the same time.

The majority of Japanese people are simultaneously believers of both Shrine Shinto and Buddhism. The number of Sectarian Shintoists is about ten million. In North America, Shinto exists mainly among some people of Japanese descent.

The center of Japanese myths consists of tales about Amaterasu Omikami (usually translated as "Sun Goddess"), the ancestress of the Imperial Family, and tales of how her direct descendants unified the nation under her authority. At the beginning of Japanese mythology, a divine couple named Izanagi and Izanami, the parents of Amaterasu, gave birth to the Japanese islands as well as to the deities who became ancestors of various clans. Here we can see an ancient Japanese notion to regard the nature around us as offspring from the same parents. This view of nature requires us to reflect on our conduct toward the pollution of the earth.

The same myth also tells us that if we trace our lineage to its roots, we find ourselves as descendants of *kami* (deities). In Shinto, it is common to say that "man is *kami's* child." This means that, as we see in the above mentioned myth, man has life given through *kami* and therefore his nature is sacred. Reinterpreting this myth more broadly in terms of our contemporary contacts with people of the world, we must revere the life and basic human rights of everyone, regardless of race, nationality and creed, the same as our own.

At the core of Shinto are beliefs in the mysterious power of *kami* (*musuhi*—creating and harmonizing power) and in the way or will of *kami* (*makoto*—sincerity or true heart). Parishioners of a Shinto shrine believe in their tutelary *kami* as the source of human life and existence. Each *kami* is

"*Then she commanded her August Grandchild, saying:*
"*This Reed-Plain-1,500-autumns-fair-rice-ear Land is the region which my descendants shall be lords of. Do thou, my August Grandchild, proceed thither and govern it. Go! and may prosperity attend thy dynasty, and may it, like Heaven and Earth, endure for ever.*"

from *The Divine Edict of Amaterasu Omikami to Her Grandson*, described in Japanese myth, when he descended from the Plain-of-High-Heaven to Japan with many deities. (Transl. by W. G. Aston, *Nihongi*, London, George Allen & Unwin, reprinted 1956, p.77)

This myth, blessing the eternality of the imperial line, is today interpreted by Shinto believers as a myth blessing the eternality of all humans including the Japanese people who have the imperial line as their center. Within Shinto we believe in the endless advance of descendants within this world, and we must work hard in order to realize this.

believed to have a divine personality and to respond to sincere prayers. Historically, the ancient tutelary *kami* of each local community played an important role in combining and harmonizing different elements and powers. After the Meiji Restoration (1868), Shinto was used as a means of spiritually unifying the people during the period of repeated wars. Since the end of World War II, the age-old desire for peace has been reemphasized.

Shinto in the world today

Since the Industrial Revolution, advanced countries including Japan have undergone rapid modernization in pursuit of material comforts and convenience. Unfortunately, these efforts have resulted in producing well-known critical global issues. To cope with such issues, Shinto leaders have begun to be aware of the necessity of international cooperation and mutual aid with other peoples. In this connection, there are several challenges facing Shinto.

1. Accumulation of experience in international life, which even today is not common in Japan.

2. Acquisition of new ethical standards to join a new spiritual and cultural world community, e.g. transforming the "in-group consciousness" which is one of the characteristics of the Japanese people. Today we need to care not only for the people within our own limited group, but also for unknown people outside our own group.

3. Changing the patterns of expression for international communication. As a cultural trait, Japanese people tend to express matters symbolically rather than logically. These efforts sometimes result in misunderstanding by others.

4. Cultivation of capable Shinto leaders equipped with a good command of foreign languages and cultures.

In spite of these difficulties, Shinto has the following merits for working positively with interfaith dialogue and cooperation.

1. Shinto's notion of *kami* emphasizes belief in many deities, and its doctrine does not reject other religions, so it is natural for Shinto to pay respect to other religions and objects of worship.

2. Within Shinto, it is thought that nature is the place where *kami* dwell, and we give thanks for the blessings of nature. This attitude toward nature may be of use to religious people considering environmental problems.

3. Within Japan, there is a tradition of carefully preserving and cultivating religions which originate in other countries. Within its boundaries, various religions have practiced cooperation and harmonious coexistence.

However, the emphasis of these three points is not suggesting that, at the present time, Shinto seeks a simple syncretism. Shinto leaders, while intent on the peaceful coexistence of all people, wish to preserve Shinto's distinctive features and strengthen its religious depths.

About 20 years ago, Shinto leaders, together with people of other religions, initiated various activities for the purpose of international religious dialogue and cooperation. Since the first assembly of The World Conference on Religion and Peace was opened in Kyoto in 1970, important figures within the Shinto world have participated both in Japan and abroad in the meeting of WCRP, IARF and others. Jinja Honcho, the Association of Shinto Shrines which includes about 99 percent of Shinto shrines, initiated in 1991 an International Department for the purpose of international exchange and cooperation.

One noteworthy movement in Japan is the "offer a meal movement." Supporters of this movement give up one meal (usually breakfast) at least once each month, and donate the equivalent expense through their religious organization. This money is used by the organization for international relief and other activities. This movement was begun in 1970s by the new religion Shoroku-Shinto-Yamatoyama; believers of Misogikyo (Sectarian Shinto) and Izumo Taisha (Shrine Shinto) have been doing the same for several years. Among Buddhists, Rissho Kosei-kai has actively advanced the same movement. While it is not easy to continue this practice, the participants have said "At first we thought this was for the sake of others, but actually we noticed this is the way to strengthen our own faith."

The following declaration was presented at the tenth anniversary of the founding of the Association of Shinto Shrines, and since that time has been recited at the beginning of many meetings of Shrine Shinto.

1) Let us be grateful for *kami's* grace
and ancestors' benevolence,
and with bright and pure *makoto* (sincerity or true heart)
perform religious services.

2) Let us work for people and the world,
and serve as representatives of the *kami*
to make the society firm and sound.

3) In accordance with the Emperor's will,
let us be harmonious and peaceful,
and pray for the nation's development
as well as the world's coexistence
and co-prosperity.

from *The General Principles of Shinto Life*,
proclaimed in 1956 by the Association of Shinto Shrines
(Transl. by Naofusa Hirai from the original declaration)

A PORTRAIT OF
The Bahá'í Faith

Dr. Robert H. Stockman

Director of Research, Bahá'í National Center, Wilmette, Illinois

*T*he Bahá'í Faith is an independent world religion now in the 150th year of its existence. According to the *Encyclopedia Britannica Yearbook* it is the second most widely spread religion in the world, with five million members residing in 232 countries and dependent territories, and national spiritual assemblies (national Bahá'í governing bodies) in 165.

The Bahá'í Faith began in Iran. Its history is intimately connected with the lives of its leading figures:

'Alí-Muhammad, titled *the Báb*. Born in southern Iran in 1819, in 1844 he announced that he was the promised one or Mahdi expected by Muslims. He wrote scriptures in which he promulgated a new calendar, new religious laws and new social norms. Opposed by Iran's Muslim clergy and ultimately by its government, thousands of the Báb's followers were killed; in 1850 the Báb himself was put to death.

Mírzá Husayn-'Alí, titled *Bahá'u'lláh*. Born in northern Iran in 1817, Bahá'u'lláh became a follower of the Báb in 1844 and was imprisoned for his beliefs. In 1853 he had a vision that he was the divine teacher the Báb had promised; he publicly declared himself as a messenger of God in 1863. He spent the rest of his life in exile and prison, where he wrote over 100 volumes of scripture.

'Abbas Effendi, titled *'Abdu'l-Bahá*. Son of Bahá'u'lláh, 'Abdu'l-Bahá was born in 1844 and accompanied his father on his exile to Palestine. Bahá'u'lláh appointed 'Abdu'l-Bahá his successor, the exemplar of his teachings, and the interpreter of his revelation. Under 'Abdu'l-Bahá the Bahá'í Faith spread beyond the Middle East, India, and Burma to Europe, the Americas, southern Africa and Australasia. He died in 1921.

Shoghi Effendi Rabbani. Grandson of 'Abdu'l-Bahá and his successor, Shoghi Effendi was born in Palestine in 1897 and received an Oxford education. As head of the Bahá'í Faith from 1921 until his death in 1957, Shoghi Effendi translated the most important of Bahá'u'lláh's scriptures into elegant English, wrote extensive interpretations and explanations of the Bahá'í teachings, built the Bahá'í organizational system and oversaw the spread of the Bahá'í Faith worldwide.

The Bahá'í scriptures constitute the books, essays and letters composed by Bahá'u'lláh, 'Abdu'l-Bahá, and Shoghi Effendi. Together they composed nearly 60,000 letters, a significant portion of which is available in English; the contents of this scriptural corpus is encyclopedic in nature. The Bahá'í teachings are those principles and values promulgated in the Bahá'í scriptures, and touch on nearly every aspect of human life.

Central Bahá'í teachings are: the *oneness of God,* that there is only one God and that God is actively concerned about the development of humanity; the *oneness of religion,* that God sends messengers such as Abraham, Moses, Zoroaster, Krishna, Buddha, Christ, Muhammad, the Báb and Bahá'u'lláh to humanity to educate it in morals and in social values; and the *oneness of humanity,* that all humans come from the same original stock and deserve equal opportunities and treatment.

The teachings also include: a detailed discussion of the spiritual nature of human beings, prayers and religious practices to foster spiritual growth, a

*"Be generous in prosperity,
and thankful in adversity.
Be worthy of the trust of thy neighbor,
and look upon him with a bright and
friendly face.
Be a treasure to the poor,
an admonisher to the rich,
an answerer of the cry of the needy,
a preserver of the sanctity of thy pledge.
Be fair in thy judgment,
and guarded in thy speech.
Be unjust to no man, and show all
meekness to all men.
Be as a lamp unto them that walk
in darkness, a joy to the sorrowful,
a sea for the thirsty,
a haven for the distressed,
an upholder and defender of the victim
of oppression.
Let integrity and uprightness distinguish
all thine acts.
Be a home for the stranger,
a balm to the suffering, a tower of
strength for the fugitive.
Be eyes to the blind,
and a guiding light unto the feet
of the erring.
Be an ornament to the countenance of
truth, a crown to the brow of fidelity,
a pillar of the temple of righteousness,
a breath of life to the body of mankind,
an ensign of the hosts of justice,
a luminary above the horizon of virtue,
a dew to the soil of the human heart,
an ark on the ocean of knowledge,
a sun in the heaven of bounty,
a gem on the diadem of wisdom,
a shining light in the firmament
of thy generation,
a fruit upon the tree of humility."*
BAHÁ'U'LLÁH, *Gleanings from the Writings
of Bahá'u'lláh*, p.285

strong emphasis on the importance of creating unified and loving families, and a prescription for solving the social ills of human society.

The *Bahá'í community* consists of those people who have accepted Bahá'u'lláh as God's messenger for this day and who are actively trying to live by, and promulgate, the Bahá'í teachings. The community has no clergy and a minimum of ritual. Independent investigation of truth, private prayer and collective discussion and action are the favored modes of religious action. Usually Bahá'í communities have no weekly worship service; rather, a monthly program called *feast* is held that includes worship, consultation on community business, and social activities.

Through a process that involves no campaigning and nominations, each local community elects annually by secret ballot a nine-member *local spiritual assembly*. The assembly coordinates community activities, enrolls new members, counsels and assists members in need, and conducts Bahá'í marriages and funerals. A nine-member *national spiritual assembly* is elected annually by locally elected delegates, and every five years the national spiritual assemblies meet together to elect the *Universal House of Justice*, the supreme international governing body of the Bahá'í Faith. Worldwide there are about 20,000 local spiritual assemblies; the United States has over 1,400 local spiritual assemblies and about 120,000 Bahá'ís.

The Bahá'í view of the challenges facing humanity

The Bahá'í scriptures emphasize that the challenges facing humanity stem from two sources: age-old problems that could have been solved long ago had humanity accepted and acted on the moral and spiritual values given it by God's messengers; and new challenges stemming from the creation of a global society, which can be solved if the moral and spiritual principles enunciated by Bahá'u'lláh are accepted and followed. Chief among these principles are:

1. Racial unity. Racism retards the unfoldment of the boundless potentialities of its victims, corrupts its perpetrators and blights human progress. Bahá'u'lláh's call that all humans accept and internalize the principle of the oneness of humanity is partly directed at destroying racist attitudes.

2. Emancipation of women. The denial of equality to women perpetrates an injustice against one half of the world's population and promotes in men harmful attitudes and habits that are carried from the family to the workplace, to political life, and ultimately to international relations. Even though he lived in the 19th-century Middle East, Bahá'u'lláh called for the equality of women and enunciated their full rights to education and work.

3. Economic justice. The inordinate disparity between rich and poor is a source of acute suffering and keeps the world in a state of instability, virtually on the brink of war. Few societies have dealt effectively with this issue. The Bahá'í scriptures offer a fresh approach, including such features as a new perspective concerning money, profits, work and the poor; an understanding of the purpose of economic growth and the relationships between management and labor; and certain economic principles, such as profit sharing.

4. Patriotism within a global perspective. The Bahá'í scriptures state that citizens should be proud of their countries and of their national identities, but such pride should be subsumed within a wider loyalty to all of humanity and to global society.

5. Universal education. Historically, ignorance has been the principal reason for the decline and fall of peoples and the perpetuation of prejudice. The Bahá'í scriptures state that every human being has a fundamental right to an education, including the right to learn to read and write.

6. A universal auxiliary language. A major barrier to communication is the lack of a common language. Bahá'u'lláh urged humanity to choose one auxiliary tongue that would be taught in all schools in addition to the local native language, so that humans could understand each other anywhere they go on the planet.

7. The environment and development. The unrestrained exploitation of natural resources is a symptom of an overall sickness of the human spirit. Any solutions to the related crises of environmental destruction and economic development must be rooted in an approach that fosters spiritual balance and harmony within the individual, between individuals, and with the environment as a whole. Material development must serve not only the body, but the mind and spirit as well.

8. A world federal system. The Bahá'í scriptures emphatically state that for the first time in its history, humanity can and must create an international federation capable of coordinating the resources of, and solving the problems facing, the entire planet. A high priority needs to be given to the just resolution of regional and international conflicts; responding to urgent humanitarian crises brought on by war, famine or natural disasters; forging a unified approach to environmental degradation; and establishing the conditions where the free movement of goods, services and peoples across the globe becomes possible.

9. Religious dialogue. Religious strife has caused numerous wars, has been a major blight to progress, and is increasingly abhorrent to the people of all faiths and of no faith. The Bahá'í view that all religions come from God and thus constitute valid paths to the divine is a cornerstone of Bahá'í interfaith dialogue. Bahá'u'lláh calls on Bahá'ís to consort with the followers of all religions in love and harmony. Because Bahá'ís share with other religionists many common values and concerns, they frequently work with local interfaith organizations.

The Bahá'í response to the challenges facing humanity

Bahá'ís have responded to the challenges facing humanity in two ways: internally, by creating a Bahá'í community that reflects the principles listed above and that can serve as a model for others; and externally, to help heal the damage that inequality, injustice and ignorance have done to society.

The international Bahá'í community contains within it 2,100 ethnic groups speaking over 800 languages. In some nations minority groups make up a substantial fraction of the Bahá'í population; in the United States, for example, perhaps a third of the membership is African American, and Southeast Asians, Iranians, Hispanics and Native Americans make up another 20 percent. Racial integration of local Bahá'í communities has been the standard practice of the American Bahá'í community since about 1905. Women have played a major, if not central, role in the administration of local American Bahá'í communities, and of the national community, since 1910. American Bahá'ís have been involved in education, especially in the fostering of Bahá'í educational programs overseas, since 1909.

Worldwide, numerous Bahá'ís have become prominent in efforts to promote racial amity and equality, strengthen peace groups, extend the reach

"*Love is the most great law that ruleth this mighty and heavenly cycle, the unique power that bindeth together the divers elements of this material world, the supreme magnetic force that directeth the movements of the spheres in the celestial realms. Love revealeth with unfailing and limitless power the mysteries latent in the universe. Love is the spirit of life unto the adorned body of mankind, the establisher of true civilization in this mortal world, and the shedder of imperishable glory upon every high-aiming race and nation.*"

'ABDU'L-BAHÁ,
*Selections from the Writings of
'Abdu'l- Bahá*, p.27

"*The unity of the human race, as envisaged by Bahá'u'lláh, implies the establishment of a world commonwealth in which all nations, races, creeds and classes are closely and permanently united, and in which the autonomy of its state members and the personal freedom and initiative of the individuals that compose them are definitely and completely safeguarded. This commonwealth must, as far as we can visualize it, consist of a world legislature, whose members will, as the trustees of the whole of mankind, ultimately control the entire resource of all the component nations, and will enact such laws as shall be required to regulate the life, satisfy the needs and adjust the relationships of all races and peoples. . . . In such a world society, science and religion, the two most potent forces in human life, will be reconciled, will cooperate, and will harmoniously develop.*"

SHOGHI EFFENDI,
World Order of Bahá'u'lláh,
pp.203–204

"*The source of all learning is the knowledge of God, exalted be His glory, and this cannot be attained save through the knowledge of His Divine Manifestation. The essence of abasement is to pass out from under the shadow of the Merciful and seek the shelter of the Evil One.*

The source of error is to disbelieve in the One true God, rely upon aught else but him, and flee from His Decree. True loss is for him whose days have been spent in utter ignorance of his self.

The essence of all that we have revealed for thee is Justice, is for man to free himself from idle fancy and imitation, discern with the eye of oneness His glorious handiwork, and look into all things with a searching eye.

Thus have We instructed thee, manifested unto thee Words of Wisdom, that thou mayest be thankful unto the Lord, thy God, and glory therein amidst all peoples."

BAHÁ'U'LLÁH

and effectiveness of educational systems, encourage ecological awareness and stewardship, develop new approaches to social and economic development, and promote the new field of conflict resolution. The Bahá'í Faith runs seven radio stations in less developed areas of the world that have pioneered new techniques for educating rural populations and fostering economic and cultural development. The Faith also conducts about 740 schools, primarily in the third world, as well as 203 other literacy programs. Bahá'í communities sponsor 700 development projects, such as tree-planting, agricultural improvement, vocational training and rural health-care. The Bahá'í international community is particularly active at the United Nations and works closely with many international development agencies. Many national and local Bahá'í communities have been active at promoting interreligious understanding and cooperation.

PRAYER

O my God! O my God!
Unite the hearts of thy servants,
and reveal to them Thy great purpose.
May they follow Thy commandments and abide in Thy law.
Help them, O God, in their endeavor,
and grant them strength to serve Thee.
O God! Leave them not to themselves,
but guide their steps by the light of Thy knowledge,
and cheer their hearts by Thy love.
Verily, Thou art their Helper and their Lord.

BAHÁ'U'LLÁH,
Bahá'i Prayers, p.204

PART 2: RELIGIONS OF THE WORLD

A PORTRAIT OF
Buddhism

Dr. Geshe Sopa *and* Ven. Elvin W. Jones

Ven. Geshe Sopa is Professor in the Department of South Asian Studies, University of Wisconsin-Madison. The Ven. Elvin W. Jones is co-founder and associate director of Deer Buddhist Center, near Madison, Wisconsin.

*B*uddhism as we know it commenced in Northeast India about 500 BC through the teaching of Prince Siddartha Gautama, often known subsequent to his experience of "enlightenment" as Sakyamuni. Sakyamuni traveled around and taught in the Ganges basin until his death at the age of 84. From there Buddhism spread through much of India until its total disappearance from the land of its origin by the end of the 13th century. This disappearance occurred as a consequence of several centuries of foreign invasions leading ultimately to the conquest of India by successive waves of conquerors who had been unified under Islam.

By the time of its disappearance in India, Buddhism had spread through much of Asia where it has been a dominant faith in Southeast Asia in Sri Lanka, Thailand, Vietnam, Cambodia, Burma and Laos; in Central and East Asia in China, Korea, Japan, Tibet and Mongolia; and in numerous Himalayan areas such as Nepal, Sikkim, Butan and Ladak. It is estimated that today there are a little over 250 million Buddhists in the world. In the USA alone there are about five million, the majority of whom are Asian immigrants or their descendents. However, in recent years, numerous Americans of English and European descent have also adopted Buddhism.

From the start, the teaching of the Buddha was a middle way. In ethics it taught a middle way avoiding the two extremities of asceticism and hedonism. In philosophy it taught a middle way avoiding the two extremities of eternalism and of annihilation. The single most important and fundamental notion underpinning Buddhist thought was the idea of "contingent genesis" or "dependent origination" (*pratitya-amutpada*). Here the thought is that every birth or origination occurs in dependence on necessary causes and conditions; however, not everything so asserted can function as a cause—in particular, any kind of eternal or permanent whole. Consequently, the Buddhist idea of "contingent genesis" came to be characterized by three salient features, i.e., unpropelledness, impermanence and consistency. "Unpropelledness" signifies that origination or genesis is not propelled by an universal design such as the thought or will of a creator. "Impermanence" means that the cause of an effect is always something impermanent and never permanent. Finally, "consistency" requires that the genesis or effect will be consistent with and not exceed the creative power of the cause. For example, it is on the basis of the quality of consistency that the Buddhist denies that any kind of material body can provide a sufficient material cause for the production of a mind. Thus, on account of this primary philosophical underpinning of contingent genesis, Buddhism has produced a quite large etiological rather than theological literature.

Taking as his basis the idea of contingent genesis in general, Sakyamuni taught a specific theory of a twelvefold dependent genesis accounting for the particularized birth of a person or personality which naturally occurs in some kind of existence which is not free of various forms of suffering or ill. The spectrum of naturally occurring births which are characterized by ill is called the "round of transmigration" (*samsara*), and the force impelling this transmigration and unsatisfactory condition of attendant births was taught by Sakyamuni to be action under the sway of afflictors or afflicting elements

"...As the previous... Buddhas like a divine skillful wise horse, a great elephant, did what had to be done, accomplished all tasks, overcame all the burdens of the five aggregates controlled by delusion and karma, fulfilled all their aspirations by relinquishing their attachments, by speaking immaculately divine words and liberating the minds of all from the bondage of subtle delusions' impression, and who possess great liberated transcendental wisdom, for the sake of all that lives, in order to benefit all, in order to prevent famine, in order to prevent mental and physical sicknesses, in order for living beings to complete a buddha's 37 realizations, and to receive the stage of fully completed buddhahood...I... shall take the eight Mahayana precepts..."
"One-Day *Mahayana* Vow Ritual," trans. Library of Tibetan Works and Archives

"Perfect Wisdom spreads her radiance... and is worthy of worship. Spotless, the whole world cannot stain her.... In her we may find refuge; her works are most excellent; she brings us safety under the sheltering wings of enlightenment. She brings light to the blind, that all fears and calamities may be dispelled... and she scatters the gloom and darkness of delusion. She leads those who have gone astray to the right path. She is omniscience; without beginning or end is Perfect Wisdom, who has emptiness as her characteristic mark; she is mother of the bodhisattvas.... She cannot be struck down, the protector of the unprotected, ... the Perfect Wisdom of the Buddhas, she turns the Wheel of the Law.
"Astasahasrika Prajnaparamita-sutra," *The Buddhist Tradition,* ed. by W.M. Theodore De Bary

such as nescience, attraction, aversion and so forth. In the language of Buddhism, this action is called *karma;* the afflictors are called *klesa;* and the resultant ills are called *dukha.* The Buddha called the reality of suffering (*dukha*) the truth of suffering, and called this action—conjoined with afflicting elements (*karma* and *klesa*)—the truth of the cause of suffering. These two truths constitute the first of the Four Noble Truths which were the principal teaching of Sakyamuni and the principle object of understanding of the Buddhist Saint.

Sakyamuni also taught the possibility of freedom or emancipation from suffering or ill through its cessation. Likewise, he taught a path leading to this cessation. These two, cessation and path, constitute the third and fourth of the Four Noble Truths. Thus, we have suffering and its causes and the cessation of suffering and its causes; these are the Four Noble Truths of suffering, its causes, cessation and path. Through the cessation of suffering and its causes one obtains *nirvana* which is simply peace or quiescence, and the cause of the attainment of this peace is the path of purification eliminating action under the sway of the afflictors. The Buddha taught that of all the afflictors contaminating action, the chief is a perverse kind of nescience which apprehends a real or independent self existing in or outside of the various identifiable corporeal and mental elements which constitute a person or personality. Thus, the cultivation of the path of purification hinges on the reversal of this mistaken apprehension of a real soul or ego or selfhood. This Buddhist view that there is no real or enduring substratum to the personality is called *anatma.*

Sakyamuni's most precise and important articulation of the Four Noble Truths was his formulation of a twelvefold causal linkage generating each and every particular instance of birth of a person. This twelvefold causal nexus begins with nescience and ends with old age and death. This nescience is in particular the perverse ignorance which grasps a real selfhood. Conditioned by this kind of nescience, actions are performed which deposit inclinations and proclivities upon the unconscious mind. These proclivities are later ripened by other factors such as grasping and misappropriation and thereby bring about unsatisfactory results through birth and death. With, however, the correct seeing of the reality of no-self, this nescience may be stopped, and thereby the whole chain of causation leading to unsatisfactory birth is brought to an end. In this way the twelvefold causal linkage is not only a theory of the genesis of a personality but also a theory of its potential for deliverance from every kind of ill.

Thus it is said in Buddhist scripture:

"Gather up and cast away.
Enter to the Buddha's teaching.
Like a great elephant in a house of mud,
conquer the lord of death's battalions.
Whoever with great circumspection,

practices this discipline of the Law,
abandoning the wheel of births,
will make an end to suffering."

"Gather up and cast away" refers to the gathering together of virtuous or wholesome qualities and the abandonment of non- virtuous or unwholesome qualities in the personality. Thus the same scripture says:

"Not to do evil,
to bring about the excellence of virtue,
completely to subdue the mind,
this is the teaching of the Buddha."

On his deathbed, the Buddha had exhorted his disciples to work on their own salvation with diligence; hence these teachings are sometimes characterized as a doctrine of individual emancipation.

About five to six hundred years after the passing away of the teacher Sakyamuni, another formulation of the Buddhist doctrine and practice gained a wide circulation in India. This later propagation is associated with the great Buddhist teacher Nagarjuna. Taking his stand on the fundamental Buddhist idea of contingent genesis, Nagarjuna argued that if every instance of genesis is a contingent genesis, then continued analysis will show that every kind of permanent and even the impermanent causes proposed either by Buddhists will be non-absolutes and non-ultimates and that consequently causality itself is in some sense illusory. In this sense even true phenomena like causality are just empty of any kind of ultimate nature. Nagarjuna carried his analysis to cover permanent non-originating phenomena like space as well. The nonexistence of all phenomena as ultimates or absolutes is the Buddhist idea of emptiness (*sunyata*), which provided a great impetus to another kind of religious aspiration aiming at the emancipation not only of one's own individual life-stream but those of all sentient life from the round of unsatisfactory birth and rebirth. He especially demonstrated the absence of any final or absolute difference between *samsara* and *nirvana,* even though phenomenally they are and will always remain opposites. Thereby, Nagarjuna opened wide the way for the pursuit of the non-attached *nirvana* taught to be achieved by the Buddhas along with numerous other sublime qualities of knowledge belonging to perfect enlightenment. From earliest times the Buddhist had already distinguished between the path of purification trodden by Sakyamuni himself, already known as the *Bodhisattva* path, and that taught and followed by numerous of his disciples. Now the Buddha's own path was encouraged for all. By its followers this later path was called *Mahayana,* or greater vehicle, whereas the former came to be called the *Hinayana,* or smaller vehicle. The *Mahayana* was synonymous with the path of a *Bodhisattva* or one who, moved by great compassion, developed the aspiration to perfect enlightenment for the sake of others. This aspiration was called *Bodhicitta,* or the mind to enlightenment, and provided the motivation for the cultivation of the *Mahayana* path. This *Mahayana* path was also taught extensively in the *Prajnaparamita-sutras* or *Perfection of Wisdom Scriptures* which also gained wide circulation in India through the efforts of Nagarjuna.

About 500 years later still another very important development occurred in Indian Buddhism. This development is associated with the brothers Asanga and Vasubandhu. This led to a great systematization of the *Mahayana* and in particular to another less radical interpretation of the meaning of the *Prajnaparamita-sutras* than that associated with Nagarjuna, whose school continued on and is generally called the *Madhyamika* or Middleist School; Asanga's is called the *Cittamatra* or Mind-only School.

Also around this time, a special kind of Buddhist esoteric scripture and practice gained wide currency. They constituted four classes or levels which moved from outer ritual action through inner meditative action to a full fledged esoteric path of spiritual attainment. These scriptures were known as the *tantras,* and their practice was called the diamond vehicle or the secret *mantra* vehicle. Espousing the practice of the *Mahayana,* they added many ritual methods together with numerous profound and difficult *yoga* or meditation practices and techniques. The *tantras* saw themselves as fulfilling the practice of the *Mahayana* as well as providing an accelerated path to its realization. The vehicle of the *tantras* is often called the vehicle of the effect because straightaway it envisages the final result of the path and imaginatively dwells upon and rehearses that until it becomes not an imagined but an accomplished result. The *Mahayana* being wisdom and method, the *tantras* add to the general wisdom and method of the *Mahayana* its own very special varieties.

Thus in India along with four classes of *tantras,* four main philosophical schools developed, each with a number of subschools, i.e. the *Vaibhasika, Sautrantika, Madhyamika* and the *Yogacara.* The former two are schools of the *Hinayana,* and the latter two are schools of the *Mahayana.* The *Vaibhasika* early developed 18 subschools, two of which are of particular importance—the *Sthaviravada,* which is the immediate ancestor of the *Theravada,* the principal Buddhism of Southeast Asia, and the *Sarvastivada,* which is the basis of monasticism in Tibet and the Tibetan community today. The *Madhyamika* provides the chief viewpoint of Tibetan Buddhism today, and the *Yogacara* has had profound and far reaching influences on the Buddhism of China, and through China on Korea and Japan. Some secret *mantra* practices were transmitted into China and from there to Japan where they survive today, and the practices of all

four levels of *tantra* are still alive in the Tibetan community.

From India by way of Central Asia, Buddhism began its penetration into China around the first century CE. There it encountered the already developed systems of Confucianism and Taoism. The later in particular provided the terminology and numerous seemingly analogous concepts for subsequent centuries of effort devoted to the translation of Buddhist scriptures into Chinese and the establishment of Buddhist practice in China. By the eighth century, Chinese Buddhism reached its mature form with its two main theoretical schools of *Tien-tai* and *Hua-yen,* together with its two popular schools of Pure Land and *Ch'an* (Japanese: Zen). These sinicised forms of Buddhism began their spread to Korea mainly from the fourth century on and commenced spreading from Korea to Japan from the middle of the sixth century.

Although some important Buddhist development occurred a century earlier, Buddhism began to be strongly cultivated in Tibet in the eighth century. In this century Indian and various Sinitic Buddhist developments collided in a debate held by the Tibetan king at Samyas, the first Buddhist monastery founded in Tibet. Tibetan history records that the Indian faction won this debate, and it is clear that afterwards Tibet looked to India throughout its prolonged subsequent period of importation of Buddhism. As a consequence, Tibet remains a great repository of a vast body of important literature which later perished in India itself. From Tibet, Buddhism was afterward spread into Mongolia and throughout the Himalayan region.

Now, in the aftermath of World War II and the collapse of Western colonial establishments in Asia, the modern efforts of numerous Asian countries to make a transition from agrarian to industrial societies has led and still leads often to the establishment of military dictatorships or to socialist totalitarian regimes. Buddhism has generally fallen upon difficult times particularly at the hands of Marxist-Leninist regimes, for whereas Buddhism does not see any natural conflict between itself and modern science, its middle way philosophy is staunchly opposed to dialectical materialism. In fact, two of the worst atrocities of nearly genocidal proportions to be perpetrated in modern times have taken place in two such countries, Cambodia and Tibet, the later continuing—and this is hard to believe—for over 30 years.

Buddhist leadership nonetheless has continued to press for freedom and democracy, for peace and non-violence as these will be the best safeguard for the natural human wish to avoid suffering. Here, it is particularly indicative to note that two of the most recent Nobel Peace Prize winners have been Buddhists—H. H. Holiness the 14th Dalai Lama of Tibet, and Daw Aung San Suu Kyi, of Burma.

"*For the last several years I have been looking at the world's problems, including our own problem, the Tibetan situation. I have been thinking about this and meeting with persons from different fields and different countries. Basically all are the same. I come from the East; most of you are Westerners. If I look at you superficially, we are different, and if I put my emphasis on that level, we grow more distant. If I look on you as my own kind, as human beings like myself, with one nose, two eyes, and so forth, then automatically that distance is gone. We are the same human flesh. I want happiness; you also want happiness. From that mutual recognition we can build respect and real trust for each other. From that can come cooperation and harmony, and from that we can stop many problems.*"

THE 14TH DALAI LAMA OF TIBET

"*By the next century the population of the countries giving aid will total around 800 million; the populations of countries needing aid will reach around 5.3 billion. Thus the ratio is about 1 to 7. . . . The Buddha described three kinds of hungry spirits: those with no possessions, those with few, and those with great wealth. The first group is miserable, having nothing to eat. Those in the second have little and also deserve sympathy. Those in the third, however, have great wealth and more than enough food, yet turn a deaf ear to people in dire necessity. It is believed that this last group goes to hell.*

We in the developed nations must not allow ourselves to become wealthy hungry spirits. Let each of us do as much as we can to help seven people in need."

KINZO TAKEMURA,
excerpted from an editorial in *Dharma World*,
Jan./Feb. 1993

Zen

*I*n the 6th century CE, Bodhidharma, the semi-legendary figure from whom all Zen schools trace their ancestry, brought to China that Buddhist practice which we call Zen. The word itself is a Japanese transliteration of a Chinese transliteration of a Sanskrit word meaning meditation. Thus, Zen is that school of Buddhism which emphasizes meditation (*zazen* = sitting meditation) as a primary practice for calming and clearing the mind and for directly perceiving reality. According to the texts the Zen that Bodhidharma taught and practiced can be summed up as:

"*A special transmission outside the scriptures;
No dependence upon words and letters;
Directly pointing at one's own nature;
Attaining Buddhahood.*"

Zen eventually reached Japan where the Soto school was established by Eihei Dogen (1200–1255) who considered Zen not as a separate school but simply as Buddhism. In the early 1960s Shunryu Suzuki Roshi came to San Francisco to minister to the local Japanese congregation. Out of his contacts with Western students, Zen Center of San Francisco was born. Many other centers have since opened elsewhere in North America and in other countries.

THE ZEN CENTER, San Francisco

A Dual Awakening Process

Dr. Ahangamage T. Ariyaratne

"The word *sarvodaya* was coined by Mahatma Gandhi to describe a new social order, which he envisioned as being very different from the capitalist and communist systems prevalent at that time. Literally it means "the welfare of all." With my Buddhist outlook, when I came across the word *sarvodaya* I interpreted it as "the awakening of all." . . . I cannot awaken myself unless I help awaken others. Others cannot awaken unless I do. So it is an interconnected and interdependent dual process of awakening oneself and society that we have chosen in the *Sarvodaya* [organization, of which he is Director] . . . . Lord Buddha's admonition to us was [to serve]

*by helping those who suffer physically
to overcome physical suffering,
those who are in fear to overcome fear,
those who suffer mentally to overcome mental suffering,
Be of service to all living beings.*

This is *sarvodaya* in the most profound sense. Transcending all man-made barriers of caste, race, religion, nationality and other ways of separating human beings, *Sarvodaya* serves all. *Sarvodaya* works to remove the causes of human physical suffering, anxiety and fear. Working for interreligious and interracial harmony, eradicating poverty and empowering the poor, promoting peace by religious education and spiritual development programs, engaging in every kind of peace-making process, taking nonviolent action against human rights violations and other forms of injustice, are all part of the *Sarvodaya* portfolio of activities."

excerpted from his acceptance speech
for the Ninth Niwano Peace Prize,
printed in *Dharma World*, July/August 1992

Christianity: Origins and Beliefs

The Rev. Thomas A. Baima, S.T.L.

A Catholic Priest and Director of Eastern Christian and Non Christian Relations for the Office for Ecumenical and Interreligious Affairs of the Archdiocese of Chicago; member of the Board of Trustees of The Council for a Parliament of the World's Religions.

Because the range of communities within Christianity is so wide, we invited members of several distinct traditions to provide essays on specific topics for this section of Part 2. To assist readers in identifying and understanding the diversity within Christianity, others essays located in Part 2C include a detailed summary of the main characteristics of 15 "families" plus descriptions of several movements or branches. In the essay below, Father Baima provides an introduction to the origins, basic beliefs and interfaith relations of Christianity. –Ed.

*T*he origin of Christianity begins in the heart of God. The Divine nature is Love. Love is not something that comes from God. Love is God and God is love. If a Christian were to name the Divine in English, the best term would be simply "God-Love."

Within God-Love, before time, came an urge to create. This urge was not for pleasure, since God-Love is beyond such things. Rather it was, as Archbishop Joseph Raya says, for the multiplication of love. God created for this reason alone, that love might grow. Divine love by its very nature shares itself.

Made in the image and likeness of God-Love, humanity had the essential quality or condition that makes loving possible, free will. Some humans chose to reject the offer of close relationship with God-Love. This rejection, which we will call sin, entered human experience and remains a permanent part of it. Sin is separation or a false autonomy, false because it is not possible to be or exist independently of God. This false autonomy is the basis of human rejection of God-Love.

The separation between humanity and God-Love required divine action to overcome it. As a permanent part of human nature nothing we could do of our own power could heal the separation. A new offer of relationship by God-Love was required.

So God-Love selected one of the nations of the earth to be a sign and instrument of this divine action. That nation was the Hebrew people. Through a process of self-disclosure, God-Love guided Israel out of slavery into an experience of rescue. God-Love guided Israel through the naming of sin in the Ten Commandments and the calling to virtue through the commands to pray, celebrate sacred ritual and act with compassion.

The guiding and forming of Israel created a sign and instrument which could extend and express God-Love.

Throughout almost 2,000 years of faithfulness and struggle, this one people, guided by prophets, priests and kings, was the light of God-Love among the nations.

Then God-Love chose to graft onto this one people all the nations. In a small village in the northern part of Palestine, a young woman became pregnant even though she was a virgin. Though no man had ever touched Mary—Life grew within her. Nine months later "a child was born, a son given, upon whom dominion rested. And the prophet had called him 'wonder-counselor, God-hero, Father forever and Prince of Peace.' " Mary named him Jesus—"God saves."

It is here that Christianity, which began eternally in the heart of God, is made visible in the person and event of Jesus. We who are his disciples have come to see the fullness of revelation from God-Love, of God-Love in him. For this reason we call him Lord, Son of God, Savior. And it is in the teaching of Jesus that we learned something new about the inner life of God. Jesus called the one God—Father, Son and Holy Spirit. Within the Godhead there exist relationships of love. God is personal, not merely as a way to relate to us, but in the very divine being. We would not know this about God had not the Son taken flesh in Jesus of Nazareth and revealed it to us.

In addition to this revelation of the inner life of God, the Lord Jesus taught a way of life that made it possible for God-Love to be experienced as a reality in the world. After his earthly ministry the Lord returned to his Father. He empowered and designated a few of the disciples to carry the teaching on. Thus it has come to us, handed on by living witnesses.

These living witnesses or apostles went out from Jerusalem and founded local assemblies of faith. Like Israel of old, these assemblies were the sign and instrument of the Lord Jesus in that place. It was by the example of love that others became attracted to Christianity. It was through prayer and life within the assemblies that the living witnesses were able to go forth and preach. And it was through incorporation into these assemblies that an individual came to know the Lord Jesus; receive formation in the Teaching, sanctification in prayer and guidance in the Christian life.

Within these assemblies believers entered into worship of God—Father, Son and Holy Spirit. Through the singing of psalms, hymns and inspired songs, through the breaking of bread and the prayers, they met the Lord Jesus who sanctified their inner life. Through devotion to the teaching of the apostles, they came to know the revelation of God which Jesus had disclosed in himself.

The primary elements of the Teaching are:
There is one God who is almighty, whom Jesus called Father. This one God is the Creator of heaven and earth. Jesus is the divine and human, only Son of this Father, and as we call God Lord, we call Jesus Lord, for the Father is

in him and he is in the Father. The miracle of Jesus' virgin birth attests to this. Jesus suffered at the hands of the Roman Governor, Pontius Pilate, giving his life in the process. He died and was buried as we all shall be. But he did not remain in the tomb, for God raised him up out of death. His suffering and death broke the chains of sin for all who died before his coming, again making God-Love available to them. He rose from the dead, making life with God now and forever our blessed hope. He ascended, returning into the presence of God-Love from which he came. He sent the Holy Spirit to create the assembly of believers and to be its constant guide in faith, hope and love. He will return to bring time to an end, to judge the living and the dead and to complete creation with the inauguration of the eternal kingdom of, with and in God-Love.

These assemblies of faith, formed and guided by the Spirit, also taught a way of conduct based not on law, but virtue. The Lord Jesus taught that all sin in life could be overcome and rooted out of human experience by the avoidance of the negative behavior and the substitution of a corresponding virtue. These virtues are seen as active gifts of the Holy Spirit to the believer. Love, joy, peace, patience, kindness, goodness, faithfulness and self-control are the spiritual means to a Christian life.

This simple foundation of doctrine and virtue has been reflected on over the centuries in the development of our understanding. Through prayer, holy women and men have penetrated to the depths of these mysteries guided by the Holy Spirit of God-Love. The assemblies look to four sources for insights to develop the living faith carried in the mind of the whole people of Christ. First is Scripture, second the oral tradition, third is reason and the fourth is experience. Scripture includes the Hebrew Scriptures interpreted through the New Testament. Tradition is the preaching, teaching and ritual which guides the assembly in prayer life, work and worship. Reason is the application of disciplined thought to understand more fully the mystery. Experience focuses on the changes within us which doctrine makes. These are the sources of theological reflection.

Faith is handed on through life in the assembly, sometimes through preaching and sometimes through sacred rites. Baptism and Eucharist are the signs and means of entrance into and nourishment of the assembly's life. Confession of sins and anointing with oil heal the spiritual and physical life of the body while marriage and ordination create, lead and guide the family and the assembly.

APPROXIMATE CENSUS OF CHRISTIANS

- Catholics: 900 million
- Orthodox: 125 million
- Protestants and Pentecostals: 622 million

NOTE: See also the articles about Christian "families" and branches in Part 2C.

In Christianity today, almost 2,000 years after the ascension of the Lord Jesus, divisions exist. John Wesley, one of the great reformers in England, spoke of a fully balanced Christianity having four components mentioned above—Scripture, Tradition, Reason and Experience—as the bases of religious knowledge. We could consider the divisions within Christianity to be a function of favoring one or more of these components over the others. Political, economic and other human considerations aside, the division in the Church has resulted from the development of different theological schools which emphasize the different components. For example, the Orthodox are known for the emphasis on the Tradition and Experience; the Catholics on Tradition and Reason; the Protestants on Scripture and Reason; and Pentecostals on Scripture and Experience.

These differences in emphasis have led to differences in the formulation of doctrine, the number and status of the sacred rites or sacraments, and the authority of the ordered ministries. These emphases have brought each Christian community a deeper insight into faith but also have limited their fellowship with the rest of Christianity.

Interfaith relations

Christians also differ in their relation to non-Christians. These relations are characterized by three positions:

1) The **exclusive position** holds that a saving relationship with the Lord Jesus is the *only* way to salvation. In this perspective, those who lack this will suffer forever, excluded from God-Love.

2) The **pluralist position** sees Christianity as merely one path to God among other religions which also offer the possibility of salvation. This view sees salvation as universal and knowledge of God as relative to culture and tradition.

3) Between them is the **inclusive position.** While holding to the belief that the fullness of revelation came in the person of Jesus and that he is the ordinary way to right relationship with God, here it is believed that God-Love can work beyond this. Hence a Christian may esteem truth where he/she sees it, and we will know it is the truth when it agrees with Jesus and the teaching and example received from him. The revelation of God-Love is fully disclosed in Jesus.

This description of Christianity can in no way capture the breadth, height and depth of the religion. But it is our hope that this summary has presented a glimpse of our life.

A PORTRAIT OF
Christianity in the World Today

Dr. Dieter T. Hessel

The second essay on Christianity, addressing the critical issues and wisdom, is written by a Presbyterian minister and ethicist. Dr. Hessel is also director of the ecumenical Program on Ecology, Justice and Faith, and is editor of After Nature's Revolt *(Fortress Press, 1992), as well as of* The Egg: An Eco-Justice Quarterly.[1]

The primary challenges and issues facing humanity

*A*mong **perennial** challenges are the quest for meaningful human existence and the struggle for social justice and peace. Greater scientific and technological power over nature tempts humans to ignore creaturely limits and to make themselves the center of value. Human efforts to achieve inordinate security and comfort actually oppress and destroy other life, offending the Source of existence and warping right relationships in earth community. Today, the rich/poor gap has become harsher. More than a billion people lack enough to eat, while another billion misuse resources and overconsume. Militarization brings mass death to the "meek" even as it allows the militarily powerful to retain unjust advantage over the earth's resources for a wealthy few.

Pressing **new** issues face humanity, including the degradation of the environment on a global scale and the negative impact of exploding human population growth on social systems and other species. The world's religions and governments have also been surprised by a new public health crisis worsened by AIDS, and by the breakdown of public and private morality, as well as by the failures of common educational systems, in commodified societies. Meanwhile, counterrevolutionary forms of cultural/religious fundamentalism foster crusading intolerance of other faiths or ethnic groups and threaten minority rights. Mature religion and politics, to the contrary, will foster multicultural appreciation, religious tolerance, civil liberties, gender equality and racial justice.

How may Christianity respond to these issues?

*F*irst, **rethink and reinterpret faith for these times.** Pertinent Christian faith expresses reverence for the Creator, Sustainer and Redeemer of the cosmos, and corresponding respect for all of the creatures whom God loves and enjoys. Such faith guides compassionate and courageous human living. The norm for spirited humanity is set by Jesus of Nazareth, "pioneer of faith" and "Son of God," whom Christians perceive as Reconcilor of the world and Sovereign of life. His prophetic and healing public ministry inaugurates the Kingdom of God. Everyone is invited to enter this commonwealth, a community of *shalom* and sharing intended to encompass all known races, cultures, species, places. The church's role is to be the ecumenical social body of the crucified-risen Christ, celebrative of God's design, concerned for the well-being of all. Christian worship through word and sacrament and social witness in each locale visibly signify God's reign already operative but not yet fulfilled in history.

Second, embody an ethic of covenant faithfulness. A Christian ethics that is: a) based on the biblical story of God's love for creation and covenant with human creatures (*humus* = "from earth"), and b) responsive to the needs of the time, will foster and embody these values:

- love for human beings everywhere who are equally "created in the image of God," and respect for basic human rights,
- care for the well-being of near and distant neighbors, both human and otherkind, on this home planet,
- justice to the oppressed as well as generosity toward the deprived,
- prophetic denunciation of sin toward neighbor and nature, and idolatry or corruption in personal life and public affairs,
- frugality of lifestyle—neither strictness nor laxity—so that there may be sustainable sufficiency for all,
- nonviolent action to resist exploitation, and cooperative habits of coping with social conflict,
- renewal of community life and cultivation of civil processes for the common good.

Third, examine ambiguities of religious life: Christianity in the late modern era has partially embodied but often contradicted its faith affirmations and moral imperatives. Transformative faith leading toward biophilic harmony has been obscured by domineering or distorting tendencies. Christians have proclaimed "the grace of our Lord Jesus Christ, the love of God and the communion of the Holy Spirit," while acquiescing to racist, sexist, classist, naturist and ecclesiastical practices of domination. The church's emphasis on human rights worldwide has fostered liberation of the oppressed, but is in fragmentary ways captive to individualism, ethnocentrism and popular moralism.

On every continent, Christian communions have been coopted by the forces of destructive nationalism, and even now the ecumenical church remains shamefully divided over issues of gender justice and reproductive rights, added to ancient divisions over faith and order. Moreover, most local congregations lack racial and class heterogeneity, or constructive relations with other faith communities and popular movements for social change.

Nations with Christian majorities have relied on military force much more than on peacemaking initiatives and cooperative development. Western economic ethics has favored democratic capitalism over policies and practices of social solidarity and ecological integrity.

Newly awakened ecumenical concern for "integrity of creation" is still very anthropocentric and has just begun to explore intrinsic values in nature, or sacred dimensions of the evolutionary story.

Priestly celebrations of grace within nature will see earth, water and wind as sacramental, along with bread, wine and spirit. Prophetic responses to these times will seek "eco-justice"—social and economic equity coupled with ecological integrity and cooperative peacemaking for the sake of earth and people.

Wisdom in Christianity

Christians characteristically ask *not* "What is the good?," but "What purposes and patterns of conduct are in keeping with being faithful *people of God*?" Since Pentecost, Christian communities have understood themselves to be people of "The Way" (Acts 4:32–35; 18:24–26). The Christian Way is viewed as consistent with the expectations of the Noachic and Sinai covenants. A Christian ethical spirituality—"Live your life in a manner worthy of the gospel of Christ"—is expressed in the communion meal and baptism, as well as in public preaching and social practice. The individualistic, bureaucratic and technocratic acids of modernity have corroded commitment to this way; intentional Christian communities, though often ignored by mainline churches, have been primary bearers of the tradition.

People of the Way have vision, values and virtues that are consistent with the basic themes, though not legal details, of the Hebrew *covenant* story. Today, Christians and Jews alike are rediscovering wisdom dimensions of covenant ethics, keyed to the rest-and-play Sabbath purpose of creation's seventh day. For example, Exodus 23, Leviticus 19 and 25, plus Deuteronomy 15 summarize covenant laws that contain the implicit ecological and social wisdom of herding tribes and primitive agrarians living close to the land. Faithful people give animals frequent "time off" and let the land lie fallow at least once every seven years. Neither neighbors nor nature are to be exploited. Earthkeeping humans are responsible for making sure that people, animals and the land have their times of rest, peace and restoration (Ex. 20:8–11; 23:10–12). It is a grand jubilee tradition (Lev. 25 & 26, Luke 4:16–22) with much contemporary relevance.

Covenant teaching fosters an ethic of environmental care coupled with social justice. Moral responsibility toward land and beasts must be matched by justice toward the poor. An appropriate response to poverty, therefore, involves more than alms-giving; it entails debt relief, gleaning opportunities, equitable redistribution of land, as well as care for "strangers, widows and orphans."

Yet, despite deep appreciation of nature and reverential descriptions in the Psalms, in Job, in Jesus' Sermon on the Mount, and despite Isaiah's hopeful vision of *shalom*, which includes a restored creation, scripture is punctuated with sad stories of land coveting and defilement. Some striking biblical examples of eco-injustice are the tale of Naboth's vineyard (I Kings 21), Solomon's order to cut down the beloved cedars of Lebanon to aggrandize Jerusalem (I Kings 5:6–11; Ps. 104:16), and the people's lament at becoming powerless tenant farmers after the return from exile (Neh. 5:3–5). Wherever human beings are unfaithful to the eco-social requirements of God's covenant, their idolatrous behavior has devastating consequences (Jer. 9:4–11); the land mourns, even the birds die (Hos. 4:3). Even so, there is hope for renewal of the covenant; God continually acts with justice and mercy to redeem creation.

Covenant ethics is concerned with right relationships within the whole web of created interdependency. It views Jesus Christ as the normative clue to faithful and fitting life. "Faithful" means loyal to the cause of God who

---

"*The Lord said to Moses on Mount Sinai, 'Say to the people of Israel, When you come into the land which I give you, the land shall keep a sabbath to the Lord. Six years you shall sow your field, and six years you shall prune your vineyard, and gather in its fruits; but in the seventh year there shall be a sabbath of solemn rest for the land, a sabbath to the Lord; you shall not sow your field or prune your vineyard.'*"

LEVITICUS 25: 1–4

"*And he [Jesus] came to Nazareth, where he had been brought up; and he went to the synagogue, as his custom was, on the sabbath day. And he stood up to read; and there was given to him the book of the prophet Isaiah. He opened the book and found the place where it was written,*

'The Spirit of the Lord is upon me, because he has anointed me to preach good news to the poor. He has sent me to proclaim release to the captives and recovering of sight to the blind, to set at liberty those who are oppressed, to proclaim the acceptable year of the Lord.'"

LUKE 4: 16–21

"*Blessed are you poor, for yours is the kingdom of God. Blessed are you that hunger now, for you shall be satisfied. Blessed are you that weep now, for you shall laugh. . . .*

But woe to you that are rich, for you have received your consolation. Woe to you that are full now, for you shall hunger. . . .

But I say to you that hear, Love your enemies, do good to those who hate you, bless those who curse you, pray for those who abuse you. . . . And as you wish that men would do to you, do so to them."

LUKE 6: 20–31
(The Sermon on the Mount)

---

makes covenant with creation after the flood, through the exodus, and at the incarnation. "Fitting" means practical human action consistent with the kingdom vision and covenant values. Responsible action "fits in" with everything that is going on and that is needed to solve problems.[2]

The *cross,* the central symbol in the new covenant story, signifies God grappling with human sin, accepting and overcoming life's persistent suffering and perpetual perishing, and ultimately creation's comprehensive renewal, including harmonious human living with myriad species of animals and plants (as envisioned by the prophet Hosea 2:18–22). That is not all it means, but Christians can perceive Jesus' crucifixion- resurrection as the deed that reconciles human beings to God, each other and the world of creation—*at-onement* with nature and society, *atunement* to what God is doing with us and all other creatures. The gracious, enabling work of Christ brings responsive communities of faith into right relation with God, other people and the larger ecological-social environment with its bio-diversity.

But "developed" and "developing" societies alike have yet to face the limits nature places on polluting economic growth and material consumption, and to adopt an ethic and practice of eco- justice that would keep the earth, achieve justice, build community. This ethic comes into sharp focus in terms of four norms: ecologically *sustainable* or environmentally fitting enterprise; socially *just participation* in obtaining sustenance and managing community life; *sufficiency* as an equitable standard of organized sharing that requires basic consumption floors and ceilings, and *solidarity* with other people and creatures—companions, victims and allies—in earth community. Observance of each ethical norm reinforces the others, serving the common eco-social good by joining what is socially just with what is ecologically right.

The **covenant theology tradition,** going back to Augustine, and behind him to both testaments, has prominence in the preceding portrait of Christianity. But there are several other important Christian approaches which can be viewed as having complementary rather than competing effects on Christian witness in the contemporary world.

One of these is the **wisdom tradition** of Job, the Psalms, Proverbs, Ecclesiastes, and the New Testament gospel and epistles of John. Practical folk wisdom among Christians carries on the tradition, which is also folded into Biblical covenant faith and ethics, as we have seen. Suffice it to add here that from the Wisdom perspective, Jesus is understood to be the incarnate Word of God, **logos** of life and reason—from the beginning to the end. The prologue to the book of *John* views the logos as involved immanently in the whole of God's creation, enlivening all living things while enlightening all that have such capacity.

Another approach is offered by **mature evangelical** Christianity (as distinct from crusading fundamentalism).

It recognizes that to start and stay on a path of *sustainable sufficiency for all* requires spiritual conversion—change of heart and repentance—moving toward sanctification that must be reinforced in a faithful, nurturing community. Saving grace is the joyous message so characteristic of 19th century Protestant hymnody. The crucial result of Christ's redemptive work is to restore human "mutability"—our ability to respond to God's call and to grow and change toward maturity. This is not possible by human willing alone. The gracious, saving work of Christ is necessary for the flourishing of responsible human activity.

Another Christian approach is the **sacramental tradition,** fostered by Catholic mystics, and supported in Anglican and Orthodox liturgy. It "ecstatically experiences the divine bodying forth in the cosmos, and beckons us into communion" (as Rosemary Radford Ruether writes in *Gaia & God,* HarperCollins, 1992). "We must start thinking of reality as the connecting links of a dance in which each part is equally vital to the whole, rather than [using] the linear competitive model in which the above prospers by defeating and suppressing what is below." The resulting ethical spirituality knows the value and transcience of selves in relation to the great Self, the living interdependence of all things, and the joy of personal communion within the matrix of life—a sacred community.

Passionist Fr. Thomas Berry, a contemporary interpreter of the sacramental tradition, recently discussed the question, "What are the conditions for entering into a Viable Future?"

First condition: Recognize that the universe is a communion of subjects, not a collection of objects. (A theology of stewardship misses the point that communion—deep rapport—is the primary experience.) Earth community **is** the sacred society where we have complementary manifestations of the divine.

Second condition: Appreciate that the earth is primary; humans are derivative. So earth-healing comes first. All professions, business, education and religion must focus on the well-being of the whole community.

Third condition: Come to grips with the fact that in the future nothing much will happen that humans are not involved in, given our numbers and power. This requires human subjectivity in contact with the subjectivity of the world. "All human activities must be judged primarily by the extent to which they generate and foster a mutually enhancing human/earth relationship."

Adequate theological and ethical responses to the environmental challenge will encompass (in a wholistic way) both created reality **and** human subjectivity. William French of Loyola University, Chicago emphasizes the "need to move beyond dualistic thinking that suggests we must choose between focusing on subjectivity or creation, freedom or natural necessity, historical consciousness or ecological sensitivity." (in *Journal of Religion* 1992) Just as subject-centered theology need not turn against creation, critical creation-centered theology need and should not reject the importance of human subjectivity or constructive historical projects.

Adequate theology and ethics will pay close attention to the "view from below" even as it also learns to listen to nature. The feminist insight is catching hold that "Domination of women has provided a key link, both socially and symbolically, to domination of earth; hence the tendency in patriarchal cultures to link women with earth, matter and nature, while identifying males with sky, intellect and transcendent spirit. . . . The work of eco-justice and the work of spirituality are interrelated, the outer and inner aspects of one process of conversion and transformation . . . [involving] a reordering to bring about just and loving interrelationships between men and women, between races and nations, between groups presently stratified into social classes, manifest in great disparities of access to the means of life."[3] Poor and indigenous communities of people who are most affected by economic exploitation and environmental destruction have important things to teach us about living in harmony with nature and caring for place. Such communities have priority justice claims on religious, educational, business and political organizations.

Finally, in response to modern physics, biology and ecology, we should note the maturing of a more philosophical and interdisciplinary style of Christian **process thought**, as fostered by John Cobb. His thought in *The Liberation of Life* (1981, with biologist Charles Birch) asserts the need for an organic or ecological view of God and reality that does not construe God as a substance isolated from the world. God is inherently related to the world, indwelling all eco-social systems, which by their nature are intrinsically interconnected communities. Rev. Carol Johnston, a student of Cobb, notes that, "When relations are conceived as inherent, then the person is both influenced by relations with others and influences

them. In this context, justice is a matter of the quality of relationships . . . characterized by freedom, participation and solidarity. Recognition of inherent relatedness establishes the need to take marginalized people and externalized ecosystems into account. . . . All entities have a right to be respected appropriate to their degree of intrinsic value and to their importance to the possibility of value in others."[4]

To cultivate a renewed spirituality that undergirds an ethic of care for earth community is the special obligation of religious leaders, clergy and lay, in these times. Otherwise, many more people will suffer from environmental degradation and social injustice, while numerous special places and wondrous otherkind will not be saved; sooner or later they also will fall to the utilitarian logic of the developers.

Authentic spirituality features awe, respect, humane pace, justice and generosity, **not** intensively efficient use of all being, as goes the instrumental logic of modern life and business. Authentic spirituality loves the suffering ones, aspires toward harmony with the wilderness, shows deep respect for the dignity of animals, plants, mountains and waters. Such religion celebrates spirit in creation, inculcates an ethic of genuine care for vulnerable people, creatures, eco-systems, as it appropriates the wisdom of nature and of long-standing communities.

In this web of life, religious people will praise and participate in the "economy of God" on this planetary home, foster loving deeds of eco-justice, build communities that model sufficiency, join with others to envision and move toward reverential, sustainable development (and foster corporate responsibility consistent with this goal). They will also explore urban and rural dimensions of ecology, encourage appropriate technologies at home and abroad, participate in community organizations that are working for environmental and economic justice, while they express integrity in both individual and institutional lifestyle, consistent with a spirituality of creation-justice-peace. ⊛

"If I speak in the tongues of men and of angels,
but have not love, I am a noisy gong or a clanging cymbal.
And if I have prophetic powers, and understand all mysteries
and all knowledge, and if I have all faith so as to remove
mountains, but have not love, I am nothing. . . .
Love is patient and kind;
love is not jealous or boastful;
it is not arrogant or rude.
Love does not insist on its own way;
it is not irritable or resentful;
it does not rejoice at wrong, but rejoices in the right.
Love bears all things, believes all things, hopes all things,
endures all things. Love never ends . . . .
So faith, hope, love abide, these three;
but the greatest of these is love. Make love your aim. . . ."
PAUL, THE APOSTLE,
I Corinthians 13

NOTES
1. *The Egg* is published at the Center for Religion, Ethics & Social Policy, Cornell University. Dieter Hessel also served the national staff of the Presbyterian Church (U.S.A.) for 25 years as coordinator of social education and of social policy development. His most recent book is *The Church's Public Role: Retrospect and Prospect;* Wm. B. Eerdmans, 1993.
2. See Charles McCoy, "Creation and Covenant: A Comprehensive Vision for Environmental Ethics," in *Covenant for a New Creation,* Carol S. Robb and Carl J. Casebolt, eds.; Orbis Books, 1991.
3. Ruether, *Gaia & God.*
4. "Economics, Eco-Justice, and the Doctrine of God," in Dieter T. Hessel, ed., *After Nature's Revolt;* Fortress Press, 1992. Also see Herman Daly and John B. Cobb, Jr., *For the Common Good: Redirecting the Economy toward Community, the Environment, and a Sustainable Future;* Beacon Press, 1989.

A PORTRAIT OF
African American Christianity

Dr. David D. Daniels

Associate Professor of Church History, McCormick Theological Seminary, Chicago, Illinois

African American Christianity is a religious community within global Christianity, located in the United States of America among the descendents of the African slaves who were violently transported to the Americas beginning in the 1500s. While it has always believed the common creeds of the Christian Church, it also recognizes that religion must be embodied in social structures and practices, and it demands correspondence between these social embodiments of faith in God with personal confessions and lives of faith.

The African American Church emerged in colonial British North America during the revolutionary fervor of the late 18th century. At that time, African Americans discerned the need for assuming responsibility for their religious lives within the Christian faith rather than totally entrusting their religious existence to their oppressors, the slaveholders of European national origins. The other major issue which promoted the emergence of African American Christianity was the institutional racism which shaped most American congregations. In these congregations, parishioners were segregated by race, and African Americans were denied the right to official religious leadership, including the office of minister.

Historically, the African American Church has struggled to create social space where a just system could be erected that affirms the human dignity of African Americans and their humane relationships with others. Currently, African American Christianity is an interdenominational movement with members in communions ranging from Roman Catholicism to Baptist and Pentecostal.

African American churches confess faith in God the Creator, accenting God's creation of all races from a common humanity. African Americans opened their congregations to all Christians regardless of race, and campaigned to end discrimination against persons because of race. During the late 19th and early 20th centuries, the African American Church buttressed its faith in God the Creator by confessing the essence of relationships as "The Fatherhood of God and the Brotherhood of Man." The Civil Rights Movement of the 1950s and 1960s, led by the Rev. Martin Luther King, Jr., communicated the strength of African American Christian faith and demonstrated its resolve to embody its faith within social structures. The congregations spearheaded a national interreligious campaign which struggled to reshape American society; its goal was to dismantle the system of legalized segregation which denied God as the creator of all races and the image of God in all humanity.

African American Christians, as other Christians, confess faith in the province of God. During the eras of slavery and segregation, African Americans remained confident that God was acting in history to overthrow slavery and segregation. They held in creative tension a firm belief in both personal and social salvation. The African American Church is shaped by God's revelation in Jesus Christ. Jesus is worshipped in song, prayer and life as the revelation of God's solidarity with the poor and oppressed through the historical Jesus' identification with poor, the outcast, women and the oppressed of the first century CE.

LIBERATION,
by Archbishop Desmond Tutu

"*African and Black Theology must be concerned—and vitally concerned—with liberation because, as we have shown, liberation is a serious preoccupation at the present time, and it is not seen as being an alternative to personal salvation in Jesus Christ. No, it is seen in Africa as the inescapable consequence of taking the Gospel of Jesus Christ seriously. Only a spiritually, politically, socially and economically free Africa, where Christianity today is expanding faster than anywhere else in the world, can make a distinctive contribution to the life of the body of Jesus Christ and to the world community as a whole....*

from *Hope and Suffering,* p.76

"When you lift your hands outspread in prayer I will hide my eyes from you. Though you offer countless prayers, I will not listen. There is blood on your hands . . . cease to do evil, learn to do right, pursue justice and champion the oppressed, give the orphan his rights, plead the widow's cause."

GOD, speaking in Isaiah 1:15–17

"Is not this what I require of you as a fast: to loose the fetters of injustice, to untie the knots of the yoke, to snap every yoke and set free those who have been crushed? Is it not sharing your food with the hungry, taking the homeless poor into your house, clothing the naked when you meet them and never evading a duty to your kinsfolk?"

GOD, speaking in the Book of Isaiah

"Inasmuch as ye have done it to the least of these my brethren, ye have done it to me . . . . Inasmuch as ye have not done it to the least of these my brethren, ye have not done it to me." JESUS, in Matthew 25

The African American Church identifies racial injustice as the social impact of sin. The impact of slavery and segregation as forms of racism is evident in the structuring and legalizing of an inferior or less- than-human status of African Americans, beneath their God-given status and creation as human beings. The African American Church weds God's goodness to the African American practice of Christian love, along with strong demands for justice; these are seen as keys to the social embodiment of faith in God the Creator and glimpses of the justice of God in society.

Racism, specifically slavery and segregation, is named as the curse of the earth, a violation of God's model of human interaction, a model which reflects God's justice and love which is to be reflected in human relationships. Racism is problematic because it reduces persons who are its victims to objects of labor. It arrogantly uncreates what God created, the humanity of its victims, thus blaspheming God. Racism violates creation by treating people as less than human and legalizing such treatment. The issue goes beyond the denial of inalienable human rights, inhumane labor, restriction of freedoms or cruel treatment. At its core is the attempt to destroy the image of God in persons, annihilating the personhood of its victims. Ultimately, racism mars both the oppressed and the oppressor through its confusion of human authority with the prerogatives and authority of the Creator. Racism also undermines the bonds of human community and corrupts the religions and governments which sanction it and other forms of injustice.

Interreligious dimensions

*I*n addition to the interreligious dimension of the Civil Rights Movement, African American Christianity has indirectly created religious communities with Judaism and Islam through African Americans who adopted Jewish and Islamic beliefs and practices.

From African American Christianity there emerged in the 1890s a new movement which was led by converts to Judaism. While these converts borrowed heavily from Judaism to develop their expression of it, their core remained African American Christianity. Even the early names of their organizations within African American Judaism reflected Christian forms: Church of God and Saints of Christ; Church of the Living God. Other names, reflecting themes of identity were Ethiopian Hebrews and the Moorish Zionist Temple. During the late 20th century, dialogues with the world Jewish communities led African American Judaism to incorporate more aspects of Global Judaism.

In the 1910s there emerged a new movement within Islam led by converts from African American Christianity. Like African American Judaism, it relied on African American Christianity for its form, but borrowed heavily from Islam. This religious community is represented by such organizations as the Moorish Science Temple, the Nation of Islam and the American Muslim Mission.

The African American Church has provided an historic witness to the justice and sovereignty of God within the world community, identifying with many movements around the world committed to the liberation of peoples from oppression. It has historically had dialogue with religiously-inspired movements such as the Hindu-inspired decolonization campaign in India led by Gandhi and the Islam-inspired Palestinian liberation movement. Each endeavor worships God by bringing correspondence between the embodiment of faith in social structures and humane relationships, with personal confession and lives of faith.

Native American – Christian Worship

In North America, as in many countries, there is a considerable range of experience and interaction between Christians of many denominations and indigenous peoples from a wide variety of tribal and religious communities. In many cases, indigenous people are reclaiming parts of their heritage and combining them with parts of the Christian message.

The following description is an example of a way of understanding a shared, interfaith worship experience between Native American Christians and other Christians. It is included here as an example of cross-cultural understanding and worship. The goal, as with other interfaith and intercultural experiences, is to show respect for and to understand the gifts, the rituals and the meanings found in unfamiliar traditions—*as the believers themselves experience it.*

This explanation is excerpted from the service booklet for "A Celebration of Native American Survival," held at the National Cathedral on October 12, 1992. Derived from a longer article written by the Right Reverend Steve Charleston, a Native American Christian Bishop, titled "Planning with Native Americans for a Shared Worship Experience," this explanation was previously printed in "Eco-Letter" of the North American Coalition on Religion and Ecology, Fall–Winter 1992. *–Ed.*

UNDERSTANDING THE WORSHIP EXPERIENCE

The Circle

For Native American people, and for their theology, the Circle is the symbol that expresses its unique identity as a people. It expresses the sense of wholeness, of harmony, unity and mutual interdependence that is at the heart of Native civilization. The Circle is a powerful metaphor for the special insights and gifts that Indian and Eskimo people bring into the Christian faith as part of their ancient cultural heritage.

The Drum

In Indian country, the term "drum" means more than just the physical instrument itself. It implies also the singers who are seen as an organic part of the music; they are also the instrument of the drum. The drum, a perfect representation of the Circle, embodies the heartbeat of the body of Christ.

The Four Sacred Directions

Within the Circle, the points of the spiritual compass indicate the four sacred directions of God's creation. These directions represent the eternal balance of the harmony and goodness of the world. They can be illustrated by different colors, depending on the tribal tradition.

Our Mother, the Earth

Here is a very precious part of Native American theology; it is one that must be accorded great respect. Speaking of the Earth is not done casually in Native worship; rather, the living Earth shows the nurturing, sustaining power of God in all its warmth and beauty.

Cedar, Sage, Sweet Grass and Tobacco

Many tribes have a form of incense to purify the place of prayer and worship. Any of these four can be used individually or collectively as incense during a service.

Native Hymns

A great many traditional Christian hymns have been translated into Native languages. One hymn, "Many and Great, O God, are Thy Works," is actually a Dakota hymn, translated into English, and a part of some hymnals.

A PORTRAIT OF
Confucianism

Dr. Douglas K. Chung

Professor in the Grand Valley Sate University School of Social Work, in Grand Rapids, Michigan; Dr. Chung is writing a book on the understanding and application of religious traditions in social work.

"The moral law begins in the relationship between man and woman, but ends in the vast reaches of the universe."

CONFUCIUS,
Doctrine of the Mean 12

Confucianism is the philosophy of a way of life, although many people also consider it a religion. Chinese, Korean and Japanese philosophical systems synthesize elements of three traditions: Confucianism, Taoism and Buddhism.

Confucianism derives its name from Kung Fu Tzu, or Confucius. Confucius (551–479 BC) is renowned as a philosopher and educator, although he is less known in his roles as a researcher, statesman, social planner, social innovator, and advocate. Confucius was a generalist with a universal vision. The philosophical method he developed offers a means to transform individuals, families, communities and nations into a harmonious international society.

The overall goal of Confucianism is to educate people to be self-motivated, self-controlled and able to assume responsibilities with the dual aim of cultivating the individual self and contributing to the attainment of an ideal harmonious society. Confucius based his method on the assumption that lawlessness and social problems result from the combination of unenlightened individuals and a social structure without norms.

The Confucian belief system is based on several basic principles:

1. In the beginning, there is nothing.

2. The Great Ultimate (*Tai Chi*) exists in the *I* (change). The Great Ultimate is the cause of change and generates the two primary forms: the Great *Yang* (a great energy) and its counterforce, the Great *Yin* (a passive form). *Yang* and *Yin* symbolize the energy of the tension within any system of counterforces: positive and negative, day and night, male and female, rational and intuitive. *Yang* and *Yin* are thus complementary, and in their interaction, everything that is—from quanta to galaxies—comes to be. And everything that exists—all systems—coexist in an interdependent network with all other systems.

3. The dynamic tension between *Yin* and *Yang* forces in all systems result in an endless process of change—of production and reproduction and the transformation of energy. This is a natural order, an order in which we can see basic moral values. Human nature is inherently good. If a human being goes along with the Great Ultimate (*Tao*) and engages in rigorous self-discipline, that person will discover the real self (the nature of *Tao*) and enjoy the principle of change. And since all systems exist in the interdependent network, the person who knows this truth also cares.

4. There are four principles of change:

a. Change is easy.
b. Change is a transforming process due to the dynamics between *Yin* and *Yang*. Any change in either part (*Yin* or *Yang*) will lead to a change in the system and its related systems. The transforming process has its own cycle of expansion and contraction.
c. Change carries with it the notion of constancy and changelessness; that there is change is a fact that is itself unchanging.
d. The best transformation promotes the growth and development of the individual and the whole simultaneously—it strives for excellence for all systems in the interdependent network.

5. Any search for change should consider the following factors:

a. The status of the object in the interdependent network—that is, what is the system and what are this object's role, position, rights and duties in the system?

b. Timing within the interrelated network—that is, is this the right time to initiate change?

c. The mean position or the Golden Path in the interrelated network situation; the mean position is regarded as the most strategic position from which one can deal with change. *Tao* (Truth) exists in the mean (*Chung*).

d. The respondence of *Yin* and *Yang* forces—that is, are the counterforces willing to dialogue or compromise?

e. The integration between the parts and the whole—that is, the system in its economic, political and cultural realms.

6. There is an interconnected network of individual existence, and this pattern of interdependent relationships exists in all levels of systems, from individual, through family and state, to the whole world. The whole is dependent upon the harmonious integration of all the parts, or subsystems, while the parts require the nurture of the whole. The ultimate unit within this framework is the universe itself.

Self is a here-and-now link in a chain of existence stretching both into the past and into a future to be shaped by the way an individual performs his or her roles in daily life. One's humanity is achieved only with and through others.

Individual and social transformations are based on self-cultivation, the personal effort to search for truth and to become a life-giving person. Searching for and finding the truth will lead to originality, the creative ability to solve problems, and development. The process will also enable individuals and systems to be life-giving and life-sharing—to possess a *Jen* (love) personality. Wisdom, love and courage are inseparable concepts.

7. Organizational effectiveness and efficiency are reached when systematically interconnected individuals or subsystems find the truth—and stay with it. Existence consists of the interconnected whole. Methods that assume and take account of connections work better than methods that focus on isolated elements. Organizational effectiveness can be improved through a rearrangement of the relationships between the parts and the whole.

In other words, a balanced and harmonious development within the interdependent network is the most beneficial state for all. Self-actualizing and collective goals should always be integrated.

These principles of Confucian social transformation are drawn primarily from *I Ching, The Great Learning, Confucian Analects* and *The Doctrine of The Mean*.

Thus, in contemporary terms, Confucianism can be defined as a school of social transformation that is research oriented and that employs a multidimensional, crosscultural, multilevel and comprehensive approach applicable to both micro and macro systems. It is a way of life—or an art of living—that aims to synchronize the systems of the universe to achieve both individual and collective fulfillment.

Two major schools of Neo-Confucianism eventually emerged: the rationalists, who emphasized the "inner world" (philosophy), and the idealists, who emphasized practical learning in the "outer world" (social science). The leading exponent of the rationalists was Chu Hsi (1033–1107 AD) and that of the idealists was Wang Yang-Ming (1472–1529 AD). The rationalists held that reason is inherent in nature and that the mind and reason are not the same thing. The idealists held that reason is not to be sought from without; it is nothing other than the mind itself. In ethical application, the rationalists considered the flesh to be a stumbling block to the soul. The idealists, on the other hand, considered the flesh to be as the soul makes it.

Neo-Confucianism in Korea was led by Lee T'oegye (1501–1570) who emphasized a philosophy of inner life and moral subjectivity.

When the Chinese came into contact with Indian Buddhism around the first century AD, the pragmatic side of Confucianism responded and they developed a kind of spiritual discipline called *Ch'an* (meditation). This *Ch'an* philosophy was eventually adopted in Japan, around AD 1200, under the name Zen. Zen is thus a unique blend of the philosophies and idiosyncrasies of three different cultures. It is a typical way of Japanese life, and yet it reflects the Buddhism of India, the Taoists' love of naturalness, and the pragmatism of the Confucian mentality.

Confucianism is thus a strong influence in China, Korea, Japan and the countries of Southeast Asia as well as among people of Far Eastern descent living around the world. More and more Western people are able to appreciate Confucianism through international contacts and through its literature.

Confucianism in the world today

*P*ostindustrial social change has led to human crisis in social networks. The effects of this are seen in any social system: in volunteerism, social support, social care and in the self-help movement.

Postindustrial Confucians today are carrying the vision of Confucianism by applying the Confucian model of social transformation to reach the goal of a Great Harmonious Society. In *Great Learning* Confucius prescribed seven steps of a general strategy of social transformation to achieve the ideal society.

1. The investigation of things (variables). Find out the way things are and how they are related.

2. The completion of knowledge. Find out why things are the way they are; that is, why the dependent variable was related to other variables. This is the reality of things, the truth, *Tao*. And since everything exists in an

interrelated network, discovering this truth empowers a person to transform his or her attitude.

3. The sincerity of thought. One should be sincere in wanting to change or to set goals that are a commitment to excellence and the truth, Tao, which is the source of self-motivation, the root of self-actualization and the cornerstone of adequate I-Thou and I-Thing relationships. The most complete sincerity is the ability to foreknow.

4. The rectifying of the heart. The motivation for change must be the right one, good for the self as well as for the whole. It is a cultivation aimed at virtue, a moral self achieved through the intuitive integration of Jen (humanity, benevolence, perfect virtue, compassion, and love), *Yi* (righteousness), *Li* (politeness, respect), and wisdom (from steps 1, 2 & 3). Only such a self has the real freedom to be free from evil, to have moral courage and the ability to be good.

5. The cultivation of the person. There must be life-long integration between the "knowledge self" (steps 1 & 2) and the "moral self" (steps 3 & 4) through self-discipline (education) and self-improvement. This is the key to helping self and others.

6. The regulation of the family. One should use self-discipline within the family by honoring parents, respecting and caring for siblings, and loving children. One should understand the weaknesses of those one likes and appreciate the strength of those one dislikes to avoid prejudice and disharmony in the family.

7. The governance of the state. The state must provide public education, set policies to care for vulnerable people, make policies rooted in public opinions, appoint and elect capable and moral persons as public officials and employees, and apply the principles of "mean" management. This sort of public administration should lead to the ideal harmonious state. The practice of these seven steps is a self-cultivated discipline that seeks the truth, *Tao,* as the practitioner enacts individual and social changes for an improved and more harmonious world.

The most persistent form of the Confucian worldview sees the person as an integral part of a cosmos dominated by nature. Contentment and material success come only through acceptance of the rightness of the person adjusting himself or herself to the greater natural world to which that person belongs.

Under the impetus of a contemporary revitalization of Confucianism, Confucian economic ethics has become an important force for initiating socio-economic change in China, Japan, Hong Kong, Korea, Singapore and Taiwan. Contemporary Confucianism is a component in the process of social transformation in much of eastern Asia.

Confucius described the ideal welfare state in *Li Chi* (the Book of Rites) as follows:

When the Grand course was pursued,
a public and common spirit ruled all under the sky;
they chose people of talents, virtue and ability;
their words were sincere,
and what they cultivated was harmony.
Thus people did not love their parents only,
nor treat as children only their own.
An effective provision was secured for the aged till their death,
employment for the able-bodied,
and the means of growing up to the young.
They showed kindness and compassion to widows/ers,
orphans, childless people, and those who were disabled by
disease, so that they were all sufficiently maintained.
Males had their proper work, and females had their homes.
(They accumulated) articles (of value),
disliking that they should be thrown away upon the ground,
but not wishing to keep them for their own gratification.
(They labored) with their strength,
disliking that it should not be exerted,
but not exerting it (only) with a view to their own advantage.
In this way (selfish) scheming was repressed
and found no development.
Robbers, filchers and rebellious traitors did not show
themselves, and hence the outer doors remained open,
and were not shut.
This was (the period of) what we call the Grand Union

(pp.365–66).

After the successful integration of Buddhism into Neo-Confucianism, many contemporary Confucians have issued a challenge for another religious integration among five of the major world religions: Buddhism, Christianity, Confucianism, Islam and Taoism. For this to come about, more Asians need to read the Bible and the *Qur'an,* and more Westerners need to know about the *I-Ching* and the *Qur'an.* Such a global dialogue would certainly help facilitate a new global understanding of religions.

REFERENCES

Chung, K. (1992). "The Confucian Model of Social Transformation," in *Social Work Practice with Asian Americans,* edited by Furuto, Biswas, Chung, Murase and Ross-Sheriff. Newbury Park, Cal.: Sage Publications.

Confucius (1971). *Confucian Analects: The Great Learning and The Doctrine of the Mean* , trans. J. Legge. New York: Dover Publications.

Confucius (1967). *Li Chi* , trans. J. Legge. New York: University Books.

Integration of the religions

Dr. Douglas Chung

*T*he Chinese came in contact with Indian thought, in the form of Buddhism, around the first century AD. This event, comparable to the spread of Christianity in the Western world, was marked by three characteristics in particular:

First, the translation of the Buddhist *sutras* stimulated Chinese philosophers and led them to interpret the teachings of the Indian Buddha in the light of their own philosophies. The impact of this study led to the establishment of the Hua-yen and Tien-tai schools of Buddhism in China and the Kegon school in Japan.

Second, under the influence of their familiar, pragmatic Confucian ways of thought, the Chinese creatively responded most to the practical aspects of Buddhism's spiritual discipline, which the Chinese called *Ch'an* (meditation). The *Ch'an* philosophy was eventually adopted by Japan around AD 1200 under the Japanese term Zen. Zen is therefore a blend of the mysticism of Buddhism, the natural philosophy of Taoism, and pragmatic Confucianism—a well-integrated religion or philosophy.

Third, traditional Chinese scholars, both Confucian and Taoist, felt that their cultural foundation had been shaken by the challenge of Buddhism. They reexamined their own philosophies and worked out a way to apply the *I-Ching*—and thus *Yin-Yang* theory—to integrate Buddhism into a new Chinese culture. The *I-Ching*, or *Book of Changes*, describes universal ontology, the processes by which things evolve, principles of change, and guidelines for choosing among alternatives of change. This ancient book of omens and advice is the oldest of the Chinese classics. Confucius used it as an important text in instructing in methods of personal and social transformation.

There are different interpretations of *I-Ching*. The major ones include: Cheng Yi (1050), *I-Ching, the Tao of Organization;* Chih-hsu Ou-i (1599–1655), *The Buddhist I-Ching;* Liu I-ming (1796), *The Taoist I-Ching: I-Ching Mandalas, A Program of Study for the Book of Changes,* translated by Cleary. These different interpretations are a good example of how Buddhism, Taoism and traditional Confucianism were blended into the Neo-Confucianism that profoundly affected the premodern Chinese, Korean, Japanese and Vietnamese dynasties. The Neo-Confucian school attempted a synthesis of Confucianism, Buddhism and Taoism, which culminated in the philosophy of Chu Hsi (1033–1107 AD), one of the greatest of all Chinese thinkers. It guides people to learn the truth (*Tao*) in order to solve problems, which leads one in turn to be harmonious with *Tao*-truth (unification), the core of Confucianism and Taoism. Most Chinese integrate three cultural traditions: Confucianism, Taoism and Buddhism. Under the influence of the *I-Ching* the Chinese are equipped with a *both-and* mentality that seems to integrate religious diversity with less difficulty than the *either-or* tendency of Western mentality.

Both Confucianism and Taoism share the same ontology from *I-Ching* while Buddhism also came to use *I-Ching* to interpret Buddhist thought. They use different approaches, however, to reach the unification with *Tao*/Brahman. Confucians emphasize a rational approach, Taoists focus on an intuitive approach and Buddhists favor a psychological approach. Confucianism favors education and the intellectual approach, while Taoism tends to look down on education in favor of intuitive insight into Nature. Buddhists are interested in changing human perception and thus stress detachment; they tend to participate in the world affairs accordingly.

Huang Te-Hui (1644–1661 AD) of the Ching Dynasty founded the Hsien-Tien-Tao in China. Huang integrated the three main belief systems of Confucianism, Taoism and Buddhism to form the Hsien-Tien-Tao. I-Kuan-Tao (Integrated *Tao*) evolved from the Hsien-Tien-Tao. Chang Tien-Jan was recognized as a master of I-Kuan-Tao in 1930. Various I-Kuan-Tao groups moved to Taiwan in 1946 and 1947, where the headquarters of the I-Kuan-Tao encompasses all the groups into one organization. Today, I-Kuan-Tao priests preach an integrated religion drawn from Confucian, Buddhist, Taoist, Christian and Islamic canons. The concept of oneness of all religions is the major theme, and the mission is to integrate all religions into one.

This religious group was among the first in contemporary society to start interfaith dialogue and interfaith integration. However, many people in Taiwan viewed the I-Kuan-Tao religion as a heresy, and it was officially banned for many years by the government prior to 1987. Since it was granted official recognition, I-Kuan-Tao of Taiwan has expanded internationally. It now has organizations in South Korea, Japan, Singapore, Malaysia, Thailand, Indonesia, the Philippines, Australia, the United States, Canada, Brazil and Paraguay.

A PORTRAIT OF

Hinduism

Dr. T. K. Venkateswaran

Professor of Religious Studies (Emeritus), University of Detroit

Introduction

*H*induism is the oldest and perhaps the most complex of all the living, historical world religions. It has no one single identifiable founder. The actual names found for the religion in the Hindu scriptures are Vedic Religion, i.e. the Religion of the *Vedas* (Scriptures) and *Sangtana Dharma*, i.e. the Universal or Perennial Wisdom and Righteousness, the "Eternal Religion." Hinduism is not merely a religion, however. It encompasses an entire civilization and way of life, whose roots date back prior to 3000 BCE, beyond the peoples of Indus Valley culture. Yet, since the time of the *Vedas*, there is seen a remarkable continuity, a cultural and philosophical complexity and also a pattern of unity in diversity that evolved in the course of its history, also a demonstrated propensity for deep integration and assimilation of all new and external influences.

Main sources of religious knowledge

*S*criptures: (1) The four *Vedas*—*Rig, Yajur, Sama* and *Atharva Vedas*—are seen as *Sruti*, "Heard," as Revelation and "not human-originated," though human beings, wise and holy sages, seers and prophets were the human channels of the revealed wisdom. They "heard" in their hearts the eternal messages and "saw" and symbolized various names and forms of the One, Sacred, ultimate Reality, Truth, God from different perspectives and contexts. The Hindu gods and goddesses, worshipped with different names and forms and qualities are, in reality, many aspects, powers, functions and symbols of the only One all-pervasive Supreme Being, without a second. The *Upanishads*, later portions in the *Vedas*, teach that salvation/liberation is achieved in an experiential way and that oneness with the supreme Reality, *Brahman*, is possible; the supreme goal, *Brahman*, is also the One Self, the higher Self found in all. The philosophy and spiritual practice is known as Vedanta.

(2) The *Agamas* (Further Scriptures) teach union with God as the Lord, the Highest Person, *Brahman* seen in the process of action.

Supplements to the Scriptures: (1) *Smritis* (works of Hindu Law, etc.). (2) The two epics: the *Ramayana* and the *Mahabharata* (along with the *Bhagavad Gita* in the latter, seen almost as an autonomous scripture) and the various *Puranas*.

Basic beliefs, values, paradigms and teachings

*T*he One all-pervasive supreme Being is both immanent and transcendent, both supra-personal and highest person (God), who can be worshipped as both Father and/or Mother of the universe.

The universe undergoes endless cycles of creation, preservation and dissolution. All souls are evolving and progressing toward union with God and everyone will ultimately attain salvation/liberation.

Karma is the moral and physical law of cause and effect by which each individual creates his/her own future destiny by accepting responsibility and accountability for one's own thoughts, words and deeds, individual and collective.

The individual soul reincarnates, evolving through many births and deaths, until all the *karmic* results, good and bad, are resolved. One can and should strive to attain liberation from this cycle of constant births and deaths in this very life, by pursuing one of the four spiritual paths to God—realization, the ways of Knowledge, Love and Devotion, Selfless Action and Meditation.

Four aims or goals in life are arranged hierarchically: The *joy* cluster (sensual, sexual, artistic, aesthetic joys, compatible with ethics), the *economic and social fulfillment* cluster, the *morality* cluster (duties, obligations, right action, law, righteousness, general virtues and supreme ethical values, etc.), and the *spiritual goal of salvation/liberation* (union and oneness with God). All the elements that are usually seen as exclusive or antagonistic in life are brought together in this holistic model, in which every goal has its own place.

Each individual passes through several stages in his/her journey through life toward the spiritual goal. The four classical stages in life are: (1) the student, (2) the house-holder, (3) retirement to the woods for spiritual pursuits and (4) renunciation (optional). Within each stage are specific goals which provide a practical model for the organization of life.

Divine aspects and elements of God, the "presence," are invoked through ritual symbolism and prayers in consecrated images and icons for purposes of worship. God also "descends," periodically, in incarnations and historical personalities such as Rama and Krishna.

All life is sacred and is to be loved and revered, through the practice of nonviolence, realizing that there is unity and inter-dependency among all forms of life and all aspects of the universe. Exemplary spiritual teachers (*Gurus*) who themselves are liberated in this life help the spiritual aspirants with their knowledge and compassion.

No particular religion (including Hinduism) teaches the only, exclusive way to God and salvation, above all others. All authentic, genuine religious paths and traditions lead to the One God and are facets of God's love and light, deserving proper respect, mutual tolerance and right understanding.

Hindu sub-traditions (Sampradayas)

The One Brahman is conceived and symbolized according to divine functions as Brahma (the Creator), Vishnu (the Sustainer and Preserver) and Shiva (the Destroyer of evils and the Dissolver of the universe). This is referred to as the Hindu Trinity.

Within the Great Tradition of Hinduism are four main, living sub-traditions, called *sampradayas*: (1) Shaivites (2) Vaishnavites (3) Shaktas and (4) Smartas. The differences are based upon conceptions and worship of the central name, form, symbols, liturgies, mythologies and theologies of the One God, Lord and highest Person, as Vishnu, Shiva, Shakti (the Divine as Mother), etc. Smartas worship, equally, several personal manifestations of the supreme Reality and philosophically emphasize the ultimate identity-experience of the individual self with the supreme Self, which is also Brahman.

Hinduism has a vast network of sacred symbols. Some are drawn from sacred geography like the Ganges River, others are drawn from plants, bird and animal life; other symbols include profound polyvalent (multi-level meanings) symbols such as the sacred sound-syllable *Om* (also written as *AUM*) which contains all reality, and Shiva's icon as the "Cosmic Dancer," fulfilling all the divine functions.

In the above Hymn of Origins, several ultimate questions are raised: What is time? What is the nature of potency, *karma* (action-influence)? How to understand the mystery of division and differentiation through naming, language into being, non-being, death, immortality and so forth? How to transcend the boundaries of conceptual thought?

Only the highest Spirit knows the full truth of the origins of creation and existence. The quest for the original undivided unifying "Field" and ground cannot be purely conceptual, but has to be experiential, through meditation and spiritual *yajna*. The hymn leads one to the farthest reaches of the frontiers of modern science and cosmology and shows the profundity of what lies beyond anything that can be conceived and spoken of.

"The Knowledge of Akshara the immutable unchanging ground of all relative existence and expressions, brings integrity, stability and fulfillment to the goals of life. One, whose awareness is not opened up, to realize that Akshara, what is the use of mere words and knowledge, scriptures, etc. to him?" Rig Veda I-164-39; also Svetasvatara Upanishad IV-1

"Come together in unity. Speak in profound agreements. May your minds converge (in deep consensus). May your deliberations be uniform and united be your hearts. May you be firmly bound and united in your intentions and resolves." Rig Veda X-191, 2–4

"To one who aspires and is established in Rta, the Cosmic and Moral Order and Harmony, sweet blow the winds. The rivers flow sweet. For us, who are rooted in Rta, may the herbs and plants be as sweet as also the nights and dawns. May the earth and its soil be full of sweetness. May our Father, may the Heaven be sweet. May the plants, the sun and the cows (and animals) be full of sweetness in our life." Rig Veda I-90, 6–8

This beautiful hymn (above) is of profound value for environmental and ecological concerns and awareness. Such hymns in the *Vedas* link peace and sweetness, beauty and quality of life to the daily practice and experience of *Rta* in personal lives with sacred commitment. One of the oft-repeated definitions of God in the *Vedas* is *Rta*, which has several nuances of meanings: Cosmic and Moral Order, Balance, Harmony, the Divine Natural Law and unified Life-giving Energy and Rhythm. *Rta* is also the fundamental norm of existence. Human greed, selfish power, transgression and violation of *Rta*—individually and collectively—brings ecological and social disaster and destruction of the earth.

"May there be peace on earth, peace in the atmosphere and in the heavens. Peaceful be the waters, the herbs and plants. May the Divine bring us peace. May the holy prayers and invocations of peace-liturgies generate ultimate Peace and Happiness everywhere. With these meditations which resolve and dissolve harm, violence and conflicts, we render peaceful whatever on earth is terrible, sinful, cruel and violent. Let the earth become fully auspicious, let everything be beneficial to us."
Atharva-Veda, XIX-9

"Having entered into the earth, with My Life-giving Energy, I support and uphold all the life-forms. Having become the life-giving nectar, I nourish all the herbs and plants." Bhagavad-Gita XV-13

In the above verse, God (speaking as Krishna) indicates that the healing and nourishing functions found in the herbs and plants is divine and of divine origin. The divinity cannot be segregated from Nature nor the latter exploited by human selfishness and greed.

Approaches to interfaith dialogue and cooperation

There are several hymns in the *Vedas* and other scriptures which categorically declare that there are different approaches and perspectives to God and experience of God and ultimate reality. This also arises, necessarily, from different human contexts. The central teaching, constantly repeated is: God is One, but names and forms are many; symbols and paths are many. Thus, there arose a rich theological and philosophical pluralism within Hinduism creating an internal "parliament of sub-traditions and sub-religions," but all grounded in the unity of the *Vedas* and One Brahman. Also, multiplicity is encouraged and thrives by means of the free choice and self-determined identification with one specially-loved manifestation of God—Shiva, Krishna, Shakti, Rama and so on—in pursuing the moral and spiritual path to salvation/liberation.

Because people are at different starting points and stations, Hindu scriptures affirm and accept variety in religious experiences as a necessity and psychological reality. This wisdom is extended to other non-Hindu religions as a spontaneous and logical outflow of the same ethos. There is no historical tradition or theological necessity in Hinduism for proselytization or conversion of non-Hindus to Hinduism. All authentic religions and traditions, all over the world, rising from different historical and cultural starting points and contexts, are to be respected, accepted, appreciated and cherished.

Multiplicity brings with it differences, which one cannot destroy or do away with. Yet, the deep commonalities in structures of religious experience and in the profound moral values found in all religions are to be constantly probed and appropriated for the development of a deeper spiritual and human solidarity and fellowship, transcending the cultural and other barriers. At the same time, the distinctive theological and core-symbol elements and central rites of all religions are to be respected in dialogue and interrelations, based on correct and accurate understandings and on mutual empathy. All should work together to eliminate, in the future, horrors that have been committed in the name of God and religion. Truth values are equally important to the values of religious satisfaction.

Primary challenges facing humanity at this time

Our age has deteriorated to an age of quick fixes of meaning from sources such as science and the media; it has become an analgesic culture. Our contemporary metaphors, symbols and signals are mixed, confused and contradictory. Several examples can show that we live in a mosaic of fragmentation in consciousness, with nothing to hold the pieces together, nothing beneath to connect them and provide a meaningful substratum. We inhabit several historical ages simultaneously.

Social stability and participation in a common good has vastly eroded; we lack a broad consensus where an intricate web of mutual obligations and an accepted network of responsibilities uphold society. Family integrities are threatened.

Cultural and ecological balance and harmony in the universe are being depleted. Economic and technological progress has limits. It now seems unlikely that the wasteful affluence of the West can become available to all. Everyone should learn to endure more weal and woe equally, develop more patience, and pursue real quality of life on the planet, which is not found in the acquisitive amassing of material goods.

Uncontrolled population growth has become another global war, a war which must be won. Religious, cultural and ethnic hatreds are on the increase; horrors of unprecedented scale, violence and cruelty are being unleashed in different parts of the world. Group identities and ideologies are being sanctified and absolutized.

Holistic human development and the complete fulfillment of all needs—material, moral and spiritual—has been lost from view; physical and mental health and the quality of our lifestyles have deteriorated.

Depersonalization caused by mega-cities and technology continues to cheapen the richness and meaning of human joys and life. Computer simulations usurp relationships and are on the verge of providing the most intimate pleasures, on-line, providing virtual sex.

How do members of the Hindu community respond to these issues?

The responses of both the Hindu community and contemporary Hinduism are briefly summarized. Some of these responses are still modest.

There is a renewed and vigorous interest in restoring the rich, polyvalent Hindu myths and their moral, philosophical and spiritual impact through new artforms, media ventures, etc. Of all the peoples, Hindus never abandoned their myths through excessive de-mythologization and heavy rationalization, as happened in the West. If the body needs a house and nourishing food, provided by latest technologies, the soul equally needs an abode in which to grow. In Hinduism, the religious myths built that house and provided a unified and integrated vision on life. One cannot live with values that are only contingent and ephemeral. Hindu art and myths save one from the one-sided reductionistic understanding of reality. It should be carefully noted that myth is different from verbal dogma and ideology. They also help to raise the human consciousness to the highest levels and heal fragmentations.

The "four-fold goals" scheme and the "four-stages in life" paradigm, found in the Hindu *Dharma*, are both needed for holistic human development. These are now being carefully re-studied in their contemporary contexts with the help and insight derived from social sciences. Further relevant interpolations and applications are being generated, with universal implications. Too much emphasis on individual rights has somewhat torn the intricate and delicate network of obligations and duties that are necessary to sustain and uphold family integrity, restore a sense of community, and foster

---

WISDOM, continued

"Oh Brahman Supreme! Formless and colorless are you. But in mystery, through your power you transform your light and radiance into many forms and colors in creation. You bring forth the creation and then withdraw them to yourself. Fill us with the grace of your auspicious thoughts and vision. . . . You are in the woman, in man, you are in the young boy, in the youthful maiden. You are in the old man who walks with his staff. . . . You are in the dark butterfly, in the green parrot with red eyes. . . You are without beginning, infinite, beyond time and space. All the worlds had their origins in you." Svetasvatara Upanishad IV: 1–4

God reveals in silence through women, men, all life-forms. The above verses validate all the four stages of life and also tilt toward those usually neglected and abused—children, women and the elderly—by specific scriptural mention. God is equally present in man and woman.

"All this, whatsoever moves in this moving universe, is permeated and inhabited by God, enveloped by God. Therefore, you should enjoy (the world), only by first renouncing and disowning (the things of the world). Do not covet; whose indeed are (these) treasures (in the universe)?" ". . . In darkness are they who worship only the world. In greater darkness are they who worship the Infinite alone. Those who accept both (seen in relationship), save themselves from death by the knowledge of the former and attain immortality by the knowledge of the latter.". . . "And one who sees all beings in his own Self and his own Self in all beings, no more loathes and hates." Isa Upanishad 1,6, 9–11

The above verses teach non-possessive love and stewardship-enjoyment of things in the world.

"Everything here is verily Brahman (the supreme Sacred Divinity). Atman, the (higher) Self is Brahman. The Self has four grades (four states of consciousness). The first condition of the Self (state) is the waking life of outward cognition and consciousness (of subject-object, dualistic perception). . . . The second state is the inward dream-state cognizing internal objects. The third condition is the deep sleep state, where there are no desires for objects nor any dream-objects, only silent consciousness full of peace and bliss. The fourth (highest) grade of state of consciousness is the (complete) Self (God) in Its own pure state, the fully awakened (and integrated) life of supreme Consciousness. This (fourth) highest ineffable state of the Self is Peace, Love and Bliss, in which the fragmented world-perception disappears, which is the end of evolution, which is the One without a second and non-dual, which should be known, realized and experienced (in Life). In the oneness experience with Him (the Self) lies the ultimate proof of His reality. This Atman (Self) is (indicated, symbolized by) the eternal Word OM." Mandukya Upanishad, (most of the verses)

"They call and name the One, Indra, Mitra, Varuna, Agni and the beautiful Garutman. The Real is One, though wise sages (perceive in their minds) and name It variously." Rig-Veda I-164-46

"The wise sages shape (and symbolize) the One, with their words and expressions into many forms and manifestations." Rig-Veda X-114-5

The above and similar hymns categorically declare for the Hindu that God is One, but names and symbols are many, paths and perspectives are many, all to be respected and loved.

"In whatever way and path, humans worship Me, in that same path do I (meet) and fulfill their aspirations and grace them. It is always My Path that humans follow in all their different paths and journeys, on all sides." Bhagavad-Gita IV:11

God's Way is the Way behind all paths and religions.

"O Mother! Let all my speech be your prayer; let all my crafts and technology be your worship and be the mystic gestures of my hands, adoring you. May all my movements become your devotional circumambulations. May everything I eat or drink be oblations to you. Let my lying down in rest and sleep be protestations to you. Mother! Whatever I do, may all that become a sacramental service and worship for you." ADI SANKARA, *Hymn to the Divine Mother*

Adi Sankara of eighth century CE here worships God as the Divine Mother, exemplifying the experience of Hindus who relate to and approach God, the supreme Person, equally in male and female orientations, both as Father and as Mother. This has profound implications for the vision of equality towards and between the sexes.

world-responsibilities. This shredded fabric has thwarted the creation of abilities and energies needed to create new forms of consensus on the common good.

One of the central definitions of God (Brahman) found in the *Vedas* is *Rta,* which is manifested in the universe and also on planet earth. *Rta* also has mystery and transcendental dimensions, with many meanings, including Order, Balance, Harmony, Law, Unified Life-Energy and the principle of Intelligence. The divine *Rta* is the foundational and fundamental norm of existence, the ground of cosmic and human morality and intelligence. To be fully and really rational is also to be fully moral. *Satya* (Truth) and *Rta* are two sides to the same Divine. Divinity should not be segregated from creation and the all-embracing presence should be constantly felt. This truth, a vital part of the Hindu tradition, is being researched and re-probed to formulate sound environmental and ecological policies and programs at the highest levels. The aim is to seek to restore cultural and ecological balance and harmony, including new population-management and family planning programs with a Hindu ethos, combined with the latest scientific help.

Preventive medicine as seen and practiced in the ancient Hindu medicine-texts and life-sciences such as *Ayurveda* and *yoga*-manuals, along with the already established and well-documented mind-body connections found in those ancient texts, have spurred vast new research and applications world-wide, with future relevance for all. Renewed interest in and use of ancient meditation-systems and techniques is supported by pioneering brain-studies, consciousness research and new, mind-body behavior modifications techniques; together these are pointing toward renewed physical, mental and spiritual health in humanity.

Conclusion

The respect within Hinduism for other religions has been discussed in detail. Beyond that, Hindus everywhere are actively promoting and aggressively participating in interfaith dialogues and other interreligious projects. The constant message is: one should not delimit or circumscribe God by one's own concepts or by one's own religion or world-views.

WISDOM, continued

"May there be welfare to all beings; may there be fullness and wholeness to all people; may there be constant good and auspicious life to everyone; may there be peace everywhere. . . . May all be full of happiness and abundance; may everyone in the world enjoy complete health, free from diseases; may all see and experience good things in their lives, may not even a single person experience sorrow and misery. Om. Peace! Peace! Peace!" Daily prayers of Hindus

Prayers like the ones above and below have been offered and recited daily since ancient times. It is to be noted that the word *sarve* (all, everyone) is constantly repeated. The prayers are universal, offered for all and in the name of all, not for one group, religion, nation or collectivity; they show the inter-dependence of the welfare of one with the welfare of all, treating the whole world as a single family.

"Lead us from the unreal to the Real, from darkness to Light, and from death to Immortality. Om, Peace, Peace, Peace." from the *Upanishads*

A PORTRAIT OF
Islam

Dr. Ghulam Haider Aasi

Associate Professor of Islamic Studies and the History of Religions, American Islamic College, Chicago; Member of the Board of Trustees of the Council for a Parliament of the World's Religions.

Islam

*I*slam is the proper name of religion which Allah, the Alone God, revealed to mankind through the series of human messengers-prophets in human history and completed in His final revelation of *Al-Quran al-Karim, Kalam-Allah* (the speech of God) sent down upon the Prophet Muhammad (570–632 CE). (*Salla-Allahu alayhi wa Sallam*—May Allah's blessings and peace be upon him—abbreviated to SAAWS) Within history, Islam is embodied in the *Qur'an* and in the *Sunnah* (sayings, actions and approvals of the Prophet Muhammad) in its final and eternal form.

The term "Islam" derives from the root letters *s.l.m.* (*Ar. Sin, Lam, Mim*) which means "to be in peace," "to be secure" and "to be integral whole." Hence, Islam means one's conscious submission to the Will, Law and Guidance of Allah, the Almighty Alone God and thus to be in peace with one's own self, with all creatures and with the Creator and Originator of all that exists. The person who consciously surrenders one's whole being to God and commits oneself to pattern one's life on the divine guidance communicated and exemplified by the human messengers-prophets sent by God is called a "Muslim." The *Qur'an* describes Islam in two ways: 1) as the primordial or natural religion (*religio naturalis*) of the innate nature with which Allah created mankind (Q.30:30), and 2) as the religion which was completed and consumated in the *Qur'an*, the final and definitive Divine Writ from Allah.

Allah, the Exalted Almighty Alone God, declares in the *Qur'an* that all the universe and creation surrenders to Him either willingly or unwillingly and that all must return to him (Q.3:83). Whereas the universe surrenders to God's law by its innate nature and is endowed with order, humankind obeys the guidance of God through its divinely endowed moral choice and free will.

"Glorify the name of your Sustainer, the All-Highest, Who creates all that exists, then forms it in its best mold, determines its nature with the proper measure and guides it towards its fulfillment." (Q.87:1–3) (Tr. by M. Asad)

Allah created mankind, endowed them with an innate awareness of Him, empowered them with faculties of reason and cognition and made them to inherit the earth, testing their free choice of good and evil by their obedience to or denial of Allah's universal guidance. *Qur'an* unequivocally declares the unity, uniqueness and universality of Allah, the unity and equality of all mankind, the universality of His guidance to all mankind through the human messengers-prophets and the unity and indivisibility of the Truth. Allah created Adam, the first human being, made him and his progeny inheritors of the earth (*Khalifat-Allah fi al.Ard*), and endowed them with the requisite faculties to be His trustees on earth. His messengers-prophets, starting with Adam and culminating in the Prophet Muhammad (SAAWS), conveyed and exemplified His guidance to their communities.

Historical establishment

*M*uslims believe in the historical crystalization and establishment of Islam within the religious experience of the Prophet Muhammad (SAAWS). He actualized the Will of God as embodied in the *Qur'an* by his beautiful model, the *Sunnah,* and raised a society of true Muslims. His Companions, rightly guided *Caliphs* and *Imams,* carried out his tradition, transmitted it to the following generations and established it in history.

The Prophet Muhammad (SAAWS) was born at Makkah in Saudi Arabia in 570 CE. From a very young age he came to be known as Al-Amin, the honest and trustworthy. At the age of 25 he married a righteous widow, Khadijah, who was 15 years his senior. When he was in his 40s, he was called upon by Allah to deliver His final guidance and message, the *Qur'an,* to mankind and to bring about the *Ummah Muslimah,* the community of submitters to Allah. The Prophet Muhammad received the first revelation sent down upon him through the agency of angel Jibrail (Gabriel) while he was meditating in the cave of Hira'. It reads in translation as follows:

"Read in the name of thy Sustainer, who has created. Created man out of a germ cell. Read, for thy Sustainer is the Most-Bountiful One. Who has taught man the use of the pen. Taught man what he did not know. Nay, verily, man becomes grossly overweening whenever he believes himself to be self-sufficient: for, behold, unto thy Sustainer all must return. (Q96: 1–8; trans. by M. Asad)

In Makkah, the Prophet Muhammad called upon the Arab idolaters of his time to believe in One Alone God, Allah (*Tawhid*), to not ascribe divinity to aught beside Allah. As a result of the scathing criticism of the *Qur'an* against idolatry and its various forms of Associationism (*shirk*) the Makkan oligarchy turned to persecuting Muhammad and his followers. It became so harsh and harrying that the Prophet was commanded to migrate along with his Makkan followers to Yathrib.

This emigration of the Prophet Muhammad and his Makkan Muslims who since then were designated *Muhajirun* (migrants in the Cause of Allah) in 622 CE marked a watershed point in the history of mankind. The

Muslims' religious calendar, known as *Hijri*, is based on this most meaningful and significant event. The city of Yathrib since then came to be known as Madinah (abbreviated from Madinat al-Nabi, city of the Prophet) and it was here that the Prophet was able to establish *Ummah Muslimah*, the religio-moral and socio-political community of Muslims, commonly known as the Islamic city state of Madinah.

Within a decade this nascent and model Muslim community was successful in establishing Islam in the whole of the Arabian Peninsula; in addition, the Prophet sent missions to all the surrounding rulers and empires including both the superpowers of the time, the Persian Sasanid and the Byzantian Roman Christian empires. Just months before his death, the Prophet Muhammad addressed all mankind during his Farewell Pilgrimage to Ka'bah, in Makkah and made the eternal message of Allah universally known and established. Some of the salient parts of this historic address are the following:

"O, mankind, listen to what I say: I do not know whether I will meet you ever at this place after this year. O, mankind, verily your lives, your honor and your property are inviolable and sacred like this day and this month until you meet your Sustainer. You will definitely meet your Sustainer and He will ask you of your deeds. . . . Whoever is entrusted with any trust, he must return the trust fully. Verily, all usury is abolished but you have your capital. Wrong not and you shall not be wronged. Allah has decreed that there is to be no usury. . . . You have rights over your women and they have rights over you. . . . Listen and understand, O, mankind, I am leaving with you the Divine writ, the Qur'an *and the* Sunnah *of His Prophet. If you stick to it you will never go astray. This is a self-evident fact. You must know every Muslim is a brother to another Muslim. All Muslims constitute one brotherhood. One is only permitted to take from a brother what he gives willingly, so wrong not yourselves. O, Allah, be witness I have conveyed."*
(Ibn Hisham, Sirat al-Rasul)

After the death of the Prophet Muhammad in 10H/632 CE, the *Ummah* was first led by the four rightly-guided Caliphs (10–40H/632–661 CE), followed by the dynastic rulers. Both the historical spread of Islam and unprecedented expansion of Muslim rule through all the continents known at the time, within less than a century after the death of the Prophet, changed not only the map of the world but also transformed the destiny of human history and world civilization. By 711 CE, Islam had crossed Gibraltar in the west, Caucasus in the north, Sudan in the south and reached India and China in the east. Muslim *Caliphantes* ruled most of the world, from Al-Andalus, Spain (711–1492 CE) to Asia and Africa, at the period when Europe and the West was still in its dark and Middle ages. Islam made lasting contributions to human civilization and transformed ancient regional civilizations into a world civilization. The so-called Western civilization would never have emerged had there not been the integrating Islamic civilization across the European Dark and Middle ages and the Renaissance.

This *pax Islamica*, however, was never immune from internal disintegration or from external repulsions and reconquests. The Christian reconquest of Spain, the Inquisition and the Crusades set a course of historical conflict between the West and the Muslim world of which European Colonialism and Western Neo-imperialism have been the historical corollaries. Despite all these geo-political changes and socio-economic conflicts, Islam continued to spread, gaining adherents in all parts of the world. Today, Muslims total over a billion and their geographical spread is throughout all the continents. The historic spread of Islam has never been due to its early conquests alone; rather, its appeals are the egalitarian bonding of all believers into universal brotherhood (*Ummah*) and providing them with the spiritual truth of God-consciousness (*Tawhid* and *Taqwa*) that transforms their lives to be meaningful and purposeful.

Main sources

*F*or Muslims the essential sources for all aspects of life are: (a) the *Qur'an*; (b) the *Sunnah* and *Hadith*; (c) *Ijma* (traditional consensus of the Companions of the Prophet and teachings of the *Imams* for the Shi'ah); and (d) *Ijtihad* (reasoning and analogical deduction based on the *Qur'an* and *Hadith* to derive solutions for new problems).

(a) **The Qur'an.** Muslims believe in the *Qur'an* as verbatim revelation from Allah, sent down upon Muhammad through the agency of the angel Gabriel during Muhammad's prophethood, 610–632 CE. The whole *Qur'an* was sent down upon the Prophet piecemeal, was memorized, written and publicly transmitted upon its revelation. Its uniqueness as an inimitable miracle and eternal definitive words of God, its historical preservation, regular and authentic transmission and dissemination are essential beliefs of Islam. It comprises 114 *surahs* (chapters) which are designated as Makkan or Madinan according to the place of their descent upon Muhammad.

(b) **Sunnah** and **Hadith.** The second universal source of Islam is the *Sunnah* which comprises sayings, actions and approvals of the Prophet Muhammad. Their reportage in narration is called *Hadith*. Six collections are recognized as authentic by the Sunni Muslims; the Shi'ah recognize Al-Kulini's collection, entitled "AL-Kafi," as earliest and authentic.

(c) **Ijma.** Sunni Muslims believe in the consensus of the Muslim scholars and the community as the third source of Islamic law whereas the Shi'ah take the teachings and interpretations of the *Imams* as binding.

(d) **Ijtihad.** This names the total effort of a religious scholar to discover both the intent of the Islamic law and the correct answer to a new problem in light of the first two material sources called *Nass* (divine text), through a well-defined systematic procedure of *Qiyas* (analogical deduction).

Beliefs and observances

A: Articles of Faith (*Arkan al Iman*)

*M*uslims believe in six articles of faith which are derived from revealed sources, the *Qur'an* and the *Sunnah*. (Q.2:285; 4:136, 150–152)

(i) Belief in **One Alone God, Allah**. He is Unique, Infinite, Transcendent, Creator and Sustainer of all that exists. "Nothing is like unto Him." (Q.42:11) He Alone is worthy of worship. All else is His creature and servant. He is Unique both in his essence (*Dhat*) and in His attributes (*Sifat*). "His are the beautiful names (99 beautiful names described in the *Qur'an*) and all that is in the heavens and the earth glorify Him . . . ." (Q.59:24; 7:180; 17:110; 20:8)

(ii) Belief in the **eternal life of Hereafter** (*Al-Akhirah*). Muslims believe in the end of the world, in Ressurrection, in the resurrection of whole person after death (*al-Ba'th*), in the Day of judgment (*Yawm al-Hisab*) and in eternal Hell and Paradise.

(iii) Belief in **angels**. Muslims believe in angels as creatures of Allah, eternally busy in His service, glorification and Praise. ". . . they never disobey God what he commanded them to do and do what they are ordered." (Q.66:6; 16:50)

(iv) Belief in **Revelations from God**, commonly known as belief in the Books from God. Muslims believe that Allah revealed His messages and guidance to different messengers at different times and places. These include the scrolls of Abraham, the *Torah* to Moses, Psalms to David, *Injil* to Jesus, culminating in the *Qur'an* to the Prophet Muhammad.

(v) Belief in **human messengers-prophets of God**. Muslims believe that Allah chose certain human beings as His prophets and messengers to convey His guidance and to exemplify it for their people. Every peoples have a prophet from among themselves who conveyed the guidance and norms of God to them in their own language. Muslims believe that the series of prophets starts with Adam and includes Abraham, Noah, Moses, Jesus, and culminates in Muhammad, who is the Seal of the office of Prophethood. The office of Prophethood is indivisible. May God's blessing and peace be with all of them. (Q.10:47,14:4, 16:36, 21:25, 28:59, 33:40)

(vi) belief in the **Decree and Plan of God**. Muslims believe that all happens, good or evil, with the decree of God and nothing can fail His Plan. (*Qada wa Qadar*).

B. Pillars of Islam (*Arkan al Islam*)

(i) *Shahadah*: The statement of faith. A person becomes a Muslim when one out of his own will and conviction bears witness to the fact that there is no deity but Allah and Muhammad is His messenger (and final prophet and servant).

(ii) *Salat*: Every male and female adult Muslim is obliged to offer five daily worship-prayers. (Q.4:103, 2:177)

(iii) *Sawm*: Fasting during the whole month of *Ramadan*, the ninth month of Muslims' lunar calendar and abstaining from food, drink, sex and all sorts of idle and immoral acts from dawn to sunset. (Q.2:183–187)

(iv) *Zakat*: Sharing wealth. Every Muslim who has his savings for a year is obligated to pay a fixed portion of it to the needy, the poor and those who are under debt. Wealth-sharing purifies the giver's wealth from greed and stinginess and reconciles the hearts of the recipients. (Q.9:60)

(v) *Hajj*: Pilgrimage. All Muslims who can afford journey to Ka'bah, in Makkah, Saudi Arabia, both physically and financially, are obliged to perform pilgrimage once in their lifetime; it is usually made during the first ten days of the last month of the Muslim *Hijri* Calendar, *Dhu-al. Hijjah*. Pilgrimage at other times is called *"Umrah."* (Q.2:189–179, 3:97)

Schools of law

*W*ith the developing needs of the Muslim *Ummah*, the expansion of the Muslim empire and changing situations, there arose a need to derive laws from the revealed sources and to develop a systematic method for doing so. Though there were many legal opinions in the beginning, by the end of third century *Hijrah*, four schools of law were recognized as othodox among the Sunni Muslims: Hanafi, Maliki, Shafi'i and Hanbali. Among the Shi'ah, two became prominent: Ja'fariyah of the Twelver Shi'ahs of Iran and Zaydiyah (Fivers) of Yemen.

Theological schools

*A*t its earliest stage Muslim theological speculation emerged in response to internal political differences. The murder of Uthman (d.656 CE), the third Caliph, and subsequent civil wars raised important issues, including: Who is a true believer? What is the nature of faith (*Iman*) and its relation to Islam (submission to God's law)? What qualifies a person both to be the leader and member of a truly believing Community? Variant responses to these questions split the *Ummah* first into different political views and groups, then resulted in sects:

(i) *Khawarij*
The first explicit political and theological schism was of the Khawarij (Secessionists) who called for extreme piety and idealistic egalitarianism. They fought against all claimants of political rule. Some even rejected the need for any governing institution. Their pursuit of a pure society later led them to fanaticism and violence. Continuous rebellion against every goverment and ever-increasing internal dissension and disunity almost eliminated their

role and existence. Those who survived took refuge in the rugged mountains of North Africa and Yemen.

(ii) Shi'ah

The second major schism represented, in its earliest phase, primarily a socio-political critique against the rulers; later it became a permanent sect or branch of Islam. The name "Shi'ah" was given to the partisans of 'Ali (d.661 CE), the son-in-law of the Prophet, the fourth-rightly guided *Caliph* of the Sunnis and the first *Imam* of the Shi'ah. They developed the doctrine of *Imamah* over and against the Sunni Khilafah. According to this view, the legitimate successor of the Prophet was 'Ali, their first *Imam*, whose succession then continued in his descendants who are thus political and religious leaders. These *Imams* are divinely inspired, infallible and authoritative interpreters of the *Qur'an*. Later, debating the legitimacy of different Imams, Shi'ism split into numerous sects. Their main branches are:

a. *Ithna 'Ash'ariyyah* (Twelvers) believe in the 12 *Imams* and hold that a son, Muhammad al-Muntazar, was born to the 11th *Imam*, Hassan al-Askari (d.874) but went into concealment until he will reappear at the proper time to set the whole world in order. They subscribe to the legal school *Ja'fariyyah*, have been established in Iran since the *Safvid* period (1501) and constitute the largest branch of Shi'ah.

b. *Zaydiyah* consider Zayd b. Ali (d.740), the second grandson of Husayn, to be the fifth and final *Imam*. Zaydiyah follow the Zaydi school of Islamic law and are closer to Sunnis. They established themselves in Yemen.

c. *Isma'iliyah* take Ismail's (d.760) son Muhammad as the impending *Mahdi*. They split into many offshoots such as Fatimids, Qaramitah, Druz, Nizaris and Agha Khanis, continuing to present times.

(iii) Sunnis

The majority of Muslims—more than 90 percent of all Muslims in the world—identify themselves with the term *Ahl- al-Sunnah wa al-Jama'ah*, or People of the Tradition and the Community, commonly known as Sunni in distinction to unorthodox sects and groups. Among them, two main theological schools and dispositions became permanent. In their classical terms, these are known as *Mu'tazilah* and *Ash'ariyah*. The first tendency represents rationalist philosophical theology while the second emphasizes the absolute primacy and total sufficiency of the revealed texts, the *Qur'an* and the *Sunnah*.

Contemporary Movements

Most of the revivalist or reform movements—pejoratively called fundamentalist or neo-fundamentalist groups in the West—derive their thought and arguments from Ash'riyah and its sister traditional theologies.

Feasts and Festivals

Muslims observe a lunar calendar of 354 days. The two most important religious feasts celebrated by all, everywhere, are the two *Ids*:

(i) **Id al-Adha**, the feast of Sacrifice and *Hajj*, is celebrated on the tenth of *Dhu al-Hijjah*, the 12th month. Congregational worship prayer is offered in the open or in big *mosques*. Every household slaughters an animal, and meat of sacrifices is shared and distributed.

(ii) **Id al-Fitr** is celebrated on the first day of *Shawwal*, the tenth month, to give thanks for completion of the fasting of *Ramadan* and asking God's forgiveness. *Id-Salat* is offered in congregation in the open or in big *mosques*. On both *Ids*, charity is given, gifts are exchanged, open houses are maintained, visits are made to friends, neighbors, relatives and even to graveyards. Generosity, hospitality and caring are hallmarks of these feasts.

(iii) In addition to the two '*Ids* there are other optional small holidays or historical celebrations such as fasting on the tenth of the first month, vigil on *Laylat al-Qadr*, popularly on the 27th night of the fasting month of *Ramadan*, celebrating the birthday of the Prophet (Mawlid al-Nabi) on 12th of the third month and on first *Muharram*, as the *Hijri* new year day, etc. Shi'ah particularly commemorate the martyrdom of Husain (d.680), the grandson of the Prophet, during the first ten days of *Muharram*.

Sufism

One of the most enduring contributions of Islam to human spirituality is its mystical tradition and dimension generally known as Sufism, more correctly called *Tasawwuf*. It is unfortunate that, more often than not, Islam has been perceived as a political, legalistic, orthoprax and this-worldly religion due to its distinctive emphasis on the Transcendence and complete otherness of Unique and Alone God. The historical fact, however, is that it is the Islamic spiritual reality rather than Muslim imperium or an Islamic state which made Islam a universal religion. This stream of spiritual experience has been carried on by Sufis who have been the mystics and scholars of traditional Islam up to the present. Sufism sees the essence of the human in his being "of God, in the world" rather than "of the world, for God." It sees humans innately bound with God due to the primordial covenant of their souls witnessing to the fact of God's lordship. (Q.7:172)

It is human forgetfulness of God and absorption in the material world that makes them alienated from their essence. (Q.59:18–19) Hence, to gain one's real self is to be in constant remembrance of God (*Dhikr*; Q.13:28) and to detach oneself from the transitory material world. True submission (*Islam*) is to make one's heart, not just head, the real throne of God where God manifests Himself both as Transcendent and Immanent. Realizing such presence of God requires one to experience the absolute love of God, by dying in Him and living in Him. Out of their religious experiences, Sufis derived the doctrines of *Fana* (dying in God or annihilation of the human self and attributes in God) and *Baqa* (living with God and acquiring divine attributes). They systematically developed and explained the different stations and states through which every genuine mystic has to tread on the path of spiritual experience of reality. While the primary requirement for a Muslim is to abide by the rules and regulation of the Islamic law and rituals (*Shari'ah*), that observance does not guarantee the spiritual experience of God and His vision.

It is to devote and pledge oneself to God through the experienced guide that one can tread the path of spiritual reality (*Tariqah*). Within the variety of these religious-spiritual experiences, the mystics of Islam introduced their orders and provided institutions where adepts lead the initiates to experience of spiritual reality.

Islam and other religious traditions

*N*o other religious scripture addresses the issue of the religious diversity of mankind as directly as the *Qur'an*. It emphasizes the unity and universality of One Alone God, unity and equality of mankind, unity of the Truth and universality of God's guidance to all mankind through human messengers-prophets, starting from Adam and culminating in the Prophet Muhammad who is the final messenger and the mercy to all the worlds (*Rahmatan lil'alamin*, Q.21:107; 7:158; 34:28; 33:40). The *Qur'an* declares that God created all mankind as one religio-moral community (*Ummah wahidah*). It was humanity's exercise of freedom of will and claim of self-sufficiency (Q.96:6-7) that led to differentiation and to deviation from the innate nature. Then God, out of His universal grace, raised among them messengers who conveyed God's guidance to them in their own languages. (Q.16:36; cf:35:23–25; 23:44; 10:47; 14:4 and more)

Whereas each community ought to have accepted the universality of God's messages and believed in His messengers-prophets, their mutual jealousy and attempts to appropriate God's favor turned them instead to splitting the one and true religion of God and dividing into sects and mutually exclusive communities. (Q.23:51–53; 21:92–94; 30:30–32) Yet even this religious diversity with different symbols and rituals is categorized by the *Qur'an* as God-willed reality so long as it does not fall into the worship of false deities (idolatry) and does not deny universal fundamental principles of truth and morality. (10:19; 11:117–119; 16:93; 42:8).

ALL MANKIND were once one single community; (then they began to differ) whereupon God raised up the prophets as heralds of glad tidings and as warners, and through them bestowed revelation from on high, setting forth the truth, so that it might decide between people with regard to all on which they had come to hold divergent views. Yet none other than the self-same people who had been granted this (revelation) began, out of mutual jealousy, to disagree about its meaning after all evidence of the truth had come unto them. But God guided the believers unto the truth about which, by His leave, they had disagreed: for God guides onto a straight way him that wills (to be guided).
(Q.2:213 Tr. by M. Asad)

And unto thee (O Prophet) have We vouchsafed this divine writ, setting forth the truth, confirming the truth of whatever there still remains of earlier revelations and determining what is true therein. Judge, then, between the followers of earlier revelation in accordance with what God has bestowed from on high, and do not follow their errant views, forsaking the truth that has come unto thee. Unto every one of you have We appointed a (different) law and way of life. And if God had so willed, He could surely have made you all one single community: but (He willed it otherwise) in order to test you by means of what He has vouchsafed unto you. Vie, then with one another in doing good works! Unto God you all must return; and then He will make you truly understand all that on which you were wont to differ. (Q.5:48 Tr. by M. Asad)

Qur'an rejects any claim of appropriating God's truth or favor. No person, race or nation is chosen of God. Any claim on God's unilateral covenant or saving grace by any atonement is vehemently rejected by the *Qur'an*. For God all humans are equal. What characterizes one as noble is one's God-consciousness (*Taqwa*) and carrying out His norms of universal ethics.

"O' mankind, Behold, We have created you all from a male and a female and have made you into tribes and nations so that you might come to recognize one another as (interdependent and equal), verily noblest of you before God is one who is most conscious of Him, verily, God is all knowing, all aware." (Q.49:13, Tr. by M.Asad)

Islam abolished and condemns all forms of racial, tribal or national prejudices which cause one to stand by one's own people in an unjust cause over and against truth and justice. (Q.5:2, 8).

The *Qur'an* reconfirms the fact of earlier revelations from God and hence it gives to the adherents of *Torah* and *Injil*, Jews and Christians, the appellation of *"Ahl-al-Kitab,"* the people of the revealed scriptures. Though the Qur'an explicitly identifies the Jews and Christians as *Ahl-al-Kitab*, the term in its general import and implicit *Qur'anic* allusions extends to all religious traditions which might concur with identifying their religious sources as derived from one and the same Divine source. Thus the Prophet also included Zoroastrians in this category. With the spread of Muslim rule over Asia, India and Africa, some Muslim jurists later included both Hindus and Buddhists in the category of *Ahl-al-Dhimma* which, by extension, absorbed all non-Muslims who chose to be the subjects of the Muslim rule.

Islam does not identify people in terms of political, geographical, ethnic, racial or national entities, rather it categorizes them in terms of their religio-moral commitments and religious traditions. As Professor Dr. Syed Muhammad Naquib al-Attas, the Founder-Director of International Institute of Islamic Thought and Civilization, Kuala Lumpur, maintains:

"We Muslims not only tolerated non-Muslims but also opened our doors of lands and houses even, our hearts and minds to make them feel at home amongst us."

But what made Muslims the pioneers of religious coexistence was their recognition of non-Muslims as legal citizens based on rules derived from the teachings of the *Qur'an* and the *Sunnah*. And it was on these grounds that Muslims worked out the detailed legal rights and duties of non-Muslims vis-a-vis the Muslims as a part of Islamic law. Muslims were the first to recognize non-Muslims as *religio licita*, providing them legal religio-cultural autonomy. Every Muslim goverment or leader is obliged by the Prophetic command to safeguard the rights of non-Muslims with special care (*Dhimmat-Allah wa Rasulihi*).

The *Qur'an* categorically prohibits coercion in matters of religion, be it by sheer force or implicit deceptive ways. Muslims are obliged to call mankind toward submission to God by wisdom, good example and sincere exhortation, not in argument, but with kind manner (Q.2:257; 16:125). Such imperatives of the *Qur'an* provide Muslims with a clear call to humanity; Muslims repeat and try to live by the following guidelines in their interreligious dialogues and cooperations:

"Say, O followers of earlier revelation, come unto that tenet which we and you hold in common—that we shall not ascribe divinity to aught beside Him, and that we shall not take human beings for our lords beside God."
(Q.3:64. Tr. by M. Asad)

Cooperation, peace, justice and virtue

The main objective of every venture of interreligious dialogue and cooperation is to bring about justice, order and peace in the world. Cooperation in furthering virtue and justice and in ending evil and aggression is exactly one of the most distinctive imperatives of the *Qur'an* (Q.5:2&8).

A PERSONAL PLEA

While I am writing these words early in July 1993, I cannot help but express my extreme disappointment in all world bodies and conferences, including religous organizations, with regard to the situation in Bosnia-Herzegovina. In his open letter addressed to: "All of Those Who still Believe in Love and Divine Justice," my dear colleague and friend Dr. Mustafa Ceric, Supreme Head of Islamic Community in Bosnia-Herzegovina writes:

"We, the Muslims of Bosnia, have been betrayed. All that remains to us is the hope that people who believe in love and justice, particularly the religious leaders of the world's major faiths, will stand with us.

We call upon: all the Muslim *ulama* of the world in the name of Muslim altruism; on the leadership of all the Christian denominations—Catholic, Orthodox, Protestant and all others—in the name of Christian love

and mercy; on the Jewish Rabbinate in the name of supreme justice; on every Buddhist leader in the name of Buddha's Compassion; On Hindus, Confucians, Taoists, Parsis, Bahá'ís, in sum, every religious leader as well as secular humanists in the name of their principles, to help us. . . .

Let them voice love in the face of hatred, justice in the face of murder. And let them voice their religious vows here in Sarajevo, the city of mosques, churches, synagogues and temples where different faiths and traditions have always lived in peace . . . where today genocide of Bosnia's Muslims is carried out."

As I repeat this cry for justice and appeal to human conscience, my heart is rending with pain. Will the Parliament of the World's Religions, 1993, in Chicago stand to change the situation?

Islam and the parliaments of the world's religions

At the 1893 World's Parliament of Religions, Islam was not represented properly. Alexander Russell Webb, a singular American new Muslim, made a genuine effort to bring across the true teachings of Islam to the West, but to no avail. Since its historical inception to the present, Islam has been grossly misunderstood and distorted in the West. Most of the papers on Islam were read and written by Christian missionaries active in the Muslim world at the time. They not only explained away Islam, but also reasserted more stereotypes, a legacy which continues to the present. Whereas for centuries distortion of Islam and stereotypes of it were created and carried out by the missionaries and mercenary Orientalists, today this distortion continues by the Western media and by those who are antagonistic to Islam.

Muslims hope and pray that the 1993 Parliament of the World's Religions at Chicago will lay the foundations of proper understanding of Islam in the West and America, and that the Western World will see in Islam the panacea rather than the threat to the needed just world order. ✿

STATEMENT OF ACKNOWLEDGMENTS
First, All praise and thanks are due to Allah. I am also grateful to American Islamic College, both to its administration and community for providing me with the time and facilities to work for the CPWR. For the preparation of this article, I am extremely thankful to International Institute of Islamic Thought and Civilization, Kuala Lumpur, to its Founder-Director, Dr. Prof. Syed Muhammad Naquib al-Attas and to all its members for providing me the time and facilities. Special thanks are due to Ms. Nor Azimah for typing it unfailingly.

Most of all my heartfelt gratitude is due to my wife, Zubaida and to my children: Humaira, Sumaira, Irfan, Rummanah and Salman. Without their continous support and unceasing sacrifices I would have never been able to make contributions to these good causes.

Finally, I acknowledge Joel Beversluis, the Editor of this *SourceBook*, whose constant encouragement and unceasing forbearance brought this to publication.

May God Almighty bless all!

Islam in America

Dr. Aminah B. McCloud

Professor of Islamic Studies in the Department of Religious Studies at DePaul University, Chicago

*I*slam first came to North America on the souls and tongues of African traders, and then in the hearts of many African slaves. Islam comes in a more noticeable garb with immigrants in the late 19th century and with a string of influence beginning with the 20th century. There is no monolithic Islamic expression among Muslims in America since it has all the diversity of the Muslim world. By 1960 Islam was definitely an American religion with its own institutions and several generations of indigenous Muslims. Muslim children could attend Muslim schools through the high school level in almost every major city in America by 1960. Since the 1960s the Muslim presence in the public space is also evident in the spread of the domed *masajid* and Arabic calligraphy signs.

The study of Islam in America is important for a variety of reasons. It is the fastest growing religion in America. Its basic practices and beliefs are obviously different from American Protestant Christianity. Since Muslims act in concert with other Americans in a wide assortment of tasks such as the practice of medicine, industry, education and even celebrations, some knowledge of those differences is crucial. To handle the needs of their community and to promote an understanding of Islam, Muslims have formed dozens of organizations—professional, social and educational. In spite of these efforts dialogue between Muslims and other religious communities has been sparse. While there are numerous texts on Muslim–Christian relations, there are almost no texts on encounters within the American context. It is only recently that Islam has come to be seen as a legitimate part of the American religious landscape by scholars, and most of this has come through a media focus.

In America, Muslims struggle to enact the obligations of their faith. The obligation to pray five times daily (*salat*) at certain times can be problematic in the American work place or school. Often Muslims encounter the American resistance to the notion of prayer as an intimate part of one's self understanding. In the work place, Muslims often trade breaks and/or lunch times to meet the obligations of daily prayer and the congregational prayer on Fridays (*Jum'ah*).

The work place can also provide challenging social encounters with regard to dress, lifestyles, holidays and professionalism. Most Muslim women have met numerous obstacles with reference to dress and their head scarves, while some Muslim men have the same problems with the length or presence of their beards. Muslim reluctance to participate in social gatherings where the main activity is drinking and dancing has led to difficulties. Differences have often led initially to hostility, later followed by understanding and in some cases accommodation. The celebration of holidays remains an issue since Islamic celebration days appear on very few calendars; most often, Muslims must take vacation or sick days in order to participate in the festivities. On Christian holidays, however, Muslims are forced to observe closed offices and the cessation of work.

Fasting (*sawm*) also provides some difficulty for the Muslim in America. The Islamic fast is one of abstinence from food, drink and certain behaviors from sunrise to sunset for 30 days. Alertness of mind and the ability to carry out tasks is somewhat compromised during the first few days of the fast, which can make the American work load difficult. Whether the Muslim is a student or a physician, this is indeed challenging. The other part of the tradition during this month of fasting where the believer tries to make extra prayers nightly in the *masjid* also puts a strain on the Muslim who has to be at work at 8 a.m. the next morning. Students often experience the most challenge in the public school systems where they may be questioned as to the legitimacy of this religious obligation.

Muslims fulfill the obligations of the giving of charity in several different ways. *Zakat* (the formal giving of a specified amount of charity) is given to the local community for distribution to those in need at the end of the month of fasting. The more informal, day to day charitable response to misfortune or to assist in a positive venture is carried out on a person-to-person basis in and across communities.

Muslims in America have taken their diversity and in many ways have welded these cultural differences into one face of Islam. All communities are open for prayer and participation in social activities to everyone. Efforts in business and education express the variety of ethnicities and their social concerns. Muslims in America, without regard to ethnicity, remain tied to all parts of the Muslim world. Political issues emerging abroad have profound effects on Muslims in America at many levels. In many cases these communities are highlighted and sometimes maligned for political and religious differences. This is currently the fueling force for the necessity of dialogue.

The largest single contingent of Muslims in America is African American. At least 17 different communities evidence choices of Islamic philosophy and Islamic responses to American racism and theocentricity. As indigenous Americans and as ex-slaves, their move into the Islamic worldview has often been challenged as inauthentic. There remains an ongoing suspicion that these choices for Islam by up to four generations of African Americans continues to be a protest against the abuses of Christianity. While this may have been a primary impetus decades ago, it has long ceased to hold weight in current spiritual understandings and experience. African American Muslims, alongside their brothers and sisters from the Muslim world, have developed the necessary institutions and businesses for community in America.

The real need now is for greater attention to Islam in its American context. There is a critical need for awareness of the American Muslim position on American affairs as well as for dialogue on issues and concerns. ⊛

Islam in the World Today:

Situations of Minority Conflict and the Ummah's Responsibilities

Syed Z. Abedin

Director of the Institute of Muslim Minority Affairs, Jeddah, Saudi Arabia and London, U.K. (deceased May 1993)

Introduction

The world situation with respect to Muslim minority communities around the globe is getting more complex day by day. No respite appears to be in sight. We at the Institute of Muslim Minority Affairs have at the moment no propositions either. In any case, we do not see ourselves as problem solvers. Most cases of conflict in present times which involve Muslims are of a political nature and their solution calls for political initiatives on the part of governments.

What we can do and have been doing over the past ten years, in our capacity as an independent research Institute, is to formulate the right questions and to provide an accurate and objective data base for possible answers. This helps to clarify the issues. And if there is will on the part of the contending parties, the Institute's input could facilitate the search for solutions.

One reason perhaps why viable solutions have not been forthcoming is that nobody is asking the right questions.

As is well known, there are at least half a dozen situations in various corners of the globe where Muslims are presently engaged in a desperate struggle. Imminent or potential conflict situations are many times this number.

Now in all these situations, live or latent, major or minor, the Ummah is urged to intervene. These calls for active intervention are made not only by those minority Muslims who are immediately affected but also by various constituents within the Ummah. Thus the pressure on the Ummah is both domestic and foreign, internal and external.

The Ummah is thus faced with a dilemma. The dilemma consists in that even if there were consensual will on issues of minority conflict on the part of all its constituents members, resources are not inexhaustible. There is no way in which the Ummah could wage a determined, aggressive and successful campaign on all fronts where Muslims are presently engaged in conflict with others.

Let us not forget that even the United States not too long ago had to solicit material and manpower resources of over two dozen countries of the world in order to wage a successful campaign on one single front.

To make matters more complicated upholders of the Islamic cause inside the Ummah insist on making each occasion of conflict anywhere in the world, in which any number of Muslims are involved, a test case for the Ummah's Islamic commitment and its consciousness of accountability before God Almighty.

The Ummah has therefore before it two options: it could either choose to plunge into every quarrel anywhere in the world where Muslims in any number feel that they are being thwarted from getting whatever they want, and in consequence cease to be a credible world power, or it has to face the wrath of its own people, who see in the lack of alacrity on the part of the Ummah a sign of betrayal of Islam.

Verbal jihad

The Ummah's record in the past indicates that to save face it has opted for a third alternative: this third alternative for want of a better term may be described as a verbal jihad. Every now and then, when the domestic pressures build up, various spokesmen of the Ummah come forward with passionate statements directed at the offending parties.

In these event, the statements could have constituted a clever, strategic compromise between the two options noted above. But these statements, pliable though they are, end up adding further fuel to a fire that should not have been started in the first place: they alienate the non-Muslims concerned from all the constituents of the Ummah (even from the faith they profess), and raise false hopes of Ummah support among the Muslim minorities. This leads to tragic consequences.

The Ummah concept

One possible way of resolving this dilemma could be to look at the Ummah as representing not a political but primarily a religious and spiritual concept. Realistically speaking, in present times there appears to be no other way of giving viable meaning to this concept. For, if the Ummah is projected as a political entity, then there is in truth no Ummah. There are indeed 50 or more sovereign Muslim states, but they are nation states, each with its own national goals and interests, but no Ummah.

If on the other hand the term Ummah is accepted as primarily reflecting a religious and spiritual concept, then in all situations of conflict the question to ask would be: Is this a religious conflict? i.e., Are Muslims being victimized because of their religion? Are their rights to freedom of worship, belief, practice and propagation being denied?

If the consensus among the constituents of the Ummah is that, yes, it is a religious conflict, then without doubt every effort should be made to resolve it to Muslim satisfaction.

But if our investigation reveals that the real cause of the conflict is not religious but ethnic, national, economic, strategic or political and that religion is being used merely as a pretext, then like all secular conflicts, it should be amenable to negotiations, accommodation and compromise. The *Ummah's* responsibility would then be to use its good offices to facilitate such a resolution.

However, it is important to remember that the procedures adopted for doing do by the *Ummah* would be markedly different from those adopted in the case of a religious conflict. The hell-fire and brimstone strategies most often employed in religious conflicts in our time are not likely to pay much in dividends in political conflicts.

Unfortunately, this important distinction has not always been maintained by even responsible spokesmen of the *Ummah*.

Furthermore, it has also to be considered that if a conflict is truly a religious conflict, then in all good conscience it has to be conducted as one. We cannot claim commitment to a cause and then go on to pursue the cause oblivious to its value limitations. Islam is not a racial, national or ethnic concept. We are Muslims not because we all have kinship or language ties, or live in the same territory, or dress in the same way or prefer the same cuisine. We are Muslims because we together believe in certain common values. These values color (or should color) everything we do. So that without being told who we are, anybody looking at us, from our appearance and behavior, could determine that these must be followers of the faith of Islam.

In Islam there is no concept of total war. In any case, we as a people were not raised to conquer the world for God. God is capable of doing so Himself. Didn't He say in the *Qur'an* that if He had wanted to He could have made the whole world Muslim? But He did not (*Qur'an* 10:99). We were raised in order to be a witness (a model) unto what a God-conscious life of total surrender to His will is supposed to be lived like and look like.

Revenge or reconciliation?

*I*n a situation of conflict between two groups, one Muslim and the other non-Muslim, in particular in the case of actual or potential conflict between Muslim minorities and non-Muslim majorities, the crucial question to determine at the very outset is: Is the primary concern of the *Ummah* to put a nation or a community or a religion in the dock before the international community, i.e., to determine culpability first?

Or, is it to provide urgent relief to the suffering millions engaged in conflict?

It should never be forgotten that however cheap

Muslim life may have become in our time, causing its wanton loss for self-titillation or communal ego-boosting is still a cardinal sin.

It is also perhaps instructive to note here that however cynical and polarized, religiously or nationally, the world may have become, the conscience of the world community is still alive and well. Indeed, some of the most damaging indictment of government policies toward their Muslim minorities has come not from Muslims but from non-Muslims themselves, both indigenous and foreign.

And herein lies our hope

Let us build on this hope. Let not the forces of hatred and fanaticism drown our Islamic good sense. Let some people among us plumb the depths and resources of our moral and Islamic being and come up with ways of understanding and resolution.

Who knows what non-Muslim powers may also be waiting for such an opening. After all, they also well realize that, considering the present international order, the minorities that reside within their jurisdiction cannot be just wished away. In fact, looked at from the perspective of history, non-Muslim states such as Russia, China, India and Bulgaria which contain significant Muslim minorities, would not be what they are today if their national life had not been interwoven by the multiple and many hued contributions of their minority constituents.

The people of conscience in these countries have given and are giving expression to their sense of outrage at the violation of human and civil rights perpetrated in these societies. Perhaps these people are also wishing for such a gesture on our part. They have already done *their* human duty. It is now *our* turn.

Let us put aside, for a while at least, our sense of umbrage as Muslims and take our Islamic courage in hand and be the first to break this impasse, this standoff between communities and states, between the governors and the governed.

Let the world community know that we come, not to condemn nor to aggravate an already sensitive and explosive situation, but that we desire only to understand and ameliorate. Whether it be Russia or China or India or Philippines or Bulgaria or Cyprus or Burma, let the world know that we come, more in sorrow than in anger, to help find a workable arrangement that would put a stop to the bloodletting and the suffering and the humiliation and the loss of honor and dignity. And to help lift the burdens and the shackles that have oppressed the victims, and equally, the conscience of the perpetrators.

Is this too much to ask?

A PORTRAIT OF
Jainism

Dr. N. P. Jain

Former Ambassador of India to the EEC, UN, Mexico, Nepal and Belgium

This prayer is continued on the next page

A JAIN PRAYER

1. May my thoughts and feeling be such that I may always act in a simple and straight-forward manner. May I ever, so far as I can, do good in this life to others.

2. May I never hurt and harm any living being; may I never speak a lie. May I never be greedy of wealth or wife of another. May I ever drink the nectar of contentment!

3. May I always have a friendly feeling towards all living beings of the world and may the stream of compassion always flow from my heart towards distressed and afflicted living beings.

4. May I never entertain an idea of egotism; nor may I be angry with anybody! May I never become jealous on seeing the worldly prosperity of other people.

5. May I never become fretful towards bad, cruel and wicked persons. May I keep tolerance towards them. May I be so disposed!

6. May I ever have the good company of learned ascetics and may I ever keep them in mind. May my heart be always engrossed and inclined to adopt the rules of conduct which they observe.

7. May my heart be overflowing with love at the sight of the virtuous, and may I be happy to serve them so far as possible.

8. May I never be ungrateful (towards anybody); nor may I revolt (against anybody). May I ever be appreciating the good qualities of other persons and may I never look at their faults.

9. May my mind neither be puffed up with joy, nor may it become nervous in pain and grief. May it never be frightened even if I am in a terrible forest or strange places of cremation or graveyards.

Jain religion is one of the oldest religions of India and indeed of the world, dating back in its origin to around 2500 BC. Twenty-four *Tirthankaras* (Leader-prophets) beginning with Lord Rishabhanath and ending with Lord Mahavir (599–527 BC) have guided its evolution and elaboration by first achieving and then preaching.

All the *Tirthankaras* were, at one time, historical figures enjoying immense political power and high social status. And yet, at the pinnacle of material glory, when the light of *ahimsa* (nonviolence) and *aparigraha* (non-attachment) dawned upon them, they renounced all material possessions of life, set out on the path of spiritual enlightenment and eventually achieved emancipation by conquering the suffering inherent in the instinct of attachment to material illusions.

Jain religion is unique in as much as in its existence of about 5,000 years, it has never compromised on the concept of nonviolence either in principle or practice. It upholds nonviolence as the supreme religion *(Ahimsa Parmo Dharmah)* and has insisted upon its observance in thought, expression and action at individual as well as collective levels.

Reverence for all forms of life is deeply ingrained in the Jain ethos. Both in its philosophical essence as well as rituals, Jain religion invokes an intense and constant awareness of communion and interdependence not only with all living beings but indeed with all elements of nature. The holy text *Tatvartha Sutra* sums it up in the phrase *"Parasparopragha Jeevanam"* (all life is mutually supportive).

Jain religion presents a truly enlightened perspective of *equality of souls*, irrespective of differing physical forms of living creatures ranging from human beings to animals and microscopic living organisms. Humans, alone among living beings, are endowed with all the six senses of seeing, hearing, tasting, smelling, touching and thinking; thus humans are enjoined upon to give the lead for achieving oneness and harmony with all life by being compassionate, loving, tolerant, forgiving, rational and full of equanimity.

Jain philosophy envisages *harmonious coexistence between humans and nature* in creating an environment that is at once peaceful and non-polluted as well as congenial and inspiring to spiritual upliftment.

Jain religion has a clearly articulated scientific base which elucidates the interrelated properties and qualities of animate and inanimate substances; the interrelationship is described in terms of evolution and the growth of atoms in time and space as an integral part of the oneness of all life. Religious impulse is equated with the search for "Truth" (*Satya*) that: "by soul alone I am governed" (*appanam anusasayi*) and "Let *Karma* not bind you." The path of enlightenment is sought by finding the kingdom of god within one's inner self through right belief (*Samyak Darshan*), right knowledge (*Samyak Gyan*), and right conduct (*Samyak Charitra*).

Jain religion focuses primary attention on *non-attachment (Aparigraha)* towards material things of life through self restraint, fasting, abstinence from overindulgence, voluntary curtailment of one's needs and elimination of the aggressive urge. The rituals and practices prescribed for monks (*Mahavrata*) are more rigorous than those (*Anuvrata*) prescribed for ordinary followers. *Aparigraha* and *Ahimsa* taken together imply supreme respect for ecology and the conservation of the environment through avoidance of injudicious exploitation of nature or its wanton destruction.

Vegetarianism is a way of life for a Jain, taking its origin from the concept of kindness toward living creatures (*Jiva Daya*). The practice of vegetarianism is regarded as a potent instrument for the practice of nonviolence and peaceful, cooperative coexistence. Jains are strict vegetarians, consuming only one-sensed beings (vegetables) and milk products.

Anekantavada is another basic principle of Jainism which offers a wider, multiple and nondogmatic perception of human relationships. Just as a father also has the role of a husband, a brother, a boss or a cousin to different persons, life has multiple rays radiating from a single element. Relativity in thinking promotes a broader, more universal and more appreciative perspective on life.

Jainism has not only shown a spiritual way of life to its followers, but has inspired a distinct stream of culture which has enriched philosophy, literature, art, architecture and sculpture, democratic living and spiritual advancement in India. Although Jain religion did not spread abroad as widely as Buddhism, it was spread across all parts of India. Jain literature, a rich treasure, is found in Sanskrit, Prakrit, Hindi, Gujrati, Kannada and Tamil languages in varied forms of poetry, prose drama, and story. Temples at Abu, Ranakpur, Halebid, Gomak, Satrunjaya, Sametshikhar, Deogarh and Sravanabelgola are marvelous examples of art and architecture, ethically depicting serenity in a detached and dignified form.

The followers of Jainism number around ten million. Jain religion is not dogmatic or caste ridden. It is an open philosophy, whose benefits can be taken up by anyone willing to improve one's quality of life and render human conduct rational in situations both of stress and strain as well as harmony and tranquillity. Principles of Jain religion have a universal message for humanity as a whole and an abiding relevance in a rapidly changing world.

AHIMSA

Know other creatures' love for life, for they are alike ye.
Kill them not; save their life from fear and enmity.
All creatures desire to live, not to die.
Hence to kill is to sin.
A godly man does not kill.
Therefore, kill not thy self, consciously or unconsciously,
living organisms which move or move not,
nor cause slaughter of them.
He who looketh on the creatures of the earth, big and small,
as his own self, comprehendeth this immense world.
Among the careless, he who restraineth self is enlightened.

LORD MAHAVIRA

10. May my mind remain always steady and firm, unswerving and unshaken; may it become stronger every day. May I bear and endure with patience the deprivation of dear ones and occurrences of undesired evils.

11. May all living beings of the world be happy! May nobody ever feel distressed! May the people of the world renounce enmity, sin, pride and sing the songs of joy every day.

12. May Dharma (truth) be the topic of house-talk in every home! May evil be scarce! May (people) increase their knowledge and conduct and thereby enjoy the blessed fruit of human birth.

13. May disease and pestilence never spread, may the people live in peace, may the highest religion of Ahimsa (non-injury) pervade the whole world and may it bring about universal good!

14. May universal love pervade the world and may ignorance of attachment remain far away. May nobody speak unkind, bitter and harsh words!

15. May all become "heroes of the age" heartily and remain engaged in elevating the Cause of Righteousness. May all gain the sight of Truth called Vastuswarupa (Reality of substance) and may they bear with pleasure, trouble and misfortunes!

AMEN

SARASWATI MAHA MANTRA
(To the Goddess of Learning)

Oh goddess, you are living in
the mouth of Arihant.
You can destroy all kinds of sin.
A thousand, thousand flames
are burning from you and
you are distributing divine knowledge.
My sin, burn, burn, destroy, destroy.
Ksham, Ksheem, Kshoom,
Kshoum, Kshah.*
You remove all my poisons.
You are white like milk.
You took birth from nectar.
Give me wisdom.

*Ksham—seed of power for protection
and happiness.
Ksheem—seed of psychic power and goodness.
Kshoom—seed of power to remove
sadness and depression.
Kshoum—seed of power to purify *sushumna*
and contact Divine.
Kshah—seed of calling power and acceptance.

PRAYER

Highly auspicious are the adorable ones
And so are the emancipated;
The saints too are the auspicious ones
And so is the speech divine.

Best in the world are the adorable ones
And so are the emancipated;
The saints too are the best in the world,
And so is the speech divine.

Refuge do I take in the adorable ones.
And also in the emanicpated;
Saints are also the place of my refuge.
And so is the speech divine.

Thus do I pay homage and veneration
Unto the great Arhats every day
In devotion deep with the purity in mind,
In speech and in deed indeed.

THE IMMORTAL SONG

1. May the sacred stream of amity flow forever in my heart
   May the universe prosper, such is my cherished desire.
2. May my heart sing with ecstasy at the sight of the virtuous,
   And may my life be an offering at their feet.
3. May my heart bleed at the sight of the wretched, the cruel,
   the irreligious,
   And my tears of compassion flow from my eyes.
4. May I always be there to show the path to the pathless wanderers
   of life,
   Yet if they should not hearken to me,
   May I bide in patience.
5. May the spirit of goodwill enter all our hearts,
   May we all sing in chorus the immortal song of human concord.

FIGHT AGAINST DESIRES

O man! Control thyself.
Only then you can get salvation.
If you are to fight, fight against your own desires.
Nothing will be achieved by fighting against external enemies;
if you miss this occasion, it will be lost forever.
One's own unconquered soul is one's greatest enemy.

The above prayers and songs are from *Jainism—Past and Present:*
Prayers, Articles and Short Stories, published and compiled by Dr. Tansukh J. Salgia,
1984, Parma, Ohio, USA

The Jain Declaration on Nature

Dr. L. M. Singhvi

*T*he Jain tradition which enthroned the philosophy of ecological harmony and nonviolence as its lodestar flourished for centuries side-by-side with other schools of thought in ancient India. It formed a vital part of the mainstream of ancient Indian life, contributing greatly to its philosophical, artistic and political heritage. During certain periods of Indian history, many ruling elites as well as large sections of the population were Jains, followers of the *Jinas* (Spiritual Victors).

The ecological philosophy of Jainism which flows from its spiritual quest has always been central to its ethics, aesthetics, art, literature, economics and politics. It is represented in all its glory by the 24 *Jinas* or *Tirthankaras* (Path-finders) of this era whose example and teachings have been its living legacy through the millennia.

Although the ten million Jains estimated to live in modern India constitute a tiny fraction of its population, the message and motifs of the Jain perspective, its reverence for life in all its forms, its commitment to the progress of human civilization and to the preservation of the natural environment continues to have a profound and pervasive influence on Indian life and outlook.

In the 20th century, the most vibrant and illustrious example of Jain influence was that of Mahatma Gandhi, acclaimed as the Father of the Nation. Gandhi's friend, Shrimad Rajchandra, was a Jain. The two great men corresponded until Rajchandra's death, on issues of faith and ethics. The central Jain teaching of *ahimsa* (nonviolence) was the guiding principle of Gandhi's civil disobedience in the cause of freedom and social equality. His ecological philosophy found apt expression in his observation that the greatest work of humanity could not match the smallest wonder of nature.

. . . .

"There is nothing so small and subtle as the atom
nor any element so vast as space.
Similarly, there is no quality of soul more subtle than non-violence
and no virtue of spirit greater than reverence for life."

"One who neglects or disregards the existence of earth, air,
fire, water and vegetation disregards his own existence
which is entwined with them."

MAHAVIRA, 500 CE

. . .The ancient Jain scriptural aphorism *Parasparopagraho jivanam* (all life is bound together by mutual support and interdependence) is refreshingly contemporary in its premise and perspective. It defines the scope of modern ecology while extending it further to a more spacious "home." It means that all aspects of nature belong together and are bound in a physical as well as a metaphysical relationship. Life is viewed as a gift of togetherness, accommodation and assistance in a universe teeming with interdependent constituents.

excerpted by the Editor from *The Jain Declaration on Nature*

For more information or copies of the full Declaration, contact:
Bhagwan Mahavir Memorial Samiti
3 Benito Juarez Road
New Delhi 110 021, India
or

Federation of Jain Associations in North America (JAINA)
9831 Tall Timber Drive
Cincinnati, Ohio 45241 USA

NOMOKAR MOHA MANTRA
(The Universal Prayer)

Obeisance to the Arihamtas–perfect souls–Godmen

I bow down to those who have reached omniscience in the flesh and teach the road to everlasting life in the liberated state.

Obeisance to the Siddhas–liberated bodiless souls

I bow down to those who have attained perfect knowledge and liberated their souls of all *karma*.

Obeisance to the masters–heads of congregations

I bow down to those who have experienced self-realization of their souls through self-control and self-sacrifice.

Obeisance to the teachers–ascetic teachers

I bow down to those who understand the true nature of soul and teach the importance of the spiritual over the material.

Obeisance to all the ascetic aspirants in the universe

I bow down to those who strictly follow the five great vows of conduct and inspire us to live a virtuous life.

This five-fold obeisance mantra

To these five types of great souls I offer my praise.

Destroys all demerit

Such praise will help diminish my sins.

And is the first and foremost of all

Giving this praise is most auspicious—

Auspicious recitations

So auspicious as to bring happiness and bliss.

from *Jainism–Past and Present,*
by T. J. Salgia

THE WORTH OF WISDOM

"*With what shall I come before the LORD
And bow myself before God most high?
Shall I come before him with burnt-
    offerings, With calves a year old?
Will the LORD
be pleased with thousands of rams,
With myriads of streams of oil?
Shall I give my first born for my
    transgression, The fruit of my body for
the sin of my soul?
You have been told, O man, what is good,
And what the LORD requires of you:
Only to do justice, and to love mercy,
And to walk humbly with your God?"*

MICAH 6:6–8

"*God shall judge between many peoples,
and shall decide for strong nations afar off;
and they shall beat their swords into
    plowshares,
and their spears into pruning hooks;
nation shall not lift up sword against
    nation,
neither shall they learn war any more;
but they shall sit every man under his
    vine and under his fig tree,
and none shall make them afraid.*"

MICAH 4:3–4

"*How happy is the man who finds
    wisdom,
The man who gains understanding!
For her income is better than income of
    silver,
And her revenue than gold.
She is more precious than corals,
And none of your heart's desires can
    compare with her.
Long life is in her right hand,
In her left are riches and honor. . . .*"

"*The LORD by wisdom founded the earth,
By reason he established the heavens;
By his knowledge the depths are broken up,
And the clouds drop down dew.*"

THE BOOK OF PROVERBS

A PORTRAIT OF
Judaism

Rabbi Herbert Bronstein

Senior Rabbi, North Shore Congregation Israel, Glencoe, Illinois; member of the Board of Trustees of the Council for a Parliament of the World's Religions

"Hear O Israel,
the Lord Our God, the Lord is One."
And you shall love the Lord, your God,
with all your heart, with all your might, with all your soul.
And these words which I command you this day,
shall be upon your heart that you may remember,
do all my commandments
and be holy unto your God.

DEUTERONOMY (*D'Varim*) 6.4–9

*T*hough often spoken of as a "Western" religion and linked with Christianity ("Judeo-Christian tradition"), Judaism has its origins in the Middle East.

Judaism is a spirituality which indeed gave birth to Christianity, and later played a role during the emergence of Islam. But Judaism as we know it began almost 4,000 years ago among a pastoral/nomadic and later agricultural people, the ancient Hebrews.

The religion of the people Israel was and is the loving and faithful Covenant devotion to one God who revealed Divine Teaching through the mothers and fathers of the people of Israel (the Patriarchs and Matriarchs), through Moses and the Prophets and Sages whose spirituality is documented in the 22 books of the Hebrew Bible.

The goal of this Covenant consciousness in alliance with the Divine is clearly put in the ancient texts as:
    A good life for all,
through adherence to God's Teaching (*Torah*)
and Commandments (*Mitzvot*),
harmony on earth on the individual and social levels
culminating in peace and well-being for all humanity.

Thus Judaism is characterized as a religion of deed, a "Way" by which human beings are capable of understanding and responding to God's teaching.

Because over the centuries every major power that entered the Middle East (namely Egypt, Assyria, Babylonia, Persia, Greece and Rome) coveted the land of Israel (a strategic joining point of Africa, Asia and Europe), the religion of Israel changed, not in central principles or institution but in form, in response to the demands of changing conditions, including oppression and exile.

After the Roman destruction of the central Temple in Jerusalem and the end of Jewish independent existence in the Holy Land, Judaism was separated from the sacrificial cult, the priesthood disappeared, and Judaism became a religion of congregations all over the world in which Worship, Deeds of loving kindness and the Study of God's Teaching replaced the central cult of the Temple in Jerusalem. Nevertheless, Jerusalem remained a central spiritual symbol of Jewry throughout the world linked with the vision of redemption of the Jewish people from exile and oppression, and, peace for all the world (the Messianic vision).

In Judaism as it developed, prayer services emerged which recapitulated the main stories and themes of Judaism, from the universal *Creation* by the Universal God to the *Revelation* of God's Teaching to Moses and the people at Mount Sinai to the *Redemption* of Israel and all humanity. It is a way of life in which all Jews are equally responsible as "a Kingdom of Priests and a Holy People."

Over the centuries a vast body of teaching and lore has grown up, often taking the form of exegesis or interpretation of the ancient Biblical texts. This has included the elaboration of actual religious practice (the *Halacha* or "Way") and philosophical texts, stories, homilies, parable and poetry (the *Aggadah*). The vast rabbinic text known as the *Talmud* (again, "Teaching"), is second only to the Bible in importance. There is also a continual mystical stream in Judaism embodied in the various texts known collectively as *Kabbalah* (the "received" tradition) such as the *Zohar* (the *Book of Splendor or Illumination*) which teach the emanation of the Godhead into the world, the experience of communion with God in transcendence of the self and the maintenance of the cosmos through human action in Covenant with God. Again the basic mythos or narrative embodied in Judaic consciousness is *from* the universal God, Creator of all of existence *through* particular Jewish covenant existence *to* the universal redemption of all Beings and all Being from bondage.

The basic symbol of Judaism is thus a seven-branched candelabrum which embodies cosmic images of all Time and Space. It is also a symbol of the Redemption which is the goal of human existence. This symbol is reducible to Light which is expressed many times in Jewish observance: the kindling of the Sabbath and Festival lights in the home; the braided candle at the end of the Sabbath; the kindling of lights in the eight day midwinter Festival of Lights (*Chanukah*) which commemorates the rededication of the holy Temple from pollution and therefore of the sacred from profanity; the memorial lights to remember the dead; and the Eternal Light over the Ark in the synagogue which contains the *Scroll of the Torah*.

Jews celebrate the recreation of the moral order of the world and the rebirth of the soul at the beginning of the religious year (*Rosh Hashanah* and the Day of Atonement, *Yom Kippur*) a ten day period of spiritual introspection and moral resolve. The home celebration or service which relives in story and song, ritual and prayer the Exodus from Egypt at the Passover (*Pesach*) season is called a *Seder* celebration. Its themes reenergize Jewish social consciousness, Jewish hope and vision of a better day for all.

Jews are not divided into creedal denominations, strictly speaking, in the same manner as Christianity. There are "streams" of Jewish religious life which express varying responses to the encounter of Jews with the modern world. The most liberal of these is usually designated as "Reform" or "Liberal" Judaism which has responded by adapting to more western styles of worship. "Reform" leans toward the vernacular in worship and has modified considerably the forms of observance passed down by tradition.

Orthodox Judaism conceives of the entire corpus of Jewish observance, the received tradition, as equivalent to having been given by God at Sinai and therefore unchangeable except through procedures which were themselves given at Sinai.

Conservative Judaism finds its way between these two positions.

Reconstructionism is the most recent stream to emerge in modern Jewish life. It conceives of Jewish religious forms and observances as part of an historic Jewish culture or "civilization." Reconstructionism values this culture, linking its preservation with a naturalist theology. Reconstructionism has recently been hospitable to neo-mystical themes and observances.

However, this does not begin to describe the considerable varieties of Jewish religious life in all of its dimensions and degrees in our time. The number of Jews is in the world is estimated at 12,807,000, the number of Jews in North American is estimated at 5,880,000.

"The highest wisdom is kindness."
BERAKOT, 17a

"Deeds of kindness are equal in weight to all the commandments."
T. J. PE'AH, 1:1

"'Thou shalt love thy neighbor as thyself.' This is the great general rule in Torah."
T. J. NEDARIM, 9:4

"The beginning and the end thereof [Torah] is the performance of loving-kindness."
SOTAH, 14a

"If two men claim thy help, and one is thy enemy, help him first."
BABA METZIA, 32b,

"If the community is in trouble, a man must not say, 'I will go to my house, and eat and drink, and peace shall be with thee, O my soul.' But a man must share in the trouble of the community, even as Moses did. He who shares in its troubles is worth to see its consolation."
TA'ANIT, 11a

"The command to give charity weighs as much as all the other commandments put together. . . . He who gives alms in secret is greater than Moses."
BABA BATHRA, 9b

"God says: 'Both the Gentiles and the Israelites are my handiwork, therefore how can I let the former perish on account of the latter?'"
SANHEDRIN, 98b

"*In that hour when the Egyptians died in the Red Sea, the ministers wished to sing the song of praise before the Holy One, but he rebuked them saying:*
'My handiwork is drowning in the sea; would you utter a song before me in honor of that?'"   THE SANHEDRIN

"*In a city where there are both Jews and Gentiles, the collectors of alms collect both from Jews and Gentiles, and feed the poor of both, visit the sick of both, bury both, comfort the mourners whether they be Jews or Gentiles, and restore the lost goods of both.*"   T. J. DEMAI, 6:6

"*One man alone was brought forth at the time of Creation in order that thereafter none should have the right to say to another, 'My father was greater than your father.'*"   T. Y. SANHEDRIN, 4:5

"*You must not pervert the justice due the resident alien or the orphan, nor take a widow's garment in pledge. You must remember that you were once a slave yourself in Egypt, and the LORD your God rescued you from there; that is why I am commanding you to do this.*

When you reap your harvest in your field, and forget a sheaf in the field, you must not go back to get it; it is to go to the resident alien, the orphan and the widow, that the LORD your God may bless you in all your enterprises. When you beat your olive trees, you must not go over them a second time; that is to go to the resident alien, the orphan and the widow. When you pick the grapes of your vineyard, you must not go over it a second time; that is to go to the resident alien, the orphan and the widow. You must remember that you were once a slave yourself in the land of Egypt; that is why I am commanding you to do this."
LEVITICUS 24:6–22

Judaism and interfaith dialogue

There is a profound religious and historic basis to the Jewish view on interfaith dialogue.

Jewish belief encompasses a dialectic between an all embracing humane Universalism and deep commitment to a particular Jewish religious way of life and to the continuity of the Jewish people as a religious people. Between the two, namely, universal humane concern and Jewish particularism, there is, in the Judaic world view, no contradiction. And, in fact, the ideal Jewish position is integration of the two: On the one hand, the ideal Jew is deeply loyal to his own faith, way of life and people. There is, at the same time, a firm commitment in Judaism to God's universal embrace, care and love for all humanity, the ideal of loving one's fellow human being as oneself. The *Torah* teaches that all humanity is created in the image of God. In the Jewish myth of creation, one couple, Adam and Eve, are the parents of all humanity. In this view God speaks to all human beings and all human communities in various ways. All perceive the one God in their own way and take different paths to the service of the ultimate Godhead. Dialogue would therefore be an endeavor to understand, on the deepest level possible, the views and positions of the Other toward the goal of ultimate harmony between all human beings which is the Judaic affirmation of the Sovereignty of God, harmony, peace, *Shalom*.

But over the centuries Jews, as a minority in the Christian world, were subject to persecution, degradation, impoverishment, rioting and even mass death for their loyalty to their faith. "Interfaith" contact was all too often a staged disputation to prove the falsity of Jewish faith and a prelude to the burning of Jewish holy books, physical attacks and even murder of Jews, sometimes in massive numbers. Jews often confronted the choice between conversion and martyrdom. Therefore, many Jews of traditional leaning, while willing and eager to work on ameliorative civil projects with all other groups, are leery of any theological dialogue that would tend to undermine the faith commitment of Jews as a minority community. However, throughout the modern period, but most particularly in the twentieth century and particularly in pluralistic North America, Jews have been partners in Christian/Jewish dialogue as well as with Muslims and Buddhists.

Today Jews join in that trend of dialogue which is moving toward an attempt to understand the *faith of the believer* rather than simply studying simplistically about the beliefs of other faiths.

A PORTRAIT OF
Sikhism

Dr. Rajwant Singh and Ms. Georgia Rangel

Dr. R. Singh is Secretary, The Guru Gobind Singh Foundation, Maryland, and a member of the Board of Directors of North American Interfaith Network; Georgia Rangel is a member of The Guru Gobind Singh Foundation.

*F*ounded only 500 years ago by Guru Nanak (1439–1539), Sikhism is the youngest of the world religions. After a revelatory experience at the age of about 38, Nanak began to teach that true religion consisted of being ever-mindful of God, meditating on God's Name, and reflecting it in all activities of daily life. He condemned superstition and discouraged ritual. He traveled throughout India, Ceylon, Tibet and parts of the Arab world with followers of both Hindu and Muslim origin, discussing his revelation with those he met. His followers became known as Sikhs (from the Sanskrit word *shishya*—disciple.

Nanak and his nine successors are known as *gurus,* which is a very common term in all Indian traditions for a spiritual guide or teacher. In Sikhism, *"Guru"* means the voice of God speaking through someone. Sikh *gurus* were careful to prevent worship being offered to them. The last living *guru,* Guru Gobind Singh, who died in 1708, pronounced the end of the line of succession and declared that henceforth the function of the *guru* as teacher and final authority for faith and conduct was vested in the community and the Scriptures, the *Guru Granth Sahib.* It occupies the same place in Sikh veneration that was given to the living *gurus.*

The *Guru Granth Sahib* is at the heart of Sikh worship and its presence lends sanctity to the Sikh place of worship, the *gurdwara.* This holy book contains devotional compositions written by the Sikh *gurus,* recorded during their lifetimes. It also contains hymns by Hindu and Muslim religious thinkers. Written in Sanskrit, Persian, Hindi and Punjabi, the compositions are set in rhymed couplets. The *Guru Granth Sahib* is printed in *Gurmukhi* script, an alphabet adapted by the second *guru,* Guru Angad, for the Punjabi language. It has standardized pagination, all copies having 1,430 pages. The *Rehat Maryada* (Sikh Code of Conduct) published in 1945 by the SGPC of Amritsar, Punjab, India, regulates individual and corporate Sikh life.

Beliefs

*T*he seminal belief in Sikhism is found in the *Mool Mantra* with which the *Guru Granth Sahib,* begins:

*T*here is One God.
He

> *Is the Supreme Truth*
> *Is without fear*
> *Is not vindictive*
> *Is Timeless, Eternal*
> *Is not born so*
> *He does not die to be reborn.*
> *Self-illumined,*
> *By Guru's grace*
> *He is revealed to the human soul.*
> *Truth was in the beginning, and throughout the ages.*
> *Truth is now and ever will be.*

In Sikhism, time is cyclical, not linear, so Sikhism has no eschatological beliefs. Rather, just as time is seen as repeated sequences of creation and destruction, individual existence is believed to be a repeated sequence of birth, death and rebirth as the soul seeks spiritual enlightenment.

Sikhs believe that greed, lust, pride, anger, and attachment to the passing values of earthly existence constitute *haumai* (self-centeredness). This is the source of all evil. It is a person's inclination to evil that produces the *karma* that leads to endless rebirth. *Haumai* separates human beings from God.

God is All-Pervading and is the Source of all life. Sikhism believes that human life is the opportunity for spiritual union with the Supreme Being—to merge with the Ultimate Reality as a drop of water merges with the ocean and becomes one with it. Thus is one released from the cycle of death and rebirth. By God's Grace, not by one's own merits, is achieved the level of spiritual self-knowledge necessary to reach this stage of enlightenment. Any person, of whatever intellectual or economic level, may become enlightened through a life of single-minded devotion to God. Enlightenment, not redemption, is the Sikh concept of salvation.

Life cycle events are recognized in Sikhism by naming of the newborn in the *gurdwar,* the marriage ceremony, and the funeral, following which the body is cremated. Any kind of funeral monument is forbidden.

Sikhism rejects asceticism and encourages full participation in family and work day life and responsibility as the framework within which to seek God. Sikhism is founded on the principle of equality of all persons. It rejects the caste system, and inculcates in its adherents an egalitarian attitude and practice toward men and women of all races, religions and social classes.

Sikh names do not indicate gender. All Sikh men, therefore, take the additional name Singh (lion) and women take the name Kaur (princess). Guru Gobind Singh, the tenth *guru,* instructed his followers to drop their last names which in India indicate one's caste. They are to use only Singh and Kaur to show their acceptance of the universal equality of all persons. Another symbol of the Sikhs' acceptance of universal equality is the *langar*. This is a meal which is eaten together by the congregation, shared food becoming a social leveler.

In adulthood, a Sikh is initiated into full membership by the *Amrit* ceremony which was originated by the last human *guru* in 1699. At this time, the initiate promises to follow the Sikh code of conduct as an integral part of the path toward God-realization. He or she vows at that time:

To abstain from the use of tobacco and/or other intoxicants.

To never cut the hair on any part of the body.

To not eat the meat of animals killed in a religious or sacrificial manner.

To totally refrain from any sexual contact outside of marriage.

To wear the five symbols of Sikhs.

After this ceremony, the initiate is considered a part of the *Khalsa* (belonging to God) brotherhood, and is enjoined to tithe both time and income and to pray and meditate daily. He or she must live a moral life of service to mankind, in humility and honesty. The five symbols worn by the initiated Sikh are

1) unshorn hair, over which men wear a turban; 2) a comb; 3) a steel bracelet; 4) a short sword; 5) a type of knickers usually worn under a Sikh's outer clothes.

The symbols most often associated with Sikhs as a group are the characters which symbolize One God, and an arrangement of three swords (called *khanda*). (See the symbol on the book cover.)

Sikhs do not have a priestly order, nor monks, nor nuns. The Sikh "clergyman" is the *granthi*, who is encouraged to marry. Sikh congregations are autonomous. There is no ecclesiastic hierarchy. The *Akal Takhat* heads the five temporal seats of Sikh religious authority in India which debates matters of concern to the Sikh community worldwide and issues edicts which are morally binding on Sikhs. These decisions are coordinated by the SGPC which also manages Sikh shrines in India.

Formal Sikh worship consists mainly of singing of passages of the *Guru Granth Sahib* to the accompaniment of music. A passage of the *Guru Granth Sahib* is read aloud and expounded upon by the *granthi* at the conclusion of the religious service. The central prayer of Sikhs, *Ardas*, which simply means prayer, is recited by the *granthi* and the assembled congregation. This prayer gives a synopsis of Sikh history as well as being a supplication to God. Any Sikh with sufficient religious knowledge is permitted to conduct *gurdwara* worship in the absence of a *granthi*. All are welcome to religious services and to participate in the *langar* served after.

There are no denominations in Sikhism, but in the United States, in particular, there is grouping along language and cultural lines. The majority of Sikhs in the U.S. are immigrants of Indian origin, speak Punjabi, and have distinct customs and dress that originate in Punjab, India. Since the 1960s, however, there has existed a group, generally called American Sikhs, whose leader is Yogi Harbhajan Singh. American Sikhs are easily distinguished from others by their all white attire and by the fact that turbans are worn by both men and women. This group now numbers about 5,000. The majority of American Sikhs, who refer to their group as 3HO (Healthy, Happy, Holy Organization) know only limited Punjabi. Indian Sikhs and American Sikhs are mutually accepting and visit one another's *gurdwaras*. Sikhs of Indian origin number approximately a half million in North America and approximately 21 million throughout the world.

Interfaith dialogue

*I*nterfaith dialogue and cooperation have been a part of Sikhism since the time of Guru Nanak, its founder. He did not attempt to convert the followers of other faiths but, rather, urged them to rediscover the internal significance of their beliefs and rituals, without forsaking their chosen paths. He indicated that because of human limitations, each group grasps only a narrow aspect of God's revelation. The Sikh *gurus* were opposed to any exclusive claim on truth which a particular religion might make.

Just as this indicates a pluralistic acceptance of the legitimacy of all faiths, and that all are valid, it indicates, too, an acceptance of all groups and individuals. Guru Arjan said:

"All are co-equal partners in the Commonwealth with none treated as alien." (*Guru Granth Sahib*, p.97)

Numerous examples show how this attitude has evidenced itself in Sikh history:

When compiling the manuscripts that would make up the *Guru Granth Sahib*, Guru Arjan included hymns written by both Hindu and Muslim religious thinkers. It is the only scripture which includes and sanctifies texts of people belonging to other faiths, whose spirit conformed to the spirit of Sikhism.

There are, in the *Guru Granth Sahib*, hymns written by persons considered by Hindus to be untouchables.

The holiest of Sikh shrines, the Golden Temple at Amritsar, has four doors, each facing a cardinal direction. This was done to indicate that all are welcome. The cornerstone of the Golden Temple was laid by a Muslim holy man.

The ninth *guru*, Guru Tegh Bahadur, died championing the rights of Hindus to practice their own religion.

In modern times, the lesson of equality that is taught by the *langar*, the meal eaten together by Sikh congregations, extends beyond caste-obliteration to the acceptance and toleration of people of all races, creeds and nationalities. Sikhs do not disparage other faiths, nor claim sole possession of the truth. Sikhs do not attempt to convert adherents of other faiths.

In North America, Sikh congregations belong to local interfaith associations and participate fully in efforts such as environmental protection campaigns, issues affecting children, AIDS, food and other help for the homeless and displaced. In India, particularly, there are many free clinics operated by Sikhs which accept persons of all religions and castes as patients. In some North American cities, Sikhs have continued that tradition.

Since the intrinsic spirit of Sikhism is pluralistic, it has much to contribute towards interfaith and inter-community accommodation. It is a willing partner in the emergence of a pluralistic world community that preserves the rights of human dignity and freedom for all human beings. In witness of this attitude, the *Ardas* recited at the end of a Sikh religious service ends with the words "May the whole world be blessed by your grace."

Responses to social problems

Gender Equality: Sikhism recognizes each human being as a valuable creation of God, having a divine spark. Every human being has a right to live life free of religious, political and economic exploitation. The Sikh *gurus* vehemently condemned the caste system in India which had divided the whole society into many hereditary castes and subcastes. The lowest caste, the untouchable, was the most exploited of all, even to the extent of being barred from temples, as were all women, of all castes.

In the time of the *gurus,* as is true in many places even now, women of all social levels were treated as property and grossly exploited. Rejecting the idea of female inequality, Guru Nanak said:

"Man is nourished in the womb and born from a woman; he is betrothed and married to a woman. Friendship is made with women and civilization originates from a woman. When a wife dies, another wife is sought because family affairs depend upon a woman. Why call her bad, from whom are born kings? From a woman another woman is born; none is born without a woman."

Guru Nanak specifically forbade the practices of widow *sati* (self-immolation on the pyre of her husband). He encouraged the remarriage of widows, which was unheard of in his time. He was gravely concerned about the practice of female infanticide. Not only is it forbidden to Sikhs, but a Sikh cannot associate with anyone who kills his female children. In the name of equality, Guru Nanak abolished the custom of the bride's family giving the groom dowry, since this encourages men to think of women as commercial commodities.

In Sikh society, a woman occupies a position equal to men and is not prevented from fulfilling her potential through education, religion or profession.

Environmental concerns: Conservation, preservation, restoration and enrichment of environment have become major global issues at all political, social and ethical levels. Into his beautiful creation, God has placed man with the power to enhance or destroy. Modern technology and man's greed and unconcern have made the potential for destruction of species, the fertility of the land, of the viability of our waters, indeed of the world itself, a very real possibility. The Sikh Scriptures say:

"Air the vital force,
water like the father,
and earth like the great mother.
Day and night are like nurses
caring for the whole world in their lap."

If air is our vital force, it is a sin, as well as self-destructive, to pollute it. If we consider water to be our progenitor, dumping industrial wastes in it is unforgivable disrespect. As we destroy the ozone layer, the cycle that manufactures chlorophyll in green plants is damaged or interrupted; since plants are part of the air-producing cycle, we strangle ourselves.

Sikhism seeks to give to humankind a progressive and responsible philosophy as a guide to all of the world's concerns. Recognizing that there is a part of the divine in all that He created, we must recognize the interdependence of all generations, species and resources. We must preserve what was passed to us and pass it on in a healthy and robust condition.

Service to humanity

A cornerstone of the Sikh faith is the concept of *seva*, the selfless service of the community—not just the Sikh community, but the community of man. Bhai Gurdas, the early Sikh theologian, whose *Vars* (poems) are highly respected by Sikhs, says: "Service of one's fellows is a sign of divine worship." What one does in selfless service is considered to be real prayer. When one prays or meditates, it is often done for the good of one's own soul or to supplicate for one's own imagined needs. A Sikh who, with no thought of reward, serves others, performs the truest form of worship, whether he is feeding the homeless or bringing company and compassion to an AIDS sufferer.

"Among the lowly, I am lowliest of the low.
My place is with them. What have I to do with the great?"
(*Guru Granth Sahib, p.15*)

Sikhs are instructed to pray, before they eat, that a needy person will come and share their food. This attitude toward each person's role in achieving social justice motivates Sikhs to actively participate in ensuring that the poor in the world community, as well as in the local community, are fed, clothed and sheltered, and motivates them to be part of finding long-term solutions.

A PORTRAIT OF
Taoism

Dr. Douglas K. Chung

Professor at Grand Valley State University School of Social Work, Grand Rapids, Michigan

*L*i Erh (6th century BC) commonly known as Lao Tzu (the Old Master), was a contemporary of Confucius. He was the keeper of the imperial library, but in his old age he disappeared to the west, leaving behind him the *Tao Te Ching* (*Book of Tao and Virtue*).

Taoism derived its name from this profoundly wise book, only about 5,000 words in length. It can be used as a guide to the cultivation of the self as well as a political manual for social transformation at both the micro and macro levels. The philosophy of Taoism and its belief in immortals can be traced back to the Yellow Emperor, Huang-Ti. That is why Taoism is often called the "Huang-Lao" philosophy.

Taoism believes *Tao* to be the cosmic, mysterious, and ultimate principle underlying form, substance, being, and change. *Tao* encompasses everything. It can be used to understand the universe and nature as well as the human body. For example, "*Tao* gives birth to the One, the One gives birth to Two, and from Two emerges Three, Three gives birth to all the things. All things carry the *Yin* and the *Yang,* deriving their vital harmony from the proper blending of the two vital forces." (*Tao Te Ching* , ch. 42).

Tao is the cause of change and the source of all nature, including humanity. Everything from quanta to solar systems consists of two primary elements of existence, *Yin* and *Yang* forces, which represent all opposites. These two forces are complementary elements in any system and result in the harmony or balance of the system. All systems coexist in a harmonious interdependent network. The dynamic tension between *Yin* and *Yang* forces in all systems results in an endless process of change: production and reproduction and the transformation of energy. This is the natural order.

Tao and virtue are said to be the same coin with different sides. The very title *Tao Te Ching* means the canon of *Tao* and Virtue. Lao Tzu says, "The Highest Virtue is achieved through non-action. It does not require effort," because virtue is natural to people. This is what is meant by "*Tao* creates and Virtue sustains" (ch. 51).

Taoists believe that *Tao* has appeared in the form of sages and teachers of humankind, as, for example, Fu Hsi, the giver of the Pa Qua (eight trigrams) and the arts of divination to reveal the principles of *Tao*. The *Pa Qua* is the foundation of the *I Ching* and represents the eight directions of the compass associated with the forces of nature that make up the universe. There are two forms of the *Pa Qua*: the *Pa Qua* of the Earlier Heaven (the *Ho To*), which describes the ideal state of existence, and the *Pa Qua* of Later Heaven (*Lo Shu*), which describes a state of

disharmonious existence. The path of the Return to the *Tao* is the process of transforming Later Heaven into Earlier Heaven. In other words, it is the process of a reunification with *Tao*, of being transformed from a conflicting mode to a harmonious mode.

The conflicting mode is the destructive or waning cycle of the Five Elements (metal, wood, earth, water and fire). The destructive cycle consists of metal destroying wood (axes cutting trees); wood dominating earth as the roots of the trees dig into the ground (power domination); earth mastering water and preventing the flood (antinature forces); water destroying fire (antinature causes pollution that destroys the beauty of the world); and fire melting metals (pollution).

Taoists believe that through both personal and social transformation we can convert the destructive cycle of the Five Elements into a creative cycle of the Five Elements—to change from a conflicting mode of life into a supportive way of living. The creative cycle of the Five Elements is this: metal in the veins of the earth nourishes the underground waters (purification); water gives life to vegetation and creates wood (nourishment); wood feeds fire to create ashes forming earth (nature recycling). The cycle is completed when metal is formed in the veins of the earth. The path of the Return to the *Tao* is the core of Taoism and is clearly needed in light of today's concerns about energy and the environment.

Taoism believes in the value of life. Taoists do not focus on life after death, but rather emphasize practical methods of cultivating health to achieve longevity. Therefore, Taoism teaches people to enhance their health and longevity by minimizing their desires and centering themselves on stillness. Taoists firmly believe that human lives are in our control. For example, Lao Tzu promotes *Chi Kung* (breathing exercise) to enhance life (ch. 5, 20, 52). He offers three methods of life enhancement: 1) keeping original "oneness;" that is, to integrate energy, *chi*, and spirit; 2) maintaining one's vital energy in order to retain the flexibility and adaptability a newborn baby has; 3) persisting in practice for longevity (ch. 10, 52, 59). To practice *Chi Kung* is to practice the path of the Return to the *Tao* on an individual level to integrate physical, emotional, and spiritual development for health and longevity.

Taoism advocates nonaggressive, nonviolent, peaceful coexistence of states. For example, Lao Tzu describes an ideal state as one in which people love their own country and lifestyle so much that, even though the next country is so close the citizens can hear its roosters crowing and its dogs barking, they are content to die of old age without ever having gone to see it (ch. 80). Lao Tzu regards weapons as the tools of violence; all decent people detest them. He recommends that the proper demeanor after a military victory should be the same as that at a funeral (ch. 31).

Taoism advocates a minimum of goverment intervention, relying instead on individual development to reach a natural harmony under *Tao*'s leading. To concentrate on individual development is to practice the path of the Return to the *Tao* on a macro level. Lao Tzu writes:

"The Tao *never does anything, yet through it all things are done." (ch. 37)*

"If you want to be a great leader, you must learn to follow the Tao. *Stop trying to control. Let go of fixed plans and concepts, and the world will govern itself. The more prohibitions you have, the less virtuous people will be. The more weapons you have, the less secure people will be. The more subsidies you have, the less self-reliant people will be." (ch. 57).*

"Act without doing, work without effort. Think of the small as large and the few as many. Confront the difficult while it is still easy; accomplish the great task by a series of small acts. The Master never reaches for the great; thus she achieves greatness. When she runs into a difficulty, she stops and gives herself to it. She doesn't cling to her own comfort; thus problems are no problem for her." (ch. 63)

"Prevent trouble before it arises. Put things in order before they exist. The giant pine tree grows from a tiny sprout. The journey of a thousand miles starts from your first step." (ch. 64)

Lao Tzu's view of social distribution is this:

*"*Tao *adjusts excess and deficiency so that there is perfect balance. It takes from what is too much and gives to what isn't enough. Those who try to control, who use force to protect their power, go against the direction of the* Tao. *They take from those who don't have enough and give to those who have far too much" (ch. 77).*

Basically, Taoists promote a way of life that exhibits six characteristics (Ho, 1988): (1) determining and working with the Tao when making changes; (2) basing one's life on the *laissez faire* principle—let nature follow its own course as its guideline for change; (3) modeling one's life on the sage, on nature, and thus on the *Tao*; (4) emphasizing the *Tao*'s strategy of reversal transformation; (5) focusing on simplicity and originality; (6) looking for intuitive awareness and insight and deemphasizing rational and intellectual efforts. These characteristics are the essential Taoist guidelines for personal and social development.

Taoism in the world today

The people of the world today are confronted with the problems of environmental pollution, fragmentation, competition, dehumanization, and no common agreement on what constitutes an ideal society. In this world of conflict and unrest, a world that is nevertheless interdependent, Taoists still search to provide natural ways of solving problems. They gain the strength to transform their own lives and thereby to fulfill their mission. They try to help individuals as well as societies to transform from a way of life based on conflict to a harmonious way of life.

The practitioners of Taoism and those who are influenced by its philosophy include environmentalists, naturalists, libertarians, wildlife protectors, natural food advocates or vegetarians, and many physicists. More and more Westerners are able to appreciate Taoism through international contacts and Taoist literature.

Dr. Eva Wong, the director of studies at Fung Loy Kok Taoist Temple, is a member of the state of Colorado's Interfaith Advisory Council to the governor. She translated *Cultivating Stillness: A Taoist Manual for Transforming Body and Mind* (1992). She also offers graduate-level courses on Taoist and Buddhist philosophy at the University of Denver. Fung Loy Kok Taoist Temple has two branch temples in the United States and four temples in Canada. These temples offer various study programs and activities, including scripture study, lectures, meditation, classes in chi-kung, cooking, retreats, *kung-fu*, and training in traditional Lion Dance.

Chungliang A. Huang formed the Living Tao Foundation to promote *Tao* sports and to publish various books related to Tao. Many people practice *chi-kung*, *Tai-chi chuan* and acupuncture daily even without knowing that they are practicing Taoism.

REFERENCES

Capra, F. (1991). *The Tao of Physics.* Boston: Shambhala.

Chang, P. T. (1986). *The Inner Teachings of Taoism.* Boston: Shambhala.

Cheng Yi (11th century). *I Ching The Tao of Organization,* trans. T. Cleary (1988). Boston: Shambhala.

Chung Tzu, trans. J. Legge (1971). New York: Ace Books.

Cleary, T., trans. (1990). *The Tao of Politics: Lessons of the Masters of Huainan.* Boston: Shambhala.

Cleary, T., trans. (1989). *The Book of Balance and Harmony.* San Francisco: North Point Press.

Cleary, T., trans. (1989). *I Ching Mandalas: A Program of Study for The Book of Changes.* Boston: Shambhala.

Graham, A. C. (1989). *Disputers of the Tao Philosophical Argument in Ancient China.* La Salle, Ill.: Open Court.

Ho, J. Y. (1988). *Lao Tzu's Taoism.* Taipei: Wu Nan Publishing Co.

Huang, C. A. & Lynch J. (1992). *Thinking Body, Dancing Mind: Taosports for Extraordinary Performance in Athletics, Business, and Life.* New York: Bantam Books.

I-Ching Mandalas: A Program of Study for The Book of Changes, trans. T. Cleary (1989). Boston: Shambhala.

Kongtrul, J., trans. (1987). *The Great Path of Awakening.* Boston: Shambhala.

Lao Tzu (5th century BC). *Tao Te Ching,* trans. C. H. Wu (1966). New York: St. John's University Press.

Lao Tzu (5th century BC). *Tao Te Ching,* trans. S. Mitchell (1988). New York: Harper & Row Publishers.

Liu I-ming (1796). *The Taoist I-Ching,* trans. T. Cleary (1986). Boston: Shambhala.

Ma, C. J. (1988). *Chinese Chi Kong.* Hong Kong: China Books Press.

Min, C. (1988). *Yen Hsin Scientific Chi Kong.* Hong Kong: China Books Press.

Republic of China Yearbook, 1990-91. Taipei: Kwang Hwa.

Watts, A. (1976). *Tao: The Watercourse Way.* London: Jonathan Cape.

Wong, E. (1989). *Fung Loy Kok Week, 1988.* The Taoist Tai Chi Society of Colorado.

Wong, E., trans. (1992). *Cultivating Stillness: A Taoist Manual for Transforming Body and Mind.* Boston: Shambhala.

Wong, E., trans. (1990). *Seven Taoist Masters: A Folk Novel of China.* Boston: Shambhala.

A PORTRAIT OF

Zoroastrianism

Dr. Pallan R. Ichaporia

Chair of the Research and Preservation Committee of the Federation of Zoroastrian Associations of North America

The Opening Prayer

*"In humble adoration,
with hands outstretched,
I pray to Thee, O Lord,
Invisible benevolent Spirit:
Vouchsafe to me in this hour of joy,
All righteousness of action,
all wisdom of the Good Mind,
That I may thereby bring joy
to the Soul of Creation."*

Yasna 28.I, from the *Gathas*

*"Unto Thee, O Lord, the Soul of
Creation cried:
'For whom didst Thou create me,
and who so fashioned me?
Feuds and fury,
violence and the insolence of might
have oppressed me.
None have I to protect me save Thee;
Command for me, then,
the blessings of a settled,
peaceful life.'"*

Yasna 29.I, from the *Gathas*

An ancient monotheistic religion

Zoroastrianism is the first revealed monotheistic religion of the world. The date of its founding is lost in antiquity, but general consensus places it between 2000 to 1800 BCE. Its founder, Zarathushtra or Zoroaster (as called by the Greeks), flourished on the East Iranian Plateau. Zarathushtra saw the God (Ahura Mazda—the Wise Lord), felt conscious of His presence, and heard His words, which are recorded in the five Songs or Poems he composed. These are called the *Gathas*. One easily understands Zarathushtra by seeing the Prophet's zeal in the *Gathas* and the visible manifestation of his meeting the God.

Primary beliefs

Zoroastrians believe in the One Supreme, Omnipotent, Omniscient God, called Ahura Mazda. He is to be understood through his six divine attributes: *Vohu Mana* (Good Mind), *Asha* (Truth, Righteousness), *Spenta Armaity* (Correct Thinking, Piety), *Xsthra Vairya* (Divine Domain), *Haurvatat* (Perfection, Integrity) and *Ameratat* (Immortality). His attributes are also found in each and every human being who must work as a co-worker of God to defeat evil and bring the world to perfection. This can be achieved by good thoughts, good words and good deeds.

Angels known as the *Yazatas* work endlessly to aid humans in bringing the world to perfection. All the natural elements like air, water and lands are to be kept pure. Their pollutions are to be prevented at all cost. This makes Zoroastrianism the first true ecological religion of the world. After death, the immortal soul of the departed person is judged according to all the good deeds done by him or her in this world; the soul then enjoys the pleasures of paradise or undergoes the tortures of hell.

There is also belief in the appearance of the last savior, called Sosayant, and of the final day of judgment with the resurrections of all who have died (these last two are later beliefs).

Main sources of religious knowledge

The primary source is the *Gathas of the Prophet*; this is followed by *Hapatan Haiti*, the seven chapters written by the Prophet's disciples. These scriptures are called *Old Avesta* as their language differs from the later scriptures, called the *Younger Avesta*. Together they are known as the *Avestan*. The *Younger Avesta* consists of the *Yasna* (without the *Gathas*, containing 72 chapters), *Vispered*, *Vendidad* and the *Yasts*. The original *Avestan* scriptures were written in 21 books called *the Nasks*, from which only one complete *Nask—Vandidad*—has survived the ravages of time. The *Gathas* and the rest of the scriptures survived because they formed part of the long *Yasna* liturgical ceremony, which was passed from generation to generation by oral tradition.

Rituals

*T*he most important ritual which every Zoroastrian has to undergo is the *Navzote* or *Sudraposhi Ceremony*, which is for new initiates (ages 7 to 15 years) entering the Religion. Generally the rituals are divided into two classes: (1) Those like the *Yasna* ceremony, to be performed in the Zoroastrian Fire-Temples, and (2) Those to be performed anywhere outside the Zoroastrian Temples, like *Jashan* (thanksgiving) ceremony.

The word *fire temple* is a misnomer as the Zoroastrians do not worship the fire. The fire is kept as a symbol of purity, acting as the focal point (like the *Kebla* of the religion of Islam) for prayers.

A minority religion

*T*he Zoroastrians are the smallest minority of all religions, having undergone the severest persecutions for centuries in Iran at the hands of its conquerors, after the fall of the last Sasanian Zoroastrian Empire. At one time the number of the community ran into millions (650 CE). A small band of the community had migrated to India (between ninth and tenth centuries CE) to avoid harassment and persecution; called the Parsees, these now number fewer than 60,000 in India and 2,500 in Pakistan. Still fewer have survived in Iran (10,000), and some have settled in the West, mostly in North America (12,000) and in Europe (7,000); there may be 3,000 in other parts of the world. With such a small total number of the community there are no fixed denominations as such, although the Iranian Zoroastrians and the Parsees have different cultures and mother tongues, which developed due to long separation. ✿

ZOROASTRIANISM IN THE WORLD TODAY

Dr. Jehan Bagli

Founding member of the Zoroastrian Association of Quebec, Editor of Gavashni and first Editor of FEZANA Journal

Current approach to interfaith dialogue

*T*hroughout its long history, the Zarathushtrian tradition has experienced numerous social environments shaped by various ruling dynasties, in different eras in early Iran. Consequently, from early times the adherents have learned to coexist with people of different beliefs. This has built within the tradition a strong sense of tolerance for other faiths and other religious viewpoints, an attribute which is firmly intertwined with the teachings of the first revealed religion of mankind.

The basic tenets of the faith proclaim respect for creation of nature and of equality for all human beings; these are the fundamental cornerstones of the tradition. With these axioms in focus, Zarathushtrians consistently make a concerted effort to learn and comprehend the nature and beliefs of other faiths. The migration of Zarathushtrians from Iran to India around 936 AD put them within the milieu of the Hindu society. Here they emerged as the most intellectual, honest and hard-working minority of the world. Despite imbibing the knowledge and customs of other faiths, they have for the past 3,500 years maintained the integrity and identity of their faith with glowing success.

Followers of an Ancient Faith in a Modern World

Robinton M. Rivetna

President of the Federation of Zoroastrian Associations of North America; member of the Board of Trustees of the Counil for a Parliament of the World's Religions.

. . . Zoroastrian ideas have played a vital role in the development of western religious thought. Some theological concepts shared by Zoroastrianism with Judaism and Christianity are:

- Belief in one supreme and loving God
- Heaven and Hell, and individual judgement
- Ultimate triumph of good over evil
- A strict moral and ethical code
- The Messiah to come for the final restoration
- Resurrection, final judgement and life everlasting
- The words *satan, paradise, amen* are of Zoroastrian origin

The interchange of Zoroastrian thought with Judaeo-Christian ideology first took place when Cyrus the Great defeated the Assyrians and released the Jews from Babylonian captivity. They heralded Cyrus as their messiah, as prophesied two centuries earlier in Isaiah 45:1–3. The Old Testament is replete with references to the Persian emperors Darius, Cyrus and Xerxes, all of whom were Zoroastrians.

Excerpts continue on next page

. . . Zoroastrian rituals and prayers are solemnized in the presence of a flame. A flame, scrupulously tended with sandalwood and frankincense, is kept burning in the inner sanctum of every Zoroastrian temple, and often, in every Zoroastrian home. Zoroastrians revere fire as a visible symbol of the inner light, the inner flame that burns within each person. It is a physical representation of the Illumined Mind, Light and Truth, all highly regarded in the Zoroastrian doctrine. Zoroastrianism, despite its prehistoric origins, has vehemently denounced idolatry in any shape or form.

The *Fravashi* or *Farohar* is the presence of *Ahura Mazda* in every human being. It is the Divinity in Humanity. It is the conscience. The *Fravashi* is immortal and does not die with the person, but lives on forever. The *Fravashi* is ever present to guide and protect the person. It is the duty of a person in making the choice between good and evil, to seek guidance from his *Fravashi*.

Excerpts on this and the previous page are from *Followers of an Ancient Faith in a Modern World*, by Rohinton M. Rivetna, published by the Federation of Zoroastrian Associations of North America (FEZANA).

For more information, contact:
FEZANA
626 West 56th Street
Hinsdale, Illinois 60521 USA

Primary challenges and issues

At this time the major challenge that faces humanity in the world is a breakdown in true respect and tolerance for other human beings. Much of this is motivated by materialism and greed, but conflicts are frequently perpetrated in the name of religion, under false pretenses. The understanding that all humans emerge from the same creating force has been totally overshadowed by dogmatic and egotistic endeavors, without regard for needs of the others.

The other major issue in our highly technocratic society is the lack of regard for the elements of creation. In the interest of bettering living conditions, the relationship between humanity and the creation has reached the all-time low. The concept of the preservation of the creation, with humans as its stewards and as co-workers with the creator, promoted by various religious traditions, has totally disappeared. Exploitation of our non-renewable resources, pollution of our waters with chemical wastes, and excessive deforestation are some of the most serious infractions by the human society towards the elements of creation.

Community response

There is a great renaissance of spiritual awareness among the Zarathushtrian community in North America. Attempts are being made to disseminate the message of the prophet to the youth and to adults to make them aware of these injustices that are perpetrated in the name of religion. The Federation of Zoroastrian Associations of North America is making all efforts to spread awareness of the Zarathushtrian religion through interfaith dialogue with other religious groups and to make our sentiments known.

"*O Ahura Mazda, and O Spirit of Truth:*
Do you grant me and my followers such strength and ruling power.
That with the help of the Benevolent Mind,
we may bring to the world, restful joy and happiness,
of which, Thou, O Lord, art indeed the first Possessor."

Yasna 29.10, from the second chapter of the *Gathas;*
passages from the *Gathas,* here and above, were prepared by D. J. Irani in
"An Elementary Introduction to the *Gathas,*"
talks given to children and young adults in 1936

A PORTRAIT OF
The Christian Family Tree

The Rev. Epke VanderBerg

Protestant minister, member of the Episcopal family and of the Grand Rapids Interfaith Dialogue Association.

Because the Christian religion has so many communities and denominations, branches and offshoots, we present in this essay, and in the articles following it, many of the families, movements and branches with a presence in North America. In the first essay, Epke VanderBerg provides an outline of 15 "families" of Christians.

The several movements and organizations—both Christian and from other traditions—described following the first essay do not provide a complete list. Due to constraints of time and access, some significant groups are missing; those that are included are here in part because of their roles in the 1893 Parliament, in interfaith relations, or in the 1993 Parliament. They are presented here in simple alphabetical order, and speak for themselves. –Ed.

*L*ooking back down the many branches of Christianity, we see a tree called Jesus the Christ. But, even beyond this trunk, Christianity is rooted firmly in God's call of Abraham in the land of Ur. From the time of Jesus into the 20th century, the roots divided and multiplied, dipping into soils and water foreign to its beginning, affecting color and character. Throughout its history, however, it never forgot its beginning, even though its memories of who Jesus was and what he taught, waxed and waned through time and place.

The following summaries describe the major branches of Christianity, focusing on their growth into North America. The descriptions provide the reader with some primary characteristics and a method of categorization. If there are errors in it, they are due to the writer who tried to summarize here the work of J. Gordon Melton in *The Encyclopedia of American Religions* (vols. 1 and 2, Triumph Books, 1989, New York), and to the Editor who condensed it even further. Readers are encouraged to explore Melton's much more detailed and fascinating work for descriptions of well over 1,000 religious movements and groups in North America.

*W*estern Liturgical Family: The four oldest Christian families are the following: the Eastern Orthodox tradition, the non-Chalcedonian Orthodox tradition, the Western Catholic tradition and the Anglican tradition. A strong liturgical life characterizes these Christian families, along with true-creeds, sacraments, language and culture, which find their expression in their liturgy. Most of these families observe seven sacraments: baptism, eucharist, holy orders, unction, marriage, confirmation and penance. Two other characteristics mark these churches: allegiance to creeds and belief in Apostolic succession.

Even though these churches evolved from one common beginning, they unfolded into separate entities with Christianity's spread into other cultures.

The Eastern Orthodox family, its authority centered in the cities of Antioch, Alexandria and Constantinople, split from the Western Catholic tradition in 1054 AD. The Western Catholic tradition, based in Rome and entrenched in Western Europe, exercised strong political and religious authority. The Anglican tradition in England broke with Rome in the 16th century when Henry the VIII saw opportunity for an independent church that would give him his desired divorce and financial freedom for battle. *The Thirty Nine Articles of Religion* and *The Book of Common Prayer* established it as a separate liturgical tradition. In the immigration to North America and after the American Revolutionary War, the Anglican Church became known, in 1787, as the Protestant Episcopal Church in the U.S.

*E*astern Liturgical Family: Political, cultural and doctrinal differences separated the Eastern Orthodox churches from the Roman churches in 1054. Thereafter, and not having a Pope, this family was governed by Patriarchs who have equal authority and are in communion with each other. Even though the family does not demand celibacy of its priests (as long as they are married before their ordination), monks, who are celibate, are the only members who attain the office of bishop. This family does not recognize the authority of the Bishop in Rome, nor that part of the Chalcedonian Creed that says that the Holy Spirit proceeds from the Son.

A number of groups fall into this family:

Nestorians: This group, recognizing Christ's two natures, does not believe that Christ had two equal natures and that Mary bore only the human nature of Christ—she did not bear God [Mary is not *theotikos*].

Monophysites: This group believes that Christ is of one person (*mono*) and of one nature (*physis*); it rejects the two-nature position of the Nestorians.

The Armenians: Established in Armenia as a bishopric in 260, this group customarily celebrates Holy Communion only on Sunday, using pure wine [without water] and unleavened bread. Infants are served immediately after baptism. Under persecution by the Turks in 1890, many moved to North America. Controversy soon followed: would the pro-Soviet dominance of Armenia govern or would the Armenian nationalists?

Syrian Churches: under the leadership of Jacob Baradeus (followers were often called Jacobites), who was a monophysite, the Syrian churches spread throughout the Mediterranean region and beyond.

Coptic Churches of Egypt and Ethiopia: Formerly one of the largest Christian groups in the world, this group diminished through persecution. Today, found mainly in Egypt, its numbers are increasing. The Ethiopian Church differs from the Coptic on several points: 1) accepts Apocrypha as Scripture, 2) venerates the Sabbath along with Sunday, 3) recognizes Old Testament figures as saints, and 4) observes many Old Testament regulations on food and purification.

*L*utheran Family: Martin Luther, in cooperation with German princes, brought about the first successful breach with the Roman Catholic Church. Even though October 31, 1517 is often thought to be the start of the Lutheran Church, a more persuasive argument may be made for the year 1530 in which the Augsburg Confession was published. This confession became the standard that congregations used to justify their independent existence and distinguished the churches that used written confessions as "confessing churches." Luther taught that salvation is by grace through faith, rather than works and faith, and that the Bible is the rule of faith and sole authority for doctrine. Luther, in distinction from other Reformation churches, placed greater emphasis on the sacramental liturgy and understood the eucharist as consubstantiation (Christ present but elements not changed) in distinction from the Roman Catholic tradition of transubstantiation (elements changed into Christ's essence). Luther's translation of the Bible into the German vernacular (1532–34) became the standard for the German language and sparked the use of the vernacular in the Lutheran liturgy. Through Luther, many new hymns came into use and changed the complexion of the liturgy.

*R*eformed-Presbyterian Family: The force behind this family is John Calvin, a Frenchman, who established the Reformed church in Geneva, Switzerland in the 1540s. The Reformed churches distinguish themselves from the other Christian families by their theology (Reformed) and the church government (Presbyterian). Calvin, an intellectually brilliant student, derived his Reformed theology from the major premise of God's sovereignty in creation and salvation. He taught that God predestined some to salvation and that atonement is limited to those whom God has elected. Today, a strict or lenient interpretation of predestination separates many Reformed churches. On the continent, the churches were known as Reformed; in the British Isles they came to be known as Presbyterian. The Reformed churches were one with other Protestant churches in adherence to the authority of the early Christian creeds and believing in the Trinity, salvation by grace through faith, and that the Bible is the sole authority for faith and doctrine (in opposition to the Roman Catholics' position of salvation by faith and works, and of authority in the Bible and tradition). These churches did not concern themselves with apostolic succession, but concerned themselves with the pure preaching of the Gospel (predominantly a teaching function) and in the pure administration of the sacraments (baptism and eucharist). In the eucharist, God, who is present, can be apprehended by faith; this is in opposition to the Lutherans and Roman Catholics who maintain God's special presence in the elements.

*P*ietist-Methodist Family: Three groups of churches fall under this category: the Moravian Church, the Swedish Evangelical churches and the Methodist (Wesleyan) churches. As a movement of pietism, these churches reacted to Protestantism as practiced in the late 17th century. They reacted to the rigidity and systematic doctrine of the scholastic Lutheran and Calvinist theologians. Not wishing to leave their established churches, they wanted a shift from scholasticism to spiritual experience. They advocated a Bible-centered faith, the experience of the Christian life, and giving free expression of faith in hymns, testimony and evangelical zeal. Through the early work of Philip Jacob Spener and August Hermann Francke, and using home studies, their work rejuvenated the Moravian Church in 1727, influenced John Wesley and helped establish the Swedish Evangelical Church. In their work they were open to traditional practices and beliefs and sought life within the forms of the traditional churches.

Methodists are characterized by their dissent from the Calvinist teachings on predestination and irresistible grace. In 1784, at a Christmas conference, the Methodists in America formed the Methodist Episcopal Church. Its history in North America reflects the history of other denominations, including their relationships to Old World governments, ecclesiastical affiliations, and changing North American political patterns.

*H*oliness Family: Through the influence of John Wesley's teaching of perfection, the holiness movement uses Matthew 5:48 as its theme: "Be ye perfect as my father is perfect." It is distinct from modern Wesleyism and other Protestant churches by how it understands the framework of holiness and perfection. They have traditionally separated themselves from Christians who did not strive high enough for perfection. Wesley, however, seeing the practical problems with perfection or sinlessness, then stressed love as the primary theme for Christians while the holiness movement continued to stress sinlessness. Holiness, or the sanctification experience, is the end work of a process that starts with accepting Christ as one's personal savior (being "born again"). Having accepted Christ, one then grows in grace with the help of the Holy Spirit. The second work of grace comes when the Holy Spirit cleanses the heart of sin and provides the power for living the Christian life. Living the life of holiness results in banning certain forms of behavior as inappropriate for the Christian. This tendency resulted in the adoption of a strict set of codes of behavior. However, groups of churches, depending upon their understanding of holiness—whether it comes instantaneously or later—established their own independent churches.

Pentecostal Family: Today's Pentecostal family is usually traced back to the work of Rev. Charles Parham and his experience at Bethel Bible College in 1901. However, the movement has also had a long history replete with the experiences usually associated with it. What makes this family distinct from other Protestant churches is not their doctrinal differences: it is their form of religious experience and their practice of speaking in tongues—glossolalia. Tongue speaking is a sign of baptism by the Holy Spirit, a baptism that often is accompanied by other forms of spiritual gifts such as healing, prophecy, wisdom and discernment of spirits. Pentecostals seek the experience, interpret events from within it and work to have others share in it. Those who do not manifest the experience are thought often to be less than "full of the Spirit." Pentecostal worship services appear to be more spontaneous than the traditional churches; however, Pentecostal services repeat a pattern of seeking the experience and showing the desire to talk about it. Because it is shaped by cultural forces, Pentecostalism appears in different forms, emphasizes different gifts, yet collects similar minds into its community. Neo-Pentecostalism, however, is a recent phenomenon, and has occurred predominantly in established churches that have found room for this movement.

European Free-Church Family: While Luther and Calvin advocated a fairly close relationship with the state, 16th century radical reformers from within the Roman Catholic Church advocated a complete break with the state church. Their doctrines resembled many of the Protestant doctrines, but their ecclesiology differed. They thought the visible Church to be a free-association of adults who had been baptized as believers (as opposed to being baptized as infants) and who avoided worldly ways. The free-church family is thought to have started on December 25, 1521 when one of the leaders celebrated the first Protestant communion service, a service format that is followed by much of Protestantism. From this group evolved the Mennonites, the Amish, the Brethren, the Quakers and the Free Church of Brethren. Because many of them shunned allegiance to the government, they suffered persecution. Suffering persecution, many of them moved to North America and established congregations there.

Baptist Family: As a free association of adult believers, Baptists make up the second largest religious family on the American landscape. Though they may also be related to the continental free-church family, American Baptists seem more related to British Puritanism. In general, they teach that the creeds have a secondary place to Scripture, that baptism is by immersion and administered only to believing and confessing adults, that the Lord's supper (not understood as a sacrament, but as an ordinance) is a memorial, that salvation is a gift of God's grace, and

that people must exercise their free will to receive salvation. Even though they are a free association, they have organized themselves into various groupings, depending upon emphases of creed and the necessity for control, and at times by differences in theological perspectives due to the American phenomenon of regionalism (e.g., Southern and Northern Baptist conventions).

Independent Fundamentalist Family: Following the lead of Englishman John Nelson Darby (1800–1882), Independent Fundamental families distinguish themselves from Baptists by their belief in dispensationalism. The Fundamentalists believe the Bible is a history of God's actions with people in different periods. Because of apparent Biblical contradictions, they resolve those differences by assigning Biblical passages to different dispensations. By failing to meet God's commands, God's economy establishes new paths to follow, which in the present dispensation, leads to the final dispensation in which Christ is recognized as the supreme universal authority. This dispensational framework has resulted in much speculation about prophecy of the Last Times. Another distinguishing feature of this family is the belief that the Church is only a unity of the Spirit, and not of organization. The Fundamentalist family frequently uses the Scofield Reference Bible as their major source for doctrine.

Adventist Family: The feature that distinguishes the Adventist family from other Christian groups is their belief in the expectation or imminent return of Christ when Christ will replace the old order of the world with an order of joy and goodness. When Christ comes again, he will establish a millennial (a thousand-year) reign in which unbelievers will have a second chance to accept Christ's Lordship. Even though a belief in the imminent return has long roots, it was heightened with the work of William Miller, a poor New York farmer. He believed that Biblical chronology could be deciphered, a belief that prompted him to predict Christ's return between March 21, 1843 and March 21, 1844. The 50,000 people who followed these teachings, and who experienced the non-return, retrenched. Rather than seeing a literal return of Christ that failed, one group advocated a spiritualized return—following the teachings of Charles Taze Russel—in which the event is understood as a "heavenly or internal event." The Adventist Family shares many of the Baptist teachings, from which much of the family has its genesis. Some of the more distinctive teachings of the family (but not all) are the following: 1. the imminent return of Christ, 2. denial of a person's immortality, 3. Old Testament laws are effective, including the observance of the Sabbath (Saturday), 4. rejection of the belief in a Hell, 5. Christ's death counters the death penalty of Adam passed to his children by inheritance, 6. that the Church is the suffering body of Christ and offers a spiritual sacrifice of atonement to God, and 7. that God's name is

Yahweh. Some of the more well-known families that have evolved from the millennial expectation are the Seventh Day Adventists, Church of Jesus Christ of the Latter-Day Saints, the Jehovah Witnesses, British Israel Movement, and the WorldWide Church of God.

The Liberal Family: Because yesterday's liberal may be today's conservative, the word "liberal" can be somewhat ambiguous. Most often, however, they are identified as being against the mainstream theistic position of the dominant culture in Western society. The Liberal family, depending upon orientation, finds itself somewhere among the three positions of unitarianism, universalism and atheism. Unitarianists think that God is one, that the Trinity does not exist; the universalists think that all will be saved, that Hell does not exist; the atheists reject the idea of a transcendental God. Liberalism's American origins developed in reaction to New England's Calvinism. However, the genesis of Liberalism is most often thought to rest in the work of Michael Servetus, martyred by John Calvin in Geneva. Liberals have championed human rights, the need for education and the high worth of every person. By removing God from cosmic calculations, life's answers could only come from two other sources: human feelings—as in the position of Transcendentalists—and human reason—as in the Rationalist position. Early 18th century liberals advocated that people could improve the world through reason. Nineteenth century liberalism, seeing the results of scientific thought, expanded the above with evolution, science and materialism, seen as necessary for uncovering the essential (Monotheistic) laws of the universe.

*L*atter-Day Saints Family: Joseph Smith, in the fervor of revivalist movements sweeping New York in the early 19th century, received at the hands of an angel in 1827 gold plates written in what he described as a reformed Egyptian language. By means of two crystal-like stones, the *Urim* and *Thummim*, this translation has been become known as the *Book of Mormon*. The *Book of Mormon* claims to be the history of two tribes, the Jeredites and the Israelites. The Jeredites moved to North America after the Tower of Babel; the Israelites moved to North America after the destruction of Jerusalem in the 6th century BC. Joseph Smith published a number of other works including the *Book of Moses*, the *Book of Abraham* and the *Book of Commandments* (now called the *Doctrine and Covenants*). The early history of Mormonism includes persecution, schisms and violence, culminating in the murder of Joseph Smith in Carthage, Illinois, June 27, 1844. In the ensuing power struggle, Brigham Young moved his group to Salt Lake City, Utah, where he established the dominant branch of Mormonism. One other major branch resides in Independence, Missouri, claiming Joseph Smith III (son of Joseph Smith) as successor to his father. This group is known as the Reorganized Church of Jesus Christ of Latter-day Saints.

Several major Mormon beliefs are the following: 1. affirmation of a trinitheism (not Christian trinity) of the Father, Jesus and Holy Spirit, 2. denial of original sin and the necessity of obedience to certain articles of faith for salvation, 3. a specific church hierarchy, 4. the Word of God consists of the Bible, the *Book of Mormon* and the *Pearl of Great Price,* 5. revelation is open and added to the *Doctrine and Covenants* when received, and 6. the future Kingdom of Zion will be established in North America—either in Independence, Missouri or Salt Lake City, Utah.

*C*ommunal Family: Citing references to the early Christian Church, the communal family desires to share all their worldly possessions with other members of the group. Communalism made a serious start in the fourth century with the development of monasticism, a movement that thought the Western Catholic tradition brought everyone into the church rather than seeing the Church as the body of true believers. Monasticism thought the principle of equality could be achieved through poverty and renunciation of the world. Francis of Assisi, thinking that monasticism did not represent true poverty (monastic orders had become very wealthy), advocated poverty of use as method of reform. The Roman Catholic Church did not accept his vision, but saw it as a threat. The Taborites and the Munsterites, shortly after the Reformation, set up several communal communities, but, for a variety of reasons, failed. After 1860, visionaries and reformists began the most active era in the drive to build communes. In North America, the most famous and successful of these communities is the Hutterite community. Having a similar background to Russian Mennonites, today these people have established and maintain well over 300 communities.

*C*hristian Science-Metaphysical Family: Concerned with the role of the Mind in the healing process, the Christian Science and the New Thought movement drew on the metaphysical traditions of the 19th century that suggested the presence of spiritual powers operating on the mind and body. Swedenborg, a prolific writer, suggested the priority of the spiritual world over the material and that the material became real in its correspondence to the spiritual. The Christian Bible, he also taught, must be interpreted spiritually. In the late 1800s, Mary Bakker Eddy (the founder of Christian Science) and Emma Curtis Hopkins (the founder of New Thought) built on the methodology of Swedenborg. Disease, they taught, is the result of disharmony between mind and matter. New Thought, however, is distinct from Christian Science. New Thought governs itself through ordained ministers, most of whom are women; developed a decentralized movement; emphasized prosperity (poverty is as unreal as disease); and emphasized the universal position that all religions have value.

A PORTRAIT OF
Swedenborgianism

The Rev. George F. Dole

About Swedenborgians

Swedenborgians first formed a separate church in London in 1789 on the basis of acceptance of the theological views promulgated by Emanuel Swedenborg (1688–1772). Distinctive features of its belief include a strong insistence on the divinity of Christ as the outcome of a process of struggle between his divine and his human heritages, an interpretation of Scripture as essentially symbolic rather than literal, and an emphasis on living an upright and useful life. Swedenborg repeatedly stated that the Lord provided the means of salvation in every religion.

There are some 4,000 members of Swedenborgian churches in the U.S. and Canada, and approximately 60,000 worldwide, about half being native South African.

Charles C. Bonney, a Chicago Swedenborgian, proposed the 1893 Parliament, formulated its goals and policies on Swedenborgian principles, and delivered its opening address.

In the world today

The older branch of the Swedenborgian church in the U.S. is a member of the National Council of Churches, and has felt that it has a particular contribution to make in the area of theological dialogue. Local congregations and clergy are normally active in local interfaith councils. Our Boston congregation has initiated regular "clergy breakfasts" which involve representatives of any and all faiths in consideration of current societal issues, and other churches have welcomed presentations by other faiths.

In general, we regard current problems less as new developments than as the surfacing of human evils which have been ignored or glossed over in the past. We would take very seriously Jesus' statement that such evils proceed out of the human heart; and while we support efforts toward social justice as our small size permits, we are convinced that fundamental changes in attitude are essential to any secure and lasting improvement of the human condition. We see these changes as the "rebirth" enjoined in the Gospels, and we see that "rebirth" not as a single dramatic event, but as a lifelong process.

"... *true worship consists of fulfilling uses and therefore in expressing caring in action. If people believe that serving the Lord consists only of regular church attendance, listening to sermons and praying, and that this is adequate, they are sadly mistaken. Real worship of the Lord consists in fulfilling uses, and uses, while we are living in this world, are for each of us properly to fulfill his or her function in his or her position. This means putting our hearts into service to our country, our community and our neighbor; it means acting with candor toward our associates and performing our duties with care according to our several abilities.*"
EMANUEL SWEDENBORG,
Arcana Coelestia, 7038.

"*No one should be instantly persuaded about the truth—that is, the truth should not be instantly so confirmed that there is no doubt left. The reason is that truth inculcated in this way is "second-hand" truth—it has no stretch and no give. In the other life, this kind of truth is portrayed as hard, impervious to the goodness that would make it adaptable. This is why as soon as something true is presented by open experience to good spirits in the other life, something opposite is presented soon thereafter, which creates a doubt. So they are enabled to think and ponder whether it is true, and to gather reasons and thereby lead the truth into their minds rationally. This gives their spiritual sight an outreach in regard to this matter, even to its opposite.*"
ibid., 7298[2]

"*[As a highly complex and organized form], heaven ... cannot be made up of the people of one religion [only], but of the people of many religions.*"
EMANUEL SWEDENBORG,
Divine Providence, 3261[0]

"*There is only one life, and it comes from the Lord alone. Angels, spirits and mortals are only recipients of life. This has been made known to me from so much experience that there is not the slightest doubt left. ... Our appropriation of the Lord's life comes from his love and mercy toward the whole human race, from the fact that he wants to give himself and what is his to each individual, and that he actually does so to the extent that we accept it—that is to the extent that we are involved in lives of goodness and lives of truth, as images and likenesses of him.*"
EMANUEL SWEDENBORG,
Arcana Coelestia, 3742

A PORTRAIT OF
Theosophy

Dr. John Algeo

President-elect of the Theosophical Society in America

About Theosophy

*T*he modern Theosophical movement dates from the founding of the Theosophical Society in New York City in 1875 by Helena Petrovna Blavatsky, Henry Steel Olcott, William Quan Judge and others. The movement, however, views itself as a contemporary expression of a tradition going back to the Neo-Platonists of Classical antiquity (hence the name) and earlier.

Primary Theosophical concepts are:

(1) the fundamental unity of all existence, so that all dichotomies—matter and spirit, the human and the divine, I and thou—are seen as transitory and relative distinctions of an underlying absolute Oneness;

(2) the regularity of universal law, cyclically producing universes out of the absolute ground of being; and

(3) the progress of consciousness developing through the cycles of life to an ever-increasing realization of Unity.

Theosophy is nondogmatic, but many Theosophists believe in

- reincarnation
- *karma* (or moral justice)
- the existence of worlds of experience beyond the physical
- the presence of life and consciousness in all matter
- the evolution of spirit and intelligence as well as matter
- the possibility of conscious participation in evolution
- the power of thought to affect one's self and surroundings
- free will and self-responsibility
- the duty of altruism, a concern for the welfare of others.

*T*hese beliefs often lead to such practices as meditation, vegetarianism and care for animal welfare, active support of women's and minority rights, and a concern for ecology.

Knowledge of such ideas and practices derives from the traditions of cultures spread over the world from antiquity to the present in a "perennial philosophy" or "ancient wisdom," held to be fundamentally identical in all cultures. But it also derives from the experiences of individuals through the practice of meditation and the development of insight. No Theosophist is asked to accept any opinion or adopt any practice that does not appeal to the inner sense of reason and morality.

Theosophy has no developed rituals. Meetings typically consist of talks and discussion or the study of a book, although they may be opened and closed by brief meditations or the recitation of short texts. There are no privileged symbols in Theosophy, but various symbols from the religious traditions of the world are used, such as the interlaced triangles and the ankh.

Today there are three main Theosophical organizations. Membership statistics are not available for all of them, but the American section of the society with international headquarters in Madras, India, has a membership of about 5,000. There are associated groups in about 50 countries.

WISDOM IN THE THEOSOPHICAL TRADITION

"*It is well known that the first rule of the society is to carry out the object of forming the nucleus of a universal brotherhood. The practical working of this rule was explained by those who laid it down, to the following effect:*

"He who does not practice altruism; he who is not prepared to share his last morsel with a weaker or poorer than himself; he who neglects to help his brother man, of whatever race, nation or creed, whenever and wherever he meets suffering, and who turns a deaf ear to the cry of human misery; he who hears an innocent person slandered, whether a brother Theosophist or not, and does not undertake his defense as he would undertake his own—is no Theosophist."

H. P. BLAVATSKY,
"Let Every Man Prove His Own Work," 1887,
CW 8:170–71

"*There is but one way of ever ameliorating human life and it is by the love of one's fellow man for his own sake and not for personal gratification. The greatest Theosophist—he who loves divine truth under all its forms—is the one who works for and with the poor.*"

H. P. BLAVATSKY,
"Misconceptions," 1887, *CW* 8:77

Theosophy in the world today

INTERFAITH DIALOGUE AND COOPERATION

*T*he first Object of the Theosophical Society is (in one wording) "To form a nucleus of the Universal Brotherhood of Humanity without distinction of race, creed, sex, caste, or color"; and the second is "To encourage the study of comparative religion, philosophy and science." As those objects indicate, Theosophy is dedicated to increasing cooperation among human beings and understanding among their cultures and religions.

Theosophy holds that all religions are expressions of humanity's effort to relate to one another, to the universe around us, and to the ultimate ground of being. Particular religions differ from one another because they are expressions of that effort adapted to particular times, places, cultures and needs. Theosophy is not itself a religion, although it is religious, in being concerned with the effort to relate. Individual Theosophists profess various of the world's religions—Christian, Jewish, Moslem, Zoroastrian, Hindu, Buddhist; others have no religious affiliation.

The Theosophical Society has, from the time of its founding, promoted dialogue and cooperation among the religious traditions of humanity, since we regard them all as varying expressions of a basic human need and impulse. The Society itself is an expression of the faith that human beings, however diverse their backgrounds, can communicate and cooperate.

PRIMARY CHALLENGES AND ISSUES FACING HUMANITY

*H*umanity is faced by a range of seemingly insuperable problems: uncontrolled population growth, diminishing resources, exploitation of one group by another, ancient animosities, passion for revenge, racial antagonism, religious prejudice, territorial ambition, destructive use of the environment, oppression of women, disregard of the rights of others, greed for wealth and power, and so on. In the Theosophical view, all these are secondary or derivative problems—the symptoms of a disease. The primary, original problem, the cause of the disease, is the illusion of separateness, the notion that we are unconnected, independent beings whose particular welfare can be achieved at the expense of the general good.

The primary challenge facing humanity is therefore to recognize the unity of our species and in turn our ultimate unity with all life in the universe. Despite the superficial cultural and genetic differences that divide humanity, we are a remarkably homogeneous species—physically, psychologically, intellectually and spiritually. Biologically, we are a single human gene pool, with only minor local variations. Psychologically and intellectually, we respond to stimuli in fundamentally the same way. Linguistically, behind the surface variations of the world's tongues, our underlying language ability is remarkably uniform. Spiritually, we have a common origin and a common destiny.

Neither is the human species isolated from the rest of life in the universe. We are part and parcel of the totality of existence stretching from this planet Earth to the farthest reaches of the cosmos in every conceivable dimension. When we realize our integral connection with all other human beings, with all other life forms, with the most distant reaches of space, we will realize that we cannot either harm or help another without harming or helping ourselves. We are all one, not as metaphor, but as fact.

Individual Theosophists engage in social, political and charitable action as they are moved by their consciences and sense of duty to become so engaged. They are urged by the Theosophical tradition to realize the concept of Unity in practical responses to the challenges we face, and urge that all human

"The Society was founded to teach no new and easy paths to the acquisition of "powers"; . . . its only mission is to re-kindle the torch of truth, so long extinguished for all but the very few, and to keep that truth alive by the formation of a fraternal union of mankind, the only soil in which the good seed can grow."
H. P. BLAVATSKY,
"Spiritual Progress," 1885, *CW* 6:333

"The path of right progress should include the amelioration of the individual, the nation, the race and humanity; and ever keeping in view the last and grandest object, the perfecting of man, should reject all apparent bettering of the individual at the expense of his neighbor."
H. P. BLAVATSKY,
"The Struggle for Existence,"
1889, *CW* 11:151–52

"If Theosophy prevailing in the struggle, its all-embracing philosophy strikes deep root into the minds and hearts of men, if its doctrines of Reincarnation and Karma, in other words, of Hope and Responsibility, find a home in the lives of the new generations, then, indeed, will dawn the day of joy and gladness for all who now suffer and are outcast. For real Theosophy is Altruism, and we cannot repeat it too often. It is brotherly love, mutual help, unswerving devotion to Truth. If once men do but realize that in these alone can true happiness be found, and never in wealth, possessions or any selfish gratification, then the dark clouds will roll away, and a new humanity will be born upon earth. Then, the Golden Age will be there, indeed."
H. P. BLAVATSKY,
"Our Cycle and the Next,"
1889, *CW* 11:202

"There are three truths which are absolute, and which cannot be lost, but yet may remain silent for lack of speech:

[1] The human soul is immortal, and its future is the future of a thing whose growth and splendor has no limit.

[2] The principle which gives life dwells in us and around us, is undying and eternally beneficent, is not heard or seen or smelt, but is perceived by the one who desires perception.

[3] We are each our own absolute law-giver, the dispenser of glory or gloom to ourselves, the decreer of our life, our reward, our punishment.

These truths, which are as great as is life itself, are as simple as the simplest human mind.

Feed the hungry with them."
MABEL COLLINS,
The Idyll of the White Lotus, 1884 [rev.]

From the unreal, lead us to the Real.
From darkness, lead us to Light.
From death, lead us to Immortality.
Peace unto all the world.

UPANISHADS

O hidden Life,
    vibrant in every atom,
O hidden Light,
    shining in every creature,
O hidden Love,
    embracing all in oneness,
May all who feel themselves
    as one with thee
Know they are therefore one
    with every other.

ANNIE BESANT

beings should feel by virtue of their humanity. Collectively and as Theosophists, however, we do not regard it as our special calling to be social, political or charitable activists. Theosophy addresses the cause rather than the symptoms of the human disease. Theosophy seeks to make humanity aware, intellectually, affectively and experientially, of our unity with one another and with the whole universe. From such awareness will flow naturally and inevitably a respect for differences, a wise use of the environment, the fair treatment of others, a sympathy with the afflictions of our neighbors, and the will to respond to those afflictions helpfully and lovingly.

"Help Nature and work on with her; and Nature will regard thee as one of her creators and make obeisance." [sl. 66]

"Sow kindly acts and thou shalt reap their fruition. Inaction in a deed of mercy becomes an action in a deadly sin.

Shalt thou abstain from action? Not so shall gain thy soul her freedom. To reach Nirvâna one must reach Self-Knowledge, and Self-Knowledge is of loving deeds the child." [sl. 135-36]

"To live to benefit mankind is the first step." [sl. 144]
H. P. BLAVATSKY,
The Voice of the Silence, 1889

"Behold the truth before you: A clean life, an open mind, a pure heart, an eager intellect, an unveiled spiritual perception, a brotherliness for one's co-disciple, a readiness to give and receive advice and instruction, a loyal sense of duty to the Teacher, a willing obedience to the behests of TRUTH, once we have placed our confidence in, and believe that Teacher to be in possession of it; a courageous endurance of personal injustice, a brave declaration of principles, a valiant defense of those who are unjustly attacked, and a constant eye to the ideal of human progression and perfection which the secret science (Gupta-Vidya) depicts—these are the golden stairs up the steps of which the learner may climb to the Temple of Divine Wisdom."
H. P. BLAVATSKY,
1890, *CW* 12:503

"There is a road, steep and thorny, beset with perils of every kind, but yet a road, and it leads to the very heart of the Universe: I can tell you how to find those who will show you the secret gateway that opens inward only, and closes fast behind the neophyte for evermore. There is no danger that dauntless courage cannot conquer; there is no trial that spotless purity cannot pass through; there is no difficulty that strong intellect cannot surmount. For those who win onwards, there is reward past all telling—the power to bless and save humanity; for those who fail, there are other lives in which success may come."
H. P. BLAVATSKY,
1891, *CW* 13:219

A PORTRAIT OF
The Unification Church

Dr. Frank Kaufmann

Executive Director, Inter Religious Federation for World Peace

The Unification Church is best understood in the context of the larger work of Reverend Moon and Mrs. Moon. In addition to heading the Unification Church, Reverend Moon and Mrs. Moon have founded and support dozens of initiatives for world peace in all spheres of human endeavor. Of special note are the Inter-Religious Federation for World Peace, The International Federation for World Peace and the Women's Federation for World Peace. These are surrounded by a constellation of cultural, educational, relief and humanitarian projects. Two important elements must be considered in order to develop an accurate grasp of the Unification Church: (1) The teachings which guide the Unification community, namely the *Divine Principle,* and (2) The status of Reverend and Mrs. Moon.

Reverend Moon was born in what is now North Korea, January 6, 1920, during the period of brutal Japanese occupation. The fifth of eight children, Sun Myung Moon came from a family well respected for its great hospitality and who were referred to as "those who could live without law," a Korean phrase indicating people who were capable of guiding themselves by conscience alone. Reverend Moon's religious foundations combined the ancient traditions of Korea with the message of Christian missionaries. According to Reverend Moon, Jesus appeared to him while deep in prayer on a Korean mountainside, on Easter Sunday, 1936. Jesus asked him to complete the responsibility left unfinished since the origin of humankind. From that point the life of Sun Myung Moon changed dramatically. For nine years Sun Myung Moon researched the Bible, the natural world and the spiritual world to produce what is known today as the *Divine Principle.*

The *Divine Principle* is divided into three sections, Creation, Fall and Restoration. It teaches that God's original ideal is expressed in "the three great blessings" found in the Genesis account of human origins. To "be fruitful" is understood as the commission for each person to perfect their unique individuality by uniting mind and body and being in full union with God. These perfected individuals, man and woman, were to "multiply," forming families born of the unconditional love of a husband for his wife, of a wife for her husband. It is taught that the original human couple were thus to become "True Parents." This ever expanding family should "have dominion," namely establish a perfect ecological relationship with the natural universe. This ideal was not achieved by the first human ancestors, who instead violated God's commandment "not to eat the forbidden fruit," by engaging in physical love without receiving God's blessing to do so. This act of disobedience, in which the Archangel Lucifer participated, created the personage of Satan and bound the first human ancestors with him. Satan participates in human affairs through the perpetuation of impure love and lineage.

Salvation providence reveals God's work to re-create the conditions for, 1. the fulfillment of the original three great blessings, and 2. to liberate the descendants of Adam and Eve from their bondage to Satan. This task constitutes the mission of the Messiah, who by the fulfillment of his own responsibility obeys the commandment and fulfills the purpose of creation. Thus Jesus came both as "Adam," and as the Savior; to fulfill the three blessings, and to liberate all of humankind. The faithlessness of those around Jesus led to his crucifixion, thus preventing him from his opportunity to fulfill the three great blessings. The divine love of Jesus however, preserved the mission of Savior, allowing Jesus to provide spiritual salvation to those who believe in him and follow his teachings. Jesus promised the "second coming of Christ," knowing that the original will of God, the three blessings remained unfulfilled despite his own ministry. It is this original mission that Jesus asked Sun Myung Moon to fulfill in 1936.

In the 20th century Sun Myung Moon came as the return of Christ (at the end of WWII, in 1945), but, like Jesus, he was rejected. When this failure occurred, Reverend Moon was forced to establish a religious community which could carry out the mission of Christianity and serve as the Bride of Christ. This community became known as the Unification Church, founded in 1954. In 1960 Reverend Moon married Hak Ja Han Moon, thus fulfilling for the first time in human history the original mission of True Parents. Unification Church members and members of other religions have their marriages "blessed" by Reverend and Mrs. Moon whereby they inherit the potential to themselves become true parents.

The mission of the True Parents and Savior is to all people in all religions. The Unification "Church" does not desire to be an enduring religious body. Long before the Unification Church appeared each world religion was already instructed to await and receive the one who will end evil history and restore an unbroken relationship between God and all humanity. The Unification Church exists to teach the Divine Principle and support the effort of the True Parents to freely give the blessing.

A PORTRAIT OF
The Unitarian Universalist Church

The Rev. David A. Johnson

Pastor, First Parish in Brookline, Massachusetts

*T*he Unitarian Universalist Association is the institutional embodiment of two separate denominations (movements, faith traditions) extending back to the Reformation era and well beyond. Universalist convictions are found as early as the church father, Origen, who declared that all creation would ultimately be drawn back to its divine source, nothing and no one ultimately and forever excluded. Unitarian thought, its conviction that God is ultimately and absolutely one, has been a recurring heresy within the established church since the first century of the Christian Era.

The Roumanian-Transylvanian Unitarian Church, now more than four centuries old, stems originally from the skeptical and evangelical rationalist movements within the Roman Catholic Church and the openness engendered in the Reformation era. Its faith and struggle, and that of Socinianism in Poland and the low countries, became a fertile seed ground for the beginnings of British Unitarian thought and structure. American Unitarianism has its own primary roots in the liberal Christian movement within New England's old Puritan establishment, and the formal break that produced the American Unitarian Association in 1825.

Unitarian faith rejected Calvinist double predestination—original sin as fatally flawing all human character—and the full and absolute personhood of each member of the trinity. Unitarians affirmed the just and loving character of God, the God-given moral and reasoning capacity of people, working out one's salvation with diligence and God's grace, and above all, one God.

Universalist institutional roots are in the Radical reformation, intertwined with the histories of several Anabaptist, Separatist and Pietist movements. The Universalists first organized separately in Britain as an offshoot of the Wesleyan Methodists. What was to become the Universalist Church of America was first gathered in September of 1793, making this the 200th anniversary. Universalism in this country found its supporters chiefly from Protestants disaffected by the bitter sectarian enthusiasms of much of American Protestantism—prepared to condemn the great mass of humankind to eternal perdition. Many who could not believe in the almost universal Protestant conviction that an everlasting fiery pit awaited all who lacked a proper faith and salvation experience joined the Universalists in the heady revival era of the end of the 18th century and the beginning of the 19th.

Both the Unitarian and Universalist denominations were democratic in polity and basic organizational structures. Both rejected absolute and binding statements of faith. Both affirmed freedom of personal belief within the disciplines of democratic community, and the freedom of each congregation to shape its own faith and worship, and choose its clergy. Both became clearly unitarian in theology long before the merger of the two associations of churches in 1961. The Unitarian Universalist Association became an international association of churches in the last few years with congregations in several countries.

Because of its openness the Unitarian Universalist movement encompasses persons of liberal Christian, deist, theist, religious humanist and world religionist persuasions. When the World Parliament of Religions gathered in Chicago in September of 1893, Rev. Jenkin Lloyd Jones (a Unitarian) was the secretary and general work horse of the planning committee. Rev. Augusta Chapin (a Universalist) was the chair of the womens' religion committee. Neither denomination was intimidated by other traditions or feared contamination from the vigorous non-Christian world (as did so many others) there represented. Hundreds of Universalists and Unitarians participated in the Parliament as attendees, participants and speakers. Clearly they were there as much as anything to share, learn and inform their own faith.

Our ritual is as diverse as our congregations. Most worship shows its rootage in mainline Protestantism. However, it is no surprise to find a tea ceremony, a high holy days service, a Hindu Festival of Lights, a Muslim prayer or a Wiccan ritual in a Unitarian Universalist church. No single symbol has universal acceptance among us. For some the cross remains the central symbol, for others no symbol is acceptable. For some a grouping of world religious symbols centers worship. In recent years the flaming chalice has become the dominant symbol. It originates in the movement that spread from the martyrdom of Jan Hus in the 13th century. The symbol was originally a flame in the communion cup symbolizing the enduring flame of his faith, burning up from the chalice, both forming the shape of a cross. It has been reshaped in many forms as congregations have used and adapted it, meaning commonly today the light of knowledge and search for truth.

The Unitarian Universalist association remains a small, vigorous and growing religious body loosely connected to American Protestant Christianity, though seeing itself today predominantly as separate and different. It is a member of the International Association of Religious Freedom (69 member groups in more than 40 nations) and a new coalition of Unitarian movements worldwide. ✹

A PORTRAIT OF
Wicca

Michael Thorn

Public Information Officer, The Covenant of the Goddess, Berkeley, California

*M*odern Witchcraft (or Wicca) is the most common expression of the religious movement known as Neopaganism. According to the Institute for the Study of American Religion, Neopaganism is the fastest growing religion in the United States. Its practitioners are reviving ancient Pagan practices and beliefs of pre-Christian Europe and adapting them to contemporary American life. The result is a religion that is both old and new, both "traditional" and creative. The easiest way to grasp this "new" religion is to consider Native American religions, but with a pre-Christian European cultural setting and informed by modern American science and technology. Both Wiccan and Native American spiritual paths tend to agree on respect for all life, observation of the seasons and cycles of the life through ritual, belief in the Divine as immanent in all things (as well as transcendent); belief in the Divine as manifesting in many gods, both male and female; and the practice of magic to help with the day-to-day trials of life.

Witches focus their liturgy and worship around a Goddess and a God. Rituals and services are timed to the phases of the moon and to the Wheel of the Year (i.e. the solstices, equinoxes, and the days falling midway between these such as May Day and Hallowe'en). Most Witches treat their practice as a priesthood, somewhat akin to the mystery cults of classical Greece and Rome, involving years of training and passage through life-transforming initiatory rituals. All Witches agree on the ethical code, "An it harm none, do what ye will"; in other words, "Do what you truly believe is right, but let no one be harmed by your actions."

The Covenant of the Goddess: A brief history

*T*he Covenant of the Goddess (CoG) is the world's largest religious organization for Witches. In the 1970s there was a marked rise of interest in Witchcraft in the United States and throughout the world, reflecting a growing feminist awareness and widespread concern for the environment. These are both values strongly emphasized in modern Witchcraft. In 1975, many Wiccan elders had the idea of forming a religious organization for all practitioners of Wicca. At a Spring Equinox gathering in 1975, representatives from several covens met to draft a "covenant" among themselves. This, and the group that grew out of it, would be known as the Covenant of the Goddess. The representatives also drafted bylaws to administer this new organization. The Covenant was to be non-hierarchical and governed by consensus. It was to be an umbrella organization of cooperating Wiccan congregations (covens) with the power to confer credentials on its qualified clergy. At the 1975 Summer Solstice, the bylaws were ratified by 13 member congregations.

The Covenant of the Goddess was incorporated as a non-profit religious organization on October 31, 1975, to increase cooperation among Witches and to secure for Witches and covens the legal protection enjoyed by members of other religions. It is the largest and oldest Wiccan organization, with members in North America, Europe and Australia.

THE CHARGE OF THE GODDESS

Composed by Gerald Gardner and
Doreen Valiente
from inspiration and traditional sources

"Listen to the words of the Great Mother; she who of old was also called Artemis, Astarte, Athene, Dione, Melusine, Cerridwen, Arianrhod and by many other names.

Whenever ye have need of any thing, once in the month, and better it be when the moon is full, then shall ye assemble in some secret place, and adore the spirit of me, whom am Queen of all Witches. There shall ye assemble, ye who are fain to learn all sorcery, yet have not won its deepest secrets; to these I teach things that are yet unknown. And ye shall be free from slavery; and as a sign that ye be truly free, ye shall be naked in your rites; and ye shall dance, sing, feast, make music, and love, all in my praise. For mine is the ecstasy of the spirit, and mine also is joy on earth; for my law is love unto all beings. Keep pure your highest ideal; strive ever towards it; let naught stop you or turn you aside. For mine is the secret door which opens upon the Land of Youth, and mine is the cup of the wine of life, and the Cauldron of Cerridwen, which is the Holy Grail of immortality. I am the gracious Goddess, who gives the gift of joy unto the hearts of women and men.

Continued on next page

"Upon earth I give knowledge of the spirit eternal; and beyond death, I give peace, and freedom, and reunion with those who have gone before. Nor do I demand aught in sacrifice; for behold, I am the Mother of all living, and my love is poured out upon the earth."

"Hear ye the words of the Star Goddess; she in the dust of whose feet are the hosts of heaven, and whose body encircles the universe:

"I who am the beauty of the green earth, and the white Moon among the stars, and the mystery of the waters, and the desire of the hearts of mankind, call unto thy soul. Arise, and come unto me. For I am the soul of nature, who gives life to the universe. From me all things proceed, and unto me all things must return; and before my face, beloved of Gods and mankind, let thine innermost divine self be enfolded in the rapture of the infinite. Let my worship be within the heart that rejoiceth; for behold, all acts of love and pleasure are my rituals. And therefore let there be beauty and strength, power and compassion, honor and humility, mirth and reverence within you. And thou who thinkest to seek for me, know thy seeking and yearning shall avail thee not unless thou knowest the mystery; that if that which thou seekest thou findest not within thee, thou wilt never find it without thee. For behold, I have been with thee from the beginning; and I am that which is attained at the end of desire."

The first few years of the Covenant's existence were devoted to growth and developing cooperation among its members. In recent years CoG has turned attention and resources to community projects and social action, including health insurance, Scouting awards for our young people, emergency relief for disaster victims, promoting positive media portrayals, and interfaith outreach. The Covenant's participation in the 1993 Parliament of the World's Religions marks a new high point in our continuing efforts as a contributing member of the world's community of faiths.

What is a Witch? What is Witchcraft?

The word "Witch" comes from the Anglo-Saxon *wicce* (meaning witch), which in turn derives from an Indo-European root word meaning to bend or change or perform magic/religion. It is possibly related to the Old Norse *vitki* (meaning priest), derived from the root words meaning "wise one" or "seer." Related words are "pagan," or "heathen," meaning a country dweller on the heath, peoples who were the European equivalent of the Native Americans and other indigenous, nature-worshipping people.

Today, a Witch is a woman or man who practices a life-affirming, Earth and nature-oriented religion, honoring Divinity in female as well as (or instead of) male aspects, and practicing *Magick* (often spelled with a *k* to distinguish it from stage illusions). There are many different traditions of Witches. Some traditions are practiced by women only, and recognize only the Divine Feminine, the Goddess. Others include men and recognize a male god in addition to the Goddess. Some traditions may date back for hundreds of years or more and others have been in existence for only a few years. The strength of the Witches' religion (also called "the Craft" or "Wicca") lies in its diversity; it is a living, growing religious tradition.

Witchcraft today may be seen as the sum total of all a Witch's spiritual practices, including but not limited to meditation, ritual and ritual drama, healing, herbalism, divination, creative mythology and more. It is the goal of these practices to bring the conduct of one's life fully into accord with the Divine as it is experienced and embodied in the natural world.

Conservative reckonings estimate 200,000 Wiccans in the United States. There could be many more, who are simply private about their religion because of concerns that they may face discrimination because of their beliefs.

Wiccan concepts of divinity

The Goddess worshipped by Wiccans is seen as transcendent and immanent. She can have many names and many aspects; some Wiccans worship only the nameless single Goddess, and others worship Her under all the names by which she has been known to the ancients: Ishtar, Diana, Cerridwen, Athena, Amaterasu, Hecate, Isis, Demeter and more. In addition, the Goddess can be seen in three aspects; the Maiden, the Mother and the Crone/Wise Woman. The Moon, the Sea and the Earth can all be personified as Goddesses.

Some Wiccans include the Divine Male, the God. The Sun is often personified as a God, as is plant life; the dying and reborn Grain God is common in many agricultural myths and cultures. Some call him by names such as Apollo, Osiris, Dionysus, Odin, Pan, Tammuz and many others. ✸

PART 3

Forming a Community of Religions

"'Buddhists are not looking for a convergence of religions.'
Quoting the well known edict of the Buddhist Emperor Asoka,
Ven. Vajiragnana continued,
'Let us be prepared to accept our crucial differences without trying to throw a threadbare rope between them.
Rather let us build bridges of better understanding,
tolerance for diverse views,
plus encouragement for morality and ethical culture.
This is where harmony is to be found.' "

VEN. PANDITH M. VAJIRAGNANA
at the 1988 WCF Conference,
in *Pilgrimage of Hope* by Marcus Braybrooke,
p.79

A Pilgrimage of Hope

The Rev. Marcus Braybrooke

Formerly Executive Director of the Council of Christians and Jews and Chaplain of Magdalen Chapel, Bath, and currently Chairman of the International Interfaith Organizations Coordinating Committee and of the World Congress of Faiths.

Since the 1893 Parliament, numerous interfaith conversations, shared worship services and joint responses to a variety of issues have served as bridges to interreligious harmony. No one has charted that activity better than Marcus Braybrooke. The essay which follows is the concluding chapter of his history of the past 100 years of the interfaith movement, *Pilgrimage of Hope*. –Ed.

The interaction of people of different faiths has increased enormously in the last century. Partly, this is for technological reasons. Far more people travel to other countries, whilst television gives us easy access to information about other cultures. Large numbers of people have been uprooted from one country to another, either as refugees or immigrants.

This human interaction, which may be very personal as in the case of marriages between people of different faiths, has been accompanied by a growing desire to know about other people's religion and way of life. The study of religions has become more common in colleges and schools, and books about world religions are now plentiful. By contrast, 150 years ago, very few of the religious classics of Asia had been translated into European languages and often Asians themselves were unfamiliar with their scriptures. At the same time, partly through the missionary efforts of the churches, some knowledge of Christian teaching is widespread. There are also Christian communities, often very small, in most countries of Asia, and now Muslim, Sikh, Hindu and Buddhist centers are to be found throughout Europe and America.

Too often, the interaction is negative, hostile and violent. The recent revival of religious enthusiasm in some areas of the world has been accompanied by an increase in religious extremism and intolerance. In parts of the Muslim world, for example, the revival of Islam has led to the persecution of Bahá'ís and other religious minorities. Many minority groups, in countries across the world, feel that they suffer from discrimination. Religious differences also continue to enflame other causes of division, for example in the Punjab, in Israel and the West Bank, in Northern Ireland and in Sri Lanka.

Yet the ever-growing interaction of people of different religions has also been accompanied by the growing desire that this should be friendly and creative. I have been astonished, in my research, to discover how many groups in so many different places are seeking interreligious understanding and cooperation. Only the larger groups have been mentioned [in *Pilgrimage of Hope*] and not all of them. They are matched by numerous local groups and by the efforts of people of goodwill, who belong to no particular interfaith organization. I think of ministers of religion who proclaim their faith without adverse comments on the beliefs of others, or of teachers who treat with proper respect the different religions of their pupils, or television producers who convey with integrity the beliefs and practices of people of another faith, or of all who work for good community relations or who support the great variety of bodies which work for peace, justice, international understanding and the relief of human need. These efforts seldom attract media reports, but they need to be set in the balance when there are much-publicized accounts of interreligious conflict.

> "*Some years ago, a meeting such as this would have been unthinkable. And, let us admit, even today, each one of us is aware of the difficulties [s]he has to face within his own congregation.*
>
> *The important fact is the miracle accomplished by the Lord: **we are here**. We respect each other. None of us is prompted by proselytizing motives. Each one has come with an open heart, ready to understand and love his brethren. . . . Above all, we are anxious to find effective ways of coming into agreement with a view to help Humanity face its immense problems. . . .*
>
> *A real meeting requires each one to come out of his shell and overcome his selfishness. A real meeting requires that each one, while remaining loyal to his own conscience and to his own conviction, should aim at discovering whatever may unite us, without measuring sacrifices, and at whatever may make it possible, tomorrow, to work together for the greater glory of God and the well-being of mankind.*"
>
> DOM HELDER CAMARA
> in *Religion for Peace: Proceedings of the Kyoto Conference on Religion and Peace*

Meanings of dialogue

*T*he wide range of such efforts points to the considerable variety of what may be described, rather generally, as interreligious dialogue. Professor Diana Eck, who is Moderator of the World Council of Churches' Sub-Unit for Dialogue, has distinguished six forms of dialogue. The first is parliamentary style dialogue. She traces this back to the 1893 World's Parliament of Religions and sees it carried forward by the international interfaith organizations, although, as we have seen, their way of working is now very different from the approach of the World's Parliament. Secondly, there is institutional dialogue, such as the regular meetings between representatives of the Vatican and the International Jewish Committee for Inter-religious Consultation. Thirdly, there is theological dialogue, which takes seriously the questions and challenges posed by people of other faiths. Fourthly, dialogue in community or the dialogue of life is the search for good relationships in ordinary life. Fifthly, spiritual dialogue is the attempt to learn from other traditions of prayer and meditation. Lastly, there is inner dialogue, which is "that conversation that goes on within ourselves in any other form of dialogue."[1]

There are various levels of dialogue and it is a process of growth. An initial requirement is an openness to and acceptance of the other. It takes time to build trust and to deepen relationships. This is why some continuity in a dialogue group is helpful and why patience and time are necessary—all of which are particularly difficult to ensure at an international level. Too easily, we find ourselves imposing our presuppositions on the conversation. Christians, for example, often assume that Muslims really adopt a critical attitude to the *Qur'an* similar to that common amongst Christians in their reading of the Bible. We have to learn to enter another world that may seem alien and which has different presuppositions. We have to allow our deepest convictions to be questioned. Some Buddhists, for example, will question deeply held Christian assumptions about God and the self. It is important for those venturing into dialogue to be secure in their own faith. They need to beware of becoming marginalized in or alienated from their own religious tradition. Dialogue needs also to be of equals, that is to say of those with similar levels of scholarship and study.

At its deepest, dialogue will raise questions of truth. Rabbi Dr. Norman Solomon, Director of the Centre for the Study of Judaism and Jewish/ Christian Relations at Selly Oak, Birmingham, said in his inaugural lecture, "Dialogue admits of degrees: there is dialogue which is of value though it does not reach deep. Much of the dialogue between Jews and Christians is a matter of simply learning to be nice to each other, trying a little to understand what the other is doing, cooperating in social endeavor. . . . Many ordinary Jews or Christians lack the skills necessary to engage in a deeper, theological dialogue, and are rightly wary of setting their faith at risk in a confusing enterprise. Yet the heart of dialogue is in talk together of theologians of both faiths, for it is they whose concern is with the meaning of life at its deepest level and it is they who translate from the doctrinal formula to the underlying reality."[2]

Dialogue does not necessarily produce agreement and, if it is a search for truth, there is no desire for easy compromise. Sometimes it makes clearer where essential differences lie, exposing the various presuppositions or views of the world with which partners in dialogue are operating. Sometimes it can be painful. The American Jewish writer, Dr. Eugene Borrowitz, has said, "Only by directly confronting our deepest differences can we come to know one another fully. Despite risks, interreligious discussion needs at times to be interreligious debate. That is one way it shows its conviction that truth is ultimately one."[3]

THE DIALOGUE DECALOGUE

Ground Rules of Interreligious and Interideological Dialogue

- Dialogue to learn, to change, to grow and act accordingly.
- Dialogue to share and receive from others.
- Dialogue with honesty and sincerity.
- Dialogue comparing ideals with ideals and practice with practice.
- Dialogue to define yourself and to learn the self-definition of others.
- Dialogue with no hard-and-fast assumptions about someone else's beliefs.
- Dialogue to share with equals.
- Dialogue in trust.
- Dialogue with willingness to look at your beliefs and traditions critically.
- Dialogue seeking to understand the other person's beliefs from within.

Adapted by the Grand Rapids Interfaith Dialogue Association from Leonard Swidler's "Dialogue Decalogue"

An Experience of Interreligious Dialogue

Father Thomas Keating O.S.C.O.

Convener of the Snowmass Conference and member of Monastic Interfaith Dialogue

A report on an experience of on-going interreligious dialogue might be helpful at this point. In 1984 I invited a group of spiritual teachers from a variety of the world religions—Buddhist, Tibetan Buddhist, Hindu, Jewish, Islamic, Native American, Russian Orthodox, Protestant and Roman Catholic—to gather at St. Benedict's Monastery, Snowmass, Colorado, to meditate together in silence and to share our personal spiritual journeys, especially those elements in our respective traditions that have proved most helpful to us along the way.

We kept no record and published no papers. As our trust and friendship grew, we felt moved to investigate various points that we seemed to agree on. The original points of agreement were worked over during the course of subsequent meetings as we continued to meet, for a week or so each year. Our most recent list consists of the following eight points:

1. The world religions bear witness to the experience of Ultimate Reality to which they give various names: Brahman, Allah, Absolute, God, Great Spirit.

2. Ultimate Reality cannot be limited by any name or concept.

3. Ultimate Reality is the ground of infinite potentiality and actualization.

4. Faith is opening, accepting and responding to Ultimate Reality. Faith in this sense precedes every belief system.

5. The potential for human wholeness—or in other frames of reference, enlightenment, salvation, transformation, blessedness, *nirvana*—is present in every human person.

6. Ultimate Reality may be experienced not only through religious practices but also through nature, art, human relationships and service of others.

7. As long as the human condition is experienced as separate from Ultimate Reality, it is subject to ignorance and illusion, weakness and suffering.

Continued on next page

The distinctive character of interfaith organizations

With the growth of dialogue, the vocation of interfaith organizations needs to be distinguished, on the one hand from bodies which may be described as "universalist movements for spiritual unity"[4] and, on the other hand, from the agencies for interreligious relations of a particular religion, such as the Pontifical Council for Inter-Religious Dialogue. The work of interfaith organizations needs also to be distinguished from centers and bodies devoted to the academic study of religions.

The interfaith organizations all accept the multiplicity and particularity of the world religions. As Dr. Francis Clark puts it in his *Interfaith Directory*, "the majority of those who are involved in the worldwide interfaith movement . . . see the rich multiformity of the world's religious traditions as a positive value to be treasured and developed, and take it as a basic datum in their quest for interreligious understanding and cooperation."[5] It has been repeatedly said that no one participating in the organizations is expected to compromise their own faith commitment—the only requirement is that a person should show the same respect to the faiths of other people as he or she would hope that others would show to his or her religion. Members of interfaith organizations hold a variety of views about the relationship of religions to each other. The question of the relationship of religions to each other is very much a matter of debate within several of the world religions.

The universalist movements for spiritual unity, by contrast, are likely to presuppose or to proclaim a particular view of the relationship of religions. Because of their fear that members of the major religions will call them syncretistic, interfaith organizations have kept rather aloof from universalist movements. If, however, the distinction is acknowledged, there could in the future be a closer cooperation in some areas of work between interfaith and universalist bodies. It is perhaps particularly important that interfaith organizations enter into greater dialogue with New Age movements and also the so-called "new religions." It is understandable that whilst the interfaith organizations were themselves viewed with suspicion by the major religious communities, they were careful not to increase that suspicion by keeping company with "strange bedfellows." Now that the major interfaith organizations have an established record of achievement and a proven integrity, they may feel greater confidence in entering into dialogue with New Age and universalist groups, not least because of the gap between those who share these spiritual aspirations and many members of more traditional religious communities.

If interfaith organizations respect the integrity of the world religions, equally they do not offer a preferential position to any one religious group. This is why they are all concerned to ensure a broad range of representation, drawn from many faiths, on their controlling body and to ensure that their funding comes from a variety of sources. This also distinguishes them from agencies for interreligious relations of a particular religious community. Such agencies have to reconcile their search for good relations with other religious groups with their traditional claims to an exclusive or privileged knowledge of truth. For such agencies and their parent religions, questions of the relationship of dialogue and mission and of the truth claims of their religion are very important. Certainly members of these agencies may enter into the fullest and most open dialogue with people of other faiths, but they have to interpret their position to their fellow believers. Members of interfaith organizations, who are themselves believers, have, of course, the same questions with which to wrestle and the same task of interpretation. Yet this is not the responsibility of the interfaith organizations themselves. As the religions have seen the importance of dialogue, the number of their agencies for dialogue have increased.

In recent years, there has been a growing partnership between the interfaith organizations and these agencies, as both recognize their particular tasks. In preparation for the World Day of Prayer for Peace at Assisi, the Vatican Secretariat for Non-Christians enlisted the help of World Conference on Religion and Peace, so that those of other faiths would feel that the invitation to participate had no hidden implications. Similarly, it is the interfaith organizations which rightly can sponsor The Year of Interreligious Understanding and Cooperation, although the support of the agencies for dialogue will be vital.

Differences of emphasis in interfaith work

*A*mongst the interfaith organizations themselves, differences of emphasis can be recognized. There are those which have concentrated on building up understanding and friendship and those who feel that such understanding will grow as people of different religions cooperate in tackling the urgent problems of the world. The latter have been less concerned to discuss the theoretical relationship of religions to each other.

Those interfaith organizations, such as World Congress of Faiths and the Temple of Understanding, which have seen the building up of a fellowship of faiths as their primary task, have grappled with the question of the relationship of religions. They tend to assume a pluralist position, in which the independent validity of the world religions is acknowledged. No one religion is assumed to be superior. Rather, it is assumed that each has a contribution to make to the fuller awareness of truth. For some, the pluralist position is based on an "impelling awareness of the historico-cultural limitation of all knowledge and religious beliefs, and the difficulty, if not impossibility, of judging the truth claims of another culture or religion on the basis of one's own."[6] Such a view was particularly associated, in a previous generation, with the German theologian Ernst Troeltsch[7] and today with the British theologian and philosopher John Hick. Others put the emphasis on the infinity and ineffability of the Divine Mystery, to which all religions point. This is a view that echoes the *neti-neti* tradition of Hinduism. The Divine transcends our human thought and language and this involves a recognition of the relativity of all religious language and symbols. This "forbids any one religion from having the 'only' or 'final' word."[8] Dr. Radhakrishnan was an eloquent exponent of this position, which has also been expounded by Professor Wilfred Cantwell Smith of Harvard University. For Professor Raimon Panikkar, pluralism implies a pluralism of truth. For others, such as R. E. Whitson,[9] there is the suggestion that through dialogue there may be a growing convergence of religions in deeper understanding of the Divine—and this is one reason for seeing the interfaith movement as a "pilgrimage of hope."

The other hope that inspires the interfaith movement is that together people of all faiths may work for peace and justice and the protection of the environment. "Economic, political and especially nuclear liberation is too big a job for any one nation, or culture or religion," writes Paul Knitter of Xavier University, Cincinnati. "A worldwide liberation movement needs a worldwide interreligious dialogue."[10] This emphasis has characterized WCRP and also organizations, which are multireligious in character, which campaign on specific issues, such as the Global Forum or the World Wide Fund for Nature.

One interfaith organization?

*W*ould it be helpful for the various interfaith organizations to come together in one body? Such a suggestion was made at the first Ammerdown Conference as they began to get to know each other better,

8. Disciplined practice is essential to the spiritual life; yet spiritual attainment is not the result of one's own efforts, but the result of the experience of oneness with Ultimate Reality.

At the annual Conference in May 1986, we came up with additional points of agreement of a practical nature:

A. Some examples of disciplined practice, common to us all:

1. Practice of compassion
2. Service to others
3. Practicing moral precepts and virtues
4. Training in meditation techniques and regularity of practice
5. Attention to diet and exercise
6. Fasting and abstinence
7. The use of music and chanting and sacred symbols
8. Practice in awareness (recollection, mindfulness) and living in the present moment
9. Pilgrimage
10. Study of scriptural texts and scriptures

*A*nd *in some traditions:*

11. Relationship with a qualified teacher
12. Repetition of sacred words (mantra, japa)
13. Observing periods of silence and solitude
14. Movement and dance
15. Formative community

B. It is essential to extend our formal practice of awareness into all the aspects of our life.

C. Humility, gratitude and a sense of humor are indispensable in the spiritual life.

D. Prayer is communion with Ultimate Reality, whether it is regarded as personal, impersonal or beyond them both.

Continued on next page

We were surprised and delighted to find so many points of similarity and convergence in our respective paths. Like most people of our time, we originally expected that we would find practically nothing in common. In the years that followed we spontaneously and somewhat hesitatingly began to take a closer look at certain points of disagreement until these became our main focus of attention. We found that discussing our points of disagreement increased the bonding of the group even more than discovering our points of agreement. We became more honest in stating frankly what we believed and why, without at the same time making any effort to convince others of our own position. We simply presented our understanding as a gift to the group. ✿

"*... if we could articulate the points of agreement among the world religions, a transcultural revelation of the basic values of human life which the world religions hold in common would emerge. We would identify the spiritual heritage of the entire human family, however diversely each religion and culture celebrates it. If this consensus could then be injected, with one voice, into the socio-political arena, the world religions would be contributing an all-important spiritual dimension to the decision-making process.*

In the next generation the question may not be which religion one belongs to, but whether religion itself is of value. Those who have had some experience of transcendence must find some way to communicate the fact that the experience of the Ultimate Mystery is open to every human person who chooses to pursue the search for truth and embark on the spiritual journey—a journey which is literally without end."

THOMAS KEATING,
from "One Voice," p.127, in
Speaking of Silence, edited by Susan Walker

but on fuller acquaintance, there has come the recognition that each has its own constituency and its own special vocation. Yet, easily, the organizations could become competitive for resources. Already certain world religious leaders are in great demand to attend international interreligious conferences. Rather than creating one organization, it may be more valuable to strengthen the mechanisms for coordination and cooperation, both between interfaith organizations themselves and between such organizations and the agencies for dialogue of the religious communities. Planning for the Year of Interreligious Understanding and Cooperation in 1993 is already an occasion for greater liaison. More permanent and effective structures for coordination will be necessary in the future. The interfaith networks established in the United Kingdom and in North America may provide models.

What has been achieved?

*A*s of all efforts to change attitudes, it is hard to estimate what has been achieved in 100 years of the interfaith movement. There has been an ever widening circle of those involved in interfaith encounter. As it is a personal journey, each individual has to make the discoveries for herself or himself. Dialogue, therefore, involves a continuing process of learning and re-education. This suggests that the struggle against prejudice and intolerance is also a continuing process. At one time, I hoped that tolerance would gradually spread as people of different faiths got to know each other better. It seems, however, that certain forms of religious experience and loyalty breed intolerance, which too easily is exploited by political leaders, and that constant vigilance is necessary to curb religious extremism. Tolerance itself has its own limits and the search for interreligious cooperation means opposition to those who use religion to bolster fanaticism and to those who use religion as a cloak for power, prejudice and injustice.

Those who have entered deeply into dialogue all speak of the personal enrichment, both in terms of new friendships and of a deeper appreciation of other faiths and of their own. Many have had to sense a feeling of alienation within their own religious communities. Today, however, the religious communities have begun to appreciate the importance of interreligious dialogue and are encouraging their adherents to take part in it. This, one hopes, will bring to the religious communities the enrichment that individuals have already discovered.

In terms of the struggle for peace and a world community, the interfaith movement has done much to break down prejudice, both by encouraging personal meeting and by public education. The skills necessary to make effective contributions to conflict resolution have yet to be adequately developed. Together members of all religions need to give increasing attention to the search for shared moral values, which undergird human rights, and which can give an ethical basis to the emerging world society.[11]

When he addressed the Global Forum on Human Survival in Moscow in 1990, President Mikhail Gorbachev acknowledged that it was the alarm voiced by some scientists, which was taken up by some members of the public and then by the media, which had forced the politicians to take notice and to act. The beginnings of change lie with a few visionary individuals and a creative minority. An example of this is the way that the suggestion of international arbitration to settle disputes, made in some small peace groups in the middle of the last century, has been adopted by the nations. The prayer and work for peace in the eighties of this century seems to have created a new international atmosphere to which the politicians have responded. Increasingly members of all religions speak of the need for understanding and cooperation, rather than of the conquest of the world by

A Grassroots Model

The Grand Rapids Interfaith Dialogue Association

Dr. Lillian Sigal

Professor of Humanities and organizer of interfaith dialogue. For those thinking about initiating interfaith dialogue meetings, Dr. Sigal provides a model based on the experience of people in Grand Rapids, Michigan.

Introduction

The Interfaith Dialogue Association in Grand Rapids began as the brainchild of two women—Rev. Marchiene Rienstra, a Christian, and myself, a Jew. Marchiene and my late husband, Rabbi Phillip Sigal (a New Testament scholar), met at Calvin College, where they frequently dialogued about Judaism and Christianity. Phillip dreamt of establishing a Jewish-Christian ecumenical center. After he died, Marchiene and I determined to make his dream a reality; however, we decided to broaden its scope to include all the world religions. The seed for the Interfaith Dialogue Association was planted in 1988; it flowered as a chartered, non-profit organization in 1990; and in 1993 it is still a fledgling plant needing consistent nurturance, but betokening greater growth and outreach to fulfill its mission.

Based on my experience as co-president of IDA, I offer below suggestions and caveats for organizing, dialoguing, and developing programs for an association such as ours.

Forming a dialogue organization

We began the process of establishing IDA by first brainstorming with a cross section of leaders from the religious and academic community—both lay and clergy—to determine whether our community needed such an organization. These people strongly endorsed our concept, and many of them became members of our Board of Directors, providing us with ideas, contacts and resources to fulfill our objectives.

Subsequently, we met with a core group to create bylaws and appoint an executive committee consisting of two co-presidents, a secretary and a treasurer. We established membership dues (with option of reduced rate or no fee, depending upon financial status), a quarterly newsletter, and a brochure stating our goals and activities.

Ideas for dialogue groups

- If possible, have two groups meeting monthly on different nights to accommodate different peoples' schedules. Ideally, discussion thrives in a group of 9–12 people. However, realistically, the mailing list should be 15–18, because of absenteeism.

- Encourage members to put the dates of the monthly meetings on their calendars and to be committed to them.

- Strive to make the group as religiously and ideologically diverse and balanced as possible and include humanists.

- Meet in members' homes to enhance development of

Continued on next page

---

a single religion. Change is possible and it is made possible by the vision and creative energies of dedicated people, but continuing vigilance is necessary to ensure that changes for the better are not eroded. The interfaith movement has been a creative energy, building friendship between people of different religions and enabling them to work together for a better world. Its hopes are far from realized. It has been said that the next century will be a spiritual century or it will not be. Interfaith pilgrims need still to discover for themselves that the One God of many names is a Lover of all nations and they need to share that discovery with others so that we all may know, in our hearts, in our homes, in our nations and in our world, the "peace of God's will, the peace of our need."[12]

NOTES

1. Diana L. Eck, "What Do We Mean by 'Dialogue?,' " *Current Dialogue*, WCC, Geneva, 1987, pp. 5ff.

2. Norman Solomon, "Jewish/Christian Dialogue. The State of the Art," *Studies in Jewish/Christian Relations*, No. 1, Selly Oak, Birmingham, 1984, p. 8

3. Eugene R. Borrowitz, *Contemporary Christologies: A Jewish Response*, Paulist Press, 1980, p.19.

4. Francis Clark (ed.), *Interfaith Directory*, New Era, New York, 1987, p. viii.

5. *Ibid.*, p. v.

6. Paul Knitter, Preface to *The Myth of Christian Uniqueness*, ed. John Hick and Paul F. Knitter, SCM Press and Orbis Books, 1988, p. ix.

7. E. Troeltsch, "The Place of Christianity Among the World's Religions" in *Christian Thought*, 1923. See my *Together to the Truth*, CLS, Madras, 1971, pp. 112–113.

8. Knitter (n.6), p. x.

9. Robert Edward Whitson, *The Coming Convergence of World Religions*, Newman Press, Westminster, MD 1971.

10. Knitter (n. 6), p. xi.

11. See for example: *The Ethics of World Religions and Human Rights*, ed. Hans Küng and Jürgen Moltmann, SCM Press, 1990; my chapter, "Seeking Community" in *Belonging to Britain*, ed. Roger Hooker, The Council of Churches of Britain and Ireland, 1991; R. Traer, *Faith in Human Rights*, Georgetown University Press, Washington, DC 1990; and Hans Küng, *Global Responsibility*, SCM Press and Crossroad Publishing, New York, 1991.

12. I echo the prayer, "O God of many names" by George Appleton, used by the Week of Prayer for World Peace. I recognize, of course, that some Buddhists and others are uneasy with the use of the term "God."

Goals of IDA

1. *To eliminate prejudice* that creates tension between members of different religious traditions and ideologies.

2. *To advance understanding of religions and ideologies* by study, dialogue and sharing of religious experiences.

3. *To foster appreciation for the richness of diverse ideologies and religions.*

4. *To identify commonalities and differences among religions and ideologies* to enhance personal growth and transformation.

5. *To promote friendship and trust* among people of diverse ideologies and religions.

Overheard at a meeting

During a substantive presentation on essential beliefs and teachings of Judaism by David, the congenial group meeting at Lillian's home eagerly presented both insights and questions from their own religious perspectives. One topic was covenants; another was rites of passage. The quotes below don't detail the subjects, which varied throughout the evening, but rather show the atmosphere. Note the choice of words, the curiosity and discovery.

- Herb, a Bahá'í, said "We also make a covenant, with the Universal House of Justice." Later he began an exchange with "We would see it that . . . "
- Another in the group said "from the Jewish perspective, the covenant . . ."
- On another topic, Sayid said "It is very similar, in Islam. I read the whole *Qur'an* by the age of 13."
- Another questioned: "Do you have something like the Bar Mitzvah?"
- Renu said: "In some forms of Hinduism, it is like being 'born again,' making a spiritual commitment just before puberty." Later, she commented, "I perceive both Judaism and Islam as macho religions." This expression about her perception led to a lively exchange.
- Ed, a minister, said that "In Christianity, one of our problems is interpretation and translation. Is that a problem in Judaism?"
- Another added, "Any translation brings the agendas of the translator and the culture, and translators have power to change the religion."

Conversations, attitudes and insights like these make interfaith dialogue an enjoyable and educational experience.

personal relationships, opportunities to see and experience the cultural milieu of different members—their food, art, ritual objects, etc.

- Begin with a prayer or ritual led by a member of a different religion each time who explains its meaning.
- Discuss various festivals at seasons when they are observed.
- Generate ideas from members for a text to read in advance of each meeting. This should be done at the beginning of the year. Huston Smith's *The World Religions* was an excellent choice one year.
- Begin the first meeting with a discussion of the Dialogue Decalogue (above) to establish guidelines for meaningful and sensitive dialogue.
- Appoint a group coordinator who sends reminders of meetings.
- Appoint a group leader for each session to keep the discussion focused, to encourage full participation, to avoid monopolization of the discussion by a few members, and to faithfully follow the guidelines of the Dialogue Decalogue.
- Make one person responsible for summarizing or providing historical background for the reading material.
- Occasionally, invite an outside speaker, especially on a subject in which no group member has any expertise.
- Use the comparative method, i.e., when a theme is discussed in one religion elicit responses from members of the other religions on that theme.
- Allow time for announcements of events, religious festivals or news of interfaith activities in the community.
- Occasionally, share a potluck to provide opportunities for personal friendships to develop.
- From time to time ask members for feedback on how things are going.

Major programs

- Have an annual membership meeting with a program and a social hour to bring together the dialoguers and people on our mailing list who support us, but do not attend dialogue groups. Open these programs to the public to help advertise the organization and gain new members. The best source of members, nevertheless, is the members themselves—their friends and acquaintances.
- Have an annual conference with an outstanding figure who has contributed to interfaith dialogue. So far, we recommend Leonard Swidler, director of the Interreligious-Interideological Institute at Temple University, PA, and Huston Smith, author of *The World's Religions*. Our next conference will feature Muslim feminist Riffat Hassan, chair of Religious Studies at the University of Louisville, KY. The conferences include an interfaith panel of respondents to the keynoter and conference theme and small discussion groups of those attending the conference, facilitated by members of our organization. The funding for these conferences has been provided by three local colleges.

Conclusion

I have discovered that interfaith dialogue that is serious and not superficial involves challenges and risks, but opportunities for personal growth and spiritual enrichment. Bahá'í compares humanity to a rose garden. A garden where all the roses are white or red would be boring—the beauty of the garden resides in its variety of colors. Grassroots interfaith activity enables us to join the growing momentum—evidenced in the Parliament of the World's Religions—for global bonding to displace the hostility that religious differences have unfortunately created. Indeed, as Hans Küng has noted, "There will be peace on earth when there is peace among the world religions."

A Study Guide for Interreligious Cooperation and Understanding

Marcus Braybrooke

Marcus Braybrooke has been involved in the interfaith movement for over 25 years. For most of this time he has been an officer of the World Congress of Faiths and was for many years Editor of *World Faith Insight*. He has participated in conferences of IARF, the Temple of Understanding, WCRP and other interfaith bodies. He is chairman of the *ad hoc* International Interfaith Organizations Coordinating Committee for 1993. He has also written *Time to Meet; Children of God;* and *Stepping Stones to a Global Ethic.* As a factual foundation to this study we highly recommend *Pilgrimage of Hope* which provides a full account of the history of the interfaith movement.

The aim of these contents and suggestions for group discussion is to help readers and study groups become more aware of the growth of the interfaith movement during this century and to see how your own experiences relate to these developments. This study guide was first published as a booklet by Marcus Braybrooke of the World Congress of Faiths for use in connection with *1993: A Year of Interreligious Understanding and Cooperation,* and beyond. The author is grateful for advice and help with production from members of the World Congress of Faiths. These pages may be freely copied but please acknowledge: *1993: A Year of Interreligious Understanding and Cooperation.* Copyright Marcus Braybrooke 1992. This republication of his work (with slight modifications by the Editor) is used with permission.

Interspersed among the eight sections of the *Study Guide* are other articles about interfaith organizations mentioned in the *Guide,* reprints of some of their documents, and descriptions of several interfaith events commemorating and building upon this year of the centennial. *–Ed.*

Interfaith cooperation: Achievements and possibilities

*1*993 marks the hundredth anniversary of the interfaith movement which dates from the World's Parliament of Religions, held in Chicago in 1893. This Study Guide summarizes its development into a world-wide movement involving people from all religions.

The story of the Chicago World's Parliament and of the growth of the main international interfaith organizations is outlined and questions raised about the relation of religions to each other, their influence on war and peace and about the successes and failures of the interfaith movement. Pointing to what the interfaith movement hopes to achieve in 1993 and beyond, the guide is a quick introduction to this inspiring endeavor and is also a good basis for discussion by one-faith and interfaith groups; questions are provided.

CONTENTS OF THIS STUDY GUIDE

1. Rivalry or Cooperation?
2. Chicago, 1893
3. What Unites Us?
4. The Religious Communities Search for Peace
5. Religious Communities in Dialogue
6. Education
7. Praying Together
8. 1993 and Beyond

SCOTLAND — Commemorating 1893 in 1993

The Rev. James Paterson

Scottish interest in commemorating the 1893 World's Parliament of Religions has been given an added dimension through our realization of the contribution of a number of influential Scottish figures in the event and its planning. Significant papers came from Henry Drummond, Professor of Natural Science in the Free Church College, Glasgow and his colleague Professor Alexander Balmain Bruce. Principal William Miller of Madras Christian College gave valuable support. Lord Aberdeen, then Governor General of Canada, and Lady Aberdeen, were involved in the setting up of the Irish Village in the main Exposition.

Existing interfaith groups have used the material provided by the World Congress of Faiths to advance current interest in interfaith cooperation and understanding. The recently formed Churches' Agency for Interfaith Relations in Scotland is running a conference at Scottish Churches House, Dunblane on September 10–12. The Edinburgh Interfaith Association has a major event on October 1–2 at which the keynote speaker is Professor John Hick. The Glasgow Sharing of Faiths Group is organizing a seminar on religion and healing in October at the newly opened St. Mungo Museum of Religious Life and Art. The Museum itself promises to be a most useful venue and resource center for reflection on the meaning of the world's

Continued on next page

great religions and the history of local religious groups in Glasgow.

The Scottish Episcopal Church Committee for Relations with People of Other Faiths, among other initiatives, has promoted the WCF Study Pack "Interfaith Cooperation: Achievements and Possibilities," on an ecumenical basis. A well-publicized "Hearing" organized by the Brahma Kumaris Centre in Aberdeen on May 5th attracted an audience of some 70 people and set up an on-going group to promote on-going interfaith activities in the local area. Interest has been shown in places as far afield as Brora in Sutherland and at Staffa in Skye, where Quiraing Lodge is running a special series of meditation sessions. The Week of Prayer for World Peace (October 10–17) and One World Week (October 17–24) should generate further support.

Professor Drummond's paper on Christianity and Evolution is still relevant and has a number of phrases which indicate areas for future exploration. He stated:

"No truth can remain unaffected by Evolution . . . the Student of God's ways . . . looks at science with awe—what it contains for Christianity, or against it, he knows not. What it will do, or undo—for in the fulfilling it may undo—he cannot tell. . . . The whole field of theology is already alive . . . the opportunity now offered to theological science for a reconstruction or illumination of many of its most important doctrines has never been surpassed in hopefulness or interest."

My own view is that this applies not only to Christianity. All faiths must be open to the possibility of reconstruction and new illumination if fruitful progress in cooperation and understanding is to take place. ✿

1. Rivalry or cooperation?

*T*he hope of the interfaith movement is that religious **differences can be enriching and that each religious tradition will make its distinctive contribution to the welfare of humankind. Sadly, religious differences have often been a cause of conflict.**

In some societies, one religious tradition has been dominant and upheld by the ruling authorities. Sometimes, the practices of other religious communities were forbidden. Those who engaged in them risked punishment and even death. Elsewhere, other religions were allowed, but their followers were treated as "second class citizens," with various civil disabilities.

Sometimes, members of different religious communities have been rivals. When allied with opposing political powers, there has been active hostility and warfare—"religious wars." Elsewhere, the rivalry has been competition for adherents.

At times, the rivalry and hostility has been more hidden, where religious differences have reinforced racial, national, ethnic or class differences. Religious teaching has been exploited to foster prejudice, discrimination and communalism. Sometimes it has belittled those of another faith.

Elsewhere, people of different religious traditions may occupy the same geographical space, but with very little human meeting. There may be some commercial dealings, but each faith has its own schools and welfare institutions. People only marry within their own community. Each community may speak a different language.

In some societies, often described as "pluralist," there are several religious groupings and none has a preferential position. If the government is religiously neutral, it may be described as "secular." Other governments are clearly opposed to all religious practices.

This century has seen large scale migrations of people. Vastly improved means of communication and international travel have become available for some people. Many members of a religious tradition are now more aware of the existence of other religious traditions. There is more personal meeting.

Members of the interfaith movement believe that this encounter has creative possibilities. Indeed, peace between religious communities is essential, if there is to be peace in the world.

FOR REFLECTION AND GROUP DISCUSSION

Q. How would you characterize the religious situation of your society: (Good, Tolerable or Bad)

a. locally?

b. nationally?

Q. What is it that makes religious communities competitive?

Q. What is it that best produces cooperation? For what reason?

The Year of Interreligious Understanding and Cooperation in the United Kingdom

On January 27 the Launch event for the 1993 Year of Interreligious Understanding and Cooperation "happened" at Global Co-operation House in London, hosted by the Brahma Kumaris and planned by a multifaith committee chaired by Lord Ennals. Over 800 people attended the morning and evening sessions, with over 500 participating in the afternoon workshops on universal themes such as justice, peace and love.

A ceremony, bringing waters from the holy places of nine faith traditions to a central fountain where they later flowed together, unfolded throughout the morning, which was also punctuated by guest speakers, including Edgar Mitchell, the astronaut. Everyone present felt uplifted by the spiritual atmosphere. A multifaith concert enchanted in the evening with contributions from professional performers and local schoolchildren, highlighted for many by the interiorized and charismatic spiritual sword dance of a six year old Sikh boy.

This day was just the beginning of a

2. Chicago, 1893

Nearly 100 years ago, a Parliament of the World's Religions was held at Chicago. This is now seen to be the beginning of the interfaith movement.

Isolated figures such as the Buddhist Emperor Asoka or the Mogul Emperor Akbar or the mediaeval Cardinal Nicholas of Cusa had advocated religious tolerance. There had also been some earlier interreligious debates and disputations. The World's Parliament was new in attempting to bring together in a conference leaders of the world's religious traditions.

Held in Chicago in connection with its World Fair, the majority of the participants were Protestants from North America, although American Roman Catholics and Jews played a significant role both in the preparations and the parliament itself.

Twelve Buddhists came from Asia, including Anagarika Dharmapala from Sri Lanka, who founded the Maha Bodhi Society and Shaku Soyen from Japan, who was to introduce Dr. D. T. Suzuki to the West. There were several Hindus, including B. B. Nagarkar and P. C. Mozoomdar of the Brahmo Samaj and Swami Vivekananda, a follower of Sri Ramakrishna. Swami Vivekananda was one of the most colorful figures of the Parliament and his plea for universal tolerance won much sympathy. The only Muslim representative was an American convert. There do not appear to have been any Sikhs present. The Parliament was the first occasion when a reference to Bahá'í religious teaching was made at a public meeting in the West.

Lectures were given both on the teachings of the different religious traditions and on social problems of the day. There was much discussion about the relationship of different traditions to each other. Some claimed that their religion would ultimately become the one religion of the world—perhaps by adapting and incorporating aspects of other religions. Others hoped that a new more universal religion would emerge from the coming together of the world religious traditions. Others expected that the great religions would retain their distinct identity, although they hoped that the relations between them would reflect friendliness and charity.

Despite different views about the relationship of religions, most participants hoped that religious communities could work together to promote the peace of the world. In his opening address, Charles Bonney, who was the President of the Parliament, voiced this longing: "When the religious faiths of the world recognize each other as brothers, children of one Father whom all profess to love and serve, then, and not till then, will the nations of the earth yield to the spirit of concord and learn war no more."

The three key organizers of the Parliament each had a different purpose for it. This suggests that even if people have different philosophical presuppositions they can still work together for interreligious cooperation and understanding.

Charles Bonney hoped the Parliament would "unite all Religion against all irreligion"; and that it would "make the Golden Rule the basis of this union; (and) present to the world . . . the substantial unity of many religions in the good deeds of the religious life."

John Henry Barrows, a Presbyterian minister, whose hard work and charm as Chairman did much to ensure the success of the Parliament, believed that Christianity, by drawing on the insights of other great religious traditions, could grow into the universal faith.

Jenkin Lloyd Jones, a Unitarian minister, who was the Secretary, looked forward to a universal faith dedicated to the inquiring spirit of progress: "Let us build a temple of universal religion dedicated to the inquiring spirit of progress, to the helpful service of love."

There are groups today who hope for a future universal religion or believe that all religions are essentially the same. Some of their members share in interfaith work, but all interfaith organizations affirm and value the distinctiveness of the world religions.

FOR REFLECTION AND GROUP DISCUSSION

Q. Which of the three purposes, declared by the three organizers, would come nearest to your own?

Q. What did you hope might come out of interfaith meetings, when you first took part?

Q. Have your hopes changed during your participation in interfaith activities? What do you now hope for?

Q. Does it matter if people in the same organization have rather different motivations?

Q. Might the "Golden Rule" have a potentially significant role as a basis for cooperation?

UK year permeated with peace pilgrimages, interfaith tree planting, the opening of the St. Mungo Museum of Religious Life and Art, an Interfaith Address from the Dalai Lama, conferences, study days, national and local festivals and commemorations, many involving Marcus Braybrooke, whose energy and spirit best reflect the sacred opportunity of this Centenary Year. A Jewish/Interfaith service of thanksgiving will officially complete the celebrations and also inaugurate the next hundred years of interfaith activity.

May all the sharing and goodwill of this special year surge forward into a new and sustained era of cooperation and understanding, transforming everyone, so that the gatherings in 2093 will welcome a truly global family of faith, touching the Real and each other in every part of the world.

SANDY MARTIN,
of the Executive Committee of
The World Congress of Faiths and the Launch
coordinating committees

3. What unites us?

Despite the difference of belief and practice between and within the great religious traditions, a growing number of people seek a bond between religious believers.

There are now many local and national interfaith gatherings. Four organizations, particularly, try to link this global activity. Three of them are described below and the fourth, **The World Conference on Religion and Peace,** is described in the next section.

The oldest interfaith organization is **The International Association for Religious Freedom** (IARF), which was founded in 1900 by some of those who attended the World's Parliament of Religions. Initially most of its members were religious liberals, drawn from Unitarian churches in Britain, Hungary and North America free Christian churches in Western Europe, the Brahmo Samaj in India and the Japan Free Religious Association. As membership has increased, the spectrum of religious groups and nationalities taking part has grown enormously. The IARF now has more than 58 member groups in 22 countries.

There are many differences among members of the International Association for Religious Freedom, but all are united by a commitment to religious freedom and truthful living. IARF Congresses are held every three years and include personal sharing, worship services in the tradition of each member group, and programs on religious, ethical, political and theological issues. The IARF supports social service projects through its member groups in Eastern Europe, India, Bangladesh, the Philippines and Africa. It has representatives at the United Nations, in both New York and Geneva, and IARF members support religious freedom by writing to government officials on behalf of oppressed communities of faith.

The **World Congress of Faiths** (WCF) was founded in 1936 by Sir Francis Younghusband. In 1903, in Lhasa, Tibet, he had a decisive spiritual experience of an underlying unity of all beings. His hope was that, through WCF, members of all religious traditions would become aware of this universal experience and that "the roots of fellowship would strike down deep to the Central Source of all spiritual loveliness." The WCF, which is based in Britain, has arranged a wide variety of conferences,

International Association for Religious Freedom

The International Association for Religious Freedom is the oldest global interreligious organization and the only one with corporate memberships by constituent religious communities. For more than 90 years the IARF has worked for multicultural understanding, justice and peace, and religious freedom.

Religious communities from Europe, America, Asia and Africa contribute to the spiritual breadth of the IARF. We include liberal Christians and Unitarians, Buddhist, Shinto, Hindu, Muslim and Sikh groups, as well as tribal communities and individual members of the Jewish and Roman Catholic traditions. We are united by a commitment to religious liberty and to liberating religious practice.

Our roots are deep and diverse. The Unitarian churches in Romania date back to the 16th century Protestant reformation. The Tsubaki Grand Shrine in Japan is served by the 96th generation of its priests. The largest IARF member group, the lay Buddhist movement Rissho Kosei-kai, was founded only a generation ago but grounds its teachings in the ancient *Lotus Sutra*. Leaders of the Bramo Samaj in the 19th century laid the foundation for modern India.

The IARF brings together people from different cultures and countries, from national denominations and local congregations, from village communities and metropolitan churches, from academic institutions and religious communities. Its individual members are young and old, female and male. Its member groups come from east and west, from north and south.

IARF

- is interreligious, intercultural and interracial in composition and vision
- is recognized as a Non-Governmental Organization and accredited in category II at the United Nations in New York and Geneva, at UNESCO in Paris, and at UNICEF
- works with religious communities and secular organizations which are committed to openness and free religious inquiry, human dignity and mutual acceptance, social responsibility and service
- is guided by the Spirit of truth, which transcends time and place, and yet is revealed in and through the spiritual and moral traditions of the world.

IARF just recently moved its international offices from Germany to the new Interfaith Centre in Oxford, England:
IARF, 3 Carlton Road, Oxford OX2 7RZ UK
or, in the US, write to:
IARF, 777 United Nations Plaza, New York, NY 10017

Religious Freedom

Dr. Robert Traer

General Secretary, IARF

"*W*hat do you mean by religious freedom?" I am frequently asked this question, when I speak about the IARF. My answer is that in the IARF we mean three things.

First, by religious freedom we mean the freedom to practice our faith in peace. This is the freedom which is protected by international law and in many instances by the laws of our nations. Without this legal protection, minorities may be oppressed by the majority population or by their government.

Therefore, the IARF supports the fundamental human right of religious freedom and works to secure this right for all people. This requires that governments use their police power, if necessary, to protect the rights of all their religious communities to worship and support their traditions. This is the legal meaning of religious freedom.

Second, by religious freedom we mean freedom within religious communities. The IARF does not embrace all beliefs or practices which are described as "religious," but only those which respect helping people to learn about other faiths and to rethink traditional attitudes of opposition and hostility. It has encouraged members to appreciate one another's spiritual practices and on occasion to pray together. Rather than build up its own international organization, WCF has developed links with like-minded groups across the world and stimulated the growth of an interfaith movement, which is larger than any organization. Its journal, *World Faith Encounter*, has facilitated the growth of the interfaith movement.

The Temple of Understanding (ToU), now based in New York, was founded in 1960 by Judith Hollister. The hope, as yet unfulfilled, has been to build a "temple" that would symbolize the shared spiritual quest of all religious traditions. Meanwhile the organization has fostered the spirit of understanding. The ToU has held a series of Summit Conferences in different parts of the world and has had an international influence through contacts with delegates to the United Nations. It helped to give birth to the Global Forum on Human Survival which brings together religious leaders, politicians and scientists to try to save life on this planet. Thomas Merton, at the First

Spiritual Summit Conference, said, "We are already one, but we imagine that we are not. What we have to recover is our original unity." The Temple has affirmed "The Oneness of the Human Family, irrespective of color, sex, creed, nation or any other distinctive characteristic and also the harmonious place of the individual person in the total order of things, as a unique entity of Divine Origin, with a basic relationship to the Universe and Eternity."

The four International Interfaith Organizations all reject "syncretism," which implies an artificial mixing of religious beliefs and practices; they also reject "indifferentism," which suggests that it does not matter what you believe. None of these four organizations are trying to create one new world religion, although some other groups have that hope.

The interfaith organizations assume that most of their members will be loyal and committed members of their own faith communities. Respect for the integrity of other people's faith commitment and religious practices is essential. A few members of interfaith organizations may have no specific allegiance and describe themselves as "seekers."

Continued on 2nd following page

the fundamental human rights of persons. That is, we see religious freedom as one of the social conditions necessary for human dignity, a right which cannot be separated from other fundamental human rights. Therefore, the IARF urges religious communities to respect the freedom of their members, even as they expect other communities to respect their freedom.

Of course, this does not mean that the IARF is opposed to membership requirements or to religious discipline voluntarily undertaken by members of religious communities, nor does it mean that the IARF expects all religious communities to be egalitarian in their decision-making. It does mean, however, that religious communities are not free to ignore the fundamental human rights of their members, even when these members are voluntary participants. Beliefs which denigrate other human beings, because of their race or sex or culture or religious convictions, should not go unchallenged, and practices based on these beliefs may need to be prohibited by law. This is the ethical meaning of religious freedom.

Third, by religious freedom we mean the search together for truth. To affirm

religious freedom is to admit that we are often wrong, that we learn from one another, that we are challenged by different beliefs and practices to reflect on our own and sometimes to change them. To affirm religious freedom is not to defend our present understanding as the truth, but to confess that we come closer to the truth by opening ourselves to the experience and understanding of others.

This is why the IARF supports interfaith programs promoting understanding and cooperation. By talking and sharing in prayer and meditation with people of other faith traditions, we broaden our experience of religious life. We open ourselves to learn more about other traditions but also about ourselves, for there is much to learn by noticing how we react to the religious faith of others. This is the spiritual meaning of religious freedom.

These three aspects of religious freedom—the legal, the ethical and the spiritual—are all essential to the work of IARF. To work only for the legal protection of religious freedom would mean to ignore injustice within religious communities and to fail to admit that the truth often eludes us, even as we struggle

to do what is right. To be concerned only with freedom within religious communities, without being concerned about the rights of other communities and without admitting our own tendency to error, would be self-righteous and would cut us off from the truth that we seek to realize. To pursue the truth, without standing up for the right of others to pursue the truth in their own ways, as religious communities and individually within those communities, would be to reduce freedom to privileged piety.

Therefore, in the IARF we affirm religious freedom as a legal, ethical and spiritual quest. None of us, either individually or in our religious communities, can rightfully claim that we are the model for all others to follow. We all have much to learn, and we all fall short of our highest aspirations.

Thus, in humility, we come together—to share what we know and to learn from one another, to challenge others and to be challenged in turn, always seeking to realize more fully the vision of truth and justice in our faith, which (to our wonder) we may discover as well in the faith of others.

IARF *World* 1/93

World Congress of Faiths

WCF aims to bring people of different faith-commitments together in mutual respect and trust in order to promote better understanding between religious communities and to further dialogue between people of different convictions about religious truth and practice. It arranges conferences and is cooperating with other interfaith organizations in preparing for the Sarva-Dharma-Sammelana interfaith conference in Bangalore, August 1993. WCF is also the coordinator for the British celebrations of 1993 as a Year of Interreligious Understanding.

Among WCF's publications is *Interfaith Cooperation: Achievements and Possibilities—a Study Guide for 1993*, written by Marcus Braybrooke. A Study Pack which includes the Study Guide and leaders' notes is also available.

WCF also publishes the journal *World Faiths Encounter* three times per year as a major resource for dealing with the new questions of living in a multi-faith society. *World Faiths Encounter* covers the fascinating issues which arise from the meeting between faith-communities and faith traditions in the contemporary world. It is suitable for students of interfaith studies, local interfaith groups, educationalists, community relations workers and local practitioners in the everyday dialogue of faith. Edited by Alan Race (UK) and Professor Seshagiri Rao (USA), it is available internationally.

"By our front door we have the words of Gandhi's talisman:

'Recall the face of the poorest and weakest man whom you may have seen and ask yourself if the step you contemplate is going to be any use to him.'

Perhaps the real test of interfaith dialogue will be whether it can unite the religions in service of the needy."

from a reflection by Mary Braybrooke
in *World Faiths Encounter*,
July 1992, p.62

For more information about membership or subscriptions, contact:
World Congress of Faiths
28 Powis Gardens,
London W11 1JG, UK

Declaration on the Oneness of the Human Family

Adopted by the Temple of Understanding
at the Spiritual Summit Conference VI, in 1984;
drafted by Dr. Robert Muller, then Assistant Secretary General
of the United Nations.

A convergence of world religions towards a "Global Spirituality" might suggest the following points in common:

1. The Oneness of the Human Family, irrespective of color, sex, creed, nation or any other distinctive characteristics.

2. The harmonious place of the individual person in the total order of things, as a unique entity of Divine Origin, with a basic relationship to the Universe and Eternity.

3. The Importance of spiritual exercises, meditation, prayer, contemplation, and the inner search as links between human life and the universe.

4. The Existence of an incipient conscience at the heart of humanity which speaks for what is good and against what is bad for the human family; which advocates and fosters understanding, cooperation and altruism instead of division, struggle and indifference among nations.

5. The value of Dedicated Service to others, with a compassionate response to human suffering, with special attention to the oppressed and the poor, the handicapped and the elderly, the rejected and the lonely.

6. The Duty to give thanks and express gratitude for the abundance of life which has been given to humanity, an abundance not to be selfishly possessed or accumulated, but to be shared and given generously to those who are in need, with a respect for human dignity and a sense of social justice.

7. The need for ecumenical agencies and world religious organizations to foster dialogue and collaborative arrangements, and to bring the resources and inspirations of the religions to bear upon the solution of world problems.

8. A rejection of violence as being contrary to the sanctity and uniqueness of life and a total acceptance of the precept— "Thou shalt not kill."

9. An affiliation of the Law of Love and Compassion as the great transcending force which alone can break the nemesis of war and establish a Planet of Peace.

10. The evolutionary task of human life and society to move through the eternal stream of time towards interdependence, communion and an ever expanding realization of Divinity.

Temple of Understanding
Cathedral of St. John the Divine
1047 Amsterdam Ave. at 112th St.
New York, NY 10025 USA

Aware of the distinctiveness of the world religious traditions, members of interfaith organizations yet hope that some basis of unity exists or may be discovered. For some people, this rests upon our common humanity; for others, there is a mystical unity; still others hope that through dialogue people of different religious traditions will come closer together and grow in their understanding of the divine mystery; some stress the need of religious people to work together for peace and justice and the relief of human suffering; for others, it is enough that there should be tolerance and respect, without bothering about questions of "truth."

All these shades of opinion and many more are reflected within the interfaith organizations. For them, the search for understanding and cooperation is urgent in itself.

FOR REFLECTION AND GROUP DISCUSSION

Q. How do religious practices and beliefs agree and differ?

Q. How do you assess the ways religious people come together? What are your experiences and evaluations?

a. Socially—to meet as friends

b. To work together for good community relations and peace

c. In a shared project of social service

d. To try to understand each other's beliefs and practices

e. To seek agreement on religious belief

f. To learn about each other's ways of prayer and meditation

g. To pray together

h. To meditate together

Q. Do you belong to any of the interfaith organizations mentioned above or to other interfaith groups?

4. *The religious search for peace*

Whilst all efforts for interfaith understanding promote a climate of peace, some interfaith organizations, especially The World Conference on Religion and Peace (WCRP), have concentrated on encouraging religious people to be active in peace work.

Attempts to bring together people of different religious traditions to promote peace date back to the early part of this century. The first Assembly of the World Conference on Religion and Peace, however, did not meet until 1970. Members were aware that often religious communities had aggravated conflict. Yet it was seen to be important that leaders of the world's religious communities should affirm together their concern for peace and human dignity and that religious people should be more aware of the major issues facing humankind,

especially as they are reflected in the concerns of the United Nations. The World Conference on Religion and Peace now has chapters in many countries and there are regional as well as international gatherings. Assemblies have been held in Asia, Europe, North America, Africa and Australia. There is a carefully thought out structure to ensure a proper balance between different religious communities and nations.

There are also peace-groups within many religious communities and denominations. Increasingly these are working together and building up interfaith contacts.

It is difficult to assess the impact that religious people can have on political processes, especially as politicians seldom acknowledge those who have influenced them. Modern communications have given added weight to popular opinion. Religious leaders may play an important role in forming public opinion. They can insist on the relevance of spiritual and moral considerations. They have helped to maintain public alarm at the enormous stockpile of nuclear weapons and other means of mass destruction. They have voiced public outrage at the starvation of millions of people, as a result of hunger, war, injustice and an unfair pattern of international trade. They have upheld human dignity and protested against torture and racism. They have supported efforts to develop internationally agreed standards of human rights and have helped to monitor their application. Interreligious conferences have been among the first to warn of threats to the environment.

In local areas of conflict, religious people have often maintained contact across boundaries and despite divisions. Sometimes they have been agents of reconciliation and conflict-resolution. They have taken a lead in relief work. Sometimes, they have encouraged acts of repentance in an effort to heal deeply rooted bitterness. Yet often, too, religious people have used religious loyalties to inflame conflict and have allowed particular interests to outweigh common human and religious moral values. Some extremists stir up religious passions to gain support for their concerns.

FOR REFLECTION AND GROUP DISCUSSION

Q. Can you think of areas of conflict in your society where religious people have or are helping to solve them? List these and then share them with others.

Q. Internationally, consider areas where religious loyalties inflame conflict. Where is religious faith a power for peace?

Q. Should religious communities get involved in comment on the following issues: Human Rights? Armaments? Torture? Poverty? Environment?

Q. Is there anything that all religious people can say together on these subjects?

Q. How should we respond to those in our own religious tradition who seem to us to espouse extremism and fanaticism?

WCRP speaks on:

PEACE AND DEVELOPMENT

"Delegates from Asia, Africa and Latin America have given us all a new perspective on the arms race, as seen through the eyes of the poor. For the poor, survival is not primarily a question of the future in a nuclear world, but an urgent question of the present in a world beset with hunger, drought and disease. Our common commitment to peace is based upon the clear interrelatedness between disarmament and development."

WCRP Nairobi Declaration, 1984

CONFLICT RESOLUTION

"Whatever conscientious religious people decide in respect to the use of violence, we urge religious leaders everywhere to work ceaselessly, in the first instance, for the reduction of the level of violence in all social struggles with the final elimination of violence in favor of peaceful solutions as their firm objective. To respond to violence with violence without first seeking to eliminate its cause is to embark upon the course of unending escalation."

WCRP Leuven Declaration, 1974

DISARMAMENT

"We express our profound concern over the massive increase in military spending, which has rocketed. It seems a cruel irony that, while millions sleep with hungry stomachs, nations and their governments devote a great part of their resources to armaments, ignoring the demands of social justice. We therefore appeal to the members and leaders of our respective communities to use every political and moral influence to urge a substantial reduction in the current military

Continued on next page

The World Conference on Religion and Peace

Introduction

The World Conference on Religion and Peace (WCRP) is an international multireligious organization dedicated to reaffirming religions' moral commitments to peace and to translating their shared concerns into practical, effective action.

WCRP is based upon respect for religious differences as well as the conviction that religious persons and groups can cooperate with great value on shared commitments for peace with justice.

On local, national, regional and global levels, WCRP convenes meetings and assemblies to promote dialogue on the peace-promoting teachings of religions. This dialogue, in turn, provides a basis for commitments to common actions in eight program areas: (1) Children and Youth; (2) Conflict Resolution; (3) Disarmament; (4) Economic and Social Development; (5) Environmental Protection; (6) Human Rights; (7) Peace Education; and (8) Refugees and Displaced Persons.

The significance of multireligious cooperation for peacemaking

What roles do the world's religions have in offering guidance and helping to ameliorate strife in the modern world? Skeptics would point out that historically, and currently, religious differences often have been a component cause of conflict and warfare. While acknowledging this fact, the members of WCRP believe the world's religions can be highly constructive forces in promoting peace.

The world's religious communities possess both moral and social characteristics which equip them in unique ways to cooperate and participate in efforts designed to promote peace.

First, religions found ethical visions. They provide their adherents with forms of ethical discourse about the ultimate meaning and value of reality. These ethical visions can summon those who believe in them into powerful forms of committed action.

Second, religions possess remarkable social characteristics. Religions exist everywhere in the world; they reach into every village and town; and they are often organized at national and international levels. Taken together, the world's religious groups make up a vast network with unique capacities for communication and mobilization.

Both the moral and social characteristics of religious communities provide them with exceptional possibilities to function as powerful "agents for change" in the pursuit of peace.

Today, however, the constructive roles of individual religions for peacemaking can be strengthened greatly by cooperation among religions. Multireligious efforts can be both substantively and symbolically more powerful than the efforts of a single religious group. Moreover, cooperation among religious groups can serve to promote religious tolerance in circumstances where religious people, tragically and all too often, contribute to conflicts. These realizations led to the formation of WCRP and continue to guide its development.

As a forum for the world's religious leaders and believers, WCRP provides a potent base for a variety of peace initiatives which can address the needs and concerns of individuals, groups, governing bodies and international organizations.

Origins

The organization was formed in 1970 as a consolidation of separate movements in Japan, the United States and India. Interest in Japan began with a National Religious Conference for International Peace, convened in 1931. Following World War II and the nuclear bombing of Hiroshima and Nagasaki, cooperation grew among senior Japanese religious leaders on peace issues.

In the United States, senior religious leaders began gathering around the issues of cooperation for peace with justice in 1962. A National Inter-Religious Conference on Peace was convened in Washington, DC in 1966. A delegation of US religious leaders in 1967 undertook an exploratory mission to ascertain interest by religious groups abroad in forming a multireligious world conference on peace. They visited Geneva, Rome, Istanbul, Jerusalem, New Delhi, Saigon and Kyoto.

In 1968, religious leaders from India

formed a joint U.S./Indian committee to sponsor a symposium on peace coincident with the centenary of Mahatma Gandhi's birth. Indian political leaders also participated in the event.

The Japanese, United States and Indian interests converged at a meeting in Istanbul during 1969 where the decision was made to convene an international gathering of religious leaders at Kyoto in 1970: the First Assembly of the World Conference on Religion and Peace. World Assemblies have since been held in Louvain, Belgium (1974); Princeton, USA (1979); Nairobi, Kenya (1984); and Melbourne, Australia (1989). Another is planned for Riva del Garda, Italy, in 1994.

Organization and development

WCRP has its international headquarters at the United Nations Plaza in New York City. Additional international offices are maintained in Geneva, Melbourne and Tokyo. WCRP is recognized as a Non-Governmental Organization (NGO) having consultative status with the Economic and Social Council of the United Nations. That role enables WCRP to function as a multireligious resource and advisor for various commissions and conferences of the United Nations.

WCRP members have formed three regional conferences in Asia, Africa and Europe, and 26 national chapters in the following countries: Australia, Austria, Bangladesh, Belgium, Canada, Croatia, France, Germany, India, Indonesia, Italy, Japan, Kenya, Democratic People's Republic of Korea, Republic of Korea, Nepal, Netherlands, New Zealand, Pakistan, Philippines, Singapore, South Africa, Sri Lanka, Thailand, the United Kingdom/Ireland and the United States of America.

Leaders and other believers of the following religions regularly participate as members in WCRP: Bahá'ísm, Buddhism; Christianity; Confucianism; Hinduism; Islam; Jainism; Judaism; Shintoism; Sikhism; Taoism; Traditionalism of the indigenous cultures of Africa, the Americas, Asia, Australia and Oceania; and Zoroastrianism.

The growing WCRP network fosters activities relevant to global, regional, national and local concerns, by providing a channel for disseminating constituents' concerns throughout the world and generating support for them.

WCRP welcomes both religious organizations and individuals for membership. Contact the WCRP chapter in your country, or

WCRP/International
777 United Nations Plaza
New York, NY 10017, USA
TEL (212) 687-2163 / FAX (212) 983-0566

Excerpted and adapted from
WCRP materials by the Editor

Asian Conference on Religion and Peace

The Peace Education Center and WCRP/Japan Committee will commemorate the Year of Interreligious Understanding and Cooperation with a lecture by Marcus Braybrooke, the translation of his book *Pilgrimage of Hope,* and several seminars regarding interreligious cooperation within and without Korea. Since only a few Koreans are able to participate in the centennial events at Bangalore and Chicago, we planned these events to boost interest in interreligious dialogue throughout Korea and Japan.

In Korea, especially in South Korea, Buddhism and Christianity, along with several indigenous religions, are very prosperous, but they are often in a rivalry relationship rather than a friendly one. The Korean Conference on Religion and Peace is the most active interfaith organization in Korea, and they, in cooperation with our Center, have begun a major interfaith project during this summer in regard to environmental issues, including the joint "Declaration of Environmental Ethics" by six major religions in Korea.

SUNGGON KIM, Peace Education
Center, Seoul, Korea (founded in 1986 by the
Asian Conference on Religion and Peace)

WCRP SPEAKS, continued

expenditures of their own nations and the utilization of the funds thus saved for development around the world."
WCRP Princeton Declaration, 1979

ENVIRONMENT AND ECONOMICS

"Economic systems must be measured by ethical criteria, by how justly they provide for the well-being of all members of society, and by how they respect and use the environmental base that sustains all life."
WCRP Melbourne Declaration, 1989

HUMAN RIGHTS

"Peace is imperiled by. . . the tragic violation of human rights all over the world. . . . Religions in their historical manifestations have not always been respectful of human

rights themselves and have on some occasions purported to justify violations of human rights on religious grounds."
WCRP Kyoto Declaration, 1970

PEACE EDUCATION

"We pledge ourselves to stressing and raising to public consciousness the foundations of peace-making within our own religious traditions, through education in temples, churches, mosques, synagogues and homes. . . . As religious people of action, we must deliberately link our personal lives and daily choices to our wider work as peacemakers."
WCRP Nairobi Declaration, 1984

CHILDREN AND YOUTH

- WCRP convened the three-day international conference "The World's Religions for the World's Children" at Princeton University in July 1990.
  (See Part 4 for details.)

FOR REFLECTION AND GROUP DISCUSSION

Q. Have you participated in any —official— interreligious discussions before these?

Q. Do you know of other dialogues that have taken place?

Q. In what ways are interreligious discussions likely to be different than meetings arranged by interfaith bodies?

Q. Do you know of study and conference centers in your area?

Q. What have you learned through dialogue with someone of a different religious background from your own?

5. Religious communities in dialogue

*O*ften those who have pioneered the search for good relations between religious communities have faced misunderstanding and even hostility in their own faith community. They have been accused of compromising or "watering down" the distinctive beliefs of their own religious traditions. In fact, however, many have found that learning about other religious traditions has helped them appreciate their own more deeply.

Slowly the benefits of interfaith dialogue have become more widely recognized. Many religious and denominational bodies now have agencies to encourage such dialogue. There are some official discussions between religious organizations. For example, the Jewish world, through The International Jewish Committee on Interreligious Consultations (IJCIC), has held formal discussions with the Roman Catholic and with other churches. The Vatican has a Pontifical Council for Interreligious Dialogue and the World Council of Churches has a Unit for Dialogue with People of Living Faiths, which has arranged various consultations. Muslim groups, including the Islamic Conference of Jeddah and the World Muslim Congress, have engaged in dialogue. Buddhist organizations also take part: the Dalai Lama and several Japanese Buddhist groups; especially Rissho Kosei Kai founded by Rev. Nikkyo Niwano, have been active in encouraging interreligious understanding and in work for peace. Hindu movements have also sponsored interreligious gatherings. Many smaller groups have also taken initiatives. The Unification Church, through the Council for World Religions and other organizations, has arranged a number of interfaith consultations.

Clearly, official dialogue has a character of its own. Participants have some representative role. Much of the work is to remove misunderstanding and build up good relations, as well as encouraging practical cooperation on moral issues and social concerns. More speculative discussion about questions of "truth" may be inappropriate. Further, whilst most organizations fully respect the freedom of all who participate in consultations, the host organization may have its own agenda. This means that official interreligious discussions need to be distinguished from "interfaith" organizations, where ultimate control rests with a board or executive which is itself multifaith in composition and where funding comes from several religious communities. The growth of interreligious discussions is, however, a sign that the importance of harmony between religious communities is now seen as urgent and this is in part due to the pioneering work of interfaith organizations.

As in the family, where at times two members want to talk by themselves, so there are occasions when members of just two religious traditions wish to engage in dialogue. A particular example of this is Jewish–Christian dialogue, and a major international organization, The International Council of Christians and Jews, was formed in 1975 to foster good relations between the two faith communities. There is also growing Christian–Muslim dialogue and some Muslim–Jewish dialogue. There is considerable Christian–Buddhist dialogue both in North America and in Japan. Christians and Hindus have engaged in debate and discussion for nearly two centuries and there is some Sikh–Christian dialogue. There are now many study and conference centers in different parts of the world which promote dialogue between members of two or three religious communities.

6. Education

*T*his century has seen an enormous increase in knowledge about world religious communities. Books, films and videos are widely available. Many universities have departments for the study of religion. The academic study has been fostered by The International Association for the History of Religion (IAHR). The Shap Working Party has helped to provide material for schools.

This study has helped to provide accurate information about the religious traditions of the world. Even so, much ignorance and prejudice still exists. It has been debated whether the study should actively encourage religious tolerance or whether it should be neutral. It is also debated whether a person who is not a member of a religion can teach about it accurately and sympathetically.

There have been many debates about the pattern of religious education for children and young people. Many believers are keen that their children should be nurtured in their faith. In some countries, at least some schools have a religious foundation, where there is both instruction in a particular religion or denomination and worship according to its traditions and rites. This helps young people to grow up in a community of faith. It may, however, emphasize communal and religious divisions in a society, although a deep reverence for one's own faith should encourage respect for the faith of others.

In other schools, attempts are made to help pupils learn about the teachings of all the main religious traditions. This may encourage understanding and tolerance, but may not help pupils to grow in their own faith. In some countries, this "nurture" in one's own faith is the responsibility of church, synagogue, mosque, temple or *gurdwara* and not the task of the school. In other countries, there is no religious instruction in

SARVA-DHARMA-SAMMELANA

Bangalore, August 18–22, 1993.

"Sharing Visions of Interfaith Cooperation in the Next Century."

The theme of the Bangalore celebration of the centenary of the World's Parliament of Religions also indicates the character of the gathering. It is a people's conference. Many distinguished leaders and scholars will be coming, but it is primarily a meeting of those actively engaged in some form of interfaith work, such as those who are organizing a local group, sharing in a service project or arranging prayers for peace. Each person who comes will have a significant interfaith experience. We hope that together participants will share their successes, failures and hopes for the future. From this will emerge a clearer picture of what those who long for interfaith cooperation and understanding may hope to achieve in the years ahead.

The emphasis is therefore on participation. There will be very few platform speeches. Program I will involve an intense program group discussion, in which participants will share their visions for the future and see how they can begin to transform the present reality to match these visions. Program II will involve visits to many centers of prayer and meditation, so that participants will learn more about each other's spiritual practices. Program III will divide into workshops to look at key areas of interfaith work, such as education, service, preserving the environment and conflict resolution. In preparation, there have been many local discussions of the themes.

The occasions when all participants will come together are for prayer and meditation. Both the opening and closing ceremonies will be "liturgical"—occasions of celebration and dedication. Each morning and evening all are invited to be present as each community in turn leads the prayers. This will emphasise that the interreligious movement is a response to the Spirit and that it will grow as we wait together upon divine guidance. In our planning also we have tried to be responsive to the Spirit. The planning committee, which has the rather grandiose name of the International Interfaith Organizations Coordinating Committee, is only an *ad hoc* liaison committee. It has met in different parts of the world and in each place meetings have been open to those who have been interested. This has meant that a large number of people have had a share in the planning. The work has been done on a tiny budget, often by volunteers working from their own homes. The conference has become possible because so many people have generously responded to invitations and offered to help. All the participants have themselves had to finance their journeys to Bangalore. This emphasises that it is a people's conference, made possible only by waiting on the Spirit's guidance.

Our hope is that it will also be practical. The greatest changes will come about from the individual resolutions of those who attend as they go home inspired to new creative work for interreligious understanding and cooperation. Suggestions and recommendations will be forwarded to religious communities and interfaith organizations. There will be contributions to the proposed Declaration of Religions for a Global Ethic. The hope too is that ways can be found to build on the willingness of so many people of different religions and in different countries to work together for interreligious understanding and cooperation. One suggestion is to establish an International Interfaith Centre at Oxford for interreligious education, information, personal meeting and spiritual exploration.

The growth of extremism and communalism in parts of India have created difficulties, but have made the conference more urgent and important. The tragic increase of extremism and of violence in the name of religion in several parts of the world make all efforts for interreligious understanding and cooperation vital. My hope is that the gatherings at Bangalore and Chicago and elsewhere will both strengthen the interfaith movement and send a message of hope across the world to recall people to those spiritual values on which a world society needs to be based.

MARCUS BRAYBROOKE

Call For An International Interfaith Centre in Oxford

A centre to support the interfaith movement has long been sought. One hundred years after the 1893 World's Parliament of Religions would be a fitting moment to begin to translate this vision into reality and to provide a continuing legacy for the energies stimulated by the celebration of 1993. Such a centre might contribute to the work of institutions engaged in the study and teaching of the world's faith traditions, the teaching of religious education, and training for the ministry. Thus it is proposed that this centre be created in cooperation with colleges in the Oxford area.

The educational program of the International Interfaith Centre would consist of consultation, research, teaching and the development of educational materials. The Centre would initiate consultations among religious leaders and scholars on issues of interfaith understanding, cooperation and religious freedom. It would use these opportunities and others to create written and audiovisual materials. It would house books and archive related material with one or more of the libraries in Oxford.

For several years four international interfaith organizations—the International Association for Religious Freedom, the World Congress of Faiths, the Temple of Understanding, and the World Conference on Religion and Peace—have been working together under the auspices of the *ad hoc* IIOCC. The Centre at Oxford would support continuing cooperation among the international interfaith organizations. The Centre should also be a place of hospitality, personal support, encouragement, advice, meditation and prayer.

In its first phase, the Centre would be housed in a leased facility in or near Oxford and would be supported primarily by contributed services from participating organizations and institutions. IARF has budgeted funds for the relocation of its Secretariat to Oxford and for some initial costs. The WCF will join the IARF in sharing a leased facility in Oxford in the fall of 1993.

This proposal is being circulated for comments and support. Those interested should contact either Dr. Robert Traer, 3 Carlton Road, Oxford OX2 7RZ (44-0865-512379) or Rev. Marcus Braybrooke, 2 Bassetts, Box, Corsham, Wiltshire SN14 9ER TEL (44-0225-742827).

schools, and in some places even religious teaching at home or by the faith community is forbidden. Sometimes, minority groups have difficulty in providing religious education for their members.

If members of several different religious communities attend the same school, sometimes all are given the same course on world religions and sometimes they are divided into groups for instruction in their own religious tradition. In some countries, schools provide acts of worship or "assemblies." The question then arises whether people of different faith traditions may pray together.

Knowledge may not of itself create sympathy. Opportunities for personal meeting and friendship are important to dispel prejudice and to encourage real understanding. Many interfaith groups attach much importance to providing opportunities for young people to meet. Often they discover that they face similar problems and that in every society many young people are questioning all religious traditions and teachings. They may also discover how much people of all faiths can do together to work for a better world.

FOR REFLECTION AND GROUP DISCUSSION

Q. What are the ways in which you have learned about other religious traditions?

Q. What form does religious education take in your society?

Q. Are there ways in which you think it could be improved, or do you think a different pattern would be better?

Q. Would you encourage children of different religious traditions to pray together?

Q. Do you think enough information about the world religious traditions is easily available?

Q. How do the media in your country represent the different religious communities in your society?

Q. Do you think that the media give a balanced and fair picture?

Q. Are there enough opportunities in the colleges and universities in your country to learn about the religious traditions of the world?

Q. Are there enough opportunities for young people of different religious traditions in your area to meet and get to know each other?

7. *Praying together*

*P*eople of different religious traditions coming together in prayer and meditation can be one way that understanding may emerge amidst the diversity of experience.

In October 1986, Pope John Paul II invited other religious leaders to join him at Assisi in Italy, the home town of St. Francis, to pray together for peace. Members of each religious community represented at the gathering offered prayers for peace, drawn from their own tradition, in the presence of those of other faiths. Similar occasions have been arranged at Mt. Hiei in Japan and at Mornington Beach in Australia.

Many similar local gatherings have been held, especially during **The Week of Prayer for World Peace.** Many people regularly pray the Universal Prayer for Peace:

Lead me from Death to Life
From Falsehood to Truth
Lead me from Despair to Hope
from Fear to Trust
Lead me from Hate to Love
from War to Peace
Let Peace fill our Heart,
our World, our Universe.

At the 1893 World's Parliament of Religions, each morning began with silence and prayer and the opening and closing sessions included some hymns. Subsequent international interreligious conferences have included times of prayer. The International Association for Religious Freedom invites participants in its programs to take part, to whatever extent they wish, in the worship conducted by its different religious member groups. Mahatma Gandhi at his ashram included hymns and readings from many traditions in the evening prayer-time. Various groups, such as the Brahmo Samaj, the Bahá'ís, the Unitarians and the Universalists, include readings from the scriptures of the world in their services. The World Congress of Faiths and Temple of Understanding have arranged, on special occasions, public gatherings for people of all faiths to pray together.

Such gatherings for prayer sharply focus the question of the relationship of religious traditions. How do we balance recognition of religious diversity with acknowledgment of some common bonds? Such joint gatherings are not intended to replace the regular prayer of any faith community, but are for special occasions which stress our shared humanity and recognition of a sacred dimension to life.

Many people have found one of the best ways of learning about another religious group is to be present at times of worship, prayer and meditation. Attempts have also been made to help members of one faith tradition begin to experience the spiritual practices and traditions of another religion. A pioneer of this approach, Swami Abhishiktananda, spoke of it as a "meeting in the cave of the heart." The Quaker, Douglas Steere, spoke of "mutual irradiation." Sufis, Universalist groups and some members of "New Age" movements and others who emphasize the mystical approach to religion have also encouraged opportunities for people of different faith traditions to meditate and pray together.

There are personal occasions too when people of different religious traditions wish to meet together in prayer. Two people of different religious traditions may marry and want a blessing from each tradition, even though most faith communities do not encourage intermarriage. At a funeral, mourners may belong to more than one religious community.

These are areas on which there is no agreement, but in a fast changing world, new situations arise about which we need to think together.

FOR REFLECTION AND GROUP DISCUSSION

Q. Have there been any occasions when you have prayed with people of other faith traditions?

Q. Were there difficulties?

Q. Was there also enrichment?

Q. What effect do you think prayer has?

Q. Have you attended places of worship belonging to religious groups other than your own?

Q. Do you think there are occasions when it is helpful for people of different religious traditions to come together to pray? If so, when?

Q. Do you know of marriages in which the partners belong to different religious traditions? Discuss the possibilities and any problems there may be.

The Contribution by Religions to the Culture of Peace

UNESCO SPONSORS INTER-RELIGIOUS GATHERING

The United Nations Educational, Scientific and Cultural Organization, in conjunction with the Government of Catalonia (Generalitat de Catalunya) and the Centre UNESCO de Catalunya, a private institute in Barcelona associated with UNESCO, held an important working consultation with spiritual leaders, representatives of peace movements, interfaith organizations and scholars, on the theme, "The Contribution of the Religions to the Culture of Peace." The thrust of this gathering, held from April 13–18, 1993, was primarily practical in its deliberations and proposals. The Bosnian war added a note of extreme urgency to the session, and all the delegates were united in their anguished concern and profound sense of helplessness over this terrible tragedy.

At the first session, held at the National Palace, Dr. Janusz Symonides, the director of UNESCO's Division for Human Rights and Peace, Dr. Felix Marti of Centre UNESCO de Catalunya, and H. E. Jordi Pujol, the President of Catalonia, addressed the gathering. Professor Raimundo Panikkar delivered the keynote entitled, "Religions and the Culture of Peace," while Dr. Seyed Abedin of the Institute of Muslim Minority Affairs (London), Archbishop Angelo Fernandes (Delhi), and Prof. Samdhong Rinpoche, director of the Central Institute for Higher Tibetan Studies (Sarnath, India), who is also the speaker of the Tibetan Assembly (Parliament) in-exile, made interventions on the point of how religions are a factor for peace. The causes of war and violence, and effective ways the religions can prevent or stop conflicts were discussed by Sister Mariani Dimaranan, a human rights activist from the Philippines, Dr. John Taylor, formerly executive director of the World Conference on Religion and Peace,

Takeo Uchida of the UN University (Japan), and Archbishop Lutfi Laham of Jerusalem, as well as Rabbi Ehud Bandel of the same city.

Ven. Maga Ghosananda, a Cambodian monk, Dr. Daniel Gomez-Ibanez, Ivanka Jakik, Father Maximilian Mizzi from Assisi, Baidyanath Saraswati of the Indira Gandhi National Centre for the Arts (Delhi) pursued the elaboration of new initiatives for increasing the participation of the religions in the work of constructing the culture of peace. Dr. Daniel Gómez-Ibáñez, Executive Director of the Council for a Parliament of the World's Religions, spoke about the role of the Parliament in this effort, and Brother Wayne Teasdale, of Monastic Interreligious Dialogue, gave a presentation on the hope for a new civilization. Some very useful proposals will become part of future efforts by UNESCO and other international organizations.

BROTHER WAYNE TEASDALE

Plataforma Intercultural Barcelona

During this Year of Interreligious Understanding and Cooperation, our program includes the following:

- Participation of the Plataforma Intercultural Barcelona '92 in the Seminar on "The Contribution by Religions to the Culture of Peace," organized by UNESCO in Barcelona (Catalona), April 14–17, 1993. The Plataforma presided at the closing ceremony of the Seminar at a reception offered to representatives of different religions which coexist in Barcelona.

- Dr. Hector Vall, a member of our Plataforma, planned to present a paper at the European Meeting of the World Conference on Religion and Peace.

- The Plataforma organized a Round Table on "Religions in the culture of peace," a discussion by members of Plataforma, who represent different religions, of some of the ideas considered during the UNESCO Seminar.

- The Plataforma plans to participate in the Sarva-Dharma-Sammelana Conference in Bangalore with a paper on Ramon Llull presented by Mr. Miguel Ruiz.

- Closing our series of activities on the occasion of the year 1993 will be a ceremony commemorating the figure of Ramon Llull.

FOR REFLECTION AND GROUP DISCUSSION

Q. Do you have any plans to observe 1993 in your area or group?

Q. How do you think interfaith organizations can be more effective?

Q. What do you think should be the priorities for interfaith work in the next century?

Q. What is your vision for the world in the next century?

The International Interfaith Organizations Coordinating Committee for 1993 would much appreciate hearing from those who use this *Study Guide*. Please tell us of your experiences and your hopes. Your answers and comments should be sent to:

IIOCC
Rawmere, Raw Lane, Chichester,
West Sussex PO19 4QH. UK

8. 1993 and beyond

A century after the first World's Parliament of Religions, it is hoped that 1993 will be a year of growing awareness of our shared global humanity. In recent years there has been a rapid and widespread growth of interfaith dialogue, although there has also been renewed religious extremism and fanaticism. Many different interfaith initiatives have been taken across the world. Attempts have been made to link them, especially by the four international interfaith organizations, the International Association for Religious Freedom, the World Congress of Faiths, the Temple of Understanding and the World Conference on Religion and Peace, discussed above.

A meeting was held at Ammerdown, near Bath in England, in 1985 to see whether interfaith organizations could relate more closely to each other. It was eventually agreed to concentrate on plans to mark 1993, the centenary of the World's Parliament of Religions in Chicago, as a "Year of Interreligious Understanding and Cooperation." The hope was that the year would "celebrate a century of growing awareness of our shared global humanity and encourage a vision of just and peaceful cooperation and creativity among all people of the world."

Through the *ad hoc* **International Interfaith Organizations Coordinating Committee for 1993 (IIOCC)**, efforts have been made to encourage a great variety of groups to arrange their own events, appropriate to the theme of a "Year of Interreligious Understanding and Cooperation." The hope is that all interfaith groups and organizations, be they local or national, as well as religious bodies, will organize events which highlight the importance of interreligious understanding and cooperation.

In addition, the four organizations are arranging jointly a centennial event in New Delhi, India and a four day program in Bangalore, India entitled "Religious People Meeting Together," *"Sarva-Dharma-Sammelana."* Both events are in August 1993.

The hope is that "A Vision of Interfaith Cooperation in the Next Century" will emerge from all the gatherings. As part of the process, we seek some agreement about the present situation which, with your help, this study is intended to elucidate. What are the achievements of the interfaith movement? What are its weaknesses? What should it now seek to achieve?

This means considering the basis for interreligious cooperation as well as how to overcome prejudice and rivalry. It suggests that religious people need to consider more urgently what they can do together to promote peace and justice, to uphold human rights, to relieve suffering and to preserve the planet.

These are questions to each of us as individuals, as members of a particular religious tradition, and as members of interfaith organizations. Interfaith organizations need to consider how they can be more effective. Each has its own distinct tradition and area of work, but perhaps they would achieve more through greater cooperation. Some people have suggested a World Council of Religions; other people think this might be bureaucratic and that we should think more in terms of a movement, with close networking between different groups, instead of an organization.

What of the relations of religious communities toward each other? Many people would like to see religious leaders stress the values which they hold in common and be a more effective voice for justice and peace. Others believe that the only hope for the future is a renewal of spiritual values and an appreciation of the oneness of humanity.

1993 may be a time for all of us to attain greater interfaith understanding and cooperation.

Institute for World Spirituality

The Institute for World Spirituality exists to promote communication, cooperation and an active exchange of information among the religions of the world. It is vital for the future of our world and race to enhance and encourage this movement, which was inaugurated in Chicago in 1893. The Institute intends to contribute to this movement by means of both the written and the spoken word. We intend to engage the religions of the world in dialogue among themselves and with the human sciences, so paths of spiritual realization, healing and ascent to maturity can be compared and can strengthen one another. We describe the area of this dialogue as "spirituality," a particular moment within the length and breadth of religious phenomena, for it is our belief that here conflicts can be resolved, mutual appreciation grow and cooperation begin, and the human sciences and religious traditions can significantly enrich each other. . . .

The Institute seeks to work toward its purpose by: (1) encouraging and fostering the publication of works which directly realize its mission; (2) through conferences, institutes and retreats which will bring together spiritual teachers from the many religions with professions in the human sciences; (3) focusing attention on the future of the planet out of the stories and maxims of spiritual traditions regarding the material universe.

The first Summer Institute met at the Vivekananda Monastery and Retreat in Ganges, Michigan, on July 25 and 26, 1992.

The 1993 Summer Institute explored spirituality as the ground for encounter between four monastic traditions: the Vedanta Society (Hindu), the Benedictine (Roman Catholic), the Serbian Orthodox (Orthodox) and the Gelugpa (Buddhist). The Institute was held June 23–26 at St. Sava Serbian Orthodox Monastery in Libertyville, Illinois.

As a cosponsor of the Parliament, the Institute is offering several workshops and presentations based on its goals and resources.

For more information contact:
Robert L. Moore, President (or)
Ronald R. Kidd, Executive Director
5757 S. University, Chicago, IL 60637

adapted by the Editor from the brochure and newsletter of the Institute

The New Delhi Congress of the Inter Religious Federation For World Peace

Dr. Frank Kaufmann

Executive Director of the IRFWP

The Inter Religious Federation for World Peace (IRFWP) was founded in 1990 and has sponsored several major international, interreligious events since. Of particular note for this article is the Delhi Congress which inaugurated the centenary celebration of the 1893 Chicago Parliament in India, February 1–7, 1993.

The IRFWP was founded by Reverend Moon at the second Assembly of the World's Religions, held in San Francisco, August 1990. It came on the foundation at that time of 23 years of investment in ecumenical and interfaith work on the part of Reverend Moon. Fourteen of these years transpired on the world-wide level from New York-based headquarters. The active data base of associates who have been sponsored by these organizations to attend international interfaith gatherings is approximately 7,000 religious leaders, scholars and youth leaders.

The IRFWP, like the organizations upon which it is modeled, is guided by prominent leaders from all major world religions. Presently the IRFWP consists of six presidents, a secretary general, a four person executive committee, a 16-person presiding council, and a significantly larger advisory board. From among these approximately 60 core leaders of the Federation, four are Unificationists.

In 1985 the predecessor and current partner of the IRFWP, the International Religious Foundation (IRF), hosted the first Assembly of the World's Religions, an international gathering of over 800 religious leaders and scholars, in McAffee, New Jersey. This inaugurated an orientation toward 1993 with the commitment to hold the first three Assemblies quadrennially—the second in 1989, and the third in 1993. These Assemblies were fortified by extensive interfaith activities and programs in the intervening years. At Ammerdown in 1986, IRF offered to work collaboratively with major extant interfaith organizations but this proposal was rejected, requiring the IRF and the IRFWP to prepare independently for 1993.

Continued on next page

EXCERPTS FROM THE
New Delhi Declaration
of the IRFWP Congress

" . . . we want to note with special sadness the suffering of all people in the context of interreligious conflict, especially the suffering of Muslim women in former Yugoslavia, the suffering of Buddhist people in Tibet, the conflicts that have temporarily dimmed the light of India as a beacon of spiritual wisdom and religious toleration, and the continuing conflicts in the Middle East, in Sri Lanka, in Europe and in the Americas. In the hope that these situations might be healed:

a) we call upon believers everywhere to refuse to allow their faith to be involved with acts that violate the clear principles of their sacred traditions.

b) we call for the healing of memories that can arise as we collectively ask forgiveness for wrongs of the past so that

Continued on the next page

we may together move toward a more promising future.

c) we call upon the religious traditions to support the empowerment of women in religion and society and the protection of children which are crucial to peace in the human family.

d) we call on the religious traditions to pledge themselves to cooperate to transform those social structures and conditions that create conflict and to commit themselves to social justice.

"We have been asked by the Prime Minister of India to suggest what could be done in this land and the world. We claim no superior wisdom, but would humbly respond by suggesting:

a) that communal hatred is a poison which if left unchecked, can do deep damage to the soul of a nation, and erupt again from time to time;

b) that interreligious conflict arises where religious communities perceive great socioeconomic injustice inflicted upon them for which they fail to see effective democratic remedies;

c) that religion cannot be separated from life; and therefore it is important to urge the religious communities to affirm and teach the more positive and humane aspects of their religions in a politically, socially, economically and culturally relevant context;

d) that no one religion should dominate other religions in any country; religious people should see that majority/minority situations do not justify domination in any country; that domination by one religion in one country has consequences in other countries;

e) that, while we are all called to act, and if need be to suffer for peace and justice in one human family, we affirm the deeper and spiritual efficacy of dedicated and devout prayer by religions, by multi-religious groups, and by individual believers in bringing about peace and harmony.

f) that no religious group should do violence to the places of worship of other religions but treat them with respect as places of worship."

from the Declaration of the
New Delhi Congress, February 1–7, 1993

The New Delhi Congress

From February 1–7, 1993 the IRFWP hosted the Delhi Congress, the first major event to commemorate the 1893 Chicago Parliament of the World's Religions. Seven major components comprised the Delhi Congress: ten concurrent educational seminars of the **Religious Youth Service,** scholarly conferences sponsored by the **Council for the World's Religions** and the **New Ecumenical Research Association,** a separate scholarly colloquium by the IRFWP, experiential dimensions including daily participation in prayer and worship from all the world's religions, daily visitation to active centers of religious life in the Delhi area, and the outdoor rally and a two mile silent march for peace with which the Congress concluded.

The academic conferences and colloquium each had three groups of approximately 15–20 members presenting papers and discussing related themes. The Council for the World's Religions conference was convened by Dr. William Cenkner of Catholic University with the theme "Discovering Religious Value in Inter Religious Dialogue." The New ERA conference convened by Drs. Francis D'sa and Darrol Bryant examined "The Future of Interfaith." The IRFWP colloquium convened by Drs. Zaki Badawi and Ninian Smart addressed the theme "The Worldwide Interfaith Movement 1893–1993: Assessments and Explorations." The Religious Youth Service Global Forum had Sri Venu Goswami as its organizing chairman. Here over 250 young people were engaged under ten educational themes such as "Spirituality and Leadership for Social Change," "Environment: Developing an Interfaith Educational Approach," and others.

In all over 600 participants attended. Highlights included talks by Dr. Ninian Smart, Huston Smith, Raimundo Pannikkar, IRFWP presidents Metropolitan Paulos Mar Gregorios, and Sri Swami Chidananda of the Divine Life Society, IRFWP presiding council member Baba Virsa Singh, and many others. By many counts however, the most moving part of the entire Congress was the Peace rally and march by which the week's activities concluded.

Although the dates for the Congress had been established over a year earlier, tragic circumstances allowed the Congress to answer the desperate prayers of a nation shredded by violence in the name of religion. Just the week before the Delhi Congress, militants had torn down the Babri Masjid in Ayodya leading to violence resulting in death and tragic internal division. For this reason government officials at the highest levels attended the conference, seeking throughout the event guidelines for the restoration of peace.

A number of important and enduring documents were created for use by Indian leaders. At last on a glorious Spring morning 1,200 gathered before the Red Fort, at the site where India had declared her independence in 1948. There international religious leaders called for peace and acted for peace. After the reading of the "Delhi Declaration," and the Keynote Proclamation for Peace, Lieutenant Governor of Delhi Mr. P.K. Dave handed the IRFWP banner to Mrs. Shamila Tagore Ali Khan, granddaughter of Rabindranath Tagore, and herself in a Hindu–Muslim marriage. She flagged off the march in which the brightly clad array of all God's children then walked under *maun vrat,* a vow of silence, to the Samadhi of Ghandiji. After paying respects, the Delhi Congress ended with these 1,200 persons from all religions in silent prayer for world peace.

For more information, contact:
IRFWP
4 West 43rd St., Fifth Floor
New York, NY 10036 USA

Understanding the Parliament:

A Sign of Movement Toward a Global Ethic

Joel Beversluis

Project Editor, A SourceBook for the Community of Religions

I. Beyond belief

*I*n addition to what we might learn by participating in interreligious meetings, members and leaders of the world's faiths may also learn a great deal from both the contexts and the goals of these events and activities. Those mentioned in the previous section and those which follow—and the organizations that arrange and sponsor them—are rich and multifaceted resources for understanding the themes of pluralism, globalization and ethical responsibility. Furthermore, these global meetings and issue-oriented communiques can serve as rich case-studies of religious dynamism in response to contemporary issues and in anticipation of the challenges of the future.

Unlike the 1893 event, the 1993 Parliament was not designed to be an extravaganza of presentations and dialogue about beliefs and tradition. Today, numerous books and reference works, religion courses and a variety of media provide an abundance of information about religions. The Parliament's goals, history and program also indicate that it is much more than a centennial commemoration of the 1893 interfaith event.

The Parliament may also be one embodiment of new forms of expression of religious belief. More and more the religious life exemplified in interfaith activities includes identifying shared values and working toward a global ethic. Both intrafaith and interfaith organizations and events like the Parliament are responding to a rapidly evolving historical context, one which requires the holistic understandings that religions can provide. This context includes the changing relationships between the religions and ecology, science, business, politics and personal spirituality.

II. Beyond pluralism

*W*e are increasingly aware of the impact that pluralism is having in our lives. The title of the book of documents about the 1893 Parliament says it well—*The Dawn of Religious Pluralism*. The sun is still rising on pluralism, and we must continue to focus on its nature and issues within our communities and nations. But we can't limit our focus. More significant changes and challenges lie beyond regional and national boundaries. These include not only the transnational perceptions and loyalties of religious identity, but also the impact of globalization and of the critical global issues on the individual members of the religions, wherever they may be.

Despite their diversity, religions are themselves reflecting some new commonalities. Perceptions of interdependence and interconnectedness— those perennial religious themes—are asserting a paradigm of unity in new ways. One indication of this emerging holism is that religions are claiming a widening sphere of influence, one which reflects new insights into the connectedness of our physical, economic, political and religious selves. Then, as their concerns overlap, religions are finding common cause in wide-ranging ethical and public arenas.

On a local level, for example, the ecumenical organization in Grand Rapids, Michigan, facilitates interfaith projects on alleviation of hunger,

ECO-ETHICS AND COMMUNITY

"All ethics so far evolved rest on a single premise: that the individual is a member of a community of interdependent parts .... The land ethic simply enlarges the boundaries of the community to include soils, waters, plants and animals, or collectively: the land.... In short, a land ethic changes the role of Homo sapiens *from the conqueror of the land-community to plain member and citizen of it. It implies respect for his fellow-members, and also respect for the community as such."*

ALDO LEOPOLD,
A Sand County Almanac,
pp.239, 240

"A number of philosophers and social scientists have pointed out that the history of human morals is a story of a developing sense of community that begins with the family and tribe and then gradually extends outward embracing the region, the nation, the race, all members of a world religion, and then all humanity. The sense of community involves an awareness of kinship, identity, interdependence, participation in a shared destiny, relationships to a common good. It gives rise to the moral feelings of respect and sympathy, leading to a sense of moral obligation...."

Continued on next page

> "*There are an increasing number of environmentalists who believe that unless humanity's sense of moral community is dramatically expanded to include not only future generations of human but also other life forms and even ecosystems, there is little hope of achieving the alteration in human behavior necessary to deal with our environmental problems. The environmental crisis is a crisis in our understanding of and commitment to community.*"
> JOHN C. ELDER
> and STEVEN C. ROCKEFELLER,
> *Spirit and Nature,* p.144

> "*He accepts as being good: to preserve life, to promote life, to raise to its highest value life which is capable of development; and as being evil: to destroy life, to injure life, to repress life which is capable of development. This is the absolute fundamental principle of the moral.*
>
> "*A man is ethical only when life, as such, is sacred to him, that of plants and animals as well as that of his fellow man, and when he devotes himself helpfully to all life that is in need of help.*"
> ALBERT SCHWEITZER,
> *Out of My Life and Thought: An Autobiography,* trans. C. T. Campion, p.158

locally and internationally, homelessness, AIDS education, and political/religious study tours to Central America.

What is the effect on religions and in the popular mind when interreligious organizations and international events like the Parliament address global ethical issues such as ecology, political violence and hunger? When their objectives transcend theological and cultural dialogue and move to the formulation of cooperative responses to those critical issues, it may be that a substantive change in religious identity and expression is underway.

III. Toward a global ethic

The 1993 Chicago Parliament asks a large number of representatives from numerous religions to consider new interpretations and expressions relating to "critical issues." To accomplish this, the Council for the Parliament of the World's Religions and the Institute for 21st Century Studies, an internationally respected think tank, cosponsored the publication of *What Shall we Do?* This book is a deliberate attempt to bring the religions and science into dialogue by focusing attention on a number of interrelated critical issues, including poverty, population growth, hunger, the global environment and varieties of development.

Presentations about critical issues are also significant components of the Parliament's program. One explicit focus of the Parliament is the persistence of religious intolerance and its contributions to war. Among the Parliament's goals is contributing thoughtful, truthful and clear analysis in an atmosphere of peace and cooperation. Combined with calls to action, this program is intended to challenge individuals and institutions to reconsider their perceptions about the world, themselves and people of other religions.

The pragmatic question "what shall we do?" and the focus on ethical responsibility suggests the wide-ranging challenge that the Parliament is posing to the religions. Yet these emphases by religious leaders, scientists and advocates of change are not unique to the Chicago Parliament.

The same concern is evident in numerous other ecumenical and interreligious conferences, as Marcus Braybrooke demonstrates in his recent *Stepping Stones to a Global Ethic* (excerpts of which follow). Braybrooke notes that since the 1960s "emphasis has also fallen on encouraging practical cooperation on moral issues and social concerns. Indeed," he writes, "the search for shared moral values may be more appropriate to official discussions than more speculative dialogue about questions of truth." He then identifies three urgent tasks of the interfaith movement: first, "repentance of the rivalry and hostility which have soured religious relations through the centuries. Secondly, religious people should fearlessly unmask the misuses of religion. . . . Thirdly, the emphasis has to be on the search for a global ethic [since] interfaith organizations have shown that people of many religions, whilst disagreeing about beliefs, can agree on the importance of peace and justice, of social action to relieve suffering and on efforts to save the planet."

A close look at the charters and declarations from such meetings (many are reproduced in *Stepping Stones,* and some are presented below) reveals that these movements are now contextualizing their earlier commitments to seeking peace and justice within the preconditions of ecological wisdom and an ethic of sustainability. Another common thread among the statements is the conviction that what is of primary importance for the future of humanity and of the earth is transformation—changes of heart and corresponding changes of behavior. Far from putting their trust in technology, governments or economic systems, the participants from religious, scientific and non-governmental agencies have all identified *change of heart* as a necessary characteristic of the next phase of personal, corporate,

PART 3: FORMING A COMMUNITY OF RELIGIONS

religious and cultural history. Thus it is becoming clear that the world needs the language, power, ideals and skills of the religious and spiritual traditions.

IV. In a world looking for answers

Beyond the statements of conferences and well-intentioned advocates of change, there are many other expressions of these widening concerns. One interfaith dialogue led to the book *Spirit and Nature: Why the Environment is a Religious Issue,* edited by Steven C. Rockefeller and John C. Elder; the book is selling widely. Theologian John B. Cobb, co-author of *For the Common Good,* which also addresses global moral issues, wrote that "*Spirit and Nature* shows us that the major forces shaping the spirituality of our day are themselves being reshaped by awareness of what human beings are doing to our planet" (as a blurb on the book cover).

New images are also helping to shape both religious and secular perceptions and thus have power to energize personal change. Everyone recognizes the NASA photographs of the blue-green planet, which forever changed humanity's perception of the earth. There is, however, a gripping dark side to this symbol which also has transformative power. The swirls of pollution that are now evident in NASA photos of sky and sea foreshadow the nightmare of a world gone brown from pollution or black with death due to the destruction of the ozone layer. The potential loss of earth life is inspiring a renewed awareness of our relationship to the earth, to other humans and species, and to the cosmos. As a result, many people are demanding answers from the religions.

Storytellers are also creating or revitalizing myths for the changing world and its crises. Eco-theologian Thomas Berry and physicist Brian Swimme, among others, point out the need for new creation stories with believable scientific and anthropological underpinnings. Symbolic and evocative stories with cosmic reference points, they say, will enable changes in world views and personal consciousness appropriate to the needs of our time.

Whether consciously or unconsciously, most people have, or are seeking, a personal vision of the future to help shape their responses to the present. Proposals come from many directions. Some religious and secular scenarios depict the future in apocalyptic doomsday terms which lead to apathy or disengagement from the challenges of this world. Other world views, such as those with an optimistic belief in the dawning of a new and brighter world, may also lead to disengagement; and the secular materialism promoted by commerce leads to self-absorption and a focus on present pleasures.

Speaking to all of these, the pragmatic vision of the Parliament is that religious humans are indeed capable of envisioning a better future, which may indeed come, *and* that we are personally responsible for creating it. All of us, whether we come from the quietist or otherworldly religions or from the engaged, this-worldly traditions, can benefit from this lesson.

V. Envisioning a ceremony of pluralism in the global community

These changing times and the religious responses to them suggest the possibility of new forms of religious expression and interreligious ceremonies. For this writer, they conjure up the image of men and women clothed in the brightly colored garb of many traditions, outdoors near the market of a mythical village, the global "city on a hill." The participants have gathered to learn more about each other's beliefs, to observe each other's rituals, and, for some, to worship together. But they are also gathered to address common threats to their community's life-support systems. Participants will suggest and perhaps "sanctify" a set of ethical propositions, and they will identify cooperative action. As they encounter each other in this sacred public square, a consciousness of the community of religions is forming among them.

This new ceremony does not anticipate a convergence among religious traditions toward a monolithic world religion, nor does it propose governments administered by religious leaders. Rather, it provides for a synthesis and application of the wisdom and gifts found within religious traditions. It suggests that the community will agree on and promote certain principles: treating others as each one would be treated, protecting the rights and dignity of others, demonstrating concern for victims, showing regard for the welfare of other species, and living in harmony with the earth.

Some religious traditions will not participate in this ceremony because participation might be interpreted as suggesting that religions are parallel paths, an interpretation that violates their beliefs. Others will resist the implication that religions have substantial political, economic or ecological responsibilities. Not all will agree on the analyses and prescriptions offered. Nevertheless, the absence or dissent of some confirms the diversity within the community of religions. The lesson of pluralism is that this diversity will not be denied and cannot be overlooked. Yet we must continue in dialogue, and together must face present realities and future possibilities.

International Coordinating Committee on Religion and the Earth

THE EARTH CHARTER

During the past several years the International Coordinating Committee on Religion and the Earth (ICCRE) has cooperated with the World Council of Churches, the World Conference on Religion and Peace, the World Wide Fund for Nature, the South American Conference on Religion and Ecology and other international and interfaith organizations in formulating this Earth Charter. The Charter was designed to help people live in harmony with each other and with the earth.

As a distillation of charters written around the world—in New York, Geneva, India, Africa, the Philippines and Brazil—by members of many religious traditions, the Earth Charter has been widely recognized as a document of substance. It was endorsed at the Parliamentary Earth Summit in Rio and adopted at the state level in Minnesota; New Jersey will consider doing the same later this year. The Charter also contributed to the Preamble for the founding constitution of the newly organized International Green Cross.

The principles articulated in the Earth Charter are also providing the basis for an intersectoral initiative that ICCRE is about to launch with business, education, religion and the arts to create actions and programs that will move us toward a more environmentally responsible society. Additionally, the Charter will be used in efforts by many organizations to lobby the United Nations for the proclamation of an Earth Charter as part of their 50th anniversary celebrations in 1995.

NANCY MOSHÉ, Coordinator;
Daniel Martin, Director

ICCRE
P.O. Box 67
Greenwich, Connecticut 06831-0767 USA
Voice and Fax: (914) 238-5032

The Global Forum of Spiritual and Parliamentary Leaders on Human Survival

In October 1985, while the United Nations was celebrating its 40th anniversary, a core group of religious and political leaders met for the first time in a village north of New York City. Ten spiritual leaders, two each from five major religions, and eight elected officials from parliaments on five continents came to Tarrytown to explore the possibility of a dialogue that intermingled their perspectives.

The politicians were members of the Global Committee of Parliamentarians on Population and Development. The spiritual leaders were invited by the Temple of Understanding, an organization devoted to building understanding among the different religions. The lawmakers tended toward practical solutions while the spiritual leaders emphasized morality and ethics.

From their differing viewpoints new possibilities emerged. In the end, the religious and political leaders decided that their dialogue had become so meaningful that it must be continued and expanded. They called upon colleagues worldwide to join them in a conference on global survival.

The Oxford and Moscow Forums

The first Global Survival Conference in April 1988 drew nearly 200 spiritual and legislative leaders to the historic university city of Oxford, England, for five days. Among the participants were cabinet members, speakers of parliaments, Mother Teresa, the Dalai Lama, the Archbishop of Canterbury, High Priest of Togo's Sacred Forest, Cardinal Koenig of Vienna and Native American Chief Oren Lyons. They conferred with experts on the issues, including astronomer Carl Sagan, Soviet scientist Evguenij Velikhov, Gaia scientist James Lovelock, Kenyan environmentalist Wangari Maathai, and Cosmonaut Valentina Tereshkova. *Earth Conference One: Sharing a Vision for Our Planet,* by Anuradha Vittachi (Shambhalla), provides an eloquent description of this meeting.

A second meeting of the Global Forum was hosted in the (former) Soviet Union in January 1990 by a unique and historic alliance of scientists, faith communities, the first freely elected Supreme Soviet, and the International Foundation for the Survival and Development of Humanity. More than 1,000 spiritual and parliamentary leaders, scientists, artists, journalists, businessmen and young people from 83 countries came to the Moscow forum. President Mikhail Gorbachev hailed it as "a major step toward the ecological consciousness of humanity."

National Global Forums have also been held in Indonesia, in the Phillipines, and in Japan for a Shinto International Workshop on Global Survival and Peace.

The Parliamentary Earth Summit

Cosponsored by the National Congress of Brazil and the Global Forum, The Parliamentary Earth Summit gathered in Rio de Janiero during the first weekend of the United Nations Conference on Environment and Development (June 1992). Parliamentarians from more than 100 countries, members of their official national delegations to UNCED, met with extraordinary leaders from many different fields of human endeavor.

Value Change for Global Survival

Another general assembly was held in Kyoto, Japan from April 17–23, 1993. Through the Global Forum process of dialogue and interaction, leaders are given the opportunity to influence not only each other but to extend their spiritual and political influence for peaceful, positive change to the communities they serve worldwide. To represent these communities, the Forum involves scientists, environmentalists, artists, leaders from business and industry, educators and journalists.

adapted and excerpted from Global Forum
publications by the Editor

Akio Matsumura, Executive Director;
Dr. Kusumata P. Pedersen and
Cecile J. Reyes, Joint Secretaries
Global Forum
304 East 45th St., 4th Floor
New York, NY 10017 USA
(212) 953-7947; fax: (212) 557-2061

THE EARTH CHARTER: A Religious Perspective

Preamble

I am because we are.

The crisis we face today is a spiritual one:

We have forgotten who we are
We have lost our sense of wonder
We have degraded the Earth
We have exploited our fellow creatures

And we have nowhere else to go.

In our ignorance we have disrupted the balance of life. Now the air we breathe hurts us and the water we drink poisons us.

All things are bound together:

If we lose the sweetness of the waters,
we lose the life of the land.
If we lose the life of the land,
we lose the majesty of the forest.
If we lose the majesty of the forest,
we lose the purity of the air.
If we lose the purity of the air,
we lose the creatures of the Earth.

Not just for ourselves but for our children—now and in the future.

But a new spirit is being born, and a new awareness of our place in this delicate balance. This spirit calls us to:

- a transformation of our hearts and minds
- concrete changes in our way of life
- the renewal of our religions
- the creation of a global society

Today:

We remember who we are
We reclaim our sense of wonder
We acknowledge our responsibility
We commit ourselves to the Earth

We turn toward each other in friendship

We turn again together towards home.

SPIRITUAL PRINCIPLES

INTERDEPENDENCE

The Earth is an interdependent community of life. All parts of this system are interconnected and essential to the functioning of the whole.

THE VALUE OF LIFE

Life is sacred. Each of the diverse forms of life has its own intrinsic value.

BEAUTY

Earth and all forms of life embody beauty. The beauty of the Earth is food for the human spirit. It inspires human consciousness with wonder, joy and creativity.

HUMILITY

Human beings are not outside or above the community of life. We have not woven the web of life; we are but a strand within it. We depend on the whole for our very existence.

RESPONSIBILITIES

Human beings have a special capacity to affect the ecological balance. In awareness of the consequences of each action, we have a special responsibility to preserve life in its integrity and diversity and to avoid destruction and waste for trivial or merely utilitarian reasons.

RIGHTS

Every human being has the right to a healthy environment. We must grant this right to others: both those living today and the generations to come.

ETHICS FOR LIVING

SUSTAINABLY

Human beings must live in a way that meets the needs of the present without compromising the ability of future generations to meet their own needs.

JUSTLY

Sufficiently

In a world of great disparities between rich and poor, justice demands that every human being be able to obtain the basic needs of life.

In Participation

Justice demands universal participation in all aspects of a sustainable society through legal and institutional structures.

In Solidarity

Sustainability with justice will only be achieved through an ethic of global solidarity, which includes the rights of future generations.

PEACEFULLY

The sacredness of life demands the practice of nonviolence; differences must be resolved by consultation rather than conflict. War and the production of weapons destroys the environment as well as human life.

SIMPLY

To establish economic justice, people in the industrialized world must learn to live more frugally. Simplicity of life fosters both inner freedom and outer sustainability.

KNOWLEDGEABLY

Environmental education and free access to information are essential for global awareness and skillful care of the Earth.

HOLISTICALLY

Human life, to be fully human, must include physical, intellectual, moral and spiritual development within the community of all life.

PROGRAM AREAS

Our concern for all life expresses itself not only in our prayers and in statements of principles, but in actions in our personal, professional and political lives. We, representatives of the world's religious communities, recommend action in the following program areas. We also call upon our members to develop actions around these areas, and to promote and implement them in their personal and professional lives.

LOCAL AND INDIVIDUAL LEVEL

1. Education

The promotion of environmental education as an integral and compulsory part of school curricula.

Continued on next page

2. Health

The promotion of environmental education as a mandatory component of all health care, both in medical schools and in medical practice.

3. Food Production

The promotion of sustainable farming systems as the basis of all agricultural food production, including the preservation and integration of indigenous methods and indigenous foods.

4. Food Consumption

The promotion of food consumption that is lower on the food chain (less energy consuming), as well as food that is organically, humanely and locally produced.

5. Energy

The promotion of sustainable patterns of energy consumption through net reduction, increased efficiency and minimal use of fossil fuels.

6. Transport

The promotion of transport forms that are less energy consuming and less polluting.

7. Wildlife

The protection and, where necessary, the restoration of biological diversity, and the revival of the traditional peaceful coexistence between people and wild animals.

8. Family and Community

The promotion of the "extended family" or similar forms of community as the basic unit for integrated and environmentally balanced living.

9. Population

The promotion of population education toward the reduction of birth rates, and the related appreciation of economic and social factors.

10. Grassroots Movements

The promotion of grassroots movements to protect the environment from vested interests of all kinds (i.e. the Chipko Movement in India).

11. Religious Traditions

The promotion of religious traditions and practices that foster concern and responsibility for the environment, and the challenging of those that do not. This would include the protection and restoration of many of the indigenous values and practices which have a particular contribution to make in this area.

12. Regional Policies

The promotion of regional policies and legislation that would consider not only local effects, but also the impact on the rest of the world.

13. Local Government

The development of local government policies and structures for the promotion of the above programs.

INTERNATIONAL LEVEL

1. International Wealth

The redistribution of land, wealth and natural resources for the good of many. This will require a restructuring of the present economic system that would include the promotion of "quality of life indicators," rather than simply measures of quantity, and address the issue of debt and world trade agreements.

2. A Transnational Approach

The establishment of procedures and mechanisms that would permit a transnational approach to environmental issues and disputes, including standards, accountability and enforcement.

3. Transnational Sharing

The promotion of appropriate technology exchange: new technology from the industrialized countries and indigenous technology from the poorer nations.

4. Finances

The creation of a "world fund" for the protection of the environment: money to be raised through projects like "energy taxation," an "Earth stamp," etc.

5. Transnational Corporations

The limitation of the power of transnational corporations, as well as the encouragement of their enormous ability to foster justice and sustainability.

6. Militarization

The promotion of complete disarmament, the termination of all weapon production and trade, and the ending of military technology transfer.

7. Science

The encouragement of scientists to be environmentally responsible and to use their knowledge and skill to help alleviate environmental problems.

8. Media

The promotion of mass / electronic media for the development of ecological attitudes, values and skills.

9. Women and Children

The promotion of full and equal participation of women in all government and nongovernmental organizations, in decision-making, implementation, administration and funding at international, national and community levels. The protection of women and children as the most vulnerable to environmental and economic injustice.

10. Indigenous Peoples

The support of indigenous peoples in their efforts to protect their natural environments, and the recognition of the special contribution of indigenous peoples in providing vital wisdom and leadership in resisting the forces that are destroying the earth.

11. Biotechnology

Contribution to the ethical process involved in the development and application of biotechnology and genetic engineering.

12. Wilderness

The promotion of protection of remaining habitat (forests, wetlands, rivers, estuaries, etc.) through wilderness preservation and sustainable life practices.

Stepping Stones to a Global Ethic

Marcus Braybrooke

As readers of this book will have noted, the name of Marcus Braybrooke is prominent among those who have published materials about interfaith dialogue and activities. *Stepping Stones to a Global Ethic,* his most recent effort, includes the following essays published as most of chapters 1 and 2; this book, like his *Pilgrimage of Hope,* was published with the centennial of the Parliament clearly in mind. Much of the book consists of declarations and charters, ranging from the "The Universal Declaration of Human Rights" to the declarations of conferences and assemblies of international, interreligious organizations. These excerpts are part of his introduction to them. –Ed.

The Search for a Global Ethic

"A Global Village" has become a common way to describe our world society, where instant communication and modern means of travel have created a world community. A characteristic of many villages is that the inhabitants share a similar world view, a culture, an ethic and perhaps a religion. In many villages, of course, there are often minorities, and today large numbers do not share in the opportunities of the Global Village. The Global Village excludes millions of poorer people in the way that Greek civilization excluded the slaves on whom the economy depended. Yet even those who are illiterate are affected by the decisions of world trade. A distant stock market can decimate the value of a cash crop even more decisively than a plague of locusts.

Despite reservations about some of the implications of the term, the question which now faces the inhabitants of the Global Village is whether a world society needs a world view, a culture, an ethic and a religion. Prince Philip, in his Preface to Hans Küng's *Global Responsibility,* says that it has proved possible to arrive at a broad consensus about the facts of life on earth. Scientific discourse, like trade, is international. It has, however, Prince Philip continues, "so far at least proved impossible to overcome the jealousies, rivalries and the destructive consequences of competing religions and ideologies."[1]

Is it possible that a world ethic will emerge? Hans Küng himself says that "the one world in which we live has a chance of survival only if there is no longer any room in it for spheres of differing, contradictory and even antagonistic ethics." He concludes his book with this summary:

"No human life without a world ethic for the nations; no peace among the nations without peace among the religions; no peace among the religions without dialogue among the religions."[2]

Continued on next page

The Declaration of the Sacred Earth Gathering

Rio de Janeiro, 1992

The planet earth is in peril as never before. With arrogance and presumption, humankind has disobeyed the laws of the Creator which are manifest in the divine natural order.

The crisis is global. It transcends all national, religious, cultural, social, political and economic boundaries. The ecological crisis is a symptom of the spiritual crisis of the human being, arising from ignorance [greed, lack of caring and human weakness]. The responsibility of each human being today is to choose between the forces of darkness and the force of light. We must therefore transform our attitudes and values, and adopt a renewed respect for the superior law of Divine Nature.*

Nature does not depend on human beings and their technology. It is human beings who depend on Nature for survival. Individuals and governments need to evolve "Earth Ethics" with a deeply spiritual orientation or the earth will be cleansed [of all destructive forces].

We believe that the universe is sacred because all is one. We believe in the sanctity and the integrity of all life and life forms. We affirm the principles of peace and nonviolence in governing human behavior towards one another and all life.

We view ecological disruption as violent intervention into the web of life. Genetic engineering threatens the very fabric of life. We urge governments, scientists, and industry to refrain from rushing blindly into genetic manipulation.

We call upon all political leaders to keep a spiritual perspective when making decisions. All leaders must recognize the consequences of their actions for the coming generations.

We call upon our educators to motivate the people towards harmony with nature and peaceful coexistence with all living beings. Our youth and children must be prepared to assume their responsibilities as citizens of tomorrow's world.

We call upon our brothers and sisters around the world to recognize and curtail the impulses of greed, consumerism and disregard of natural laws. Our survival depends on developing the virtues of simple living and sufficiency, love and compassion with wisdom.

We stress the importance of respecting all spiritual and cultural traditions. We stand for preservation of the habitats and lifestyle of indigenous people and urge restraint from disrupting their communion with nature.

The World Community must act speedily with vision and resolution to preserve the Earth, nature and humanity from disaster. The time to act is now. Now or never.

*Alternative reading:
"the superior law of the Divine manifest in nature and the created order."

For nearly a century those in the interfaith movement have sought to encourage such dialogue among the religions. From small beginnings, interreligious dialogue now engages a growing number of people in all religions. A sketch of the development of the worldwide interfaith movement is given below [in his book, *Stepping Stones to a Global Ethic*]. Part of the dialogue has been on ethical matters. At a number of interfaith conferences, statements have been made affirming some shared values and sometimes making specific suggestions about moral behavior. . . .

There are many questions. Do these statements draw deeply on the teachings and traditions of the world religions or have texts been found to give a cloak of religious respectability to ideas which derive from the enlightenment and the modern world? Human rights, for example, is in one sense a recent concept, but some would claim that it derives from the age-old moral teaching of the religions.

Does the apparent agreement in such statements mask the deep differences between religions? This book is not the place to speculate on the possibility of an emergent world religion to accompany a world society. Religions are complex entities and ethical behavior is related to beliefs. These differ widely between religions. Is it possible to hope that the world religions may share values if they do not share beliefs?

How representative of their faith communities are those who produced or endorsed these statements? Even within religious traditions, there are sharp differences about belief, practice and behavior. Is it not therefore a chimera to suggest that there can be agreement between religions? Do not the statements merely represent an agreement between "liberals" of different

Traditional Circle of Indian Elders and Youth

COMMUNIQUÉ NO. 12
Haida Gwaii
Queen Charlotte Islands
Skidegate — Massett
June 14, 1989

The Traditional Circle of Indian Elders and Youth issue this communique following their Council at Haida Gwaii, land of the Haida Nation. As an introduction to the concepts that were discussed, we would like to present a statement from Haida Chief Skidegate (Lewis Collinson), made in March 1966:

"People are like trees, and groups of people are like forests. While the forests are composed of many different kinds of trees, these trees intertwine their roots so strongly that it is impossible for the strongest winds which blow on our Islands to uproot the forest, for each tree strengthens its neighbor, and their roots are inextricably entwined."

"In the same way the people of our Islands, composed of members of nations and races from all over the world, are beginning to intertwine their roots so strongly that no troubles will affect them."

"Just as one tree standing alone

would soon be destroyed by the first strong wind which came along, so is it impossible for any person, any family or any community to stand alone against the troubles of this world."

Sharing native philosophy

All peoples are part of the Creation, and have common rights and responsibilities toward Mother Earth. There are some important aspects of our ways which can be shared with those interested in understanding traditional knowledge and philosophy.

It is important to respect the fact that some ceremonial knowledge is sacred and private, meant only for the medicine societies that are responsible for those particular functions. All people are beneficiaries of these ceremonies. It is a great offense to exploit sacred knowledge. Proper performance and participation is the duty of designated traditional religious leaders. Many of these ceremonies are site-specific in their respective indigenous nations.

Aspects of Native philosophy that can be shared include principles of life and relationships to the natural world. We

are one with the continual process of Creation. People are equal partners with the plants and animals, not their masters who exploit them.

Today the four colors of the family of people—red, white, black and yellow—need to better understand our relationship to Mother Earth in order to assure the survival of people, plants and animals. There are many commonalities inherent to our survival. By sharing our philosophy we can promote harmony and balance.

Family lifestyle— a shared responsibility

Men and Women have an equal responsibility to restore the strength of the family, which is the foundation of all cultures. Parents become partners in nurturing the spiritual, cultural and social health of the family. This partnership should be based upon mutual respect.

Our cultures can teach parents how to work together in peaceful and constructive ways, how to deal with each other and how to use good words to resolve problems. Through these religions? Often those who are deeply committed to interfaith exploration find themselves out of sympathy with their fellow believers.

In any case, if the religions do agree, what practical difference will this make? Religious influence has seldom made peace and has often aggravated conflict. Many people are disillusioned with religions and are not willing to base their behavior on the teaching of a particular religious tradition. Yet, as Prince Philip says, "The motivation for altruism seems to originate in a personal attachment to an ideology or to a religion. The evidence suggests that people are influenced in their behavior by moral conviction and ethical concepts."[3] Even so, many are reluctant to be told what to do by a religious authority. The ethical teaching of a faith community needs to commend itself as life-enhancing. In Hans Küng's words: "The fundamental criteriological ethical question can be formulated: What is good for human beings? . . . the basic ethical criterion is: Humans should not live inhumanly." Religions should, he suggests, be able to agree that "the good for human persons is what helps them to be truly human."[4]

Supposing such agreement is possible between the religions, how then is the world ethic communicated to the citizens of the world? More particularly, how are people best educated in moral values, especially young people?

The search for a new world ethic raises many questions and implies a far-reaching program. Whilst some of these questions will be discussed a little more fully below, they will not be [fully] answered. The documents may provide raw material for such answers or at least be a litmus test for theories. Some people belonging to different faith traditions have been able to agree on some ethical issues. Is their work a sign of hope for the future?

Continued on next page

TRADITIONAL CIRCLE OF INDIAN ELDERS AND YOUTH, continued

ways our children will have a productive and caring life. This life will include cultural education, spiritual fulfillment, creative expression and a positive self-image for all members of the family.

Parents must be role models for the children and for their nieces and nephews. Parents have to demonstrate the value of trust, respect and honor. Parents also have to exhibit discipline, moderation and fairness in their own actions. As time has proved, children will do as the parents do, not necessarily what parents tell them to do. These changes cannot happen without the individual's commitment to disciplining themselves in their daily lives. When personal comfort and immediate gratification become more important than our children, then we are headed for serious problems.

Each nation has Original Instructions on how to live. These traditions can give families strength and consistency to deal with the realities of modern life.

Grandparents and community Elders must have a significant role in the education of our youth. Their

experience, concerns and perspectives are important. Children are part of a larger extended family clan which gives them a unique place in the world, and connects children to their culture.

Children need the security of a home, a connection to their community and a relationship to their traditional environment. Children are the future of our nations, and must be taught their Native language, spirituality and identity. In order for our children to survive in the world, they need a firm understanding and belief in the basic principles of sharing freedom and respect of individuality.

Food

One important aspect that our families need to address urgently is a change to a more healthy diet. Diseases such as diabetes and cancer are epidemic among our people. Poisons in many modern foods, from preservatives to pesticides, can cause great harm to the body, mind and soul. We need to return to more wholesome traditional foods that are nutritious and

Continued on next page

The American Indian Institute *and the* Traditional Circle of Indian Elders and Youth

The relationship between the American Indian Institute and the Traditional Circle of Indian Elders and Youth is the result of creative interaction between traditional leaders of Indian nations from the Four Directions and American Indian Institute personnel. The process was begun in 1973 and culminated in 1977 with the formation of the Traditional Circle of Indian Elders and Youth at a council of traditional Indian leaders which took place at the headwaters of the Missouri River in Montana. The resulting coalition based upon trust is unprecedented in cross-cultural relationships.

This coalition is expressed in Indian imagery as a "two-circle" concept. The American Indian Institute and the Traditional Circle of Indian Elders and Youth work together as equal but independent partners committed to common goals. In the history of North American cross-culture relationships this non-hierarchical organizational structure is unique in both function and spirit.

The Traditional Circle of Indian Elders and Youth is a spiritual circle open to all Indian people. Its purpose is to nurture a grassroots renewal of traditional values and lifeways among Native peoples, to ensure the continuity of Native wisdom and to bring that wisdom to bear upon the threats to land and life that are increasing with each passing day. The Circle is a repository of indigenous wisdom and values, and the Circle gatherings and projects represent a means of reinforcing and strengthening that wisdom within the participating delegations and extending it through them to grassroots communities as well as across cultures.

The official support group and administrative agency for the Traditional Circle of Indian Elders is the American Indian Institute, which is the heart of the non-Indian Circle. Its connection with the Traditional Circle of Indian Elders is in its support function, and in shared ideals and commitments. Each is separate but there is a spiritual binding force which is stronger than written documents and signed agreements. The relationship embodies freedom and the ideals of the Iroquois Confederacy two-row wampum: support and cooperation but no interference.

The support of the Institute to the

Continued on next page

Traditional Circle of Indian Elders and Youth is given freely. Neither partner has a self-serving agenda. The goal is the welfare of traditional Native people first and the welfare of all people through the joint effort of the two partners; neither side will dishonor that goal.

An important function of the American Indian Institute is to seek funds to assist the Circle of Elders and Youth in its meetings and work, and to provide a tax-free mechanism through which those funds may be channeled to the work of the Circle.

Another important aspect of the work of the Institute is to provide administrative and organizational support to the programs and activities of members of the Elders Circle. For example, each year the Elders Circle holds an international Council lasting six or seven days, in a different location each year. The staff of the Institute, in cooperation with the Indian host community, makes all arrangements including notification of participants and dissemination of the communiqués issued to report on the deliberations of the Elders. The same services apply to the Youth and Elder education programs, and to domestic intercultural programs as well as cross-cultural dialogue in international conferences such as the Global Forum.

Another responsibility of the American Indian Institute is to assist the Elders Circle in projecting the traditional voice across cultures on Indian terms.

The Traditional Circle of Indian Elders and Youth continues to be a beacon of hope for Native people specifically, and for all people generally. The collaboration of the Elders Circle with the American Indian Institute has been responsible for igniting that beacon and for projecting it in ever-widening circles both domestically and worldwide. Its promise and potential have only begun to be realized.

The organizational structure which has brought this about is unorthodox. It is the result of a conviction that the challenges of our day need fresh thinking and new human resources organized in innovative ways. It also results from a conviction that the ancient wellspring of indigenous wisdom, overlooked by the larger society through 500 years of coexistence, has new relevance for a new era.

ROBERT STAFFANSON,
Executive Director

**The American Indian Institute
P.O. Box 1388,
Bozeman, Montana 59715
Telephone (406) 587-1002**

The Interfaith Movement: The Present Reality

*T*he hope that religious people could together affirm certain moral principles was in the minds of some of those who attended the World's Parliament of Religions in Chicago in 1893. Charles Bonney, whose idea the Parliament was, said that one object was "to make the Golden Rule the basis of the union (of religions) and to present to the world . . . the substantial unity of many religions in the good deeds of the religious life."[5] At the Parliament the contribution of religion to peace and social issues was fully covered.

Regarded now as the beginning of the interfaith movement, the Chicago World's Parliament has come to symbolize the aspirations of all who believe that religious people should be friendly and cooperative to one another and work together for human welfare and peace. The Parliament's immediate impact, however, was more ephemeral. The Parliament drew American public attention to the teachings and practices of religions other than Christianity. It also gave an impetus to the emerging study of world religions.

The momentum for interreligious understanding and cooperation has steadily gathered pace since the 1893 Parliament, although no continuing organization emerged from the World's Parliament of Religions. At first slowly and recently quite rapidly, interfaith groups have been established in many places. Some are quite small, meeting in a home. Other interfaith organizations are national bodies and some are international, seeking to coordinate global interfaith concern.

. . . .

It is hard to assess the impact that religious people can have on political

---

economical. Families need to raise more of their own food, which if properly grown according to time tested cultural patterns, will help to restore the health, strength and happiness of our families.

Significance of women

The Natural Law gives women the responsibility of bringing new life into the world. Everyone must be born from the womb. Mothers must protect the lives they have helped to bring into this world.

The Traditional Circle of Elders and Youth wishes to affirm women in their sacred responsibilities, and to express its gratitude and encouragement to women everywhere who struggle to nurture and protect life in the face of many obstacles.

In our traditional ways, the woman is the foundation of the family. It is the mother who provides spiritual direction and inspiration to the husband and children. The opportunities for women to help their families rise to higher levels of spiritual consciousness are unlimited. A man can become a powerful force for good in the world when he is spiritually supported by a discreet and loving mate.

In order for women to carry out their responsibilities, a home atmosphere of respect, security and harmony is essential. A mother who is secure in the center of the family circle will be a source of strength to all. Abuse and repression have no place in a traditional family.

An environmental ethic, based upon tradition

Today we are faced with a serious challenge to restore world environmental harmony. We realize that the Earth is our Spiritual Mother, a living entity that maintains life, and that any threat to the environment endangers us all. We face a crisis of life for this living planet we call Mother Earth.

In our traditional ways we treat the Earth with the respect due the source of our spiritual and cultural well-being. We were warned of a time when people would ignore the fundamental Natural Law, and that they would choke in their own waste.

In our traditional ways we do not

processes, especially as politicians seldom acknowledge those who have influenced them. Modern communications have given added weight to popular opinion. Religious leaders may play an important role in forming public opinion. They can insist on the relevance of spiritual and moral considerations. They have helped to maintain public alarm at the enormous stockpile of nuclear weapons and other means of mass destruction. They have voiced public outrage at the starvation of millions of people, as a result of hunger, war, injustice and an unfair pattern of international trade. They have upheld human dignity and protested against torture and racism. They have underpinned efforts to develop internationally agreed upon standards of human rights and have helped to monitor their application. Interreligious conferences have been among the first to warn of threats to the environment.

In local areas of conflict, religious people have often maintained contact across boundaries and divisions. Sometimes they have been agents of reconciliation and conflict resolution. They have taken a lead in relief work. Sometimes they have encouraged acts of repentance in an effort to heal deeply rooted bitterness. Yet often, too, religious people have used religious loyalties to inflame conflict and have allowed particular interests to outweigh common human and religious moral values. Some

extremists stir up religious passions to gain support for their concerns.

Slowly the value of interfaith dialogue has become more widely recognized. In 1966, the Second Vatican Council's decree *Nostra Aetate* transformed the Catholic Church's attitude to people of other religions. A Secretariat for Non-Christians was established, which is now called The Pontifical Council for Inter-Religious Dialogue. At much the same time, the World Council of Churches established a Unit for Dialogue with People of Living Faiths, which has arranged various consultations. Many religious and denominational bodies now have agencies to encourage such dialogue. There are some official discussions between religions. Clearly, official dialogue has a character of its own. Participants have some representative role. Much of the work is to remove misunderstanding and build up good relations, but emphasis has also fallen on encouraging practical cooperation on moral issues and social concerns. Indeed the search for shared moral values may be more appropriate to official discussions than more speculative dialogue about questions of "truth."

The Gulf War and the Salman Rushdie affair have emphasized the practical importance and urgency of interfaith understanding. No longer can anyone dismiss religion as obsolescent or irrelevant to world affairs. But

---

TRADITIONAL CIRCLE OF ELDERS, continued

view the lands as a collection of resources that require development. Instead we view these resources as living entities to be honored with ceremonies of thanksgiving. We are at a point where we must act to save the Earth for all cultures. Our prophecies have come true. The time of warning is past. We are now faced with a common issue of survival.

The consequences of defying the Natural Law will be borne by those who rely most upon these good laws. We have a responsibility to help the world understand how their political, economic and recreational decisions impact the health and welfare of the environments in which indigenous nations live.

The Natural Law is absolute. It can be swift and cruel if not respected. People can make a difference. We must ensure that all cultures, all nations, all peoples begin immediately to protect the vanishing bounty of Mother Earth. We have to change greed into sharing, material wealth into spiritual well-being, and individual enterprise into collective will to assure that there will be a clean and safe home for future generations.

We need a coalition of indigenous nations and environmental groups to work more cooperatively to save our Mother Earth. Conciliation is the key to survival. Peace is the goal. Peace between humans and the environment. This peace will allow us to respect our different cultures as well as respect the spiritual powers of the Earth and all living things.

We cannot separate ourselves from the Earth. We cannot continue to abuse our Mother. The future welfare of Mother Earth rests squarely in our hands. We must all become caretakers of the Earth.

To begin with, we need to save those Elders who cannot speak for themselves —the trees. The redwoods are under attack. The rainforests are being destroyed at an unbelievable rate. The maple dies from the top down from the killing effect of acid rain.

The very air we breathe can now hurt us. The oxygen we need is the breath of life from our Mother Earth. She produces this air from the trees and rainforests throughout the world. "Progress" now threatens those trees that help us live. A better understanding of our philosophy

can create appreciation and a commitment for our responsibility to the life forces of Creation.

Our health is at risk. A safe supply of water—the essential blood of Mother Earth—must be protected. Good foods like the Three Sisters of Corn, Beans and Squash must be grown free of toxic chemicals. Otherwise we are committing a form of suicide. By eating food with the life taken out of it (commercially processed) we contaminate ourselves.

The Earth is alive and must be protected from further abuse by both individuals and multinational corporations. They violate the Natural Law. It is a sacred trust that must be restored for the sake of future generations of all people. Selfishness and greed must be halted to end the plunder of the gifts of Creation. A unity of the principles of sharing and caring must exist in all people. The survival of all children of Mother Earth depends upon our united actions.

Together we can end the Holocaust against the environment. Mother Earth

Continued on next page

many wonder whether the future belongs to the interfaith movement or whether we are likely to see increasing religious rivalry. Some indeed picture the next century being dominated by renewed conflict between Christendom and the world of Islam. It is only three hundred years ago that the Turks were at the gates of Vienna.

To meet the contemporary challenge, the interfaith movement needs to become more practical. Religious rivalries destroy lives. If the interfaith movement is successfully to oppose the forces of religious extremism, there needs first to be repentance of the rivalry and hostility which have soured religious relations through the centuries.

Secondly, religious people should fearlessly unmask the misuses of religion. Too often religion has been used to cloak abuses of power. Religious people need to make clear that their commitment to the search for truth and the defence of human rights is stronger than their group loyalty costly as this may be.

Thirdly, the emphasis has to be on the search for a global ethic. The discovery of those who attended the first meeting of the World Conference on Religion and Peace in Kyoto, Japan, in 1970 was that "the things which unite us are more important than the things which divide us."[6] The interfaith organizations have shown that people of many religions, whilst disagreeing about beliefs, can agree on the importance of peace and justice, of social action to relieve suffering and on efforts to save the planet. In promoting 1993 as a "Year of Interreligious Understanding and Cooperation," they hope to show the importance of interfaith work not only in combating extremism and communalism but in harnessing the energies of all people of faith and of good will to tackle the urgent problems of the world.

NOTES

1. Prince Philip, Preface, p. xiii, in Hans Küng, *Global Responsibility: In Search of a New World Ethic*, SCM Press and Crossroad Publishing Company, 1991.
2. Ibid., p.138.
3. Ibid., p. xii.
4. Hans Küng, in *World Faiths Insight*, February 1989, p. 15.
5. Charles Bonney, quoted in my *Pilgrimage of Hope*, SCM Press and Crossroad Publishing Co. 1992, p.26. The material in this section is drawn from this book.
6. The Kyoto Declaration. Statement of the First Assembly of the World Conference on Religion and Peace held at Kyoto, Japan, in October 1970.

TRADITIONAL CIRCLE OF ELDERS, continued

needs all of us to pay attention to the Natural Law. Indigenous people need help from all cultures, religions and nations to restore the harmony of our home planet.

Indigenous rights to the land

Indigenous people around the world have a birthright and a responsibility to their ancestral lands. They have an identity that is based upon the land. They have a sovereign right to protect the natural world from exploitation. If the nations remain truthful to their traditional philosophy and values toward the land, their future is secure. People need to rediscover the Natural Law which in turn will allow them access to the land without destroying it.

Our cultures are based upon two important premises that involve land. First, we believe that the Earth is our Spiritual Mother, created to support us provided we live by the Original Instructions of our Creator. Second, our diverse cultures get their individual identities from the land. This creates an essential relationship to our ancestral lands that must be preserved.

Our cultural and spiritual identity is dependent upon a land base. The land provides us with sustenance, shelter, inspiration and a responsibility to respect all elements of that land. The land is a sacred trust held in common for the benefit of the future of our nations.

Land is not an economic resource to be sold. We can no longer continue to base our economic future on the extraction and exportation of its natural resources. Access to resources is subject to the Natural Law. If we destroy the land we will have no sustenance, no home and no future for the next generations. If we destroy the resources, we have broken our sacred trust. Our nations need to set parameters for land usage with spiritual laws guiding our decisions. We need a commonsense approach to help the people benefit from the resources of the land, while assuring the long-term health of those resources.

The people, the clans and the Nations are entrusted with sovereignty over the land. It is a collective right that has spiritual consequences. Abuse of this responsibility will lead to the destruction of our nations, our cultures and all of our resources. We have been led astray by the profit motives of the industrial age. We must remember why we were given the land in the first place. Each tribal culture has a land use ethic which must be restored.

The land has been inherited from a long line of our ancestors. They have passed on the trust to us. We hold the land, not for financial gain but for the sake of future generations, so that they will have a home, a land base, a secure future. We have to instill in them a deep respect for all the gifts of Creation.

Religious rights of indigenous people

It appears that the canoe of the indigenous peoples' spirituality still sits in the shadows of the religious ships of the western world. We all rock gently on the sea of life, and share a common destiny in the protection of the well-being of Mother Earth.

Increasingly, the world is beginning to recognize the integrity of indigenous religions. Our spiritual visions are gaining equality and support in international affairs.

Yet, our religions suffer from exploiters that include scholars who attempt to refute our spiritual visions; individuals who appropriate our beliefs for their own gain; people who deal in the removal of human remains and sacred objects from our sacred places and medicine societies.

We must remind all people that the practice of our spiritual ways requires certain elements. We need access to

The National Religious Partnership for the Environment

*T*he National Religious Partnership for the Environment is comprised of four major faith groups and denominations representing over 100 million people. In July 1993, these groups—the U.S. Catholic Conference, the National Council of Churches of Christ, the Consultation on the Environment and Jewish Life and the Evangelical Environment Network—initiatied a three year, $5 million mobilization on behalf of environmental integrity and justice.

The National Religious Partnership for the Environment began to take form in response to an Open Letter to the Religious Community issued in January 1990 by 34 internationally prominent scientists. Of the peril to the planetary environment they wrote, "Problems of such magnitude and solutions demanding so broad a perspective must be recognized from the outset as having a religious as well as a scientific dimension. . . . Efforts to safeguard and cherish the environment need to be infused with a vision of the sacred."

Struck by the initiative, several hundred religious leaders of all major faiths from all five continents responded, "This invitation to collaboration marks a unique moment and opportunity in the relationship of science and religion. We are eager to explore as soon as possible concrete, specific forms of action."

On June 2nd and 3rd, 1991, a small group of religious leaders convened for scientific briefings, conversations with members of Congress, and consideration of future initiatives. At the end of the gathering, measuring sentiments within their respective denominations, they concluded, "We believe a consensus now exists, at the highest level of leadership across a significant spectrum of religious traditions, that the cause of environmental integrity and justice must occupy a position of utmost priority for people of faith."

Continued on next page

TRADITIONAL CIRCLE OF ELDERS, continued

sacred sites, which must be protected. We need access to sacred animals, which must be kept from regulatory interference. We need the return of sacred objects, many of which are now in museums, historical societies, universities and private collections.

Sacred objects are the national patrimony and the religious right of our nations. No one has the right to keep these objects from our people. To continue to do so is a violation of our human rights. Sacred items must be respected at international borders so that we can be allowed to practice our religion wherever we travel.

The remains of our ancestors must be returned to those nations that ask for their reburial. Associated grave goods should also be returned so that our dead can rest in peace. To continue to deny our nations the religious right to care

properly for the dead is an uncivilized act.

The religious rights of indigenous people are being restricted by federal, state / provincial and local governments. Policies of these agencies and cultural institutions must be changed to eliminate any discrimination toward our religions. Correctional institutions must recognize the religious right of Native inmates. The curative powers of our ceremonies and religious ways can be very important in human development. Native inmates must have access to our spiritual practices and sacred objects necessary to carry out the ceremonies. This is especially true for children in social service or youthful offender institutions.

It is time that the religious practices of the Native nations receive the same consideration and respect as the other

established religions of the world, especially in our own lands.

In closing, the Traditional Circle of Indian Elders and Youth hopes that all people will make an effort to incorporate traditional values into their lives. We believe that there is an urgent need to change the destructive ways that are harmful to the peaceful and natural way of life. With this Communique the Traditional Circle of Indian Elders and Youth reaches out to the world for support and cooperation in restoring the balance and harmony of all life, and in protecting Mother Earth.

"Daalang gii giinahl sudaas naa gi dang gyust'aa sqawdaagii uu daalang gahl kil 'laa gaa. Howa. Gaa gang at t'aa ts'ii."

(Thank you for listening to the words that have been spoken. Howa. Step carefully as you go.)

This led to an extraordinary array of programming in the American religious community. In July 1991, the Episcopal Church agreed upon and funded its first program on environment and sustainable development. Bishops of the U.S. Catholic Conference approved their first pastoral statement on environment in November of 1991. Also that autumn, the National Council of Churches of Christ established an office on environmental and economic justice and the United Church of Christ hosted an environmental summit for people of color. In March, 1992, over 100 senior leaders from all four branches of Jewish life met and set priorities for a communal environmental program. And in April 1991, World Vision U.S.A. hosted a major environmental conference for evangelical Christian leaders.

Fresh from this year of heightened activity, representatives of major denominations brought word of the religious community's growing commitment and partnership with the scientific community to the U.S. Congress.

About the mission to Washington

*I*n May 1992, 50 religious leaders and 50 Nobel laureate and other scientists convened in Washington, DC to hear scientific updates on global environmental conditions and reports on activities within their respective communities. They met to seek common ground and vision in response to global environmental challenges and to plan strategies together for action by their respective communities. The "Mission to Washington" was a unique, perhaps unprecedented, gathering of eminent representatives from a diverse world of religion, science and government in close consultation.

At the conclusion of the Mission to Washington the senior religious leaders formally established the National Religious Partnership for the Environment. The Partnership's upcoming initiatives include, among others, the annual distribution of environmental kits to 53,000 congregations; major consultations on issues of environmental justice and international development; conferences for leaders of the historic African-American churches and Orthodox Christian churches; development of seminary and religious education curriculum; theological scholarship and major public policy campaigns.

The Partnership will have a central communications office which seeks to document the activities of the religious community and to help active congregations work with one another. Its recent publication, the *Directory of Environmental Activities and Resources in the North American Religious Community,* begins to build such a network. The *Directory* includes sections on national and regional organizations and their programs, hundreds of congregational contacts as well as an extensive resource section with listings of audiovisual aids, educational materials, congregational and personal lifestyle information, theological / liturgical guides and newsletters. Copies of the Directory can be obtained by sending a check for $14.90 to the Joint Appeal c / o Kutztown Publishing, P.O. Box 346, Kutztown, PA 19530. The Partnership urges interested congregations to contact the office to join this growing network. This process is evidence of how local, individual action can lead to strengthened resolve and commitment at the highest level.

The task before us is both quantitative and qualitative: to build a base of commitment to individual and institutional action which is exponentially broader, more deeply motivated, and in service to a more comprehensive environmental vision integrating ecology and equity. The more fully we let this challenge into our hearts, the more certain we'll find ourselves moved to take the right steps. Its deepest reward, beyond its immediate effects, can be very personal and touching. From being passive witnesses to nature's destruction, we become faithful stewards of Creation's integrity, and discover how our faith is renewed in ways we never quite anticipated. That is the work that lies ahead. Together, we will move forward.

National Religious Partnership for the Environment
1047 Amsterdam Avenue
New York, NY 10025

A Historical Note about The Joint Appeal in Religion and Science

The Summit on Environment, sponsored by the Joint Appeal in Religion and Science, grew out of a collaboration which began in January 1990 with an Open Letter to the Religious Community sent by 34 internationally renowned scientists. Of the peril to planetary environment they wrote, "Problems of such magnitude and solutions demanding so broad a perspective must be recognized from the outset as having a religious as well as a scientific dimension."

Struck by the initiative, several hundred religious leaders of all major faiths from all five continents responded. The Summit on Environment was held on June 2nd and 3rd at the American Museum of Natural History and the Cathedral of St. John the Divine. It was a next step in an ongoing partnership and an effort to support the American religious community as it moves forward to act upon the vision of environmental justice and a sustainable future.

Preserving and Cherishing the Earth: A Joint Appeal in Religion and Science

An Open Letter to the Religious Community from the Scientific Community   January 1990

The Earth is the birthplace of our species and, as far as we know, our only home. When our numbers were small and our technology feeble, we were powerless to influence the environment of our world. But today, suddenly, almost without anyone's noticing, our numbers have become immense and our technology has achieved vast, even awesome, powers. Intentionally or inadvertently, we are now able to make devastating changes in the global environment—an environment to which we and all other beings with which we share the Earth are meticulously and exquisitely adapted.

We are now threatened by self-inflicted, swiftly moving environmental alterations about whose long-term biological and ecological consequences we are still painfully ignorant: depletion of the protective ozone layer; a global warming unprecedented in the last 150 millennia; the obliteration of an acre of forest every second; the rapid-fire extinction of species; and the prospect of a global nuclear war which would put at risk most of the population of the Earth. There may well be other such dangers of which we are still unaware. Individually and cumulatively, they represent a trap being set for the human species, a trap we are setting for ourselves. However principled and lofty (or naive and shortsighted) the justifications may have been for the activities that brought forth these dangers, separately and taken together they now imperil our species and many others. We are close to committing—many would argue we are already committing—what in religious language is sometimes called "Crimes Against Creation."

By their very nature these assaults on the environment were not caused by any one political group or any one generation. Intrinsically, they are transnational, transgenerational and transideological. So are all conceivable solutions. To escape these traps requires a perspective that embraces the peoples of the planet and all the generations yet to come.

Problems of such magnitude, and solutions demanding so broad a perspective, must be recognized from the outset as having a religious as well as a scientific dimension. Mindful of our common responsibility, we scientists—many of us long engaged in combatting the environmental crisis—urgently appeal to the world religious community to commit, in word and deed, and as boldly as is required, to preserve the environment of the Earth.

Some of the short-term mitigations of these dangers—such as greater energy efficiency, rapid banning of chlorofluorocarbons or modest reductions in nuclear arsenals—are comparatively easy and at some level are already underway. But other, more far-reaching, long-term and effective approaches will encounter widespread inertia, denial and resistance. In this category are conversion from fossil fuels to a nonpolluting energy economy, a continuing swift reversal of the nuclear arms race and a voluntary halt to world population growth—without which many other approaches to preserve the environment will be nullified.

As with issues of peace, human rights and social justice, religious institutions can be a strong force here, too, in encouraging national and international initiatives in both the private and public sectors, and in the diverse worlds of commerce, education, culture and mass communications.

The environmental crisis requires radical changes not only in public policy, but also in individual behavior. The historical record makes clear that religious teaching, example and leadership are able to influence personal conduct and commitment powerfully.

As scientists, many of us have had profound experiences of awe and reverence before the universe. We understand that what is regarded as sacred is more likely to be treated with care and respect. Our planetary home should be so regarded. Efforts to safeguard and cherish the environment need to be infused with a vision of the sacred. At the same time, a much wider and deeper understanding of science and technology is needed. If we do not understand the problem, it is unlikely we will be able to fix it. Thus, there is a vital role for both religion and science.

We know that the well-being of our planetary environment is already a source of profound concern in your councils and congregations. We hope this appeal will encourage a spirit of common cause and joint action to help preserve the Earth.

SIGNED BY

Carl Sagan
  Cornell University, Ithaca, NY

Richard L. Garwin
  IBM Corp., Yorktown Heights, NY

Hans A. Bethe
  Cornell University, Ithaca, NY

Elise Boulding
  University of Colorado, Boulder, CO

M. I. Budyko
  State Hydrological Institute, Leningrad

S. Chandrasekhar
  University of Chicago, Chicago, IL

Paul J. Crutzen
  Max Planck Institute for Chemistry, Mainz, West Germany

Margaret B. Davis
  University of Minnesota, Minneapolis, MN

Freeman J. Dyson
  Institute for Advanced Study, Princeton, NJ

Gyorgi S. Golitsyn
  Academy of Sciences of the U.S.S.R. Moscow, U.S.S.R.

Stephen Jay Gould
  Harvard University, Cambridge, MA

James E. Hansen
  NASA Goddard Inst. for Space Studies, New York, New York

Mohammed Kassas
  University of Cairo, Cairo, Egypt

Henry W. Kendall
  Union of Concerned Scientists, Cambridge, MA

Motoo Kimura
  National Institute of Genetics, Mishima, Japan

Thomas Malone
  St. Joseph College, West Hartford, CT

Lynn Margulis
  University of Massachusetts, Amherst, MA

Peter Raven
  Missouri Botanical Garden, St. Louis, MO

Roger Revelle
  University of California, San Diego La Jolla, CA

Walter Orr Roberts
  Yorktown Heights, New York, National Center for Atmospheric Research, Boulder, CO

Abdus Salam
  International Centre for Theoretical Physics, Trieste, Italy

Stephen H. Schneider
  National Center for Atmospheric Research, Boulder, CO

Nans Suess
  University of California, San Diego La Jolla, CA

Continued on next page

"Efforts to safeguard and cherish the environment need to be infused with a vision of the sacred."

from the Open Letter from the scientists
to the religious community

"This invitation to collaboration marks a unique moment and opportunity in the relationship of science and religion. We are eager to explore as soon as possible concrete, specific forms of action."

from the response by several hundred
religious leaders

Statement by Religious Leaders at the Summit on Environment

June 3, 1991, New York City

On a spring evening and the following day in New York City, we representatives of the religious community in the United States of America gathered to deliberate and plan action in response to the crisis of the Earth's environment.

Deep impulses brought us together. Almost daily, we note mounting evidence of environmental destruction and ever-increasing peril to life, whole species, whole ecosystems. Many people, and particularly the young, want to know where we stand and what we intend to do. And, finally, it is what God made and beheld as good that is under assault. The future of this gift so freely given is in our hands, and we must maintain it as we have received it. This is an inescapably religious challenge. We feel a profound and urgent call to respond with all we have, all we are and all we believe.

We chose to meet, these two days, in the company of people from diverse traditions and disciplines. No one perspective alone is equal to the crisis we face—spiritual and moral, economic and cultural, institutional and personal. For our part, we were grateful to strengthen a collaboration with distinguished scientists and to take stock of their testimony on problems besetting planetary ecology. As people of faith, we were also moved by the support for our work from distinguished public policy leaders.

What we heard left us more troubled than ever. Global warming, generated mainly by the burning of fossil fuels and deforestation, is widely predicted to increase temperatures worldwide, changing climate patterns, increasing drought in many areas, threatening agriculture, wildlife, the integrity of natural ecosystems and creating millions of environmental refugees. Depletion of the ozone shield, caused by human-made chemical agents such as chlorofluorocarbons, lets in deadly ultraviolet radiation from the Sun, with predicted consequences that include skin cancer, cataracts, damage to the human immune system, and destruction of the primary photosynthetic producers at the base of the food chain on which other life depends. Our expanding technological civilization is destroying an acre and a half of forest every second. The accelerating loss of species of plants, animals and microorganisms which threatens the irreversible loss of up to a fifth of the total number within the next 30 years, is not only morally reprehensible but is increasingly limiting the prospects for sustainable productivity. No effort, however heroic, to deal with these global conditions and the interrelated issues of social justice can succeed unless we address the increasing population of the Earth—especially the billion poorest people who have every right to expect a decent standard of living. So too, we must find ways to reduce the disproportionate consumption of natural resources by affluent industrial societies like ours.

Much would tempt us to deny or push aside this global environmental crisis and refuse even to consider the fundamental changes of human behavior required to address it.

But we religious leaders accept a prophetic responsibility to make known the full dimensions of this challenge, and what is required to address it, to the many millions we reach, teach and counsel.

We intend to be informed participants in discussions of these issues and to contribute our views on the moral and ethical imperative for developing national and international policy responses. But we declare here and now that steps must be taken toward: accelerated phaseout of ozone depleting chemicals; much more efficient use of fossil fuels and the development of a non-fossil fuel economy; preservation of tropical forests and other measures to protect continued biological diversity; and concerted efforts to slow the dramatic and dangerous growth in world population through empowering both women and men, encouraging economic self-sufficiency and making family education programs available to all who may consider them on a strictly voluntary basis.

We believe a consensus now exists, at the highest level of leadership across a significant spectrum of religious traditions, that the cause of environmental integrity and justice must occupy a position of utmost priority for people of faith.

Response to this issue can and must cross traditional religious and political lines. It has the potential to unify and renew religious life.

We pledge to take the initiative in interpreting and communicating theological foundations for the stewardship of Creation in which we find the principles for environmental action. Here our seminaries have a critical role to play. So too, there is a call for moral transformation, as we recognize that the roots of environmental destruction lie in human pride, greed and selfishness, as well as the appeal of the short-term over the long-term.

We reaffirm here, in the strongest possible terms, the indivisibility of social justice and ecological integrity. An equitable international economic order is essential for preserving the global environment. Economic equity, racial justice, gender equality and environmental well-being are interconnected and all are essential to peace. To help ensure these, we pledge to mobilize public opinion and to appeal to elected officials and leaders in the private sector. In our congregations and corporate life, we will encourage and seek to exemplify habits of sound and sustainable householding in land use, investment decisions, energy conservation, purchasing of products and waste disposal.

Commitments to these areas of action we pledge to one another solemnly and in a spirit of mutual accountability. We dare not let our resolve falter. We will continue to work together, add to our numbers and deepen our collaboration with the worlds of science and government. We also agreed this day to the following initiatives:

1. We will widely distribute this declaration within the religious community and beyond. We have established a continuing mechanism to coordinate ongoing activities among us, working intimately with existing program and staff resources in the religious world. We will reach out to other leaders across the broadest possible spectrum of religious life. We will help organize other such gatherings as ours within individual faith groups, in interfaith and interdisciplinary formats, and at international, national and regional levels.

2. We religious leaders and members of the scientific community will call together a Washington, DC convocation and meet with members of the Executive and Congressional branches to express our support for bold steps on behalf of environmental integrity and justice. There too we will consider ways to facilitate legislative testimony by religious leaders and response to local environmental action alerts.

3. We will witness firsthand and call public attention to the effect of environmental degradation on vulnerable peoples and ecosystems.

4. We will call a meeting of seminary deans and faculty to review and initiate curriculum development and promote bibliographies emphasizing stewardship of Creation. We will seek ways to establish internships for seminarians in organizations working on the environment and for young scientists in the study of social ethics.

5. We will prepare educational materials for congregations, provide technical support for religious publishers already producing such materials, and share sermonical and liturgical materials about ecology.

6. We will establish an instrument to help place stories on environment in faith group and denominational newsletters and help assure coverage of the religious community's environmental activities in the secular press.

7. We will urge compliance with the Valdez Principles and preach and promote corporate responsibility.

8. We will encourage establishment of one model environmentally sound and sustainable facility within each faith group and denomination. We will provide materials for environmental audits and facilitate bulk purchasing of environmentally sound products.

It has taken the religious community, as others, much time and reflection to start to comprehend the full scale and nature of this crisis and even to glimpse what it will require of us. We must pray ceaselessly for wisdom, courage and creativity. Most importantly, we are people of faith and hope. These qualities are what we may most uniquely have to offer to this effort. We pledge to the children of the world and, in the words of the Iroquois, "to the seventh generation," that we will take full measure of what this moment in history requires of us. In this challenge may lie the opportunity for people of faith to affirm and enact, at a scale such as never before, what it truly means to be religious. And so we have begun, believing there can be no turning back.

SIGNED BY

Bishop Vinton R. Anderson
  President, World Council of Churches

Rabbi Marc D. Angel
  President, Rabbinical Council of America

The Most Reverend Edmond L. Browning, Presiding
  Bishop and Primate of the Episcopal Church

Reverend Joan Campbell
  General-Secretary, National Council of Churches
  of Christ

The Reverend Herbert W. Chilstrom
  Bishop, Evangelical Lutheran Church
  in America

Father Drew Christiansen, S.J.
  Director, Office of International Justice & Peace,
  United States Catholic Conference

Ms. Beverly Davison
  President, American Baptist Church

Reverend Dr. Milton B. Efthimiou
  Director of Church and Society
  Greek Orthodox Archdiocese of North
  and South America

Bishop William B. Friend
  Chairman of the Committee for Science and
  Human Values
  National Conference of Catholic Bishops

Dr. Alfred Gottschalk
  President, Hebrew Union College–
  Jewish Institute of Religion

Dr. Arthur Green
  President, Reconstructionist Rabbinical
  College

His Eminence Archbishop Iakovos
  Primate, Greek Orthodox Archdiocese of North
  and South America

The Very Reverend Leonid Kishkovsky
  President, National Council of Churches
  of Christ

Chief Oren Lyons
  Chief of the Turtle Clan of the
  Onondaga Nation

Dr. David McKenna
  President, Asbury Theological Seminary

The Very Reverend James Parks Morton
  Dean, Cathedral of St. John the Divine

Dr. W. Franklyn Richardson
  General Secretary, National Baptist
  Convention

Dr. Patricia J. Rumer
  General Director, Church Women United

Dr. James R. Scales
  President Emeritus, Wake Forest University

Dr. Ismar Schorsch
  Chancellor, Jewish Theological Seminary

Dr. Robert Schuller
  Pastor, The Crystal Cathedral

Dr. Robert Seiple
  President, World Vision U.S.A.

Bishop Melvin Talbert
  Secretary of the Council of Bishops
  United Methodist Church

Dr. Foy Valentine
  Former Executive Director
  Christian Life Commission
  Southern Baptist Convention

(Affiliations for identification purposes only)

The North American Coalition on Religion and Ecology

OVERVIEW of NACRE

The North American Coalition on Religion and Ecology (NACRE) is an ecumenical/interfaith environmental education organization, headquartered in Washington, DC, designed to help the North American religious community enter into the environmental movement in the 1990s with more informed understanding of the environmental crisis and a dynamic sense of ecological mission as well as to assist the wider society to understand the essential ethical and value-dimension of the environmental movement. The vision of NACRE is summed up in the phrase "Caring for Creation."

Mission

1. NACRE *helps to envision* a society which truly cares for the natural environment (creation). NACRE encourages people to visualize a world that is both sustainable and regenerative. To accomplish this on practical and theoretical levels, NACRE calls for an ongoing ECO-3 "Trialogue," one in which religion (ecumenism), science (ecology) and society (economics) clarify and agree on values for a new global ethic which promotes sustainability at all levels of responsibility through private citizens, corporations and governments.

2. NACRE *strives to communicate* its "Caring for Creation" vision by developing practical resource materials for environmental education, by organizing conferences that communicate to leaders and the public and by developing new uses of media for interactive ecological collaboration. Through its "Race to Save the Planet" resources and workshops it equips leaders to act as stewards of creation and agents of eco-justice.

3. NACRE *works to transform* our culture by developing coalitions of concerned religious, scientific and environmental leaders locally, nationally and internationally (through the Consortium on Religion and Ecology-International). These leadership groups are empowered to embody this new environmentally sensitive ethic in practical models and strategies of eco-action and in their use of the *regeneration process*.

HISTORY

In 1986, a group of some 35 ecumenically minded North Americans, including NACRE's president, Donald B. Conroy, Ph.D., assembled in northern Virginia. They were searching for a community of support for the Christian and interfaith understanding of the ecological movement. Those who attended the meeting wanted to establish a framework that would articulate environmental implications mainly within the Christian tradition.

A number of key leaders later voiced concern that a strong religious–environmental movement should involve other faith traditions beyond Christianity especially in view of the 1986 Assisi gathering of leaders from the five major faiths including followers of Islam, Buddhism and Hinduism. This was further widened to include other traditions when NACRE joined the UN Environmental Sabbath Committee.

With these considerations in mind, the North American Conference (now Coalition) on Religion and Ecology was chartered in the spring of 1989.

Some Resources from NACRE

- *Eco-Letter*
  Members receive NACRE's quarterly newsletter plus two special reports
- *Rio and Beyond: The Earth Summit*
  Summarizes and analyzes UNCED and the parallel NGO '92 Global Forum, and informs readers about next steps
- *Race to Save the Planet*
  Viewer's Guide and Facilitator's Resource Guide
- *Introductory Packet*
  Environmental Education and Ministry

CONSORTIUM ON RELIGION AND ECOLOGY-INTERNATIONAL

The Consortium on Religion and Ecology-International (CORE-International) is an intercontinental (international) network established by NACRE (North American Coalition on Religion and Ecology) and SACRE (South American Conference on Religion and Ecology) in 1991.

Statement of purpose

The purpose of CORE-International is to communicate among continental and intercontinental (international) organizations and research centers to promote efforts surrounding sustainability and the process of The Earth Summit primarily through ecosocial economic indicators and the ECO-3 framework.

The ECO-3 framework is the dialogue ("trialogue" because it is between three different interests) between three major groups: environmentalists and scientists, public policy analysts and economists, and ethicists and those concerned with the spiritual dimensions of earth and human harmony.

CORE-International's criteria for membership

Criteria for membership of non-governmental organizations is the following: (1) the organization must be continental or intercontinental (international) in scope; (2) the organization must agree to work for a new global environmentally sensitive order through ethical values and economic indicators (including ecological and sociocultural realities); (3) the organization must support the goals of eco-ethical principles and ecosocial and economic indicators at the UN Conference on Environment and Development and its follow through.

For more information about NACRE's program and a variety of resources for local, regional, continental and international levels, write to:

**Dr. Donald B. Conroy, Chairman
NACRE/CORE-International
5 Thomas Circle, NW
Washington, DC 20005**

from NACRE publications, adapted by the Editor

Monastic Interreligious Dialogue

Brother Wayne Teasdale

Member of the Board of MID, author of many articles and books, and a Catholic monk

Formerly known as the North American Board for East–West Dialogue, Monastic Interreligious Dialogue is a Roman Catholic organization that grew out of the Second Vatican Council's call for Christians to seek contacts with representatives of other traditions. This Council urged discussions, dialogical relationships and collaboration with members of other religious traditions. Before the end of the Council, Vatican II established the Secretariat for Non-Christian Religions, with Cardinal Pignedoli as its first president, to facilitate its mandate on interreligious dialogue and collaboration.

Cardinal Pignedoli approached the Benedictine Order and asked if monastics could assume some responsibility in the area of establishing and promoting dialogue with the religions of Asia, notably with representatives of Hinduism, Buddhism and Zen. Cardinal Pignedoli's insight was that dialogue between East and West could be carried out on a very deep level through the encounter of monks and nuns from the traditions involved, since they share the monastic dimension in common. In a letter to the then Abbot Primate of the Benedictine Order, Rembert Weakland—now the Archbishop of Milwaukee—Cardinal Pignedoli revealed his intention in making this request of the Benedictine Confederation. He observed: ". . . the existence of monasticism at the heart of the Catholic Church is in itself a bridge connecting all religions" (June 12, 1974).

The Abbot Primate turned to an existing organization of the Benedictine Confederation called Aide Inter-Monastique, an organization founded in the 1920s to support the growth of monasteries in the developing countries, to accept the responsibility for activating dialogical contacts with members of the Asian traditions. AIM established DIM or Dialog Inter-Monastique, and the North American Board for East–West Dialogue was founded in January 1978 with nine members, representing Benedictine and Cistercian (Trappist) monasteries and convents.

The Board changed its name to Monastic Interreligious Dialogue in December 1991 in recognition of the broader mission of dialogue, which also embraces Islam and Judaism. MID comes under the authority of the Abbot Primate in Rome, and the Pontifical Council for Interreligious Dialogue at the Vatican, the new designation for the Secretariat for Non-Christian Religions. MID now has 15 members, with about 70 contact persons, one from each monastery/convent in the United States and Canada. These contact persons are the links between the various monastic houses and MID. MID also produces a publication called the *Bulletin*, which is edited by Father James Connor, OCSO, at Abbey of Gethsemani (Trappist, Kentucky 40051). Through the *Bulletin*, MID maintains its network of several thousand supporters around the world.

Since its inception, NABEWD/MID has pursued the work of interreligious dialogue and collaboration through conferences, workshops, videos, books, seminars, exchanges and lecture series. One of the most fascinating and successful programs of MID is the Intermonastic Dialogue Exchange with the Tibetans. Thomas Merton had opened up encounters with the Dalai Lama and Tibetan Buddhist monasticism in his fateful trip to India in 1968. MID has built a solid relationship with the Tibetans going back some 14 years, but initiated by Merton. The Dalai Lama has remarked that he never realized that Christians were spiritual until he met Merton. Much has happened since that first encounter, and both traditions are becoming more aware of the spiritual treasures residing in each other.

MID also continues exploring contacts with Hindus, Sufis and Jews in formal and informal gatherings. The Parliament of the World's Religions is one such avenue in these ongoing efforts at exploration, an effort that will also occasion further dialogue with representatives of the various Buddhist schools. MID became a co-sponsor of the Parliament of the World's Religions some two and a half years ago, and two members of MID have been and are actively involved with the Council for a Parliament of the World's Religions, serving on a number of its committees. Support for the Parliament may well become a permanent feature of MID.

The North American Interfaith Network

The NAINetwork is a non-profit association with a membership of more than 60 interfaith organizations and agencies throughout the United States and Canada. NAIN builds communication and mutual understanding among its members, and with the offices of religious or denominational institutions pertaining to interreligious relations in North America.

NAIN affirms humanity's diverse and historic spiritual resources, bringing these to bear on contemporary global, national, regional and local issues. Without infringing on the efforts of existing organizations, NAIN facilitates the *networking* possibilities of these large organizations. NAIN provides a coalition model for cooperative interaction based on serving the needs and promoting the aspirations of all member groups.

NAIN traces its history through many converging lines, names and efforts over the past 25 years. The Network was born in the late 1980s, and began by developing a directory of interfaith groups. Increased membership merited Directory revision in 1990. It has fostered two major interfaith conferences in accord with its purpose of building communication, and held its first full Membership Meeting in Berkeley in 1992. As a co-sponsor of the Parliament of the World's Religions, NAIN will host workshops on interfaith networking, communication and understanding.

For more information, membership, or a copy of the Directory, contact:

Ms. Elizabeth Espersen,
Executive Co-Chair
P.O. Box 1770
Dallas, TX 75221
TEL (214) 969-1977

Interfaith Manifesto of the City of God

Based on the teachings of Lord Krishna, as understood by His Divine Grace Kirtanananda Swami Bhaktipada, Founder of the City of God, West Virginia

Global Urgency for Interfaith Understanding

As the 20th century draws to a close, there is an unfortunate rise in cultural and religious exclusivity and fundamentalism around the world. Today, for the first time in history, peoples of all religions, cultures and races live together—neighbor to neighbor—all over the planet. Interfaith understanding and respect is no longer a luxury. It is an urgent necessity. Unless the peoples of the earth begin to understand, respect and even celebrate the diverse cultural and spiritual expressions of others, there can be no hope for peace in the 21st century.

Vision Statement

The vision of the City of God is to uncover and disseminate the universal spiritual principles which underlie the various faith traditions of contemporary society.

The City of God recognizes that all bonafide spiritual traditions are reflections of the One Absolute Truth. By creating a forum to communicate and experience the teachings of different traditions we can find the beauty of the Oneness of the Love of God, where all contradictions are resolved. Interfaith understanding leads to peace among neighbors, while bigotry leads to violence, riots, hate and resentment.

Mission Statement

The City of God's mission is to establish a linking network of priests, rabbis, lamas, pastors, brahmins, monks, imams, swamis and native elders who can communicate on a deep spiritual level, thus sharing in each other's love for the Absolute and for the great Earth Family of all nations and all species.

We are committed to creating a positive change in society, expanding cooperation among peoples of faith, and offering to people at large the highest goals attainable in life—without discrimination because of race, language, social background and religious tradition.

To this effect, the City of God promotes public events, publishes educational materials and sponsors interfaith conferences where interaction at different levels can occur.

Organizational Creed

We believe that God is the cause of all causes and all that is. We believe that every living being is His part and parcel, in quality one with Him, but quantitatively infinitesimal. All beings are spiritually equal because they are made of the same spiritual energy. All beings are children ("all our relations") of the Great Mother Earth.

Transformation of Consciousness

Interfaith awareness does not develop just by book knowledge of other traditions. By providing a place and proper circumstances where diverse people can meet and associate, the City of God helps individuals to break the barriers of exclusivity and superiority of one belief over another through a transformation of consciousness.

Spiritual Birthright

It is the birthright of every human being to have the opportunity to learn about the Supreme Spirit of the Universe. No one should be denied the right to practice their own religion, or to change their religion if the individual cannot find spiritual satisfaction by following a particular tradition.

Personal and Social Responsibility

It is our personal and social responsibility to promote interfaith dialogue in the world, and to facilitate a network of culturally/religiously diverse individuals willing to cooperate together for the good of all people.

A World of Resources

The planet is rich in cultural traditions and diversity. Bigotry and fundamentalism lead to a rejection or deprecation of the beautiful cultural and spiritual expressions of others. To utilize the tremendous resources of the earth's peoples for the good of the Whole, we want to promote a united interfaith effort to uncover and broadcast knowledge of the world's cultures and religions.

The Environment

There is a direct relationship between the continuing misuse of resources, exploitation of the earth, and the root cause of these mistakes: misunderstanding of the laws of God and God's Nature.

Those who ignore the laws of God/Nature remain ignorant of the consequences of irresponsible behavior toward the precious and fragile environment which all creatures of the earth share.

The City of God thus promotes a universal and nonsectarian understanding of the laws of God/Nature, which will help people to act for the highest quality of life for themselves and generations of children to come.

Service to the Peoples of the Earth

Ultimately, the test of our love for God is how we love, respect and care for our fellow brothers, sisters and relatives of all races, cultures and species.

The hungry, homeless and sick among the peoples of the earth must be helped by our interfaith projects, both materially and spiritually. Otherwise, such projects have no real value.

The peoples of the earth in this context include "all our relations" of all species—humans, animals, plants, etc.

For more information, contact:
City of God
RD 1, Box 230
Moundsville, WV 26041

Spiritual Response to the Changing Times

Brahma Kumaris
World Spiritual University

An educational organization working at all levels of society for effective and positive change; affiliated as an NGO with the United Nations, the University carries out a wide range of educational programs through 1,500 centers in over 50 countries.

"Respect, understanding and tolerance enable us to celebrate life in all its diversity. Living by these values develops a deeper spirituality in our vision towards each other. Sharing these values establishes the common ground on which we all live as one human family."

Is it just a dream? When we believe in and begin to harness the power of vision, dreams become a reality. Our shared vision of a better world is perhaps the one thing that can unite us across the divides of religion and culture and restore the most basic spiritual values within our lives.

The development of spiritual values is part of the long-standing support that the Brahma Kumaris World Spiritual University (BKWSU) has given to interfaith work in the world. The process of education offered by the Spiritual University has been to provide the essential tools to discover and release what is eternally present within the consciousness of every human being.

This educational process, includes meditation that brings the realization of the original pure state of the soul, free from any limitation in understanding or awareness. It encompasses the whole of one's day, the whole of one's lifestyle, regardless of age, religious, cultural or ethnic background. It provides a foundation, as people engage in the risky but highly rewarding process of interfaith dialogue that involves listening, understanding and communicating from the heart, in an attempt to heal the pain and divisions that have characterized our world for so long.

Brahma Baba, the founder of the Brahma Kumaris World Spiritual University, had a vision that a day will come when religious leaders of the world will come together in Mt. Abu, the spiritual home of the Brahma Kumaris. In view of this, the university now feels it obligatory on its part to organize an international interfaith event in 1994 to follow up the enthusiasm that is being generated through the centennial celebrations this year.

The International Interfaith Conference—"Spiritual Response to the Changing Times," will be held from October 20,1994, through October 24, in Mt. Abu, Rajasthan, India. The format of the conference will allow participants to come up with practical solutions/responses to the critical issues facing humankind based on the teachings of one's own tradition.

Workshop themes will include:

- Family Life: Spiritual response to the problems of disintegration and degeneration
- Neglect of moral and spiritual education in academic institutions
- Violence, crime, communal riots or "ethnic cleansing"
- Spiritual response to the environmental crisis
- Health and happiness
- The danger posed by demographic explosion
- Discrimination against women
- The negative influence of the media
- Spiritual truths, compatible with science or common logic
- Religious amity, cooperation and harmony
- Promotion of values in profession, public and household life in the face of various challenges
- Human relations and behavior
- Problems of the youth, adolescents and children
- Meditation and spiritual knowledge

"... we, the people of the world, are yearning for peace and a better world for ourselves and our children. How is it, that with all the human skill and talent that exists, with all the achievements in technology, there is still grinding poverty, massive arms expenditure and a grave deterioration of the environment?

There is so much to be done and so many willing hands and hearts to do it.

What is needed is the spirit of cooperation and goodwill, the attitude of love and respect towards each other, the practice of positive and creative thinking, the application of moral and spiritual values in daily life, as well as action based on a shared vision of a better world.

Now is the time to call on the will and clear vision of the people.

"A vision without a task is but a dream
A task without a vision is a drudgery
A vision with a task can change the world!"

excerpted from The Mt. Abu Declaration, formulated at the Mt. Abu Summit held at the International Headquarters of the Brahma Kumaris in Mt. Abu, Rajasthan, India, February 8–11, 1989

Environmental Sabbath/Earth Rest Day

and the United Nations Environment Programme (UNEP)

Established in 1987 by the United Nations Environment Programme and its advisory board and planning committee, the Environmental Sabbath/Earth Rest Day provides a way to meld spiritual values with environmental science. Many churches, temples, synagogues, mosques and other institutions have adopted the first weekend in June each year as a special time to remember the needs and value of the earth through worship and liturgy, education and personal commitment. Other organizations have built upon UNEP's resource base to develop programs of their own that extend throughout the year.

Among the publications produced for these activities is *Only One Earth*, a substantial resource guide containing scientific environmental data, action guides and declarations from religious bodies in response to contemporary environmental deterioration. The booklet also includes selected scriptures, prayers and reflections from many of the world's religious traditions which suggest the historic wisdom of the traditions regarding the earth. (Many of these texts have been used throughout this *SourceBook* to shed light on how members of the religions may respond to environmental issues.)

· In his letter about the Environmental Sabbath/Earth Rest Day addressed to religious and spiritual leaders—and to all who can use *Only One Earth*—Dr. Noel J. Brown, Director of the United Nations Environment Programme explains:

The need for establishing a new spiritual and ethical base for human activities on Earth has never been greater —as the deterioration of our Planetary Home makes the protection of the human environment a new global imperative.

In his address to the world's scientists, politicians and spiritual leaders at the Global Forum last January [1990], the Secretary-General of the United Nations was to dramatize the urgency of our situation when he called for fundamental changes in societal attitudes. In his words, "For that change, we need to draw, not only upon the intellectual, but also the spiritual resources of the world community." He was also to call for a new loyalty, "an earth patriotism as strong as any national patriotism to relieve the distress of our ailing and exhausted Planet."

Clearly, this is a vital and auspicious moment for Humanity to *reassert our compassion, care and respect for our Earth.* Thanks to the perspective provided from space, we are now able to conceive the Planet as a whole—and ourselves as a global species, with a shared inheritance and a common responsibility. We need now, however, to infuse that vision with a genuine sense of affection, optimism and hope, and to this end, we invite our religious and spiritual leaders to join us in this quest, regardless of the community we represent.

In this connection, we *invite you to inspire anew our shared responsibility to care for the soil, water and air which sustain life,* and the many living creatures which manifest life in all its variety and glory, as you speak about our mutual home—our Earth.

About the United Nations Environment Programme

UNEP is the international organization given authority to monitor and control the global environment, responding to the problems that transcend national boundaries. It is the world leader in dissemination of global environmental information. Within the United Nations, UNEP oversees the environmental work being done by all other agencies to ensure that an ecological perspective is incorporated in development projects supported by the U.N.

In addition to the Environmental Sabbath/Earth Rest Day, UNEP played a major role in the Montreal Protocol on ozone depletion; the Rio Earth Summit (UNCED) and recent developments since Rio; the Global Environmental Monitoring System offering early warning alerts on immediate and potential dangers; INFOTERRA, a global computer network; and the annual *State of the Environment* report.

Further information is available from
United Nations Environment Programme
DC2-803, United Nations
New York, NY 10017 USA

"*All human societies are built on fragile ecological foundations. Without clean air, fresh water, productive soil and a sustaining web of life,* Homo sapiens *can neither survive nor prosper. In a few short decades we are eroding those foundations beyond repair. By the year 2000, if present trends continue, one third of the world's productive land will have eroded or turned to dust. One million species may have been driven to extinction, the sharpest setback to life on earth since our remotest ancestors first appeared on the planet. And the world's climate will almost certainly change, with enormous, but incalculable consequences. In each case, human activities will be to blame.*"

excerpted and adapted from the UNEP Profile in *Only One Earth* and other publications, by the Editor

Universal Prayers

These prayers and all of the prayers and reflections on the next seven pages from nine religions were originally published in *Only One Earth* by the United Nations Environment Programme in 1990. The Environmental Sabbath/Earth Rest Day is a program of the United Nations Environment Programme in conjunction with representatives of religious traditions (see previous page).

The Universal Prayers on this page are deliberately given "secular" language, making them useful either as they are for those who so choose, or modified for a particular congregation's use in a celebration of care and appreciation for the creation. In the prayers below, a reader repeats the bold, italic phrase beween responses from the congregation. –*Ed.*

A CALL TO PRAYER

We who have lost our sense and our senses—our touch, our smell, our vision of who we are; we who frantically force and press all things, without rest for body or spirit, hurting our earth and injuring ourselves: we call a halt.

We want to rest. We need to rest and allow the earth to rest. We need to reflect and to rediscover the mystery that lives in us, that is the ground of every unique expression of life, the source of the fascination that calls all things to communion.

We declare a Sabbath, a space of quiet: for simply being and letting be; for recovering the great, forgotten truths; for learning how to live again.

A PRAYER OF AWARENESS

Today we know of the energy that moves all things: the oneness of existence, the diversity and uniqueness of every moment of creation, every shape and form, the attraction, the allurement, the fascination that all things have for one another.

Humbled by our knowledge, chastened by surprising revelations, with awe and reverence we come before the mystery of life.

A PRAYER OF SORROW

Reader
We have forgotten who we are.

We have forgotten who we are.
We have alienated ourselves from the unfolding of the cosmos.
We have become estranged from the movements of the earth.
We have turned our backs on the cycles of life.

Reader

We have sought only our own security.
We have exploited simply for our own ends.
We have distorted our knowledge.
We have abused our power.

Reader

Now the land is barren,
And the waters are poisoned,
And the air is polluted.

Reader

Now the forests are dying,
And the creatures are disappearing,
And the humans are despairing.

Reader

We ask forgiveness.
We ask for the gift of remembering.
We ask for the strength to change.

Reader

Silence

A PRAYER OF HEALING

Reader
We join with the earth and with each other

To bring new life to the land,
To restore the waters,
To refresh the air.

Reader

To renew the forests,
To care for the plants,
To protect the creatures.

Reader

To celebrate the seas,
To rejoice the sunlight,
To sing the song of the stars.

Reader

To recall our destiny.
To renew our spirits.
To reinvigorate our bodies.

Reader

To create the human community.
To promote justice and peace.
To remember our children.

Leader:
We join together as many and diverse expressions of one loving mystery: for the healing of the earth and the renewal of all life.

Meditation

A PRAYER OF GRATITUDE

Reader
We rejoice in all life.

We live in all things.
All things live in us.

Reader

We live by the sun.
We move with the stars.

Reader

We eat from the earth.
We drink from the rain.
We breathe from the air.

Reader

We share with the creatures.
We have strength through their gifts.

Reader

We depend on the forests.
We have knowledge through their secrets.

Reader
We have the privilege of seeing and understanding.
We have the responsibility of caring.
We have the joy of celebrating.

Leader:
We are full of the grace of creation.

We are graceful.
We are grateful.
We rejoice in all life.

Buddhist Prayers

LOVING KINDNESS

May every creature abound in well-
  being and peace.
May every living being,
  weak or strong, the long and the small
  The short and the medium-sized,
  the mean and the great
May every living being,
  seen or unseen, those dwelling far off,
Those near by, those already born,
  those waiting to be born
May all attain inward peace.

Let no one deceive another
Let no one despise another in
  any situation
Let no one, from antipathy or hatred,
  wish evil to anyone at all.
Just as a mother, with her own life,
  protects her only son from hurt
So within yourself foster a limitless
  concern for every living creature.
Display a heart of boundless love
  for all the world
In all its height and depth and broad
  extent
Love unrestrained, without hate
  or enmity.
Then as you stand or walk, sit or lie,
  until overcome by drowsiness,
Devote your mind entirely to this,
  it is known as living here life divine.

THE RAIN CLOUD

It is like a great cloud rising above the world,
Covering all things everywhere—
A gracious cloud full of moisture; lightning-flames flash and dazzle
Voice of thunder vibrates afar, bringing joy and ease to all.
The sun's rays are veiled, and the earth is cooled;
The cloud lowers and spreads as if it might be caught and gathered;
Its rain everywhere equally descends on all sides,
Streaming and pouring unstinted, permeating the land.
On mountains, by rivers, in valleys,
In hidden recesses, there grow the plants, trees, and herbs;
Trees, both great and small, the shoots of the ripening grain,
Grape vine and sugar cane.
Fertilized are these by the rain and abundantly enriched;
The dry ground is soaked; herbs and trees flourish together.
From the one water which issued from that cloud,
Plants, trees, thickets, forests, according to need receive moisture.
All the various trees, lofty, medium, low, each according to its size,
Grows and develops roots, stalks, branches, leaves,
Blossoms and fruits in their brilliant colors;
Wherever the one rain reaches, all become fresh and glossy.
According as their bodies, forms, and natures are great and small,
So the enriching rain, though it is one and the same,
Yet makes each of them flourish.
In like manner also the Buddha appears here in the world
Like unto a great cloud universally covering all things;
And having appeared in the world, for the sake of living,
He discriminates and proclaims the truth in regard to all laws.
The Great Holy World—honored One among the gods and humans,
And among all living beings proclaims abroad this word:
"I am the *Tathagata**, the Most Honored among humans;
I appear in the world like this great cloud,
To pour enrichment on all parched living beings,
To free them from their misery to attain the joy of peace,
Joy of the present world and joy of *Nirvana* . . .
Everywhere impartially, without distinction of persons . . .
Ever to all beings I preach the Law equally; . . .
Equally I rain the Law—rain untiringly.

from the *Lotus "Sutra"*
*the "Thus-Gone" (*Tathagata*)

Christian Prayers

A CALL TO PRAYER

The earth is at the same time mother,
She is mother of all that is natural, mother of all that is human.
She is the mother of all, for contained in her are the seeds of all.
The earth of humankind contains all moistness,
all verdancy, all germinating power.
It is in so many ways fruitful.
All creation comes from it.
Yet it forms not only the basic raw material for mankind,
but also the substance of the incarnation of God's son.

HILDEGARD OF BINGEN

A PRAYER OF AWARENESS

God is the foundation for everything
This God undertakes, God gives.
Such that nothing that is necessary for life is lacking.
Now humankind needs a body that at all times honors and praises God.
This body is supported in every way through the earth.
Thus the earth glorifies the power of God.

HILDEGARD OF BINGEN

A REFLECTION ON OUR PRESENT PLIGHT

The high, the low, all of creation,
God gives to humankind to use.
If this privilege is misused,
God's Justice permits creation to punish humanity.

HILDEGARD OF BINGEN

A PRAYER OF GRATITUDE

Most High, all powerful, good Lord,
to you all praise, glory and honor
and all blessing;
to you alone, Most High, they belong
and no man is worthy of naming you.
Praised be you, my Lord,
with all your creatures,
especially My Lord Brother Sun,
who brings day, and by whom
you enlighten us;
he is beautiful, he shines with great
splendor;
of you, Most High, he is the symbol.

Praised be you, my Lord,
for Sister Moon and the Stars:
in the heavens you formed them,
clear, precious and beautiful.

Praised be you, my Lord,
for Brother Wind
and for the air and for the clouds,
for the azure calm and for all climes
by which you give life
to your creatures.

Praised be you, my Lord,
for Sister Water,
who is very useful and humble,
precious and chaste.

Praised be you, my Lord,
for Brother Fire,
by whom you enlighten the night:
he is beautiful and joyous,
indomitable and strong.

Praised be you; my Lord,
for Sister our Mother the Earth
who nourishes us and bears us,
and produces all kinds of fruits,
with the speckled flowers
and the herbs.

FRANCIS OF ASSISI,
Canticle of the Sun

Hindu Prayers

THE WATERS, WHO ARE GODDESSES

They who have the ocean as their eldest
flow out of the sea,
purifying themselves, never resting.

Indra, the bull with the thunderbolt,
opened a way for them;
let the waters,
who are goddesses,
help me here and now.

The waters of the sky or those that flow,
those that are dug out
or those that arise by themselves,
those pure and clear waters
that seek the ocean as their goal—
let the waters,
who are goddesses,
help me here and now.

Those in whose midst King Varuna
moves, looking down upon the truth
and falsehood of people,
those pure and clear waters
that drip honey—
let the waters,
who are goddesses,
help me here and now.

Those among whom King Varuna,
and Soma, and all the gods drink
in ecstasy the exhilarating nourishment,
those into whom
Agni Of-all-men entered—
let the waters,
who are goddesses,
help me here and now.

from the RIG VEDA

THE WATERS OF LIFE

Waters, you are the ones who bring us the life force.

Help us to find nourishment so that we may look upon great joy.

Let us share in the most delicious sap that you have,
as if you were loving mothers.

Let us go straight to the house of the one for whom
your waters give us life and give us birth.

For our well-being let the goddesses be an aid to us,
the water be for us to drink.
Let them cause well-being and health to flow over us.

Mistresses of all the things that are chosen,
ruler over all peoples,
the waters are the ones I beg for a cure.

Soma has told me that within the waters are all cures
and Agni who is salutary to all.

Waters, yield your cure as an armor for my body,
so that I may see the sun for a long time.

Waters, carry far away all of this that has gone bad in me
either what I have done in malicious deceit
or whatever lie I have sworn to.

I have sought the waters today;
we have joined with their sap.
O Agni full of moisture,
come and flood me with splendor.

A PRAYER FOR BLESSING

May the axe be far away from you;
May the fire be far away from you;
May there be rain without storm;
Lord of Trees, may you be blessed;
Lord of Trees, may I be blessed.

PRAYER FOR PEACE

Supreme Lord, Let there be peace in the sky
and in the atmosphere,
peace in the plant world and in the forests;
Let the cosmic powers be peaceful;
let Brahma be peaceful;
Let there be undiluted and fulfilling peace everywhere.

ATHARVA VEDA

Jewish Prayers

And God saw everything that He had made, and found it very good.

And He said: "This is a beautiful world that I have given you.
Take good care of it; do not ruin it."

It is said: Before the world was created,
the Holy One kept creating worlds and destroying them.
Finally He created this one, and was satisfied.
He said to Adam: "This is the last world I shall make.
I place it in your hands: hold it in trust."   *Gates of Prayer* . . . p. 655

Let the heaven rejoice, let the earth be glad.
Let the sea and all it contains roar in praise.   Psalm 96

Let the sea roar, and all its creatures; the world, and its inhabitants.
Let the rivers burst into applause,
let the mountains join in acclaim with joy.
The Lord is coming to sustain the earth.
He will sustain the earth with kindness,
its people with graciousness.   Psalm 98

How wonderful, O Lord, are the works of your hands!
The heavens declare Your glory,
the arch of sky displays Your handiwork.
The heavens declare the glory of God.
In Your love You have given us the power to behold the beauty of Your
world, robed all its splendor. The sun and the stars, the valleys and hills,
the rivers and lakes all disclose Your presence.
The earth reveals God's eternal presence.
The roaring breakers of the sea tell of Your awesome might;
the beasts of the field and the birds of the air bespeak Your wondrous will.
Life comes forth by God's creative will.
In Your goodness You have made us able to hear the music of the world. The
raging of the winds, the whisperings of trees in the wood, and the precious
voices of loved ones reveal to us that You are in our midst.
A divine voice sings through all creation.   *Gates of Prayer* . . . p.652

Environmental responsibility

The earth is Adonai's and the fullness thereof.   Psalm 24:1

God acquired possession of the world and apportioned it to humankind
but God always remains the Master of the world.   Rosh Hashanah 31a

All that [we] see—the heaven, the earth, and all that fills it—
all these things are the external garments of God.
                    Shneur Zalman of Liadi, Tanya, chapter 42

In the hour when the Holy One created the first human being,
God took the person before all the trees of the garden of Eden,
and said to the person:
"See my works, how fine and excellent they are!
Now all that I have created, for you have I created. Think upon this,
and do not corrupt and desolate my world; for if you corrupt it,
there is no one to set it right after you."   Ecclesiastes Rabbah 7:28

The land is for our use

And God said: "Behold, I have given
you every herb yielding seed, which is
upon the earth, and every tree in which
is the fruit of a tree yielding seed—to
you shall it be for food."
                    Genesis 1:29

God blessed them; and God said to
them: "Be fruitful and multiply, and re-
plenish the earth, and subdue it; and
have dominion over the fish of the sea,
and over the fowl of the air, and over
every living thing that moves on the
earth."   Genesis 1:28

Reforestation— reclaiming the land

One day he, Honi the circle-drawer,
was journeying on the road and he saw
a man planting a carob tree; he asked
him, "How long does it take [for this
tree] to bear fruit?" The man replied,
"70 years." He then further asked him,
"Are you certain that you will live
another 70 years?" The man replied,
"I found [ready grown] carob trees in
the world; as my ancestors planted
these for me, so I too plant these for my
children."

                    Taanit 23a,
                    Rabbi Yochanan Ben Zakai

Environmental land usage

Six years shall you sow your field, and
six years shall you prune your vineyard,
and gather in the produce thereof. But
the seventh year shall be a Sabbath of
solemn rest, Sabbath unto the Lord, you
shall neither sow your field, nor prune
your vineyard."

                    Leviticus 25:3-4

The Holy One blessed be God said to
the children of Israel: "Sow for six years
and leave the land at rest for the seventh year, so that you may know the
land is Mine!"   Sanhedrin 39a

Moslem Reflections

*F*ollowing is a Moslem prayer for rain, called "Prayer for *Istesquaa*," . . . begging God for rain.

O God! The Creator of everything!
You have said that water is
the source of all life!
  When we have needs,
You are the Giver
  When we are sick,
You give us health.
  When we have no food,
You provide us with your bounty.

And so God, presently,
we have no rain. We need water.
Our water resources are dry;
we need you to help
us with rain—
rain for our field, our orchards
and our animals.
We need water for ablution
and general cleanliness
to prepare for worshiping You,
O Lord.

Our confidence, O Lord,
is in you and your unlimited mercy
and compassion.

Please, Merciful God,
provide us with rain.

provided by
Dr. Mohammed Mehdi, Secretary General,
National Council on Islamic Affairs

*U*nder Islam, everything is created by Allah (God) and therefore everything is sacred, useful and has its place in the general scheme of things and in the interest of man.

The protection of God's creation is therefore the duty of the Muslim and God will reward all who protect his creation.

God has created the skies, the earth, the sun and the moon, the rivers and the mountains. God has created the animals and vegetables, the birds, the fish and all that exists between the earth and sky!

The totality of the environment is God's creation and man's responsibility to protect.

The Holy *Qur'an* declares, "We have created everything from water." Hence the importance of water resources for human life. The survival of human life also depends upon agriculture and animal husbandry. Hence the Muslim obligation to be kind to animals and grateful for the availability of the rivers and the rain. Indeed, there are special prayers for rain in which Muslims express appreciation for God's bounty and beg Him to continue it by providing the faithful with rain.

The relationship of the Muslim to God is a direct and simple one. A Muslim calls upon his Creator for everything! When he is sick, he prays for God to provide him with health. If he is poor and hungry, he begs God for food and support, and so on. Hence, the permanent link between man and the environment through God and prayers to the Creator.

Islam is a religion which started in the deserts of Arabia with a universal message. Its concern for the environment is a universal concern, cutting across national, religious and geographical barriers. Its major commandments are directed, not to the Muslims, but to the human race. Hence its call upon "people" (not the Arabs nor the Muslims) to conserve the natural resources which are God's gift to mankind.

There are many verses from the Holy *Qur'an* and *Hadith* (statements by the Prophet) urging people to be kind to the land, to the rivers, to the air and not to abuse the fertile valleys. Kindness to "those who cannot speak" (animals) is urged by the Prophet again and again.

In his letter of recommendation, the First Muslim Khalifa, Abu-Baker, ordered his troops, "Do not cut down a tree, do not abuse a river, do not harm animals and be always kind and humane to God's creation, even to your enemies."

Muslim commitment to the sanctity of life is most pronounced during the *Hajj* to Mecca where the pilgrims are not permitted even to kill an insect.

Under Islam, the individual is responsible for the "good" and for the "bad." *En Ahsantutn, Ahsantum le- Anfosekum wa en Asaatumfa-lahaa,* (If you do good things, you do that for yourselves, and if you do wrong things, that is for you, too!) Hence, the responsibility for the protection of the environment is an individual responsibility in the first place and a "collective" obligation of the society secondarily.

Native American Prayers

A CALL TO PRAYER

O Great Spirit,
Whose breath gives life to the world
  and whose voice is heard in the soft breeze
We need your strength and wisdom
May we walk in beauty.

May our eyes
  ever behold the red and purple sunset
Make us wise so that we may understand
  what you have taught us
Help us learn the lessons you have hidden
  in every leaf and rock
Make us always ready to come to you
  with clean hands and straight eyes
So when life fades, as the fading sunset
  our spirits may come to you without shame.

A PRAYER OF AWARENESS

Now Talking God
With your feet I walk
I walk with your limbs
I carry forth your body
For me your mind thinks
Your voice speaks for me
Beauty is before me
Above and below me hovers the beautiful
I am surrounded by it
I am immersed in it
In my youth I am aware of it
And in old age I shall walk quietly
The beautiful trail.

Bahá'í Reflections

With respect to environment . . .
We cannot segregate the human heart from the environment outside us and say that once one of these is reformed everything will be improved. Man is organic with the world. His inner life molds the environment and is itself also deeply affected by it. The one acts upon the other and every abiding change in the life of man is the result of these mutual reactions.

Nature is God's will and is its expression in and through the contingent world. It is a dispensation of Providence ordained by the Ordainer, the All-Wise. The earth is but one country, and mankind its citizens.

Look not upon the creatures of God except with the eye of kindliness and of mercy, for Our loving providence hath pervaded all created things, and Our grace encompassed the earth and the heavens.

. . . it is not only their fellow human beings that the beloved of God must treat with mercy and compassion, rather must they show forth the utmost loving-kindness to every living creature. . . . The feelings are one and the same, whether ye inflict pain on man or on beast.

Blessed is the spot, and the house, and the place, and the city, and the heart, and the mountain, and the refuge, and the cave, and the valley, and the land, and the sea, and the island, and the meadow where mention of God hath been made, and His praise glorified.

from Bahá'í Sacred Writings

Taoist Reflections

Trees and animals,
humans and insects,
flowers and birds:
these are active images
of the subtle energies
that flow from the stars
throughout the universe.
Meeting and combining with each other
and the elements of the Earth,
they give rise to all living things.
The superior person understands this,
and understands that her own energies
play a part in it.
Understanding these things,
she respects the Earth as her mother,
the heavens as her father,
and all living things as her brothers
and sisters.

Those who want to know the truth of
the universe should practice . . .
reverence for all life;
this manifests as unconditional love
and respect for oneself
and all other beings.

LAO TZU
(translated by Brian Walker)

Sikh Reflections

Guru Nanak, the Founder of Sikhism, very aptly said:

"Air is the Vital Force, Water the Progenitor
The Vast Earth the Mother of All:
Day and Night are nurses,
fondling all creation in their lap."

Nature is not only source of life, beauty and power,
but it is also an inspiration of strength in formulation of our character.

Man is composed of Five Elements.
According to Sikh Scripture, *Guru Granth Sahib*,
these five elements of nature teach us valuable lessons:

Earth teaches us	: Patience, Love
Air	: Mobility, Liberty
Fire	: Warmth, Courage
Sky	: Equality, Broadmindedness
Water	: Purity, Cleanliness

We have to imbibe these fine traits of Nature
in our personality for fuller, happier, and nobler lives.

For the sake of posterity, those countless generations
of unborn children to come, let us save this Earth.
Let us not misuse our privileges.
Please don't let the song of birds die.
Don't let the water babies perish.
Don't let magnificent animals become extinct.
Above all, don't let human beings die of starvation
and man made disasters.

Live and Let Live

The World House

As the Reverend Dr. Martin Luther King, Jr. once said, we live in a "world house." The interfaith community is in a unique position to offer guidance on how we can live together in peace and respect for the diversity of our world house. NCCJ presents the thoughts and prayers of 12 different religious communities in metropolitan Chicago—each presented in their own way and in their own words.

AMERICAN INDIAN

*T*he sacred hoop of any nation is but one of many that together make the great circle of creation. In the center grows a mighty flowering tree of life sheltering all the children of one mother and one father. All life is holy.

People native to this land have long lived by the wisdom of the circle, aware that we are part of the Earth and it is part of us. To harm this Earth, precious to God—to upset the balance of the circle—is to heap contempt on its Creator. Therefore, with all our heart and mind, we must restore the balance of the Earth for our grandchildren to the seventh generation.

> compiled from the wisdom of Black Elk, Chief Seattle
> and many other American Indian spiritual leaders
> **Anawim Center, Native American Indians of Chicago**

BAHÁ'Í

*T*he primary question to be resolved is how the present world, with its entrenched pattern of conflict, can change to a world in which harmony and cooperation will prevail.

World order can be founded only on an unshakable consciousness of the oneness of mankind, a spiritual truth which all the human sciences confirm.

Acceptance of the oneness of mankind is the first fundamental prerequisite for reorganization and administration of the world as one country, the home of humankind. Universal acceptance of this spiritual principle is essential to any successful attempt to establish world peace. It should therefore be universally proclaimed, taught in schools and constantly asserted in every nation as preparation for the organic change in the structure of society which it implies.

> **The Promise of World Peace,**
> **a statement by the Universal House of Justice**
> **to the Peoples of the World, October 1985**
> **Spiritual Assembly of Bahá'ís of Chicago**

JUDAISM

*I*n Jewish tradition, there are many deeply held values that govern a nation's conduct in war, so that the subsequent peace may be based on dignity and justice. We are told:

"Rejoice not when your enemy falls and be not glad in your heart when (he) stumbles." (Pirke Avot)

"Who is the greatest hero? The one who changes an enemy into a friend." (Avot D' Rabbi Natan)

National Conference of Christians and Jews

THE WORLD HOUSE

*D*uring the Persian Gulf War in 1991, the interfaith community of metropolitan Chicago recognized that, regardless of perspective, one day the war would end and that everyone had to live peacefully with their neighbors. The interfaith community recognized that it was in a unique position to offer guidance to the community at large on how to live together in peace and with respect when hostilities had ceased. The following texts were published in a pamphlet by the National Conference of Christians and Jews in cooperation with representatives from 12 religious traditions in order to help people from every community begin to think in terms of those values they wished to live by once the war was over.

> NCCJ; used with permission

Among its various programs, NCCJ also publishes a full-color Interfaith Calendar to promote a greater understanding of the rich heritage of religious diversity in America.

For more information, contact:
National Conference of Christians and Jews
Chicago and Northern Illinois Region
360 N. Michigan Ave., Suite 1009
Chicago, IL USA
TEL   (312) 236-9272
FAX   (312) 236-0029

"How great is peace? Even in time of war, peace must be sought." (Sifre Deuteronomy)

"When besieging a city to capture it, one may not surround it on all four sides . . . (so that) anyone who wishes to flee may escape." (Mishneh Torah)

"Peace without truth is false." (Mendel of Kotzk)

Chicago Board of Rabbis

CATHOLIC CHRISTIANITY

"But I say to you that listen, Love your enemies." (Luke 6:27) Because Jesus' command to love our neighbor is universal, we hold that the life of each person on this globe is sacred.

Communion with God, sharing God's life, involves a mutual bonding with all on this globe. Jesus taught us to love God and one another and that the concept of neighbor is without limit. We know that we are called to be members of a new covenant of love. We have to move from our devotion to independence, through an understanding of interdependence, to a commitment to human solidarity. That challenge must find its realization in the kind of community we build among us. Love implies concern for all—especially the poor—and a continued search for those social and economic structures that permit everyone to share in a community that is a part of a redeemed creation (Rom 8:31–33).

Economic Justice for All (#326 and #365)
National Conference of Bishops November 18, 1986
Catholic Archdiocese of Chicago

ANGLICAN CHRISTIANITY

O God, you made us in your own image and redeemed us through Jesus your Son: Look with compassion on the whole human family; take away the arrogance and hatred which infect our hearts; break down the walls that separate us; unite us in bonds of love; and work through our struggle and confusion to accomplish your purposes on earth; that, in your good time, all nations and races may serve you in harmony around your heavenly throne; through Jesus Christ our Lord. Amen.

Episcopal Diocese of Chicago

ZOROASTRIANISM

In this worldly abode of ours,
May communication drive away mis-communication
May peace drive away anarchy
May generosity drive away selfishness
May benevolence drive away hostility
May compassionate words prevail over false protestations
May truth prevail over falsehood.

From the *Dahm Afringan* prayer
Federation of Zoroastrian Associations of North America

BUDDHISM

We are what we think.
All that we are is arises with our thoughts.
With our thoughts we make the world. . .

"Look how he abused me and beat me,
How he threw me down and robbed me."
Live with such thoughts and you live in hate.
"Look how he abused me and beat me,
How he threw me down and robbed me."
Abandon such thoughts, and live in love.
In this world
Hate never yet dispelled hate.
This the law,
Ancient and inexhaustible.

The Dhammapada
Buddhist Council of the Midwest

ISLAM

Is he who knoweth that what is revealed unto thee from thy Lord is the truth like him who is blind? But only men of understanding heed;

Such as keep the pact of Allah, and break not the covenant;

Such as unite that which Allah hath commanded should be joined (taking care of their mutual duties), and fear their Lord, and dread a woeful reckoning;

Such as persevere in seeking their Lord's countenance and are regular in prayer and spend of that which We bestow upon them secretly and openly, and overcome evil with good. Theirs will be the sequel of the (heavenly) Home,

Gardens of Eden which they enter, along with all who do right of their fathers and their helpmates and their seed. The angels enter unto them from every gate,

(Saying): Peace be unto you because ye persevered. Ah, passing sweet will be the sequel of the (heavenly) Home.

And those who break the covenant of Allah after ratifying it, and sever that which Allah hath commanded should be joined, and make mischief in the earth: theirs is the curse and theirs the ill abode.

Allah enlargeth livelihood for whom He will, straiteneth (it for whom He will); and they rejoice in the life of the world, whereas the life of the world is but brief comfort as compared with the Hereafter.

The Qur'an (13:19–26)
Muslim Community Centers of Chicago

HINDUISM

O Lord, lead us from the unreal to the Real,
Lead us from darkness to Light,
And lead us from death to Immortality.

May all be free from dangers,
May all realize what is good,
May all be actuated by noble thoughts,
May all rejoice everywhere.

May all be happy,
May all be free from disease,
May all realize what is good,
May none be subject to misery.

May the wicked become virtuous,
May the virtuous attain tranquility,
May the tranquil be free from bonds,
May the freed make others free.

May good betide all people,
May the sovereign righteously rule the earth,
May all beings ever attain what is good,
May the worlds be prosperous and happy.

May the clouds pour rain in time,
May the earth be blessed with crops,
May all countries be freed from calamity,
May holy men live without fear.

May the Lord, the destroyer of sins,
The presiding Deity of all sacred works, be satisfied.
For, He being pleased, the whole universe becomes
   pleased,
He being satisfied, the whole universe feels satisfied.

Swami Yatiswsarananda, Universal Prayers
Vivekananda Vedanta Society

ORTHODOX CHRISTIANITY

*L*ord our God it is truly just and right to
the majesty of Your holiness to praise You and to offer
to You our spiritual worship. We entreat You Lord to,
   Remember us and grant us profound and lasting peace.
Speak to our hearts good things concerning all people, so
that through the faithful conduct of our lives we may live
together peacefully and serenely. As Your children, may
we come to understand that we are all brothers and sisters
to one another, created in Your Image and Likeness. We
call upon You, the God of Peace, to enlighten us to treat
all people with the very same dignity, freedom and
respect which You will for all humans to enjoy; for You
have revealed to us that dignity is the essence of life itself
and from it alone do we obtain the right to call ourselves
Your children.
   Remember us, O Lord and all Your people. Pour out
Your rich mercy upon us. Be all things to all, You, who

know each person. Receive us all into Your kingdom.
Declare us to be sons and daughters of the light and of the
day. Grant us Your peace and love, Lord our God, for
You have given all things to us. Amen.

Greek Orthodox Diocese of Chicago

PROTESTANT CHRISTIANITY

O Thou whose love embraces every child of
the world, forgive our easy labels and simple answers.
As Thou hast created every living organism in
complexity and beauty, give us grace to see each other
as people with many needs and hopes and dreams. In
some way touch us with the spirit of Jesus, whose love
embraced everyone and whose sympathy knew no
bounds.
   In times of stress and disappointment, through every
dark valley and every moment of limited vision, be Thou
our stay. And when we come through those moments,
stop us, O God, that we may remember on whose grace
we have depended, and we may give Thee the thanks and
praise.
   This prayer and all prayers we are able to make because
Thou hast first put the spark of divinity within us. Amen.

Church Federation of Greater Chicago

SIKHISM

*S*ays Nanak:

There are many dogmas, there are many systems,
There are many spiritual revelations,
Many bonds fetter the self (mind):
But Release is attained through God's Grace;
Truth is above all these,
But even higher is life lived in Truth.
All God's creatures are noble,
None are base.
One Potter has fashioned all the pots,
One Light pervades all Creation.
Truth is revealed through Grace,
And no one can resist Grace.

Siri Rag, Ashtpadiyan, p.62

*A*dds Tegh Bahadur:

Oh saints (seekers of Truth), real peace is achieved
through God,
The virtue of studying the scriptures,
Lies in contemplating the Name.

Gauri, p.220

*W*e all pray for peace in the world, through
peace of mind.

PART 4

Looking Toward the 21st Century

A. New Voices Are Being Heard

B. Warnings, Declarations, Visions and Strategies

C. The Next Generations

D. What Can I Do?
Personal Ethics and Responses

*"There is a hue and cry for human rights—
human rights, they said, for all people.
And the indigenous people said:
What of the rights of the natural world?
Where is the seat for the buffalo or the eagle?
Who is representing them here in this forum?
Who is speaking for the waters of the earth?
Who is speaking for the trees and the forests?
Who is speaking for the fish—for the whales—
for the beavers—for our children?
We said: Given this opportunity to speak in this international forum,
then it is our duty to say that we must stand for these people,
and the natural world and its rights;
and also for the generations to come."*

CHIEF OREN LYONS,
of the Onondaga Nation and the Iroquois Confederacy,
in his account of speaking to the United Nations in Geneva

"Our world is in travail. It takes no special sensitivity to realize how pervasive is the stress to which the fabric of our contemporary lives is subjected. Over and over again, violence tears apart what, often, it has taken centuries to fashion.

And yet violence is not the substance, it is the symptom. Something new is waiting to be born. We are experiencing the birth pangs of a new age, of a new hope. We are present at that sacred moment when new life is about to emerge from the womb of the past. What struggles to arise out of the past might become our shared future of mutual hearing and understanding, of mutual openness, of unprecedented willingness to acknowledge and accept others in all their differentness. The questions which address themselves to each of us are: Will we recognize the mystery of this possibility? Will we be open to its opportunities: Are we willing to help it be pulled into the light of tomorrow? Will we turn away preoccupied or cynical, or will we step forward to assist? These are not merely questions. They are the agenda of tomorrow, they are the exciting, irresistible invitation to each of us to abandon prejudgement and stubborn refusals to deeply hear one another. They are the program and the means to make that leap of faith with each other which will move humanity and our earth into the new era of reconciliation and hope."

RABBI HERMAN SCHAALMAN

Indigenous Peoples

Before the community of religions can look with wisdom toward the future, we must recognize the mistakes of the past and present. Among those mistakes has been a general disregard by the strong for those with less power, softer voices, low-tech weapons, or poor defenses. We have labeled them *other*—*other* races, classes, religions, sexes, species, ages—and often disregarded their rights and needs.

The earth itself has had no voice during the centuries of exploitation. Now, however, the *people of the land,* as many indigenous peoples refer to themselves, are speaking out, for themselves and for the earth.

Others who have been dispossessed —of land, of power, of a voice, of a future, or of an intrinsically wholistic value—are also being heard. They have much to say and to teach as we reconsider our path into the 21st century. *–Ed.*

CENSUS OF INDIGENOUS PEOPLES

According to the *Gaia Atlas of First Peoples,* 250 million or more indigenous people (four percent of the global population) live in more than 70 countries. Adding the distinct indigenous peoples of Africa (not counted in *The Gaia Atlas* because they don't fall within the definitions of that book) the census can be doubled.

"*In the long hundred years since the white man came, I have seen my freedom disappear like the salmon going mysteriously out to sea. The white man's strange customs which I could not understand, pressed down on me until I could no longer breathe. And when I fought to protect my land and home, I was called a 'savage.' When I neither understood nor welcomed the white man's way of life, I was called lazy. When I tried to lead my people, I was stripped of my authority.*"

CHIEF DAN GEORGE, Vancouver

"*In many ways, the contemporary state of indigenous peoples mirrors the future of us all if we continue to treat the earth and its peoples as we have treated them.*"

JULIAN BURGER

For the next several pages, extensive excerpts have been used from *The Gaia Atlas of First Peoples: A Future for the Indigenous World,* by Julian Burger with campaigning groups and native peoples worldwide.

*T*his book [*The Gaia Atlas*] is written in the belief that individuals can contribute to greater justice for indigenous peoples. Part, although not all, of the blame for the destruction of indigenous communities can be laid at the door of the rich. Governments, banks and companies have often pursued policies and backed regimes that are unfavorable to indigenous peoples, mainly to supply market demand. It is the consumer's hands on the chain saw. But ordinary people are not powerless. We may each have a small voice, but when harmonized with others, we can make powerful institutions listen.

The Gaia Atlas of First Peoples is the product of a collaboration of many different individuals and groups . . . . An overriding objective has been to reflect faithfully the concerns of first peoples—perhaps an impossible task given the range of their different experiences. At all stages—planning, writing and editing—native peoples have been closely involved.

from the *Author's Note* by Julian Burger, p.10.

The First Peoples

Facing threats to their survival

*N*othing has been so destructive to indigenous peoples as what we call progress. Mines, dams, roads, colonization schemes, plantations, cattle ranches and other expressions of "economic development" have forced indigenous peoples from lands they have occupied for centuries and severely damaged local environments. Deforestation, desertification and degradation of fragile, marginal lands first affect indigenous peoples, the traditional inhabitants. (Burger, p.75)

In Australia, a country designated by the white pioneers as *terra nullius* (or, uninhabited), there were some 500 distinct peoples with different languages and well-defined territories. A century later, the population had been reduced to one-fifth.

The colonizers came with a sword in one hand and a Bible in the other, "To bring light to those in darkness, and also to get rich," as the soldier-chronicler Bernal Diaz del Castillo put it. Impervious to the highly developed spiritual awareness of the people, they sought to convert them— often on pain of death—to an alien religion. (Burger, p.76)

When forest is cleared for settlement, agriculture, grazing, mining, dams, logging, or to supply fuel, there are three interrelated repercussions. Indigenous peoples lose their land and their role as forest managers; the land is over-exploited and given little chance to recover; and uncontrolled forest fires release carbon dioxide, causing the "greenhouse effect" and adding to climate problems. (Burger, p.90)

Attitudes Of The First People

According to indigenous law, humankind can never be more than a trustee of the land, with a collective responsibility to preserve it. The predominant Western world view is that nature must be studied, dissected, and mastered, and progress measured by the ability to extract secrets and wealth from the Earth. The First World has dominated the Earth to enrich itself in many cases. First peoples do not consider the land as merely an economic resource. Their ancestral lands are literally the source of life, and their distinct ways of life are developed and defined in relationship to the environment around them. First peoples are people of the land. . . . all first people know the extent of their lands, and they know how the land, water, and other resources need to be shared. They understand only too well that to harm the land is to destroy ourselves, since we are all part of the same organism. They sense, too, that the Earth will survive long after human beings. (Burger, p.23)

In many parts of the world indigenous societies classify soils, climate, plant and animal species and recognize their special characteristics. . . . The Hanunoo people of the Philippines, for example, distinguish 1,600 plant species in their forest, 400 more than scientists working in the same area. . . Nearly 75 percent of 121 plant-derived prescription drugs used worldwide were discovered following leads from indigenous medicine. Globally, indigenous peoples use 3,000 different species of plants to control fertility alone. The Kallaywayas, wandering healers of Bolivia, make use of 600 medicinal herbs; traditional healers in Southeast Asia may employ as many as 6,500 plants for drugs. . . . (Burger, p.32)

Militarization

Most of our contemporary conflicts directly affect indigenous peoples. The superpowers see their homelands as "empty territory"— testing grounds for nuclear and chemical weapons. Newly independent states wanting to establish their borders and develop their economies incorporate tribal territories as part of their nation-building efforts. Sometimes indigenous territories have been invaded and occupied for strategic and economic reasons. And when conflicts break out the superpowers are often involved.

Of the 120 or more wars in the world today, 72 percent are conflicts between central state governments and a distinct nation of peoples living within its borders. (Burger, p.108)

COSTS FROM MILITARIZATION

- Almost all nuclear tests have taken place on indigenous lands and waters. . . The radiation released during nuclear testing damages the environment, contaminates the staple foods of indigenous people, and increases the risk [and incidence] of birth defects, miscarriages, sterility, cancer and other diseases.
- The USA, Britain and France have exploded over 215 nuclear bombs in the South Pacific. . . After the atomic explosions on the Polynesian island of Bikini in the 1950s, 70 out of 1,093 people died of cancer in three years.

"We understand that many of these racialist attitudes are subconscious and not premeditated, but nevertheless they reflect how deeply dominant ideology has penetrated society."

MAPUCHE INDIAN

"We do not wish to destroy your religion, or take it from you. We only want to enjoy our own."

RED JACKET, Iroquois

"The white man's advanced technological capacity has occurred as a result of his lack of regard for the spiritual path and for the way of all living things. The white man's desire for material possessions and power has blinded him to the pain he has caused Mother Earth by his quest for what he calls natural resources."

THOMAS BANYACYA,
Hopi village leader

"Let me ask you this— why are there only eight inches of top-soil left in America, when there once were some 18 inches at the time of the Declaration of Independence in 1776? Where goes our sacred earth?"

HOBART KEITH,
Oglala Sioux

"At first I thought I was fighting to save rubber trees, then I thought I was fighting to save the Amazon rain forest. Now I realize I am fighting for humanity."

CHICO MENDEZ

"I am trying to save the knowledge that the forests and this planet are alive, to give it back to you who have lost the understanding."

PAULINHO PAIAKAN,
a leader of the Kayapo of Brazil

"We define our rights in terms of self-determination. We are not looking to dismember your States and you know it. But we do insist on the right to control our territory, our resources, the organization of our societies, our own decision-making institutions, and the maintenance of our own cultures and ways of life."

GEOFF CLARKE,
National Coalition of Aboriginal
Organizations of Australia,
addressing ILO, 1988

"Our nations have a natural and rightful place within the family of Nations of the World. Our political, legal, social and economic systems developed in accordance with the laws of the creator since time immemorial and continue to this day."

Union of British Columbia Chiefs
to UN Working Group
on Indigenous Populations, 1987

"We hereby demand yet again recognition of our humanity and our land rights. Hear us, White Australia, we are the spirit of the land. Our name is humanity. Our aims are self-determination and justice. We will not be defeated. We are our history, we are our culture, we are our land. We are now."

Declaration of the People of
Musgrave Park, Australia, 1982

GLOBAL VOICES OF INDIGINOUS PEOPLES

"We are on the one hand the most oppressed people on the globe. On the other hand, we are the hope for the future of the planet. The peoples that surround us now are beginning to experience in the 20th century that there are limitations to the kinds of economic organization that define their societies."

JOHN MOHAWK,
Haudenosaunee writer

- Global military expenditure equals the total debt of the developing countries.
- Since the military annexation of Tibet, a Buddhist state with a central belief in nonviolence, by China, there are now well over 100,000 Tibetan refugees.
- China gives more military support to other nations than the USA or [former] USSR. . . Tibet, bordering India, is a key part of China's defenses, and China now keeps one-quarter of its nuclear force in the area.
- Over one million people have been displaced because of violence in Guatemala.
- There are well over 14 million international refugees, many of them displaced indigenous people.

These are some of the costs identified by Burger on pp.110–112

Alternative Visions and the Future

"Now we shall not rest until we have regained our rightful place.
We shall tell our young people what we know.
We shall send them to the corners of the earth to learn more.
They shall lead us."

Declaration of the Five County Cherokees

*I*ndigenous peoples are not passive victims. Nor have they ever been. In the past they resisted colonialism through negotiation, political protest, civil disobedience or force of arms. Sometimes they succeeded, sometimes they won partial guarantees of their territory, and sometimes they were overwhelmed by numbers and superior military technology. But the resistance has not stopped. Today's movement is part of this continuing process, and the struggle to survive as a people is as urgent as ever.

Today's indigenous peoples are adopting modern and creative political techniques—using the media, joining forces, and gaining support from the wider community. Recently, indigenous peoples have scored some important victories. (Burger, p.136)

There are over 1,000 indigenous organizations worldwide—most of them established in the last 20 years. The forces of change—political, social, economic and global have lent impetus to this new movement. . . . New international laws, too, offer a legal and moral framework for indigenous peoples. The right to self-determination is now enshrined in two covenants of the United Nations. And there are international laws on genocide and racial discrimination. (Burger, p.138)

Indigenous peoples are one of the most persistent voices of conscience, alerting humankind to the dangers of environmental destruction. And as the world searches for alternative strategies to deal with global problems, it is turning more and more to indigenous peoples. Much of their respect for nature, their methods of resource management, social organization, values and culture are finding echoes in the writing of scientists, philosophers, politicians, and thinkers. (Burger, p.166)

The Old Way Culture

In a despondent mood on a warm grey afternoon I asked Talk With Loons if the Old Way is forever gone from this land, if the few aged Healers and Grandmothers are the last vestiges of a way of life in its death-throes. I didn't know whether she'd answer directly, as her way was more often that of subtle Raven. For a few long minutes she became absorbed in reflection, during which she directed me with her eyes to observe the prairie about us. Then her gaze lost its focus as it seemed to flow into and dwell within the panorama before us, and she spoke:

'Is there still life in the Rocks,
does Father Sun still visit the dawn,
does the She-Swallow diving at our heads in defense of her young
on the limb above still Walk the Path?
The Old Way was not born with our species
and it will not be buried with our species.
As we sit here, the Grasses in the fullness of their bloom
whisper teachings that were secret to us yesterday.
As long as the Grass shall grow,
as long as the Rocks are here to speak,
the Old Way survives.' "

TAMARACK SONG

from *Gissis Mikana: The Sun Trail, a Guide to Spirit and Empowerment*, in manuscript.
The author is founder of the Teaching Drum Outdoor School.
She Who Talks with Loons was (most likely) Canadian Cree-Ojibway-Metis.

"The realization that other forms of life depend on trees and other green plants came late in the afternoon of my life. When I realized that the green form of life can live without us but that we cannot live without it, I committed myself to its preservation. I knew then that destroying it is suicidal. I knew then that plants, and the soil in which they grow, are more precious than silver and gold. But because of their abundance we take them for granted, we cut them, burn them, poison them and treat them with little respect. When their number reaches the minimal critical point, disasters follow, and we rush to prayers, grain silos, and international fora. We act as if we have discovered something completely unexpected."

WANGARAI MAATHAI, environmentalist from Kenya;
helped develop the Green Belt Movement founded by the National Council
of Women of Kenya to curb desertification.
In *Earth Conference One*, by Anuradha Vittachi, Shambhala Publications,
1989, pp.20–21

"We see it like this: it is as if we are all in a canoe traveling through time. If someone begins to make a fire in their part of the canoe, and another begins to pour water inside the canoe, or another begins to piss in the canoe, it will affect us all. And it is the responsibility of each person in the canoe to ensure that it is not destroyed. Our planet is like one big canoe traveling through time."

AILTON KRENAK,
Brazilian Union of Indian Nations (UNI)

"We need to start educating the West. . .teaching them some social alternatives which place priority on humankind—not profits, not political power, not bombs, but on humanity."

JOHN MOHAWK

"The concept of development in a developing country is not necessarily the same as that understood by one belonging to a 'developed' country. In a developing country the idea of development is closely linked with the wish for freedom—freedom to run one's own affairs the way one knows and believes, based on familiar traditions and ways of life. Freedom is in fact development, whether material progress and wealth are realized to the extent expected or not."

FRANCIS BUGOTU,
Solomon Islands

"It seems to us that from the earliest times, man's natural state was to be free as our grandfathers told us and we believe that freedom is inherent to life. We recognize this principle as the key to peace, respect for one another and the understanding of the natural law that prevails over all the universe. Adherence to this law is the only salvation of our future on the planet, Mother Earth."

CHIEF OREN LYONS,
Onondaga

Unless otherwise stated, all of the the above quotations from indigenous peoples are excerpted with permission from *The Gaia Atlas of First Peoples* by Julian Burger

Mestiza Legacy

The ships have left the harbour,
    the ghosts remain.
Whips, leather long ago,
    crafted now in silence
and absent looks.

The ships have left the harbour,
    the ghosts remain.
The child looks to her mother for strength;
    Mother has no time.

    Mother is cleaning
    always cleaning,

    with water,
    with spit,
    with blood;

cleaning,
always cleaning.

    This is a ceremony
    which is no ceremony;

    it is meaning without healing,
    it is death without joy,
    it is life without sorrow,
    it is dance without spirit;

    it is only clean.

The ships have left the harbour,
    the ghosts remain.

The child looks to her father for love,
    he is hunting, always hunting;

    with hands
    with feet

    his body
    exposed

to the elements.

The hunter tangled in the net he never saw,
wounded by the bullet
he cannot find,
choked by the tears
that will not come
he hunts.

There is no time for love;
a liquid fire dance burns.

This is a dance
which is no dance.

    It is meaning without healing,
    it is death without joy,
    it is life without sorrow,
    it is dance without spirit;

it is only ceremony.

The ships have left the harbour,
    the ghosts remain.

The child looks to herself for healing,
finds meaning in
dances, ceremonies.

She finds no life,
she finds no death.

She must go to the harbour
where the ghosts remain.

MAGDALENA GÓMEZ

Education for Justice and Awareness

"An enormous effort will be needed to create awareness in the marginalized masses, both in the developed and the underdeveloped countries, to prepare them to fight their way out of their sub-human situation, and also prepare them not simply to become as bourgeois and as selfish as those whom today they condemn.

An enormous effort is also needed to create awareness in those who are privileged, both in rich countries where there are poor groups which they allow to remain, and where there is neo-colonialism which they support whether they realize it or not, and in under-developed countries where the privileged create and profit from internal colonialism. It is very difficult to create awareness in the privileged. The teacher must have great virtue, be kind but truthful, gentle but firm.

But if the effort is not made the scandal will continue and the rich will go on getting richer and the poor poorer. The spiral of violence will get worse, injustice will increase, the resistance of the oppressed or the young in the name of the oppressed will continue and repression will become more and more brutal.

When will governments and the privileged understand that there can be no true peace until justice has been established?"

DOM HELDER CAMARA,
The Desert is Fertile, pp.47–48

The Encounter

YOU'RE A WHAT?
YOU DON'T LOOK IT.

Tears come by way of rage;
it is the only honest feeling I have left.

BUT YOU DON'T EVEN HAVE AN ACCENT,
AND YOU'RE SO INTELLIGENT.

A ceremony of guilt
rises through the land,
the white man loves me now.

SOME OF MY BEST FRIENDS
ARE PUERTO RICANS,
AND JESUS CHRIST, CAN THEY COOK!

I sell books and movies,
my presence moves fashions down the racks.

THEY ARE VERY RELIGIOUS,
EVEN THE ONES WHO DON'T GO TO CHURCH
HAVE THE HOLY MOTHER IN THEIR BEDROOMS,
BLEEDING CHRIST HEADS IN THEIR LIVING ROOMS,
ALTARS ON THEIR DRESSERS, T.V.'S AND TOILET
TANKS.

The blood of my ancestors runs
through the stems of the sugarcane;
that is the sweetness.
A drop of blood hides in each coffee bean;
that is the bitterness.
The blood of my ancestors is sold
as pieces of silver and stone,
     straw hats,
     t-shirts,
     pottery;
we are the rage,
the extra change,
the latest rising market;
we and the rest of the spics that spic spanish
will be 51% of the Catholic Church by the year 2000.*

We are the language of correctness;
we are the cocktails passed and sipped
among the righteous.

* in the U.S. –Ed.

We bond you with the affluent
who blow the coins of affirmative action
out of their noses
who sneer when we won't bend
to pick them up.

Speaking the praise of our nations
with forked tongues
bellies fatten with conceit,
a gluttony of correctness;
our daughters were not invited
to meet with your sons.

YOU DON'T LOOK IT.
YOU DON'T EVEN HAVE AN ACCENT.
YOU SPEAK SUCH GOOD ENGLISH.
DO YOU SPEAK THE REAL SPANISH?
YOU LOOK IRISH.
YOU LOOK JEWISH.
YOU LOOK ANGLO.
YOU LOOK LIKE MY COUSIN.
YOU LOOK LIKE MY MOTHER.
YOU LOOK LIKE AN AMERICAN.

A ceremony of guilt
burns and smokes across the land;
the true pipe has not been passed.
It is hidden, sacred, safe.

We cannot smoke;
our mouths are broken.
We are learning to speak again;
we know that one day you will hear.

There are still fish living in our waters,
there are still coconuts on our trees,
there are still babies in our wombs,
there is still salt in the sea,
there is still a smile on the moon,
there is still blood to flow.
And when it does
it will look just like yours.

But when I look at you,
you don't look it.

MAGDALENA GÓMEZ,
of Puerto Rican descent,
also gives dramatic readings of her poetry.

In a Dream I Had a Wolf Come to Me

In a dream I had a wolf come to me
and say how he's tired
of his followers being killed.
He said they need space
to run around and space
from humans, space

from pollution, space
from construction.

We are free spirits
and cannot be tamed
or kept in captivity.

The wolf gave
one giant howl to the full moon.
And left me to just a memory
of his black fur
and his great thought.

BRETT JOHNSON
7th grade

Who Lives in the "Global Village?"

Donella H. Meadows

If the world were a village of 1,000 people, it would include:

- 584 Asians
- 124 Africans
- 95 East and West Europeans
- 84 Latin Americans
- 55 Soviets (including for the moment Lithuanians, Latvians, Estonians and other national groups)
- 52 North Americans
- 6 Australians and New Zealanders

The people of the village have considerable difficulty in communicating:

- 165 people speak Mandarin
- 86 English
- 83 Hindi/Urdu
- 64 Spanish
- 58 Russian
- 37 Arabic

That list accounts for the mother tongues of only half the villagers. The other half speak (in descending order of frequency) Bengali, Portuguese, Indonesian, Japanese, German, French and 200 other languages.

In this village of 1,000 there are:

- 329 Christians (among them 187 Catholics, 84 Protestants, 31 Orthodox)
- 178 Moslems
- 167 "non-religious"
- 132 Hindus
- 60 Buddhists
- 45 atheists
- 3 Jews
- 86 all other religions
- One-third (330) of the 1,000 people in the world village are children and only 60 are over the age of 65. Half the children are immunized against preventable infectious diseases such as measles and polio.
- Just under half of the married women in the village have access to and use modern contraceptives.
- This year 28 babies will be born. Ten people will die, 3 of them for lack of food, 1 from cancer, 2 of the deaths are of babies born within the year. One person of the 1,000 is infected with the HIV virus; that person most likely has not yet developed a full- blown case of AIDS.
- With the 28 births and 10 deaths, the population of the village next year will be 1,018.
- In this 1,000-person community, 200 people receive 75 percent of the income; another 200 receive only 2 percent of the income.
- Only 70 people of the 1,000 own an automobile (although some of the 70 own more than one automobile).
- About one-third have access to clean, safe drinking water.
- Of the 670 adults in the village, half are illiterate.

The village has six acres of land per person, 6,000 acres in all, of which

- 700 acres are cropland
- 1,400 acres pasture
- 1,900 acres woodland
- 2,000 acres desert, tundra, pavement and other wasteland
- The woodland is declining rapidly; the wasteland is increasing. The other land categories are roughly stable.

The village allocates 83 percent of its fertilizer to 40 percent of its cropland—that owned by the richest and best-fed 270 people. Excess fertilizer running off this land causes pollution in lakes and wells. The remaining 60 percent of the land, with its 17 percent of the fertilizer, produces 28 percent of the food grains and feeds for 73 percent of the people. The average grain yield on that land is one-third the harvest achieved by the richer villagers.

In the village of 1,000 people, there are:

- 5 soldiers
- 7 teachers
- 1 doctor
- 3 refugees driven from home by war or drought

The village has a total budget each year, public and private, of over $3 million — $3,000 per person if it is distributed evenly (which, we have already seen, it isn't).

Of the total $3 million:

- $181,000 goes to weapons and warfare
- $159,000 for education
- $132,000 for health care

The village has buried beneath it enough explosive power in nuclear weapons to blow itself to smithereens many times over. These weapons are under the control of just 100 of the people. The other 900 people are watching them with deep anxiety, wondering whether they can learn to get along together; and if they do, whether they might set off the weapons anyway through inattention or technical bungling; and, if they ever decide to dismantle the weapons, where in the world village they would dispose of the radioactive materials of which the weapons are made.

DONELLA MEADOWS is the principal author of the controversial and influential (nine million in print, in 29 languages) The Limits to Growth (1972). Also based on a global computer model, that book's reassessment and sequel, Beyond the Limits, was published last year by Chelsea Green.

The preceding text is most of one side of a large poster published for the Earth Summit in Rio de Janeiro in June 1992. The other side bears a photo portrait of Gaia, in full color against black space. Value Earth Poster, 27"x 39", is $7 postpaid from Value Earth c/o David Copeland, 707 White Horse Pike, C-2, Absecon, NJ 08201. Used with permission.

Liberation Stories . . .

Bärbel von Wartenberg-Potter

From her position in the World Council of Churches, where she could observe women of numerous religions and races, Bärbel von Wartenberg-Potter gained special insights into their lives and the challenges they face. The essay which follows is Chapter 7 in *We Will Not Hang Our Harps Upon the Willows*. The author interprets one of the stories about Jesus in a way that demonstrates his special support for women. She also renders a loving and global portrait of women's struggles, and of their victories.

*D*uring my ecumenical wandering-year, women have shared many stories with me, and many images and circumstances of women's lives are in my mind's eye. I have retained them in my heart and in my head. Many of them, of course, I have been able to keep alive through the unerring eye of my camera. Now that all these pictures are as it were spread out before me, they combine to explain our women's story, brimful of fear, distortion, crying needs, brutality and failure. Yet at the same time there are stories and pictures of liberation, healing, acceptance, walking-tall, courage, determination, joy at being alive, the will to live, sisterhood. Something has happened there, giving rise to a movement, a movement in the direction of becoming free.

Because I read the Christian tradition with feminine eyes nowadays, I recognize in our own women's story (as many women have done before me) the biblical story of the healing of the crippled woman. And so I put all the pieces of my discovery of the women's world together until those many stories, alongside the biblical story, become one complete story, or picture, in which all of us feature somewhere, as those who are crippled, healing, made whole, giving thanks.

"One Sabbath Jesus was teaching in a synagogue and there was a woman there possessed by a spirit that had crippled her for 18 years. She was bent double and quite unable to stand up straight" (Luke 13:10–13).

*F*or centuries, we women have been possessed by a spirit that used to cripple us. Throughout history it fed itself on the privilege of male interpretation and culture. It thrived on life's harsh constraints humiliatingly inflicted especially on women. We ourselves also fed it with our internalized weakness and lack of self-worth, with the talents we decided not to make available, with the sacrifices made (though not of our own free will), with the magic cloak that makes our real self invisible. We did not count, we just faded into the dark of history, in childbirth, kitchens and sitting rooms. The evil spirit of female weakness caused us to be bowed down and bent double.

Continued on next page

In a Dream I Get a Peek

into the future. I look in terror
as I see the destruction.

The earth looks like
it's been burnt to a crisp

with hardly any vegetation
left to see. And there's no sign

of life whatsoever, and
no atmosphere at all.

With a large explosion,
it is the end of the world

as a line of fire goes blazing across
the whole earth.

JEFF MARCHAND
8th grade

Last Night a Frog Spirit Spoke to Me

Last night a frog spirit spoke to me.
He did not speak through words
but through thoughts. Nor did I speak.
He spoke only good—no bad,
for his soul would not let it.
Nor was he the leader of frogs
he was a messenger.

He spoke of the future and of the past
but none of the present
for he was a foreseer
He spoke of many dreams
only a few of which could
or would come true.

JOSH CLAYTON
7th grade

The Mysterious Flower

In a dream a bat
appeared in front of me
and told me that a single rose
is a real mysterious,
dark, loving flower,
and that we should teach
each other how to love
one another like
a bushel of roses.

ANDREA SWANSON
6th grade

For more information about the poems by children, see the article by Therese Becker in Part 4C

And so I see before my eyes:

- The women in Thailand; knee-deep in water, they are planting rice, bent double all their life to produce a little food, so that they may survive, they and the children, so that they need not flee to the big city.

- The mother in Soweto, bent double with grief over her child, shot down. She had brought it into the world hoping for better times.

- The women in industry at the assembly lines of the multinationals, their backs bent over the small components they have to assemble, and which give no meaning to their lives as women.

- The women behind the veils of a piously prescribed chastity, their eyes with shame averted in the face of curiosity. That is how it has always been and always will be, say the Mullahs. And those without any veils at all, on naked display in Manila, vulnerable and exposed before lustful stares—and not just stares. Money will buy anything.

- The mother with four children, looking for shelter in a sewer, as long as it does not rain. A few rags protect her, that is all; until the next rain.

- The woman refugee, with bag and baggage; the husband happens to be on the wrong side in the war. Her meager possessions—a cooking pot, a blanket—dwindling as she flees, and the unknown country will bring yet more humiliations.

- The woman giving birth on the pavement in an Indian city; worn out, her puny baby in a plastic bag in the midst of dust and stench. Who is going to bother about them?

- The water-carriers; from miles away they are hauling the precious liquid in jars on both shoulders—to do the laundry for strangers. Maybe there will be some left for their own washing.

- The desperate one, her hands covering her face. Her husband has gone, away to the city, leaving her without saying good-bye, without any promises. The burden of field work, looking after the animals, the children, now lies on her shoulders alone. He ran away out of desperation, leaving her alone with no way out.

- The seamstresses, row upon row of them; sewing luxurious dresses for a pittance. Hardly a word is spoken, though there would be so much to say; the whirring of the sewing machines is the only sound to be heard; so much sweat for the beauty of other women in Europe and America adorning themselves without giving it a second thought. Where are they, the sisters?

- The bearers of heavy baskets full of sand and stones; they are staggering under them day in and day out, for a few measly rupees, with the supervisor behind them. To satisfy his lust, he will not hesitate to pick one out—any quiet corner will do.

- The black maid in the white lady's house in Capetown, where she washes and cleans, makes children who are strangers laugh, bowed down with yearning for love and human closeness. Her own children back in the homeland are starving.

- The old woman, rummaging through stinking rubbish, looking for anything of value, anything edible, perhaps, that she might pull out of the muck. What is left of human worth? How can one retain one's self-respect—after that?

- The woman living in fear of her husband's beatings. He is unemployed and spends his last cent on drink at his local. When he comes home, he shouts, and beats her, and forces his daughter into bed with him. And she has to stand there and watch, biting her fingers till they bleed, sobbing: O my God!

- Those who are hiding; horror just outside the door, they are listening for the soldier's footsteps, for the plunging of bayonets into the front door, for steps and shouts. Hiding will be no good; defenseless they will be slashed open.

- The forgotten one, Camille Claudel, lover and source of inspiration of the great, master Rodin, the giant. Her sculptures are beautiful, majestic, playful, as good as his. Together they created many things over the years. He remained famous, she died in misery, her work long ignored, until recently.

That is how I see her in my mind's eye— with her fear of the future, of being alone, of being deserted, with the fear that drains the marrow from her bones, turning her into a mere shadow of herself. No God, no Goddess looks upon her. Woman, who are you, so bent double and unable to stand up straight?

"When Jesus saw her he called her and said:
'You are rid of your trouble.' Then he laid his hands on her."

Something flows across, a wave of love and power, recognition and becoming whole, healing for body and soul. Someone has seen her, at long last. Her eyes encounter a human face. She stands up straight, a daughter of God, put at the same level with her whole-maker, with the others!

Where God is at work through the hand of the sister, the brother, where we help each other, lovingly touch each other, desolateness fades away and we raise each other up.

Those scenes, too, I see before my eyes:

- In front of me there is a picture of Chinese women workers, putting arms around each other during the afternoon break. It gives strength for the next round of work and living.

- Unforgettable is for me the scene in a beauty salon of the psychiatric clinic in Havana: a disturbed patient with tousled head makes another one beautiful—painting her fingernails red, giving her a magnificent hair-do, so that she can carry herself with beauty into the darkness of insanity.

- Or the woman doctor in the bush, injection needle against the child's skin, fighting against fever, blindness; life-giving touch.

- Or the women's refuge in a West German city, where the telephones keep ringing and cries for help meet with a response: a bed, protection, safe accommodation and counseling for the next steps.

- A woman and a man—for a little while the outside world is forgotten, touching, only you and I, before life invades and separates again.

- Together the African women pound the yam roots to pulp, in a rhythmic one-after-another, full of community, in a common bond against hunger.

"Then at once she straightened up and began to praise God."

She stands up straight and needs someone whom she can thank. We women are today standing up straight and are beginning to live, to think, to act. The

Spirit that used to cripple us is withdrawing, has left us. The pictures I see before me also include these:

- The rebellious nuns of America, who will no longer allow themselves to be pushed around by regulations decreed from "the very top," because they have changed from being minors into thinking human beings who cannot go back again. They are acting on their own responsibility, in the light of their own faith.

- The peace women in England, taking root in the face of missile bases, their feminine determination making those in command unsure of themselves. They are standing upright.

- Women who break bread and share the cup with each other, though often still in secret. Since Jesus raised us up, who can possibly stop us? What is holiest of all, given into women's hands.

- The babushka sneaking into church, kneeling before the priest and secretly bringing her grandchild for baptism. The laughter of her gold teeth lighting up her pious face, she is the truly indestructible woman, who has been walking tall and upright for decades. One day the priests will at last bow down in homage to her and her faithfulness. She has time and can wait.

- The women of Kenya, planting trees against the desert and against hunger, united with each other as "women of the world for development and the environment." They just make simple beginnings—planting, tending future forests, the life of generations yet to come. However much their work makes them bend down, they are walking tall.

- The women who will no longer accept what male language, male symbols, a purely male religion would want to dictate to them. They are discovering the secret roots of female piety and bring to light a new language of the faith in a frightened church.

- Women working at conveyor belts are organizing themselves, walking out of the places that used to cripple them, speaking of their self-worth, their wages.

- Women against the bank, words against gold. Has anyone ever seen such a thing? How they are carrying placards, the women for South Africa, calling for a boycott, and depositing the golden calf outside the bank, where it belongs.

- Mothers in the Pacific: after nuclear tests they have given birth to jelly-fish babies, a formless bag, breathing. Now they are shouting it from the rooftops: you spoilers of our seas, our fish, our beaches, our children. Test your bombs in Paris, store them in Washington, bury your nuclear waste in Tokyo, if it is so safe!

- The African mother, her baby on her arm, addressing 3,000 church people from all over the world, speaks to the glory of God of giving birth, of blood and sweat, of life as a gift entrusted to us by God. She will send her daughter into the future walking tall.

- The old Indian woman, surrounded by women who had come from far to hear her share the age-old wisdom of her people, who are historically on the side of the losers. She addresses those listening to her as daughters and granddaughters, and her voice trembles, but she walks upright and praises Mother Earth.

- My own mother, an old woman, 76 years young, who once a week gets together with two of her daughters—also grey already—to teach them to play the guitar, in order that the human race will not forget how to sing . . .

*T*he history of all these women will have to be written afresh, by all of them together, arising out of their experience. It must become part of the history of our human race, in which future generations will be able to recognize the courage and faith of their fore-mothers and -fathers, and be guided by them so that they may go on living and working. Today we are looking for the point of contact in the story of the women. We will never again allow the biblical stories and all other liberation stories to he taken away from us.

Many women and men draw inspiration and strength from a song from the early days of the women's movement. The first to raise the demand for "Bread and Roses" were women workers, when they began to resist the imposition of harsh working conditions and through this simple formulation held on to a great goal for the human family. Again and again it is the simple things that are the goals for which to work, to struggle, to love, to pray, to argue and to sing. And where women become free, where they are being liberated from meaningless and crippling slavery, the whole of humanity will become more free.

from *We Will Not Hang Our Harps on the Willows,*
pp. 79–85

The Convergence of Science, Religion and Values

Erika Erdmann

Library research assistant for neuroscientist and Nobel laureate R. W. Sperry for nine years, and co-author, with David Stover, of Beyond a World Divided *(Shambhala, 1991), which examines the contributions of Roger Sperry to the bridging of the chasm between facts and values, between science and religion.*

The excerpts which follow are from a paper submitted by Erika Erdmann to the Parliament of the World's Religions and to the New Independent Commission on Global Governance, by invitation of Dr. Robert Muller, who assisted in creating this condensation. These new voices in neuro-science are doing pioneering work; others in physics and in the earth sciences are doing equally interesting work which takes seriously the perspective of wholism and the need for interdisciplinary study and integration. –Ed.

*H*umanity's attempts to progress toward a more humane future are blocked by two mutually exclusive world views. One segment of our population pursues facts at the expense of values, while another sector is preoccupied with values at the expense of facts. These two worlds, the world of science and the world of religion, are separated by a deep, harmful and unnecessary chasm which has lasted too long. . . .

If the founders of the world's religions were with us now, they would implore us to benefit from new facts, new knowledge, and new insights as well as from wisdom and teachings of the religions. They would ask us to break down the walls into which we imprisoned their words and to free the spirit from which they were spoken—the spirit of true concern for the fate of humanity in the universe.

This is indeed being attempted by the work of the Institute on Religion in an Age of Science (IRAS), in Chicago, which combines great thinkers from both science and religion.*

Reading the article "Bridging Science and Values: A Unifying View of Mind and Brain" by Roger W. Sperry was a revelation to me. Here a neuroscientist of world renown, a Nobel laureate, merged intuition, vision, values, poetic expression, scientific expertise and original thinking into a majestic whole.

As a neuroscientist, Sperry provoked his contemporaries through his conviction that "mind moves matter in the brain," not as an outside agent, but as an emergent with new and superior powers. Before he revolted against the neglect of consciousness in science, subjective experience had generally been considered by scientists as an ineffective byproduct of physico-chemical activity in neurons (with harmful results for a meaningful life). Sperry elevated its importance to that of a leading agent. Only ten years after he had written his pathbreaking papers on the subject in the late sixties, the entire field of behavioral science was turned around. Consciousness, previously considered a subject unsuitable for scientific attention, became a predominant target of research. . . .

That religion should adjust to science has been demanded by other pioneers. Sperry for his part demands that science must also be changed. Instead of concentrating on the smallest possible building blocks in nature alone, and recreating from them a meaningless and purposeless world, Sperry draws attention to the essential role that the concept of "emergence" plays in reality.

Emergence occurs whenever two or more entities in combination create a new entity with new laws and properties formerly nonexistent in the universe. Thus, when subatomic particles combine into atoms, when atoms combine into molecules, when molecules combine into more complex structures, each time new creations occur with formerly nonexistent effects on the world.

Sperry calls these new effects and their role in our world "downward causation." Downward causation occurs through the gradual emergence of life, of consciousness, of purpose, of values, and the enormous power exerted by all these new phenomena, which disappear when reduced to their previous components. They are, however, quite real when seen as wholes; they are part of our world, and an increasingly important part of reality. Scientific logic cannot explain them away.

Values have thus become part of a new world view, combining science and religion. They have become the most powerful factors of our world. As Sperry states in this quotation which has become a classic:

"Human values, viewed in an objective, scientific perspective, stand out as the most strategically powerful causal control force now shaping world events. More than any other causal system with which science now concerns itself, it is variables in human value systems that will determine the future."
ROGER SPERRY,
in *Bridging Science and Values:
A Unifying View of Mind and Brain*, p.8

---

* A worldwide organization founded in 1954.

Another contact is The Chicago Center for Religion and Science, founded in 1988, dedicated to relating religious traditions and the best of scientific knowledge.

CCRS/LST, 1100 East 55th St., Chicago, IL 60615-5199 USA

World Scientists' Warning to Humanity

Union of Concerned Scientists

A non-profit partnership organization of leading scientists and committed citizens which addresses the most serious environmental and security threats facing humanity. UCS conducts technical studies, promotes education of both the general public and world leaders about the issues, and seeks to influence public policy.

This comprehensive statement has been endorsed by over 1,680 members or fellows national or international science academies, including 104 Nobel laureates. The signers include a substantial number of the senior officers from organizations such as the Third World Academy of Sciences, the Brazilian Academy of Sciences, the Royal Society of London, the Chinese Academy of Sciences, the Pontifical Academy of Sciences and others. They come from 71 countries, including all of the 19 largest economic powers, all of the 12 most populous nations, 12 countries in Africa, 14 in Asia, 19 in Europe and 12 in Latin America.

Introduction

Human beings and the natural world are on a collision course. Human activities inflict harsh and often irreversible damage on the environment and on critical resources. If not checked, many of our current practices put at serious risk the future that we wish for human society and the plant and animal kingdoms, and may so alter the living world that it will be unable to sustain life in the manner that we know. Fundamental changes are urgent if we are to avoid the collision our present course will bring about.

The environment

The environment is suffering critical stress:

The Atmosphere

Stratospheric ozone depletion threatens us with enhanced ultraviolet radiation at the earth's surface, which can be damaging or lethal to many life forms. Air pollution near ground level, and acid precipitation, are already causing widespread injury to humans, forests and crops.

Water Resources

Heedless exploitation of depletable ground water supplies endangers food production and other essential human systems. Heavy demands on the world's surface waters have resulted in serious shortages in some 80 countries, containing 40 percent of the world's population. Pollution of rivers, lakes and ground water further limits the supply.

Oceans

Destructive pressure on the oceans is severe, particularly in the coastal regions which produce most of the world's food fish. The total marine catch is now at or above the estimated maximum sustainable yield. Some fisheries have already shown signs of collapse. Rivers carrying heaven burdens of eroded soil into the seas also carry industrial, municipal, agricultural, and livestock waste—some of it toxic.

Soil

Loss of soil productivity, which is causing extensive land abandonment, is

"*To a large extent, the future lies before us like a vast wilderness of unexplored reality. The God who created and sustained the evolving universe through eons of progress and development has not placed our generation at the tag end of the creative process. God has placed us at a new beginning. We are here for the future.*"

SIR JOHN TEMPLETON

For more information, contact:
UCS
26 Church St.
Cambridge, MA 02238

a widespread byproduct of current practices in agriculture and animal husbandry. Since 1945, 11 percent of the earth's vegetated surface has been degraded—an area larger than India and China combined—and per capita food production in many parts of the world is decreasing.

Forests

Tropical rain forests, as well as tropical and temperate dry forests, are being destroyed rapidly. At present rates, some critical forest types will be gone in a few years, and most of the tropical rain forest will be gone before the end of the next century. With them will go large numbers of plant and animal species.

Living Species

The irreversible loss of species, which by 2100 may reach one third of all species now living, is especially serious. We are losing the potential they hold for providing medicinal and other benefits, and the contribution that genetic diversity of life forms gives to the robustness of the world's biological systems and to the astonishing beauty of the earth itself.

Much of this damage is irreversible on a scale of centuries, or permanent. Increasing levels of gases in the atmosphere from human activities, including carbon dioxide released from fossil fuel burning and from deforestation, may alter climate on a global scale. Predictions of global warming are still uncertain with projected effects ranging from tolerable to very severe— but the potential risks are very great.

Our massive tampering with the world's interdependent web of life—coupled with the environmental damage inflicted by deforestation, species loss and climate change—could trigger widespread adverse effects, including unpredictable collapses of critical biological systems whose interactions and dynamics we only imperfectly understand.

Uncertainty over the extent of these effects cannot excuse complacency or delay in facing the threats.

Population

The earth is finite. Its abilty to absorb wastes and destructive effluent is finite. Its abililty to provide food and energy is finite. Its ability to provide for growing numbers of people is finite. And we are fast approaching many of earth's limits. Current economic practices which damage the environment, in both developed and underdeveloped nations, cannot be continued without the risk that vital global systems will be damaged beyond repair.

Pressures resulting from unrestrained population growth put demands on the natural world that can overwhelm any efforts to achieve a sustainable future. If we are to halt the destruction of our environment, we must accept limits to that growth. A World Bank estimate indicates that world population will not stabilize at less than 12.4 billion, while the United Nations concludes that the eventual total could reach 14 billion, a near tripling of today's 5.4 billion. But, even at this moment, one person in five lives in absolute poverty without enough to eat, and one in ten suffers serious malnutrition.

No more than one or a few decades remain before the chance to avert the threats we now confront will be lost and the prospects for humanity immeasurably diminished.

WARNING:

We the undersigned, senior members of the world's scientific community, hereby warn all humanity of what lies ahead. A great change in our stewardship of the earth and the life on it is required if vast human misery is to be avoided and our global home on this planet is not to be irretrievably mutilated.

What we must do

Five inextricably linked areas must be addressed simultaneously:

1. **We must bring environmentally damaging activities under control to restore and protect the integrity of the earth's systems we depend on.**

We must, for example, move away from fossil fuels to more benign, inexhaustible energy sources to cut greenhouse gas emissions and the pollution of our air and water. Priority must be given to the development of energy resources matched to third world needs—small scale and relatively easy to implement.

We must halt deforestation, injury to and loss of agricultural land, and the loss of plants, animals and marine species.

2. **We must manage resources crucial to human welfare more effectively.**

We must give high priority to efficient use of energy, water and other materials, including expansion of conservation and recycling.

3. **We must stabilize population. This will be possible only if all nations recognize that it requires improved social and economic conditions, and the adoption of effective, voluntary family planning.**

4. **We must reduce and eventually eliminate poverty.**

5. **We must insure sexual equality, and guarantee women control over their own reproductive decisions.**

The developed nations are the largest polluters in the world today. They must greatly reduce their overconsumption, if we are to reduce pressures on resources and the global environment. The developed nations have the obligation to provide aid and support to developing nations, because only the developed nations have the financial resources and the technical skills for these tasks.

Acting on this recognition is not altruism, but enlightened self-interest: whether industrialized or not, we all have but one lifeboat. No nation can escape from injury when global biological systems are damaged. No nation can escape from conflicts over increasingly scarce resources. In addition, environmental and economic instabilities will cause mass migrations with incalculable consequences for developed and undeveloped nations alike.

Developing nations must realize that environmental damage is one of the gravest threats they face, and that attempts to blunt it will be overwhelmed if their populations go unchecked. The greatest peril is to become trapped in spirals of environmental decline, poverty and unrest, leading to social, economic and environmental collapse.

Success in this global endeavor will require a great reduction in violence and war. Resources now devoted to the preparation and conduct of war—amounting to over $1 trillion annually—will be badly needed in the new tasks and should be diverted to the new challenges.

A new ethic is required—a new attitude towards discharging our responsibility for caring for ourselves and for the earth. We must recognize the earth's limited capacity to provide for us. We must recognize its fragility. We must no longer allow it to be ravaged. This ethic must motivate a great movement, convincing reluctant leaders and reluctant governments and reluctant peoples themselves to effect the needed changes.

The scientists issuing this warning hope that our message will reach and affect people everywhere. We need the help of many.

We require the help of the world community of scientists—natural, social, economic, political;

We require the help of the world's business and industrial leaders;

We require the help of the world's religious leaders; and

We require the help of the world's peoples.

We call on all to join us in this task. ✴

Wilderness and the Natural Law

Traditional Circle of Indian Elders and Youth

COMMUNIQUÉ NO. 11
Denver, Colorado
September 11, 1987

Statement reflecting the position of the Traditional Circle of Indian Elders, delivered on their behalf by Chief Oren Lyons to the 4th World Wilderness Congress

*N*eyawenhha Scano
(Thank you for being well).

Greetings to the conveners of the Fourth World Wilderness Congress; greetings to the esteemed delegates to this conference; greetings to the traditional elders, Magqubu Ntombela from Zululand, South Africa and to my traditional Native American elders from North America; and greetings to those assembled here in common cause to preserve and conserve the natural world for future generations.

Greetings from the Traditional Elders Circle, the Chiefs, Clan Mothers, Faithkeepers, men, women and children, even those on the cradle boards; We send greetings to you.

*M*y relations:

We have been asked for our perspective on the theme of this conference, the **worldwide conservation of wilderness.** I shall do my best to do this. I am sure that there will be many things left unsaid and not presented. I apologize for this and admit my ignorance of the cultures and wisdoms of the indigenous people and nations unknown to me throughout this hemisphere and the world. One thing I have been finding out is that among the indigenous nations throughout the world, we do understand the natural law, and have fashioned our societies and nations to support and adhere to this great spiritual law.

I have often been asked to speak on behalf of native peoples in North America because I am educated in my brother's culture and society. I understand his language better than I understand my own. Because of that I am able to communicate with you our collective thoughts. I have been instructed on what to say, and it stays with me.

It is important for you to understand that our societies often choose speakers to convey the thoughts of the people. The words that I speak may be the collective position of the people of the Onondaga Nation, the Onondaga Council of Chiefs, the Grand Council of Chiefs of the Haudenosaunee, or the Traditional Elders Circle of North America, the good minds.

It is not my thoughts nor my wisdom that you are hearing but the collective thoughts and wisdoms of the indigenous peoples who have always been here in these lands from time immemorial.

Their knowledge is profound and comes from living in one place for untold generations. It comes from watching the sun rise in the east and set in the west from the same place over great sections of time. We are as familiar with the lands, rivers and great seas that surround us as we are with the faces of our mothers. Indeed we call the earth ETENOHA, our mother from whence all life springs.

*M*y relations: so then let us begin.

We will start with the word *wilderness*, derived from the word *wild*. For us there is no word for wild, it is not in our vocabulary. The closest we come to that is **free**; so then we speak of freedom in the natural order of things with the inherent rules and obligations of freedom: respect and recognition of the sovereignty of the individuals whether they be human beings, the animal nations or the living forests.

For us our lands did not become wild until our brothers from across the great eastern sea arrived upon our shores, and then our lands became wild and untamed —even called the wild west. Previous to that, this continent we called the Great Turtle Island was a land of peace and plenty, so we do not perceive our habitat as wild but as a place of great security and peace, full of life.

My relations: listen to what we say.

Our grandfathers spoke of the crystal clear waters of the springs, streams, rivers and lakes and great inland seas. They spoke of the fresh pure waters. The first law of life: water.

They spoke of ancient trees, grandfathers of another age, trees so huge it took six men to circle their trunks.

They spoke of forests so vast, leaves so thick that sunlight barely found its way to the forest floors, and a squirrel could travel from the great eastern sea to the Mississippi River without touching the ground.

They spoke of flowers and medicines that grew in profusion along with the fruits, nuts and berries that fed not only the human families but also the animal nations that abounded and prospered in these vast lands.

They spoke of fish so abundant that in spawning season the streams and rivers were so full you could run on their backs.

They spoke of the passenger pigeons so plentiful that their roosting places were stripped of limbs, their combined weight breaking those limbs. So plentiful that they darkened the sky for hours as they migrated north and south.

They spoke of vast herds of game: deer, elk and massive herds of buffalo that roamed the entire continent— powerful and endless.

But they did end, and so we received our first lesson.

My relations: listen as we continue:

The lesson we learned was that man wanted to dominate, and what he couldn't dominate he destroyed. That mankind was capable of destroying life—the natural world life and his own. Our people were so closely aligned and intertwined with the order of the natural world that we suffered the same fate as the trees, and the wolves, our spiritual relatives.

It taught us that mankind could be motivated to exploit the natural resources and the environments that these resources provided, to a point of total depletion and extinction of the animal and fish life.

It illustrated to us that there were people who were ignorant of the natural law, or who chose to deliberately ignore it. It caused our people to gather together in alarm, and to hold to our bosoms the principles of the great natural law, and to protect our ceremonies that celebrated

these principles and insured the existence of the generations to come.

My relations: The natural law as we understand it is the ultimate authority upon these lands and waters. It is the prevailing law of life and the order of life upon this earth we call our Mother.

It is the law the Creator put here; set down here deliberately, firmly and with finality to govern all life in this creation.

That is the way we understand it. The Great Creator planted life upon this earth. He planted all of the nations of life from the grasses to the trees, from the insects to the elephants, from the tiniest life in the waters to the great whales in the seas.

And he planted the families of mankind in the four great sacred colors of black, white, red and yellow.

He gave instructions to these great nations of life from the grasses to the whales, and they continue to follow these original instructions. Up to this very moment to the best of their abilities they carry out their duties; they live in a state of grace. They do no wrong.

For us, the human beings, he gave additional responsibilities. He gave us hands to work with; he gave us intellect and the power of reason; he gave us options to choose our paths to do what is right or to do what is wrong. He gave us the foreknowledge of death and he gave us the insight into life after death. These are responsibilities more than gifts, and he gave each of us a mission in this life that is ours alone. These are responsibilities to be cherished and shared for the benefit of *all* life.

My relations: this is what we believe; since you asked, we shall continue:

We are sharing this with you so that you may understand us better; these are our cosmologies. Your stories may be different but we believe that we all received the same instructions in the beginning.

The natural law is a spiritual law. Its powers are both light and dark. We are blessed and we prosper if we live by the law. It is dark, terrible and merciless if we transgress the law. There is no discussion with the law; there is only understanding and compliance. Its tenets are simple:

A respect for all life, for all life is equal.

Thanksgiving ceremonies for the special forces of nature.

A Thanksgiving ceremony for the thundering Grandfathers who water the earth and the people, who freshen the springs, streams, lakes and rivers.

A Thanksgiving ceremony for the four winds who bring the seasons and sow the seeds of life.

A Thanksgiving ceremony for the corn, beans and squash that sustain our lives and give strength to our bodies.

A Thanksgiving ceremony to our Grandmother, the moon, who raises and lowers the tides of the great salt seas, who gives us light at night, and who marks the cycles of the female life and the season.

A Thanksgiving ceremony for our mighty uncle the sun, who unites with our mother the earth to bring forth life in all our seasons; who brings us light each day as we wait in the morning to greet him.

A Thanksgiving to the stars who give us direction at night in their infinite wisdom, most of which we have forgotten. We give thanks for their beauty and for the dew they bring in the night.

A Thanksgiving to those spiritual beings assigned to help the human beings carry out our duties.

A Thanksgiving ceremony to the Great Creator, the master of all life, for the creation and all that we have been given to enjoy and to protect so that seven generations from this day our children will enjoy the same things that we have now.

Listen to the howl of our spiritual brother the wolf, for how it goes with him, so it goes for the natural world.

My relations: so now we will continue:
So we have gathered here from the four directions of the earth to report on how it is where we come from. The news is heavy and there seems to be a determined effort to destroy life on the planet. How did this come about, and what are some of the problems facing us and the natural world?

What is the relationship between a fast food hamburger and rainforests in Central and South America?

We as consumers should know but we do not, and more to the point, even if we did know these connections and understand them, it is very questionable that we would give up the convenience of these fast foods for the long-term process of conserving the wilderness and saving our environment.

The discussion then resolves around the values of the societies responsible for the attitudes of its people. What are these societies teaching their children?

Rainforests are cut down for timber and to clear the lands for farming and ranching. Ranching lands are seeded for cattle grazing, a cash crop. The local people do not eat the meat. It is often shipped north to become the hamburgers we talked about earlier. The people give up subsistence farming for wages, and the land use is changed. Cheap labor on one end, more profit on the other end. At the same time the manufacture of Styrofoam releases chemicals into the earth that affect the ozone layer, the thin lifesaving protection of life on the earth.

The rainforests are the lungs of the earth. Trees recycle carbon monoxide back into oxygen; clean air that all life breathes in common, thus continuing the life giving elements and maintaining the constant atmospheres and temperatures around the earth. If we continue to cut these trees at the present rate we will have cleared a space as large as India within 30 years. The natural law is simple in this case; we will suffer in exact ratio to our transgressions; the damage done may be permanent in mankind's existence.

My relations: we shall continue:
The scenario is the same in Central and South America —first the timber companies come to clear the great forests, and the lands are used for cash crops. These crops need help to grow because the cleared lands are fragile, so fertilizers are introduced. These chemicals cost money, so soon the farmer is paying more for chemicals than his cash crops can be sold for, and he finds himself working for the chemical companies. Soon he gives up and abandons the land as it turns to dust, and as the timber companies march into virgin rainforests, he follows to continue the cycles. This process is called *progress,* and sometimes *economic development.*

The natural law is clear in this case; if you destroy the process of the life cycles of the rain forests, that affects climate around the world. Then you will affect life as we now know it. The balance is delicate. The Mayans farmed these lands for untold centuries by working *with* this balance, and so they prospered. They are called people of the corn, and they lived in the jungles of these huge rain forests in harmony. They lived with the law in respect and understanding, and so they prospered.

There are great dams being built in these same areas, and they have caused the rivers to cease their annual overflowing to bring silt and fertility to the lands that they overflowed. The lands lose their fertility and life suffers. We understand that the World Bank, who most often financially supported these projects, is now rethinking its policies, and I for one am grateful. The natural law is clear in this case. Damage done quickly takes a long time to repair or renew. Thus, we may cut a tree with a chainsaw in ten minutes but it will take a hundred years for that tree to grow back. So who suffers? Our children. We are profiting at their expense. We are deliberately changing life in the future, and we must question our motivations.

The great seas are the same as the earth.
Man has lived off the abundance of the sea from time immemorial. Its great resources have sustained life, and songs of joy and contentment have lifted our hearts up to this time. The energy it produces has galvanized civilizations and cultures throughout the world. But we, even now, endanger our lives by imprudent exploitation without regard for the laws of nature, and again, we will suffer the consequences.

My relations: you have asked us what we think, and so we will continue:
The herring is gone from the North Sea; it is gone from the diet of the people, the result of overfishing. How did this happen? It happened because we either did not understand the natural law or we deliberately chose to ignore it. We could say that technology caused the demise

of the great schools of herring but technology is a tool. Technology doesn't think, ponder or reason. That is the province of mankind. So we must agree that the destruction of the herring was a conscious decision of mankind. What then is the motivation? The answer is simple: profit. Profit at our expense, for we are all deprived including the fish life that also sustained itself on this once great natural resource. Technology unleashed our greed. There were many nations involved in this great kill; they fished in competition and rivalry.

They developed fishing nets that allowed larger and larger catches. The great seine nets were the final blow to the herring, and coupled with the giant trawlers now prowling the seas they were able to catch in one day what previously took a month of fishing. So it is not technology to blame, it is the attitude of the fisherman. The results are the same; we have lost a great resource. It is the law that we suffer.

Brothers: There are many more examples of mankind's folly, and I use the word *man* advisedly because western thinking as we see it has exploited the women as well. Men have excluded women from decision making, and thus flawed the partnership that *is* the natural law. Male and Female is fundamental to life; partners in work to be done. By excluding the female mankind has again denied a resource of compassion and understanding that balances the competitive nature of the males. We as men should not fear our mates: we should listen to their counsel. They may be the last reservoir of life. They are just now beginning to fight for life. Mankind should stop and listen to their song. As we plunge ahead to build empires and race for supremacy we should stop and listen to their song of life. For without the female there is no life.

My relations: we come to the close of this short discussion.

Do not take offense as we present the examples of what we consider flawed thinking. The examples abound:

Acid rain has already killed half the forests of Germany. Acid rain is killing life in the rivers, streams and lakes of northeastern America. It is killing the chief of the trees, the maple, as our prophecies foretold.

Great famines are sweeping the earth, particularly in Africa where the natural law is exacting the price of transgressions against it, and life suffers without relief.

Water is contaminated at the expense of our children. Toxic waste dumps are time bombs of death as they slowly work their way into the fresh water veins of our lands.

The Indian nations of North America have been particular victims of uranium mining and toxic piles of waste tailings have contaminated the people, aborting life in pregnant mothers and causing defects upon our children who are born in these areas.

How can we meet here to discuss the economic problems of wilderness and life without talking about the monster most responsible for the problems of the earth today, and that is the gigantic military complexes of the two most powerful nation states in the world. Soldiers outnumber teachers and doctors by wide margins. And row upon row of deadly bombs, weapons and aircraft wait for the moment of global war.

It is hypocritical for countries to profess the cause of peace when their economies are based upon the sales of military hardware. Something is wrong when arms to developing nations outnumber economic aid three-to-one.

We are seeing our prophecies come to be, one by one. Our gardens in the Mohawk Nation territories are stunted and refusing to grow from the dark cloud of pollution that daily rains down upon us. We were told that this would happen, and so it has.

Ninety years ago there were 13 cities with a population of over one million. Today there are 200 cities over one million, with Mexico City in the forefront with 18 million, and we know the problems of that city.

Respect should be given those indigenous nations who still carry on their ceremonies; still following the ancient laws of nature with songs and ceremonies.

We cannot give up. We must follow the spiritual law set down for us so long ago. We are not defeated if we do not allow ourselves to be manipulated like yo-yos on a string by cosmetic politicians whose interests are not for the natural world or the people.

I heard today that economic growth is a necessity and conservation is a consideration of importance—we disagree. Conservation is life, and economic growth is a matter of interpretation.

So, my friends and colleagues, here we are at this time in history with a task that we cannot leave to our children.

With a choice that takes courage, fortitude and a will inspired by an understanding of the great spiritual law of our mother earth. Take heed to the words of our Grandfathers who instructed us to *"Take care how you place your moccasins upon the earth, step with care, for the faces of the future generations are looking up from the earth waiting their turn for life."* So the decision is simple. Obey the natural law, or perish.

Dah Nay To.

Evangelical Christianity and the Environment

"Humans are called to a special task of caring for creation in a shepherdly manner, since they reflect God's image in a unique way."

*T*his was among the conclusions of a worldwide forum held at Au Sable Institute near Mancelona, Michigan, USA in August 1992. In contrast to the conclusion of some that evangelical Christians disregard environmental and social issues, the 60 evangelical leaders from eight countries and five continents attending this conference expressed vigorous biblical and Christian responses to these issues.

One major outcome of this forum of evangelical Christians was the formation of the International Evangelical Environmental Network for the purpose of disseminating information among evangelical Christian individuals and organizations having environmental and development concerns.

The Forum was held in the context of study of local flora, fauna, geography and geology of the area, and began with a challenge to evangelical churches by co-convener Calvin DeWitt (Au Sable Institute Director and Professor of Environmental Studies at the University of Wisconsin-Madison, USA) who reviewed seven specific degradations to which creation is currently subjected. Other papers and discussion focused on the theological and biblical frameworks, spiritual dimensions of the environmental movement, sustainable development, population, over-consumption, poverty, missions, technology, and the environmental effects of military preparations and war. Part III of the report outlines tasks for the Christian community and individuals, including political engagement and education.

"Addressing theological foundations . . .[the] theologians and ensuing discussions affirmed God as Creator—fully distinct from Creation—but fully involved in Creation. . . . [The final report of the Forum] acknowledges that God's deep involvement in Creation comes 'from the triune God's free love and grace. God the Son, as the eternal Word, gives form to all creatures, and became human flesh, with which are creatures are interconnected; while God the Spirit breathes energy into all.'

"Recognizing that the creation account begins by showing the threefold relationship between God creation and humanity, the forum affirms the responsibility of humans for the care of the Earth and its creatures. . . . 'All creatures are deeply intertwined with and dependent on each other, and humans have no right to destroy or despoil other species.' The report affirms that 'all God's creatures are valuable in and of themselves, apart from any usefulness to humans.' "

excerpted and adapted by the editor from a news release and the Summarizing Committee Report

For more information or for copies of the full text of the news release or of the Summarizing Committee Report, contact:

Chris Sugden, IEEN Secretariat, Oxford Centre for Mission Studies, P.O. Box 70, Oxford, OX2 6HB UK

or

Calvin DeWitt, IEEN Secretariat, Au Sable Institute 731 State Street, Madison, WI 53703 USA TEL/FAX: (608) 255-0950

The Au Sable Institute also provides a wide variety of documents including "A Christian Land Ethic," and other resources and services, including academic study, internships and conferences.

The Belgic Confession: Knowing God Through Creation

Guido de Brés

1561; revised 1566 and 1619; it was used during and since the Reformation as a major teaching document in Protestant churches.

ARTICLE 1:
The Only God

We all believe in our hearts
and confess with our mouths
that there is a single
and simple
spiritual being,
whom we call God—
eternal, incomprehensible, invisible
unchangeable, infinite, almighty,
completely wise, just and good,
and the overflowing source of all good.

ARTICLE 2:
The Means By Which We Know God

We know him by two means:

First, by the creation, preservation,
and government of the universe,
since that universe is
before our eyes like a beautiful book
in which all creatures,
great and small,
are as letters to make us ponder
the invisible things of God:
> his eternal power
> and his divinity.

As the apostle Paul says in Romans 1:20,
All these things are enough to convict men
and to leave them without excuse.

Second, he makes himself known to us
more openly by his holy and divine Word,
as much as we need in this life,
> for his glory
> and the salvation of his own.

from the Psalter Hymnal
of the Christian Reformed Church

On the Urgency of a Jewish Response to the Environmental Crisis

Issued by the Consultation on the Environment and Jewish Life, Washington, DC

March 10, 1992

*W*e, American Jews of every denomination, from diverse organizations and differing political perspectives, are united in deep concern that the quality of human life and the earth we inhabit are in danger, afflicted by rapidly increasing ecological threats. Among the most pressing of these threats are: depletion of the ozone layer, global warming, massive deforestation, the extinction of species and loss of biodiversity, poisonous deposits of toxic chemical and nuclear wastes, and exponential population growth. We here affirm our responsibility to address this planetary crisis in our personal and communal lives.

For Jews, the environmental crisis is a religious challenge. As heirs to a tradition of stewardship that goes back to Genesis and that teaches us to be partners in the ongoing work of Creation, we cannot accept the escalating destruction of our environment and its effect on human health and livelihood. Where we are despoiling our air, land and water, it is our sacred duty as Jews to acknowledge our God-given responsibility and take action to alleviate environmental degradation and the pain and suffering that it causes. We must reaffirm and bequeath the tradition we have inherited which calls upon us to safeguard humanity's home.

We have convened this unprecedented consultation in Washington, DC to inaugurate a unified Jewish response to the environmental crisis. We pledge to carry to our homes, communities, congregations, organizations, and workplaces the urgent message that air, land, water and living creatures are endangered. We will draw our people's attention to the timeless texts that speak to us of God's gifts and expectations. This Consultation represents a major step towards:

- mobilizing our community toward energy efficiency, the reduction and recycling of wastes, and other practices which promote environmental sustainability;
- initiating environmental education programs in settings where Jews gather to learn, particularly among young people;
- pressing for appropriate environmental legislation at every level of government and in international forums;
- convening business and labor leaders to explore specific opportunities for exercising environmental leadership;
- working closely in these endeavors with scientists, educators, representatives of environmental groups, Israelis and leaders from other religious communities.

*O*ur agenda is already overflowing. Israel's safety, the resettlement of Soviet Jewry, anti-semitism, the welfare of our people in many nations, the continuing problems of poverty, unemployment, hunger, health care and education, as well as assimilation and intermarriage— all these and more have engaged us and engage us still.

But the ecological crisis hovers over all Jewish concerns, for the threat is global, advancing and ultimately jeopardizes ecological balance and the quality of life. It is imperative, then, that environmental issues also become an immediate, ongoing and pressing concern for our community.

SIGNED BY

Rabbi Marc D. Angel
    President, Rabbinical Council of America
Shoshana S. Cardin
    Chairperson, Conference of Presidents of Major American Jewish Organizations
Rabbi Jerome K. Davidson
    President, Synagogue Council of America
Dr. Alfred Gottschalk
    President, Hebrew Union College-Jewish Institute of Religion
Dr. Arthur Green
    President, the Reconstructionist Rabbinical College
Rabbi Irwin Groner
    President, The Rabbinical Assembly
Walter Jacob
    President, Central Conference of American Rabbis
The Honorable Frank R. Lautenberg
    United States Senate
Marvin Lender
    President, United Jewish Appeal
The Honorable Joseph I. Lieberman
    United States Senate
Sheldon Rudoff
    President, Union of Orthodox Jewish Congregations of America
Rabbi Alexander M. Schindler
    President, Union of American Hebrew Congregations
Dr. Ismar Schorsch
    Chancellor, The Jewish Theological Seminary of America
Arden Shenker
    Chairman, National Jewish Community Relations Advisory Council
The Honorable Arlen Specter
    United States Senate
Alan J. Tichnor
    President, United Synagogue of America

Caring for the World

Robert Prescott-Allen

Writer and senior consultant to IUCN and UNEP on integrating environmental conservation and economic development, for the World Conservation Strategy.

Because the concept of a "world ethic of sustainability" is of fundamental importance for reconstructing the relationship between humanity and nature, a summary of the ethical principles proposed by the World Conservation Strategy Ethics Working Group is also presented. Both the excerpt by Robert Prescott-Allen and the principles are from *Spirit and Nature* by Steven C. Rockefeller and John C. Elder; the principles were adapted somewhat by Steven C. Rockefeller, a member of the Working Group. –Ed.

*I*n a wink of time we human beings have grown from being just regular critters, lost in the evolutionary crowd, to being monsters of the universe. In monster movies cute, creepy crawlies like insects and spiders are blown up to screen-filling proportions to terrorize the inhabitants of quaint little towns like Middlebury, Vermont. But in the real world it is humanity that is blown up to planet-filling proportions. In the two centuries or so since the Industrial Revolution, human numbers have multiplied by eight and energy use and resource consumption have risen even faster. People now consume, control or destroy almost 40 percent of the plant energy of the land and 25 percent of *all* plant energy, the ultimate source of food for all animals and almost all organisms.

As a result, quite unwittingly and ignorant of the consequences, we are reshaping earth, replacing forests with farmland, farmland with wasteland, filling rivers, lakes, and seas with sediments and pollutants, unbalancing the atmosphere, subtracting species and draining gene pools, changing climate, indeed changing earth faster, perhaps faster than it has changed ever before. We are revising creation. All this destructive effort has brought affluence to a mere fifth of the world. The remaining four-fifths struggle against increasing squalor and misery. We are alienating the whole of nature to meet human needs, yet human needs are not being met. Simply put, our relationship with earth is unsustainable.

So here we are, we citizens of Middlebury and other prosperous places, behaving like creatures from another planet. What should we do? We must make a daring change, a change to sustainability. But how?

Principles of a World Ethic of Sustainability

1. The ethical principles of sustainability affirm those bonds among all people and between people and the earth that protect the community of life and the rights of individuals. These principles are based on the recognition that people are an interdependent part of nature and the larger community of life and that ecological stability and the achievement of social justice are interconnected. While these principles emphasize interdependence and community, they respect biological and cultural diversity.

2. All members of the human family have the same fundamental rights, including the right: to life and security of person; to freedom of thought, inquiry, expression, conscience, religion, assembly and association; to an education that empowers them to exercise responsibility for their own well-being and for life on earth; to an opportunity for a sustaining livelihood, including access to the resources needed for a decent standard of living within the limits of the earth; to political enfranchisement, making possible participation in government decisions that directly affect their welfare.

3. The earth should be respected at all times, which means: to approach nature with awareness, gratitude, humility, compassion and care; to protect its essential ecological processes and life support systems; to be frugal and efficient in resource use; to conserve bio-diversity; to be guided by the best available knowledge, both traditional and scientific; and to work cooperatively to build local communities and a world society governed by policies that ensure sustainability.

4. Every life form possesses intrinsic value and warrants respect independently of its worth to people. Human development should not be at the expense of the survival of other species. People should safeguard the habitats of endangered species. They should treat all creatures decently and protect them from cruelty, avoidable suffering and unnecessary killing.

5. The resources of the earth and the costs of fundamental development should be generously shared, especially among regions that are poor and those that are affluent. Development of one society should not be at the expense of other societies or the integrity of nature.

6. The protection of human rights and the rights of nature are a worldwide responsibility of each person and all societies, transcending all geographical, cultural and ideological boundaries.

7. Each generation should conserve and expand the heritage of values that it has received from the earth and human culture so that future generations may receive this heritage more securely and widely shared than before. Each generation should leave to the future a world that is freer, more just and as rich in renewable resources as the one it inherited.

8. In the face of moral dilemmas, further development of these principles for living sustainably should be pursued under the guidance of careful experimental inquiry and a spirit of compassion.

from *Spirit and Nature: Why the Environment is a Religious Issue;* pp.128–129, by John C. Elder and Steven C. Rockefeller

Caring for the Earth: A Strategy for Sustainable Living

The first edition of the *World Conservation Strategy* was published in 1980 by the International Union for Conservation of Nature and Natural Resources (IUCN), with the advice and support of the United Nations Environment Programme (UNEP) and the World Wildlife Fund (WWF).

An expanded and updated edition, *Caring for the Earth: A Strategy for Sustainable Living*, was published in 1991 by a partnership including the same three groups plus numerous other sponsoring and collaborating organizations. The following excerpts are from the official *Summary*, also published in 1991, which outlines in 24 pages the principles and concepts included in the 228 page *Strategy*. More information is available from IUCN, 1196 Gland, Switzerland. Used with permission of IUCN-The World Conservation Union/UNEP/WWF (1991). Copies may be purchased from Island Press in the USA (1-800-828-1302) and in the United Kingdom from IUCN (44 223-277-894). –Ed.

A message to the world

*H*umanity must live within the carrying capacity of the Earth. There is no other rational option in the longer term. Unless we use the resources of the Earth sustainably and prudently, we deny people their future. We must adopt lifestyles and development paths that respect and work within nature's limits. We can do this without rejecting the many benefits that modern technology has brought, provided that technology itself works within those limits.

. . . World population may double in 60 years, but the Earth will be unable to support everyone unless there is less waste and extravagance, and a more open and equitable alliance between rich and poor. Even then the likelihood of a satisfactory life for all is remote unless present rates of population increase are drastically reduced.

Our new approach must meet two fundamental requirements. One is to secure a widespread and deeply-held commitment to a new ethic, the ethic for sustainable living, and to translate its principles into practice. The other is to integrate conservation and development: conservation to keep our actions within the Earth's capacity, and development to enable people everywhere to enjoy long, healthy and fulfilling lives.

A new strategy of care

*I*n the past 20 years, the world has been deluged with reports, action plans and other prescriptions to cure our environmental ills. International conferences, ministerial declarations, government policy documents, political manifestos, campaigns by "green" groups and somber scientific pronoucements have all pointed in the same direction.

So—what's new about *Caring for the Earth?* Two points need to be made: it is founded on an ethic of care for nature and for people; and it is a strategy of mutually reinforcing actions at individual, local, national and international levels.

Caring for the Earth is both an analysis and a plan of action. It is intended as a broadly-oriented but practical guide to the policies we must adopt and the actions we must undertake. It is divided into three parts.

Part I defines the principles of a sustainable society and recommends 60 actions. . . .

Part II describes 62 additional actions required to apply the principles set out in Part I to the more familiar sectors of environment and policy. These are energy; business, industry and commerce; human settlements; farm and range lands; forest lands; fresh waters; and oceans and coastal areas.

Part III deals with implementation and follow-up.

Who should use the Strategy?

*T*his *Strategy* is aimed at everybody. But its particular targets are those who will decide on the next essential steps. We address national leaders, ministers of government departments, heads of national agencies and intergovernmental organizations. Because the powers of governments, while indispensable, are not unlimited, we also address leaders of business and industry and the great range of local, national and international non-governmental bodies. This *Strategy* will have a chance of success only if caring and thinking people read it, understand its message, demand action—and opt for sustainable living.

We urge every reader to measure his or her personal behavior and lifestyle against these actions, and to assess the policies and practices of the citizens' groups, communities, firms and nations to which he or she belongs. . . .

An ethic based on respect and care for each other and the Earth is the foundation for sustainable living. . . .

"The benefits and costs of resource use and environmental conservation should be shared fairly among different communities, among people who are poor and those who are affluent, and between our generation and those who will come after us. . . ."

"Global and shared resources, especially the atmosphere, oceans and shared ecosystems, can be managed only on the basis of common purpose and resolve. The ethic of care applies at the international as well as the national and individual levels." (p.11)

Sustainability: A question of definition

Caring for the Earth uses the word "sustainable" in several combinations, such as "sustainable development," "sustainable economy," "sustainable society" and "sustainable use." It is important for an understanding of the *Strategy* to know what we mean by these terms.

If an activity is sustainable, for all practical purposes it can continue forever.

When people define an activity as sustainable, however, it is on the basis of what they know at the time. There can be no long-term guarantee of sustainability, because many factors remain unknown or unpredictable. The moral we draw from this is: be conservative in actions that could affect the environment, study the effects of such actions carefully and learn from your mistakes quickly.

The World Commission on Environment and Development (WCED) defined "sustainable development" as "development that meets the needs of the present without compromising the ability of future generations to meet their own needs."

The term has been criticized as ambiguous and open to a wide range of interpretations, many of which are contradictory. The confusion has been caused because "sustainable development," "sustainable growth" and "sustainable use" have been used interchangeably, as if their meanings were the same. They are not. "Sustainable growth" is a contradiction in terms: nothing physical can grow indefinitely. "Sustainable use" is applicable only to renewable resources: it means using them at rates within their capacity for renewal.

"Sustainable development" is used in the *Strategy* to mean *improving the quality of human life while living within the carrying capacity of supporting ecosystems.*

A "sustainable economy" is the product of sustainable development. It maintains its natural resource base. It can continue to develop by adapting, and through improvements in knowledge, organization, technical efficiency and wisdom.

> "*Economic growth is part of development, but it cannot be a goal in itself; . . . some [development goals] are virtually universal. These include a long and healthy life, education, access to . . . a decent standard of living, political freedom, guaranteed human rights and freedom from violence." (pp. 5–6)*

> "*A national program for achieving sustainability should involve all interests and seek to identify and prevent problems before they arise. . . ." (p. 10)*

The Cosmology of Religions

Dr. Thomas Berry

Eco-theologian, anthropologist, philosopher, monk and scholar of Teilhard de Chardin. Father Thomas Berry's books and vision, while rooted in the Catholic Christian tradition, challenge religions and our culture as well to consider a new story of the universe and of our place in it.

*T*he universe is the primary sacred community; all human religions are participants in the religious aspect of the universe itself. With this recognition, we are moving from the theology and anthropology of religions to the cosmology of religions. In the past 50 years in America there has been intense interest in the sociology and psychology of religions, and even more interest in the history of religions, yet these all fall within the general designation of the anthropology of religions.

Because none of these have been able to deal effectively with the evolutionary story of the universe or with the ecological crisis, we are led on to the cosmological dimension of the religious issue both from our efforts at understanding and from our concerns for survival.

What is new about this sense of the universe's religious mode of being is that the universe itself is now experienced as an irreversible time-developmental process, not simply as an abiding season-renewing universe. Not so much cosmos as cosmogenesis.

Our recent knowledge of the universe comes primarily through the empirical, observational sciences rather than from intuitive processes. We are listening to the earth tell its story through the signals that it sends to us from outer space, through the light that comes to us from the stars, through the geological formations of the earth and through a vast number of other evidences of itself that the universe manifests to us.

In its every aspect the human is a participatory reality. We are members of the great universe community. We participate in its life. We are nourished, instructed and healed by this community. In and through this community we enter into communion with that numinous mystery on which all things depend for their existence and activity. If this is true for the universe entire, it is also true in our relations with the earth.

From its own evidences we now know the story of the universe as an emergent process in its fourfold sequential story; the galactic, the earth, the life and the human story. These constitute for us the primordial sacred story of the universe.

The original flaring forth of the universe carried the present within its fantastic energies as the present expresses those original energies in their articulated form. This includes all those spiritual developments that have occurred in the course of the centuries. In its sequence of transformations, the universe carries within itself the comprehensive meaning of the phenomenal world. In recent secular times this meaning was perceived only in its physical expression. Now we perceive that the universe is a spiritual as well as a physical reality from the beginning.

This sacred dimension is especially evident in those stupendous moments of transformation through which the universe has passed, in these 15 billion years of its existence. These transformations include moments of great spiritual as well as physical significance—the privileged moments in the Great Story. The numinous mystery of the universe now reveals itself in a developmental mode of expression, a mode never before available to human consciousness through observational processes.

Yet all this means little to our modern western theologians who have shown little concern for the natural world as the primary bearer of religious consciousness. This is one of the basic reasons why both the physical and spiritual survival of the planet have become imperilled.

Presently we in the West think of ourselves as passing into another historical period or undergoing another cultural modification. If we think that the changes taking place in our times are simply another in the series of historical changes we are missing the real order of magnitude of the events taking place. We are at the end of an entire biological era in Earth history. We are now in a religious-civilizational period. In virtue of our new knowledge we are changing our most basic relations to the world about us. These changes are of a unique order of magnitude.

Our new acquaintance with the universe as irreversible developmental process is the most significant religious, spiritual and significant scientific event since the beginning of the more complex civilizations some five thousand years ago. But we are bringing about the greatest devastation the earth has ever experienced in the four and a half billion years of its formation. Norman Myers, a specialist in the biosystems of the planet, estimates that we are causing an extinction spasm that is liable to result in the greatest setback to the abundance and variety of life on earth since the first flickerings of life some four billion years ago.

We are changing the chemistry of the planet, disturbing the biosystems, altering the geological structure and functioning of the planet—all of which took billions of years of development. In this process of closing down the life systems of the planet we are devastating a sacred world, making the earth a wasteland, not realizing that as we lose the more gorgeous species, we thereby lose modes of divine presence, the very basis of our religious experience.

Because we are unable to enter effectively into the new mystique of the emergent universe available to us through our new modes of understanding we are unable to prevent the disintegration of the life systems of the planet taking place through the misuse of that same scientific vision. Western religion and theology have not yet addressed these issues or established their identity in this context. Nor have other religious traditions done so. The main religious traditions have simply restated their beliefs and their spiritual disciplines. This new experience of the religious being of the universe and of the planet earth is not yet perceived on any widespread scale within academic, theological or religious circles.

We cannot resolve the difficulties we face in this new situation by setting aside the scientific venture. Nor can we assume an attitude of indifference toward this new context of earthly existence because it is too powerful in its effects. We must find a new way of interpreting the process itself, because, properly interpreted, the scientific venture might even become one of the most significant spiritual disciplines of these times. This task is particularly urgent just now because this new mode of understanding has such powerful consequences on the very structure of the planet earth. We must learn to respond to its deepest spiritual content or we will be forced to submit to the devastation that lies before us.

The assertions of our traditions cannot by themselves bring these forces under control. We are involved in the future of the planet in its geological and biological survival and functioning as well as in the future of our human and spiritual well-being. We will bring about the physical and spiritual well-being of the entire planet or there will be neither physical nor spiritual well-being for any of our earthly forms of being.

The traditional religions have not dealt effectively with these issues or with our modern cosmological experience because they were not designed for such a universe. Traditional religions have been shaped within a predominantly spatial mode of consciousness. The biblical religions, although they have a historical developmental perspective in dealing with the human spiritual process, perceive the universe itself from a spatial mode of consciousness. Biblical religions only marginally provide for the progress of the divine kingdom within an established universe that participates in the historical process. They seem to have as much difficulty as any other tradition in dealing with the developmental character of the universe.

Although the antagonism toward the idea of an evolutionary universe has significantly diminished, our limitations as theologians in speaking the language of this new cosmology is everywhere evident. Much has been done in process theology in terms of our conceptions of the divine and the relations of the divine to the phenomenal world, but little has been done in the empirical study of the cosmos itself as religious expression.

To envisage the universe in its religious dimension requires that we speak of the religious aspect of the original flaming forth of the universe, the religious role of the elements, the religious functioning of the earth and all its components. Since our religious capacities emerge from this cosmological process, the universe itself may be considered the primary bearer of religious experience.

Thinking about the emergent universe in this way

provides a context for the future development of religious traditions. Indeed all the various peoples of the world, insofar as they are being educated in a modern context, are coming to identify themselves in time and space in terms of the universe as described by our modern sciences, even though none of us have learned the more profound spiritual and religious meaning indicated by this new sense of the universe.

This story of the universe is at once scientific, mythic and mystical. Most elaborate in its scientific statement, it is nevertheless among the simplest of creation stories and, significantly, the story that the universe tells about itself. We are finally overcoming our isolation from the universe and beginning to listen to it in some depth. In this we have an additional context for the religious understanding of every tradition. Through listening to the universe we also gain additional depth of spiritual understanding that was not available through our traditional insights. Just as we can no longer live simply within the physical universe of Newton so we can no longer live spiritually within the limits of our earlier traditions.

The first great contribution this new perspective on the universe makes to religious consciousness is the sense of participating in the creation process itself. We bear within us the impress of every transformation through which the universe and the planet earth have passed. The elements out of which we are composed were shaped in the supernova implosions. We passed through the period of stardust dispersion resulting from this implosion-explosion of the first generation of stars. We were integral with the attractive forces that brought those particles together in the original shaping of the earth. Especially in the rounded form of the planet we felt the gathering of the components of the earthly community and we experienced the self-organizing spontaneities within the megamolecules out of which came the earliest manifestations of the life process and the transition to cellular and organic living forms. These same forces that brought forth the genetic codings of all the various species were guiding the movement of life on toward its latest expression in human consciousness.

This sacred journey of the universe is also the personal journey of each individual. We cannot but marvel at this amazing sequence of transformations. Our reflexive consciousness, which allows us to appreciate and to celebrate this story, is the supreme achievement of our present period of history. The universe is the larger self of each person since the entire sequence of events that has transpired since the beginning of the universe has been required to establish each of us in the precise structure of our own being and in the larger community context in which we function.

Earlier periods and traditions have also experienced their intimacy with the universe, especially in those moments of cosmic renewal that took place periodically, particularly in the springtime of each year. Through these grand rituals powerful energies flowed into the world. Yet it was the *renewal* of the world or the sustaining of an abiding universe, not the irreversible and non-repeatable *original* emergence of the world that was taking place. Only such an irreversible self-organizing world such as that in which we live could provide this special mode of participation in the emergent creation itself. This irreversible sequence of transformations is taking shape through our own activities as well as through the activities of the multitude of component members of the universe community.

It is not a straight line sequence, however; the component elements of the universe move in pulsations, in successions of integration-disintegration, in spiral or circular patterns, especially on earth in its seasonal expressions. On earth, in particular, the basic tendencies of the universe seem to explode in an overwhelming display of geological, biological and human modes of expression, from the tiniest particles of matter and their movement to the vast movements of the seas and continents, with the clash and rifting of tectonic plates, the immense hydrological cycles, the spinning of the earth on its own axis, its circling of the sun and the bursting forth of the millionfold variety of living forms.

Throughout this confused, disorderly, even chaotic process, we witness an enormous creativity. The quintessence of this great journey of the universe is the balance between equilibrium and disequilibrium. Although so much of the disequilibrium falls in its reaching toward a new and greater integration, the only way to consistent creativity is through the breakdown of existing unities. That disturbed periods of history are the creative periods can be seen in the dark ages of Europe as well as in the period of breakdown in imperial order in China at the end of the Han dynasty around the year 200 AD.

So too religiously, the grand creativity is found in the stressful moments. It was in a period of spiritual confusion that Buddha appeared to establish a new spiritual discipline. The prophets appeared in the disastrous moments of Israel. Christianity established itself in the social and religious restlessness of the late Roman Empire. Now we find ourselves in the greatest period of disturbance that the earth has ever known, a period when the continued existence of both the human and the natural worlds are severely threatened. The identity of our human fate with the destiny of the planet itself was never more clear.

In terms of liturgy, a new sequence of celebrations is needed based on those stupendous moments when the great cosmological transformations took place. These moments of cosmic transformation must be considered as sacred moments even more than the great moments of seasonal renewal. Only by a proper celebration of these moments can our own human spiritual development take place in an integral manner. Indeed these were the decisive moments in the shaping of human consciousness as well as in the shaping of our physical being.

First among these cosmic celebrations might be that of the emergent moment of the universe itself as a spiritual as well as a physical event. This was the beginning of religion just as it was the beginning of the world. The human mind and all its spiritual capacities began with this first shaping of what was to become the universe as we know it. A supremely sacred moment, it carries within it the high destinies of the universe in its intellectual and spiritual capacities as well as in its physical shaping and living expression.

Also of special import is the rate of emergence of the universe and the curvature of space, whereby all things hold together. The rate of emergence in those first instants had to be precise to the hundred billionth of a fraction. Otherwise the universe would have exploded or collapsed. The rate of emergence was such that the consequent curvature of the universe was sufficiently closed to hold the universe together within its gravitational bondings and yet open enough so that the creative process could continue through these billions of years, providing the guidance and the energies we need as we move through the dangers of the present into a more creative and perhaps more secure future.

This bonding of the universe whereby every reality attracts and is attracted to every other being in the universe was the condition for the rise of human affection. It was the beginning and most comprehensive expression of the divine bonding that pervades the universe and enables its creative processes to continue.

It might be appropriate then if this beginning moment of the universe were the context for religious celebration, perhaps even for a special liturgy; it should be available, in a diversity of expressions, to all the peoples of the planet as we begin to sense our identity in terms of the evolutionary story of the universe rather than in purely physical terms or in mythic modes of expression. Although it seems difficult, at first, to appreciate that these are supreme spiritual moments, these and other transformative moments did help establish both the spiritual and the physical contours of the further development of the entire world.

Among these supreme moments we might list the supernova explosions that took place as the first generation of stars collapsed into themselves in some trillions of degrees of heat; this process generated the heavier elements out of the original hydrogen and helium atoms, and then exploded into the stardust with which our own solar system and planet shaped themselves. New levels of subjectivity came into being, new modalities of bonding, new possibilities for those inner spontaneities whereby the universe carries out its self-organization. Along with all this came a magnificent array of differentiated elements and intricate associations. The earth, in all its spiritual as well as its physical aspects, became a possibility.

To ritualize this moment would provide a depth of appreciation for ourselves and for the entire creative process. Such depth is needed because the entire earthly process has become trivialized, leaving us with no

established way of entering into the spiritual dimension of the story that the universe is telling us about itself.

The human is precisely that being in whom this total process reflects on and celebrates itself and its numinous origins in a special mode of conscious self-awareness. At our highest moments we fulfill this role through the association of our liturgies with the supreme *liturgy* of the universe itself. Since the earliest times of which we have information, the human community has been aware that the universe itself is the primary liturgy. Human personality and community have always sought to insert themselves into space and time through this integration with the great movement of the heavens and the cycles of the seasons, which were seen as celebratory events with profound numinous significance. What is needed now is integration with a new sequence of liturgies related to the irreversible transformation sequence whereby the world as we know it has come into being.

We could continue through the entire range of events whereby the universe took shape, inquiring about the religious meaning and celebrating a great many of the mysteries of the earth. The invention of photosynthesis is especially important in this context. Then the coming of the trees, later the coming of the flowers, one hundred million years ago; and finally the birth of the human species.

Only such a selective sequence of religious celebrations could enable the cosmology of religions to come into being. If the sacred history of the biblical world is recounted with such reverence, how much more the recounting of the sacred history of the universe and of the entire planet earth.

We find this difficult because we are not accustomed to think of ourselves as integral with, or subject to, the universe, to the planet earth, or to the community of living beings; especially not in our religious or spiritual lives which identify the sacred precisely as that which is atemporal and unchanging even though it is experienced within the temporal and the changing. We think of ourselves as the primary referent and the universe as participatory in our own achievements. Only the present threats to the viability of the human as a species and to the life systems of the earth are finally causing us to reconsider our situation.

This leads us to a final question in our consideration of the various religious traditions, the question of the religious role of the human as species. History is being made now in every aspect of the human endeavor not within or between nations, or ethnic groups, or cultures; but between humans as species and the larger earth community. We have been too concerned with ourselves as nations, ethnic groups, cultures, religions. We are presently in need of a species and interspecies orientation in law, economics, politics, education, medicine, religion and whatever else concerns the human.

If until recently we could be unconcerned with the species level of human activities, this is no longer the situation. We now need a species economy that will relate

Seeking the True Meaning of Peace

From June 25 to 30, 1989, an unusual conference met in Costa Rica to explore the meaning and implications of the concept of *Peace*. Present at the conference were a large number of persons concerned with various aspects of this highly pertinent topic. Participants gained new appreciation for the very real connections between such factors as population pressures, ecological crises, development and resource use, religious teachings and spirituality, and international political activity.

Noteworthy among the participants were Oscar Arias, (former) President of Costa Rica, His Holiness Tenzin Gyatso, the 14th Dalai Lama of Tibet, and Monsignor Roman Arrieta, Archbishop of San Jose; also participating were Robert Muller, Chancellor of the University for Peace and former Assistant Secretary-General of the United

Nations, Jaime Montalvo of the University for Peace, and Rodrigo Carazo, former President of Costa Rica and founder of the University for Peace.

In addition, other distinguished guests and more than 500 persons of various creeds, professional training, political orientation and nationalities—including representatives of indigenous populations—came together to study, reflect, visualize new content for the idea of *Peace*, and take action that would have impact throughout the planet.

THE DECLARATION

In preparation for the conference, a commission of representatives from the Foreign Ministry of the Government of Costa Rica and the University for Peace carried forth an international consultation and drafted the *Declaration of Human Responsibilities for Peace and*

Sustainable Development. This document is a sophisticated attempt to identify universally acceptable principles, based upon diverse philosophical and religious wisdom as well as recognizing the requirements of the ecological systems of the earth. The Declaration was enthusiastically considered and adopted by the participants in the conference, and is now being distributed by the government of Costa Rica, by the University for Peace, and by conference attendees as an instrument for reflection and commitment.

Endorsements and uses

Since the conference, the Declaration was presented in October 1989 to the General Assembly of the United Nations and was formally adopted through a presidential decree of the government of

Continued on next page

THE COSMOLOGY OF RELIGIONS, continued

the human as species to the community of species on the planet, and that will ultimately be an integral earth economy. Already the awareness is beginning to dawn that the human is overwhelming the entire productivity of the earth with its excessive demands, using up some 40 percent of the entire productivity of the earth. This leaves an inadequate resource base for the larger community of life. The cycle of renewal is overburdened, to such an extent that even the renewable life systems are being extinguished.

We could say the same thing for medicine; the issue of species health has come into view and beyond that the health of the planet. Since human health on a toxic planet is a contradiction, the primary objective of the medical profession must be to foster the integral health of the earth itself. Only then can human health be adequately attended to.

We can in a corresponding manner outline the need for a species, interspecies and even a planetary legal system as the only viable system that can be functionally effective in the present situation. As in economics and medicine, the planet itself constitutes the normative reference. There already exists a comprehensive participatory governance of the planet. Every member of the earth community rules and is ruled by the other members of the community in such a remarkable manner that the community as a whole and its individual members have prospered over the centuries and millennia. The proper

role for the human is to articulate its own governance within this planetary governance.

What remains is the concept of a religion of the human as species in the larger earth and universe communities. This concept implies a prior sense of the religious dimension of the natural world within the cosmos. Just as we can see the earth in economic, biological and legal modes of being, so might we think of the earth as having a religious mode of being. Although this concept is yet to be articulated effectively in the context of our present understanding of the great story of the universe, the ideas seem to be explicit in many of the scriptures of the world.

In general, however, we have thought of the earth as joining in the religious expression of the human rather than the human joining in the religious expression of the earth. This has caused difficulties in most spheres of human activity. We have consistently thought of the human as primary and the earth as derivative; in the future, and in a cosmology of religions, we must understand that the earth is primary and the human is derivative. Only when the cosmos is acknowledged as the matrix of all value will we be able to solve the ecological crisis and arrive at a more comprehensive view of who we are in the community of the earth. ⊛

Previously published in *Pluralism and Oppression: Theology in a World Perspective*, ed. Paul Knitter, Annual Volume #34, published by College Theology Society, pp. 99–113

Preamble to the Declaration of Human Responsibilities for Peace and Sustainable Development

Considering that both the report of the World Commission on Environment and Development[1] and the United Nations Environmental Perspective to the Year 2000 and Beyond[2] have recognized the imminent danger threatening the existence of the Earth as a result of war and environmental destruction;

Recognizing that the world has been evolving from a group of separate communities towards interdependence and the beginnings of a world community, a process reflecting global concerns, common goals and shared ideals;

Recalling that, according to the Universal Declaration of Human Rights, recognition of the inherent dignity and of the equal and inalienable human rights of all members of the human family is the foundation of freedom, justice and peace in the world;

Considering the aspirations of all the members of the human family to realize

their potential to the maximum through the cultural, social, political and economic development of individuals and of communities, recognized in the Declaration on the Right to Development[3] as an inalienable human right;

Recognizing the necessity of ensuring the full and equal participation of women and men in the decision-making processes relating to the promotion of peace and development;

Bearing in mind that the international community has proclaimed that people have a sacred right to peace[4] and has recommended that national and international organizations should promote peace;[5]

Observing that the international community has recognized the fundamental right of human beings to live in an environment of a quality that permits a life of dignity and well-being;[6]

Bearing in mind the challenge posed by the growing imbalances in the dynamic relationship between population, resources and the environment;

Considering that the General Assembly has established that all human rights and fundamental freedoms are indivisible and interdependent;[7]

Aware that the attainment of those rights has been recognized as being the responsibility of individuals as well as of state;[8]

Concerned because the efforts of human society thus far have not been sufficient to achieve the full recognition of those rights;

Considering that the United Nations has emphasized that wars begin in the minds and through the actions of human beings[9] and that the threats to continuing development and the conservation of the environment arise from diverse but interrelated forms of human behavior;[10]

Bearing in mind that the General Assembly has determined that, in order to ensure the survival of natural systems and an adequate level of living for all, human activity should be reoriented towards the goals of sustainable development;[11]

Considering that the present generation, having reached a crossroads where new challenges and decisions must be faced, bears the

immediate responsibility for its own development and for the survival of future generations, so that they may consciously constitute a single world, just, peaceful and based on cooperation with nature;

Convinced, therefore, that there is an urgent need for a greater awareness of the unity of life and of the special character of each of the expressions of life, and for a more profound human sense of responsibility and a reorientation of human thoughts, feelings and actions;

Considering that this Declaration can contribute to the achievement of this reorientation and can inspire many practical applications at the level of the individual, the family and the community as well as at the national and international levels;

In accordance with all the foregoing considerations, the Government of Costa Rica offers the present Declaration of Human Responsibilities for Peace and Sustainable Development as an instrument for reflection and compromise.

SEEKING PEACE: DECLARATION, continued

Costa Rica as an instrument for reflection and commitment. As a statement of universal principles, the document can have many applications in forums ranging from religious and ethical studies to economics and political science.

By linking the pursuit of peace with the concepts of sustainability, personal responsibility and interdependence, the Declaration's insights bring a holistic perspective to ecology and environmental studies, and have important implications for the development of personal and planetary resources. The values it promotes have implications for economic aid programs, as well as for international policies and cooperation. Its greatest value, however, is its focus on the universal responsibility of each individual, so it is through personal reflection and commitment that the Declaration will have its most significant impact.

For more information, contact:

Dr. Abelardo Brenes
University for Peace
P.O. Box 199-1250 Escazu
Costa Rica, Central America

Also available from the University for Peace is a book of its proceedings, keynote speeches and other documents based on the conference for $24.00 plus certified air mail ($4.50 for the Americas, $6.50 for Europe and $8.00 for Asia, Africa and Australia).

NOTES

1. Accepted by General Assembly resolution 42/187 of 11 December 1987.

2. Adopted by General Assembly resolution 42/186 of 11 December 1987.

3. General Assembly resolution 41/128 of December 1986.

4. Declaration on the Right of Peoples to Peace, General Assembly resolution 39/11 of 12 November 1984.

5. Declaration on the Preparation of Societies for Life in Peace, General Assembly resolution 33/73 of 15 December 1978.

6. Report of the United Nations Conference on the Human Environment (the Stockholm Declaration), 16 June 1972.

7. General Assembly resolution 37/199 of 18 December 1982.

8. See World Charter for Nature: General Assembly resolution 37/7 of 28 October 1982, and resolution 38/124 of 16 December 1983.

9. Declaration on the Preparation of Societies for Life in Peace: General Assembly resolution 33/73 of 15 December 1978; Constitution of the United Nations Educational, Scientific and Cultural Organization, preamble, paragraph 1.

10. General Assembly resolutions 37/7 of 28 October 1982; 42/186 of 11 December 1987 and 42/187 of 11 December 1987.

11. General Assembly resolutions 42/186 of 11 December 1987 and 42/187 of 11 December 1987.

Declaration of Human Responsibilities for Peace and Sustainable Development

Chapter I.
Unity of the World

Article 1. Everything which exists is part of an interdependent universe. All living creatures depend on each other for their existence, well-being and development.

Article 2. All human beings are an inseparable part of nature, on which culture and human civilization have been built.

Article 3. Life on Earth is abundant and diverse. It is sustained by the unhindered functioning of natural systems which ensure the provision of energy, air, water and nutrients for all living creatures. Every manifestation of life on Earth is unique and essential and must therefore be respected and protected without regard to its apparent value to human beings.

Chapter II.
Unity of the Human Family

Article 4. All human beings are an inseparable part of the human family and depend on each other for their existence, well-being and development. Every human being is a unique expression and manifestation of life and has a separate contribution to make to life on Earth. Each human being has fundamental and inalienable rights and freedoms, without distinction of race, color, sex, language, religion, political or other opinion, national or social origin, economic status or any other social situation.

Article 5. All human beings have the same basic needs and the same fundamental aspirations to be satisfied. All individuals have the right to development, the purpose of which is to promote attainment of the full potential of each person.

Chapter III.
The Alternatives Facing Mankind and Universal Responsibility

Article 6. Responsibility is an inherent aspect of any relation in which human beings are involved. This capacity to act responsibly in a conscious, independent, unique and personal manner is an inalienable creative quality of every human being. There is no limit to its scope or depth other than that established by each person for himself. The more activities human beings take on and become involved in, the more they will grow and derive strength.

Article 7. Of all living creatures, human beings have the unique capacity to decide consciously whether they are protecting or harming the quality and conditions of life on Earth. In reflecting on the fact that they belong to the natural world and occupy a special position as participants in the evolution of natural processes, people can develop, on the basis of selflessness, compassion and love, a sense of universal responsibility towards the world as an integral whole, towards the protection of nature and the promotion of the highest potential for change, with a view to creating those conditions which will enable them to achieve the highest level of spiritual and material well-being.

Article 8. At this critical time in history, the alternatives facing mankind are crucial. In directing their actions towards the attainment of progress in society, human beings have frequently forgotten the inherent role they play in the natural world and the indivisible human family, and their basic needs for a healthy life. Excessive consumption, abuse of the environment and aggression between peoples have brought the natural processes of the Earth to a critical stage which threatens their survival. By reflecting on these issues, individuals will be capable of discerning their responsibility and thus reorienting their conduct towards peace and sustainable development.

Chapter IV.
Reorientation Towards Peace and Sustainable Development

Article 9. Given that all forms of life are unique and essential, that all human beings have the right to development and that both peace and violence are the product of the human mind, it is from the human mind that a sense of responsibility to act and think in a peaceful manner will develop. Through peace-oriented awareness, individuals will understand the nature of those conditions which are necessary for their well-being and development.

Article 10. Being mindful of their sense of responsibility towards the human family and the environment in which they live and to the need to think and act in a peaceful manner, human beings have the obligation to act in a way that is consistent with the observance of and respect for inherent human rights and to ensure that their consumption of resources is in keeping with the satisfaction of the basic needs of all.

Article 11. When members of the human family recognize that they are responsible to themselves and to present and future generations for the conservation of the planet, as protectors of the natural world and promoters of its continued development, they will be obliged to act in a rational manner in order to ensure sustainable life.

Article 12. Human beings have a continuing responsibility when setting up, taking part in or representing social units, associations and institutions, whether private or public. In addition, all such entities have a responsibility to promote peace and sustainability, and to put into practice the educational goals which are conducive to that end. These goals include the fostering of awareness of the interdependence of human beings among themselves and with nature and the universal responsibility of individuals to solve the problems which they have engendered through their attitudes and actions in a manner that is consistent with the protection of human rights and fundamental freedoms.

Let us be faithful to the privilege of our responsibility.

The Earth Summit (UNCED)

On December 22, 1989, the United Nations General Assembly called for a global meeting that would devise strategies to halt and reverse the effects of environmental degradation "in the context of increased national and international efforts to promote sustainable and environmentally sound development in all countries."

Also known as the Earth Summit, the United Nations Conference on Environment and Development was held in Rio de Janeiro, Brazil, from June 3 to 14, 1992. After two years of preparations, the 178 governments at the Conference reached agreement on three texts: Agenda 21, a comprehensive strategy for global action on sustainable development; the Rio Declaration on Environment and Development, outlining the rights and responsibilities of governments in this area; and a statement of principles to guide the sustainable management of forests worldwide.

Agenda 21

Underlying Agenda 21 is the notion that humanity has reached a defining moment in its history. We can continue our present policies which serve to deepen the economic divisions within and between countries; which increase poverty, hunger, sickness and illiteracy worldwide; and which are causing the continued deterioration of the ecosystem on which we depend for life on Earth.

Or we can change course. We can improve the living standards of those who are in need. We can better manage and protect the ecosystem and bring about a more prosperous future for us all.

"No nation can achieve this on its own," states Mr. Maurice Strong, Secretary-General of the Conference, in the preamble to Agenda 21. "Together we can—in a global partnership for sustainable development."

from the press summary of Agenda 21 and Earth Summit press releases

More details and publications about ratification, implementation and monitoring of the conventions, as well about other ongoing developments are available from:
UNCED Information Programme, DPI
Room S-894, United Nations
New York, NY 10017 USA
TEL: (212) 963-4295
FAX: (212) 963-4556

The Rio Consensus

Parliamentary Earth Summit

June 5–7, 1992
Palado Tiradentes, Rio de Janeiro, Brazil

*W*e, the 300 parliamentarians and spiritual leaders, associating ourselves with scientists, business leaders, environmental activists, artists and journalists, have met at the Parliamentary Earth Summit conference, held under the auspices of the National Congress of Brazil and the Global Forum of Spiritual and Parliamentary Leaders on June 5–7, 1992.

Our purpose has been to discuss *value change* as it relates to the global environmental crisis.

We have reached an enthusiastic consensus on the following:

One: sustainable development

*W*e have heard powerful testimony from those on the front lines of the environmental crisis: those whose health has been damaged, whose homes have been destroyed, who see little future for themselves and their communities. We have listened to many impassioned statements of particular and local issues of great urgency. In these testimonies, three concerns have been held up over and over again by the majority of participants:

CHILDREN

*T*hroughout our meeting children themselves have been present and have offered their own statements. Children of the street have spoken in words such as these: "I am 16 and I have lived in the street for eight years." "We are often beaten by the police." "Most of my friends have been killed, and I do not know if I myself will live another year." "To get out of this, I need support—a home and a school." Children from more fortunate circumstances also have spoken with purity and eloquence of their hopes and visions for the future and their wish that nature be protected.

Our discussion can best be summed up in the words of one presenter who said, *"Any society which cannot care for its children cannot regard its development as in any sense sustainable."* We therefore commit ourselves to action for the well-being of the world's children, knowing that only those things for which we have taken responsibility will come about.

We call upon the Global Forum and the newly established International Green Cross to mobilize their networks of different sectors to mount an effective campaign at all levels to alleviate the plight of children in general and street children in particular—through advocacy and information exchange, and in cooperation with UNICEF, nongovernmental organizations and our own governments.

POVERTY

*I*t was our unanimous opinion that the problems of poverty, population growth and environmental degradation are inextricably intertwined, and that these problems can only be solved through global action at the international and national levels, guided by principles of equity. For those who cannot meet the most basic needs of life, preservation of their environment becomes tragically difficult. Those from "developing" countries have called for a full appreciation by those in the "developed" world of their total reality, and to form their understanding and their policies accordingly. The immense contribution of women to economies in rural areas must be acknowledged and programmatically supported.

FREEDOM

*F*reedom and democratic government, as well as open public discourse, is a prerequisite for sustainable development. Women, and all ethnic and cultural minorities must have full participation in governing processes for sound environmental policy to be created.

For competition in business to foster a morally positive efficiency, the public must have free access to information about the operations and policies of business and industry.

Two: values

VALUES AND TRANSFORMATION

*W*e affirm in a strong consensus—parliamentarians no less than any others—that *the environmental crisis has an inner, spiritual dimension.* The root causes of external problems are moral and psychological. Unless we address this aspect of the problem, there will be no long-term solution. "Sustainability" cannot be defined only in material terms.

We therefore call for the integration of values into public discourse and into policy-making processes where it is often absent, suppressed or ignored.

We also share a recognition of the need for our own transformation, individually and collectively. We have heard a note of repentance and a call for renewal of leadership. We acknowledge the need to question ourselves, and to re-investigate our existing value systems, personal and traditional.

The International Green Cross should be guided by spiritual values and work to prevent war, which causes extraordinary environmental damage, as for example, in Kuwait.

SPIRITUAL VALUES

*W*e have heard an extraordinary common witness from spiritual leaders of diverse traditions who have expressed a shared vision, repeatedly referring to these same fundamental insights.

The world and all life within it is a gift or a divine creation. The presence of God is in all things. Compassion and love spring from experiencing this divine presence. This compassion and love for our fellow humans—and for all living things, who are members of one family—will empower us to act to heal ourselves and the Earth. Without this healing, nothing can be done.

We acknowledge the especially powerful affirmation by indigenous peoples of this understanding of all nature as a family or community of related beings, each of which is conscious. Indigenous peoples have preserved this vision and their environmental values against great odds, and now begin to be heard as a voice of conscience.

Three: The International Green Cross

*A*t our meeting we set the beginning of a historic process in motion by deciding to establish the International Green Cross as a people-based international nongovernmental organization to promote programs at the national and international levels, and to protect and preserve the natural environment from damage caused by human action.

We have invited Mr. Mikhail Gorbachev, who originated this proposal at our meeting in Moscow in January 1990, to be the first President of the

---

The Earth Summit: A Critique

"Three of the biggest causes of environmental destruction were not criticized at all—multinational corporations, the military, and inappropriate development models. A myriad of other problems were not dealt with because they are too controversial, including the unsustainable consumption patterns of the richest peoples of the planet, and the fact that one billion people have no access to freshwater supplies. Instead of discussing policies that lead to pollution, the governments signed 'tailpipe' solutions such as checking carbon dioxide emissions and cataloging rare species in the world's remaining forests. . . .

"What then are the solutions? First of all we have to stop working with and creating more huge international institutions, top heavy with theoreticians and Northern experts, to solve problems that should be dealt with by local communities.

"Second, we have to realize that public concern over the environment has spawed a massive 'greenwash' campaign by corporations and governments to develop new 'green' products and policies, rather than stopping the production of too many goods that are consuming and destroying resources and that have brought us to the environmental crisis that we have today."

excerpts from an article by
Pratap Chatterjee in the *Food First* Newsletter,
"News and Views" (Fall 1992)

International Green Cross. He has commended our initiative in a message to our meeting in the following words.

"I reaffirm my commitment to the goals of the international environmental movement. I support the initiative for creating the International Green Cross. Our foundation and I personally are ready to participate most actively in its work."

The conference Secretary General, Akio Matsumura, under the guidance of Honorary Chairman Javier Perez de Cuellar, has been empowered to form a preparatory group to work with Mikhail Gorbachev in drafting the charter, structure, and operational plan of the International Green Cross to be presented for approval at the Kyoto meeting of the Global Forum in April 1993.

Four: dialogue and global community

*I*n our dialogue we have been moved and impressed by a new openness to one another of members of the different sectors, with their widely differing approaches, of members of different religions, of those from nations of the South and of the North. We have asked each other for understanding and have received a generous response.

We have also found a ringing spontaneous affirmation of the validity of the Global Forum concept of dialogue and cooperation between the "two pillars" of parliamentary and spiritual leaders joined by scientists, journalists, artists and business leaders.

Here in Rio we have found ourselves in a new quest for solidarity and a universal ethic, as we have realized that we are indeed part of a global civilization. The process leading to this historic gathering, encompassing the United Nations conference itself and all related activities, has made the world into a community in a new way. All over the world people are now joined by their concern about the environment.

And for these two weeks the city of Rio de Janeiro actually has become a "global village." We see in this an image which we hope may foretell the future.

"The critical issue is to understand, criticize and transform the attitudes of greed, hatred and domination in whatever context they appear, seeking to get at the deeper social and psychological roots of the egocentricity at work in these attitudes. The contemporary search by humanity for its spiritual center acquires clear direction today when it is focused on the effort to find creative alternatives to a way of life that emphasizes egoism, having and subjugation. The spiritual quest of our time is for a faith and ways of living that at once liberate the self and the other, creating an authentic community with nature as well as among people."

from *Spirit and Nature*, edited by John C. Elder and Steven C. Rockefeller, p.147

"The world needs a clear, decisive, moral lead. It needs a lead that will be full of idealism, even with a touch of the romantic; it needs a lead that will help people to dream of a future full of hope and peace, and will inspire them to turn a dream into a goal. The world does not need the tired arguments of the politicians who hope for peace by bullets. Nor the discredited hopes of those who look for peacekeeping forces and justified warfare. A new generation of church leaders is emerging: They will bring a fresh approach and a new way of thinking and they will be more open to new ideas drawn from the heart of the Gospel."

ANGLICAN PACIFIST FELLOWSHIP

The New Consciousness

Dom Bede Griffiths

*W*e are entering a new age. The European civilization which we have known for the past 2,000 years is giving way to a global civilization, which will no longer be centered in Europe but will have its focus more in Asia, Africa and South America. Christianity will no longer be a separate religion but will be seen in the context of the religious traditions of humankind as a whole.

As we enter this new civilization, the meeting-place of East and West, and of the nations of the world, will be science. The changes in contemporary Western science have provided a new outlook on life for humanity as a whole. The central point is the new understanding of the universe which is no longer perceived as consisting of solid bodies moving in space and time but rather, according to quantum theory, as a field of energy pervaded by consciousness. Western scientists, for the first time, have seriously faced the fact that if they want to understand the universe, they have to understand their own consciousness. A leader in this development was David Bohm for he was one of the first scientists to take seriously the place of consciousness in scientific understanding.

The new understanding of science and consciousness provides, as it were, a platform on which religions can meet. We are beginning to see that we can now interpret the religious traditions, particularly the myths and symbols of all the scriptures, within the context of a world where science and consciousness interrelate.

In this new global civilization, Christianity, as I understand it, will be seen in relation to Hinduism, Buddhism, Taoism, Sufism and the primordial religious traditions—the Australian, the Native American, the African and so on. A new consciousness is emerging, moving beyond the rational mind with its awareness of separate entities and its dualistic approach. We are beginning to discover the unitive consciousness which goes beyond dualistic awareness.

David Bohm speaks, as a theoretical physicist, of unity and interconnectedness in what he calls the implicate order, prior to the world of separate entities which is our normal experience. The implicate order is constantly unfolding, giving rise to the explicate order of particular forms and structures. This is where the new scientific understanding of the universe meets with the non-dualist traditions of Hinduism, Buddhism and so on. As we move beyond the present religious forms and structures we begin to see that, behind and beyond their diversity, there is an underlying unity. All the religions are expressing symbolically something which cannot be expressed in rational terms.

Any attempt to express fully that which is beyond expression is bound to fail. The new *Catechism of the Catholic Church* attempts to put the content of the Catholic faith into rational discursive terms. The aim is illusory because the *content* of the Catholic faith, in common with that of the other great religious traditions, transcends all rational, discursive thought. When he had finished his great theological work, the *Summa Theologica*, St. Thomas Aquinas realized that all he had written was as straw in comparison to his mystical experience. He was fully aware that no image or concept is remotely adequate to the fullness of the faith.

Within Christianity the focus will be on the mystery of faith, which Jesus called the mystery of the Kingdom of God and St. Paul called the mystery of Christ. A mystery cannot be expressed rationally or logically, but it can be symbolized. All scientific theories and all religious doctrines are in fact symbolic structures. In each religion the symbolic structures work by

Dom Bede Griffiths

Born Alan Richard Griffiths in 1906 in England, Dom Bede Griffiths had been invited to participate in the Parliament as a major spiritual leader but was unable to accept the invitation due to his declining health. Nevertheless, he was very supportive of the Parliament's aims, especially of the value of pluralism and of mutual responsibility for the Earth. Father Bede, also known as Swami Dayananda, or Bliss of Compassion, died on May 13, 1993.

As a Catholic Christian monk, Dom Bede Griffiths had gone to India in 1955 to establish a monastic community and, as he wrote to a friend, "to seek the other half of my soul." He discovered this "other half" in the awakening of his intuitive, mystical life, and it is this life within the *cave of the heart* that was India's gift to him. His gift to us is his harmonization in his teachings, his many books, and in his life, of the religious and mystical with the scientific, of the East with the West, of the past with the future.

The Dalai Lama of Tibet recently wrote of Father Bede Griffiths:

"[He] is one of the foremost thinking Christians of this century. I have had the great pleasure of meeting Father Bede Griffiths on a few occasions and the discussions we had were most stimulating and profound. Throughout his life and in his work as a Benedictine monk, his vision has guided him to open the hearts and minds of mankind to gain understanding and acceptance of all the major religions with respect and dignity, to gain a sense of peace and unity and to further the cause of goodwill for all people."

This article, expressing Bede Griffiths' prophetic vision, is his acceptance speech for the John Harriott Memorial Award. It was dictated in Shantivanam Ashram in Tamil Nadu, India. The last article written and published during his lifetime, "The New Consciousness" was printed in *The Tablet* (of London) on January 16, 1993; printed with permission.

compiled by the Editor
with assistance from
Brother Wayne Teasdale

A Culture of Peace

Towards a Universal Civilization with a "Heart"

Brother Wayne Teasdale

Christian monk and sannyasi *in the lineage of Father Bede Griffiths, author of books and numerous essays on mysticism, Christian Vedanta and other topics, and member of the Board of Monastic Interreligious Dialogue.*

There is a longing that stirs deep within all of us, innate to the human family, found in every nation, culture, every religious tradition, in the ancient myths, in poetry, song and historical experience. It is the inspiration behind them all—the desire for the paradisal state of life, the beatitude of the perfect society. Whether it is conceived as a garden of heavenly delights, a pure utopian state, or a more realistic process that brings transformation of society gradually over many years through a deliberate approach, the desire itself is real; it's in touch with something ultimate, something that is as mysterious as it is inviting.

In this essay I am suggesting that a universal society of a higher order than is presently the case is not only possible, but perhaps inevitable! I will try to show how the culture of peace is related to the emergence of a new civilization, what the foundation of this global society is, and what its characteristic elements are, especially the roles of nonviolence and spirituality.

Remembrances of paradise

All the myths about the original state of the human condition speak of it in terms that convey a kind of intimacy with the Divine, with Ultimate Reality and mystery. This is clear not only in the Bible, but is also true of the Hindu tradition, especially in the Bhakti school, but also, more generally, in every other school of Hindu mysticism. It is equally true of Greek mythology as it is of the experience of indigenous societies of Africa, Australia and the Americas. It is true, in its way, of Buddhist, Jewish and Islamic or Sufi mysticism, as it is of Taoism, Confucianism, Shintoism and Shamanism. In all these forms there is present the faint memory of beatitude as a real experience of intimacy with the Source of Being.

Continued on next pages

---

opening the human mind to the transcendent Reality, to the truth. The symbolic structures within the religions each have their unique value but all have limitations because they are socially and culturally conditioned.

The unique value of Christianity is its profoundly historic structure. That to me is a key point. Christ is not an *avatara*. The Incarnation is a unique historic event and Jesus a unique historic person. In gathering all things, all of humanity and all matter, into one in himself, he transforms the world, bringing the cosmos, its matter and its processes, back to its source in the transcendent Reality whom he called *Abba,* Father. This is unique. At the same time, one of the main limitations of institutional Christianity is its exclusivism, which stems from its cultural background in ancient Judaism. This exclusivism particularly will have to be transcended as we move more and more deeply into the mystery of Christ. We are in a position now to be open to all the religious traditions of the world, being aware of their limitations but also, most importantly, realizing their unity in the depth-dimension which underlies them all; and that, of course, is the mystical dimension.

Many people today are discovering the mystical dimension in religion. In Christianity, once we get beyond the doctrinal systems, we have a long tradition of mystical wisdom beginning with St. John and St. Paul, going through Clement of Alexandria, Origen and the Greek Fathers, and on to St. Augustine; and later St. Thomas Aquinas and Meister Eckhart. And now we can relate that to the traditions of Tibetan Buddhism, Hinduism and the other great religions.

The Christian Gospel as originally proclaimed was: "Repent, for the kingdom of heaven is at hand." At that time the old structures were breaking down and the kingdom of God was emerging. The Apocalypse would put it, "I saw a new heaven and a new earth. The old heaven and the old earth had passed away. And a Voice said, 'Behold, I make all things new.'" That is always happening.

I think that is exactly where we are today: the breakdown of the old civilization and of the whole order which we knew, and, within that, the rebirth of meaning, penetrated by a new consciousness. Science today recognizes that all order comes out of chaos. When the old structures break down and the traditional forms begin to disintegrate, precisely then in the chaos, a new form, a new structure, a new order of being and consciousness emerges.

The old is always dying and the new is emerging, and that which is new socially and culturally transforms the old. This is really an apocalyptic age. Within this context we can take the forms of Christian symbolism, but we can also take forms like the coming of the Buddha Maitreya or the last *avatara* of Kali. Every religion looks forward to a time when the end will come and the new birth will take place. So in a very wonderful way we are at the birth of a new age and a new consciousness. ✿

As the ancient cultures became more stable and were informed by the spirit of their original revelation experiences, they evolved societies that were essentially pacific or deeply peaceful and in a state of inner harmony. This pacific quality is evident in the great pre-Vedic Harappa culture of the Indus Valley. This culture is probably the prototype[1] of the one that arose from the Aryan-Dravidian union. We still do not know the age of the Harappa-Mohenjo-Daro civilization, but the discovery of two seals with the image of a deity seated in the meditation *asana*[2] (posture), suggests a high degree of spiritual awareness coming from the practice of meditation and an attitude of contemplative interiority. It may be that the Harappans were the progenitors of the rishic seers of Indian antiquity, and perhaps were the recipients of a primordial revelation from which they learned the cosmic and social harmony that is enshrined in the Vedic notion of *rta*.[3]

Similar to the notion of rta, on a social and political level in Chinese history and civilization, is the Confucian ideal of *Ta-t'ung*, the "Great Society," or "Great Commonwealth"[4] It can also be translated as the "Great Unity in Common," or simply as the "Great Harmony." I prefer the latter two expressions. China knew centuries of civil peace when her empire was socially and politically cohesive, centuries in which crime and corruption were nearly nonexistent, when relationships within the family, the state and the society were harmonious. These periods of China's golden ages, for example, the Tang dynasty (618-906 AD), were the consequence of the *Ta-t'ung*, when it prevailed.

We also marvel at the example of tolerance and enlightened government of the Buddhist emperor Ashoka, of the Maurya Empire in India, who reigned from 268–233 BC. His example is often cited as constituting a brilliant star in the constellation of ancient rulers.

In the West, we have the seemingly perfect blueprints of Plato's *Republic* and Thomas More's *Utopia*—"seemingly perfect" because both of these attempts, though originating in spiritual wisdom, still are somewhat abstract, untried, and so, theoretical, even though they portray societies where genuine justice exists. But it was St. Augustine who, in his monumental *City of God*, his philosophy of history, describes the perfect Christian society, whose foundation is peace, as "the tranquillity of order."[5] He elaborates this order in its highest sense: "The peace of the celestial city (the City of God, Heaven) is the perfectly ordered and harmonious enjoyment of God, and of one another in God."[6] The harmonious order of human society derives from its heavenly archetype, and the basis of the latter realm is this mystical relationship with the divine Source, which is also the end for each of us.

There is also the extremely ancient Tibetan legend of Shambhala, a mystical kingdom hidden away somewhere in or beyond the Himalayas, where a perfect utopia exists. Many of Tibetan Buddhism's secret or esoteric writings are attributed to Shambhala, including the texts associated with the Kalacakra initiation. The Dalai Lama is said to have once remarked: "If so many Kalacakra texts are supposed to have come from Shambhala, how could the country be just a fantasy?"[7]

Whether or not these legends refer to real places, however, they are found in most cultures, and we must garner their spirit, their deep spiritual truth, and apply it to our own attempts at building a new civilization. For all of these myths and treatises are inspired by an intuition that we are meant for something better.

The Parliament vis-a-vis a universal society

*A*ll memories of paradise and the attempts to create it in this world again point to the possibility and, indeed, the urgency of moving toward this *something better*, this new civilization. I believe that we have a unique opportunity today to introduce the possibility of such a new

In My Dream

I see a door into another world,
and as I pass through this door
I see wonders and beauty galore.
I see love, peace and happiness.
I am amazed by all I see:
no prejudice, no lies, no hate,
only good, nothing bad or evil;
and in the instant before I awake
I see how Eden must have been.

COLLEEN MC GARGAL
8th grade

Baby Earth

In a dream I see a small boy's heart
reaching out to the earth,
and all our troubles are being taken out
on such a small child

Who cannot understand his feelings,
who just needs
to be held and cared for.

Although the boy can see the world
and its troubles,
they cannot see him.

ANGIE DOMIENIK
8th grade

The Beautiful God

In a dream I see a beautiful god
watching over his world.
There he is with the golden moon.
I see him put out his hand.
He touches mars and moves it a little.

I see a jaguar run and jump,
and as he jumps
the god gives him wings.
The jaguar flies away.

Then it starts to rain
warm purple rain drops on my head,
and all the animals come out and jump.
And as they jump,
the god gives them wings.

Then the god looks at me
and gives me wings.
Then I soar through the air
with the animals.

SHYLA WALKER
4th grade

global order as the child of enlightened values and wisdom. The introduction of a new universal civilization as well as its dissemination require the permanent collaboration of the world's religions. For just as there can be "no peace on Earth unless there is peace among the religions," as Hans Küng[8] has rightly observed, no advance to an enlightened global order is possible unless these same religions decide to work together. That much seems obvious. How to achieve this kind of sustained cooperation is less obvious.

The logic of our global life and situation with all its complexity and all the international problems we face as a planet, the fact of interdependence on all levels, and our precious and rich pluralism have brought us to this intense moment of focus in history. We are compelled and challenged to leap beyond, transcend, even outgrow our old limits, and become a *new humanity*. This new humanity receives its direction and inspiration from the discovery of our common, larger identity in what Thomas Berry, the eloquent ecological thinker calls the *Earth Community*,[9] a natural commonwealth of species united in the one planetary world, *living* in genuine harmony with one another and with the Earth itself.

I see great potential for the Parliament of the World's Religions to become a significant instrument and catalyst for a new civilization by focusing world attention upon it. In many ways, the Parliament of 1893, in historical terms, was a prophetic act because—just by happening—it pointed to the need for the religions to have a forum in which they can discover, through trial and error, their common voice and acceptance of a *universal responsibility*[10] for the Earth.

The Parliament in our time represents an historical promise, a unique opportunity to forge ahead towards a deeper sense of our identity as the *Community of Religions* within the Earth Community itself. From this profound realization—that religions constitute a larger reality of community than any one tradition standing alone—we can begin to place the stones in the edifice of the new, enlightened civilization. The Parliament of the World's

The Seville Statement on Violence

A scientific statement which says peace is possible because war is not a biological necessity, this statement was written by an international team of specialists in 1986, for the United Nations-sponsored International Year of Peace and its followup. Based on scientific evidence and endorsed by scientific and professional organizations around the world, the statement was adopted by UNESCO in 1989. –Ed.

Statement on Violence

Believing that it is our responsibility to address from our particular disciplines the most dangerous and destructive activities of our species, violence and war; recognizing that science is a human cultural product which cannot be definitive or all encompassing; and gratefully acknowledging the support of the authorities of Seville and representatives of the Spanish UNESCO, we, the undersigned scholars from around the world and from relevant sciences, have met and arrived at the following statement on violence. In it we challenge a number of alleged biological findings that have been used, even by some in our disciplines, to justify violence and war. Because the alleged findings have contributed to an atmosphere of pessimism in our time,

we submit that the open, considered rejection of these misstatements can contribute significantly to the International Year of Peace.

Misuse of scientific theories and data to justify violence and war is not new but has been made since the advent of modern science. For example, the theory of evolution has been used to justify not only war, but also genocide, colonialism and the suppression of the weak.

We state our position in the form of five propositions. We are aware that there are many other issues about violence and war that could be fruitfully addressed from the standpoint of our disciplines, but we restrict ourselves here to what we consider a most important first step.

IT IS SCIENTIFICALLY INCORRECT to say that we have inherited a tendency to make war from our animal ancestors. Although fighting occurs widely throughout animal species, only a few cases of destructive intra-species fighting between organized groups have ever been recorded among naturally living species, and none of these involve the use of tools designed to be weapons. Normal predatory feeding upon other species cannot be equated with intra-species violence. Warfare is a particularly human phenomenon and does not occur in other animals.

The fact that warfare has changed so

radically over time indicates that it is a product of culture. Its biological connection is primarily through language which makes possible the coordination of groups, the transmission of technology and the use of tools. War is biologically possible, but it is not inevitable, as evidenced by its variation in occurrence and nature over time and space. There are cultures which have not engaged in war for centuries, and there are cultures which have engaged in war frequently at some times and not at others.

IT IS SCIENTIFICALLY INCORRECT to say that war or any other violent behavior is genetically programmed into our human nature. While genes are involved at all levels of nervous system function, they provide a developmental potential that can be actualized only in conjuction with the ecological and social environment. While individuals vary in their predispositions to be affected by their experience, it is the interaction between their genetic endowment and conditions of nurturance that determines their personalities. Except for rare pathologies, the genes do not produce individuals necessarily predisposed to violence. Neither do they determine the opposite. While genes are co-involved in establishing our behavioral capacities,

Religions, along with the United Nations, the nation states, the individual religious traditions, and non-governmental and international organizations could become an essential institution of this global society and a *vehicle* for its actualization on a global scale. We have a historic responsibility in our time to cast light on this unique and unprecedented opportunity. Thus the prophetic direction of the first Parliament can be realized by the second in our time.

The Parliament of the World's Religions should emerge as a permanent international institution from the centennial deliberations in Chicago because it is desperately needed. There is, I believe, a certain necessity to its birth, urged on us and directed by the Spirit. The time has come for this powerful idea to flower into historic incarnation before our open hearts, despite our disbelieving minds. If it happens, the Parliament will be not simply the event of 1993, nor of the decade, nor even of the 21st century, but its birth might well be the definitive event of the next several millennia!

Nonviolence and the culture of peace

I am convinced that we must become aware of the culture of peace that is slowly developing within the larger context of the new global civilization. It is unquestionably fundamental to it, one of its enduring pillars. More basic still, and essential to the growth and deep rootedness of the culture of peace and the new civilization, is the value and attitude of nonviolence. As Mahatma Gandhi, Martin Luther King and the Dalai Lama well understood, one of the most effective tools in educating for peace is teaching nonviolence.

To set the stage for the introduction of nonviolence as a serious option on a global scale, particularly as we enter into the next century, The Seville Statement on Violence[11] presents the highly significant conclusions of an international group of scientists and researchers. Endorsed by UNESCO, The Seville Statement offers great and solid hope to the world by underscoring the *good news* that violence is *not* innate to the human species, that it is a

---

THE SEVILLE STATEMENT ON VIOLENCE, continued

they do not by themselves specify the outcome.

IT IS SCIENTIFICALLY INCORRECT to say that in the course of human evolution there has been a selection for aggressive behavior more than for other kinds of behavior. In all well-studied species, status within the group is achieved by the ability to cooperate and to fulfill social functions relevant to the structure of that group. *Dominance* involves social bondings and affiliations; it is not simply a matter of the possession and use of superior physical power, although it does involve aggressive behaviors. Where genetic selection for aggressive behavior has been artificially instituted in animals, it has rapidly succeeded in producing hyper-aggressive individuals. This indicates that aggression was not maximally selected under natural conditions. When such experientially-created hyper-aggressive animals are present in a social group, they either disrupt its social structure or are driven out. Violence is neither in our evolutionary legacy nor in our genes.

IT IS SCIENTIFICALLY INCORRECT to say that humans have a *violent brain*. While we do have the neural apparatus to act violently, it is not automatically activated by internal or external stimuli. Like higher primates and unlike other animals, our higher neural processes

filter such stimuli before they can be acted upon. How we act is shaped by how we have been conditioned and socialized. There is nothing in our neural physiology that compels us to react violently.

IT IS SCIENTIFICALLY INCORRECT to say that war is caused by *instinct* or any single motivation. The emergence of modern warfare has been a journey from the primacy of emotional and motivational factors, sometimes called *instincts*, to the primacy of cognitive factors. Modern war involves institutional use of personal characteristics such as obedience, suggestibility and idealism, social skills such as language, and rational considerations such as cost-calculation, planning and information processing. The technology of modern war has exaggerated traits associated with violence both in the training of actual combatants and in the preparation of support for a war in the general population. As a result of this exaggeration, such traits are often mistaken to be the causes rather than the consequences of the process.

We conclude that biology does not condemn humanity to war, and that humanity can be freed from the bondage of biological pessimism and empowered with confidence to take the transformative tasks needed in this

International Year of Peace and in the years to come. Although these tasks are mainly institutional and collective, they also rest upon the consciousness of individual participants for whom pessimism and optimism are crucial factors. Just as *wars begin in the minds of men*, peace also begins in our minds. The same species who invented war is capable of inventing peace. The responsibility lies with each of us.

SEVILLE, May 16, 1986

SIGNERS

David Adams, Psychology
S.A. Barnett, Ethology
N.P. Bechtereva, Neurophysiology
Bonnie Frank Carter, Psychology
José M. Rodríguez Delgado, Neurophysiology
José Lewis Díaz, Ethology
Andrzej Eliasz, Individual Differences Psychology
Santiago Genovés, Biological Anthropology
Benson E. Ginsburg, Behavior Genetics
Jo Groebel, Social Psychology
Samir-Kumar Ghosh, Sociology
Robert Hinde, Animal Behavior
Richard E. Leakey, Physical Anthropology
Taha H. Malasi, Psychiatry
J. Martin Ramírez, Psychobiology
Federico Mayor Zaragoza, Biochemistry
Diana L. Mendoza, Ethology
Ashis Nandy, Political Psychology
John Paul Scott, Animal Behavior
Riitta Wahlstrom, Psychology

learned behavior, and that, consequently, it can and must be left behind as humans, in effect, unlearn it.

All of us know that we must come to grips with the escalating problem of violence, both in society and in ourselves. It is especially critical that we confront it as it emanates from communities of faith in conflict. Everything would seem to depend on getting violence under control; one way to do this —a way which serves the culture of peace and brings us nearer to the universal civilization—is to make a solid commitment to nonviolence among religions, nations, groups and persons. In committing ourselves to nonviolence in our individual intentions and actions, and, collectively, through the Parliament and our religious institutions, our international organizations and our governments, we are making a quantum leap forward.

Teilhard de Chardin spoke eloquently of the eventual emergence into a higher, planetary consciousness. I believe that we have arrived at the very threshold of this exciting process. We require only the radical, childlike courage and wisdom to walk through that door! In passing through this threshold we assume the responsibility of what is essentially a new commandment for us; that commandment is nonviolence.

Nonviolence is the active living out of peace and the very essence of a culture of peace. It is infinitely more effectual to *be* a concrete example of peace than merely to talk about it. Nonviolence means a sensitivity towards all life, a respect and reverence for it, without exception. Nonviolence—*ahimsa*—is rich and all-embracing as a virtue, an attitude, a habit and a value. It is at once an active commitment to nonharming in any form, whether physical, emotional, intellectual, social, economic, political and spiritual. It is also the disposition of gentleness, of humility, of selflessness, and yet includes moral clarity, firmness, patience, perseverance and openness. Nonviolence is all of these and more. In its ultimate depth of reality, nonviolence is love! Thus it is necessarily not only the basis of a culture of peace—the way to teach peace in the deepest sense—but also the basis of the new universal society, the civilization of love.

With these goals, the North American Board for East-West Dialogue (now called Monastic Interreligious Dialogue) developed and signed the "Universal Declaration on Nonviolence" with the Dalai Lama.[12] Its primary intention is to be a first step towards a new civilization where violence has no place, and nonviolence, as a value and a practice, is preeminent.

The shape of the new civilization

In this space I can offer only the barest of outlines of the future global society: It will require a new metaphysics, cosmology, theology, ethics, and, of course, a new way to conduct economics and politics. On the social level, in the relationship of the various religious traditions to one another, and in the interest of peace among the traditions, this planetary society will be established firmly on the insight that the community of religions is the primary religious organization of humankind.

Spirituality is the soul of this civilization, and what will animate it. For it is spirituality that unites us all on the deepest level, and each one of us has some kind of personal spirituality. As a universal tradition of wisdom and an individual process of inner development, as the unfolding and flowering in relationship to Ultimate Reality and as the fruits of this inner process reflected in one's life, spirituality is the foundation of the new civilization's culture and vitality. The spirituality of humankind emphasizes the mystical awareness of unity as the essence of enlightenment, whether conceived or experientially understood as *Advaita, Nirvana, Dzogchen, Satori, Fana* or the *Unitive Life.* This intense and ultimate awareness of unity is the ground of genuine solidarity in the evolving universal tradition of wisdom.

The moral[13] foundations of the new civilization include the values of love, compassion, nonviolence, empathy, respect for pluralism, justice, courage, respect for human rights, and for the rights of all species, and solidarity. The new civilization also relies upon personal commitment to universal responsibility, especially as this embraces the total Earth Community, its environmental needs and values, the guarding of justice and making peace.

The social, political, material and economic foundations[14] of a new culture lie in the balance between the individual's rights and those of the Earth Community. The common well-being is the basis of personal well-being, but personal well-being guides the interpretation of communal welfare. Society exists for the person—for his or her protection and development, but equally, the person has a responsibility to the Earth Community always to consider the larger welfare of the whole, and always to live in harmony with it.[15]

A universal order of sannyasa

Finally, I'd like to offer one last vision: the creation of a universal "order" of *Sannyasa,* an order of mystics or contemplatives coming from all the great world religions that possess a mystical life and teaching. This would not be a new form of elitism, for it would be open to all who have the desire and the potential for spiritual development within and, perhaps, beyond their traditions and to those who are open to integrating insights and experiences from other traditions.

In the Sanskrit of the Hindu tradition, *sannyasa* means renunciation: of desire, wealth, power, sex and oneself. The purpose of this great renunciation that the renunciate, monk, or nun makes is to be free to go in quest of the Absolute. In an essential way, the *sannyasi* stands beyond all formal religion while still being loyal to and rooted in his or her own tradition. In this usage, "beyond" religion means that the *sannyasi* knows interiorly that Ultimate Reality cannot be circumscribed by theological formulations. In the inner awareness he or she transcends the limits of understanding. So, in this essential way, the *sannyasi* is "beyond."

Since the 17th century there has been a Christian form of *sannyasa* and it has been growing steadily in India during the course of this century. This proposal suggests the extension of *sannyasa* to the other traditions as a spiritually uniting medium, though not a formally synthetic act of integration. Its primary purpose would be to promote peace among the members of the community of religions, not confusion or syncretism. A universal order of *sannyasa* could, thus, be profoundly beneficial to interreligious dialogue, encounter and reconciliation.

A civilization with heart

Solutions to humankind's problems must originate in and flow from the heart, from an *inner change* of attitude and direction. Although the intellect

Universal Declaration on Nonviolence: The Incompatibility of Religion and War

This document is an attempt to set forth a vision of non-violence within the context of an emerging global civilization in which all forms of violence, especially war, are totally unacceptable as means to settle disputes between and among nations, groups and persons. This new vision of civilization is global in scope, universal in culture, and based on love and compassion, the highest moral spiritual principles of the various historical religions. Its universal nature acknowledges the essential fact of modern life: the interdependence of nations, economies, cultures and religious traditions.

As members of religious groups throughout the world, we are increasingly aware of our responsibility to promote peace in our age and in the ages to come. Nevertheless, we recognize that in the history of the human family, people of various religions, acting officially in the name of their respective traditions, have either initiated or collaborated in organized and systematic violence or war. These actions have at times been directed against other religious traditions, groups and nations, as well as within particular religious traditions. This pattern of behavior is totally inappropriate for spiritual persons and communities. Therefore, as members of world religions, we declare before the human family, that:

Religion can no longer be an accomplice to war, to terrorism or to any other forms of violence, organized or spontaneous, against any member of the human family. Because this family is one, global and interrelated, our actions must be consistent with this identity. We recognize the right and duty of governments to defend the security of their people and to relieve those afflicted by exploitation and persecution. Nevertheless, we declare that religion must not permit itself to be used by any state, group or organization for the purpose of supporting aggression for nationalistic gain. We have an obligation to promote a new vision of society, one in which war has no place in resolving disputes between and among states, organizations and religions.

In making this declaration, we the signatories commit ourselves to this new vision. We call upon all the members of our respective traditions to embrace this vision. We urge our members and all peoples to use every moral means to dissuade their governments from promoting war or terrorism. We strongly encourage the United Nations organization to employ all available resources toward the development of peaceful methods of resolving conflicts among nations.

Our declaration is meant to promote such a new global society, one in which nonviolence is preeminent as a value in all human relations. We offer this vision of peace, mindful of the words of Pope Paul VI to the United Nations in October 1965: "No more war: war never again!"

Signatories: Thomas Keating, Johanna Becker, Wayne Teasdale, Dom Bede Griffiths, Raimundo Panikkar, Katherine Howard, Pascaline Coff, Theophane Boyd, Ruth Fox, Timothy Kelley, and other members of the North American Board for East-West Dialogue.

His Holiness the Dalai Lama

Promulgated and signed on April 2, 1991 at Santa Fe, NM, USA

Resolution on Tibet

This resolution is proposed by Monastic Interreligious Dialogue/North American Board for East-West Dialogue for consideration at the Parliament of the World's Religions. While there are many troubled spots in the world deserving the attention and resolve of the religious community, and which might be included in *The SourceBook,* the Tibetan struggle for justice is a *nonviolent* moral resistance. As the world community pursues a culture of peace and condemns injustice, we need to encourage models of nonviolent response to situations of conflict wherever they occur. –Ed.

We have observed the intense suffering of the Tibetan People that has been inflicted on them for more than four decades. It is with great concern, empathy, a deep sense of responsibility and solidarity that we, on this important historical occasion, express our collective outrage at the brutal and callous actions of the Peoples' Republic of China in Tibet. These actions include genocide, torture, starvation, forced abortion and sterilization, continuation of subhuman living conditions and systematic violation of the human rights of the Tibetan People as well as deforestation and dumping of nuclear waste on Tibetan lands. Such actions are thoroughly reprehensible and morally repugnant to all people within the religions, and even to those with no religion.

Therefore, considering the situation in Tibet to be totally unacceptable, we call for the complete and immediate restoration of the legitimate rights of the Tibetan People; the return of the Dalai Lama to Lhasa in Tibet with his exiled government and all those who wish to return with him; and for the immediate and total cessation of China's massive population transfer into Tibet. We regard Tibet's freedom as necessary in order to protect her people and their precious culture.

A CULTURE OF PEACE, continued

will make its contribution, our problem is not one of understanding. We all grasp the crisis of our planet in its many facets. Our problem, rather, is one of *will*: the capacity to change before it's too late for our beloved Earth. Together, the religions have the immense *challenge* of *inspiring* this *will* to change in the human family. Building the culture of peace is a major step toward a new civilizational reality that is truly global in scope, universal in culture, and informed by our ultimate values. The culture of peace is the ambience of this new global society, this civilization with a heart.

We are all collaborators in the construction of this civilization possessed of a heart. In this great labor, the emergence of a permanent forum for the world's religions is an absolute necessity and an urgent responsibility to which, I believe, the Spirit calls us in our time of monumental transition. In view of this necessity and responsibility, the existing interfaith organizations should work together with the religions and other organizations, disciplines and institutions, to see to it that the Parliament or some similar entity becomes a permanent reality. We must seize the initiative to make it happen.

Let us realize the historic opportunity we are being offered; the emerging forum of the world's religions will provide a place for all of us who wish to serve the Earth Community. The question comes to this: can we model in ourselves, for the sake of the world, that quality of dynamic change so indispensable to our planet? Much depends on the answer we give to this question. ✪

NOTES

1. See Mircea Eliade, *Yoga: Immortality and Freedom, Bollingen Series* , Princeton Univ. Press, 1969, pp.353–358.

2. *Ibid.,* pp.355–356.

3. For a profound and comprehensive study of *rta,* see Jeanine Miller, *The Vision of Cosmic Order in the Vedas,* Routledge & Kegan Paul, London, 1985.

4. Dun J. Li, *The Essence of Chinese Civilization,* Von Nostrand, New York, 1967, p.109. See also K'ang Yu-wei (1858–1927), a modern Confucian thinker, especially his *Ta-t'ung shu (Book of Great Unity),* Peking, 1956.

5. S. Augustinus, *De Civitate Dei,* bk. 19, ch. 13.

6. *Ibid.*

7. Edwin Bernbaum, *The Way to Shambhala: A Search for the Mythical Kingdom Beyond the Himalayas,* Tarcher, Los Angeles, 1989, p.27.

8. Hans Küng, "No Peace in the World without Peace among Religions, *World Faiths Insight,* New Series 21, Feb. 1989, p.14.

9. Thomas Berry, *The Dream of the Earth,* Sierra Club Books, San Francisco, 1988 *cf.* ch. 2, "The Earth Community," pp.6–12.

10. The term "universal responsibility" is the Dalai Lama's. He has been and is popularizing it. See, for instance, his, *The Global Community and the Need for Universal Responsibility,* Wisdom Pub., Boston, 1992.

11. The Seville Statement on Violence was written in 1986 by an international group of scientists for the UN, and was adopted by UNESCO in 1989. See *The Seville Statement on Violence: Preparing the Ground for Peace,* ed. David Adams, UNESCO, Paris, 1991.

12. All documentation relating to the Universal Declaration on Nonviolence is with Sister Katherine Howard, OSB, Committee for the Universal Declaration, St. Benedict's Convent, St. Joseph, MN 56374-0277, USA.

13. Some beginnings have been made here by the UN and various interfaith organizations, *i.e.,* The International Association for Religious Freedom, Temple of Understanding, Anuvrat Global Organization, World Conference on Religion and Peace, Monastic Interreligious Dialogue, etc. These groups, and others, have all generated documents or statements of principles. See Marcus Braybrooke's *Stepping Stones to a Global Ethic,* SCM Press, London, 1992.

14. Two important books here are E. F. Schumacher's *Small is Beautiful: Economics as If People Mattered,* Harper & Row, San Francisco, 1973, and the less known, but significant work by Gerald and Patricia Mische, *Toward a Human World Order,* Paulist Press, 1977.

15. Mention should also be made of the role of the media, especially journalism, which must exercise a greater sense of responsibility, always keeping in mind the common good of the entire Earth Community. It cannot be a tool of special interests, nor operate in isolation from the guiding values of a universal society. The media has to become more accountable to the community through a process of self-regulation, that is, imposed on it by its own standards of enlightened journalism.

Zones of Peace *and* Round Tables of Reconciliation

Ivanka Vana Jakic has presented the following proposals in many forums. The first proposal is that a new international convention be established by UNESCO to authorize the establishment of International Zones of Peace, enabling countries, nations and ethnic groups to nominate their own selected sites for special protection. It is further proposed that countries and religious institutions endorse and support this proposal in its national and local implementation; the Parliament of the World's Religions is invited to give it further consideration and to act upon it.

The proposal has already received blessing and endorsement from many religious and spiritual leaders throughout the world. A resolution of support was adopted by the International Conference on Peace and Nonviolent Action, organized by ANUVIBHA, February 1991, in India. Several other peace and interfaith organizations have adopted it as a project worthy of support. –Ed.

ZONES OF PEACE

Many of the world's most precious cultural, historical, sacred and natural sites are in imminent danger of destruction, and must be preserved to maintain and enrich mankind's global heritage. We therefore propose setting aside the most cherished locations of all the world's peoples by designating them official Zones of Peace. These would include virtually all of UNESCO's World Cultural and Natural Heritage sites, with the addition of holy and pilgrimage locations. The program would provide for strong nonviolent enforcement of the sites' security.

International Zones of Peace will be protected by international law, much like embassies, as part of the birthright of all the world's citizens. National Zones of Peace will be guarded as the treasure of proprietary nations. In a similar manner, regional and local Zones of Peace will be established, safe from violence, aggression and all forms of desecration.

Zones of Peace will be demilitarized in times of peace as well as war, and therefore will be nuclear-free. They will serve as sanctuaries, havens characterized by a commitment to conflict resolution through dialogue rather than force. Zones of Peace will honor environmental balance, and will be safe from human abuse and degradation.

from "Zones of Peace: An International Initiative";
the above material is only the Overview
of the proposal presented to the UNESCO Seminar
on the Contribution of Religions to the Culture of Peace

ROUND TABLES OF RECONCILIATION

Inspired in particular by the war in the former Yugoslavia, as well as by efforts among religious leaders to resolve it, Ivanka has also proposed to the UNESCO Seminar and to the Parliament an initiative for the evolution of Round Tables of Reconciliation. Comprised primarily of religious leaders, but also including secular representatives when appropriate, these forums would directly address ethnic and religious conflicts caused in part by minority/majority distrust. The process, which could apply on international, national and local levels, would include adherence to nonviolence and the techniques of mediation and conflict resolution. –Ed.

For more details about either proposal, including pilot projects, contact:

Ivanka Vana Jakic
4004 SW 328th St.
Federal Way, WA 98023

"Reason, justice and compassion are small cards to play in the world of politics, whether international, national or tribal, but someone has to go on playing them. If you hold on to your belief in reason and compassion despite all political maneuvering, your efforts may in the end produce results. A determined effort to do what seems objectively right may sometimes eventually transcend the vicissitudes of politics."

SIR BRIAN URQUHART
A Life in Peace and War,
Widenfeld and Nicholson, 1987, p. 196

*"The conditions required for a Zone of Peace are conditions that most thoughtful people and leaders would like to establish in our communities, nations and world.
By creating small manageable areas of peace we can teach ourselves how to create a culture of peace; we can highlight the difficulty of maintaining any peace in a world where a general commitment to justice, equity, security and spiritual freedom are lacking; we can plant seeds of peace that can engulf the whole planet."*

Ivanka Vana Jakic,
from "Zones of Peace:
An International Initiative"

International Year of Reflection: Nonviolence in the Nuclear Age

Pamela Meidell

Director, Nevada Desert Experience

August 6, 1994–August 6, 1995

When the former archbishop of Brazil, Dom Helder Camara, visited the Nevada (Nuclear) Test Site in 1986, he said, "This is the site of the greatest violence on earth, therefore, it should be the site of the greatest nonviolence on earth." Again at the gates of the Test Site in 1991, he called on people everywhere to work toward a new millennium with no weapons of mass destruction, and enough food, clothing, shelter and education for everyone on the planet. Inspired by this vision, the Nevada Desert Experience proposes an International Year of Reflection on Nonviolence in the Nuclear Age, from August 6, 1994 to August 6, 1995.

We hope that this year can be a turning point for humanity where we can change our reality by laying down our swords and turning them into plowshares, by dismantling all nuclear weapons and beginning to cultivate a culture of peace.

Declaration of Remembrance

In 1995, the people of the earth will remember the 50th anniversary of the beginning of the Nuclear Age on July 16, 1945.

We will remember the image of the first mushroom cloud of the Trinity atomic test rising above the earth in Alamogordo, New Mexico.

We will remember the words of Robert Oppenheimer, director of the Manhattan Project, "I am become Death, the Destroyer of Worlds."

We will remember "Little Boy" and "Fat Man," the bombs that destroyed the Japanese cities of Hiroshima and Nagasaki on August 6 and 9, 1945.

Fifty years later, the people of the earth will remember the terrible destructive power and violence latent within us and made manifest in the bomb. We will meet this power of destruction by drawing on the rich sources of our human spiritual traditions and the deep wells of faith, beauty, humor and creativity in the human spirit to nurture the growth of a culture of nonviolence, health and peace.

We will remember the cost to all life of our commitment to death.

We will remember the indigenous peoples, on whose lands we mined for uranium, tested our nuclear weapons, and fill with nuclear waste that will be toxic for thousands of years.

We will remember the Downwinders, the Atomic Veterans and all radiation victims, knowing that in a global community, we are all downwinders.

We will remember the deserts of New Mexico, Nevada, Lop Nor, Muralinga, Algeria, Rajasthan and Kazahkstan where the atomic violence creates deserts in our hearts and souls; we will remember the islands of Muroroa, Christmas, Johnston, Bikini, Eniwetok and Novaya Zemlya where the atomic destruction makes us islands of ourselves.

We will remember the earth, whose waters, soil and air we contaminate in the name of security.

We will remember our children and grandchildren whose toxic radioactive inheritance we cannot keep from them.

We will remember our history so that we will not repeat it.

The Call to Reflection and Action

To prepare for this remembrance, the Nevada Desert Experience and Pax Christi USA call on the people of the United States and the world to reflect deeply on how the Nuclear Age and our commitment of human genius and material resources to the violence of developing nuclear arsenals has bankrupted out society, maimed our souls and robbed us of hope. We ask God's help as we face this darkness in ourselves, and seek to restore our souls and disarm our hearts of all that makes for violence and war.

We offer the people of the earth tools we can use to examine the history of the Nuclear Age prior to the Spring 1995 Review Conference at the United Nations of the (Nuclear) Non-Proliferation Treaty. To make this treaty more equitable and to extend it would halt the spread of nuclear weapons and reduce violence and tensions in our world.

Therefore, we call on the people of the earth to ponder in our hearts what we can do, and then to do it.

Therefore, we call on our religious leaders and spiritual teachers to think and reflect on this matter and to lead us in our thinking and acting.

Nuclear Age Study Guide

To assist this reflection process, Nevada Desert Experience and Pax Christi USA are preparing a year-long study guide for small groups, available from Pax Christi by August 6, 1994. (Pax Christi USA, 348 E. 10th St., Erie, PA 16503; or call (814) 453-4955 for more information.)

The Atomic Mirror Pilgrimage

50th Anniversary Interfaith Pilgrimage of Remembrance, Repentance and Renewal:

Sunday, July 16, 1995–August 6, 1995

The International Year of Nonviolence will culminate in a three-week pilgrimage that will retrace the route of humanity's first atomic bomb from New Mexico to Japan in the same three weeks it took to move from the first nuclear test on July 16 to the first use of an atomic weapon in warfare on August 6.

The pilgrimage will begin in Chimayo, New Mexico, then travel to Los Alamos, site of the Manhattan Project to create the bomb. We will journey to Albuquerque (and the National Atomic Museum), and through Laguna and other pueblos where uranium was mined, on the way to Alamogordo, New Mexico, site of Trinity, the world's first atomic explosion. We will the proceed to Las Vegas and the Nevada Test Site, where the U.S and Great Britain have tested nearly 1,000 nuclear weapons since 1952, and on to San Francisco, where in 1945, "Little Boy" was loaded on a ship to Hawaii. We will continue to the Marshall Islands, site of U.S. testing in the Pacific, winding up in Hiroshima, Japan on August 6, 1995.

People may participate for various lengths of time and in various ways. To become a cosponsor or for more information, please contact Pamela Meidell, Nevada Desert Experience/S. California Office, P.O. Box 220, Pt. Heuneme, CA 93044-0220 or the Rev. Shari Young, 110 Pacific #138, San Francisco, CA 94111. Current co-sponsors of the project include Nevada Desert Experience and Pax Christi USA.

Nevada Desert Experience is an interfaith group, with Franciscan origins, working since 1982 to stop nuclear weapons testing in Nevada through a campaign of prayer, dialogue and nonviolent direct action.

Declaration of Mutual Acceptance by the Community of Religions

The following declaration is a draft of a resolution written by Brother Wayne Teasdale and sponsored by Monastic Interreligious Dialogue. Its goal is to provoke thought, discussion, resolution and action—both at the Parliament and afterward—addressing the specific need for acceptance of and respect for each other's religious traditions. *–Ed.*

*O*ur common awareness and our collective wisdom have brought us to this realization:

We proclaim for our time and the ages to come, a mutual tolerance, acceptance and respect among all the religions of the world. The countless wars in history and even today, rooted in ignorance, intolerance and an appalling lack of acceptance, show the compelling need for this statement of commitment.

Human intolerance comes from fear of differences in language, customs, rites and symbols. Ultimately, all external fears are driven by our own self-fear of the contradictions within each one of us. All fear disturbs our sense of security; thus we reject differences in order to maintain an intellectual security and contentment. Here lies the basis of all religious conflict.

Acceptance of others begins with self-acceptance, and self-acceptance requires genuine self-knowledge. It means confronting our fears and weaknesses, and integrating our contradictions. Mutual acceptance between and among religious traditions must begin with this self-acceptance in its members, particularly in its leaders.

The awareness of our deep unity and interdependence inspires us to take this historic step on the great occasion of the second Parliament of the World's Religions. Each faith tradition possesses a special, even mystical knowledge of this unity. Now, that precious wisdom must be applied toward the transformation of past attitudes of intolerance and hatred which have produced so many terrible wars.

We recognize that the world's religions are no longer simply isolated traditions competing with one another, but belong to a greater Community of Religions. In this commonwealth, each religion preserves and celebrates its uniqueness while collaborating with the others in the work of building a new civilization with a heart!

We rejoice in our rich diversity of expression, a brilliant tapestry of experience, insight and creativity, joyfully accepting each and every religion. We commit ourselves to teach this value and skill of openness. In another application of the Golden Rule, we declare: Let us accept others with sincerity and enthusiasm, just as we wish for ourselves.

This quality of acceptance grows through the practice of dialogue. It evolves from mere tolerance to open acceptance, to fondness and love, and, finally, into communion. It is this gift of communion—the fruit of mutual knowledge and trust—that is the goal of the Community of Religions and of a civilization with a heart. We call upon all peoples everywhere to embrace this value of living dialogue and acceptance with us.

Declaration on Indigenous Peoples

This draft of a resolution is an initiative of Monastic Interreligious Dialogue regarding our religious and cultural understanding and acceptance of indigenous peoples of the earth, who are now speaking of their experience and beliefs. This proposal is made to the Parliament of the World's Religions and to other bodies for their consideration, adoption and action. *–Ed.*

*I*n the last five centuries, the Indigenous Peoples of the Western Hemisphere, and in more recent centuries, in the Eastern Hemisphere, have been and still are living in oppressive conditions. Their cultures and lands have been seriously damaged. They have been exposed to deadly diseases and reduced to grinding poverty.

We call upon all states with native peoples to respect their human rights, including the right of self-determination within existing national states, the right to manage their own territories, their resources and social structure, the right to form and develop their own distinctive institutions, and the right to preserve their unique way of life and culture which can teach us so much about sustainable living and about the spiritual dimension of the Earth Community.

We also urge the United Nations to recognize a special status for the indigenous populations of the world and to grant them representation in that global forum as well as in all of its specialized agencies.

Nonviolent Response to Violence in Bosnia-Herzegovina

Joel Beversluis

*R*eaders of this *SourceBook* are probably distraught over the warfare and continuing violence in Bosnia-Herzegovina. We are equally upset over the failures of international diplomacy and threats of military intervention to restore the peace. As of this writing (late July 1993), discussion in the media and political circles tends to revolve around whether NATO or the United States should begin bombing or other military actions.

Is there room midst this pain and debate for a nonviolent response that serves the culture of peace? Can human rights and justice be restored through nonviolent means? How is the "civilization with a heart" expressed?

The United Nations' goal of peacekeeping without the use of military action is being sorely tested here as well as in other troubled spots—the Middle East, Cambodia, and Somalia, to name a few. Yet that goal must be reinforced; casualties and failures notwithstanding, the United Nations must preserve its peace-keeping function.

CITIZEN WITNESSES

Growing numbers of citizens from many countries and religions are discovering the simple truth that diplomacy for peace and intervention for human rights are the right and responsibility of the people, and not the domain only of nation-states and international agencies. More and more committed citizens are engaged in peacemaking, ecological preservation, disaster relief and solidarity movements. These activities operate independently of the nation-states and sometimes stand in opposition to their policies, as with the Witness for Peace program of intervention and public disclosure in Central America. Citizens' movements are also developing creative strategies for conflict resolution, the pursuit of justice and approaches to sustainable development. These groups are modeling strategies for the development of a culture of peace.

The motivations for these autonomous actions are often spiritual, and their structures are often based in religious organizations, embodying religious responses to humanitarian and ecological crises.

MEDIA AND THE RELIGIONS

The record shows that the media do not pay much attention to these citizens' activities. Instead of seeing them as pioneering attempts to implement the highest values of religious and political will, they are often dismissed as fringe protests, out of touch with mainstream thought.

It is time to modify the common perception that the power and influence for good resides primarily in the politicized diplomatic and military responses of the nation-states. Organized religions and the establishment media might also learn how to support and participate in these nonviolent and idealistic challenges to the destructive impulses of our societies.

We Share One Peace

*O*ne example of a nonviolent response to the violence in Bosnia-Herzegovina is the peace encampment called "We Share One Peace", coordinated by "Blessed are the Peace-Makers" (Beati i Costruttori di Pace), of Italy.

A first action in December 1992 brought 500 people from Italy and other parts of the world into the territories at war to assert the urgent need for recognition of the rights of all people to life and well-being. This example of popular diplomacy was promoting a peaceful solution to the conflict and demonstrating that the search for peace is not the exclusive function of governments, but rather belongs to all peoples, as is stated in the International Law of Human Rights. Two Chicagoans among the 500 unarmed internationals noted that the death toll dropped from 20 civilians a day to five, during their brief stay.

In late July and August 1993, a second effort brought another international and interreligious group of more than 1000 persons together for a massive, nonviolent civilian witness against war. Camps were planned in and near Sarajevo, which has a Muslim government, in Ilidza, which has a Serbian government, and in Kiseljak, which has a Croatian government. The first week of the encampment was to include an interreligious ceremony.

Other activities of the peace encampment were the provision of greatly needed resources to non-combatants; some delegates were also prepared to initiate dialogue with combatants, with the heads of religious communities and with civil and military representatives. The participants were also planning to urge the United Nations to allow an unarmed force mainly composed of conscientious objectors to be posted alongside the UNO forces with the aim of reducing tensions, defending the ordinary people, and helping to prepare for genuine peace negotiations.

ARE CURRENT POLITICAL RESPONSES A BETRAYAL OF THOSE WHO ARE VIOLATED?

Dr. Mustafa Ceric, Supreme Head of the Islamic Community in Bosnia-Herzegovina, provides one answer on page 72 of this book.

Clearly, international inaction and disengagement from the issues is a betrayal not only of suffering humans but also of our standards of human rights. True nonviolent responses are not passive, however, and do not shy away from analyzing and speaking the truth.

Furthermore, those who work for peace without taking sides, who are providing material assistance to the victims of all combatants and who are willing to risk their lives in solidarity with those who are suffering, are expressing the power of nonviolence. They are also embodying fundamental truths of the religions.

LA POMPA

Tito
Paco
Cheo

warriors in shorts
skin the color of cinnamon sticks
bare feet dancing on hot pavement
t-shirts hung like flags on the fence

Tito
Paco
Cheo

liberate the neighborhood
with Mr. Mendoza's pliers

la pompa
gushes the river of relief
toddlers pull off their diapers and run
    from the heat
into paradise

the children howl
as liquid ice hits their naked backs

the children of la senora Pentecostal
watch from across the street
dry from the wind
of their mother's breath
as she prays for the souls
of the little motherless savages

Tito
Paco
Cheo

whisper and laugh
about the girls they will get
who tease them with lollipops
and rolling eyes

Abuela pulls her shopping cart
filled with leche
        platanos
        batatas
        arroz
        aguacate
        y bacalao

she redirects the stream
with her eyes

Tito
Paco
Cheo

have seen the candles
she keeps in teacups
have seen the power
of her hand
across fevers

broken hearts
    and spirits of the dead

abuela is nobody to mess with
she keeps candy
in the pockets of her bata
and a stick by her door

la calle is flooded with giggles
and stamping feet
the dogs chase their tails in delight
the cats look with suspicion
from behind garbage cans
they cannot relax

Pasote drives by in his cadillac
he owns the streets
but not the people
he rolls up his windows
and shrinks behind the glass

Tito
Paco
Cheo

laugh and tell him to eat his crack

Don Pedro
emerges from the door
of the social club
where he rules the domino table
and pays for the beers
for those who can't

he left Borinquen
when he was twenty
to send for his novia
so she would live like a queen
she left him for an American tourist
the bochinche is
she sells cheap furniture
on lay away
somewhere out in Queens

Tito
Paco
Cheo

hear the siren
it is an ambulance
they calm la pompa
out of respect
the ambulance
does not stop on their street
they laugh at the speed
and guess the drivers
are going to lunch

Mariela's girls play chinese jump rope
in their bathing suits
and run to her for sips of orange juice

Continued on next page

Children Appeal to World Policymakers:
DON'T COMPROMISE
OUR FUTURE!
"*We are speaking on behalf of the young people. We are here because we have a right to be involved in these decisions. . . . Your pursuit of diplomatic compromises is compromising our future.*

We have a right to demand a safe future for ourselves and all generations to come. What is required is a fundamental change in attitudes, values and lifestyles, particularly in the developed nations. We insist that . . . you make decisions which reflect intergenerational equity and a concern for the environment. Remember that we will inherit the consequences of your decisions. We will not sign the Montreal Protocol—you will. You will not bear the brunt of ozone depletion—we will.

We demand that you think in the long term. . . . Have the courage to put aside your short-term national concerns and act in the interests of our common well-being.

Will you protect our future?"

Read by Susannah Begg, 17, of Australia at the June 1990 meeting in London where nations agreed to phase out production of the chemicals that destroy Earth's protective ozone layer.
Printed in *Our Children Their Earth*, UNEP, p.23

Negrito pulls his hands
the size of tobacco leaves
from the pockets of his linen slacks
he holds a knife
and picks up the cross
he is carving for abuela
in thanks for saving
his little Rosita
from la melancolía
that drained her body
of light

Doña Ramona
sits on the stoop
and smokes a cigar
the kind her Juan enjoyed
before the police
mistook him for a burglar
in his own home
the sandwich he was eating
was not loaded

Tito
Paco
Cheo

hear Mr. Softee
from three blocks away
its tune sends mothers
running to their windows
throwing down quarters
wrapped in handkerchiefs
into little hands that open
like flowers in the rain

La Pompa is forgotten

Tito
Paco
Cheo

are followed to the truck
by a swarm of dancing braids
and smiles

nobody cuts the line
rainbow sprinkles
for everybody

Mr. Mendoza
finds his pliers
resting on the curb
goes to la pompa
and looks up to be sure
the sun is indeed going down

the cry of liberation
turns to a quiet whisper

the children are busy
with sweetness

Tito
Paco
Cheo

offer licks to the children
whose mothers are at work
whose fathers returned to the fields

there is enough for everyone

Mr. Mendoza looks for Don Pedro
invites him for un palito
and rests his pliers on the table
where he shuffles the dominoes

Tito
Paco
Cheo

their t-shirts
flags on the fence
wave in the breeze
of simple joys.

MAGDALENA GÓMEZ

"*Each second we live in a new and
unique moment of the universe,
a moment that never was before and
will never be again. And, what do we
teach our children in school?
We teach them that two and two
make four, and that Paris
is the capital of France.
When will we also teach them
what they are?
We should say to each of them:*

*Do you know what you are?
You are a marvel. You are unique.
In all the world there is no other child
exactly like you. And look at your
body. What a wonder it is. Your legs,
your arms, your cunning fingers,
the way you move! You may become
a Shakespeare, a Michelangelo,
a Beethoven.
You have the capacity for anything.
Yes, you are a marvel.*"

PABLO CASALS

The Shield Within

I carry an inner shield
that no one can see
unless I let them—
it's woven from time,
a snow-capped mountain, the sun,
a star and a whale.

My snow-capped mountain: knowledge
true, stupendous, towering
ready to explode!
It is burning with the desire to be more
to learn more.
Quietly, gently, the snow calms
this anxiety rushing.

My sun—no ordinary sun,
but one of great importance
shedding rays of love and spirituality
penetrating
the souls of all creatures
of all beings.

Me, a star, an artist.
My star brings on a wonderful calm.

My whale to me
is a mysterious marvel,
a giant soul
filled with wisdom beyond
a conscious reach.

ALINA CLARK
8th grade

The Right Hand

I am holding
a beautiful planet.
I feel the warmth
from her soil,
the breeze
from her sky,
and her soft flowing
plasma; two moons
peer out of her surface
splitting the soil
in new directions:
blood flows around her,
in rivers so deep,
while I, the right
hand, help to hold her
in place, for if I let go
she would perish.

BRIAN URBANOWICZ
11th grade

Listen to the Children

Therese Becker

Poet, teacher, photograper, journalist, advocate for the creative process. Therese Becker is currently compiling a book of children's poems and descriptions of the excercises she uses to evoke them, titled When a Child Sings.

I began working with children through the Michigan Council for the Arts, Creative Writers in the Schools program in the spring of 1986, and I've been learning from them ever since. I read everything they write as a result of the exercises that I put them through and I am continually stunned at the deep wisdom that emerges when they listen to themselves.

I've never forgotten a statement made by Oakland University Professor Margaret Kurzman: "If you don't become who you are, then what you might have contributed to the world will never have a chance to be." I instantly knew it was true. Everything I do in a classroom is directed toward fostering self-trust which produces self-esteem. I also encourage journal writing (the more you write, the more you can write), and reading and writing as necessary twins in the writing process.

I've worked with grades K through 12 and with children who are labeled "learning disabled," "average," "the smart students," "the trouble makers," and the "gifted and talented"; I've found that every group has its own barriers to overcome, but when the writing is finished you can't tell one group's work from another.

Learning to trust the self seems, at first, quite simple, but it is more difficult than one might imagine. Almost everything in our society seems set up to make us believe that our answers lie somewhere outside of ourselves instead of within. The poet Rainer Maria Rilke said, "What is happening in your innermost self is worthy of your entire love," and that love is real power and the bricks in the path to freedom.

One of my most successful exercises is having students take a trip inside their hand. When they do this with their imagination, anything can become something else. Recently, a ninth grade girl wrote in her hand exercise, "when I look into my hand, I see nothing but an empty space where my soul used to sit." She then went on to tell about the criticism she's received for being different. It was an incomplete piece, so I encouraged her towards exploration by asking questions evoked by the original piece of writing. Should she fight for her soul, and is that something that artists and writers had to do if they were to pursue their art in any true way? I also asked her if different was really less or was it more. I believe it's more, and we must encourage and honor our differences if the planet and species is going to survive.

Listening to children has taken me right to the heart of their spiritual and moral struggles. Although I can encounter a great deal of violence in their work, it has restored my faith in the human race, rather than destroyed it. The bottom line in every school I visit is that our children want to love the earth and each other, and they particularly yearn to become who they are. As Gandhi said, "If we are to attain real peace in this world, we will have to begin with the children." Listen to the children and applaud.

"Listening to children has taken me right to the heart of their spiritual and moral struggles."

When I Look into My Hand

I see rivers, streams,
and oceans with little islands
and trees on them: Lonely
and confusing, mystifying
and dangerous.

In the oceans the whales
and dolphins swim freely,
but then man comes.

In the rivers fish swim gracefully,
but then man comes
and pollutes in the water.

In streams the water
glistens and sparkles,
but then man comes.

MELISSA ROLAND
8th grade

My Hand

is extended into space,
but it is not a hand—
it is a colony:
prosperous, magnificent.
Spectacularly structured
tunnels rise above.

Where do they lead?
To another star?
To my own room?
They are the tunnels
of imagination,
of power.

ALINA CLARK
8th grade

My Home

The palm of my hand
is the house of feelings.
I live in the commonest path
which is the longest
which is my joy.

The shortcut is my anger.
I barely ever take that path.
Then over the bridge
I travel and feel lonely.

I'll travel to the hills
and feel loved:
then I'll go home.

ELIZABETH FREEMAN
6th grade

The State of the World's Children

James P. Grant

Executive Director of UNICEF

My Poem for the World

I wish the world could be free
and have no illegal things.
I wish I could just close my eyes
and have heaven float
and God could have the power to release
the men who are not free.

I wish we could go wherever
we wanted to on a cloud.
I wish we could help everyone.

God, if we fall,
catch us, lift us up
to where we belong.

MARY MC LAUGHLIN
3rd grade

Hold hands until dawn.
Hold hands until the bell rings.
Hold hands until the stars come out.
Be friends, hold hands.

Until the sun is high, hold hands.
Holding hands makes you feel
warm and safe.
Hold hands forever.

ZOE WARD
3rd grade

"Our children are living messages that we send into a world we'll never see."
ANONYMOUS

*A*mid all the problems of a world bleeding from continuing wars and environmental wounds, it is nonetheless becoming clear that one of the greatest of all human aspirations is now within reach. Within a decade, it should be possible to bring to an end the age-old evils of child malnutrition, preventable disease and widespread illiteracy.

As an indication of how close that goal might be, the financial cost can be put at about $25 billion a year. That is the UNICEF estimate of the extra resources required to put into practice today's low-cost strategies for protecting the world's children. Specifically, it is an estimate of the cost of controlling the major childhood diseases, halving the rate of child malnutrition, bringing clean water and safe sanitation to all communities, making family planning services universally available and providing almost every child with at least a basic education.

In practice, financial resources are a necessary but not sufficient prerequisite for meeting these needs. Sustained political commitment and a great deal of managerial competence are even more important. Yet it is necessary to reduce this challenge to the denominator of dollars in order to dislodge the idea that abolishing the worst aspects of poverty is a task too vast to be attempted or too expensive to be afforded.

To put the figure of $25 billion in perspective, it is considerably less than the amount the Japanese Government has allocated this year to the building of a new highway from Tokyo to Kobe; it is two to three times as much as the cost of the tunnel soon to be opened between the United Kingdom and France; it is less than the cost of the Ataturk Dam complex now being constructed in eastern Turkey; it is a little more than Hong Kong proposes to spend on a new airport; it is about the same as the support package that the Group of Seven has agreed on in 1992 for Russia alone; and it is significantly less than Europeans will spend this year on wine or Americans on beer.

Whatever the other difficulties may be, the time has therefore come to banish in shame the notion that the world cannot afford to meet the basic needs of almost every man, woman and child for adequate food, safe water, primary health care, family planning and a basic education.

A ten percent effort

*I*f so much could be achieved for so many at so little cost, then the public in both industrialized and developing countries might legitimately ask why it is not being done.

In part, the answer is the predictable one: meeting the needs of the poorest and least politically influential has rarely been a priority of governments. Yet the extent of present neglect in the face of present opportunity is a scandal of which the public is largely unaware. On average, the governments of the developing world are today devoting little more than ten percent of their budgets to directly meeting the basic needs of their people. More is still being spent on military capacity and on debt servicing than on health and education.

Perhaps more surprising still, less than ten percent of all international aid for development is devoted to directly meeting these most obvious of human needs. . . about $4 billion a year. This is less than half as much as the aid-giving nations spend each year on sports shoes. It could therefore fairly be said that the problem today is not that overcoming the worst aspects of world poverty is too vast or too expensive a task; it is that it has not been tried.

. . .

Promises on paper

The importance of the Convention [on the Rights of the Child], the Summit [for children], and the national programs of action that have been drawn up should neither be overestimated nor underestimated. At the moment they remain, for the most part, promises on paper. But when, in the mid-1980s, over 100 of the world's political leaders formally accepted the goal of 80 percent immunization by 1990, that, too, was just a promise on paper. Today it is a reality in the lives of tens of millions of families around the world.

One lesson to be learned from that achievement is that formal political commitments at the highest levels are necessary if available solutions are to be put into action *on a national scale*. But a second lesson is that such commitments will only be translated into action by the dedication of the professional services; by the mobilization of today's communications capacities; by the widespread support of politicians, press and the public; and by the reliable and sustained support of the international community. Most of the countries that succeeded in reaching the immunization goal succeeded primarily because large numbers of people and organizations at all levels of national life became seized with the idea that the goal could and should be achieved. . . .

To maintain the political momentum that has been generated, nothing less is now required than a worldwide strengthening of the basic needs movement to the point where it begins to exert the same kind of pressure as is today being brought to bear for the protection of the environment.

Such pressure will not be easy either to create or sustain. A movement to overcome the worst aspects of poverty, and particularly to protect children, has no obviously powerful constituency and no immediate vested interest to appeal to. The environmental and women's movements are, in varying degrees, becoming everyone's concern, for the obvious reason that almost everyone is directly touched by both of these issues. A movement to meet basic human needs will not succeed unless it, too, becomes everyone's concern. And to achieve that, the complex realities of common cause must also become more widely known and understood. None of the great issues that are assuming priority today—the cause of slowing population growth, the cause of achieving equality for women, the cause of environmentally sustained development, the cause of political democracy—will or can be realized unless the most basic human needs of the forgotten quarter of the earth's people

are met. This cause, too, must therefore become the concern of all. . . .

20 percent for basics

As the end of the 20th century approaches, there is therefore an accumulation of reasons for believing that ending the worst aspects of poverty is an idea whose time may finally have come.

New strategies and low-cost technologies are available. Specific goals which reflect this potential have been agreed upon. The commitment to those goals bears the signatures of more Presidents and Prime Ministers than any other document in history. The plans for achieving them have been or are being drawn up in most nations. And there is a growing acceptance of the idea that targeting some of these worst effects of poverty, particularly as they affect children, is an essential part of long-term development strategy.

In the wider world, the ground being gained by democratic systems means that the long-starved concerns of the poor may begin to put on political weight. At the same time, economic reforms may also create the kind of environment in which a new effort to meet basic human needs would have a much greater chance of success. Meanwhile, the powerful tide of demographic change is also beginning to turn.

For all of these reasons, a new potential now exists for moving towards a world in which the basic human needs of almost every man, woman and child are met. But it is equally clear that this attempt will not gather the necessary momentum unless the political commitment is sustained and the extra resources made available.

If advantage is to be taken of the political commitments that have been made, and of the national programs of action that have been drawn up, then those extra resources must begin to become available in the next 12 months to two years. . . . UNICEF strongly supports the United Nations Development Programme's suggestion that at least 20 percent of government spending should be allocated to these direct methods of meeting priority human needs. If implemented, such a restructuring of government budgets would enable the developing nations as a whole to find several times the $25 billion a year that is needed to achieve the agreed goals.

. . .

In the decade ahead, a clear opportunity exists to make the breakthrough against what might be called the last great obscenity—the needless malnutrition, disease and illiteracy that still casts a shadow over the lives and the futures of the poorest quarter of the world's children.

It is almost unthinkable that that opportunity to reach these basic social goals should be missed because the political commitment is lacking or because the developing world and the donor nations cannot, together, find an extra $25 billion a year.

. . . It is time that challenge replaced excuse. If today's

obvious and affordable steps are not taken to protect the lives and the health and the normal growth of many millions of young children, then this will have less to do with the lack of economic capacity than with the fact that the children concerned are almost exclusively the sons and daughters of the poor—of those who lack not only purchasing power but also political influence and media attention. And if the resources are not to be made available, if the overcoming of the worst aspects of poverty, malnutrition, illiteracy and disease is not to be achieved in the years ahead, then let it now be clear that this is not because it is not a possibility but because it is not a priority.

Conclusion

*I*n 1992, many specific tragedies have again assaulted the very idea of childhood in such places as Somalia and the former Yugoslavia. The response to these tragedies, wherever they occur, is a major part of the work of UNICEF and is addressed in many other UNICEF publications and statements during the course of the year.

But for more than ten years, the *State of the World's Children* report has concentrated on issues which profoundly affect far larger numbers of children but which do not constitute the kind of news event which qualifies for the world's attention. This is tragedy which does not happen in any one particular place or time; it happens quietly in poor communities throughout the developing world. It is therefore not news, and so it slips from the public eye and from the political agenda. But it is nonetheless a tragedy far greater in scale than even the greatest of the emergencies which so often command the world's, and UNICEF's, concern. No famine, no flood, no earthquake, no war has ever claimed the lives of 250,000 children in a single week. Yet malnutrition and disease claim that number of child victims *every week*. And for every one of those children who dies, many more live on with such ill health and poor growth that they will never grow to the physical and mental potential with which they were born.

When little or nothing could be done about this larger-scale tragedy, then neglect was perhaps understandable. But slowly, quietly, and without the world taking very much notice, we have arrived at the point where this tragedy is no longer necessary. It is therefore no longer acceptable in a world with any claim on civilization. The time has therefore come for a new age of concern.

Political and economic change in the world is beginning to create the conditions which, however difficult, offer new hope for overcoming the worst aspects of world poverty, particularly as they affect the world's children. The cost of providing health and education services in the developing world remains relatively low, and the gradual stabilization in the numbers of infants being born means that further investments in basic services can now begin to increase the proportion of the population served. Meanwhile, the technologies and strategies for controlling malnutrition, disease and illiteracy have been tried and tested and now stand waiting to go into action on the same scale as the problems they can so largely solve.

The convergence of all of these different forces means it is now possible to achieve one of the greatest goals that humanity could ever set for itself—the goal of adequate food, clean water, safe sanitation, primary health care, family planning and basic education, for virtually every man, woman and child on earth.

In 1990, this new potential for specific action against these worst aspects of poverty was formulated into a set of basic social goals which accurately reflect that potential and which have been formally accepted by the great majority of the world's political leaders. A start has been made, in many nations, towards keeping the promise of those goals.

We therefore stand on the edge of a new era of concern for the silent and invisible tragedy that poverty inflicts on today's children and on tomorrow's world. Whether the world will enter decisively into that new age depends on the pressure that is brought to bear by politicians, press, public and professional services in all nations. And among the readers of this report, there is hardly any individual or organization that could not now become involved.

Excerpted from the official Summary of the 1993 report, issued by James P. Grant, the Executive Director of UNICEF. For the full text of the 1993 *State of the World's Children*, contact any UNICEF office or write to the Division of Information, UNICEF House, 3 UN Plaza, New York, NY 10017 USA. The report is also published by Oxford University Press.

The World's Religions
for the World's Children

Prior to the World Summit for Children, held at the United Nations in September 1990, a Conference on The World's Religions for the World's Children was held at Princeton, USA. Organized by the United Nations Children's Fund (UNICEF) and by the World Conference on Religion and Peace, it was attended by 150 people from 40 countries drawn from 12 major religions. The participants agreed that there is still time to reclaim the environment for our children and as a heritage for succeeding generations. And they said that "despite differences in our traditions, our practices, our beliefs, and despite our inadequacies" they would work together to influence their nation's political leaders and their own religious communities so that children's basic needs will be given priority. To this end they issued the following Declaration and an action plan with specific goals for the 1990s.

Princeton, New Jersey, July 25–27, 1990

Conscious of the plight of vast numbers of children throughout the world, we representatives of 12 religions from 40 countries participating in the World's Religions for the World's Children conference, meeting in Princeton, New Jersey, USA, July 25–27, 1990, speak with common voice. We commend the United Nations for its efforts in creating and adopting the Convention on the Rights of the Child. We urge its ratification and adherence in practice by all governments. We commend those government leaders who have recognized the urgency and priority of addressing the needs and rights of children. Cognizant of the efforts of earlier generations represented by the 1924 League of Nations Geneva Declaration on the Rights of the Child, and the United Nations 1959 Declaration on the Rights of the Child, we are aware of the difficulty of moving from the statement of rights to their realization. Our common voice resounds despite differences in our traditions, our practices, our beliefs, and despite our inadequacies. Our religious traditions summon us to regard the child as more than a legal entity. The sacredness of life compels us to be a voice of conscience. We speak hereby to heads of state and government, to the United Nations, to our religious communities and to all, throughout the world, who have held a child in love, with joy for its life, with tears for its pain.

Recognizing the rights of the child

The Convention on the Rights of the Child, which acknowledges the rights of the world's children to survival, protection and development, is rooted in the Universal Declaration of Human Rights which recognizes the inherent dignity and the equal and inalienable rights of all members of the human family. We recognize that, lamentably, such rights are not universally respected or legally guaranteed, nor are they always accepted as moral obligations.

As religious men and women, however, we dare to assert that the state of childhood, with its attendant vulnerability, dependence and potential, founds a principle that the human community must give children's basic needs priority over competing claims—and a "first call"—upon the human and material resources of our societies. Such a principle needs to be both recognized and accepted as a guide for relevant actions in human communities.

Spirit

The spirit is still here
somewhere in the sky,
somewhere in the trees.
But who knows where?
No one you see.

Does Nature? Does the wind?
Do the trees? All we know
is the spirit is somewhere
in there.

JESSICA DENNIS
7th grade

To My Students

You danced on the page,
reinvented yourselves,
opened the ancient doors
and bright birds of every color
flew out to greet me.

You showed me how well you hear
the earth's music,
the music in yourselves
and each other.

You will be with me always
an invisible necklace
of water and light—
a distant song in my ear.

Remember, the journey
is everything;
the key is trust:
the world is waiting
for you to name it
and you will.

THERESE BECKER
Previously published in
Louisville Review: *Spring 1990*

The Wild Man's Heart

It is the same dream.
It is the wild man's heart, prancing.
It is the wild wings of a flying eagle.

They will dance—
the wild man and his heart:
prancing on, and on.
It is love.

BILL THIRY
7th grade

Asking the Stars

I was sneaking around,
asking the stars: "may I,
may I behold you?"
"You may far child, you may."

"Who are you might I ask?"
And they answered, "The moons,
the moons, yes, the moons."

And then they said to me:
"And you are a true genesis
in your own way, a type of god,
not a big god, but a god."

ROBERT JONES
7th grade

Peace

As you enter the wild depths
Phantoms below,
You notice the whale's call,
As if wanting help
Or maybe telling us
We should live in peace.

God must have made them
  for a purpose.
Maybe they are the peacemakers.
Their voices are mysterious
like a fog horn on the misty dock.

There's so much violence
In the world,
So much chaos,
So much terror.
If we are to survive
This imperfect world,
We must listen
Listen to the peace.

GABRIEL MYLIN
6th grade

Society's responsibility to children

The survival, protection and development of children is the responsibility of the whole world community. However, for countless girls and boys there is no survival, no protection, no chance for development. Societies are morally bound to address the obscene conditions which result in the death of 14 million children during every year, two thirds from preventable causes, and the other conditions of abject poverty that result in wasted bodies, stunted physical development or permanent handicaps. Existing health care knowledge and technology, promptly and persistently applied, have the potential to make dramatic improvements in child survival and health with relatively moderate financial costs. Such possibilities underscore our obligations. To fail to make such efforts for the well-being of children is morally unconscionable.

Societies are also bound to rectify the gross injustices and violations which children suffer, such as child abuse, sexual and labor exploitation, homelessness, victimization due to war and the tragic consequences of family disintegration, cultural genocide, social deprivations stemming from intolerance based upon race, sex, age or religion, to name but a few. Addressing these issues will require fundamental structural change.

Societies are obliged to confront the broad constellation of human forces and failures which affect children. The social and international order necessary for the full realization of children's rights does not exist. Our interdependent political and economic systems can be restructured and refined to provide children their basic needs. The world has the resources to provide the basic needs of children. Wars, in which children are increasingly the victims and even the targets of violence, need not be the inevitable expression of human conflict. Our readiness to resolve conflict through violent means can be changed. Development cannot succeed under the illusion that our resources are inexhaustible or uniformly self-renewing. While our air, water and soil are polluted, we still have the chance to reverse the most devastating trends of environmental degradation. What will we bequeath to our children? The dangerous forces that impact upon children jeopardize the full realization of freedom, justice and peace.

The grim realities we confront demand our outrage because they exist; they demand our repentance because they have been silently tolerated or even justified; they demand our response because all can be addressed, some of them quite readily.

Responsibilities of governments and international organizations

We religious women and men gathered in Princeton urge governments and relevant international organizations to fulfill their responsibilities to children through at least the following:

To sign, ratify, fully implement and monitor compliance with the Convention on the Rights of the Child.

To undertake those actions which would have a dramatic impact upon child survival at very low cost.

To take vigorous and immediate action to rectify the myriad obscene injustices which children suffer, such as abuse from exploitation.

To take the steps necessary, in each country, to achieve the goals for children and development in the 1990s, as defined by the international community.

To utilize peaceful means of conflict resolution in order to protect children from the ravages of war.

To create new, or adjust existing, political and economic structures that can provide access to and distribution—for all—of both the natural resources and the products of human labor, including information, so that the claims of justice may be met.

To undertake the bold steps known to be necessary and to develop new steps to protect and reclaim the environment as the heritage for our children and succeeding generations' development.

To allocate adequate funds to undergird the global programs, addressing health, education and development.

To ensure full participation of Non Governmental Organizations (NGOs) in the implementation of appropriate actions.

To provide basic education for all children.

To reduce the burden of debt that robs a nation's children of their rightful heritage.

To support the family, help keep it intact, and provide the resources and services for the adequate care and protection of its children.

To provide resources and develop programs for the survival, health and education of women, the bearers and primary care givers of children.

To ensure the participation of women in the entire range of social governance and decision making.

To take steps to ensure that children actually receive a first call on society's resources.

Religious and spiritual responsibilities

Our consciences as religious men and women, including those of us bearing governmental and other forms of social responsibility, will not allow us to evade the responsibilities of our religious traditions. We therefore call upon religious women and men and institutions:

To order our own priorities so as to reaffirm our central claims about the sacredness of life.

To examine any of our own traditional practices that may violate the deeper spirit of our faiths and indeed the sacredness of human life.

To provide resources for families, from single parent to extended in size, so that they can fulfill their roles in spiritual formation and education.

To protect and support parents in their rights and responsibilities as the primary religious educators.

To undertake actions to promote the well-being, education and leadership roles of female children and their right to equal treatment with male children.

To engage in services of nurture, mercy, education and advocacy, and to exemplify before the world the possibilities for compassion and care.

To cooperate with all agencies of society, including other religious bodies, that have as their purpose the well-being of the children in our societies.

To advocate the ratification and implementation of the Convention on the Rights of the Child in our respective countries and communities.

To work for the protection of the unborn in accord with the teachings of our respective religious traditions.

To establish independent systems to monitor the state of children's rights.

To coordinate with other religions in the removal of religious and other forms of prejudice and conflict in all contexts.

To re-order our communities' resources in accord with the principle of the right of children to a first call on those resources.

Political will is necessary to create the social and international climate in which survival, protection and development can be achieved. We call on governments and the international community to manifest that will.

Spiritual will is necessary to establish a shared ethos in which children can flourish in freedom, justice and peace. We call on all spiritual and religious peoples and institutions to manifest that will.

"*We can easily forgive a child who is afraid of the dark; the real tragedy is when men are afraid of the light.*"
PLATO

"*You have to ask children and birds how cherries and strawberries taste.*"
GÖETHE

The Meadow's Shadow

The morning starts up
and I arise,
Traveling wherever
the sun goes,
Bringing new sights
to my eyes.
Over the dry grasses
and over the rustling creek,
I travel the prairie
until the sunset
makes me meek.

GABRIEL MYLIN
6th grade

Mindwalking

When I am mindwalking,
exploring my inner garden,
there is so much peace within me.
Touching. Holding. Smelling.
The flowers of Happiness, Joy and Love
grow and prosper in my garden.

Insects live here too.
They fly from flower to flower
picking up more wisdom and laughter
with every stop.
These insects fly on giving
happy messages to others,
telling them of everything good
and happy, and sometimes sad.

Miracles can happen here.
They are ideas, memories,
all of which come out of a doorway,
and are released so all may hear
and experience them.

The ideas and everything else
that tumble out,
fly around like doves
who want to tell others
about what they have to tell.

LISA BROWN
8th grade

Growing Up in Earthly Danger

Dr. Noel J. Brown

The article which follows, by Dr. Noel Brown, Director, UNEP Regional Office for North America, introduces the Spring 1991 Environmental Sabbath/Earth Rest Day Guide, *Our Children Their Earth: Playing for Keeps*.

*E*nvironmental degradation is killing our children.

Children are the first victims of environmental destruction—as we have seen in the aftermath of the Gulf War—because their growing bodies and minds are more vulnerable to malnutrition and a contaminated environment.

Our children's access to the fresh food and water that a healthy environment provides depends on us as parents, guardians and governments. Children have no other recourse. The have nothing to do with the causes of environmental devastation—"They do not vote, they have no political or financial power, they cannot challenge our decisions," says *Our Common Future*, the influential report on sustainable development—yet they are the first to suffer.

Today, the earth tries to support nearly two billion children under the age of five, and of them 1.5 billion live in developing countries. These hundreds of millions of children mean even larger populations for decades to come. Most will struggle to survive in countries with minimal financial resources that can be allocated for their needs and for protection of the natural resources on which their lives are based.

This year, 14 million children under the age of five will die from common, mostly preventable diseases and malnutrition—unless we act now to protect them and the environments in which they live. Many of these deaths are from "environmental" causes—unsafe water, air pollutants and hazardous chemicals. Others are caused by the "environments of poverty." Environment is not the cause; the causes are environmental mismanagement and development that destroys earth's resource base.

The natural resources we have today are the basis for future development; so are today's children. Both tend to be undervalued by decisionmakers because "they are difficult to quantify in economic terms." And, as we see once again, in times of economic hardship, budgets for children's welfare and environmental protection are the first to be cut, everywhere.

Yet in these tough times, it is the children in many countries who are taking the lead, who are filled with hope and a belief that morality and practicality can be combined. Given a chance, they have boundless energy and open, ethical minds. They can be powerful forces for positive change in many fields, and especially in environmental protection where, as you will see in these pages, so many young people already are proving their commitment and potential leadership.

This guide [*Our Children Their Earth*] is dedicated to them and to children of all ages. It is designed as a practical and moral road map to the Environmental Sabbath, to be used in conjunction with the UNEP Sabbath booklet, *Only One Earth*.

In recent years the United Nations has given children and their environment international priority. Now it is up to us to shine a moral spotlight on what the UN has done by mobilizing our faith communities. Only we can infuse these legal and ethical texts with spiritual energy, so that they have force and vitality for the future of our earth—its children. ☸

Our Children Their Earth

*T*he Environmental Sabbath/Earth Rest Day was established in 1987 by the United Nations Environment Programme (UNEP). Its advisory board and planning committee established this annual focus as a way to meld spiritual values with environmental science. Among its publications is *Only One Earth* which contains scientific data, declarations and texts from religious bodies, and relevant scriptures from many of the world's religions. Many churches, temples, synagogues, mosques and other institutions have adopted the first weekend in June as a special time to remember the needs and value of the earth through worship and liturgy, education and personal commitment. Other organizations have built upon UNEP's resource base to develop programs of their own that extend throughout the year.

In July 1990, the United Nations gathered religious leaders from 12 faiths and 40 nations to enlist their help in easing children's suffering worldwide. The UN has developed laws guaranteeing children's rights and protecting them and the environments they are born into, for both are dying at terrifyingly rapid rates. UNEP and UNICEF supported these UN initiatives with a variety of programs.

In Spring of 1991, the Environmental Sabbath/Earth Rest Day focused on children and the environment, and produced the resource guide *Our Children Their Earth*, from which the following scriptures are drawn.

Adapted from the Spring 1991 Environmental Sabbath/
Earth Rest Day Newsletter

United Nations Environment Programme
Regional Office for North America
DC2-0803, United Nations
New York, NY 10017 USA

"If a child is to keep alive his inborn sense of wonder . . . he needs the companionship of at least one adult who can share it, rediscovering with him the joy, excitement and mystery of the world we live in." RACHEL CARSON,
from *The Sense of Wonder*

"Those who have the humility of a child may find a key to reverence for, and kinship with, all life."

J. ALLEN BOONE,
from *The Language of Science*

"When I bring you colored toys, my child, I understand why there is such a play of colors on clouds, on water, and why flowers are painted in tints."

RABINDRANATH TAGORE,
Nobel Laureate, India

"The world was not left to us by our parents, it was lent to us by our children."

AFRICAN PROVERB

Scriptures and Reflections on Children and the Earth

Bahá'í

O God! Educate these children. These children are the plants of Thine orchard, the flowers of Thy meadow, the roses of Thy garden. Let Thy rain fall upon them; let the Sun of Reality shine upon them with Thy love. Let Thy breeze refresh them in order that they may be trained, grow and develop, and appear in the utmost beauty. Thou are the Giver. Thou art the Compassionate.

ABDU'L-BAHÁ,
Bahá'í Prayers, p.35

*T*rain your children from their earliest days to be infinitely tender and loving to animals. If an animal be sick, let the children try to heal it; if it be hungry, let them feed it; if thirsty, let them quench its thirst; if weary, let them see that it rests.

From the writings of
ABDU'L-BAHÁ,
No. 130. p.158

Buddhist

*I*t's time for elders to listen to the child's voice. You see, in the child's mind there is no demarcation of different nations, no demarcation of different social systems of ideology. Children know in their minds that all children are the same, all human beings are the same. So, from that viewpoint, their minds are more unbiased. When people get older, though, they start to say, "our nation," "our religion," "our system." Once that demarcation occurs, then people don't bother much about what happens to others. It's easier to introduce social responsibility into a child's mind.

His Holiness the XIVth Dalai Lama,
TENZIN GYATSO, in *My Tibet*,
written with Galen Rowell

Christian

*O*ne generation passeth away, and another generation cometh: but the earth abideth forever.

ECCLESIASTES 1:4

*T*hey brought young children to Christ, that he should touch them: and his disciples rebuked those that brought them. But when Jesus saw it, he was much displeased, and said unto them, "Suffer the little children to come unto me, and forbid them not: for of such is the kingdom of God. Verily I say unto you, Whosoever shall not receive the kingdom of God as a little child, he shall not enter therein." And he took them in his arms, put his hands upon them, and blessed them.

MARK 10:13–16

Hindu

*T*he Hindu mind is singularly dominated by one paramount conception: the divinity of life. Regarding the creation of the universe, Hindu tradition, based on the experience of illumined mystics, asserts with deep conviction that God is the supreme creator of every thing and every being. . . . Hindus give God a favored place in our homes as mother, friend, child, even husband or sweetheart. God, being the most beloved object of life, must find a place in our family life. He must be dear and near to us. This ideal of the sweet God, lovable God, playmate God, child God has been admirably illustrated in Hinduism in the personality of Sri Krishna. So, every child can be looked upon by anyone as a baby God, and spiritual life can be quickened in this manner.

SWAMI TATHAGATANANDA,
Vendanta Society, New York

*L*et us declare our determination to halt the present slide towards destruction, to rediscover the ancient tradition of reverence for all life and, even at this hour, to reverse the suicidal course upon which we have embarked. Let us recall the ancient Hindu dictum: "The earth is my mother, and we are all her children."

Dr. KARAN SINGH
at the World Wide Fund for Nature gathering
of religious leaders, Assisi, Italy

Jewish

*J*ust as you found trees which others had planted when you entered the land, so you should plant for your children. No one should say, "I am old. How many more years will I live? Why should I be troubled for the sake of others?" Just as he found trees, he should add more by planting even if he is old.

MIDRASH TANCHUMA,
KEDOSHIM 8

A person's life is sustained by trees. Plant them for the sake of your children.

From SEDER TU BISHEYAT,
the Festival of Trees,
Central Conference of American Rabbis

Moslem

*T*he Prophet [Mohammed] was very concerned about wasting and polluting water. Even when we were very young, our mothers taught us that whoever soils the river, on the day of judgment that person is going to be given the responsibility of cleaning the river. So we were really learning about preserving the purity of water from childhood.

SHEIKH AHMAD KUFTARO,
Grand Mufti of Syria,
in *Shared Vision*, 1990

Native American

*W*e are taught to plant our feet carefully on Mother Earth because the faces of all future generations are looking up from it.

OREN LYONS,
Chief Joagquisho of the Haudenosaunee
(Iroquois) Confederation

*T*each your children what we have taught our children, that the earth is our mother. Whatever befalls the earth, befalls the children of the earth. If we spit upon the ground, we spit upon

ourselves. This we know. The earth does not belong to us; we belong to the earth. One thing we know, which the white man may one day discover, our God is the same God. You may think now that you own Him as you wish to own our land, but you cannot. He is the God of all people, and His compassion is equal for all. This earth is precious to God, and to harm the earth is to heap contempt on its Creator. . . . So love it as we have loved it. Care for it as we have cared for it. And with all your mind, with all your heart, preserve it for your children, and love it . . . as God loves us all.

CHIEF SEATTLE
of the Squamish, *circa* 1855

Sikh

*F*or the sake of posterity, those countless generations of unborn children to come, let us save this Earth. Let us not misuse our privileges. Please don't let the song of birds die. Don't let the water babies perish. Don't let magnificent animals become extinct. Above all, don't let human beings die of starvation and man-made disasters.

From the World Wide Fund
for Nature gathering of religious leaders
at Assisi, Italy

*A*ir is the Vital Force,
Water the Progenitor.
The Vast Earth,
the Mother of All:
Day and night are nurses,
fondling all creation
in their lap.

GURU NANAK,
founder of Sikhism

The Convention on the Rights of the Child

Children are especially vulnerable to rights violations. Each day nearly 35,000 children die from lack of food, shelter or primary health care. About 30 million children live in the world's streets, and another 20 million have been displaced, physically disabled or otherwise traumatized by armed conflict.

The United Nations Convention on The Rights of the Child is an international treaty establishing an international legal framework for the civil, social, economic and political rights of children. Unanimously adopted by the UN General Assembly on November 20, 1989, as of February 1993, 129 countries have ratified the Convention so far. Drafted over a ten-year period by the 43 nations that are members of the United Nations Human Rights Commission, the Convention is the most comprehensive international expression of children's rights. By gathering them into a single legal instrument, the Convention represents an unprecedented international consensus.

The Convention commits all ratifying nations to recognize that children have special needs and encourages all governments to establish standards for their survival, protection and development. *Survival* means the right to food, shelter and essential health care. *Protection* includes sheltering children from abuse and from involvement in war, and gives them the right to a name and nationality. *Development* guarantees the right to a basic education and provides special care for handicapped children.

The preamble recalls the basic principles of the United Nations Charter and specific provisions of relevant human rights treaties such as the Universal Declaration of Human Rights as well as other statutes and proclamations. It reaffirms the fact that children, because of their vulnerability, need special care and protection, and it places special emphasis on the primary caring responsibility of the family and extended family.

The Convention also reaffirms the need for legal and other protection of the child before and after birth, the importance of respect for the cultural values of the child's community, and the vital role of international cooperation in securing children's rights. It also includes provisions never before recognized in an international treaty, requiring countries to:

- do everything possible to ensure child survival;
- pursue "full implementation" of the child's right to the highest level of health possible by working to provide primary health care, to educate mothers and families about breast feeding and family planning, and to abolish harmful practices such as the preferential treatment of male children; and
- work toward achieving universal primary education, and take measures to reduce drop-out rates and encourage regular school attendance.

The World Summit for Children

Nearly one year later, in September 1990, a unique summit meeting was held at the United Nations in an extraordinary effort to address the problems of the world's children. With 72 heads of state and government, the World Summit for Children was the biggest gathering of national leaders in the history of humankind. It also was the first time that leaders from around the globe had met for a single, common purpose —to give children priority on governmental agendas in the 1990s.

The World Summit's goals were to:

- draw attention to major problems affecting children— debt, war and other hostilities, environmental deterioration, drugs, and AIDS;
- give children "first call" on society's resources;
- accelerate implementation and monitoring of the Convention on the Rights of the Child; and
- encourage people and their governments to "do the doable" —mass, low-cost, available means of action.

"We do this not only for the present generation but for all generations to come. There can be no task nobler than giving every child a better future."

from the Declaration
of the World Summit for Children

Excerpted and adapted by the Editor from *Our Children Their Earth*, pp.21–22, from the UNICEF *Backgrounder*, and from the Convention on the Rights of the Child.

For the complete text and an unofficial summary of the main provisions of the Convention, contact:
UNICEF
777 United Nations Plaza
New York, NY 10017 USA
TEL (212) 687-2163

A World Core Curriculum

Dr. Robert Muller

Now serving as a Chancellor (Emeritus) at the University for Peace in Costa Rica, Dr. Muller spent nearly four decades working at the United Nations where he rose to the rank of Assistant Secretary-General. Dr. Muller is now promoting a number of important projects aimed at achieving his lifetime objective: peaceful coexistence among human beings. The author of many books, and considered by many to be the "father of global education," he was recently awarded the prestigious Albert Schweitzer International Prize for the Humanities for his lifelong dedication to the cause of world peace. –Ed.

*W*e have reached a point in human evolution when we must ask ourselves some very fundamental questions regarding the meaning of life and evolution itself. If we assume that all we have learned, all that is happening, all we are trying to do makes little sense, then there is no hope and the human species might as well destroy itself and disappear. If, on the contrary, we assume that some cosmic force or law or God or Creator in the universe has put in the human species certain objectives, functions, expectations and destinations, then it is our duty to ascertain on a contemporary scale what these objectives are.

By giving us capacities to see, to hear, to feel, to think, to dream, to teach and to invent, the universe gives us an indication of what is expected of us: It wants us to know and to understand the maximum range possible of what the universe is all about. We are driven to know more and more of our globe and of Creation, including the art of recombining cosmic forces through energy, matter and life itself. Humanity has become the manager of this planet, a cosmic agent, a very advanced phenomenon in the universe. We are made to feel the thrill and benefits of this task, of being alive, of being human, i.e., a specially valuable, advanced, sensitive force or cell in that universe in which the consciousness of the universe and of time constantly grows.

If this is the case or if we suppose it to be so, then our next great evolutionary task will be to ascertain what this cosmic or divine pattern means and to prepare for it the right institutions, people, values, guidelines, laws, philosophy, politics and ethics. This immense, unprecedented task is dawning upon us everywhere, piercing the core of our earlier beliefs, values and institutions. The present essay is one of these global perceptions born in someone who has been nurtured by world forces for more than a third of a century in the Earth's first universal organization.

Let me tell you how I would educate the children of this planet in light of my 33 years of experience at the United Nations and offer you a world core curriculum which should underlie all grades, levels and forms of education, including adult education.

The starting point is that every hour, 6,000 of our brothers and sisters die and 15,000 children are born on this globe. The newcomers must be educated so that they can benefit from our acquired knowledge, skills, and art of living; enjoy happy and fulfilled lives; and contribute in turn to the continuance, maintenance and further ascent of humanity on a well-preserved planet.

Alas, many of the newly born will never reach school age. One out of ten will die before the age of one and another four percent will die before the age of five. This we must try to prevent by all means. We must also try to prevent that children reach school age with handicaps. It is estimated that ten percent of all the world's children reach school age with a handicap of a physical, sensory or mental nature. In the developing countries, an unfortunate major cause is still malnutrition.

Thirdly, an ideal world curriculum presupposes that there are schools in all parts of the world. This is not yet the case. There are still 814 million illiterates on this planet. Humanity has done wonders in educating its people: We have reduced the percentage of illiterates of the world's adult population from 32.4 percent to 28.9 percent between 1970 and 1980, a period of phenomenal population growth. But between now and the year 2000, 1.6 billion more people will be added to this planet and we are likely to reach a total of 6.1 billion people in that year. Ninety percent of the increase will be in the developing countries where the problem of education is more severe. As a result, the total number of illiterates could climb to 950 million by the bimillenium.

With all these miseries and limitations still with us, it remains important, nevertheless, to lift our sights and to begin thinking of a world core curriculum. I would organize such a curriculum, i.e., the fundamental lifelong objectives of education, around the following categories:

I. Our Planetary Home and Place in the Universe

II. Our Human Family

III. Our Place in Time

IV. The Miracle of Individual Human Life

I. Our planetary home

The first major segment of the curriculum should deal with our prodigious knowledge of planet Earth. Humanity has been able, of late, to produce a magnificent picture of our planet and of its place in the universe. From the infinitely large to the infinitely small, everything fits today into a very simple and clear pattern. Astrophysicists tell us how stars and planets are born and die. We know the physics, atmospheres and even soils of other planets. Thanks to human-made satellites we have a total view of our globe, of our atmosphere, of our seas and oceans and land masses. We know our complicated climate. For the first time ever, we possess a soil and land map for the entire planet. We know our mountains. We know our total water resources. We know our deserts. We know our flora and fauna. We know part of the crust of our Earth into which all nations have agreed to dig holes of at least 1,000 meters. Our knowledge reaches far down into the microbial, genetic and cellular worlds, into the realm of the atom and its particles and subparticles. We have an incredible, beautiful, vast picture of our place in the universe. If a teacher wishes to give children a glimpse of the tremendous expanse of our knowledge, all he or she has to do is to have them visit, on the same day, an astronomical observatory and an atomic bubble chamber!

We can now give children a breathtaking view of the beauty and teeming, endless richness of Creation as has never been possible before. It should make them glad to be alive and to be human. It should also prepare them with excitement for the vast number of professions which have arisen from that tremendous knowledge and its related and consequent activities.

Moreover, as it is vividly described in the story of the Tree of Knowledge, having decided to become like God through knowledge and our attempt to understand the heavens and the Earth, we have also become masters in deciding between good and evil: Every invention of ours can be used for good or bad. Outer space technology can be used for peace or for killer satellites, aviation for transportation or for dropping bombs, the atom for energy or for nuclear destruction, etc.

This gives the teachers of this world a marvelous opportunity to teach

ENVIRONMENTAL STUDIES

"*The religious and moral dimension of environmental studies is fundamental for three principal reasons.*

1. All religions, including humanism and scientific rationalism, imply a view of the relation of man to nature, the content of which affects the way the environment is treated.

2. Policy decisions themselves involve evaluations of nature and the environment which may properly be considered moral.

3. Environmental problems of pollution, the conservation of resources, the preservation of nature itself, the growth of population globally and locally, and of migration and aggregation into burgeoning urban complexes, cannot be set apart from social and economic questions which have an undisputed moral dimension."

R.P. Moss, "Environmental Studies," in
A Dictionary of Religious Education,
edited by John M. Sutcliffe, p.124

PEACE STUDIES

"Peace Studies has become a viable teaching prospect for two reasons:

1. It fits into the pattern of topic studies that emerged in the era of expansion and experiment as an alternative to the subject based approach and

2. The intensity of political confrontation coupled with rapid development of weapons technology in the nuclear, electronic, chemical and biological fields has produced a new level of consciousness about the urgency that permeates issues of peace and conflict.

At the same time it is ironic that it is this very sense of urgency that makes Peace Studies a controversial item in schools and colleges since it can be used as a cover for manipulation by devotees of any part of the political spectrum. Total academic integrity that demonstrably seeks to equip pupils with the capacity to analyze both existing and potential alternative values in the topic are a teacher's only defense when such accusations fly.

Peace Studies cannot be soundly built on a revulsion from War/Conflict Studies. The topic is as inexorably bound to these as Feminist Studies are to the doctrine of man. Indeed, analysis of conflict helps to define aspects of Peace Studies from inner mental conflict of the individual, through family tensions to neighborhood animosities, on through class and ethnic antipathies to terrorism and to conflicting interests and ideologies at the international level. Each level of conflict has a corresponding "peace" with distinctive features that deserve close study. In each case there is also the recurring issue of whether one is talking of containing conflict as a form or peace or is reserving the word "peace" for a genuine resolution and removal of conflict.

Continued on next page

children and people a sense of participation and responsibility in the building and management of the Earth, of becoming artisans of the will of God and of our further human ascent. A new world morality and world ethics will thus evolve, and teachers will be able to prepare responsible citizens, workers, scientists, geneticists, physicists and scores of other professionals, including a new one which is badly needed—good world managers and caretakers.

II. The human family

*T*here is a second segment in which humanity has also made tremendous progress of late: Not only have we taken cognizance of our planet and of our place in the universe, but we have also taken stock of ourselves! This is of momentous importance, for henceforth our story in the universe is basically that of ourselves and of our planet. For a proper unfolding of that story, we had to know its two main elements well: the planet and ourselves.

We have learned so much about humanity since the end of World War II. As a matter of fact, a proper global education or world curriculum would have been impossible 30 years ago because there were no world statistics! Today we know how many we are, where we live, how long we live, how many males, females, youth and elderly there are. We also know ourselves qualitatively: our levels of living, of nutrition, of health, of literacy, of development, of employment, etc. We even have records of our progress: We know how many literates are being added to this planet each year; we know that by eradicating smallpox the number of blind in the world was reduced by half, etc. Incidentally, it was no small achievement to have accommodated two billion more people on this planet within a short period of 30 years! As a result of many international efforts, we have an unprecedented inventory and knowledge of humanity. That fundamental, up-to-date knowledge must be conveyed to all the children and people of the world.

We enter the global age with 176 nations,[1] 5,000 languages and scores of religions. Other entities are rapidly expanding in response to new global demands, namely world organizations, multinational corporations and transnational associations. All these groups are being studied and heard in the United Nations and its agencies. What this all means is as yet little understood. The theory of group formation, or entities, or sociobiology of the human species from the world society to the individual is still a rather primitive science.

The first task of the United Nations and of educators is to build bridges, peace and harmony between these groups, to listen to their views and perceptions, to prevent them from blowing each other up and endangering the entire planet, to seek what each group has to contribute, to understand their legitimate concerns, cultures, values, denominators and objectives, and to grasp the meaning of the vast and complex functioning of life from the largest to the most minute, from the total society to the individual, from human unity to an endless and more refined diversity.

What will be important in such a curriculum is the dynamic aspect of the relations between humanity and the planet: We now have good inventories; we know the elements of the great evolutionary problems confronting us, but we barely stand at the beginning of the planetary management phase of human history—demographic options, resource management, environmental protection, conflict resolution, the attainment of peace, justice and progress for all, the fulfillment of human life and happiness in space and in time. The United Nations and its specialized agencies offer the first examples of attempts at global management in all these fields and must therefore occupy a cardinal place in the world's curricula. The earlier we do this, the better it will be for our survival, fulfillment and happiness.

III. Our place in time

When I joined the United Nations in 1948, there was very little time perspective. The word "futurology" did not even exist. Some nations who had five-year economic plans were derided, because it was believed that no one on this planet could plan for five years ahead. How the world has changed since then! Today every nation is planning for at least 20 years ahead. Something similar is happening with regard to the past: In the 17th century, Bishop Usher calculated that the Earth was 6,000 years old; then the French naturalist Buffon estimated that it was at least several hundred thousand years old. Today we know that our planet is more than 4½ billion years old and we have developed a vast knowledge of our paleontological and archaeological past.

Thus humanity is forced to expand its time dimension tremendously both into the past and into the future: We must preserve the natural elements inherited from the past and necessary for our life and survival (air, water, soils, energy, animals, fauna, flora, genetic materials). We also want to preserve our cultural heritage, the landmarks of our own evolution and history, in order to see the unfolding and magnitude of our cosmic journey. At the same time, we must think and plan far ahead into the future in order to hand over to coming generations a well-preserved and better managed planet in the universe.

It will take great vision and honesty to achieve the harmony and fulfillment of our journey in the universe and in time. We have come to the point when the prediction of Leibnitz is coming true. He had forecast that scientific enquiry would be so thrilling for humanity that for centuries we would be busy discovering, analyzing and piercing the surrounding reality, but that the time would come when we would have to look at the totality and become again what we were always meant to be: universal, total beings. The time for this vast synthesis, for a new encyclopedia of all our knowledge and the formulation of the agenda for our cosmic future, has struck.

IV. The miracle of individual life

It is becoming increasingly clear that in this vast evolutionary quantum change the individual remains the alpha and the omega of all our efforts. Individual human life is the highest form of universal consciousness on our planet. Institutions, concepts, factories, systems, states, ideologies, theories have no consciousness. They are all servants, instruments, means for better lives and the increase of individual human consciousness. We are faced today with the full-fledged centrality, dignity, miracle, sanctity or divinity of individual human life, irrespective of race, sex, status, age, nation, or physical or mental capacity.

Pablo Casals, the musician and poet, expressed this in very moving and emotional terms at the United Nations: "The child must know that he or she is a miracle, a unique miracle unmatched since the beginning of the world and until the end of the world."

Education of the newcomers is basically the teaching of the miracle of life, the art of living, and of human fulfillment within our immense knowledge of space and time. It is to make each child feel like a king or queen in the universe, an expanded being aggrandized by the vastness of our knowledge. It is to make each human being feel proud to be a member of a transformed species.

And here I would complete my core curriculum for the individual with the four segments so dear to the former Secretary-General of the United Nations, U Thant:

RE [Religious Education] may relate to Peace Studies in two ways.

1. Peace Studies may be included as a topic within an RE syllabus, considering the relationship of religion to society and the various belief systems as they interpret the human situation. The need for and capacity of religious groups to challenge society is important although often lost within the context of state or civic religions.

2. RE can make a contribution to a peace studies program. An important stage in this is to overcome common misconceptions and even prejudices about the involvement of religion in war and its causes throughout history. It is profitable in contrast to consider religious resources for peace. In both approaches to the relationship of RE and Peace Studies the contribution of major religious figures to the cause of peace will play a significant part.

James Green, "Peace Studies," in *A Dictionary of Religious Education* edited by John M. Sutcliffe, p.254

VALUES EDUCATION

"Values Education is an inescapable part of any educational system, though it may not always be openly acknowledged as such. Its presence may be observed in anthropological accounts of young people growing up in primal societies, e.g., Samoa or the early colonial period in Africa, through to the sophisticated system of modern states, e.g. France, China, USA or USSR. Primal and sophisticated alike have a common expectation that young people will take their place as responsible adults to their own benefit and that of their community. . . .

Aims. There are three aims that mark off polarities in Values Education [VE]:

1. to produce conformity to existing values;

2. to produce dedication to radical change;

3. to foster a capacity for critical appraisal of both existing and potential values.

Historically one is unlikely to find a pure example of any of these so they are best used as *types* or markers by which to review and assess one's own work in VE. One has to keep in mind that the capacity for critical appraisal needs to be applied to alternative as well as existing values for it is not difficult to show that radical change is often demanded on the basis of views which their exponents cannot or do not critically examine. Indeed today's radical critics have often become tomorrow's tyrants enforcing a new conformity.

Where all adults are able to take part in the political process and even more where there is a variety of culture and interest-groups in one society, the most appropriate aim is to maximize the capacity for critical appraisal of all existing and alternative values and to enable openness to the existing and alternative values that survive such appraisal.

James Green, "Values Education,"
in *A Dictionary of Religious Education,*
edited by John M. Sutcliffe, p.356

Good physical lives: knowledge and care of the body; teaching to see, to hear, to observe, to create, to do, to use well all our senses and physical capacities.

Good mental lives: knowledge; teaching to question, to think, to analyze, to synthesize, to conclude, to communicate; teaching to focus from the infinitely large to the infinitely small, from the distant past to the present and future.

Good moral lives: teaching to love; teaching truth, understanding, humility, liberty, reverence for life, compassion, altruism.

Good spiritual lives: spiritual exercises of interiority, meditation, prayer and communion with the universe and eternity or God.

An immense task and responsibility thus behooves all teachers and educators of this planet: It is no less than to contribute to the survival and good management of our planetary home and species, to our further common ascent into a universal, interdependent, peaceful civilization, while ensuring the knowledge, skills and fulfillment of the flow of humans going through the Earth's schools.

A world core curriculum might seem utopian today; by the end of the year 2000 it will be a down-to-earth, daily reality in all the schools of the world.[2]

NOTES

1. Membership as of December 1992

2. Excerpted from a paper written by Robert Muller that first appeared in *New Era,* the magazine of the World Education Fellowship in January 1982. Now included in *Essays on Education: A Vision for Educators,* by Robert Muller, edited by Joanne Dufour. Published by World Happiness and Cooperation, P.O. Box 1153, Anacortes, WA 98221 USA

EDUCATION 2000: A Holistic Perspective

Global Alliance for Transforming Education

The excerpts which follow are from the vision statement of GATE published in August 1991.

Preamble

We are educators, parents and citizens from diverse backgrounds and educational movements who share a common concern for the future of humanity and all life on Earth.

We believe that the serious problems affecting modern educational systems reflect a deeper crisis in our culture: the inability of the predominant industrial/technological worldview to address, in a humane and life-affirming manner, the social and planetary challenges that we face today.

We believe that our dominant cultural values and practices, including emphasis on competition over cooperation, consumption over sustainable resource use, and bureaucracy over authentic human interaction have been destructive to the health of the ecosystem and to optimal human development as well.

As we examine this culture-in-crisis, we also see that our systems of education are anachronistic and dysfunctional. In sharp contrast to the conventional use of the word *education*, we believe that our culture must restore the original meaning of the word, "to draw forth." In this context, *education* means caring enough to draw forth the greatness that is within each unique person.

The purpose of this Statement is to proclaim an alternative vision of education—one which is a life-affirming and democratic response to the challenges of the 1990s and beyond. Because we value diversity and encourage a wide variety of methods, applications and practices, it is a vision toward which educators may strive in their various ways. There is not complete unanimity, even among those of us who endorse this document, on all of the statements presented here. The vision transcends our differences and points us in a direction that offers a humane resolution to the crisis of modern education.

Principle I. Educating for human development

We assert that the primary—indeed the fundamental—purpose of education is to nourish the inherent possibilities of human development. Schools must be places that facilitate the learning and whole development of all learners. Learning must involve the enrichment and deepening of relationships to self, to family and community members, to the global community, to the planet, and to the cosmos. These ideas have been expressed eloquently and put into practice by great educational pioneers such as Pestalozzi, Froebel, Dewey, Montessori, Steiner and others. . . .

We call for a renewed recognition of human values which have been eroded in modern culture—harmony, peace, cooperation, community, honesty, justice, equality, compassion, understanding and love. . . .

Principle III. The central role of experience

We affirm what the most perceptive educators have argued for centuries: education is a matter of experience. . . .

Continued on next page

Educating for Global Citizenship: An Outline

PHILOSOPHY AND PURPOSE

Each of us—whether we realize it or not— *is* a global citizen. The purpose of education for global citizenship is to facilitate the awareness of our own roles in the global ecology, including the human family and all other systems of the earth and universe.

CONDITIONS AND GOALS

Studies are interdisciplinary and reinforced across the curriculum. It is *not* just a subject called "global education."

Principles and values may be deduced by the student from the study of successful ecological systems and of human cultural and religious experience, and from deliberate personal experience and reflection.

The goal is transformation of mindsets through an ongoing cycle of study, experience, reflection and response.

The process should always cultivate critical thinking and creative responses.

UNIVERSAL VALUES

1) Harmony (balance, wellness, attunement, personal growth)

2) Love (compassion)

3) Understanding (respect for diversity, wisdom, cooperation)

4) Equality

5) Responsible Action (service, honesty)

6) Search for truth and truthfulness

7) Self-transcendence (search for meaning)

COMPONENTS

1) The conditions for peace and techniques of conflict resolution

2) Developing visions of change and acting creatively toward their realization

3) Multicultural education for cultural literacy and interaction

4) Learning about both cooperation and new models of leadership

5) Human rights and needs: justice issues, population issues (hunger, health, education, sustainable development)

6) Interdependence and the scope of our responsibility

7) Earth literacy (ecology, our environments, future focus)

8) Economic and political interrelationships

9) World religions and world views

10) The congruence of personal and global well-being

compiled by the Editor from a workshop of the Global Alliance for Transforming Education

And education should acquaint the learner with the realm of his or her own inner world through the arts, honest dialogue and times of quiet reflection—for without this knowledge of the inner self, all outward knowledge is shallow and without purpose.

Principle IV. Holistic education

We call for wholeness in the educational process, and for the transformation of educational institutions and policies required to attain this aim. Wholeness implies that each academic discipline provides merely a different perspective on the rich, complex, integrated phenomenon of life. Holistic education celebrates and makes constructive use of evolving, alternate views of reality and multiple ways of knowing. It is not only the intellectual and vocational aspects of human development that need guidance and nurturance, but also the physical, social, moral, aesthetic, creative and—in a nonsectarian sense—spiritual aspects. Holistic education takes into account the numinous mystery of life and the universe in addition to the experiential reality.

Holism is a reemerging paradigm, based on a rich heritage from many scholarly fields. Holism affirms the inherent interdependence of evolving theory, research and practice. Holism is rooted in the assumption that the universe is an integrated whole in which everything is connected. This assumption of wholeness and unity is in direct opposition to the paradigm of separation and fragmentation that prevails in the contemporary world. Holism corrects the imbalance of reductionistic approaches through its emphasis on an expanded conception of science and human possibility. . . .

Principle VII. Educating for a participatory democracy

We call for a truly democratic model of education to empower all citizens to participate in meaningful ways in the life of the community and the planet . . .

Principle VIII. Educating for global citizenship

We believe that each of us—whether we realize it or not—is a global citizen. . . . We believe that it is time for education to nurture an appreciation for the magnificent diversity of human experience and for the lost or still uncharted potentials within human beings. Education in a global age needs to address what is most fully, most universally human in the young generation of all cultures. . . .

Since the world's religions and spiritual traditions have such enormous impact, global education encourages understanding and appreciation of them and of the universal values they proclaim, including the search for meaning, love, compassion, wisdom, truth and harmony. Thus, education in a global age addresses what is most fully and universally human.

Principle IX. Educating for earth literacy

We believe that education must spring organically from a profound reverence for life in all its forms. We must rekindle a relationship between the human and the natural world that is nurturing, not exploitive. This is at the very core of our vision for the 21st century. The planet Earth is a vastly complex, but fundamentally unitary living system, an oasis of life in the dark void of space. Post-Newtonian science, systems theory and other recent advances in modern thought have recognized what some ancient spiritual and mythological traditions have taught for centuries: The planet, and all life upon it, form an interdependent whole. . . .

We call for education that promotes earth literacy to include an awareness of planetary interdependence, the congruence of personal and global well-being, and the individual's role and scope of responsibility. . . . Earth education is an integrative field including politics, economics, culture, history, and personal and societal change processes.

Principle X. Spirituality and education

We believe that all people are spiritual beings in human form who express their individuality through their talents, abilities, intuition and intelligence. Just as the individual develops physically, emotionally and intellectually, each person also develops spiritually. Spiritual experience and development manifest as a deep connection to self and others, a sense of meaning and purpose in daily life, an experience of the wholeness and interdependence of life, a respite from the frenetic activity, pressure and overstimulation of contemporary life, the fullness of creative experience, and a profound respect for the numinous mystery of life. The most important, most valuable part of the person is his or her inner, subjective life—the self or the soul.

The absence of the spiritual dimension is a crucial factor in self-destructive behavior. Drug and alcohol abuse, empty sexuality, crime and family breakdown all spring from a misguided search for connection, mystery, and meaning and an escape from the pain of not having a genuine source of fulfillment.

We believe that education must nourish the healthy growth of the spiritual life, not do violence to it through constant evaluation and competition. One of the functions of education is to help individuals become aware of the connectedness of all life. Fundamental to this awareness of wholeness and connectedness is the ethic expressed in all of the world's great traditions: *"What I do to others I do to myself."* Equally fundamental to the concept of connectedness is the empowerment of the individual. If everyone is connected to everyone and everything else, then the individual can and does make a difference.

By fostering a deep sense of connection to others and to the Earth in all its dimensions, holistic education encourages a sense of responsibility to self, to others and to the planet. We believe that this responsibility is not a burden, but rather arises out of a sense of connection and empowerment. Individual, group and global responsibility is developed by fostering the compassion that causes individuals to want to alleviate the suffering of others, by instilling the conviction that change is possible and by offering the tools to make those changes possible.

Conclusion

As we approach the 21st century, many of our institutions and professions are entering a period of profound change. We in education are beginning to recognize that the structure, purposes, and methods of our profession were designed for a historical period which is now coming to a close. The time has come to transform education so as to address the human and environmental challenges which confront us. ⊛

For the full document or for more information, contact:
GATE
P.O. Box 21
Grafton, VT 05146 USA
TEL: (802) 843-2382 FAX: (802) 843-2300

The Shap Working Party on World Religions in Education

The Shap Working Party on World Religions in Education is a group of people who are actively interested in all stages of education. Founded in 1969 at the Shap Wells Hotel, Cumbria, UK, it now has connections world wide, especially in other parts of Europe.

The Shap World Religions approach is one which places the emphasis upon understanding the nature of religious beliefs and practices, and the importance which these have in the lives of believers.

What this means in practice is such things as understanding the following:

- A religion's world view, what people believe and how this forms a basis for the values they cherish and the lives they lead;
- What believers do when, for example, they worship, go on pilgrimage or fast, and why they undertake such practices;
- The stories which believers tell to express or interpret their beliefs;
- The social aspects of religion; such community rules as the requirement to wear the turban, make the *Hajj*, eat or avoid certain foods;
- How believers are expected to behave and why; their conduct in such matters as forgiveness, love, honesty; their attitudes towards peace and war, the family, sexuality, the punishment of crimes; and the way they arrive at their views on these kinds of issues;
- The experiential element; what their religion means to believers, how it motivates, inspires and supports them.

In other words it is concerned with understanding what it means to be a Christian or Muslim, for example, in terms of beliefs, practices, values and how they see the world; what it means to take a religious commitment seriously.

What is the place of Christianity in this approach? Christianity is one of the major religions in the world. It is the one which has most influenced the values of British society. On any reckoning a religious education which does not pay considerable attention to it must be regarded as inadequate.

Isn't it likely that children will leave school believing that all religions are the same? Religious traditions share many human values such as love, peace and justice. These similarities should be given proper attention. However, the distinctive features of religions must be taught. Such beliefs, practices and values are important elements in developing the identities of individuals and communities. It is essential that children should understand them.

Wouldn't the result of this approach be to make children confused after studying several religions? We would argue that if there is confusion, it results from bad teaching by people lacking a Religious Studies qualification who have to compete with other areas of the National Curriculum for a place on the timetable and for resources. Where these conditions are reversed, in schools where headteachers and governors value religious education, and skilled teachers are given support and encouraged to do the job for which they have been trained, it is clear that the study of religion can be interesting, enjoyable, relevant and valuable to pupils as young people growing to adulthood in a mature democracy. In such schools we do not find confusion. Those students who possess a religious faith tend to find their understanding of it sharpened and enriched. The rest become aware of the importance which it has for individuals and societies.

The anxiety we share with parents, religious leaders and politicians, as well as teachers, is about the absence of religious education in many schools. We want to highlight the lack of properly qualified teachers and of inservice training, especially for teachers in primary school. Even the teaching of Christianity poses severe problems for teachers in a society where many people are skeptical of the worth of religious belief, usually Christian. To teach it requires professional training and academic knowledge. We deplore situations where there is no religious education or where Christianity is not taught. We use our energies and skills to rectify them.

But why have any religious education in school? The case for a broad-based study of beliefs and values is grounded in the education which all children require and deserve. This should be one which cherishes those aspects of life which make us human and ensures that they are given proper recognition in the curriculum. Through such an education, children are enabled to understand their place in their community in local, national and global terms, and to discover and aspire to reaching their full human potential in a mature democracy.

Chair: Mary Hayward;
President: Ninian Smart;
Vice-Chair: Paul Williams

PUBLICATIONS

The annual Shap Journal, *World Religions in Education,* and the Calendar of Religious Festivals are the principal publications, appearing in July. Themes of journal issues include: Women in Religion (1988); Humankind and the Environment (1989); Religion and Story (1990/91); Religious Education and the Creative Arts (1991/92); Religion and Truth (1992/93).

The most recent book is *Teaching World Religions,* Clive Erricker, ed., with Alan Brown, Mary Hayward, Dilip Kadodwala and Paul Williams (Heinemann, 1993). This handbook offers distinctive approaches to world religions in the classroom and an exploration of world views; includes detailed resource lists.

Shap produces other books as needed; details of publications currently available may be obtained from:

Alan Brown
The National Society's RE Centre
23 Kensington Square, London W8 5HN
UK
TEL: 071 937 4241

For further information about the Information Service and the conferences, contact:

Owen Cole
Shap Publicity Officer
WSIHE, College Lane, Chichester
PO 19 4PE UK
TEL: 0243 781 455

Association of Professors and Researchers in Religious Education

This interfaith organization, which currently includes Jews and Christians, welcomes educators and colleagues from all faith traditions. The Association provides a number of services:

- Co-publication of *Religious Education*, the quarterly Journal of the Religious Education Association and the Association of Professors and Researchers in Religious Education
- Task Force Groups related to Religious Education and: Adult Education, Electronic Technology, Evaluation, History of Religious Education, Multicultural and Multiethnic Religious Education, Ethnography as Methodology, and Gender
- An annual meeting of APRRE, held in conjuction with six denominational meetings
- the quarterly *Bulletin* of the Council of Societies for the Study of Religion, of which APRRE is a member
- Doctoral Student Recognition of outstanding papers
- Travel Grant Endowment Fund for Association members
- Student Caucus to discuss a range of ideas and issues
- A new directory of Association membership

For more information, contact:
Padraic O'Hare
Executive Secretary, APRRE
10 Phillips Street
Medway, MA 02053 USA

Multifaith Resources

The Rev. Dr. Charles R. White

President of Multifaith Resources, Presbyterian minister, and a founder and former Director of North American Interfaith Network

Year by year throughout North America, in both Canada and the United States, there is increasing cultural and religious diversity. The rich tapestry of traditions which are encountering each other in our open societies present opportunities to learn about and cooperate with people who are different from ourselves. This requires that religion and culture be taken seriously throughout the society—in schools along with places of work and service. It also means that people of diverse traditions need to respect and cooperate with each other. Churches and other religious institutions can provide leadership in this direction.

Multifaith Resources provides helpful aids to persons of many traditions who are working to respond to a variety of human needs while promoting and enhancing interfaith understanding and cooperation. While Multifaith Resources is clearly based on Christian principles, its goal is to respect the integrity of other religious traditions. An educational ministry conducted by the Rev. Dr. Charles R. White, we encourage and support expression of thoughts and actions which are consistent with the highest values found in each of the world's religions.

Services and supplies

- The *Multifaith Calendar,* published by Canadian Ecumenical Action in Vancouver, B.C., and other materials such as annotated bibliographies of resources helpful in interfaith dialogue
- Multifaith religious education materials published by the widely-respected Christian Education Movement in England; videos on world religions from the Hartley Film Foundation and others
- North American subscriptions to *World Faiths Encounter,* the journal of the World Congress of Faiths
- Locating and providing almost any resource which may be needed in interfaith situations
- Workshops which help equip teachers, chaplains, administrators, pastors and others to provide leadership in the pluralistic society
- Consultations with groups and organizations seeking to become more inclusive in their understanding and practices
- Catalog listing all of the resources available (cost: $3.00, prepaid; cost can be applied to any order of $25.00 or more)

For more information or to purchase supplies, contact:
Multifaith Resources
P.O. Box 128
Wofford Heights, CA 93285
PHONE/FAX: (619) 376-4691

What Can I Do?

A Response to Those Who Despair
About the State of the World

Dr. Willis W. Harman

Director of the Institute of Noetic Sciences, Sausalito, California; Dr. Harman was formerly Senior Social Scientist at SRI International and is emeritus professor of Engineering–Social Systems at Stanford University.

*A*nyone who is sanguine about the global future probably doesn't understand. The problems of a progressively degraded environment, ravaged resources, uncontrolled man-made climate change, chronic hunger and poverty, persistent ethnic and religious conflicts, ever-increasing militarization of societies, and systemic maldistribution of wealth and opportunity seem sufficiently overwhelming, and the political responses so pathetic, that despair seems a reasonable response.

In the context of this Parliament of the World's Religions it seems important to remind ourselves of the creative response which can be found at the core of the esoteric understanding in any one of the world's religious traditions. But first we need to make explicit a number of principles, none of which can be defended in this short space.

Six principles for creative action

1. Each of us can discover within ourselves a *deep sense of purpose;* the deepest yearning of each of us is to make sense of our lives, to know that our lives have meaning. The ultimate learning is that we are spiritual beings in a spiritual universe, that ultimate cause is not to be found in the physical world but in spirit, and that meaning comes through contributing creatively to the whole.

2. The *present world order is not sustainable in the long term.* The world has become unmanageable; fundamental change is required, at the level of the most basic underlying assumptions. We are all reluctant to realize this fact. But like the first step of the "12-step" programs for addiction, we can make no advance without this recognition.

3. Part of our collective confusion comes from the fact that *the scientific worldview which is at the heart of the modern world order, and is taught throughout the modern world from kindergarten to university, explicitly denies the validity of the discovery described in the first principle.*

4. *We intuitively know what are the characteristics of a sustainable and glorious society.* We know what is required at a family and community level, and we only have to extend that to the whole world. This sounds simplistic; the goal *is* simple—it's just getting there that is not.

5. *Each of us can discover our particular role.* There is a place in the system where we uniquely fit, a place where our unique gifts and the demands of the situation fit together perfectly. We may find that place partly through following intuition; partly through trying things and seeing what "wants to happen"; partly by watching for "meaningful coincidences."

6. *Each of us can say "yes" to that role.* There is a new pattern of understanding and valuing which is emerging from the various social movements and deliberations of recent decades. That "new paradigm"— which draws on the perennial wisdom of the world's spiritual traditions— affirms that all things are parts of a single, ultimately spiritual whole, and

"The boat people said that every time their small boats were caught in storms, they knew their lives were in danger. But if one person on the boat could keep calm and not panic, that was a great help for everyone. People would listen to him or her and keep serene, and there was a chance for the boat to survive the danger. Our Earth is like a small boat. Compared with the rest of the cosmos, it is a small boat indeed, and it is in danger of sinking. We need such a person to inspire us with calm confidence, to tell us what to do. Who is that person? The Mahayana Buddhist sutras tell us that you are that person. If you are yourself, if you are your best, then you are that person. Only with such a person— calm, lucid, aware— will our situation improve. I wish you good luck. Please be yourself. Please be that person.

THICH NHẤT HANH,
from "Please Call Me by My True Names,"
in *The Path of Compassion,*
edited by Fred Eppsteiner,
Buddhist Peace Fellowship

that each of us, as a part of that whole, has access to an "inner knowing" which can guide us to ultimately meaningful action.

Elements of a personal program

How can one play one's part in all this? The following three elements comprise an effective personal program:

1. *Personal transformation (inner work).* Many guides to inner transformation are available; ultimately one has to work with what feels intuitively right. *Intention* is the key requirement for discovering within oneself the inner wisdom and deep sense of purpose that will lead to making an effective contribution. The right way will appear. It may be within an established religious tradition, or it may not—or it may be for a time one and later on the other. It will probably involve a meditative discipline, prayer or yoga. It may or may not be with a personal spiritual teacher.

2. *Local action (outer work).* Whole-system transformation involves the transformation of all parts of the system; we can contribute anywhere. Wherever we are in the system is a good place to start—our families, our jobs, our communities. All creative action is with a small group, locally—although the effects may ripple out worldwide. Taking action is essential: it provides "grounding" through which we receive feedback. Action leads to experience, and "all experience is feedback." The guidance of deep intuition as it develops in our inner work, together with feedback from our outer work, will direct us toward discovering our particular role—the place in this whole-system evolution where we uniquely fit.

3. *Global re-perception (inner work).* Modern society, like all societies that have ever existed, rests on some set of basic assumptions about who we are, what kind of universe we are in, and how we relate to one another and to the whole. The present world order is not long-term sustainable because its worldview is not accurate. But we have complicity in that order because we "buy into" the underlying belief system. It is not comfortable to discover that the experienced reality we come to through deep inner work is not that of the materialistic scientific worldview. The re-perception of a sustainable worldview reveals neither the manipulative rationality that passes for knowledge nor the prevailing ethic of acquisitive materialism, and it does not lead to the conventional belief system of economic rationality. Yet it is necessary to come to this realization if we are to clear the path to our own intuitive wisdom and make a meaningful contribution to the whole. There is no resolution of our global dilemmas short of changing these collective beliefs, beginning with ourselves.

ACTION AND PRAYER

"*Righteous action among the people saves prayer from becoming an escape into self-satisfied piety.*

Prayer saves righteous action among the people from self-righteousness.

Righteous action saves prayer from the hypocrisy among the pious which the children of this world will never fail to spot.

Prayer saves righteous action from the fanatical ideologizing through which those who are committed to change become bad representatives of their own commitment.

Righteous action saves prayer from pessimism. Prayer saves righteous action from resignation.

Action keeps prayer in the realm of reality; prayer keeps action within the realm of truth."

EBERHARD BETHGE,
Am gegebenen Ort

"*It is not difficult to hear God's call today in the world about us.*
It is difficult to do more than offer an emotional response, sorrow and regret.
It is even more difficult to give up our comfort, break with old habits,
let ourselves be moved by grace
and change our life, be converted."

PRAYER

"*What is the point of your presence if our lives do not alter?*
Change our lives,
shatter our complacency.
Make your word flesh of our flesh,
blood of our blood,
and our life's purpose. Take away the quietness of a clear conscience.
Press us uncomfortably.
For only thus that other peace is made, your peace."

DOM HELDER CAMARA,
The Desert is Fertile, pp.17 and 19

Planetary Therapy
Twelve Steps of Ecological Spirituality

Albert LaChance

Author, therapist, poet and environmentalist; founder, with his wife, of the Greenspirit Center in New Hampshire.

The materials below are excerpted from *Greenspirit: Twelve Steps in Ecological Spirituality*, by Albert LaChance, which has a foreword by Thomas Berry. The book is a detailed description of a 12-step process of cultural therapy. These excerpts are from the Preface and Introduction. –Ed.

"The industrial world is a kind of entrancement, a pathology. It's addictive. We become addicted to automobiles. It's paralyzing, because once we're totally caught up in it, we think we can't do anything about it. We have a type of religious commitment to the industrial world."

THOMAS BERRY, in *Earth Conference One* by Anuradha Vittachi (Shambhala Books, 1989)

*T*here is only one problem: everything! We like to talk about the ecological problem, the nuclear problem, the drug problem, the family problem, the violence problem, the alcohol problem, the species extinction problem, and so on as though each of these were separate and distinct pathologies, each unrelated to the other. There's really only one problem. It's the way we live. The Earth has only one problem. It's the way we live. We suffer from a deep, cultural pathology.

Industrial culture has a bad chemical dependency problem. Internally, within our bodies, we call it the drug and alcohol epidemic. Externally, outside our bodies, it's the pollution problem—the two faces of one problem, a toxic human on a toxic planet. . . . We need to move into recovery *as cultures*. We need to de-toxify the planet! *Greenspirit* is that final stage of recovery. *Greenspirit* is a cultural thereapy and therefore a planetary therapy.

"The massive overconsumption of the middle and upper classes is merely a symptom of a deeper disease. That disease is materialism in its truest sense."

JEREMY RIFKIN, in *The Emerging Order*, written with Ted Howard

THE TWELVE STEPS OF ECOLOGICAL SPIRITUALITY

1) We admit that we are powerless over an addicted society, that our lives and all of life have become degraded.

2) We come to acknowledge the existence of an Originating Mystery accomplishing the evolution of the universe. We accept that, if allowed, this Originating Mystery will reveal to each of us our natural relationship to self, to others, to other species, to the Earth and to the Universe.

3) We decide to surrender our lives and our wills to this Originating Mystery, whatever we choose to name it.

4) We examine ourselves, listing all our attitudes and actions that damage the created order, thereby stopping or impeding the emergence of this Originating Mystery.

5) We acknowledge to ourselves, to that Originating Mystery and to another person, the specifics of our illusory thinking, attitudes and behavior.

6) We become entirely willing to have all habits of illusion removed from our thoughts, our attitudes and from our behavior.

7) In humility, we request that this Originating Mystery remove all our habits of illusory thought, attitude and behavior.

8) We make a list of all persons, all other species and all the life systems of the planet we have harmed, and we become ready to do everything in our power to heal them all.

9) We make a strenuous effort to heal all phases of the created order—human, animal, or planetary—injured by our illusory thinking, attitudes or action.

10) We continue on a daily basis to go on examining our thinking and our actions as to whether they foster or impede the emergence of life. Where they impede this emergence, we admit it and become willing to be changed.

11) We continue through physical-mental-spiritual disciplines to so change ourselves as to improve our own ability to foster the emergence and health of the whole created order.

12) Having experienced a reawakening to self, to humanity, to all species, to the planet and to the universe, we try to spread this awareness to others and to practice these disciplines in all phases of our lives.

Greenspirit was published in the USA in 1991 by Element, Inc., 42 Broadway, Rockport, MA 01966; and in Great Britain in 1991 by Element Books Limited, Longmead, Shaftesbury, Dorset, UK.

How May I Help?

Nonviolent Social Change in the Gandhian Tradition

Dr. Guy de Mallac

A founder of The Ways of Peace and Service and the United Peace Network, Dr. de Mallac is also professor emeritus at the University of California—Irvine, in the School of Humanities.

*A*s we know from previous essays, the people of this planet face major global issues. One temptation for any individual is to be overwhelmed by their magnitude, so overwhelmed that one does nothing . . . which is very much against authentic spiritual endeavor, and very much against the Gandhian spirit.

The correct view is that every step (however minor) counts. Every step matters—every step that I take, trying to be of service, to be of help. Every such step contributes to fulfilling the purpose of my life. Albert Schweitzer wrote that "The purpose of life is to serve and to show compassion and the will to help others." A key statement on the Volunteer Commitment Card of the Alabama Christian Movement for Human Rights in 1960 translates that attitude or principle into a suggested practice: "Seek to perform regular service for others and for the world."

Let us now see what Nonviolence can contribute toward finding concrete ways in which one can help.

1. Nonviolence—another name for loving, dynamic outreach

*F*ollowing in the footsteps of his mentor Leo Tolstoy, Mahatma Gandhi felt there are two global forces at work in the world:

(1) the Law of Love, and (2) the Law of Violence or Aggression. He felt Love is stronger and can prevail, given our best efforts.

For those who feel that the word "love" has been unduly cheapened, we might substitute synonyms for it: "Nonviolence" (although, like the Sanskrit word "*a*-himsa," *non*-violence is a negative definition, conveying: *not* hurting, or the failure to do violence). Or, with Carl Rogers we might talk of "unconditional positive regard." Again, we might say, "loving, dynamic outreach."

Whatever term we use, we must realize the existence in ourselves and others of a positive force based on warmth, understanding, love, cooperation. Attuned to that force within ourselves, we reach out and turn on that force in others. This force, which reaches out to meet the other, promotes sharing and cooperation, and thus resolves conflicts. Generally speaking, love has been defined as having the following four characteristic attitudes toward the loved one(s): care, responsibility, respect and knowledge (Erich Fromm, *The Art of Loving*).

In usual practice, we tend to love in a restricted way within a set of circles: most strongly, our spouse and/or close family; then other relatives, and friends; and finally perhaps members of affinity groups or associations, and fellow countrypeople. To *universalize* love, we should reach out to all within these concentric circles as sincerely and efficiently as possible.

There are several stages in dynamic outreach: first, develop acquaintance with the member or members of the "other" group, with those who are first seen as "different" from me; then, cultivate greater awareness of those "others" as worthy of respect, as unique, as close to me; demonstrate greater sensitivity, respect and acceptance; and, finally, work toward joint goals together.

If we fail to reach out in that way, but rather insist on viewing the others as radically or forever "different" from us, then the crystallized feeling of difference or estrangement leads to such ills as racism, ethnocentrism or triumphalism; these can give rise to enmity and, in time, generate conflict and war.

Concrete suggestions for implementing nonviolence:

(1) *Practice the Law of Love:* Love all humans as brothers and sisters, with respect, promoting universal acceptance and *familyhood*. Challenge all discriminations and prejudices. Promote the dignity of human beings regardless of age, sex, race or creed. Practice strategic nonviolence as part of an active struggle: denounce injustice.

(2) *Alongside reasonable concern for self, work and serve for the welfare of all.* Practice the Golden Rule. "I can never be what I ought to be until you are what you ought to be." (Martin Luther King)

(3) *Practice thoughtful attentiveness and creative listening to the other's side.* In dealing with an opponent, search actively for common/mutual interests; on the basis of these interests, build projects to encourage the development of increasing mutual trust.

(4) *Respect other societies, cultures, races and the heritage of each.* Conduct intercultural, interreligious, interethnic, interclass and intergender exchange and interaction. Support human freedom and dignity at home by endorsing civil liberties; not granting such liberties is also a form of violence. Persistently denounce and oppose injustice.

(5) *Work for reduction in military budgets.* Actively pursue alternatives to military intervention. Support human freedom and dignity by ending foreign military intervention; interfering in another country's internal affairs is a form of violence.

(6) *Instead of supporting narrow, parochial approaches, develop broader horizons—pluralize and globalize issues.*

(7) *Foster togetherness, unity, harmony.* When two or

more individuals come together to achieve that aim, the Godhead is with them.

2. Nonviolent economics

*A*wareness of the need for nonviolent economics comes with an awareness of what Mahatma Gandhi called "the wide gulf separating the few rich from the hungry millions." If a few decades ago he was warning us that this gap was significant, how much more concerned should we not be today, knowing that this gap *has been widening markedly?* Gandhi saw a direct, causal relationship between (a) the extreme of considerable wealth and idleness and (b) the extreme of considerable poverty and crushing labor.

We need a fuller awareness of what poverty really means: its lack of access to work and basic amenities; the biological damage it causes; the heavy restrictions and waste of human potential that it brings about. We can each develop a fuller awareness of the meaning of the *absolute poverty* which is the lot of close to one billion human beings. We need to become better acquainted with the mechanisms which stop many rich individuals from even perceiving the gap between rich and poor.

Concrete suggestions for implementing nonviolent economics:

(1) *Our caring for others should lead us to insist on nothing short of full economic justice*—leaving behind traditional "charity" and handouts.

(2) Gandhi and Tolstoy urge us all *to do some necessary manual work,* to commune with all those who are condemned to especially alienating and harsh forms of manual work.

(3) *Practice frugality and a simple lifestyle.* Over the last two decades more than a dozen stimulating books have discussed intentional simplicity as part of strategies to achieve fairer distribution of available resources.

(4) *Give all a chance to work.* Especially, give the right to work to the weak, the poor and the disenfranchised so that they might achieve greater autonomy and self-sufficiency.

(5) *Learn to share, to give, to practice generosity* on a daily basis. Share resources, including land. In third world countries there is a crying need for land reform to make land available to the landless, who often are landless as a result of documented injustice. Establish a fairer and saner balance of resources, and view ourselves merely as stewards or trustees, to whom resources have been entrusted for a broader purpose, transcending the individual.

(6) *Implement appropriate or intermediate technology* as defined in E. F. Schumacher's landmark book *Small is Beautiful.*

(7) *To whatever extent is feasible, practice local or regional self-sufficiency;* support local agriculture and manufacture; practice economic and political decentralization.

(8) *Nurture the environment:* practice right ecology.

(9) *Stop designing and manufacturing weapons.* Achieve economic conversion of military jobs to *jobs with peace!*

(10) *Support cooperative approaches* to work and economic problems. Gandhi's plea was to avoid and denounce the practices of exploitive capitalism.

3. Nonviolent communication

*T*o combat violent communication (which often is synonymous with oppression) and the lack of communication, foster the more complete and effective nonviolent, cooperative communication.

Concrete suggestions for implementing nonviolent communication:

(1) Let our attitude toward the person we are communicating with be one of *Love* (care + respect + responsibility + knowledge) as opposed to an attitude of domination.

(2) Let our attitudes toward the other party be ones of *flexibility:* tolerance, humility and openness to other viewpoints—as opposed to arrogance.

(3) Let us practice *trust* in the other: regard for the other, patience toward the other, and assuming the other's goodwill—as opposed to scorn for the other and disbelief in the other's potential and goodwill.

(4) Let me have a reasonably open and *questioning* attitude toward my ideas and positions, and be prepared to view them in a new light on occasion—as opposed to a closed and dogmatic mentality.

(5) Let us be prepared to engage in a two-way process of *sharing* information, facts, ideas, opinions—as opposed to a close-minded attitude.

(6) In the process of dialoguing, let us systematically *listen* to the other party or parties and be prepared to express differences as well as commonalities. Let us consider signing up for workshops in Listening Skills and undergoing training in that area. (Mostly, we are very poor listeners).

(7) Let us engage in authentic *dialogue* which, according to the definition of that term, implies a two-way flow.

(8) Practice *cooperation* as part of the process of communication and dialogue. This supposes a willingness to view issues and problems in a more general perspective, and to pluralize or globalize the issues.

(9) Practice *consultation,* which is the process whereby we seek information, opinions, advice or guidance from others.

(10) If the above approaches have not been attempted

or have not worked and we are in a situation of exacerbated conflict, practice the various skills and approaches relevant to *conflict-solving/conflict-resolution:* negotiation; mediation; arbitration; reconciliation.

*W*ar is the ultimate breakdown in communication, and is the ultimate evil which the process of communication seeks to avoid.

4. Nonviolent government/politics (including international politics)

*R*easonable participation in the governmental process is a basis of the Gandhian doctrine of nonviolence; civic awareness and involvement in activities are viewed as important as a prayer or religious duty or act.

We must train ourselves to examine the institutions we have created. If a governing body or road repair service does not achieve what our best judgment and our moral selves want it to achieve, we must reconsider why we as citizens created such a service.

Gandhi has warned us that "the State represents violence in a concentrated and organized form." We must therefore always be on the lookout for the violence which the State and its agencies are perpetrating, claiming it is done *in our name.* It is a mistake to assume that the judiciary or the military or the government stands for justice or peace; our duty as citizens is to make sure they come closer to that ideal.

Concrete suggestions for implementing nonviolent government:

(1) Participate by making sure that through representation of our opinions, through our votes and actions, government agencies achieve their original purpose—the administration of a required service in accordance with our aims and values.

(2) Decentralize: go back to human scale.

(3) Inter-relate through adequate communication with other groups within a nation or among nations or continents.

(4) Build a society that provides for basic human needs (such as adequate housing, health, education, jobs in humane working conditions, and a safe environment). Change social structures which exploit the poor.

(5) Democratize: respect the rights and opinions of all groups, and especially of minorities.

(6) Ensure that the laws are *just.* If a given law is not just, convey our wish to have it repealed; as needed, get involved in actions to achieve that end.

(7) Democratize the international world order. Democratize relations among nations.

(8) Pluralize issues: view them in the light of the concerns of *all* parties involved; in a domestic context, this means all the groups involved; in the international context, all the nation-states involved.

5. Nonviolent education

Concrete suggestions for implementing nonviolent education:

(1) Develop education for peace and nonviolence, education in nonviolent communication, in mutual understanding and cooperation. This should be the basis for curriculum and the framework within which all educational subjects fit.

(2) Have the students/learners learn from work and learn from life. Encourage full and responsible (not just token) involvement in various crafts and in various other forms of work (such as agriculture). All should do some necessary manual work.

(3) Work on self-improvement, on achieving knowledge and mastery of self, on educating the individual character and on development of truthfulness and fearlessness. This naturally leads to spiritual training.

(4) Self-sufficiency is to be developed on the basis of students' ability to learn from life, and to cope with a variety of manual tasks. Self-sufficiency is the ability to adapt to tomorrow's knowledge and context, after aspects of today's knowledge become obsolete. Educate for tomorrow's context.

(5) Develop the crucial dimension of outreach. Learn to intuit or discover the needs of others, to meet such needs, and to do committed volunteer service for the welfare of all.

For more information, please contact:
Guy de Mallac
Center for Nonviolence
P.O. Box 1058
San Jacinto, CA 92581-1058

The Family of Abraham

Dom Helder Camara

Archbishop of Recifé, Brazil

*J*ews, Muslims and Christians know the story of the father of believers. . . Did Abraham receive great gifts? He gave a faithful return, the best he could. He served. . . . . If you feel in you the desire to use the qualities you have, if you think selfishness is narrow and choking, if you hunger for truth, justice and love, you can and should go with us. . . .

The violence of the truth

*I*n underdeveloped countries the Abrahamic minorities must try to find out and understand what is involved in a sub-human situation. "Sub-human" is an explosive word. Take it in detail.

- Find out about housing. Do the places where some people live deserve to be called houses? . . . Look at the water, drains, electricity, the floor, the roof.
- Investigate clothing, food, health, work, transport, leisure . . . .

  You should ask the right questions.

- With work, for example, does it pay a living wage sufficient to support a family; is employment guaranteed or are there frequent redundancies (layoffs)? Are trade unions encouraged, tolerated, interfered with, forbidden? What are the apprenticeship conditions? the sanitary conditions? holidays? retirement provisions? Are the laws on social conditions kept? Are human beings treated with respect?

This sort of inquiry could of course arouse suspicion, and that could have unpleasant consequences. But it is necessary to find out what the real situation is in conditions of internal colonialism. What other way is there of becoming convinced and convincing others of the huge gap between those who suffer from an almost feudal situation in which the masses have no voice and no hope? Such information would not aim at inciting anger and rebellion but at providing a solid argument for the necessity to change the structures. . . .

Its aim is to supply liberating moral pressure. For many, this in itself is dangerous and subversive. But one day it will be understood that this violence of the peaceful is greatly preferable to the explosion of armed violence. . . . Choosing the way of moral pressure is not choosing the easy way out. We are replacing the force of arms by moral force, the violence of the truth. We must believe that love can strengthen the courage of these Abrahamic minorities who want justice but who refuse to answer violence with violence. . . .

In their work of diagnosing unjust situations, in their action of liberating moral pressure these minorities must be careful to remain humble. As we know our own selfishness, we must be aware that if we were in the place of those we condemn, we might behave in the same way as they do.

excerpted from *The Desert is Fertile*,
pp.8, 9, 54–57

HOPE

"*St. Augustine says that Hope
has two lovely daughters,
Anger and Courage. . . .
In the famous Pauline statement,
of faith, hope and love,
love is the greatest (1 Cor. 13),
but Augustine praises Hope
for she tells us that
God will work God's will. . . .
Anger so that what cannot be
will not be,
and courage so that what must be,
will be.*"

DOROTHEE SOLLÉ,
from the Foreword to *We Will Not Hang Our
Harps on the Willows,*
by Bärbel von Wartenberg-Potter

THE FORCE OF TRUTH

"*Its aim is to supply liberating moral
pressure. For many, this in itself is
dangerous and subversive. But one day
it will be understood that this violence
of the peaceful is greatly preferable to the
explosion of armed violence. . . .
Choosing the way of moral pressure is
not choosing the easy way out. We are
replacing the force of arms by moral
force, the violence of the truth.*"

DOM HELDER CAMARA,
"The Family of Abraham"

The Religious Freedom Project

Dedicated to a bold promise for global peace and an end to religious violence, The Religious Freedom Project is an organization and strategy for accomplishing the end of bloodshed which is justified, excused or motivated by religious concerns by the year 2005.

Conventional thinking, which has produced the problems of today, is insufficient for solving them. Historical understanding would declare a promise of this magnitude impossible, yet this unconventional organization will not only maximize existing opportunities but also create new ones, new realities which might not otherwise occur. Strategies are focused on identifying and leveraging large global forces in time for the fulfillment of the unalterable purpose of the project.

For more information, contact:
The Reverend Eileen L. Epperson,
Executive Director
The Religious Freedom Project
23-8 Royal Crest Drive
Marlborough, MA 01752-2422

Envisioning a World Without Religious Violence

The Reverend Eileen Louise Epperson

Presbyterian minister and Executive Director of the Religious Freedom Project

*Albert Einstein wrote that
"The significant problems we face
cannot be solved at the same level of thinking
we used when we created them."*

The way we see the problem of religious violence *may be* the problem. Even our most creative, audacious thinking is bound by invisible constraints. We pray and strategize within a context in which violence is a given. We expect it. Thus, even potentially viable solutions are inadequate to deliver on our commitment to move beyond religious violence as they, too, arise within the current paradigm.

A viable program of personal and global change must begin by confronting the facts about religious violence. We must gain a clear understanding of its occurrences, of the sad irony of "religious violence," in which difference is perceived as a source of danger and fear, and of its costs: the terrible human toll, the environmental degradation and the financial waste.

Then we must gather ourselves together and boldly step into a place of not knowing, beyond our certainty, beyond the well-wrought solutions with which we are comfortable. In that uncertainty, we can begin to deliberately envision a world, a possible future, in which violent response to differentness becomes an anomaly found only in history books. Together we will invent a way of speaking which alters the direction of the present and aims it at the future. Standing in the future, as it were, we will speak that future in this moment.

This potent expression brings to life that which is spoken, calling both speaker and listener into effective action and partnership. It is a radical departure from the language of wishes, hopes or opinions, as heartfelt or reasoned as they may be. This stand-taking includes and enhances the spiritual resources with which we are familiar.

A final step is to explore the unique access to the Divine or Ultimate which is granted by different religions. We inquire into their possible value for our own journeys. Still grounded in our own faith tradition, yet having shifted our relationship to other faiths from threat to value, we will ask of the religions questions such as:

Can another religious tradition speak to my own experience, even if I do not practice that path and have no intention to do so?

Do other religions address such basic questions as "What is worth living and dying for?" in a way which can actually make a difference to me?

Can spiritual paths other than my own even contribute to the strength and depth of my chosen religion?

In a world which is safe and free from even a thought of potential violence, spiritual exploration is not only a possibility, but a joyous, natural, human expression.

Seeking Interreligious Dialogue

Marcus Braybrooke

There are many ways that we can participate in responding to the needs we perceive for interreligious understanding and cooperation. We can act through organizations and meetings but also through interpersonal relationships and inner reflection. In the excerpt which follows, from *A Pilgrimage of Hope* (p.310), Marcus Braybrooke describes six forms of dialogue identified by Professor Diana Eck (of Harvard University and Moderator of the World Council of Churches' Sub-Unit on Dialogue). The description serves this concluding section of the *SourceBook* by distinguishing several important aspects of the process of creating a community of religions. –*Ed.*

*T*he first [form of dialogue] is parliamentary-style dialogue. [Diana Eck] traces this back to the 1893 World's Parliament of Religions and sees it carried forward by the international interfaith organizations, although. . . their way of working is now very different from the approach of the World's Parliament.

Secondly, there is institutional dialogue, such as the regular meetings between representatives of the Vatican and The International Jewish Committee for Inter-religious Consultation.

Thirdly, there is theological dialogue, which takes seriously the questions and challenges posed by people of other faiths.

Fourthly, dialogue in community or the dialogue of life is the search for good relationships in ordinary life.

Fifthly, spiritual dialogue is the attempt to learn from other traditions of prayer and meditation.

Lastly, there is inner dialogue, which is "that conversation that goes on within ourselves in any other form of dialogue."

Diana Eck's article is "What Do We Mean by Dialogue?"
in *Current Dialogue*, WCC, 1987, pp.5 ff.

*"The Christian is not to become a Hindu or a Buddhist,
nor a Hindu or a Buddhist to become a Christian.
But each must assimilate the spirit of the others
and yet preserve his individuality
and grow according to his own law of growth. . ."*

VIVEKANANDA

*"If you want to nourish a bird,
you should let it live any way it chooses.
Creatures differ because they have different likes and dislikes.
Therefore the sages never require the same ability
from all creatures. . . .
The true saint leaves wisdom to the ants,
takes a cue from the fishes,
and leaves willfulness to the sheep."*

CHANG TZU

A CHRISTIAN TEACHING

In the tender compassion of our God,
the dawn from heaven
will break upon us, to shine upon
those who live in darkness,
under the shadow of death,
and to guide our feet
into the way of peace.

from the SONG OF ZECHARIAH,
Luke 1:78 & 79

A TAOIST TEACHING

I have three precious things which
I hold fast and prize. The first is gentleness; the second is frugality;
the third is humility, which keeps me
from putting myself before others.
Be gentle, and you can be bold;
be frugal, and you can be liberal;
avoid putting yourself before others,
and you can become a leader of men.
Gentleness brings victory to him who
attacks, and safety to him who de-
fends. Those whom Heaven would
save, it fences round with gentleness.
The greatest conquerors are those
who overcome their enemies without
strife.   LAO TSE

AN ISLAMIC TEACHING

There is no kind of beast on earth,
nor fowl which flieth with its wings,
but the same is a people like unto you.
Unto their Lord shall they return. . .
God is the light of the heavens and of
the earth. Hast thou not seen how all
in the heavens and in the earth ut-
tereth the praise of God?
the very birds as they spread
their wings?
Every creature knoweth its prayer
and its praise.   THE *QUR'AN*

DECIDE TO BE A SPIRITUAL PERSON

Render others spiritual

Irradiate your spirituality

Treat every moment of your life
    with divine respect

Love passionately your Godgiven,
    miraculous life

Be endlessly astonished at
    your brief, breathtaking
    consciousness of the universe

Thank God for every moment
    for the tremendous gift of life

Lift your heart to the heavens always

Be a cosmic, divine being,
    an integral conscious
    part of the universe

Contemplate with wonder
    the miraculous Creation
    all around you

Fill your body, mind, heart and soul
    with divine trepidation

Know that you are coming
    from somewhere

and that you are going somewhere
    in the universal
    stream of time

Be always open to the entire universe

Know yourself and the heavens
    and the Earth

Act spiritually

Think spiritually

Love spiritually

Treat every person and living being
    with humaneness
    and divine respect

Pray, meditate, practice the art
    of spiritual living

And be convinced of eternal life
    and resurrection

ROBERT MULLER

A NATIVE AMERICAN PRAYER

Let us know peace.

For as long as the moon shall rise,
For as long as the rivers shall flow,
For as long as the sun will shine,
For as long as the grass shall grow,
Let us know peace.

A CHEYENNE INDIAN

A HINDU PRAYER

May the winds, the oceans,
the herbs, the nights and days,
the mother earth,
the father heaven,
all vegetation, the sun,
be all sweet to us.

Let us follow the path of goodness
for all times, like the sun and the
moon moving eternally in the sky.
Let us be charitable to one
another. Let us not kill or be
violent with one another.
Let us know and appreciate the
points of view of others.
And let us unite.
May the God who is friendly,
benevolent, all-encompassing,
measurer of everything,
the sovereign, the lord of speech,
may He shower His blessings
on us. . .

Oh Lord, remove my indiscretion
and arrogance; control my mind.
Put an end to the snare of endless
desires. Broaden the sphere of
compassion and help me to cross
the ocean of existence.

excerpted from "Hindu Prayers"
in *Religion for Peace*, 1973, WCRP

ISLAMIC PRAYER

Oh God,
You are Peace.
From You comes Peace,
To You Returns Peace.
Revive us with a salutation of Peace,
and lead us to your abode of Peace.

a saying from THE PROPHET,
used in daily prayer by Muslims

A JEWISH TEACHING

In that hour when the Egyptians
died in the Red Sea,
the ministers wished to sing the song
of praise before the Holy One,
but he rebuked them saying:

"My handiwork is drowning
in the sea;
would you utter a song before me
in honor of that?"

from the *SANHEDRIN*

A BUDDHIST REFLECTION

Now under the loving kindness and
care of the Buddha, each believer of
religion in the world transcends the
differences of religion, race and
nationality, discards small differences
and unites in oneness to discuss
sincerely how to annihilate strife from
the earth, how to reconstruct a world
without arms, and how to build welfare
and peace of mankind, so that never-
ending light and happiness can be
obtained for the world of the future.

May the Lord Buddha give His loving
kindness and blessing to us for the
realization of our prayers.

from "Buddhist Prayers"
in *Religion for Peace*, 1973, WCRP

A JAIN (UNIVERSAL) PRAYER FOR PEACE

Lead me from Death to Life,
from Falsehood to Truth

Lead me from Despair to Hope,
From Fear to Trust.

Lead me from Hate to Love,
from War to Peace.

Let Peace fill our Heart,
our World, Our Universe.

SATISH KUMAR

A SIKH PRAYER

May the kingdom of justice prevail!
May the believers be united in love!

May the hearts of the believers
be humble, high their wisdom,
and may they be guided in their
wisdom by the Lord.

O *Khalsa,* say *Wahiguru,*
Glory be to God! . . .

"Entrust unto the Lord what thou
wishest to be accomplished.
The Lord will bring all matters
to fulfilment:
Know this as truth evidenced by
Himself."

excerpted from "Sikh Prayers"
in Religion for Peace, 1973, WCRP

A SHINTO PRAYER

O Most High, help to bring thy Light
into the darkened conditions of the
world! Be gracious to us thy humble
servants and bless us with illumination as to that which is Divinely relevant to the fulfilment of thy will!

O Most High, inspire thy servants
throughout the world to further efforts towards leading back thy children who are led astray to the right
way, and to live and act on the faith
of what has been taught by the
great founders of the religions!
Bless all spiritual leaders with thy
power and enable them to give
help, joy, comfort and reassurance
to those suffering, to whom they
minister!

excerpted from "Shinto Prayers"
in Religions for Peace, 1973, WCRP

A CHRISTIAN PRAYER

LORD,
Make me an instrument
    Of thy peace.

Where there is hatred,
    Let me sow love.

Where there is injury,
    Pardon.

Where there is doubt,
    Faith.

Where there is despair,
    Hope.

Where there is darkness,
    Light.

Where there is sadness,
    Joy.

O Divine Master,
Grant that I may not so much seek
    To be consoled,
    As to console;

Not so much to be understood,
    As to understand;

Not so much to be loved,
    As to love.

For it is in giving
    That we receive.

It is in pardoning
    That we are pardoned.

It is in dying
    That we awaken
    To eternal life.

ST. FRANCIS OF ASSISI
(1182–1226)

A BAHÁ'Í TEACHING

When love is realized and the ideal
spiritual bonds unite the hearts of
men, the whole human race will be
uplifted, the world will continually
grow more spiritual and radiant, and
the happiness and tranquillity of mankind be immeasurably increased.
Warfare and strife will be uprooted,
disagreement and dissension pass
away, and Universal Peace unite the
nations and peoples of the world.
All mankind will dwell together as
one family, blend as the waves of one
sea, shine as stars of one firmament,
and appear as fruits of the same tree.
This is the happiness and felicity of
humankind. This is the illumination
of man, the glory eternal and life everlasting; this is the divine bestowal."

'ABDU'L-BAHA,
The Promulgation of Universal Peace

A ZOROASTRIAN PRAYER

With bended knees,
with hands outstretched,
do I yearn for the effective expression
of the holy spirit working within me:
For this love and understanding,
truth and justice;
for wisdom to know the apparent
from the real that I might alleviate
the sufferings of men on earth. . . .

God is love, understanding,
wisdom and virtue.
Let us love one another,
let us practice mercy and forgiveness,
let us have peace,
born of fellow-feeling. . . .

Let my joy be of altruistic living,
of doing good to others.
Happiness is unto him
from who happiness proceeds
to any other human being.

RESPONSE:

We will practice what we profess.

excerpted from the Avesta prayer
in "Zoroastrian Prayers,"
in Religion for Peace, 1973, WCRP

This interfaith anthem was commissioned for performance at the Inaugural Ceremonies of the Council for a Parliament of the World's Religions held at Rockefeller Chapel on the campus of the University of Chicago on November 4, 1989. The event marked the opening of a series of interfaith services, conferences and other activities designed as part of the centennial observance of the 1893 World's Parliament of Religions, culminating in the Parliament held in the summer of 1993.

The music and text printed here are the abbreviated version of a longer (SATB) edition, which is available with full score and notations for organ, choir, cantor and narrator, from:

G.I.A. Publications
7404 So. Mason Ave.
Chicago, IL 60638 USA.

This version may be photoduplicated for use in service bulletins; if so used, the publisher requests that the entire contents, including the title, names, and copyright notices be reproduced.

CHANT FOR THE UNIVERSE
AN INTERFAITH ANTHEM

Text: Rabbi Herbert Bronstein
Ronald R. Kidd

Music: Richard Proulx, 1989

Spir - it af - firms, the

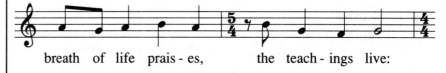

breath of life prais - es, the teach - ings live:

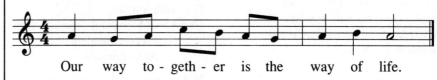

Our way to - geth - er is the way of life.

Narrator recites: Rejoicing in the richness of our differences

Assembly recites: Together we preserve as priceless treasures, as gifts to one another, the arts, the songs and traditions of all our nations, peoples, and religions.

Choir: Let the creatures of this earth give thanks! Surrounded by song, enchanted by dance. Blessed by our stories, lifted up by our temples, ancient poems of great wisdom: the sun always rises.

All repeat refrain above.

Narrator: With many hands and a single heart

Assembly: Together we reach out to the cold, to the hungry, the neglected, the hopeless.

Choir: When I see you cold, may I give you warmth. When I see you hungry, may I give you food. When I see you alone, may I give you friendship. When I see you without hope, may I give you lilacs and rivers.

All repeat refrain above.

Narrator: With knowledge and with will

Assembly: Together we labor to preserve the earth, our living home, and all the delicate intermingling channels of life; the air and the soil and the water all are our single sphere of life.

Choir: Let rivers flow, orchards yield fruit, hills and mountains grace this earth. Let rains fall, pure, to give growth to earth's gifts. May air be clean again, transporting sun and the light of the stars; And the round, cool moon appear above a universe at peace.

All repeat refrain above.

Narrator: Each one of us stands alone, with differing power and strength.

Assembly: Together we are strong in restraining the fist of violence, of vice, and of crime.

Choir: Reach out to those wounded! Reach out to those robbed! Reach out to those raped! Reach out to those maimed! Let all the suffering be gathered up in mercy: Wholeness to the injured, a new heart to the violent.

All: Spirit affirms, the breath of life praises, the teachings live: Our way together is the way of peace.

Narrator: All have known subjection and in every generation the lash of tyranny.

Assembly: Together we strive against all servitude from within and from without that all may be free to serve all people and all creatures of the earth.

Choir: Let those enslaved arise in freedom. Let all those enslaving be freed from a sad heart. Let those wrapped in their own chains, burst out into free air! No bonds from within, no bonds from without!

All: Spirit affirms, the breath of life praises, the teachings live: Our way together is the way of joy.

Narrator: Difficult as it is to hear and understand the words of the other

Assembly: Together we keep open the channels of human discourse, of science and of learning. Together we try to listen to one another.

Choir: We speak a thousand tongues, we honor the truth; We sing a million songs, the echo is one. Give me your books, teach me to hear. Give me your mind, a new galaxy swirls.

All: Spirit affirms, the breath of life praises, the teachings live: Our way together is the way of love.

Narrator: Our sages are many, our books in number beyond count:

Assembly: Together we teach one doctrine of compassion and love.

Choir: Prophet, sage, hero, saint, Bodhisattva, avatar, teacher, One blessing for all the earth, A thousand gold flames for everyone alive!

All: Spirit affirms, the breath of life praises, the teachings live: Our way together is the way of life.

Narrator: Many the paths we have taken, many the paths which point out the way.

Assembly: Our pathway together is the pathway of peace.

Choir: A wide, wide world, journeys as broad. A mountain to the sun, how many paths? Hands clasped, hearts entwined: Peace within, a highway at our feet.

All: Spirit affirms, the breath of life praises, the teachings live: Our way together is a pathway of peace.

Epilogue

Until one is committed,
there is hesitancy, the chance to draw back,
always ineffectiveness.

Concerning acts of initiative (and creation)
there is one elementary truth
the ignorance of which kills countless ideas
and splendid plans:

> That the moment one definitely commits oneself
> then Providence moves too.

All sorts of things occur to help one
that would never otherwise have occurred.

A whole stream of events issues from the decision,
raising in one's favor all manner
of unforseen incidents and meetings
and material assistance
which no one could have dreamt
would come their way.

Whatever you can do,
or dream you can, begin it.
Boldness has genius, power and magic in it.

Begin it now.

GÖETHE